The City Is

ABLAZE!

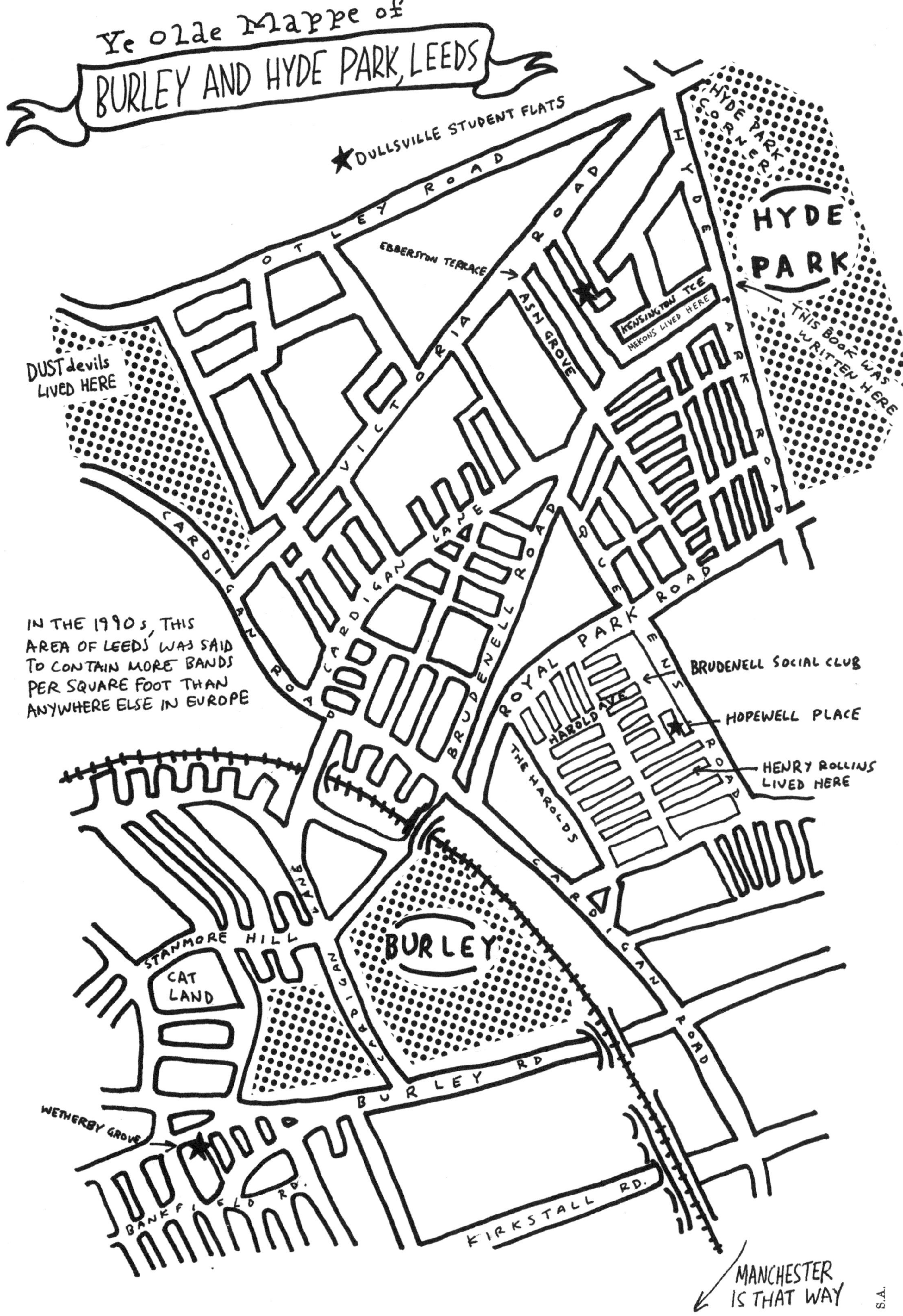
Ye Olde Mappe of
BURLEY AND HYDE PARK, LEEDS
DULLSVILLE STUDENT FLATS
OTLEY ROAD
HYDE PARK CORNER
HYDE PARK
HYDE PARK ROAD
THIS BOOK WAS WRITTEN HERE
EBBERSTON TERRACE
ASH GROVE
VICTORIA ROAD
KENSINGTON TCE
MEKONS LIVED HERE
DUST devils LIVED HERE
CARDIGAN ROAD
CARDIGAN LANE
BRUDENELL ROAD
QUEENS ROAD
ROYAL PARK ROAD
BRUDENELL SOCIAL CLUB
HAROLD AVE.
THE HAROLDS
HOPEWELL PLACE
HENRY ROLLINS LIVED HERE
IN THE 1990s, THIS AREA OF LEEDS WAS SAID TO CONTAIN MORE BANDS PER SQUARE FOOT THAN ANYWHERE ELSE IN EUROPE
LANE
STANMORE HILL
CAT LAND
CARDIGAN
BURLEY
CARDIGAN ROAD
BURLEY RD
WETHERBY GROVE
BANKFIELD RD.
KIRKSTALL RD.
MANCHESTER IS THAT WAY
S.A.

The City Is
ABLAZE!

The Story of a Post-Punk Popzine 1984 - 1994

Karren Ablaze!

Mittens On
PUBLISHING

First published in 2012 by Mittens On Publishing, 145 - 149 Cardigan Road, Leeds LS6 1LJ, UK

Reprinted with revisions, March 2013

© Karren Ablaze! 2012

All rights reserved. No part of this publication may be reproduced or transmitted in any form by any means, electronic or mechanical, including photocopying, recording or any other information storage or retrieval system, without the prior written permission of the publisher. This book is sold subject to the condition that it shall not, by way of trade or otherwise, be lent, resold, hired out or otherwise circulated without the publisher's prior consent in any form of binding or cover other than that in which it is published and without a similar condition being imposed on the subsequent purchaser

All copyright remains with the individual authors, photographers and artists. Every effort has been made to contact the owners of written work, photographs and drawings

British Library Cataloguing-In-Publication Data
A catalogue record for this book is available from the British Library

ISBN 978-0-9574270-0-6

Designed by Shaun at Whatever Happens Next

Inside front cover photo of the late Timmy Taylor of Brainiac by Tony Woolgar

Printed by Graficas Cems, Spain

START!

My 1980s were surely as magical and terrible as anyone else's teenage decade. Yet those years mark a time of unprecedented musical creativity – following the all too well-documented cultural iconoclasm of punk – and provided a colossal feast of exhilarating noise-sounds, the likes of which had never been dreamed. Hundreds of post-punk bands roamed the UK, and there were fanzines everywhere – enough to invalidate the music press, had the networks been right. In youthcultureland, it seemed as if this was what everyone did – write a zine, or play in a band. That, or put on gigs, run a zine distro, or form a chaotic freeform dance troupe (like The Much Hoolers[1]), and then form a band. Mere consumption was not an option.

Ablaze! was one of those many zines published in the UK in the late eighties and early nineties, and this book tells the story of one girl's adventures in self-publishing. It begins when childlike fingers, sticky with pritt stick, set to clunky manual typewriter keys, and then switched on the photocopier. It describes the life-changing effects of overcoming paranoia enough to produce a two-sheet teen-angst zine for friends, and moves onto how, along with a team of co-conspirators, I ended up producing huge text-dense music publications that sold to thousands. It's about the years of fun that ensued and all the people we met and befriended; protagonists and passionistas across the western world.

The main body of this book consists of selected zine pages, presented for your viewing pleasure[2]. Interspersed between them you'll find personal recollections and interviews that intertwine, overlap or fly off at tangents, held together by the thread of fanzines and DIY culture. Whilst selling the first issue of *Ablaze!* I met three new friends: Pik was a student single-handedly running a guerrilla radio station from the tops of the city's skyline; Simon Morris was in a band that teetered on the cutting edge and sometimes fell off it, only to find themselves spearheading the Mad Pride movement; and Andrew Neal was thinking of starting a zine of his own...

Then there are Three Fanzine Kings: John Robb, a Blackpool punk on the way to becoming a journalist and TV star, via screaming with bulging eyes in the trad rock-killing Membranes; Richard Johnson was a printer, ghoulishly taking over the zine world in his spare time; and Dave Haslam stayed true to his vision and found himself on an expanding adventure, with some critics – myself included – in tow.

You'll find *Ablaze!* contributors William Potter, Chris Trout, Gavin Bradbury and Andrew Johnson telling their sides of the story. Tony Woolgar, Leeds' most prolific rock photographer, contributed many images to the zine; there are examples of his work throughout, including those opposite.

And if you're thinking it's all quite boy-dominated, you'd be right – it was. But that was to change in the early nineties. Riot Grrrls Simone Ivatts, Aisha Ali, Bela Emerson, Geraldine Montgomerie and Sarah Bag recall what really happened in the Yorkshire wing of the Grrrl explosion. Lucy Cage ponders why girls are still considered to be inferior appreciators of music, Deborah Withers expounds on the transformative power of DIY, and Natalie Bradbury lets us know what it's like to do a fanzine in the twenty-tens.

Finally, there is a message from a boy from a small town, a boy who lost all hope until an old copy of a zine made him change his mind, so that he could go on to change the whole damn scene. Gary Jarman's epilogue takes us into the future.

This book has everything: fascinating letters from pop stars, a lost Pavement interview, and even a mystery – a missing person[3]. It is a tale of two cities, one that changed its name to reflect the stylistic insanity it came to represent, and one that continued to rock. It's an incomplete noise bible that might even recall elements of your own story...

Dear outcast children, this is for you.

Karren Ablaze!, Seville, March 2013

[1] The Much Hoolers was a chaotic dance troupe from Much Hoole in Lancashire. They only performed at shows by The Membranes and later on went to become the band Dandelion Adventure, pictured on the right. Photo: Tony Woolgar
[2] Apologies for pages not Included. All is not lost however – some back issues are available at www.ablazefanzine.com.
[3] Micheal Walsh – phone home.

Kill Yr

Memories of *Ablaze!* and the Leeds music scene

Ross Holloway

Ablaze! spanned the era that marked the end of punk and post-punk, and the point at which grunge, acid house and Britpop hit the mainstream. The years between 1987 and 1993, covered by ten issues of *Ablaze!*, were - broadly speaking - the era of indie pop, at a time when the term 'indie' still implied a continuation of the ideas of punk: a do-it-yourself, anti-establishment attitude.

Most musical histories of the era are written from the perspective of either London or Manchester, but this one is from Leeds - and we had our own thing going on.

Leeds is situated pretty much slap-bang in the centre of Britain, 40 miles north-east of Manchester, approximately 200 miles north of London and 200 miles south of Edinburgh. From this vantage point, music coming from elsewhere in Britain could seem either local – Manchester or Sheffield – or distant - London or Glasgow. Music from America felt no more removed from us than what was coming out of London, and in some ways, actually much closer to us than the capital.

The punk and post-punk scene in Leeds produced four bands of enduring influence and significance: Gang of Four, The Mekons, The Sisters of Mercy, and Soft Cell. Both Gang of Four and The Mekons achieved greater recognition in the USA than in their country of origin. I think there's an argument to be made that alt-country originated not in America, but in Leeds with The Mekons around 1984, when they added strains of Hank Williams and Johnny Cash to their ramshackle punk. One other Leeds band from this period must be mentioned, although their influence took time to filter through. Delta 5 were girl-led pioneers from the same University scene that spawned Gang of Four and The Mekons. They're important to the story because their scratchy, incendiary post-punk constituted a crucial forerunner to the Riot Grrrl scene.

Soft Cell were long gone, yet still hugely popular with the gothic punk working-class youth in Leeds, although never as widely adored as The Sisters of Mercy. Now Karren never liked The Sisters, and I suppose if you're going to herald the new, it helps to dismiss the old. I thought then as I do now that The Sisters were magnificent. They melded the New York cool and urban threat of Suicide, the heaviness of Hawkwind and Motorhead, the mystic Albion soul of Led Zeppelin, and bound it all together with Leeds' heritage of dark satanic mills and damp, ancient stone. An old factory chimney stack loomed over the back of the Sisters' house in Burley, just a short walk away from the ruined medieval Kirkstall Abbey. In the mid-eighties The Sisters truly were the sound of the city.

In 1986/87, my friends and I were all digging a new sound called 'grebo' - bands like Gaye Bykers on Acid, Crazyhead and The Janitors, along with some exciting new American 'noise' bands such as Butthole Surfers, Sonic Youth, and The Beatnigs. The band I was a part of, Purple Eternal, really dug the first two Gaye Bykers singles, which we couldn't help noticing were produced by Jon Langford of the Mekons, and also of The Three Johns. The Three Johns played a kind of agitprop, surrealist, drum machine-driven socialist drinking music, and we never missed an opportunity to see them play. One particularly memorable show took place at the Astoria Ballroom in Roundhay (now sadly demolished), during which the stage collapsed midway through a song. The band didn't miss a beat and finished their set on the now-sloping stage. In the audience that night was Steve Albini. Big Black were firm favourites of ours, and one didn't come across musical luminaries from Chicago in Leeds' suburban dancehalls every day, so naturally we went over to talk to him. Mr Albini was very friendly and courteous to these teenage ragamuffins babbling at him, and it turned out he was in Leeds to see Mr Langford. The same night we also met an odd girl with a great mop of vividly dyed red hair and a big smile. She looked like Robert Smith's little sister - this was Karren Ablaze!

Rollins Band, Leeds University, 1987 Photo: Tony Woolgar

Around this time we were really digging some recent releases by Henry Rollins. *Hot Animal Machine*, *Henrietta Collins and the Wife Beating Child Haters*, and *Life Time* by the Rollins Band, all of which were recorded (at least in part) by Geoff Clout at Off Beat Studios in Leeds. Geoff, later of Leeds psych-beat combo Ringo's High, was known to us for running a cassette duplication service from his house in the East Leeds suburb of Armley. During 1987 the enterprising Steve 'Weave' Hawkins put on Big Black, Swans, Butthole Surfers and Pussy Galore in Leeds, and would later bring the likes of Mudhoney and Dinosaur Jr. to the city. At the same time Flame in Hand Promotions arranged gigs for the likes of Leeds' own Chumbawamba, Dutch anarcho-punks The Ex, and a variety of American bands including Fugazi and Nirvana at the now legendary Duchess of York. All of this merely demonstrated

Idols

Leeds' Duchess of York   Photo: Tony Woolgar

how deeply Leeds was immersed in the American music scene of the time, right down to Johnny Thunders drinking in the Faversham on a Friday night with Leeds rock'n'roll reprobates the Dead Vaynes, and Patricia Morrison (once of LA's The Gun Club and now a fully-fledged Sister) holding court in another corner of the same pub. And let's not forget that the man who drew the crazy squiggles on the sleeve of Sonic Youth's *Death Valley '69* was from Meanwood - Mr Savage Pencil, or just plain Edwin Pouncey to his friends.

There were hundreds of fanzines around in those days, most being cheaply printed and distributed locally. The fanzine writer was a subcultural sub-species in itself, distinguished by a particular intense brand of geekiness, and easy to spot by their ever present rucksack brimming with publications, cardboard hitching signs, and a tendency to look down at their shoes when they were talking to you. Their fanzines existed in a cultural vortex left unfilled by the London-centric weekly music press, covering bands and scenes too marginal to demand many column inches in Sounds, Melody Maker, or the NME. Many also reflected a way of living far removed from the metropolitan music elites.

Yet fanzines did more than simply fill the void created by the complacency of the mainstream music press, in fact they had a completely different modus operandi. They were rarely courted by record companies, didn't print revisions of press releases, and didn't provide balanced reviews or polished journalism. This wilfully-opinionated stance typified fanzines, and also applied to *Ablaze!*, but whereas many other fanzines stayed small and disappeared quickly, *Ablaze!* grew and gradually became influential. Karren wrote it as she saw it and encouraged the other contributors to do the same. Re-reading the reviews now, with the benefit of hindsight, the really striking ones are those of the records and zines they didn't rate, which were almost always hilariously dismissive. The flipside of this was the passion and unconditional love

Doug Aikman, Nerve Rack

bestowed upon the music they took to. For the reader, this was thrilling and infectious, and you knew and trusted the purity of its intent.

Along with integrity there was also loyalty, which goes to explain the greater-than-strictly-merited coverage of my own band, Purple Eternal, in the pages of *Ablaze!* Karren's particular loyalty, however, was to Leeds, and to a lesser extent, Manchester (from whence she came), but more generally to the North of England. Despite the international scope of music covered and the aforementioned connections to US punk, *Ablaze!* was always concerned with the music being created all around us. Musicians weren't difficult to locate, as virtually all the Leeds bands drank in either the Royal Park or the Cardigan Arms. The bands included sharp-edged, agitprop noise merchants Nerve Rack, psychedelic noiseniks Jellyfish Kiss (who released several LPs on the infamous Shimmy Disc label – I once spotted label head honcho and producer Kramer in Maumoniat's general store while on my way to get my regular breakfast of vegetable samosas), Leeds' very own Church of the SubGenius clench Cud, shoegazers The Pale Saints and of course The Wedding Present.

My actual contributions to *Ablaze!* were limited. I hitched down to London one summer day in 1988 to interview Sonic Youth at Mute Records' offices on the eve of the release of *Daydream Nation*. Karren despatched myself and Sven in her place, as she felt she might be too starstruck to interview them properly herself. I'm not sure how she thought a couple of pimply youths, neither of whom had ever interviewed a band in their short lives, were going to do better but that was Karren for you: she put her faith in people.

After issue 6 a team coalesced around Karren at *Ablaze!* Towers. This comprised Chris Trout (AKA Lucy Nation), Gavin, and Michael Walsh, an old school friend of mine who, while he rarely put pen to paper, was such a ball of energy, witty banter and incisive repartee that he became a vital element In the chaotic mix. Between April 1989, when issue 5 emerged, through to 1993's issue 10, *Ablaze!* got slicker and glossier. The free singles went from flexidiscs to proper vinyl and the writing kept hitting home in its inimitable, irrepressible style.

Sonic Youth, Adam & Eve's, Leeds, 1986

Photo: Tony Woolgar

Issue 10 sounded the death knell for *Ablaze!*, and I tend to wonder whether its demise was due to The Sonic Youth Incident. There was a small piece in that issue that was critical of Sonic Youth's unquenchable desire to be cool. The fallout was a salvo of faxes sent to the main hubs of power across the indie world from Thurston Moore, a refutation from Karren which appeared in a mini-zine called *NO!* despatched to record shops in New York, and an eventual apology from Thurston. *NO!* was a cousin of the political pamphlets of the nineteenth century, espousing the values of Riot Grrrl whilst offering practical guidance on its possible applications. Karren then turned her attention to other matters, and the Leeds music scene sadly lost its most eloquent commentator.

Purple Eternal. L-R: Ross Holloway, Karl Berlin, Mark Webster, Daren Pickles and Sven Kleinschimdt

Had circumstances been different, I'm sure that *Ablaze!* would have carried on. There would have still been local bands for Karren to champion, and as I write this the Leeds music scene continues to thrive. Its epicentre is the Brudenell Social Club, which sits adjacent to the old *Ablaze!* HQ in Hopewell Place. When I visit, I hear a continuity of the sounds and influences that make up Leeds' distinctive guitar music heritage, but with one distinct change – there are a lot more girls on stage now than there used to be.

Karren always wrote what she truly believed and it was this unshakeable faith in the music, presented from the informed fan's point of view that made *Ablaze!* so essential, so readable and so epically, achingly fantastic. The very few music writers worth going back and reading decades later are the ones who weren't just observers, but also *participants*, and their involvement gave something back to the times in which they lived. In this tiny category of music journalists I would include Lester Bangs, Nick Kent, and Karren Ablaze! - none were afraid to kill their idols.

Karanoia
Early Zines
Morrissey pic: Ian Tilton - www.iantilton.net

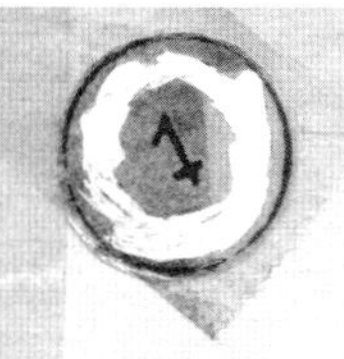

SCRITTI commune

I AM NOT A GIRL

I AM A THING THAT WRITES ON PAPER

Why start a fanzine? Why create a world?

Where I come from, children had no thoughts or feelings. At age five I knew I needed out. My dream was to live in a shed, as long as I could ensure a supply of food and something to do. Lacking that basic information on how to form relationships, the need for communication still burned in my heart. Quietly, by myself, I would create newspapers that nobody would read, and send letters to anyone who'd write back.

I didn't know how to realise my shed dream, so I took to the garage. A cheap telescope transported me millions of miles into the black night, where I gulped at the multitude of sparkly otherworlds. And for earthly company, I put the radio on. All the old sets had station names listed on a kind of wavelength roadmap, and I was fascinated by these all-but defunct services. Experimental twists of the dial revealed one that remained: Luxembourg issued a chaotic, crunched-up sound, all Euro electropop, American rock and static. At the same time, the early eighties charts were rich with intense new wave sounds, ever-increasing musical horizons, as breathtaking as the celestial realms that unfolded above the asbestos of the garage roof.

I refused to engage with eighties popular culture, but my knowledge of independent music ran deep and specialised. The evening-time mysteries of Radio One revealed themselves to me, and I dropped most other interests, disappearing to my bedroom to absorb the godlike voice and selections of John Peel. More dial-turning led to encounters with all the punk and alternative shows my aerial could snatch from the waves. In the North West UK that meant Piccadilly Radio's *Cures for Insomnia*, hosted by Mark Radcliffe, BBC Liverpool's Roger Hill, BBC Manchester's *Meltdown*, BBC Lancashire's *On the Wire*, and pretty much everything on Stockport-based pirate KFM, which seemed to focus largely on underground music.

But I didn't just listen, I broke in - barraging presenters with letters (invariably demanding that they play more by the post-punk pre-synth version of Scritti Politti, with which I was worryingly obsessed), and showing up at the studios -

WILMSLOW CHESHIRE PHONE 061-477 7536

Dear Miss Politti,
How are ya? Its 2:22a.m on Tuesday the 17th
just finished some art work for
couldn't

sometimes I was even invited. Not yet part of a network, at least I had accessed some form of communication. They acknowledged that I existed.

At school (a convent school – with real live nuns) I became a member of a small misfit community. Some of our connections revolved around a passion for what was then called alternative music, and its associated sartorial adventures.

I had no money for records, but hung around in record shops to hear new stuff, and no-one kicked me out. Under-16 bus fares cost 10p in the mid-eighties, so loitering in Manchester's city centre record stores became my Saturday afternoon paradise. In such shops I met all sorts of people, and with them various adventures would unfurl.

It was in these record shops that I found the most amazing things – fanzines. Black and white, sitting on the counter, their cover prices fell within my budget – pence! – and the fanzine writers liked it if you wrote them letters. They'd even write back, and send fliers for other zines, and for compilation tapes you could obtain by sending off a blank tape and a stamp. In this way I started to feed off the energy of the UK DIY scene, corresponding with people like Clare from Kvatch fanzine, who would later run Sarah Records, and Mark Williams, a North Wales fanzine legend and boy of many pseudonyms (generally he was named after the titles of his zines: Mark Shine, Mark Lemonade, Mark Whip Me and Go Moo; he later attained indie chart success in the band Emily). Mark and I would write to each other daily, using two stamps which we'd meticulously sellotape and re-affix to each urgently scrawled missive, to be transported back and forth by kindly - or blind - postal workers.

These were letters that made the school day go faster, letters to get up for, to run home for. Letters, in their multiplicity, that you could paper a house with. Equivalent, if their intensity and length could be translated and divided into tweet-like portions, to the quantity of communications we can enjoy right now on our shiny little screens. But back then it was all pens and paper, it was analogue and intense. You knew you could say anything to these correspondents, because they were writers who always wrote the truth.

Other people did fanzines, and I consumed them. It never occurred to me that I might become one of these higher beings, until a local radio show broadcast a piece about how to do it yourself. Two bubblingly enthusiastic youngsters declared how easy it was to self-publish, and how anyone could do it. I was writing all the time anyway. It was a way of calming myself down, endlessly scribbling in notebooks whilst hunched on the back seat of the bus, feet comfortably propped on the seat opposite, or huddled in bus stations waiting for the next one, killing time alone in the city.

Yet it would be altogether another thing to assemble something which a group of unknown others might read. To do this would mean directly engaging with all the critical voices that had bored themselves into my head, without any external supportive ones to guide me through the psychological mire. I chose to wade through this swamp of doom only because there was nothing to gain by not moving, and so much to gain by getting to the other side.

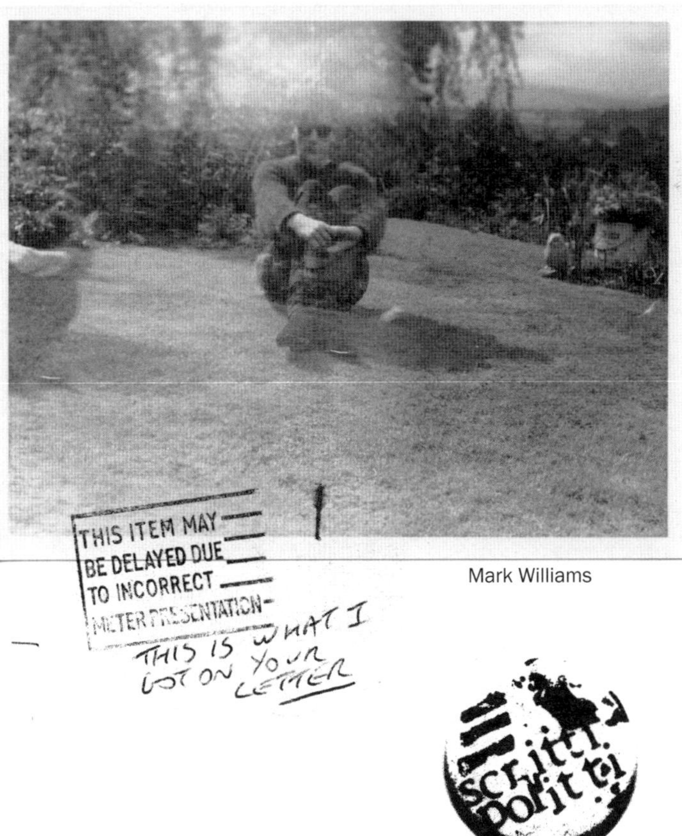

Mark Williams

Dear Karen, it's not really that I'm ignoring your letters, it's just that - and you're going to hate me for this - I'm now fearfully keen on the world. What can I say? Sorry?
John

Dear John,
I'm sick of writing that get totally ignored, but keep on writing then. And I'm now, to you, because I'm absolu desperate, I mean really, truly. You've just got to listen to me, there else I can turn to. Have I got y I doubt it. Anyway, here goes...
Please, John, Please will play the scritti politti single

HE NEW BASTED FANZINE FOR A NEW BASTED WORLD
ou wake up and dont know what's going to happen
hat time is it, what day is it?
ou've got ideas but they wont be really true and
he dreams that you dreamed wont really happen.
hey will chagge and the tangle of words thoughts
eoplle experience gets bigger and more inconciev
it turns round new corners and

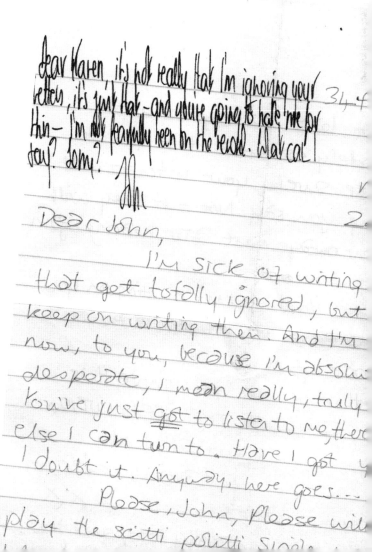

Unit 3, 104 Northenden Rd., SALE, CHESHIRE. Tel: (061) 962 8628

9th May 1984

Dear Karen

Thanks for your letter inquiring about the possibility of an interview with MARC RILEY and band for your hopefully forthcoming fanzine. The best thing would be for me and Marc to meet up at some local hostillery with yourselves and establish whether it will be a serious affair as regards the interview. No offence intended but since the publication isn't of the ground yet it could well be a complete waste of time for all concerned.

Let me know when you hope to have the first copies printed as it will be an out of date interview that will be published if it takes a while for yourselves to get everything together. The first edition is always going to be the longest to organise with all the early teething problems.

So good luck and hear from you soon.

Yours sincerely

Jim Khambatta

Jim KHAMBATTA.

I wrote three zines before *Ablaze!*. The first, produced whilst I was at school, was called *The Value of Defiance*. It was named after a Scritti Politti lyric and never came out. I was a nervous punk and didn't know how people would react to my daring to communicate. In my world, children were begrudgingly seen, never heard, and definitely not published, so it ended up in the bottom of the wardrobe.

Here, for the first time, are some of its pages. Pete Becker from Eyeless In Gaza kindly took a train up from Warwickshire to be interviewed by me, and it only seems fair that the piece should see the light of day, albeit almost 30 years late.

I'd first heard Eyeless in Gaza on *Pillows and Prayers*,[1] and must have deemed them interview-worthy.[2] They sent me a tape of their latest LP, *Rust Red September*, and although I lapped it up, I didn't ask them a single question about their music. What could I ask? I knew nothing about music except that I loved the weird sounds. It's a sign of those rich post-punk years that the intense, lovelorn, nature-hewn tones of Eyeless, with their proggy keyboards and swooping vocals, never caused me to bat an eyelid. In the sanitised future, this autumnal album sounds a lot stranger than it did back then. You can almost hear the morris dancer's bells on the bracing 'Leaves Are Dancing'. 'No Perfect Stranger' is a rare thing, a relationship song written by a guy [Martyn Bates] who oozes emotional intelligence. Hearing 'September Hills', I can imagine him energetically racing home, powered by the excitement of what he has seen, to breathlessly write it all down. Although our actual seasons have changed now, and would be more suitably represented by a Pollock than a neat tetraptych, the beauty of this album is perennial.

I agree to abide by the Rules and Conditions of membership of St. Joseph's Youth Club.

The Value of Defiance boasted an all-female team of journalists. Ruth Turnbull defended the Icicle Works from imaginary detractors, and Selma Malik praised *The Unforgettable Fire*. Jo McCarton, Justine Wolfenden and I were engaged in a plot to interview The Smiths, but all we got was a crummy letter from Morrissey. I'm not sure how I was in touch with the first two, but Jo and I were best school friends, and accompanied one another on many an escapade. Justine is the "distressed Smiths fan" you will read of shortly.

Living in Manchester, we felt that we might have some kind of access to the most significant band of that decade because they lived there too. It now seems bizarre that Jo and I, having gained entry to the BBC building where The Smiths had been sequestered, could have concluded that "half the group had gone home so there wasn't much point" in doing an interview with boring old Johnny Marr. We were both intrepid and determined people, so it's rather more likely that this would have been Johnny's own sentiment; perhaps he wasn't allowed to give audiences by himself - surely that was the eloquent singer's domain? I would really rather not think that we walked away from our chance to interrogate the maker of the defining guitar sound of the eighties through any lack of derring-do on our part.

While The Smiths meant a great deal to most lovers of original music, they meant that bit more to Mancunian adolescents. We'd play each other their records in our bedrooms, swooning to the profound melancholy of 'Reel Around the Fountain', 'Back to the Old House' or 'Suffer Little Children', and exchange tales of Smiths sightings, gasping at the news that Mozzer had been seen cycling home along the King's Road in Stretford, or spotted visiting his mum in Hale.

For me, the gig at the Free Trade Hall possessed a magic above and beyond that emitted by Manchester's most evocative quartet. It seems like the crystallisation of the finest elements of that time. I was there with Jo my best friend and Anne Marie my desk-friend – we sat together in fifth form. In the queue of trenchcoated daffodil thieves I was to meet Jaz, whose memory now remains intact enough to provide the following eyewitness report:

"I left it rather late to get tickets for the Free Trade Hall gig and the best I could do was the balcony, from which the view was akin to watching this much-anticipated event on someone else's telly from across the road through their living room window. It didn't take long to work out, however, that the 'security' (grey haired men in bow ties) were better suited to showing altogether more mature concert-goers to their seats than restricting the movements of several hundred infatuated Smiths fans, and after heading downstairs we simply walked unchallenged into the main auditorium. This was great until everyone else in the venue had the same idea, at which point things got a bit scary. Pretty quickly the crush at the front of the stage grew so great that the mass of bodies pressing against the first row of seats caused them to collapse, followed by several more behind them in short order. At one point I was knocked over and for a brief, panicky moment I wasn't able to move at all, pinned down by others who'd fallen on top of me.

Meanwhile the band carried on playing, perhaps unaware of what was unfolding [or folding] in front of them. I managed to find the people I'd gone with and moved back a few rows. It seemed at that point that everyone had escaped serious injury, although there were reports later than a girl had had her leg broken in the melee."

And Justine was there too. Justine's school required her to gain some work experience and, being extraordinarily canny, she arranged to do hers at the Free Trade Hall the week The Smiths were due to play there, so she was already installed and ingratiated with the staff by the time the band arrived. When I scrawled my interview request note to Morrissey at a bored moment during their riotous set, I thought I was being nice and polite. It did not occur to me for one moment that I was actually a brat, and that the question "Remember Manchester?" might ruffle some feathers. Justine duly added her paragraph of righteous indignation regarding the damage done to fans, fixtures and fittings that evening, and I folded the paper in four and passed it to the t-shirt seller, hoping it would somehow bring us closer to that elusive Smiths interview. When a locally postmarked, spikily-addressed envelope arrived a few days later, I had to accept that we just weren't getting one of those.

Jim Khambatta of In Tape Records was similarly circumspect about allowing the time of his business partner Marc Riley to be wasted. I was excited to discover that a record label had been started in Sale, the soulless suburb in which I lived, and even more impressed to hear that their records were being played by Peel. Foolishly they granted me an interview, the subject of which was ostensibly Marc Riley and The Creepers, and, accompanied by Jaz's sister Janet, we met up with them in the Sale Hotel. A pint of snakebite in the middle of the day rather messed with my mind, and I recall the whole thing as being quite chaotic. Janet made off with the tape so I can't even say what really happened, but the highlight was definitely this story by Marc Riley which I will now faithlessly relate from, erm, memory.

"Scritti Politti put The Fall on in Leeds a few years ago and after the gig they said 'come back to ours for something to eat.' So we started walking, and we were really hungry, thinking about this food we were going to have, thinking about chicken, and they made us walk for miles and miles, and when we eventually got there all they had was brown rice."

---

1 The flawless Cherry Red compilation LP, sold at the flawless price of 99p. It's full of tracks by the likes of The Passage, Felt, The Nightingales, and a bunch of Ben Watt and Tracey Thorn bands.

2 Although at that stage, I'd interview literally anyone. I liked to take to the streets outside school with a friend or two and interrogate any characters who looked vaguely interesting, under the pretence that we were conducting a survey.

EYELESS IN

The steps of the BBC in Manchester did at the time seem a good place to meet, but the weather had not been taken into account and the rain was getting heavy. I stood under the bus shelter worrying about the danger of appearing to be part of the queue, and I watched a couple who might have been looking for someone. It was only when I stepped from the shelter to stand nearer the building that they spoke to me. I silently followed Pete (one half of Eyeless in Gaza) and Jay into one of those cheap plastic cafés on Oxford Road....

Pete Testing testing one two

KazZZZ Do you like Scritti Politti?

Pete No they're horrible. Ha ha ha ha. No,yes I do. I think they're really good.

Kaz What are the groups influences apart from Scritti? I understand that they are one of the main ones.

Pete Well when their first single, Skank Bloc, came out we used all the information from the printed sleeve and made our own single. I suppose it was really influential to actually give information out on a record sleeve about how it was made.

Kaz So it was the information you were after, it wasn't their music which influenced you?

Pete It wasn't so much the music, it's more like a feel that you get off people about what they're doing, an area in which they're working, not particularly that I think "They're playing E, F and G notes so it must be great"... I get a good feeling about them and I have done since they started. I liked what they did initially, not as though they've done a lot of work because Green always seems to go to sleep in between his releases - he puts one record out and about three years later he wakes up and puts another one out.

Kaz No it's really not true - they were probably working quite hard in the beginning but perhaps their financial situation didn't allow them to release a lot...

Pete Plus Green was "ill", or so I heard but I don't know whether it's true or not. There's another rumour that he went to live in a cottage in Wales...

Kaz I think that is quite true actually. So who influenced your music?

Pete Oh God...nobody. I don't think any one band influenced what we were doing. When we started we were very much a product of the times, very independant, the sort of '79, '80 way of clubbing together and making your own record and distributing it yourself which is great because it gives you an idea of how you are as a person, rather than as part a big machine.

Kaz Do you still feel that people should be doing that now?

Pete I think it's still valid but you can't reach a mass audience by doing something in your front room because you don't have the capabilities money-wise....I think a way round it is to work within what's going on, using the majors to help you do what you want to do.

GAZA

Kaz So, you believe in the majors?

Pete I believe in compromise. Everybody has to believe in compromise otherwise you'd never cross a road. There's compromise involved in everything.

Kaz If there was so much compromise there'd be no revolutions.

Pete That's true but I don't think there'll be a revolution in this country, not in my lifetime anyway.

Kaz So you won't name any names of groups? (to get back to the question)

Pete At the time there were people like Cabaret Voltaire and the Human League and I liked parts of their music but there wasn't any one group that I could say "they did it for me" about...I suppose you've got to mention the pistols 'cos they were part of the Revolution (in inverted commas) at the time.

People still call it a new wave and it was in 1976, seven years ago, so it's not true anymore. We were just two people doing what we wanted to do, we weren't trying to jump on any punk bandwagon. We were very individual at the time Punk was a lot of different things to me, so that's why I felt it was valid to do something in music. But it got worse with Sid Vicious and all that, you couldn't be a punk unless you had a uniform on...I'm being cynical now!

Kaz I'm very ignorant about the history of your group...

Pete So am I!

Kaz How, where and when did it start?

Pete It was the beginning of 1980 and I tried to join a local duo already in existance in Nuneaton called but I couldn't fit in and they wouldn't have me. Martyn also tried to join playing guitar but his style was such that he couldn't fit in with what they were doing. The group suggested that we should get together and do something, so we met and it seemed to click from the word go. It grew from there and we did a few local gigs. Actually the first few music-making sessions that we did turned up as our first E.P. which we got the information for from the Scritti thing.

Kaz Do you consider live work important?

Pete It's important to us because this is the way we work and I like doing it. There was a period when I really didn't want to play live - I thought it was a bit of a cop-out, somehow selling yourself short... There's a lot of things against you, the acoustics in the hall, the sound equipment being bad and people generally not caring about who you are. I really hate that rock attitiude of not caring about people. I prefer the more personal touch, more involvement with a group of people when you feel you're advancing forward together rather than you just fighting the rest of the world, which it quite often seems to be when there's just two of us on the stage and there's all these other people telling you what to do. I do enjoy live work and I think it is important to give people a chance to see you perform.

Kaz What about the records...? (an unfinished question)

Pete It's very important to make very good records. I think the time when you can just put out any old rubbish, and hope that it would change the world has gone now. Things have moved on and people are looking for more quality in music. Still, if you can have content in the music - something that actually means something to somebody somewhere, then I think you've achieved something. There's a lot of classy records being put out with very glossy production, but they don't actually say anything, they haven't got any content. They're just like "baby I love you" or "meet me outside the..."

Kaz	What's wrong with that kind of language?
Pete	There's nothing wrong with it but it has been going round for so long that it's become a cliché. You can say those things in such a way as to make them sound new and fresh but if you just say the same old clichés all the time people become immune to it. It's like watching somebody being shot on t.v. everyday. After a while it doesn't mean anything, and it's like a song with "I love you" in it, then the next song comes on and says exactly the same thing. It's production-line pop without any kind of content in it. That's what I don't like but it's what everybody wants to do to get a hit. I don't know, I'm confused.
Kaz	I am too. I wasn't before but I am now. How many records have you done so far: which ones and on what labels?
Pete	We've put out four singles and four albums for cherry red I think so far, which nobody knows about, completely obscure...

We were supposed to be interviewing the Smiths after their appearance on the Oxford Road Show (10,2,84), and although Andy Rourke said he'd make sure our names were put on the guest-list, the receptionist refused to let us in.

Instead we spent an hour standing outside the doors, until Jonny Marr came out to sign autographs. He was very helpful and took us inside to do the interview but half the group had gone home so there wasn't much point. Well thanks Andy!

There are many differing opinions on The Smiths gig at the free Trade Hall (13,3,84). I had some very enthusiastic reviews of the event (but unfortunately in this nearly all interview issue we have no room to print then) and one of two sad reports of the evening.

I watched the beginning of the set, but after a while I wandered over to a distressed Smiths fan, who told me, in the conparative peace of the foyer, tales of gans passing out and new chairs being destroyed in the hysteria.

Apparently messages had been sent to the group after the second song, asking them to stop playing for a while so that the people who were injured, squashed or passing out could be helped.

Between us we scrawled a note to Morrissey, mentioning the possibility of an interview next time he is in Manchester (remember Manchester?), and also suggesting that he might have been able to prevent some of the damage at the gig. We handed the letter to a girl selling t-shirts and a few days later I recieved a reply:

is this man real?

Dear Karen,

I was obviously annoyed by your letter. It seems that whenever things go wrong at concerts people always blame the group.

Nobody told me about your fanzine at the ORS, so what exactly am I supposed to do?

Please don't give me the "remember Manchester" nonesense; not one living soul in Manchester ever helped the Smiths in our early days – our glorious radio stations, local press, music/media people, people from local record companies. Anything we have achieved we have absolutely earned, and we quite literally do not owe anyone anything.

I will always speak to fanzines whenever they care to speak to me. But

you are obviously entirely
unaware of our true natures and
ideals otherwise you would clearly
realise that I would have halted any
crowd unpleasantness had I been aware
of it. We have sensitive people
whose job it is to help people out of
the crowd should they need it. Frankly
I do not care about the chairs at
the free Trade Hall. Being criminally
NON-sighted, I can see no further
than 10-inches in front of me, I do
not ever recognise individuals in an
audience.

I do not want an interview with
your fanzine because you obviously
don't seriously care about me or the
Smiths. I don't enjoy being cross-
examined; there are OTHER people
to condemn, Karen ... aren't there?
Haven't we done any GOOD things??

Sadly — MORRISSEY

Karanoia '86 / I Hate Punks

Publication date: February 1987

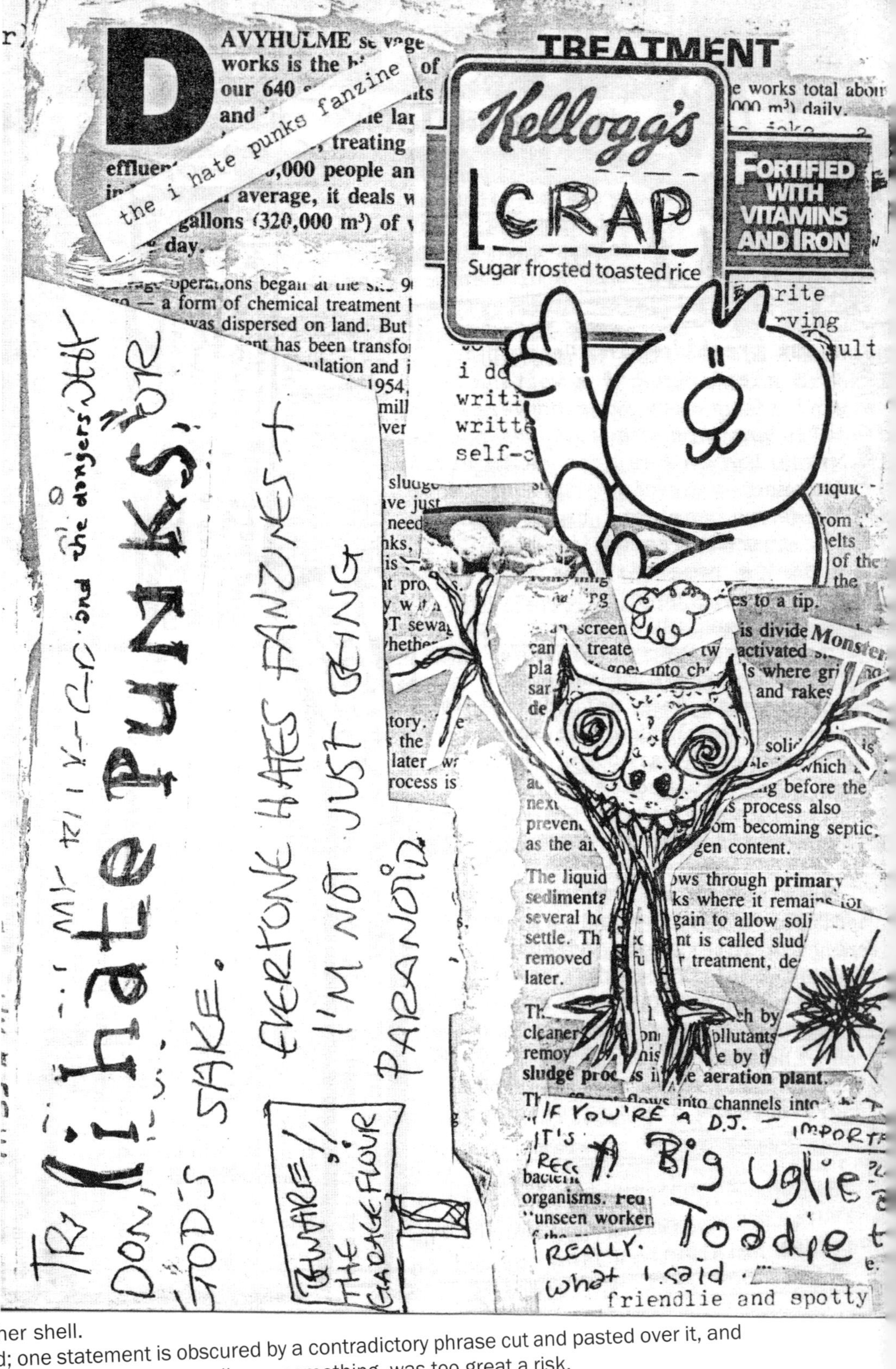

I left school at fifteen and went to a Catholic sixth form college in Moss Side for two disastrous terms. The other kids were cool but many of the staff were frightful, and after a suicide attempt I dropped out. This enabled me to enjoy the luxury of the dole for a few months, with its amazing free cash:free time ratio. I then got my ass in gear and returned to college, this time to a wonderful, and secular, Further Education establishment in Timperley, recognising it as a magic escape portal out of suburbia.

They let me do my A-levels in nine months, which was enervating and exactly what I needed. *Karanoia '86/ I Hate Punks* had been assembled in dole time, but it was this new college's stimulating and egalitarian atmosphere that enabled me to actually reveal my creation. All turned in on itself, full of double negatives and nom-de-plumes, it is the work of a girl only contemplating coming out of her shell. Everything in there is defended; one statement is obscured by a contradictory phrase cut and pasted over it, and that might be in brackets anyway. To commit, to actually say something, was too great a risk.

It opens with an interview with Piccadilly Radio DJ Tony Michaelides, or what I could remember of it as the cassette recorder had broken down. Mark Lemonade had a page to himself. There's a page slagging off my regular haunt, Cloud 9, a Manchester goth club I frequented with school friends including Clare Jackson, who contributed a cartoon. The rest is pretty much really lame gig reviews and teen angst poetry.

The amazing thing about this tiny zine was the reaction it received. In a fit of bravery I'd photocopied five copies in the college office. Damage limitation. But when I distributed them to friends in the cafeteria, a small miracle occurred. After 16 years of being ignored I was stunned to see these copies being snapped right up and then silently devoured by five sets of eyes. They even *talked* about it. Although I'd had no expectation that my lovingly-crafted work would be taken seriously, at that moment I understood that my words could have power - if I put them in print. I resolved to take advantage of this curious piece of good fortune, and marched right back to the college office to request 30 more copies. Thus began a somewhat addictive pattern of ever-increasing print runs in an exploration of how far I could take this thing - the experience of being heard.

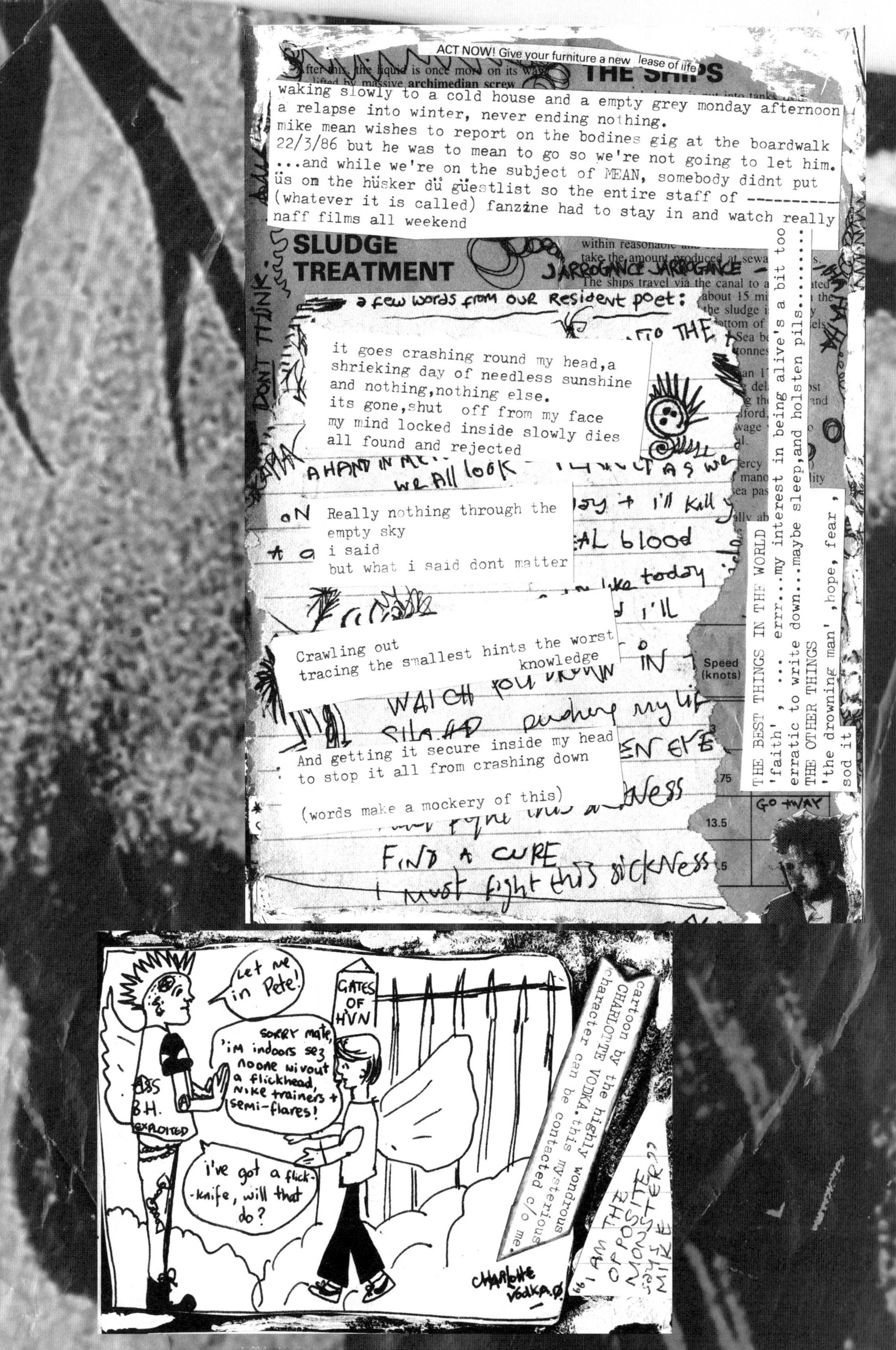
ACT NOW! Give your furniture a new lease of life
THE SHIPS
waking slowly to a cold house and a empty grey monday afternoon
a relapse into winter, never ending nothing.
mike mean wishes to report on the bodines gig at the boardwalk
22/3/86 but he was to mean to go so we're not going to let him.
...and while we're on the subject of MEAN, somebody didnt put
üs om the hüsker dü güestlist so the entire staff of ----------
(whatever it is called) fanzine had to stay in and watch really
naff films all weekend
SLUDGE TREATMENT
ARROGANCE ARROGANCE
DONT THINK
a few words from our Resident poet:
it goes crashing round my head,a
shrieking day of needless sunshine
and nothing,nothing else.
its gone,shut off from my face
my mind locked inside slowly dies
all found and rejected
Really nothing through the
empty sky
i said
but what i said dont matter
Crawling out
tracing the smallest hints the worst
knowledge
And getting it secure inside my head
to stop it all from crashing down
(words make a mockery of this)
FIND A CURE
I must fight this sickness
THE BEST THINGS IN THE WORLD
'faith' , ... err...my interest in being alive's a bit too
erratic to write down...maybe sleep,and holsten pils........
THE OTHER THINGS
'the drowning man' ,hope, fear ,
sod it
GO AWAY
Let me in Pete!
GATES OF HVN
sorry mate, 'im indoors sez noone wivout a flickhead, nike trainers + semi-flares!
i've got a flick-knife, will that do?
EXPLOITED
CHARLOTTE VODKA
cartoon by the highly wondrous CHARLOTTE VODKA.this mysterious character can be contacted c/o me.
"I AM THE OPPOSITE MONSTER" says MIKE

is an explanation required? i dont know, but i "wrote" this sometime in '86 and planned to get it printed... but then i knew how people in general (and in particular) would disapprove. so some got thrown away and some got lost, including some wondrous insights into the world arising from the dark workings of the brain of micheal mean. this is very sad and we are all worse off because of it.

in my home there is a place where the carrierbags dwell, and out from this place on this very night did seven pieces of paper emerge.this is the eighth,as unnecessary as the rest.i have nothing to say to the world in general, and only vague things to say to anybody in particular

seven pieces of paper for my imaginery friends.

much vagueness and some random particular thoughts

look out for dangerous and gentle monsters in these times they really do exist and are rewarding to observe. but some words-of-warning: the ones that are confined to the circles of plastic are safer and much more sociable (?.).especially the black circles of plastic. because real monsters can disturb your brain especially if you are nice to them

the beastie boys are OBNOXIOUS
Julian Cope is silly
but these people make songs to turn a sad dead mind into sheer life and joy

mark lemonade wrote the mark article

i wrote the rest except for the clare-honeypie cartoon (her name is not really honeypie, it is sweetie - yummyface)
and the snake poem which is fairly anonymous but well worth committing to memory.

these pages are worthless and precious

i cannot give apologies to no-one, i am not never going to hide.

love KARENA x

26.2.87

CONTACT:
34 FULMAR Drive
SALE
M33 4NH

this "fanzine" is called KARANOIA '86.

Made In Manchester

Summer 1987

Still at college, I discovered that a zine and cassette compilation would be a perfectly suitable project for my Communication Studies A-level, so from then on my study time was spent in pubs and practice rooms with Mancunian bands, doing interviews and getting tracks for the tape.

One of those bands was a clatteringly bombastic quartet from Didsbury called The Stone Roses. Singer Ian Brown and I were friendly when we both agreed that his band were amazing, but this situation was to change from my side when they altered course around the time of their second single. This interview is reprinted in *Ablaze!* 7, along with a few observations and reviews of some early gigs. I also added a bit of background to the interview itself:

"Arrived at Salisbury Ale House[1] 15 minutes late for an interview with a band that had their name scrawled in white paint all over the town (about two dozen people at the time accused me of doing it. I didn't, but I know a man who did...), who had released a single I loved, had committed many exciting rough psych rock songs to tape, had tormented me to screaming point with their detached, manic live shows, and were about to release their second single, the god-awful Sally Cinnamon. Previously I'd found Ian quite reasonable in conversation, yet when I switched on the tape recorder he adopted a determined arrogance and, along with John, proceeded to treat me with a mixture of sarcasm and contempt. Fitting treatment for a new fanzine with a readership one hundred strong? I knew not their vast intentions, or if I'd detected them in 'I Wanna be Adored' and in their blustering interview technique, I had chosen to ignore them."[2]

Another equally vibrant proposition was The Membranes, a band just as clatteringly bombastic but possessing different ambitions - coming from a DIY punk rock angle, the aim was to have as much fun as possible, and at their gigs we did. Dangerous swamp surfers Inca Babies had little to say to me; maybe I should have taken Justine along – she once told me of her plan to take them out on a picnic and feed them cucumber sandwiches. Tools You Can Trust were bashing metal and grunting pre-lingually, whilst The Bodines were crafting a unique flavour of Go-Betweens-inspired jangle pop.

With *Made In Manchester*, I was on a mission to celebrate the richness of the city's music scene, which was at the time largely ignored by the mainstream media. So many brilliant bands, and no-one was taking any notice; maybe my little A-level project zine could help in some way? Arranging meetings with local bands was fiendishly easy as most had made their addresses or phone numbers public. Everyone was so keen to get a little bit of attention, however low key, that they tolerated my deeply unimaginative questions; I wasn't exactly applying my critical faculties to the job, and mainly asked them about the provision of venues and other resources for bands in the city. My concern lay with the infrastructure – did these amazing bands have what they needed to survive?

The manager of one such venue, Colin Sinclair of the small and perfectly formed Boardwalk, furnished me with a bin bag full of demo tapes, which I lugged home on the bus and, having rescued the best one (an incredibly rare Walkingseeds demo) taped over the rest. One hundred copies of the zine-and-tape combo went out by mail order and to local record shops, and the Examining Board liked it so much they confiscated all my source materials. Maybe they knew something? In a few months I was to leave for Leeds, making a fortunate escape before the boy-dominated drug scene they called Madchester exploded in all its slack-mouthed, dead-eyed charmlessness.

The cover features the fountain which used to stand at the centre of Piccadilly Gardens, and I hold it to be the now-mythical fountain which Morrissey sung about reeling around. I'd commissioned Alison Martin to take the photo, and was dismayed to find that, at the time it was captured, the damn thing was switched off. After a little deliberation, I decided that that, like most anything, could be fixed with some well-placed Tipp-ex.

@@

SONGS ON THE TAPE:

SIDE ONE:

1. Emily - "What the fool said" (demo recorded 7.3.87 somewhere in Flint)
2. Stone Roses - "Sally Cinnamon" (demo recorded June '86 somewhere in Stockport)
3. Twang - "What's the rap?" (demo) *
4. Vee V V - "Keep beat" (recorded live at Thames poly 25.10.86)
5. Inca Babies - "Thirst" (demo)
6. Membranes - "Triple bad acid yeah"
7. Tools You Can Trust - "A brutal light"

SIDE TWO:

1. Membranes -"Spike Milligan's tape recorder" (recorded live at Lee Green Old Tiger's Head 4.4.84)
2. The Bodines - "Clear" (demo)
3. Bradford - "Saturday Insanity" (demo recorded February '87)
4. That Ted - "Will i end up soylent green?" (demo)
5. Soil - "Indifference" (demo)
6. Too Much Texas -"Infelice" (demo)
7. The Railway Children - "Another Town"

@@

All tracks appear by the nicest and kindest permission of the groups.

Wont be a free tape stuck to the front so if you want one
SAE to the address inside the front cover

1 I'd dated this as late 86 and as taking place at the Salisbury Ale House in Manchester City Centre, but I actually remember it as the City Roads Inn, and it must have been early 1987.

2 You'll find more Roses recollections later, on page 164.

Made in Manchester

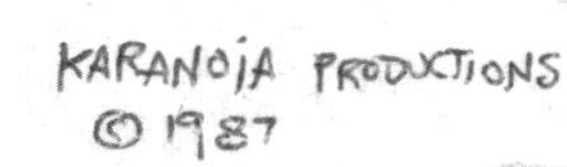

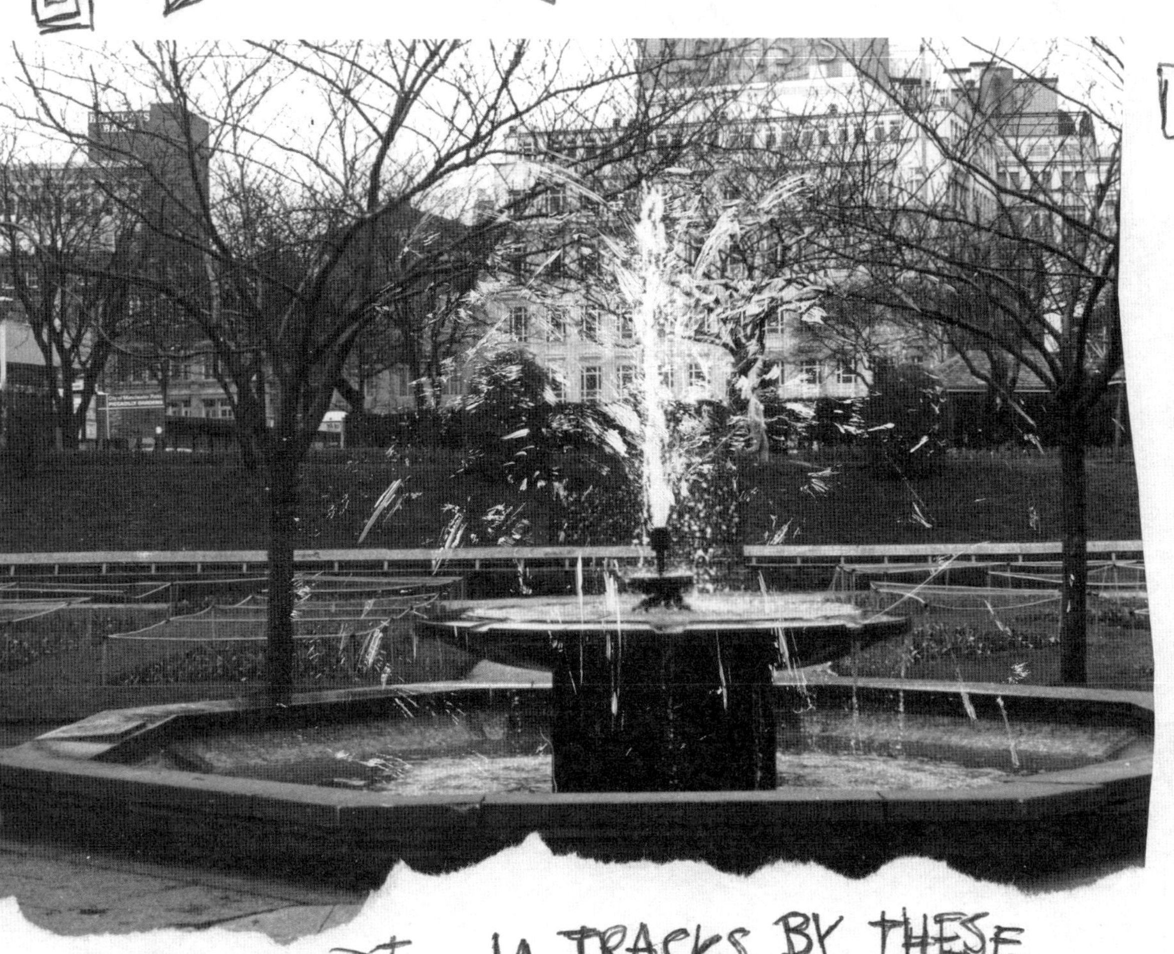

FREE TAPE · 14 TRACKS BY THESE BANDS :

INCA BABIES · SOIL · EMILY · BRADFORD · STONE ROSES · TOO MUCH TEXAS · VEE V V · RAILWAY CHILDREN · THAT TED · MEMBRANES · TWANG BODINES · TOOLS YOU CAN TRUST · * * * * * * * *

INCA BABIES

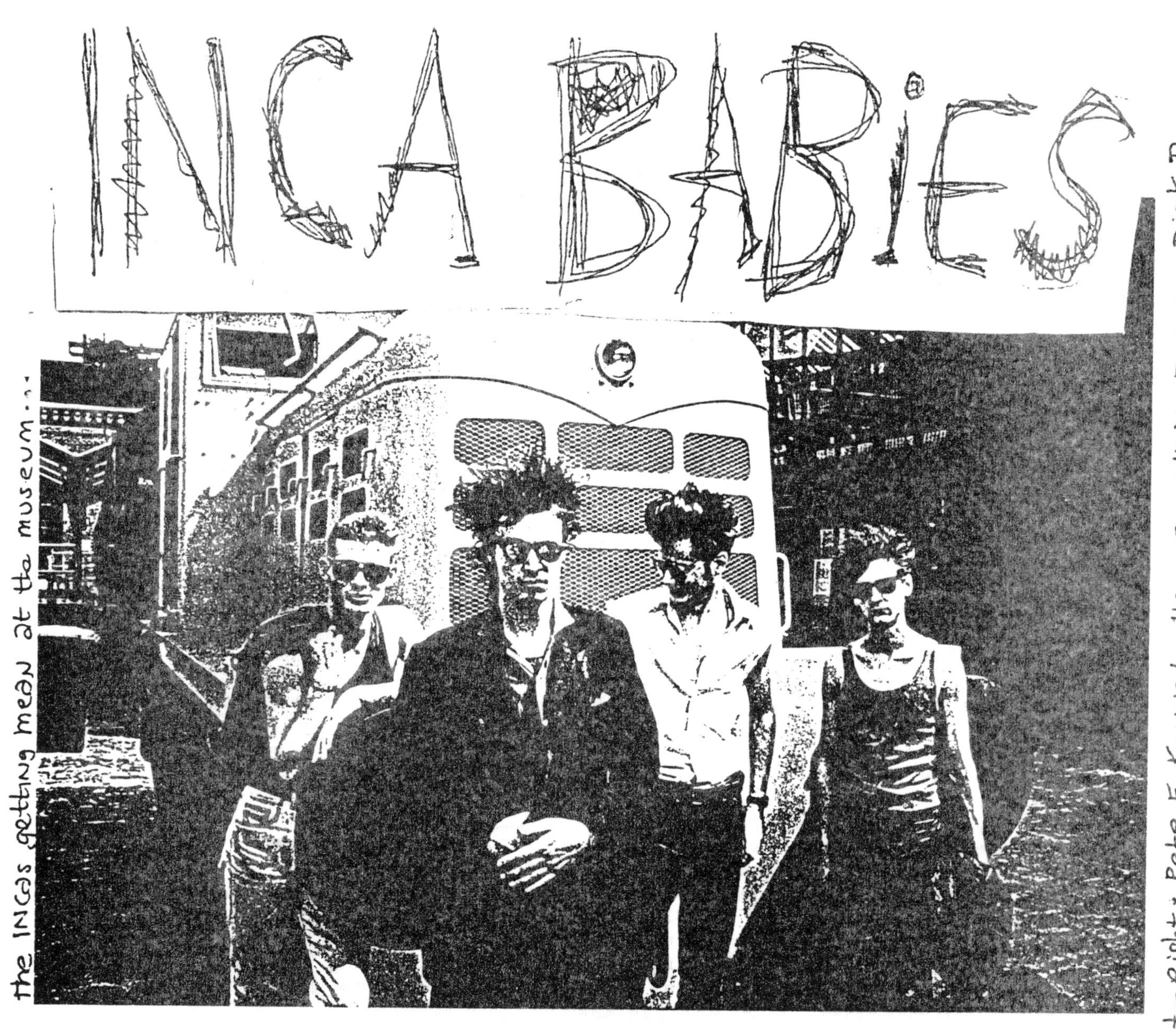

the INCAs getting mean at the museum...

...Left - Right: Pete F. Kennedy, Harry S, William Bonney, Dirk D.

In their rehearsal room at the bottom of the Boardwalk i hassled them with questions. Noise pounded through the walls so we could hardly hear what was going on.

Harry s.: Is upstairs any quieter?..no there's too many people milling about upstairs..Well, fire away!

K: D'you like any Manchester bands?

H: Yeah definitely the Fall. But most of them are the sort of shambling pop bands, anorak music, which i'm not too keen on.

K: There's not any others like the Inca Babies round here.

H: There aren't. There's a few up & coming bands...Big Ed & the Rocking Rattlesnakes are probably one of the better Manchester bands. The Slum Turkeys are okay. Manchester isn't a centre for our sort of music, although there are a lot of people that like it. People who start bands tend to do shambling anorak music.

K: How would you describe your sort of music?

H: Shambling noise !

K: Why've you had a line up change?

H: Our singer had a nervous disease so he just had to go. Now we've got Darren in and he's going the same way. No, actually he had to go back to college, which is a disease anyway.

K: What sort of things make you want to be the Inca Babies ?

D: The free beer you get on tour.

H: I think it's the fact that there aren't many bands like us There probably are in America and Europe, but in this country you could probably count the best ones on one hand. We're just waiting for our time to come round again.

Scene: Two-thirds of the Membranes & one soggy interviewer are seated around a table in what appears to be the nerve-centre of Membranes operations ...

John- You got a cold then?

Karen- yeah, it's because of all that rain...what manchester bands do you like?

J- err, iliked big flame, they were good.Most bands aren't really Manchesterbands,cos usually about half the band lives in manchester & the other half lives somewhere else any way.What other good bands are there Wallis?

Wallis -Dunno..

K-Are you the new person?

J-Yeah he's the new person.

K-How did you get him?

J-He was just wandering around and he ended up in the band.

W-I had nothing better to do.

J-He couldn't get into art school.

W-I didn't apply for art school.

J-He didn't apply for the membranes either..

K-You've been in loads of fanzines- does anyone ever get sick of it?

J-Probably,yeah.I get sick of reading interviews with me,

K-Have you had much criticism?

J-Loads,yeah.One or two fanzines spent the whole issue slagging us off which is even better than getting whole interviews-you just get a free load of publicity.It's quite funny because they totally misinterpret what we're doing which is quite good as well because we like people to misinterpret what we're doing.

K-What's the correct interpretation of what you're doing?

J-There isnt one really.We have a set idea of what we're doing and it's probably the opposite of what the music press think we are,because people like Seething Wells say we're a load of working class lads on the barricades,he said it'sa genuine proof that there's a working class art or something.We're all dead middle class so it's quite funny.

K-Do you like living in manchester?

J-It's better than living in Blackpool,except it rains all the time.

K-Does it rain more here than in Blackpool?

J-Yeah,it's the wettest city in Europe.

K-I thought it would rain more in Blackpool cos it's near the sea isn't it?

J-Manchester's in the hills though, isn't it.It's just damp in Blackpool Ithink the clouds go over Blackpool & they bump into the hills where Manchester is & it rains on Manchester...we escaped from Blackpool a couple of years ago.We've only been back about twice,it's so depressing

K-What sort of things make you want to write songs?

J-Just about everything really.That isn't a deliberately vague answer, all our songs are about everything anyway,mainly things that you do or see or things that get on your nerves.

K-Why did you leave creation?

J-Cos we didnt want to wear anoraks.

K-Honest?

J-No,we had an argument with them over this gig.We were headlining but they decided to make it a Slaughter Joe gig so we ended up going on first,& no one had actually come to see Slaughter Joe,& loads of people missed us,so we went back on at the end.There was a big row & everyone was drunk,& Slaughter Joe said he was going to break our legs,so we said"if you want to break our legs, come on stage & break our legs", which he didnt do, & then he got like a bit heavy afterwards...they didnt actually sack us from the label,but about a week later we rang up & they wouldnt speak to us,& we found out from somebody else that we werent on the label anymore. P.T.O.

Go to Page 32

Not the easiest people in the world to interview, the Stone Roses sat round a table in the Salisbury ,and for the most part treated me with a mixture of sarcasm and contempt.Perhaps this is just their way, or perhaps me getting there 15 minutes late had annoyed them...but i think that it is worth a try to break through their arrogance to see what's underneath...oh well, here goes...

K:Do you like any Manchester bands?

Ian:All of them.

K (astonished):including,say,Simply Red and Easterhouse?

I:They're me favourites.

Faced with this lack of co-operation i decide to ask them their opinions on Manchester's venues.

Rene:There's enough of them.

John:There's nothing between the Boardwalk and the Hacienda..

K:Except some trafficlights.(couldn't resist that).

J:In SIZE.

K:Colin Sinclair at the Boardwalk said he'd asked you to play there and that you turned him down...twice.

I:We dont wanna play little places like that.It makes you look like a little group if you play little places.That's why we played the uni and bigger places - so that it makes you look like a bigger group.

R:The reason we dont play the Boardwalk is that half the audience wouldn't get in- it only holds about 200- it's too small.

K:I like small places like that.There the stage is only a few inches above the rest of the place.It doesnt separate you from the band.

J:You wouldnt like it if you were stuck outside the door trying to get in.

I:I think it's a good thing that the stage separates the band and the audience,cos if you're paying to see someone you don't want to think "they're the same as me" do you?

Well, i do actually but there seems little point in pursuing it so i don't...

K:How helpful have the local press and radio been?

R:If it wasn't for Piccadilly radio we'd be playing the Boardwalk.

I:We've not done anything that the press can write about for a year.

R:We've got a lot of enemies, certain writers that we don't kiss the arse of.

I:A lot of people wont write about us cos we don't join in with local band things - we dont go to the Boardwalk and play festivals, cos we dont wanna support band in our own town.We do support bands but we dont support anyone in Manchester.We never have.

K:I heard you sacked your manager and got thrown off your record label.

R:We sacked the record label as well.

I:The record label was half ours, half the manager's and half the producer's (?!) and we didn't want to work with them anymore.

R:Cos the manager couldn't manage and the producer couldn't produce...

J:We didn't have a lot to go on really.

K:Was Gareth at the International your manager?

I:He's our manager now.

K:Who was the manager before?

I:He was called Howard Jones - he used to manage the Hacienda.

R:He tried to run us like he ran the Hacienda and they sacked him too.

K:Your new tape (demo of Sally Cinnamon and others) sounds really different.Is it because you've got a new person in the group?

I:No, it's because we've learnt how to write songs.

K:I thought the old stuff was really good.
I:It was at the time,but you've gotta move on.
K:You used to sound totally original but now it sounds...
R:..poppier by the minute.
K:Yeh.Did you plan it to be that way?
I:No,it was a natural progression.All them original songs that you like are crap cos they're all just punk songs, and now they're songs with a bit of tune, so perhaps you don't like songs that've got tunes.

Perhaps i don't then.At this point Madonna is singing very loud out of the jukebox.
I:D'you think you can hear us with that thing going?
K:Dunno.Can't you turn them down?
I:Dunno.Could throw a coat over it or something...
K:..Oh, you'll just have to shout.
I:OK.

K:Why have you only had one single out?
I:We put the single out with Thin Line and we didn't want to do anything else with them ,so we did some gigs, we did some demos, we got some record deal offers, we picked a record company and now we're on Revolver.We're just doing a single for them now.It takes a long time.
K:Who else is on Revolver?
I:They were a heavy metal label and now they've branched out into the independent market.They used to have heavy metal bands.They're based in the Midlands.

K:You took your name from "Titus Groan" didn't you?
R:No.
I:Who?
K:The book by Mervyn Peake.
I:We read that in a quiz but it wasn't true.John thought it up.
K:Why? Why are you called the Stone Roses?
J:Cos of the influences of the group - some are really soft like Simon & Garfunckel sorta thing, and some are really hard like the Pistols.
I:There's a actual book called "The Stone Roses" which we found about a year after the group started.
R:It's just coincidence.

K:What's "heart on the staves" about?
I:I can't remember.We don't do that one anymore.

K:What's a "garageflower"?
I:Garageflower? 'E thought it up.Ask 'im.
J:Same thing as a stone rose.
K:It's a good word.
J:It's TWO words.

K:When's the single coming out?
I:Sometime in February."Sally Cinnamon"-don't you like that one?
K:I wish i did.Are you planning an LP?
I:Yeah, but we don 't know when it's coming out.
K:Are you going to do any gigs?
I:The next gig's at the International on January 30th.
k:Yeah? Do you have some sort of group image? you were all wearing the same stipey shirts at the uni.
I:No, it was accidental. We all went out and bought the same shirts.We're gonna wear diamond ones at the International.

...And, sure enough, they did.The place was completely packed, which was probably something to do with the fact that nobody had to pay to get in - it seemed that half of Manchester were on the guestlist.Apart from the funny way that John seemed to be playing guitar, which really bugged me,it was a fairly brilliant gig.Don't ever miss a chance of seeing the Stone Roses live.

TRUST

toolsyoucantrust

TOOLS TO TRUST

Tools You Can Trust got their name from an advert in a 1950's magazine.As they tell me:"It just said "Spear & Jackson, Tools to trust" so we changed it to Tools you can trust.We thought it was good.It's on the telly now."

I sat in a Yate's wine lodge in town with Rob and Ben of the group.It was very early on a saturday afternoon and i was feeling ill.Through a haze of terribleness i discovered that a noisy group can be made up of very quiet people.Perhaps it should have been obvious to me, but without microphones and instruments they are nearly inaudible.

To begin with, i try to find a basis for my preconceived idea that they dont appear to be in it for the money...so:

K:Have you got jobs or is the group a full time thing?

Ben:He's got a job.

K:From what i've seen you dont seem to be too bothered about making money from the group.

Ben:Oh yeah, we are really.

K:Well a couple of your gigs that i went to were free and at one of them i bought a record off you for 50p...

Ben:Who sold that? Who sold that?!

Rob:it was probably us,we probably couldn't sell any.

Ben:Where was that- at the cornerhouse?

K:Nah,it was at the uni.

Rob:That was free cos we got paid anyway,we got a set fee.

K:And the Castlefield Carnival...

Ben:Oh that,we got 150 quid for that.

K (shocked):Why?

Ben:Cos we're good!(puts on "annoyed ratepayer voice") The council are wasting my money on these gigs!

Rob:Ah, so you were at Castlefield? We were a bit duff there.

I decide to ask them about their videos that were shown at the Boardwalk in October...

Rob:We made the videos because we had the chance to.Ikon just asked us to do it.It was good fun.The first bit was done about 3 years ago by some friends of Ben's in London.

K:Are you pleased with the results?

Rob:oh yeah.

Ben:It's dead good.

That's good.It seems to me that Tools You Can Trust like what they do and that's why they do it.They'd like more people to hear them and buy their records,but as they say:"We dont really get enough publicity or enough gigs...that's what we fall down on really."

TOOLS TO TRUST

toolsyoucantrust

TRUST

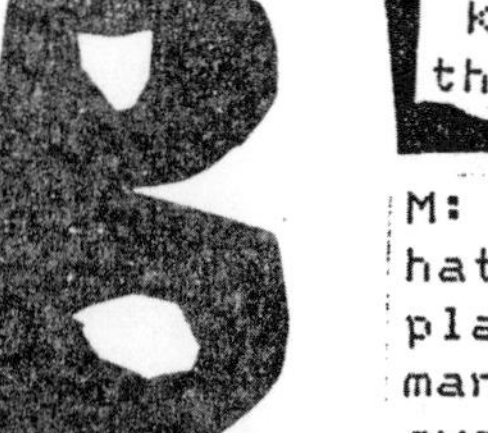

BODiNES

I interviewed Mick Bodine (better known as micheal Ryan) in a terrible building before the beginning of a party that the group were to play at.We started in the "bar",were driven downstairs to a room full of guitars because of the noise that pounded through the walls.and moved again at the threat of being locked in.We ended up in a dark chairless corner of the room where we started.Despite all the hassle that surrounded it, i was very lucky to get a Bodines interview as the group had been quite unnobtainable and, as you'll see,are required to be in London a lot of the time.That night was to be their only Manchester "gig" for a while.

K: You spent some time touring with New Order in Canada recently - did you find that you were known over there?

M: Not really.Some people had heard of us.The first night we got there somebody shouted for "Scar Tissue" which was a bit wierd.The audiences are really receptive cos they've got no preconceptions about bands, they're open to you.We went down really well over there - we don't go down that well over here when we're headlining places.

K: D'you think you could do better living elsewhere?

M: We could do better living in London, but nobody wants to live in London.It would be really practical, cos i've got to go down and stay there all next week and we've got two gigs, and interveiws and photographs ,it's just to show your face at the record company or they'll forget they've got you.I don't like London very much.It's unfriendly - it's the only place where you could stand that close to someone (holds his hand in front of his face) and they could look away from you.You'd be chatting if it was round here, or anywhere else for that matter.

K: What're your opinions on the venues round here ?

M: I think it varies.I hate the International.We've played there god knows how many times and it gets worse every time.The audiences get better but i'm just getting sick of places like that, It's so nightclubby.You have to show your backstage pass - if you walk ten yards someone jumps out from behind a pillar - they only bother the bands about it.The Boardwalk should be better than it is but no-one seems to go anymore.I went to see the Wild Swans there.I thought it'd be packed so i bought a ticket in advance, but there was only about 50 people there.I was really disappionted cos it was probably the best gig i've seen there.

K: How d'you think the local press and radio have treated you?

M: I think Piccadilly radio've been dead good - they played "Therese" in the day and they played "Heard It All" a few times in the daytime.Local press...Muze is a pathetic magazine, it's so opinionated.

There was an interview with us in there and he didn't tell us who he was from, he was trying to make out he was from some fanzine or something, and he just tore us apart in print.We were slagging the Mighty Lemon Drops off, more out of habit than anything, and he said "but they can fill out the International" - WE can fill out the International.He said we were playing the small bar at the university, but we played the night before in Rochdale and there was quite a few there, it was full at the university, and we played the Boardwalk the night after and that sold out, so that must amount to as much as the International easily.

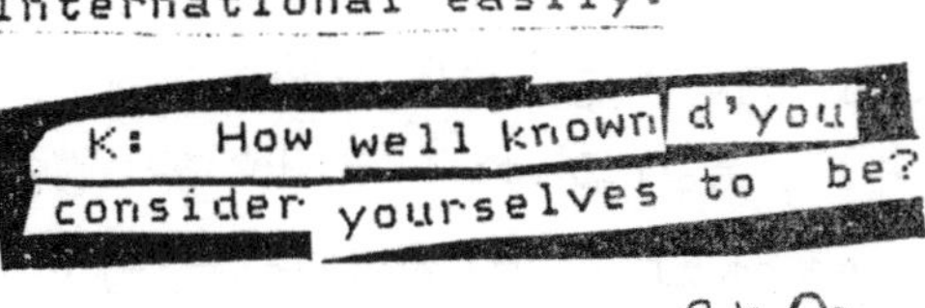

K: How well known d'you consider yourselves to be?

p.t.o.

More Bodines

M: That's really hard to tell. A friend of mine came over from London and she said we're dead well known there, but it doesn't seem like it to me - i go to the same pubs, the same places, i've just got more money to go there.

K: Reading an interview with you in Debris, i got the impression that it all happened by accident...

M: Well it did, we were doing it as a hobby. It still happens by accident. It's a pain in the arse having to arrange all the gigs so we got a manager in, and we ended up signing to Magnet and leaving Creation. We weren't getting a lot of money for recording, no more than the other acts were, and we were making better records than them so we left in the end, we were sick of it.

K: What was it like being on Creation?

M: It was alright at first but it got a bit funny after a while cos we never went down to London very much except when we played there, and we never saw eye to eye with any of the other acts on Creation and i didn't particularly like Alan McGhee. He got a bit funny...when we started arguing about things you heard things that he'd been saying about you. Before we decided to leave properly we heard that he'd phoned these people and said that we were going nowhere and that we're really shit. He said we'd never get anywhere with our attitude, but i think we might prove him wrong. I don't know, he's a turd. He was pissed off at the time cos the Marychain'd sacked him. He seemed to be going mad, he was dead ill and everything. We're uncontrolled, everybody hates us. You meet people to do with the business and they're a bit wary of us cos they've heard that you're arkward and stuff, but it's not true. It doesn't help having your press officer saying things about you smashing the record company offices up and stealing things, which was partly true, y'know, all we did was i stole a David Bowie picture, this signed Man who fell to earth poster, and he got pissy about it but we gave it him back.

K: What are your plans for '87 ?

M: We're starting the album in February so that'll be out in March. We've remixed "Therese" cos we wanted to release it on an E.P. with other tracks, we might include "Heard It All" on it as well. We just wanna get it out of the way, and record all of our present set for an album, and then we'll have a clean slate to work with, and then we'll just do a tour after that.

Membranes continued:

W-That was the same week the Pastels left cos they were involved in it too.

K-Why didnt you put the LP out on Vinyl Drip?

J-cos i cant afford to go into the studio-£1,500 is a lot of money.

K-Is it nice being on Intape?

J-It's alright yeah. I mean labels are labels, we're never at home on any label. When we were on Creation at the start, that's the closest we've ever been to being on a label with a load of other bands who were similar to us but it just got cackier & cackier...i mean he had stuff like the L Loft, well their single's alright, but the Weather Prophets...he started getting some really bad stuff on the label & we started feeling out on a limb again. On Intape they've got stuff like Frank Sidebottom which is not very close to what we're doing. I like to be on a label with similarish sorts of bands doing the same sot of things, & Creation was good at the beginning of '85 cos there was loads of noisy bands & we felt at home.

W-Five go down to the sea were on it

J-And the Moodists were on it, & the Marychain.

K-You've had a lot of line up changes havent you?

J-No, not really when you compare it to other bands. We've had the same 2 people in the band right from the beginning..

K-Is that you & Sid?

J-Yeah, & we've had Walliss this year & Stan the year before & Tills 2 years before that, & we were a 4 piece at first. It's not an awful lot of line up changes if you compare it with other bands like the Fall, they've had about 30 members. We've had about 9 people through the band over the years. We don't like being static, with one thing all the time, we like to keep changing our sound all the time, which we can do now, cos we've got Walliss who's a jazz-funk bass player- he could play bass for 7 days before he joined the band

W-14 years really..

K-Do you prefer playing live or making records?

J-I like both really, i like playing the guitar really loud through an amplifier & if someone's going to pay me to do it i'll keep doing it.

28th issue of John's wild fanzine ROX is out now; 40p & SAE from 87 Anchorsholme lane Blackpool, or buy it in a shop...just BUY IT.

RECORD SHOP SKULKERS

Maybe it doesn't happen anymore; there just aren't so many record racks to skulk around now. But back in the last century, record shops provided a free space for broke and lonesome youngsters to exist outside of the tedious glare of the mundane; they were a portal to other, more fascinating worlds.

Record shops also functioned as spaces where you could hear sounds; grown-ups with money were able to purchase the sounds and take them home, but kids with no pence had to be there at the same time and place as the sounds were coming out of the speakers if they really wanted to hear them.

For a couple of years from the release of their debut LP in 1982, I liked to spend my spare time in such retail outlets, guarding the Scritti Politti 12"s. There were several of them and they were very beautiful[1] - it was a pursuit I engaged in with great vigour. I'd wait until someone touched one of them, or even brushed their fingers on the divider with the band's name stuck on the top in Dymo tape, and then I would ask them The Question. It was not a question of any great profundity – not to regular ears anyway. Neither was it one of any acuity. The Question was simply: "Do you like Scritti Politti?" It was my very own dubious method for screening humanity. If the answer was "No" or "Who?", accompanied by a startled withdrawal of the hands, there was no need for me to continue the conversation.

But if they said yes, then all that lurking had been worthwhile. I might even have a new friend. We clearly had a great deal to talk about, and I would have no qualms about wandering home with that person. Of course I met some dodgy characters as a result. Justine Wolfenden - not dodgy - answered in the affirmative, and we have orbited around each other ever since.

I'm not sure I would recommend this as a practice for any other vulnerable teenager. Of course, you can do this with any band, but you're more likely to get locked up for it these days. And who else did this stuff anyway? I searched for a similarly deviant skulker and found Geraldine. "My prime place of hanging out for several years was Jumbo Records," she told me. "I didn't have an established taste in music nor much money and they had a sort of reduced price box, like you get in supermarkets for things that are past their best. I used to mainly skulk around this, and despite many purges of my record collection to keep it transportable, some ten pence gems remain. There's something magical about an underused vinyl record, like an unloved book or hat. I used to hide in the booth where you can listen to records without buying them, loitering, reading flyers and fanzine type things."

There must be more ex-record shop lurkers out there, deranged individuals who spent their teenage years haunting record shops, listening to music for free, and pestering the

Geraldine, master skulkstress

Jumbo Records, Leeds

Photo: Tony Woolgar

staff and patrons. Reading his epilogue to this book, it sounds like Gary Jarman might've been one.

I had this one special haunt, and it remains my all-time favourite record shop. Piccadilly Records is now situated on Oldham Street, in Manchester's bohemian Northern Quarter, but its first home was a few hundred yards away, on the outside of Piccadilly Plaza, and it was my number one top spot for skulking. Martin has worked there for 28 years, and remembers me hanging around back then. "You were just known as Scritti Politti Karren," he says. The duration of his tenure there is one testament to how cool a place it is - the staff have always been incredibly friendly, they stocked all the vinyl anyone needed, and they tolerated me and my monotonous conversation topic. I asked him if there are still people who do that now.

"There probably aren't the number of obsessives there used to be. There are still music obsessives that hang around looking for inspiration. Now, with the website, they can check things out on there, so I think that helps them to satisfy their curiosity before they come in."

I don't think that would fulfil the same emotional needs, and wonder if Martin's ever considered that there is some sort of social care function involved?

"Less so, again, than it used to be. People seem to be a wee bit more focused now. We do get people who are slightly unbalanced, but then again, even they understand that we have things to do. The eighties was a time of really big indie bands: post-punk, and then bands like The Smiths, ending up with The Stone Roses, and these were areas and bands that people became obsessed about. That's not really the case anymore, there's some amazing music around at the moment, but there's such a vast variety of it. People just seem generally to like music; there are no obvious groups to be obsessed by. You're not going to get people feeling the same way about First Aid Kit as they do about The Smiths or The Stone Roses. Those bands were relatively inventive - they weren't just good, they weren't just smart, they were original. That doesn't tend to happen so much now. Even bands like Metronomy, they're brilliant but they are a mish mash of styles."

I tell him that I'm heartened to see that there is still an array of fanzines laid out on the counter here.

"Yes, and again, that culture has changed. There are less of them, and if they are around they're probably very, very underground. We used to be inundated by fanzines of all kinds: indie fanzines, football fanzines, whatever, but that's just not the case now. People tend to want to consume music rather than create."

1 The three singles from Scritti Politti's debut album, *Songs to Remember*, were modelled on famously-branded consumer products. 'Faithless' was Dior Eau Sauvage, 'Asylums In Jerusalem' was Courvoisier brandy, and 'The "Sweetest Girl"' was Dunhill cigarettes – all strange, mysterious, grown- up things...

Ablaze!
1, 2, 3

Ablaze!

Publication date: Autumn 1987

The word *Ablaze!* appeared in my mind whilst listening to a Julian Cope record. I used it to name myself, and then the zine. Fast to produce, fast to read, this debut boasts two so-called interviews and lots of bad typing.

The Pastels played the Boardwalk and I'd ambled backstage with only two questions, but Stephen agreed to be interviewed on the spot. Getting answers was less easy due to interruptions by a boy from another fanzine and a young Smiths fan, but I can still hear Stephen's replies in his downtrodden Glaswegian drawl. The Inspiral Carpets were only too delighted to be featured; they were young, newly-formed, and rather excitable.

There's a review of my first ever Sonic Youth gig, hazardously located the night before one of my Sociology A-level exams; I didn't really know what was going on. Dave Haslam from *Debris* fanzine had put on the show, and his office was sometimes a port of call on my Saturday afternoon drifts around town. When I told him I didn't own any of their records, his eyes filled with compassion and he handed me his own battered copy of *Sister*. Still, revising left me with little time to absorb that album's storm-smashing treble-textured urgency and I felt out of my depth when I saw them play at the New Ardri Ballroom with fIREHOSE. I attended other shows under the guidance of older scenesters and before I understood the bands' work; Big Black played one of their last shows at the Boardwalk but all I saw were the hard, unyielding backs of many men, with a noise like a car crash coming from behind them. I was on much more familiar terrain with The Cure, and gave their latest LP a double-page review in which I incorrectly stated that "this group know what they're doing and they'll know when to stop."

There's also a review of Glastonbury 1987, which I attended with my best school friend, Jo McCarton. To get there, we hitched hundreds of miles through the night, and had no trouble getting past stoned security. What I don't mention was how I wandered into a field on the first afternoon and met two strange men who gave me acid and then kidnapped me. Our muddy adventures crescendoed with Julian Cope's ascent to heaven from the main stage. The mysterious men turned out to be the singer and drummer of The Janitors, a band that, having thus enchanted me, went on to receive far too much coverage in subsequent issues.[1]

Ablaze! 1 was funded by the British government - they just didn't know it. At age 16, I'd dropped out after two disastrous terms at a Catholic sixth form college and gone on the dole. It was brilliant; they gave you money every fortnight, so I was able to save up the printer's fee of £27. The first printer I gave the originals to did nothing with them; I hadn't made copies and he had my money. After an anxious few weeks I got them back and took them to a resource centre in North Wales. They were cheap and friendly, but insisted that I Tipp-Ex out any areas of black that would somehow obstruct the printing process. I still don't know why they made me do that, but it was enough to tone down the cover's blazing sun, reducing its rays to fluffy white-out wings. No matter; their low rates meant I had enough money left over to offer a free gift.

"I draw a picture and then, I climb into it. I am a whirl of colour, the noisiest girl, the terriblest exploding monster. I'm a plastic cover with nothing inside... a blank screen and I show wild pictures. You look at me in surprise, so I reply with a stare of fake sincerity, holding in all the noise and laugh. But the noise and laugh gets out anyway and I roar and run, break my body against the walls to see what I look like, and fly, and pretend I have no care..."

I think I was starting to get happy.

[1] My diary of the event included several pages of stage times and live reviews, but then the writing stopped abruptly and this drawing appeared. The central figure is Julian Cope onstage, and I'm not so sure who all the other characters are, or why I drew an axe.

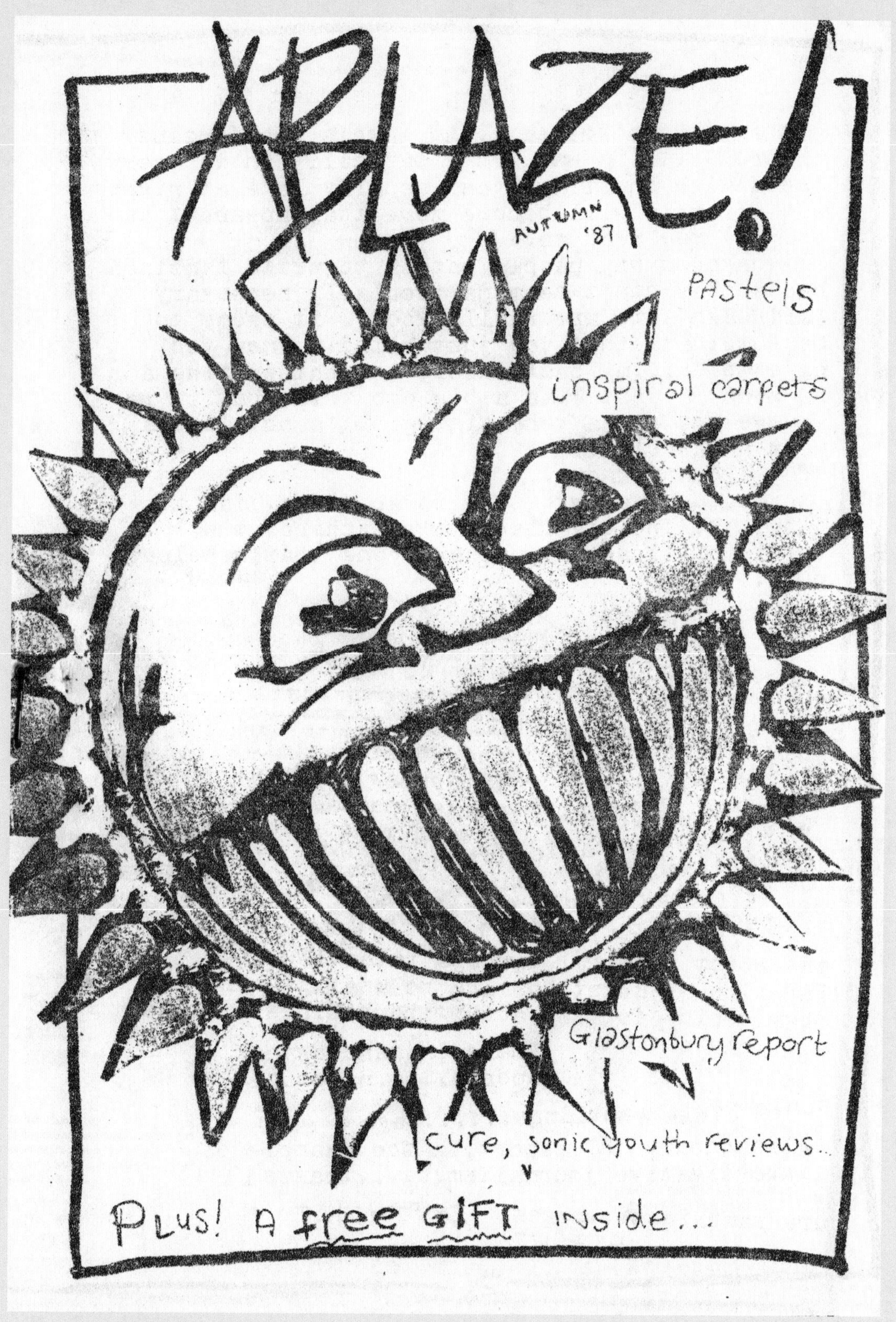
ABLAZE!
AUTUMN '87
pastels
inspiral carpets
Glastonbury report
cure, sonic youth reviews...
PLUS! A free GIFT inside...

summer '87

the city is ablaze...and here's the fanzine to prove it. it was wrote basically in $1\frac{1}{2}$ weeks typed with one finger and usually late at night but all this will become more than apparent as (or if) you read on.

i wondered why people bother to write fanzines becos they don't seem particularly necessary (although some are really good). it seems to be something that you just blindly know you have to do...my best theory is that writing a fanzine is just like a big ego trip, but if you've not got a very big ego it's not like a very good trip...

but i don't know...

thanks to mark w, steve ideal diane, ian h, deby, jo, the big black time machine, the bottle of tippex & just everyone that's helped out.....

+dave haslam!

see you,

KARREN

KARREN ABLAZE XXX

YOUR VERY OWN DEAD ACE + SPECIAL ABLAZE! GUIDE TO HOW TO KEEP WARM THIS AUTUMN....

Take your free gift in one hand and strike the coloured end against a brick or a zip or a friendie's face. bring the flaming match to the bottom righthand corner of this page (marked ✱!!) and give it a few seconds to get going. for extra effect, first sprinkle the pages with a bit of petrol...

FREE GIFT

OR, ALTERNATIVELY-
go to the boardwalk,and you will feel warm in your heart when an impoverished student approaches you with the pitiful plea "got a light?".you can hand him/her your ablaze free gift and assure yourself that this truly generous act will have benefitted a fellow human being...err,i mean student

2

the Gig everyone's writing about-

Sonic Youth New Ardri Ballroom June '87

the location- a ballroom in hulme, plastic trees and all...the kids weren't used to this...the bouncers ain't used to kids...england late 80's- baseball hats, swig american lager, a fair cross section of manchester youth gather, chat and go"yo"..

firehose worked bloody hard, no-one could deny that.manchester enjoys and yells more...no nonsense or wackyness, just pure elite rock'n'roll, competent and tight.

sonic youth, also tight tonight, played tracks off "sister", some off "evol"...moore's guitar whirling and speeding, i thought something must burst at one stage...FASTER, LOUDER...sonic youth prove they're one of the world's best. no-one sound like s.y. so don't try and tell me nothing

(Mark Whip Me & Go Moo)

gig review so far (transcribed from a beermat)-
the band havent come on stage yet. the new ardri ballroomis a gorgeous low room with a tiny stage that's surrounded by bingo lights. all floorspace is crammed with freaky people & fanzines are changing hands at a nicely rapid rate.i never washed my hair, not for ages., which pehaps i shouldn't have but it doesn't actually matter. firehose are playing "like REM meets big flame but not verrie interesting to look at." the descriptive bit comes from steve idea as i cant catually write gig review (you never guessed??.)

can't catually spell-either

S O N I C Y O U T H played with wildness & passion.
joyful dancing occured under the plastic flowers there is something very serious and important about this band but i don don't know what it is.
THE MADNESS OF FRIENDIES etc...why do they insist on saying "hello" to the taperecorder when i switch it on? it isnt a lonely taperecorder, truly, i do give it lots of attention...
THE UNFAIRNESS OF LIFE etc at 22 minutes to 1, as the strains of white cross entered my ears, i left the place in the interests of my brain.somehow it seemed sensible, although dead heartbreaking, to get to bed & get some sleep.
why do I have to be a member of the pathetic race of students? why do s.y. come to manchester the night before sociology paper 2?WHYYYYYYYYYYY???

the city is ablaze.

it is indeed

some thoughts:

GIG REVIEWS seem like pretty much totally futile things to do. in my case at least, whether i enjoy a gig or not depends more on how i feel at the time than on how well the band actually play.any report is therefore going to be dead subjective...it's like i'd prefer to see emily playing really "badly" at the boardwalk than see some group get everything technically perfect in front of thousands of people.
and due to my short attention span i tend to hate bands that go on for more than 40 minutes, unless they're really "brilliant" (and my criteria for what is brilliant is unlikely to be the same as yours becos no-one has the same musical taste as a anyone else.)
what i'm trying to say is, there's no point in me writing a proper gig review becos there's no point in anybody taking my word for what actually happened (& i cant-write reviews anyway).

never!!

A SPECIALLY SPECIAL THANK YOU TO RHYL COMMUNITY AGENCY WHO HAS ENABLED YOU TO READ THIS THING (they printed it!)

A BIG NO THANK YOU TO KARL BUSHELL.....

3

MELTDOWN PLAYLIST → Listen to Meltdown on monday nights 9-10, Radio manchester 95.1 v.h.f, 206 m.w.

1. public enemy-
rebel without a pause
2. dub sex-tripwire
3. annie anxiety-
as i lie in your arms
4. firehose-
brave captain
5. shaunie g-
mission impossible
6. phil wilson-
10 miles
7. slab- smoke rings
8. B52's- wig
9. stone roses-
sally cinnamon
10. t la rock-
this beat kicks

EMILY

emily are well into flexidiscs at the moment- they'll be in no idea! 2 (steve fanzine is a impostor) playing "what the fool said" & "the old stone bridge"...also, the sha la la label are putting "the old stone bridge" out with a tra track by a group called remember fun, and you can get that in the next issue of are you scared to get happy? they recently did a excellent gig at the boardwalk and they'll be playing somewhere in sheffield on july 24th (at the groovy fishtank actually)

this is supposed to be on page 8 or 9...

P A S T E L S

steven pastel was stood quietly cradling a tin of lager backstage at the boardwalk when i tumbled in and attempted to interview him. it was after a wonderful weekend, as the pastels had played there on both saturday an sunday, with the membranes as well on the saturday & john robb joining them on stage both nights for the encores...

i had 4 questions in my head, the 1st being:

k- how come you're so '''''' brilliant?

s-it's the glasgow water, it's a lot softer y'see, it's kind of druggy.

the candyfloss fanzine writers were there so they helped out with my near lack of quetions:

a candyfloss boy: are you into all acid 'n'all that ,or is that just a big hype?

s- i don't take it that often, my mind's okay.

a.c.b.-you mean you only take it when you get your dole checque?

s- no, i'm not on the dole, but...

a.c.b.-have you got a spare can of lager?

a.c.b.-what d'you think of girls with pink hair?

k-sod off

a.c.b.-what d'you think of no idea fanzine?

s- i've not seen it.

4

ABLAZE!

a.c.b.-have you seen a fanzine called candyfloss?

s- no.

k-who wrote that?

a.c.b.- we did.

k- last question (i forgot the other 2)-my friendie says why didnt you play "address book"?

s- oh, we cant play every thing everytime.

k-you cant, it's true right.have you enjoyed being in manchester?

s- oh yeh.

k-what did you do?

s-we played the membranes at football.

a.c.b.-everybody plays the membranes at football.

k-you cant have done that all day..

s- no, we stayed in bed in the morning.

a.c.b.-isit flattering being a sex symbol?

s-oh yeh, yeh.

a.c.b.- when are you going to get married, or is that an impossible question?

s- yes that's impossible

k- when are you goi g to come back to manchester?

s- i dont know.

k-it's dead bad, i never thought this weekend would end and it has, it it's dead sad.

a.c.b.-arrrrr wot time is it?

k- it's 11 o'clock exact. thanks for this interview.

a.c.b.-(to the taperecorder)ca dyfloss is ace right!

INSPIRAL CARPETS

i went to see the inspirals supporting crazyhead at the boardwakk in may. they played dead well, each song getting better than the one before, & i was eager to talk to them afterwards to try to find out what they're about.

the interview took place (as usual) in the board walk which was dead noissy making it impossible for me to differentiate between the voices of most members of the band when i played the tape back afterwards, specially when they all talked at once...so their replies will be presented as if the whole group said them.

the inspiral carpets are (l-r in the photo): graham ste, clint, scott, & craig.

k- how did you get to do the debris flexi?

inspiral carpets- dave haslam liked us, he liked graham's bubbling personality! some of us had previous encounters with him...he just asked us cos we had loads of money ...or he thought we had.

k- have you been doing lots of gigs?

I.C.s- yeh we've done loads. we've been on the road for 2 days. we did a gig last night in a youth club in royton.

k- d'you go out of your way to get publicity?

recently it said on the radio that we're the most self publicized band.. that was on meltdown. we dont bend over backwards but we have got a bit of scandal: one of us is a 15 year old paperboy

k- which one?

i'll give you a clue, he's got red hair.

but don't put that...say

ABLAZE!

that he's 13.

describing themselves, they say:

we're a very practical band, when we played london we took flasks & packed lunches...we only just made it to the gig. we're very well organized & well disciplined.

k- you keep going on a about the stone roses...

who does?? we don't! we never mentioned them.

k- they're your favouritest band in the whole world, arent they?

you can quote me when i say...they're alright. we bought every record they've ever done, up to "tell me "!

k- but isn't "garage full of flowers" about garage-flowers?

no, it's just that they coined the phrase and we cashed in on it. have we said anything useful yet?

the bodines thought that we were that good that they took us to london to do a gig, but we played to a bodines audience and they didnt like us.

k-are they your friends, yeh?

yeh, they're our friends. when you read write-ups on them they sound as if they don't wanna know any-body, but they're really smart to get on with & really down to earth & everything.they looked after us on ourlondon trip & bought us 2 cans of beer each, and nathan (the bodines' manager) took us to a club to treat us, but we ended up having to pay to get in!

GLASTONBURY '87

Special ABLAZE! report

the Beginning

we stumbled onto the festival site just as the sun was getting upon friday morning.we made our way through a field and over a fence ,wondering whether we had avoided the officials who would want our tickets or at least a bribe...they were lurking by a gate, distinctly out of their heads, so jo used some of her charm and explained that we didn't have any tickets, we didnt have any money and could they perhaps shut their eyes while we climbed over the gate? bribeless and giggling they opened the gate for us and let us in anyway.

rain had been thrashing down all night and the floor was soft and slippy.we searched for some friendies and crashed out in their van, prepared to sleep till the husker du set,but little sleep was to be had...so i slid down to the second stage where the chesterfields totally failed to inspire me.when myears sensed the beginning of the husker du set on the main stage i was happy to go and see them even though they very nearly bored me to bits.

that day the words you could hear people saying were like "nightmare", "awful" and husker du but rather it was to do with the fact that the ground had degenerated into a sludgebath and all feet had submerged into generously spread,smooth textured, milk chocolate coloured mud.it was funny really to observe how some people appeared to have tip-toed across this brown deep sea while others must have been swimming in it.

the markets were ace places to be, worth spending hours just browsing round.you could buy most things in the world but the ground just wantedto suck my shoes off.

God

some very strange people led me round the edges of the vast site causing me to miss the soup dragons but that was the unimportant problem in the whole world becos we got back in time to witness the greatest julian cope set ever ever.he seemed infinitely powerful,illumined by a thousand lights and taking the place of the sun as it gorgeously slipped away.the band worked like an engine in the background,supportin the pride of the singer as he mounted the microphone stand, going up and up, higher and higher and higher...he steered the spaceship stage with magical elegance,set the course for the deepest heaven and left the world helplessly elated.

12

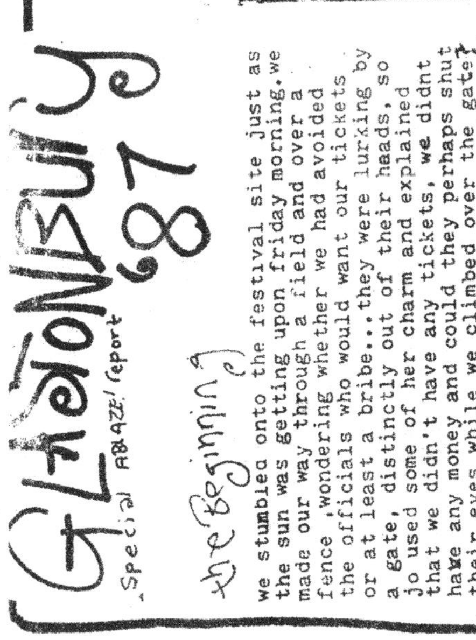

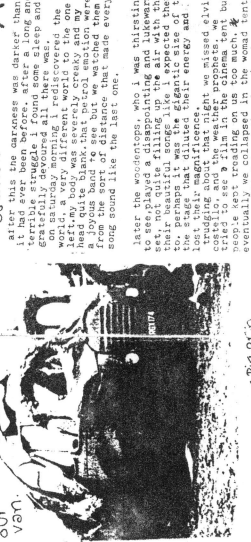

oBLivion

after this the darkness was darker than it had ever been before. after a long and terrible struggle i found some sleep and gratefully devoured all there was.

on saturday morning i rediscovered the world, a very different world to the one i left.my body was severely creaky and my head quite blank.that petrol emotion were a joyous band to see but we watched them from the sort of distance that made every song sound like the last one.

later the woodentops, who i was thirsting to see,played a disappointing and lukewarm set, not quite filling up the air with the their beautiful songs like i expected them to. perhaps it was the gigantic size of the stage that diluted their energy and lost their magnificence.

trudging about that night we missed elvis costello, and the weather prophets. we tried to see a film in the cinema tent but people kept treading on us too much. eventually we collapsed in the womad tent and snuggled into muddy sleeping bags and snored happily, dreaming of the benevolen sun who'd transformed the ground back into a solid surface once more.

Lesbian Dopeheads on Mopeds

sunday was a good day for bands, but only at the second stage. i missed the start of an excellent pop will eat itself set, then there was stump doing just the usual stuff but doing it really well (apart from cope, these were the best people i saw...had to fight with myself not to jump around).shortly after these,the gaye bikers, who were minor stars of the whole weekend, made real prats of themselves with lines like "you see that lad in the green hat over there- he's got aids".this was accompanied by equally shit music and the crowd showed their appreciation by hurling anything that could be thrown at the stage.

13

ABLAZE!

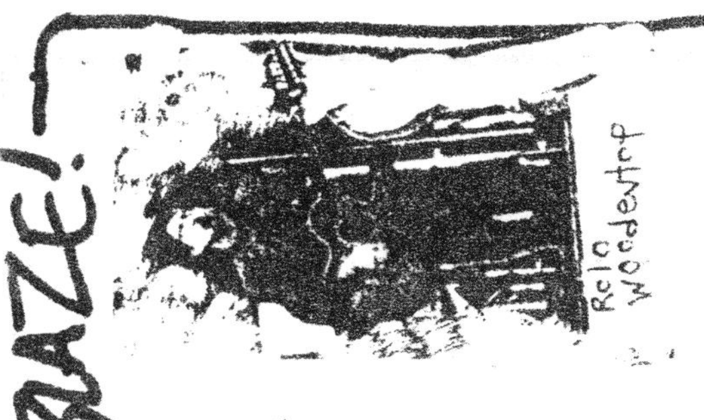

the end.

aftera lot of laffing and walking and drinkin and everyhing (and not a lot of sleep, or thought of the outside "world" which probably ceased to exist anyway) we staggered off the festival site , monday morning, midsummer '87. ...and the rain...started to pour...on our weary heads. (karren)

68 Gretney Walk
Moss Side
Manchester
August sometime...

Dear Simon,

I cant really remember what we wrote to each other last. it must have been a long time ago. I hope you're alright, I hope things are nice for you.

I'm writing becos i'm leaving manchester soon and hopefully you will give me some advice. i've got a place at leeds uni so it would be good to know where the clubs are + things like that. where to go + where to go only if you're really bored.

Leeds is the place where the 3 Johns come from isn't it, which is a good thing. Also it's not too far from here which is a better thing. I thought I was going to end up in LONDON!

What are you doing now? I don't do anything. I painted a fucking BLAZING demented SUN on the wall... it makes it difficult to sleep. I wrote some fanzines by the way: KARANOIA 86 (50 copies!) A thing with a brilliant compilation tape (100) + ABLAZE! issue 1 (200) but the bastard printer seems to have ripped me off so I have to take him to court. that should be ace. it isn't very impressive yet but just wait...

is there a club that plays Sonic Youth, Membranes, Janitors, Mel + Kim, stuff like that? it's important. see you, Love KARREN ABLAZE! x

An unsent letter to Simon Blackburn, a Leodian with whom I'd previously corresponded, and (extra-legally) married on his one visit to me in my Saturday afternoon Manchester city centre idyll. The letter indicates my deepest concerns about moving cities for the first time, and hints at a nascent megalomania with regard to increasing circulations. Simon was a student in Newcastle who fed off the post-punk paradise of the eighties. I'm sad to say that he died in the nineties, in a road accident as he travelled to his job as a nurse in the city of Bradford. Although he hadn't asked for it, I had donated my original copy of the Morrissey letter to him in a fit of Catholic asceticism.

Ablaze! 2

Publication date: December 1987

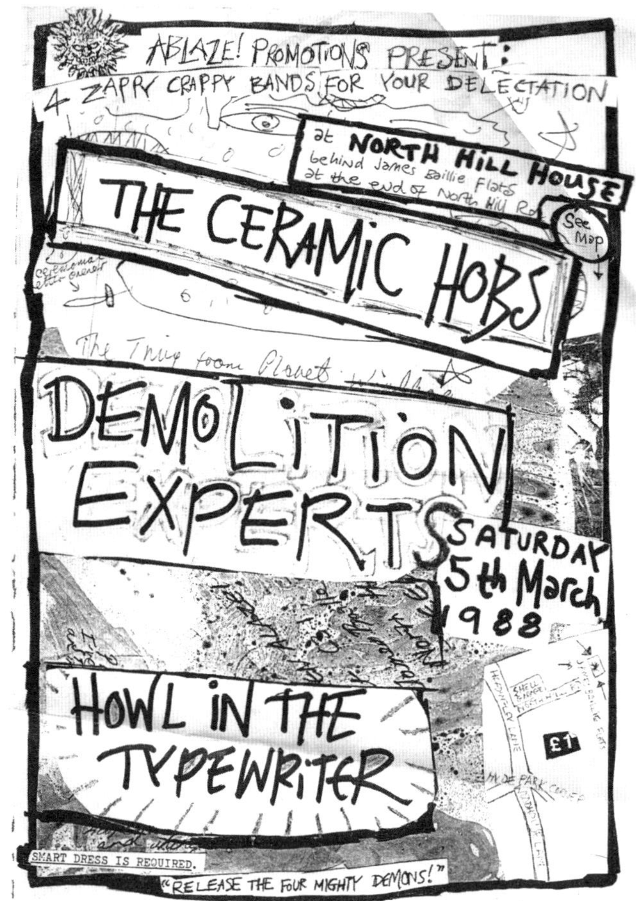

Whilst residing in James Baillie student flats in Headingley, I decided to put on a gig. Attached to the flats was this creepy old mansion that we were allowed to use, and my unerring sense of possibility led me to believe that a complex housing a few hundred first-year students would be a great venue for a Ceramic Hobs and Howl in the Typewriter show. I was wrong. Apart from friends, only two punters showed up, and *they* walked in without paying. I lived in a cell-like single room in which four of us were to sleep that night, so Pik did some tidying up. He took all the stuff that was on the floor and put it out of the way, sellotaping it to the walls and ceiling. This arrangement of things elicited the determined curiosity of my flatmates as they attempted to crane around the door to view the cutlery, photographs and slices of bread fixed in place around the room. That was about the most exciting thing that happened that year, apart from the time I ordered 47 pints of milk for the boys in Flat B.

I'd arranged the Happy Mondays interview by tracking down their manager, Phil Saxe, at his jeans stall in Manchester's Arndale Market. He gave me a home-copied tape of their first album, the John Cale-produced *Squirrel and G-Man Twenty Four Hour Party People Plastic Face Carnt Smile (White Out)*, and permitted me to meet them in their practice room, located in the basement of the Boardwalk. The walls oozed stuffing and were etched with anti-Semitic graffiti, the floor was littered with beer cans and fag packets – so tame in comparison with what they would do when their fortunes changed - and the group were sullen, intimidating and unfriendly. But it *was* teatime, so they were more-or-less sober.

A couple of issues later I would start to tie myself in knots, wrestling with questions of how music and politics interact, but for now I was innocent of such troubles, unable to see the subtleties of the Mondays' discussions of sexuality, the pictures they painted of untamed youth in the city and the misadventures they pursued. And I got nowhere near finding out how these seemingly dim-witted boys managed to create such an innovative debut album.

The interview is illegible, and anyway it gets revamped in issue 7 by way of a new improved transcription, so flip ahead to that if you want the full depressed-Mancunians-in-a-cellar experience.

The main action in this issue involves two interviews with The Janitors, the dodgy grebo band that had captured my mind at Glastonbury the previous summer. In one of those spooky coincidences, I had taken a trip to visit my friend Bela Emerson in deepest, darkest Wales, only to discover that they were playing in a nearby town. We tracked down the gig, stalked the band at their post-gig meal, and enticed them back to Bela's house for gin and scrabble. For their part, they concentrated on being sarcastic and pulling our pigtails, but unfortunately everything stayed quite above board.

I also interrogated fellow greboes, Gaye Bykers on Acid, with the same razor-blunt interview technique, and singer Mary Mary responded by being sarcastic but *not* taking the piss, which was very nice of him - however the resulting interview is too boring to include.

Having finished assembling the artwork on a bus, I took it to that venerable resource centre where they printed it for me in red, green and blue, rendering it only semi-readable. A note from the chap who printed it suggested I not stick all the original artwork together in the format of the finished product, as text and images showed through from the pages behind. This was the first of many issues where legibility suffered for various reasons. Looking back, it seems an obvious flaw, but at the time it wasn't a priority. Doing it was the thing, breathlessly and narrowly getting by. People worked hard to read it, but seemed to find it a worthwhile expenditure of effort.

I took a copy round to a boy named Luke, who lived in another wing of the student flat complex I called home, as he had expressed the wish to see it. When he saw it, he said, "Well done," which struck me as odd. I wasn't used to being praised for something I had created.

At the start of my first year at the University of Leeds, I'd been bombarded with literature seeking to prepare me for all the sex, drugs and rock'n'roll I was about to enjoy. I felt falsely-advertised to, as there was actually nowhere near enough sex. There was, however, a reasonable amount of drugs; LSD in particular was plentiful and cheap. And, having escaped Madchester at exactly the right time, Leeds provided plenty of rock'n'roll. Youthful noiseniks The Purple Eternal played a show in the student union and I was rather taken by their good looks and treacherous ways. Suddenly I had five new friends; I'd arrived in Leeds.

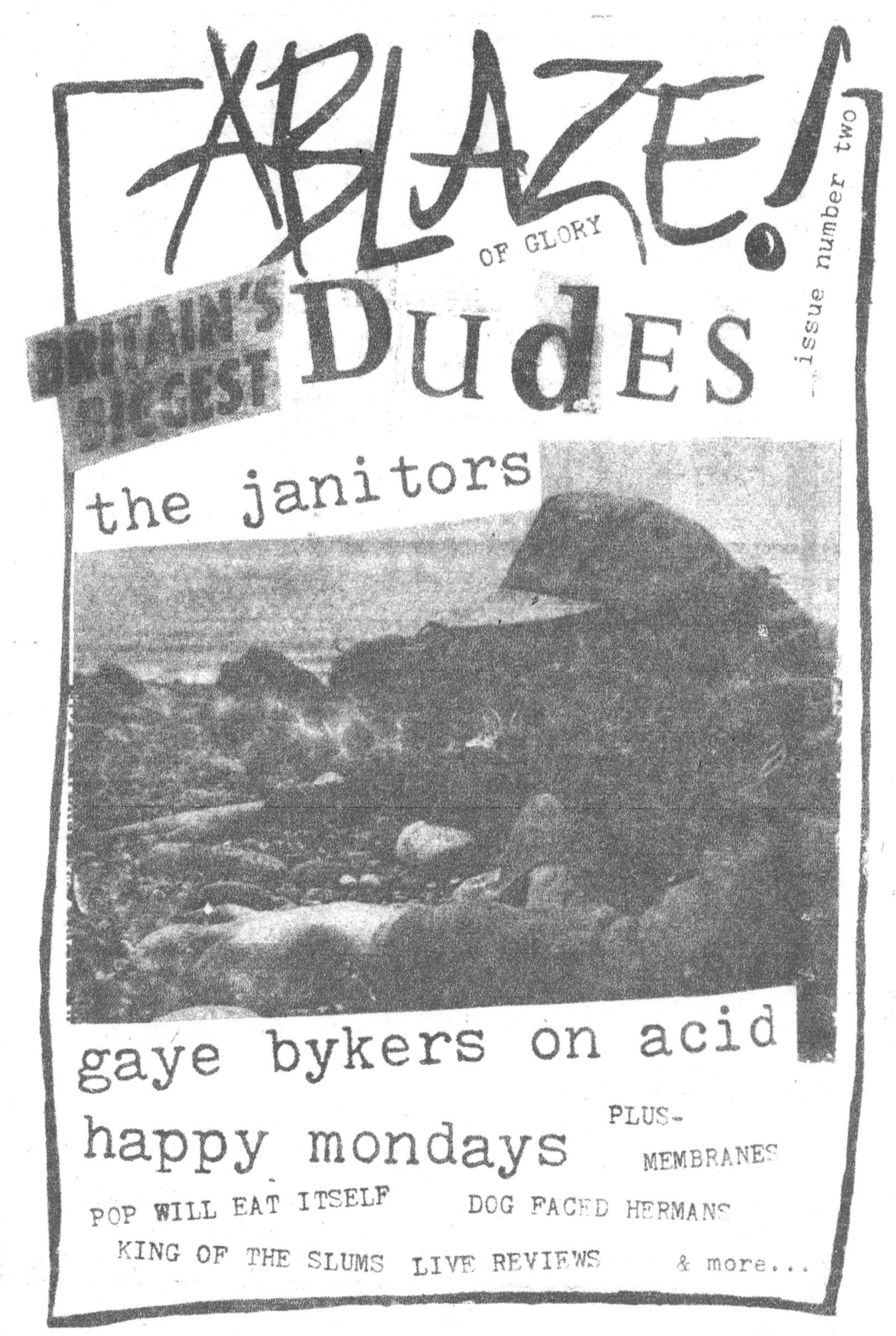
ABLAZE!
OF GLORY
issue number two
BRITAIN'S BIGGEST
Dudes
the janitors
gaye bykers on acid
happy mondays
PLUS-
MEMBRANES
POP WILL EAT ITSELF
DOG FACED HERMANS
KING OF THE SLUMS
LIVE REVIEWS
& more...

ABLAZE! BLAZE OR DIE

hello + welcome back to your favourite goth mag heh heh heh plenty scary people in this ... who all wear black ... plus this months fashion tips — starving yourself to death, deceased-look + woao!! so there's lots get your fangs into!!

SCREAM!!

NOOOOOOOOOOOO!!!

NOOOOOOOOO!!!

POOR BASTARD FRIGHTENED BY HIS OWN REFLECTION!

this new sisters of mercy LP's just what you need ... DEATH!

goff off!! DESTROY!

corespondance address-
34, fulmar dr
sale,
manchester,
m33 4nh.

thanks to mark osbourne for cover photo of the jans going for a swim.

MIKE MEAN to the rescue, just in time to save the ABLAZE! editorial from those evil imposters the GOTHS. finally put out of their misery & hopefully destroyed forever, leaving us to our noble task of mental pyromania...(?)

yeh this is ABLAZE! II, brought to you despite lots of hassle, death threats etc. not going to say happy xmas & new year & all that, it does my head in,

dont mean to sound so negative but there you go...hello 800 people, have a nice time today or something, read the stuff in here & if you like it then write me letters perhaps

bye-bye, Love KARREN x

YO DUDES corner-
ta to a million billion people, like ian h, mark w, isabela, julie, lizzie b, steve, cathryn, all friendies, specially my poor flatmates (who havent seen the kitchen table for weeks), thanks to the janitors for lifts etc, & the gaye bykers & the happiest mondays..........

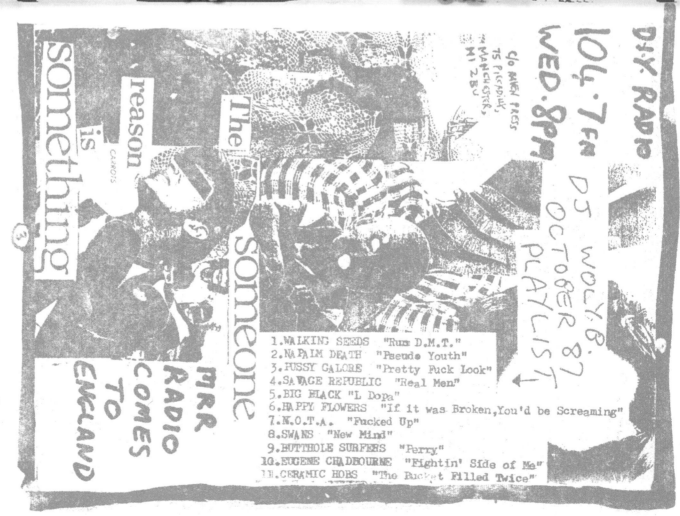

(2)

D.I.Y. RADIO

104.7FM
WED.8PM

c/o RAVEN PRESS
75 PICCADILLY,
MANCHESTER,
M1 2BU

DJ WOLY B.
OCTOBER 87
PLAYLIST

1. WALKING SEEDS "Rum D.M.T."
2. NAPALM DEATH "Pseudo Youth"
3. PUSSY GALORE "Pretty Fuck Look"
4. SAVAGE REPUBLIC "Real Men"
5. BIG BLACK "L Dopa"
6. HAPPY FLOWERS "If it was Broken, You'd be Screaming"
7. N.O.T.A. "Fucked Up"
8. SWANS "New Mind"
9. BUTTHOLE SURFERS "Perry"
10. EUGENE CHADBOURNE "Fightin' Side of Me"
11. CERAMIC HOBS "The Bucket Filled Twice"

The someone reason is something

CARROTS

MRR RADIO COMES TO ENGLAND

(3)

LOS GREBOS

a thursday night in wales...how can i explain? there was me & isabela. and there was 5 janitors...it was all a complete accident. they were trying to eat and we were trying to interview th m, and this was happening in a chinese resteraunt
the big taperecorder found a plug socket in the wall and caught mos* of their mutant mutterings
and the waitor was locking wo..ied...

Tim (½ a compact disc round his neck, between gobfulls of curry)!
go on then, fire away.
Karren; what are you into, music-wise, beer-wise, anythin' ?
Jeff- yeh what do i like to drink? special brew, tennents super, anythin'...nesquick.
Karren: what sort of music?
Jeff: anythin' obnoxious.
Isabela: that's not very descriptive.
dentover: yeh, it could be anytning in the charts.
Isabela: what's your favourite band EVER?
Dentover: what sort of question is that?
(in the argument that followed the answer to whatever sort of question it was got lost forever)
Waitor: you had 6 meals?
Tim: no that's just extra rice
Dentover: and one's a soup as well. special fried rice, that was extra between us.big boys
Tim: can i have a match please? what do i like to drink? i like a good solid rich red wine, i used to like special brew but it's knackered me - i drank too much of it so i dont drink that anymore...my favourite artist is
Somebody- bauhaus:
Tim:...micheal jackson...cos he's bad. that's the honest truth.
Dentover: he's good. he's such a naughty boy.
Tim: if it's not micheal jackson then it's julian bream the classical guitarist for a similar reason, artistically & aesthetically. i joined the band becos i worship julian bream and i thought at the time craig was the nearest guitarist i knew to julian bream...
Dentover- you told me it was nobby pike
Tim- no it was tubby sods. this isnt really denton, this is tubby sods the famous footballer & you've never even heard of him.
Dentover- yeh, mr tubby sods, played for macclesfield wanderers...

Tim- my worst hatreds are nuclear weapons,chinese foodshops in wales and young girls from manchester who dont know what questions to ask famous bands...
Isabela- you're not famous at all;!
Dentover- shhhh!
Tim- you're still young girls from manchester.
Isabela - i'm not from manchester.
Karren- and i'm not young.
Tim- you're younger than i am.
(well, i'm not a girl either- ed.)
Dentover- when do i get my go?
Isabela now.
Dentover- my favourite drink is champagne, my favourite food is s suckling child , lightly roasted over a charcoal grill, i like the special curry now & again,..
Karren- i'm bored with this question, lets do the next one. where are you from?
Dentover- hell.
Karren- can you drink beer in here?
Tim- no.
Karren- who's the sex symbol in the group? (back to the serious questions...)
Tim- we all have equilibrium of sexual status- we appeal individually to different types of women so it's a redundant question.

After some bickering about the question we agreed that there dosent have to be a sex symbol in their (or anybody's) band, they concluded that if anyone it would be steve their new "guitarist" ("you wont see him on stage, he plays by telepathy" they claim).
The "conversation" then took a more interesting turn towards the taperecorder which was showered with affectionate kisses...
Karren- anyone want to hear the next question?
(Evidently not- they'd rather talk about trivial pursuits, a levels, chunks of dead people and throwing up)
Karren- I'm not going to speak unless you want to know what the next question is.
Dentov-er- go on then.
Tim- dont throw a wobbly on us.
Karren- who's got problems here and what are they?
Tim- what, financial, sexual, philosophical..?
Karren- yeh, anything...
Dentover- i havent got any.
Tim- i cant have a piss in wide open spaces. i'm allergic to all members of the bomb party and crazyhead...

it got worse & worse, somebody left the band and no-one noticed, they decided to send messages to isabela's mum : "hello shirley's mum", followed by attempts to guess her name...
Isabela- do i look like a "shaz"??!!!

continues over→

THE JANITORS continued

Karren- what were your most harrowing experiences? ← steve's question
Somebody- what does harrowing mean?
Jeff- in harrow?
Dentover- it's the chinese word for smack
Tim- mine was discovering i was a man instead of a woman...he (Denton) was in bed with me at the time...and going to poland for a week.
Dentover- that was the best bit. i loved it.
Karren- what do you think of the "greebo" scene?
Tim- you mean grebo. it doesnt exist outside of this band and when it does it's not greebo it's grebo, and i dont know what that means.that's how they spell it in the papers these days.
Dentover- we're just going by what we can read.
Tim- we cant read much. most of it's unreadable....status quo are grebo, the original showaddywaddy are greeboes...the membranes are weedoes...and pop will eat itself are musos.

It was clear that they were running out of shit to talk about ("but we've still got to swap wigs so that everybody laughs" they protested) So we decided to take on these janitors, the most sarcastic band in the world, on our territory at their next manchester boardwalk gig...

janitors, Manchester Boardwalk

musically amazing, & in every way surprizing,this was their gig & they were in charge.the drummer drummed like the devil , brimming with contempt, bassplayer bassplayed with his eyes tight shut. floating round, the guitarer was nonchalant & the singer was not- afterwards praised as a brilliant live performer. he joked & spitted , snapped the microphonestand devoured the audience & vomited them back onto the floor, waving his track-suit-clad legs around...obnoxious as always

these janitors really excelled themselvestonight, with the sound practically perfect &the songs almost wonderful manchester seemed to love them,this audience sharing a new energy as they exchanged beercans & insults

go see this band.
rave rave etc etc...

Buy all their records as well

this is a very blank space & i dont know what to write on it becos i havent got any more photographs

BLAZE BLAZE
Burn the city down

ordinary people get blown up but margaret thatcher doesnt, not even when it's meant for her. police dont protect me. unemployment statistics are going down, due to road accidents, ferry disasters substation fires, lung cancer, youth training schemes...

if we cannot destroy the evil power that's destroying the world then it's going to destroy us, obviously. if we dont try, do we really deserve to exist?

every cell in my body is involved . i am sick becos i breathe sick air & drink from a poison bottle. my mind is pure, pure chaos.

GIGS

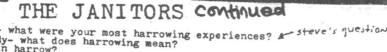

PSYCHO SURGEONS/ MEMBRANES/ POP WILL EAT ITSELF...LEEDS UNI.

The surgeons' singer didnt look very well at all, what with his head all bandaged up & a VERY pale complexion, but when he started running thru' the audience wavind a big sword we guessed he'd recovered. a good live band & they certainly got the kiddies dancing.

the membranes & a fire-eating act- another brilliant ace raging set from that 3/4/5+?-piece pop monster, so nonchalant & always & not ever singing their haircuts on massive flames that fill up the stage

p.w.e.i. filled up the whole building never mind the stage with sodding dry ice, for a while they were out of sight which was ace. honest, these dickheads would actually be quite bearable if you couldnt see them & they sang in a language that nobody understood. i wanted so much to give them highspeed beerglasses, but any injury would only get them sympathy, & who would take me seriously if they thought i had violent tendencies, not that anyone takes me seriously anyway...

BLAZE OR LIE

KING OF THE SLUMS manchester boardwalk

i knew that i would like this band so its possible that i didnt watch them with a completely open mind, they had an air of nervousness and were concerned about the sound being right -when they asked was the violin loud enough i longed for them to know that it wasnt, s it is the violin snaiso, along with the muffled vocals, that make them stand out ... they dont look like a wildly happy band, perhaps they sing about sickness and poverty

continues nowhere

UNBEND

dogfaced hermans / jackdaw with crowbar / A C Temple / Cud... Leeds astoria

getting away from the usually accepted idea of one band playing as the headliner & the others as supports, the hermans / jackdaw / a c temple package take it in turns to be 1st, 2nd & 3rd on the bill. their attempt to destroy this convention, & the order of importace it implies, explains why tonight's line up seemed a little bizzarre with the hermans, being the obvious favourites, appearing 1st and cud, as tonight's special guests, appearing last.

the (wonderfully-named) dogfaced hermans' musical imagination is refreshing like a fizzy drink scalding your throat. i heard a guitar being tortured till it cried , and sounds that would creep along awhile,...then pounce with pure viciousness into your ears. marion, the childsize frontperson, punctuated monster vocal attaks with trumpet blasts & noises from a selection of instruments at her feet. never ceasing to move, her energy inspired dancing among many of the youngsters in the sparse audience.

they were followed by jackdaw with crowbar, more fast frenzied music with loudhailer vocals they were most remembered tho' for their exciting & hypnotic visual show; 4 camera things projected a startling collage of images onto sheets hung behind the stage, managing to create a 4th degree of confusion in my head.

a c temple have a comparatively subdued sound. their influences were almost too clear - the swans, & sonic youth (specially in the kim/ thurston type duets). they look & sound very tidy - a little unchallenging but enjoyable nevertheless.

and cud...cudn't, basically. they played with an obvious sense of humour but were musically unimpressive, however i feel they should be given the benefit of the doubt, as the singer's apology for them being at their worst EVER seemed sincere. worth another look.

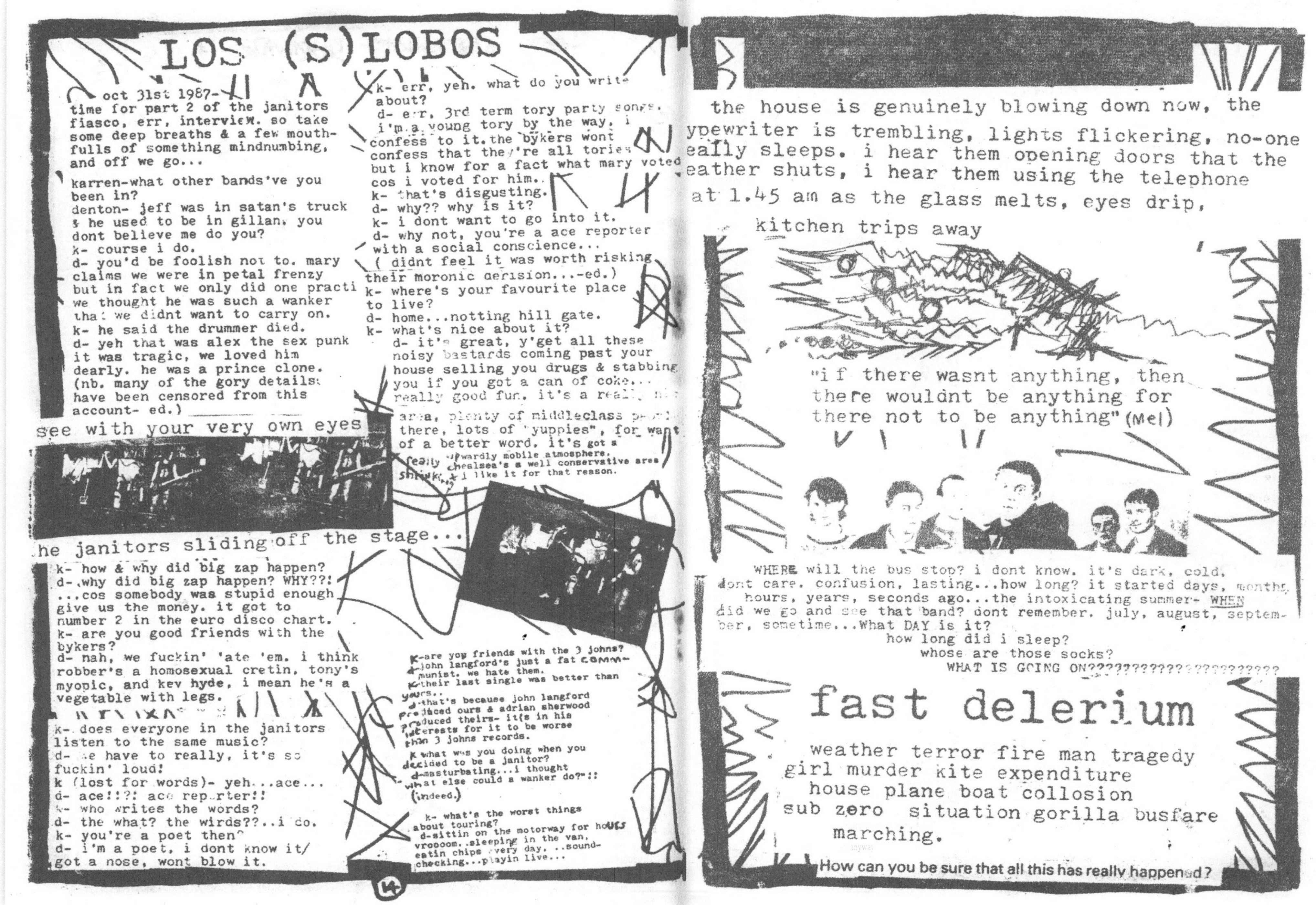

LOS (S)LOBOS

oct 31st 1987- time for part 2 of the janitors fiasco, err, interview. so take some deep breaths & a few mouthfuls of something mindnumbing, and off we go...

karren-what other bands've you been in?
denton- jeff was in satan's truck & he used to be in gillan. you dont believe me do you?
k- course i do.
d- you'd be foolish not to. mary claims we were in petal frenzy but in fact we only did one practi we thought he was such a wanker that we didnt want to carry on.
k- he said the drummer died.
d- yeh that was alex the sex punk it was tragic, we loved him dearly. he was a prince clone.
(nb. many of the gory details have been censored from this account- ed.)

k- err, yeh. what do you write about?
d- err, 3rd term tory party songs. i'm a young tory by the way, i confess to it. the bykers wont confess that they're all tories but i know for a fact what mary voted cos i voted for him.
k- that's disgusting.
d- why?? why is it?
k- i dont want to go into it.
d- why not, you're a ace reporter with a social conscience...
(didnt feel it was worth risking their moronic derision...-ed.)
k- where's your favourite place to live?
d- home...notting hill gate.
k- what's nice about it?
d- it's great, y'get all these noisy bastards coming past your house selling you drugs & stabbing you if you got a can of coke... really good fun. it's a really nice area, plenty of middleclass people there, lots of "yuppies", for want of a better word. it's got a really upwardly mobile atmosphere. chealsea's a well conservative area shrunk, i like it for that reason.

see with your very own eyes

the janitors sliding off the stage...

k- how & why did big zap happen?
d- why did big zap happen? WHY??! ...cos somebody was stupid enough give us the money. it got to number 2 in the euro disco chart.
k- are you good friends with the bykers?
d- nah, we fuckin' 'ate 'em. i think robber's a homosexual cretin, tony's myopic, and kev hyde, i mean he's a vegetable with legs.

k- does everyone in the janitors listen to the same music?
d- we have to really, it's so fuckin' loud!
k (lost for words)- yeh...ace...
d- ace!!?! ace reporter!!
k- who writes the words?
d- the what? the wirds??..i do.
k- you're a poet then?
d- i'm a poet, i dont know it/ got a nose, wont blow it.

k-are you friends with the 3 johns?
d-john langford's just a fat communist. we hate them.
k-their last single was better than yours..
d-that's because john langford produced ours & adrian sherwood produced theirs- it's in his interests for it to be worse than 3 johns records.
k what was you doing when you decided to be a janitor?
d-masturbating...i thought what else could a wanker do?"!!
(indeed.)

k- what's the worst things about touring?
d-sittin on the motorway for hours vroooom..sleeping in the van, eatin chips every day, ..soundchecking...playin live...

14

the house is genuinely blowing down now, the ypewriter is trembling, lights flickering, no-one eally sleeps. i hear them opening doors that the eather shuts, i hear them using the telephone at 1.45 am as the glass melts, eyes drip,
kitchen trips away

"if there wasnt anything, then there wouldnt be anything for there not to be anything" (Mel)

WHERE will the bus stop? i dont know. it's dark, cold, dont care. confusion, lasting...how long? it started days, months, hours, years, seconds ago...the intoxicating summer- WHEN did we go and see that band? dont remember. july, august, september, sometime...What DAY is it?
how long did i sleep?
whose are those socks?
WHAT IS GOING ON?????????????????????

fast delerium

weather terror fire man tragedy
girl murder kite expenditure
house plane boat collosion
sub zero situation gorilla busfare
marching.

How can you be sure that all this has really happened?

Ablaze! 3

Publication date: Early-mid 1988

Previous readability problems were compounded when the resource centre allowed me to operate the printing machine all by myself. This, as you'll soon see, was a Very Bad Idea.

After the disappointments of the first part of my first year I was delighted to find myself in an entanglement with another zine editor, Simon Morris of *Turnip Flag*, a Dadaist journal fuelled by nihilism and PCP. Under Simon's sinister influence my cut and paste style became more energetic, and I relished finding just the right text from *The Plain Truth*, a freely-distributed fundamentalist Christian magazine, and combining it with paper bags and pizza leaflets. Slapdash, confident – the front cover must've taken minutes – I was feeling good about it all.

I had a bad habit of failing to credit writers. This backfires - not only does it make me look like I totally heart The Shrubs and The Wonder Stuff (pieces by Mark Lemonade and Simon Eeyore respectively) but it also suggests that I go round smashing chains in people's faces (Walkingseeds review by Simon Morris). On the other hand I was unkindly keen to distance myself from Emma's adoration of Echo and the Bunnymen, a band I had eschewed in favour of the rich seam of DIY underground noise.

King of the Slums were a wonderful and preposterous group, Charlie Keigher comes on like a more Mancunian Morrissey with Sarah Curtis as his screechy Marr. Here they reveal how they funded the release of their astounding debut single *Spider Psychiatry* with insurance money after their flat "got robbed".

It was as a result of reading *Ablaze!* 3 that Ian Brown told me to fuck off. I thought I'd just made a mild comment about Sally Cinnamon being too poppy but reading it now, it seems I may have expressed the sentiment a little harshly. Or maybe not harshly enough, in view of what was to follow. For some reason I'd gone to see them at Leeds Poly with Simon and Patrick, and Ian felt moved to make this declaration. His full statement was "Fuck off, I'll give you the time of day but I won't do an interview for yer fanzine."

Paul Morley of The Slum Turkeys was feeling frustrated. His raucous Big Black-influenced band wasn't getting much attention in a city subliminally gearing up for a Madchester epidemic. But one day a little fanzine writer wandered into his lair. He declared himself uninterested in the indie schmindie flexidisc scene, but on the other hand... He casually suggested my zine might be better at A4 size, as then I could put out flexis and they wouldn't get bent. For my part, I welcomed any encouragement I could get. Someone cared, regardless of their motivation, and that's why this issue is the last of the A5s.

What we left out:
Unreadable interviews with The Shrubs, The Wonder Stuff, King of The Slums, Emily and The Slum Turkeys, which pretty much just leaves a lot of cut-and-pasted insanity.

ABLAZE!
DISTRIBUTORS
REQUIRED IN
ALL
AREAS

If you are aged 3 or over and have two or three hours to spare on any day at all you could earn extra cash by distributing ABLAZE! FANZINE in your area. Supplies will be delivered to houses within walking distance of your home. A car is not needed

I AM INTERESTED IN BECOMING A ABLAZE! FANZINE DISTRIBUTOR

Name..........

Address..........

....

.... Tel..........

If you interested in joining our team complete the above coupon and send to:
Ablaze! / 34 Fulmar Drive / Sale / Manchester / M33 4NH

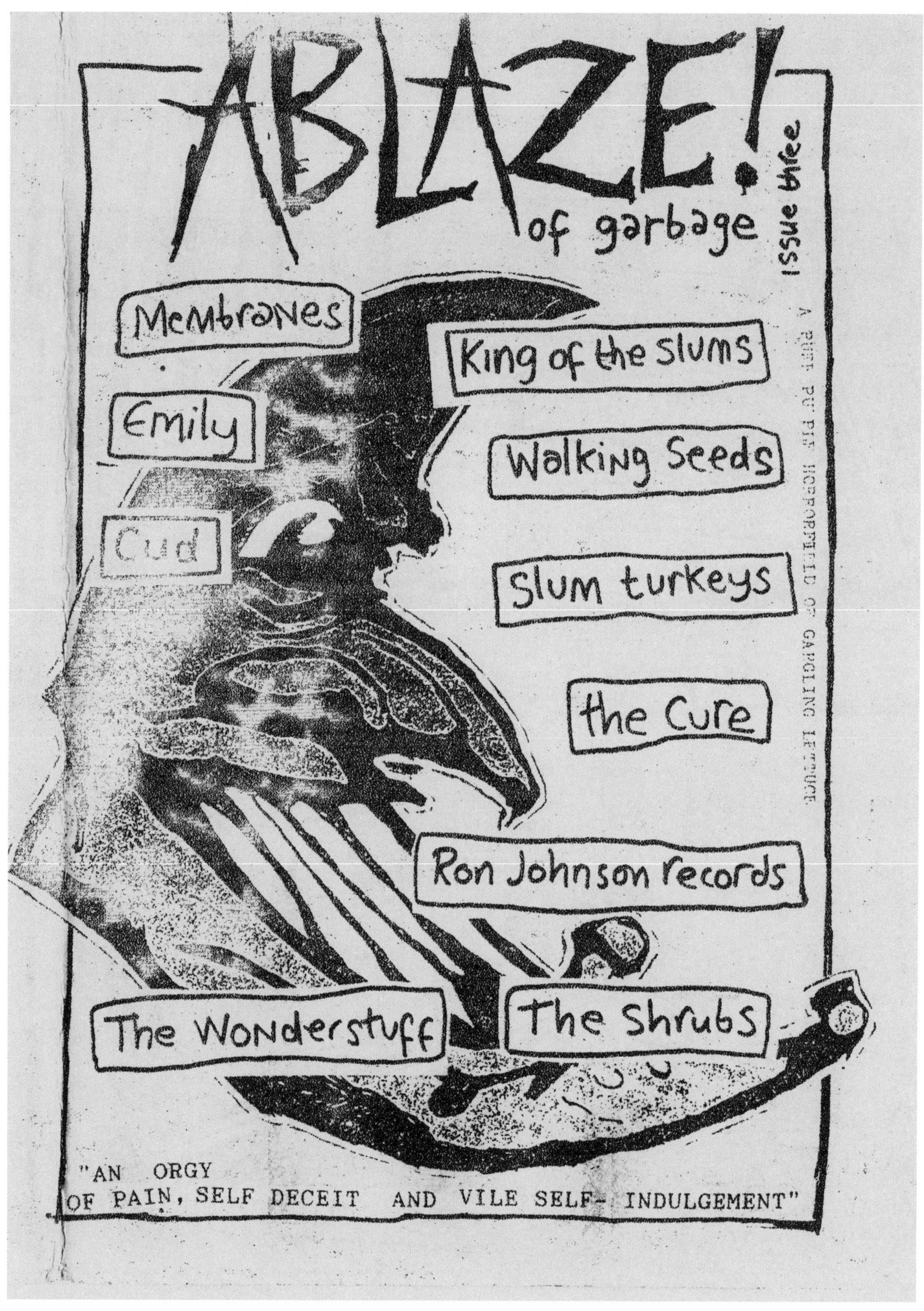
ABLAZE!
of garbage
issue three
Membranes
King of the slums
Emily
Walking Seeds
Cud
Slum turkeys
the Cure
Ron Johnson records
The Wonderstuff
The Shrubs
"AN ORGY
OF PAIN, SELF DECEIT AND VILE SELF- INDULGEMENT"

send your comments & criticisms to :

ABLAZE! PROMOTIONS
C/O 34 FULMAR DRIVE
SALE, MANCHESTER,
M33 4NH.

this is ABLAZE! Ø 333333
this is where you live
humbly presented idea
nothing too

I can keep going from dawn to dusk – no problem.

ALL ABOARD the new ABLAZE! mystery tra.

ABJUR of abundant ABNORMALITIE

JUST WRITE for god's sake!

the abode of ALL ABYSMALITY

an ABATTOIR of english language

ABOMINABLE ABUSE

A BASTARD load of ABOMINABLE ABUSE

...AND ABOUT TIME TOO.

Fish live in water

I WANT TO CHANGE MY NAME

Midnight blaze

THE MANIC PICNIC PANIC

live fast, get groovy (PARANOIA)

KARREN X

the guilty party; Mark Williams, Simon Eyore, Dave Swift, Emma Hill, Simon Turnip, Patrick DIY, JULIE SKOELY, Laura Lovechild

Paul 777, Jeane, William Potter, & anyone else who helped to write or inspire this thing.

apologies for a almost total lack of JANITORial information this issue (I'm sure you're all dead upset, but..) there hasnt been any news.EXCEPT, the single that was due for release in january has finally emerged. it's called "moonshine" and it's out on abstract records and it's a fucking work of art.

talking of works of art, this issue's **cover star** is the blazing moon, captured in all its malevolence by Neil Cookson.

Ablaze! 3, chaos issue
Created by the labour of many minds esp. mine

Gently reduces temperature, relieves toothache, headache, sore throat, feverish colds & flu.

fast-forward bread

Lots of thanks also go to Martin at Raquel studio and Rhyl community agency for letting me use their printing facilities.

thanks to Rich Holden for artwork used on pages 7 and 12. You can buy his publications, "Mesh" and "Cage IN", from 14 Woodlands Drive, Hawarden, Deeside CH5 3LA

Toad

Revolving Credit

Banana, Coconut Oil, Sucrose, Honey

produced in the face of physical + mental exhaustion for you to cast aside and ignore

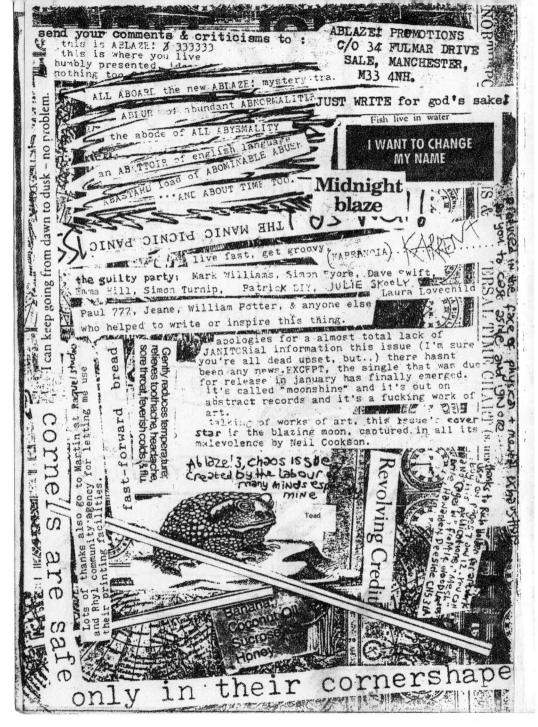

corners are safe
only in their cornershape

the audiences at Stone Roses gigs seem to me to include a significant proportion of big idiot men who like to kick up lots of havoc at the front so that fragile creatures like myself (oh yeh!) get pushed over when we try to dance...the Roses still emit the same arrogance that first attracted me to them,yet i still cannot cope with their tragic decision to learn to play their instruments and make (completely spineless, very commercially viable) pop music. i LOVE songs like "So young", "Wanna be adored", "Heart on the staves" etc but "Sally Cinnamon", everybody's favourite, happy sicky love song has always made me want to eject the contents of my stomach through my mouth...

the evening over, we snatched a few hours sleep and wandered through the day like senseless ghosts. i had to force myself awake at 8 and somehow managed to get myself over to the boardwalk where something exciting promised to happen.

I'm always happy to get a chance to see the **Inspiral Carpets** - they work hard to craft tunes that deserve a lot more attention than they've recieved so far - it's about time some bastard gets to realise this and puts out some of their stuff on vinyl...their set was packed with good songs that i longed to dance to, if only some other people would have...yeh i know...the audience (we) kept our distance, embarrassed at the intimacy of a half empty boardwalk and how it looked like the band could see us as well as we could see them... the stage was so brightly lit too, they must have felt dead exposed...

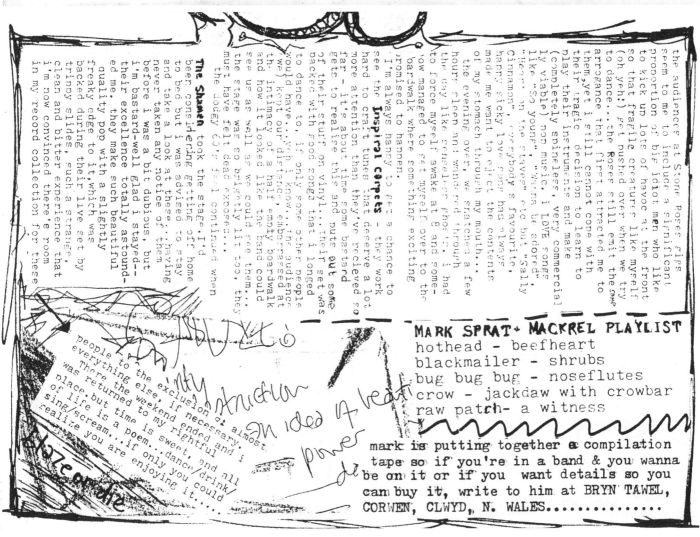

the dodgy 60's feel continued when **The Shamen** took the stage.I'd been considering getting off home to bed but i was advised to stay and take a look at these...having never taken any notice of them before i was a bit dubious, but i'm bastard-well glad i stayed--their excellence totally astounded me. they make such beautiful quality pop with a slightly freaky edge to it,which was backed during their live set by trippy slides, such a strange, clean and bitter experience that i'm now convinced there's room in my record collection for these

people to the exclusion of almost everything else, if necessary. There the weekend ended and i was returned to my rightful place.but time is sweet, and all of life is a poem...dance/drink/sing/scream...if only you could realize you are enjoying it.....

ablaze or die

an idea of beat power

MARK SPRAT + MACKREL PLAYLIST

hothead - beefheart
blackmailer - shrubs
bug bug bug - noseflutes
crow - jackdaw with crowbar
raw patch- a witness

mark is putting together a compilation tape so if you're in a band & you wanna be on it or if you want details so you can buy it, write to him at BRYN TAWEL, CORWEN, CLWYD, N. WALES...............

PIZZAS

SMALL MEDIUM

8 Can people trust what you say?

(a) I'm as straight as a die. I don't say things I don't mean.

(b) I try to be honest most of the time but sometimes it's too difficult or complicated to explain in detail.

(c) Why bother if the other fellow's happy?

OK here's a update on the Ron Johnson record company, currently by far the best label in the country and it's about time you conservative bastards realized it as well...they seem to have all the best bands signed up : THE SHRUBS, A WITNESS, NOSEFLUTES, JACKDAW WITH CROWBAR etc. (except the dull TWANG and the predictable GREAT LEAP FORWARD).Here's news on the forthcoming releases folks:

A WITNESS 12" (a four-track EP including " Raw patch", "Zip up"),a LP by out-of-control scooter club officiandos JACKDAW WITH CROWBAR (recently praised by UK's best writer Steven Wells), a studio LP by SEWER ZOMBIES (includes the brill "They died with their Willie Nelson T-shirts on"), a 12" remix by the MACKENZIE called "Really meally mouths" , and forthcoming LPs by NOSEFLUTES, TWANG, A WITNESS , GREAT LEAP FORWARD etc...

Ron's currently looking for new talent (so send them demos in), and is doing something with Greg ex-BIG FLAME, in a a band called P. DOGS...

If you wish to write to them send a SAE to : RON JOHNSON RECORDS,
15 FOREST RD. EAST,
NOTTINGHAM NG1.

and in the meantime check out the following golden oldies from the label:
"Take me aside for a midnight harange" SHRUBS LP
"I an John's pancreas" - A WITNESS LP
"Sunk by a iceburg" - JACKDAW WITH CROWBAR
"Rotting honeymoon" - NOSEFLUTES 12"

(MARK)

FOOTNOTE - Debris recently listed the noseflutes in their worst band of 87 section- i expect this is because they're not called Sonic Youth or BIG Black or a very hip hip hop act

WALKINGSEEDS Boardwalk 16/1/88

I COUGHED DURING SEX

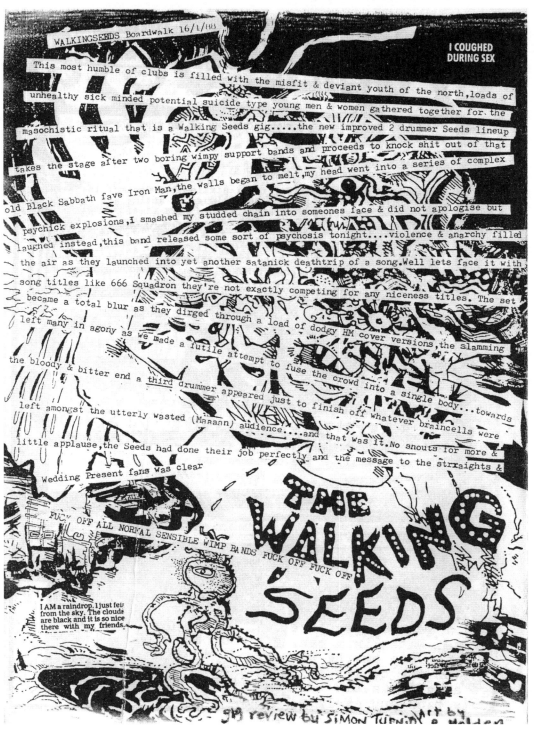

This most humble of clubs is filled with the misfit & deviant youth of the north, loads of unhealthy sick minded potential suicide type young men & women gathered together for the masochistic ritual that is a Walking Seeds gig.....the new improved 2 drummer Seeds lineup takes the stage after two boring wimpy support bands and proceeds to knock shit out of that old Black Sabbath fave Iron Man, the walls began to melt, my head went into a series of complex psychick explosions, I smashed my studded chain into someones face & did not apologise but laughed instead, this band released some sort of psychosis tonight....violence & anarchy filled the air as they launched into yet another satanick deathtrip of a song. Well lets face it with song titles like 666 Squadron they're not exactly competing for any niceness titles. The set became a total blur as they dirged through a load of dodgy HM cover versions, the slamming left many in agony as we made a futile attempt to fuse the crowd into a single body...towards the bloody & bitter end a third drummer appeared just to finish off whatever braincells were left amongst the utterly wasted (Maaaan) audience....and that was it. No snouts for more & little applause, the Seeds had done their job perfectly and the message to the straights & Wedding Present fans was clear

FUCK OFF ALL NORMAL SENSIBLE WIMP BANDS FUCK OFF FUCK OFF

THE WALKING SEEDS

I AM a raindrop. I just fell from the sky. The clouds are black and it is so nice there with my friends.

gig review by SIMON TURNIN art by

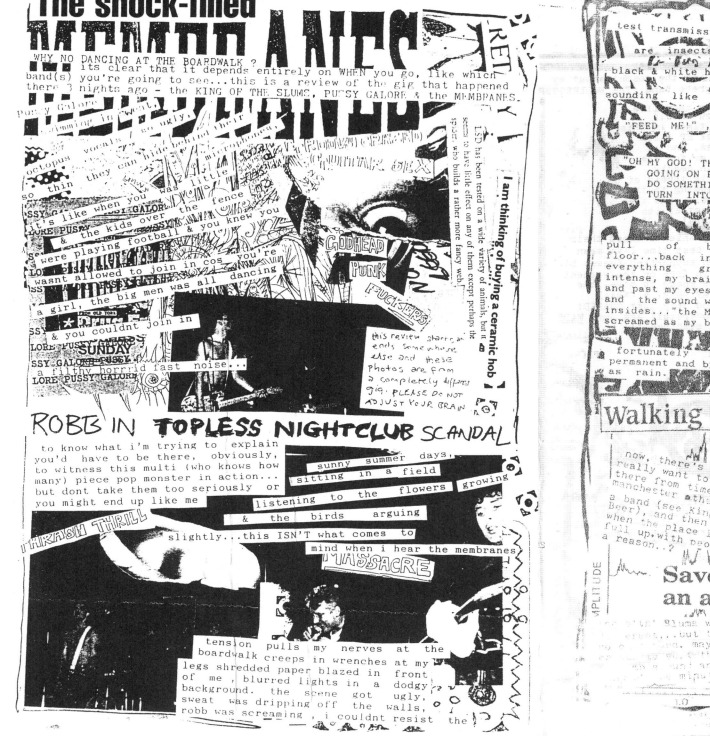

The shock-filled

WHY NO DANCING AT THE BOARDWALK ?
its clear that it depends entirely on WHEN you go, like which band(s) you're going to see...this is a review of the gig that happened there 3 nights ago - the KING OF THE SLUMS, PUSSY GALORE & the MEMBRANES.

Pussy Galore swimming in sweat,
octopus vocals / so ugly,
so thin they can hide behind their microphones,
it's like when you was little
& the kids over the fence
were playing football & you knew you
wasnt allowed to join in cos you're
a girl, the big men was all dancing
& you couldnt join in
a filthy horrid fast noise...

GODHEAD
PUNK
FUCKERS

LSD has been tested on a wide variety of animals, but it seems to have little effect on any of them except perhaps the spider, who builds a rather more fancy web.

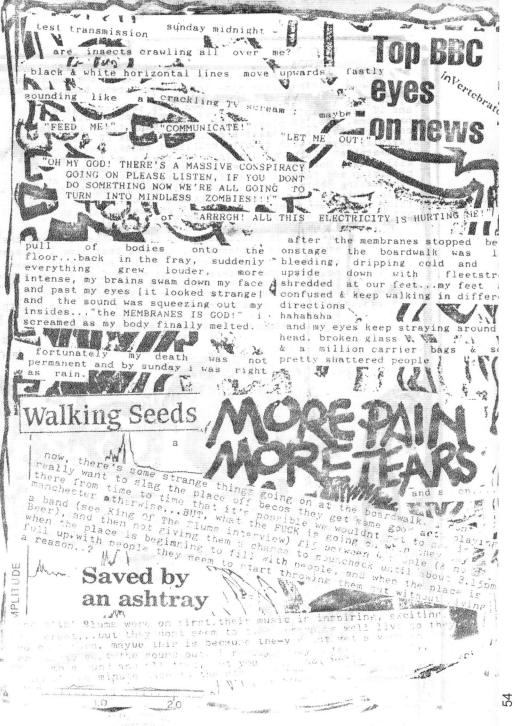

I am thinking of buying a ceramic hob

this review starts and ends somewhere else and these photos are from a completely different gig. PLEASE DO NOT ADJUST YOUR BRAIN

ROBB IN TOPLESS NIGHTCLUB SCANDAL

to know what i'm trying to explain you'd have to be there, obviously, to witness this multi (who knows how many) piece pop monster in action... but dont take them too seriously or you might end up like me

sunny summer days,
sitting in a field
listening to the flowers growing
& the birds arguing
slightly...this ISN'T what comes to
mind when i hear the membranes

THRASH THRILL

MASSACRE

tension pulls my nerves at the boardwalk creeps in wrenches at my legs shredded paper blazed in front of me , blurred lights in a dodgy background. the scene got ugly, sweat was dripping off the walls, robb was screaming , i couldnt resist the

test transmission sunday midnight -
are insects crawling all over me?
black & white horizontal lines move upwards fastly
sounding like a crackling TV scream : maybe
"FEED ME!" , "COMMUNICATE!" , "LET ME OUT!"

Top BBC eyes on news

inVertebrate

"OH MY GOD! THERE'S A MASSIVE CONSPIRACY GOING ON PLEASE LISTEN, IF YOU DONT DO SOMETHING NOW WE'RE ALL GOING TO TURN INTO MINDLESS ZOMBIES!!!"
or "ARRRGH! ALL THIS ELECTRICITY IS HURTING ME!"

pull of bodies onto the floor...back in the fray, suddenly everything grew louder, more intense, my brains swam down my face and past my eyes (it looked strange) and the sound was squeezing out my insides..."the MEMBRANES IS GOD!" i screamed as my body finally melted.

after the membranes stopped be[illegible] onstage the boardwalk was l[illegible] bleeding, dripping cold and upside down with fleetstr[illegible] shredded at our feet...my feet [illegible] confused & keep walking in differ[illegible] directions hahahaha
and my eyes keep straying around head. broken glass [illegible] & a million carrier bags & s[illegible] pretty shattered people

fortunately my death was not permanent and by sunday i was right as rain.

Walking Seeds

a MORE PAIN MORE TEARS

and s[illegible] on...

now, there's some strange things going on at the boardwalk. i dont really want to slag the place off becos they get some good acts playing there from time to time that it's possible we wouldnt get to see in manchester otherwise...BUT, what the FUCK is going on when they get a band (see King of The Slums interview) fit between 4 people (& no Beer), and then not giving them a chance to soundcheck until about 3.15pm when the place is beginning to fill with people, and when the place is full up with people they seem to start throwing them out without giving a reason..?

Saved by an ashtray

MPLITUDE

1.0 2.0

BROADCASTING MUSIC to MANCHESTER

DIY RADIO
104,7 FM

DO I NEED AN EAR OPERATION?

WEDNESDAYS 8PM–10

it is **illegal** to listen to pirate radio

This is absurd when we have now grown a brain that is for the first time capable of appreciating these wonders.

Court takes pirates off air

He said: "I was drinking like mad and spent £1,200 in one month. Now I'm back home, I won't get in trouble or my old man will rap me."

for information etc WRITE TO:
DIY radio
c/o RAVENPRESS
75 PICCADILLY
MANCHESTER
M1 2BU.

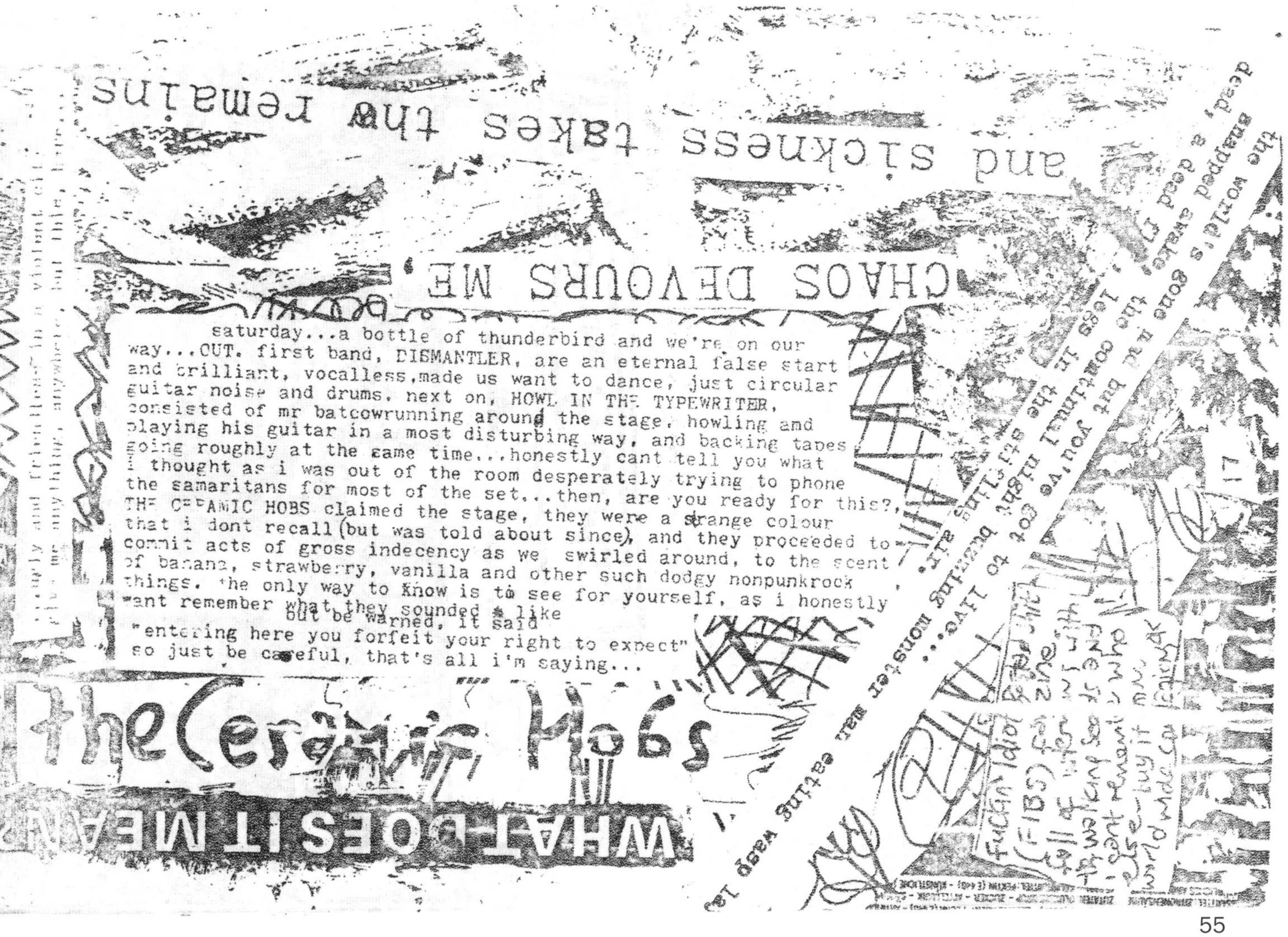

and sickness takes thw remains

CHAOS DEVOURS ME,

saturday...a bottle of thunderbird and we're on our way...OUT. first band, DISMANTLER, are an eternal false start and brilliant, vocalless,made us want to dance, just circular guitar noise and drums. next on, HOWL IN THE TYPEWRITER, consisted of mr batcowrunning around the stage, howling and playing his guitar in a most disturbing way, and backing tapes going roughly at the same time...honestly cant tell you what i thought as i was out of the room desperately trying to phone the samaritans for most of the set...then, are you ready for this?, THE CERAMIC HOBS claimed the stage, they were a strange colour that i dont recall(but was told about since), and they proceeded to commit acts of gross indecency as we swirled around, to the scent of banana, strawberry, vanilla and other such dodgy nonpunkrock things. the only way to know is to see for yourself, as i honestly cant remember what they sounded like
but be warned, it said
"entering here you forfeit your right to expect"
so just be careful, that's all i'm saying...

the Ceramic Hobs

WHAT DOES IT MEAN

DIY RADIO

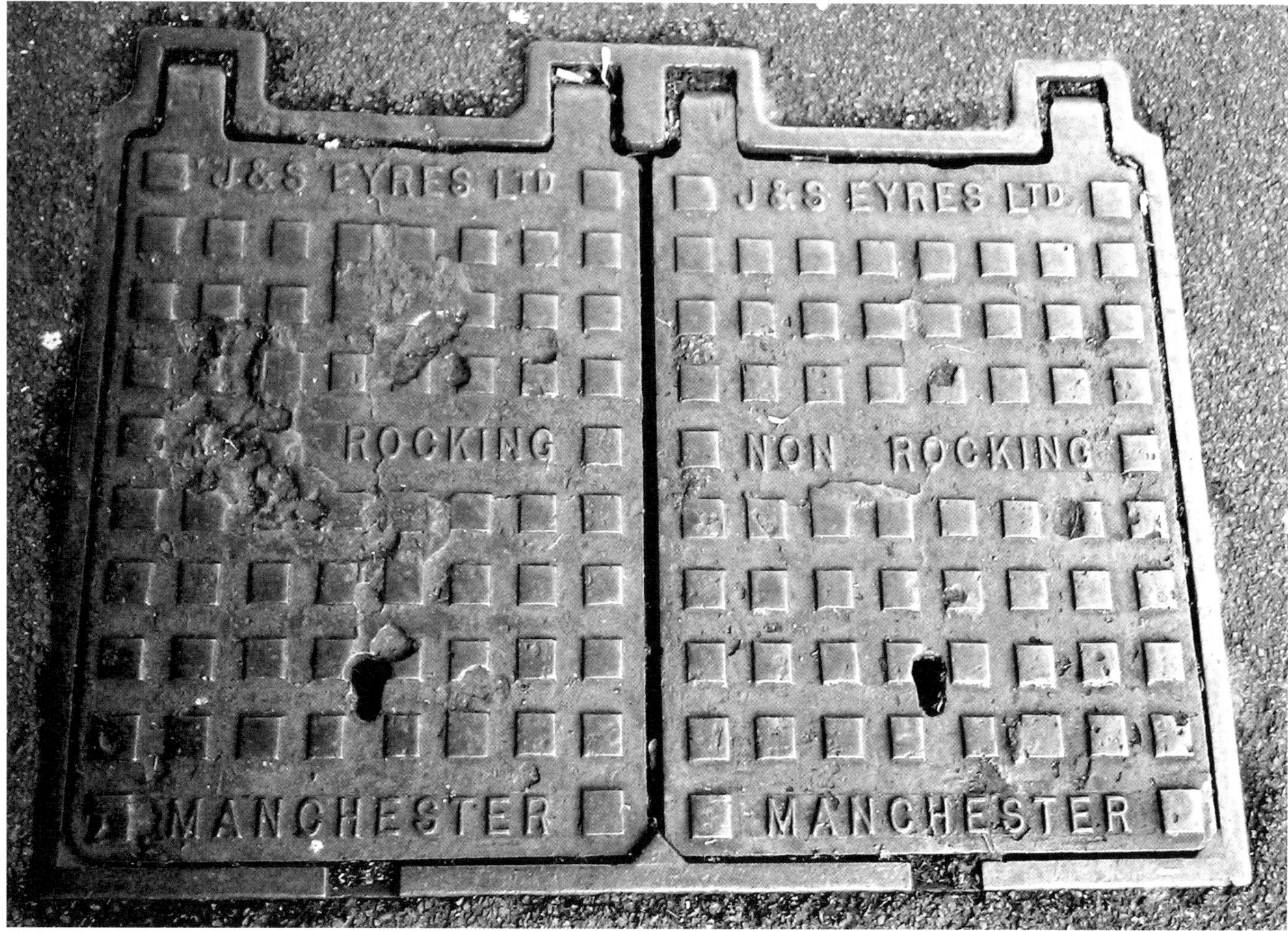

Pik was one of the first people I met through *Ablaze!*. A tall, half-French PhD student who always wore a suit, he was cool in an intelligent older punker kind of way. And he had an agenda.

One dull Sunday afternoon in the mid-1980s, equipped with a disposable camera, Pik took photographs of a pair of drain covers on which three immortal words were proudly etched: NON ROCKING MANCHESTER.

The music was there, he knew, but it needed to be shouted about from the rooftops. He was going to gigs across the North, sleeping on strangers' floors or hanging out at freezing railway stations for the first train home. Eventually he assembled a network of similarly-motivated individuals, and found a way to make the rooftops sing.

Mainstream mediocrity ran deep, and the pricks really needed kicking against. Sure, everyone listened to John Peel and went to gigs, but there was so much greatness out there, only known to those who saw it. Pik knew he couldn't buy a secret megaphone for the skies, so he decided to create his very own monster... a radio transmitter.

I cornered the fugitive in a London café and rediscovered what went on.

So you were living in Manchester doing your PhD? What was it in?

I arrived in 1982, did my degree there and my PhD started I guess in 1986. It was in engineering and biotechnology.

Did you get straight into the music scene when you got to Manchester?

Yeah, pretty quick. I grew up in a smaller town which didn't have so much music going on, and I realised after I came to Manchester that this was where the music was happening. One of the first gigs that I went to was at the Hacienda, The Birthday Party in February 1983, which was... wow. I didn't even know where the Hacienda was, but I knew who the Birthday Party were. Just after visiting the Hacienda, and seeing other bands like The Chameleons and The Fall, it became clear to me that there was some really interesting music going on here.

When did you start to get into radio?

I think it probably started when I was a kid; I got chicken pox and was given a small transistor radio to keep me quiet. I discovered all these disembodied voices and this weird music, and Radio Luxembourg - it was a medium wave only set - and so I heard different music that wasn't being played elsewhere: glam and pop and disco and black music, things that you didn't hear so much on other channels, that didn't necessarily make any sense until I was older. When you're just a kid, you don't know what the night scene is like, what these places are, and what role music plays in society. You can hear this music and these voices and styles, and later on you start to piece together the story, the puzzle of where they come from and what they mean.

You were intrigued...

Yeah, by the possibilities of a whole new world just behind this three-inch square piece of black plastic, the universes that lay behind it. Then around 1984 a group of students set up a short-lived radio station called The Rig, and I got involved on the technical side. I did a show with a guy called Tom Burke from Chicago, we were doing a US punk thing. Tom had records by his local Chicago bands, Naked Raygun, who were big at the time, and a lesser known act called Big Black. He was coming in with some of the records that I was reading about in Maximum Rock'n'Roll, and that you couldn't hear, even on Peel, and he actually he had them in his bag. It got me thinking that, not only is there music here, but real people like him and me, and record shops and record collections and an enthusiasm for this music.

What were your shows like?

Shambolic. They were live. You just went on. We got no training, none of the stuff that I later realised was kind of important. The quality wasn't very good for technical reasons, but it was a show. We had people listen to it, and you could hear people talk about it. It gave me a taste – and then we'd go and see bands together. At that time Black Flag played in Manchester. I was really into this second wave punk stuff from the US, early forms of Hüsker Dü, later on Meat Puppets, R.E.M., all those bands, a lot of bands from the east coast, west coast, and later on the Pixies. The precursors of all those things were coming through back then, supported by college radio in the States.

So how did DIY Radio start?

One of the critical things in helping that to start was that some anarchists in Bristol had produced a booklet called *Radio Is My Bomb*. For a long time they promised that this book would come out, it was going to be a partial history of free radio with some technical descriptions of how to build a transmitter. Eventually it appeared and it was a proper 80-page A4 glossy-covered stapled magazine, and it was all there. You'd get to learn about the history in different countries, with very difficult situations in Eastern Europe where it was forbidden to say certain things, let alone broadcast. And of course, the key element that had been missing for me at the time was knowing how to make one of these damn things [transmitters], so I went down to the electronic shop and bought all the bits and made some, and they worked.

How soon after you got the book did you get out there and broadcast?

Pretty quick. I think the book came out in summer 1987, I built two or three transmitters to try them out, and by October a plan was coming together about how to make it happen, and I was ready to broadcast. One of the things I did want to put out was the Maximum Rock'n'Roll radio show. MRR was [and still is] this really cruddy-looking magazine printed on 100 or so pages of newsprint which covered the punk scenes in all different countries, and reported on intense and elaborate philosophical debates such as the maximum allowable length of a guitar solo in punk songs - the answer was 1.4 seconds. And they did a weekly C60 cassette radio show. I'd got a sample copy way back at the time I'd been involved with The Rig and it seemed to me that there was a lot of stuff on there that was worth playing. There was a little bit of an overlap with some of what Peel was playing, but he was playing all kinds of different stuff, whereas this was more focused. And I wanted to broadcast that, so with that tape as programme number one, the transmitter and all the gubbins that goes with it, somewhere to broadcast from - I won't go into the details - the next question was, is there anything else that I could be putting out on this? Using a basic record player/tape recorder set up and a lot of fiddling about, it was just about possible to make a radio show, so I started trying to find other people with a similar interest and levels of energy to contribute. It was one thing to talk about it down the pub with people who like listening to stuff or people who are in bands, but they were all busy doing something else. So that's when I started reaching out to people doing fanzines.

You thought everybody doing fanzines wanted to do other stuff too?

I think they wanted to do more than just listen to records and go to gigs, and for various reasons they didn't feel the need to spend all the rest of their time playing in bands or trying to replicate what the bands were doing. They were fulfilling another role in this, what we now call an ecosystem. To make music work, get people excited, to put out new ideas, you need record shops, record labels, you need the musicians, the bands and the venues, but if you haven't got a magazine or a radio station, you're missing something. I think it worked out well with the fanzines. I wasn't doing another fanzine but I was providing the paper, if you like.

How did you find your fanzine writer DJs?

I looked through some likely fanzines at Piccadilly Records, and came across Ablaze! #1, the one with the free gift. A few days later, one early weekday evening around the end of October, I went to a gig at The Tropicana Club, which was like a knocking shop disco recycled for one evening as a live music venue. I'm not sure who was playing – possibly The Bodines... Dub Sex? The room was pretty empty, and cold, but I could see these two individuals stooping over the other punters, making their way around the gloomy room. One was unmistakably the shaven-headed figure of Dave Haslam of *Debris* magazine, the other was you. "Hiya, actually I've already got that one. I liked the free gift. Have you thought about... there's this er... new... radio station started up looking for DJs?" "Oh, I'm going to Leeds," but I got your address and sent you a note that evening - this was pre-internet and mobile phones. I met you again a few weeks later at a party at [BBC Radio Manchester DJ] Al Martin's house - passing through the kitchen to grab a drink, I saw this shock of multi-coloured hair and makeup lunging out of the corner and into the brightness of the kitchen, cassette tape in hand. It was labelled 'Songs for you to hate, b/w More songs for you to hate'.

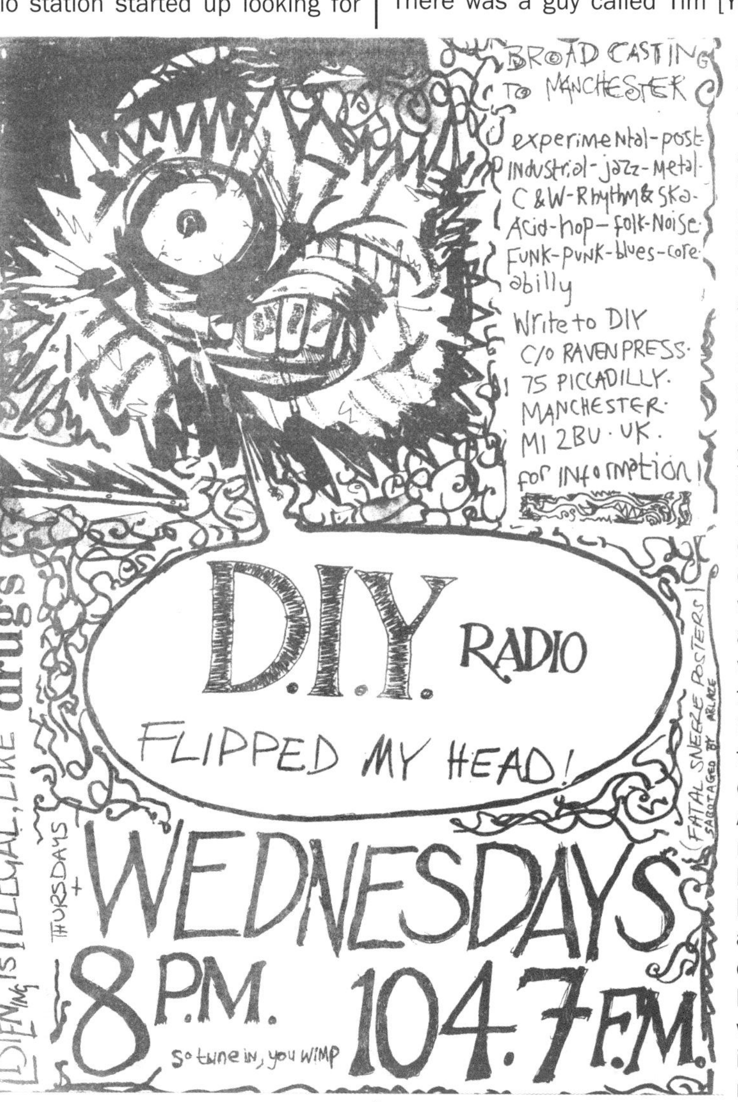

It was so much fun. Making a show was just like making a mix tape but with talking in between. And you could make your own jingles.

And not knowing who was going to hear it.

So when did DIY Radio start?

At the start of October 1987. We broadcast Wednesday nights, then later we got more people involved and broadcast on Thursday evenings as well. I had to do all the promotion for it, handing out flyers at gigs and getting some feedback there. We had some little stickers that we started putting everywhere. There were lots of other big, black pirate stations in Manchester at the time, with massive transmitters and big egos. We had a space on the dial next to them. They were louder and more popular in their communities, fulfilling a different role. You'd see our stickers alongside their posters.

How many shows were there?

The most we ever did was four hours a week, two hours on Wednesday and two hours on Thursday - it was a pop-up station. I tried to persuade people to provide a half-hour show so there would be eight shows a week, and some people, for various reasons, couldn't do every week and were more comfortable doing one every other week. So I think there were 11 or 12 different groups of people altogether. They had to provide the show on one side of a C60 cassette, and it was down to them how they produced it. And there was the MRR show.

Could people subscribe and listen to it at home?

No, it was supposed to be only for radio stations. There was a list on the inside cover of MRR detailing the stations broadcasting it, and I think we were the only one in the UK; there was maybe one other in Europe. There were a bunch in Canada, a couple in Australia and occasionally some other place. It was listed by state, so one in Arkansas, three in Iowa and then one in Manchester. So we were up there next to Sioux Falls or whatever.

Who presented the MRR show?

There was a guy called Tim [Yohannon]: "Hi, I'm Tim from MRR." They just had a couple of people presenting it and they rotated through people. They'd talk quite fast in American English, so if you were not tuned to that it was quite hard, but I think for us it was okay and the music was good stuff, and there was some slightly odd stuff there. But what I was struck by was how, one of the editions I'd had a couple of years before, I didn't know the bands, but years later they'd become more well known. The Butthole Surfers were on an early show in '84, then they came over to the UK, then you went to see them in like 1987 and thought "What on earth was that?" - we played them first. There was some KUKL in there somewhere as well; this weird girl from Iceland called B-jorn or something. And then Peel would play it six months later - but that's only because he had a six-month backlog, not because he was any less well connected. Later on at DIY we tried to cover all kinds of different music. It wasn't just the stuff I liked, indie rock, there was some metal and hip-hop. A guy called Nadeem would play some real weird-ass stuff and I'd have to get him to explain it to me afterwards.

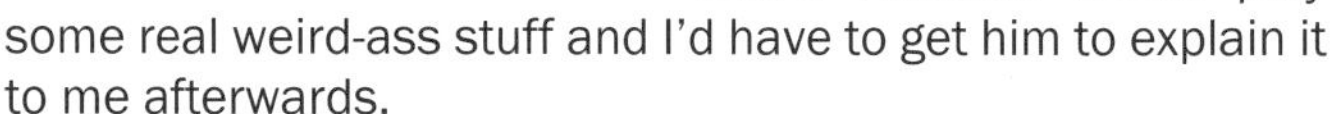

Where did the signal reach?

It went out in the city centre, and south of the city centre. It covered the student area. I did try to get more power [for the transmitter], but that wasn't the principle of the thing. It was to be low-key, low power, and not to draw too much attention to itself.

And did it?

Not really. I don't want to go into all the dark arts but we managed to avoid trouble for a long, long time, and the other stations did get closed down. It went on for about a year from when I set it up, then my studies finished and I handed it on to someone else who scaled it up, but then it petered out after that. So it was a year and a bit in all, until October 1988. It was fun but it was stressful, trying to run the whole station as one person. I realised that radio stations need several people to run them. It was one of those projects where if nothing happens, that's good, whereas normally in life you want something to happen. You didn't want to get closed down, you didn't want the thing to stop. So that was all a bit hard to deal with, just waiting for something to go wrong.

What did you do next?

I moved to Sheffield. I thought there must be someone around here interested in a similar thing, and waited around until 1992 when some students set up a student society, initially wanting to do TV, and maybe start with some radio. That had actually been my original plan in Manchester, to do TV. There was a group in London, Network 21, that I was in touch with who were doing that, and they helped me in the early days. But for TV you need a lot more money and a lot more time. The quality standard, believe it or not, is quite high, so it's really hard to meet the expectation. The BBC has spoilt us, maybe less so these days, by being too high-tech. YouTube's changed this, of course. Anyway, in Sheffield we set up a broadcast. By that time, the licensing authority had become more open to small-scale groups running radio stations, rather than just one per city, which had been the rule before. So we applied for a one-month licence, to broadcast 24 hours a day starting at the beginning of the student term – which nearly killed us - but at least we had proper resources, and a team of motivated people, an office, phones, a studio, microphones, all that stuff that helps make it a little bit easier. And then that group carried on and did nine more broadcasts like that before moving on, all in one month blocks, as Forge FM.

Once we had permission and everything we needed, the question was how do we fill all the slots? I thought "Oh, hang on, I know some people!" You picked up the offer, as indeed did some other people. Chris Trout did the very first show. He was the first person to swear on air, 12 minutes in. I was involved for the first two broadcasts and then I moved on. It was the vision of one person in particular, Paul Kewley, and I filled in some of the blanks. He had a lot of the technical knowledge and political nous to make it happen. Without him, it probably would not have happened, and there was a team of outstanding people. Then I moved to France and got involved with the same kind of radio station there, with Brume FM, which broadcast in Grenoble and Lyon.

After DIY Radio, our roles were reversed - you started to contribute to my fanzine [and I tried to start a radio station, Fervour FM].

We interviewed the Sugarcubes together, more Einar than Bjork. But she was quite close with a pushchair and the kid in it. She was there but didn't speak. She just went past, she wasn't playing.

You interviewed SH Draumar too.

There was a big thing about Iceland at the time, there were a few bands coming out. A guy called Gunar used to do some darkly humorous Icelandic scene reports, and I wrote to him and asked if he could send me something I could use. He said "Send $2 and I'll send you a cassette," and then he introduced me to some other people and I got a bunch of music and it was interesting stuff.

You also interviewed Nirvana for me (we'll talk about that later in the book!). What are your views on where fanzines fitted in?

In terms of the role that these media had in the development of music, we both saw how some bands, like Nirvana, would be very friendly to alternative media outlets. If you were from the press or TV: "We know your game," or if you were from a fanzine or an alternative station: "Oh yeah come on in we'll talk to you." There are a number of instances where I heard that, and now with the internet it's the same thing only a million times more. Without that there's something missing. Alternative media fulfil a role other media do not provide.

You mentioned the idea of an ecosystem earlier...

Yeah, there are the venues. I think in Leeds you were very lucky to have The Duchess of York as a place that was always showing stuff, probably more so than in Manchester. I mean Manchester had lots of venues but it was very chaotic and you'd have nothing for a couple of weeks then you'd have three gigs on the same night. Some places seemed a bit better co-ordinated, or maybe it was just luck. And then you had the record shops. In Manchester we had Eastern Bloc, Piccadilly Records and a few others. Piccadilly are great, friendly people and they'd always recommend stuff, and Eastern Bloc could be fantastically snooty, you couldn't get to the counter if you weren't cool enough. But they performed a role in the development of music at that time. The Madchester thing, the dance music that was happening in the late 1980s, if the record shops, the venues, the other radio stations had not all been taking part, it wouldn't have been the same.

And, you know, it's not right to overplay how much hard work it also was: printing and distributing the zines, finding like-minded people with whom to collaborate, fly-posting, editing and broadcasting the music, and generally getting our voice heard. If we'd known how hard and expensive it was going to be, well, no, we'd still have done it. It's easy to say the technology now, the iTunes-podcast-YouTube-Facebook-Twitter machine, makes it so much easier, but that's not the point.

KARREN ABLAZE !
Flat C31,
James Baillie,
N. Hill Road,
LEEDS LS6 2EN

15 Feb. 1988

Dear KARREN !

It was great to meet you 'properly' at last; rather than trying to talk to you hiding under a pinball machine which I found quite difficult. Thanx for the floor, hard as it was, and

The Gospel according to Andrew Truth

Could fanzine writing be compared to being a Jehovah's Witness? There is a shared, obsessive devotion to a cause, and a determination to convert others to your worldview. At least a fanzine writer is only obtrusive when interrupting conversations at gigs, and never resorts to door-stepping. Fanzine editors also harbour no delusions about being rewarded in an afterlife; converting a few readers to the joys of another criminally-ignored band is sufficient reward.

I speak from experience, having edited 15 issues of *Plane Truth* between 1988 and 1995, and having contributed to numerous other zines, including *Ablaze!*. So what drew a shy and introverted youngster into this world? Like 99% of people heavily involved with independent music at the time, the answer is John Peel. As a child who grew up spending an unhealthy amount of time alone indoors, the radio was a faithful companion. Being slightly too young to have been gripped by punk, it was Two Tone which really started to shape my worldview. I first tuned into Peel in May 1980, having heard he would be broadcasting a session that evening by The Beat, and that was the day my musical horizons began to be stretched. Although some of the music I heard that night was a taste it would take me some time to acquire, I had started to travel a path from which there would be no return.

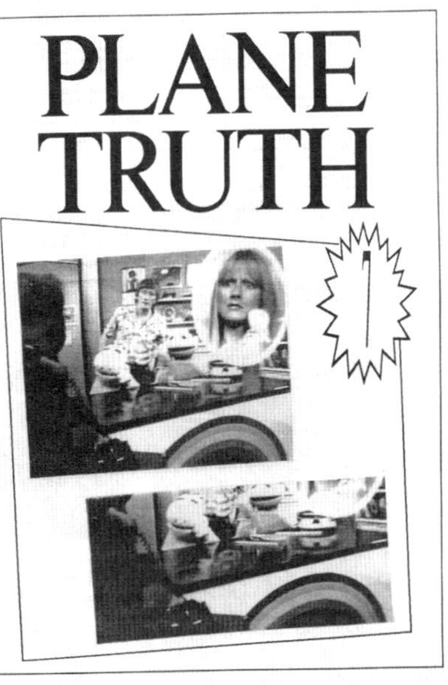

Over the next five years, Peel's dulcet tones soundtracked my evenings, interrupted only by the occasional gig when the likes of The Specials, Madness, The Beat, Dexys Midnight Runners, Echo and the Bunnymen and The Teardrop Explodes visited the municipal halls of nearby Lancashire towns. In 1985 I turned 18 and, armed with a birth certificate to prove it, I was off to the newly formed Twang Clubbe at The Caribbean Club in Preston. Each Wednesday, for the princely sum of £1, some of the leading indie bands of the era, such as Big Flame, June Brides, Age of Chance, Marc Riley and the Creepers, Membranes, Bogshed, The Nightingales and The Wedding Present would perform under a glitterball in the unlikely setting of this working men's club. All of these bands had received favourable music press coverage, and having been brought up on gigs at bigger venues, it was quite a surprise to see them sitting in the audience prior to their sets. I was quick to notice that, in general, the same people were turning up to gigs each week and that they all tended to be in bands and/or writing fanzines. That was the first intimation that this music actually was a minority interest everywhere, as opposed to my home town, Chorley, being a freakishly uncool place. Having been self-taught in my music tastes, and turning up to these gigs on my own, I was amazed when the promoter, Dave Hindmarsh, asked what I thought of the gigs and when John Robb of my favourite band, The Membranes, started talking to me on the train after a Vee V V gig. I was still prey to the hero worship of most young music fans but, suddenly, my heroes were accessible.

Naturally, I wanted to absorb all I possibly could about my favourite music so would buy any fanzine which crossed my path. My particular favourites were a Preston zine, *Noise Annoys*, and Blackpool's legendary *Rox*. However, over the next couple of years, I would get increasingly disillusioned with the many zines that consisted of lazily unedited question-and-answer interviews and generally poor writing, and it was these that were the inspiration for my first two attempts at confrontational "anti-zines" as I dubbed them: *Snailtank* and *FiBS*. It was only when I encountered *Ablaze!* for the first time that I was reminded it was possible to balance perceptive interviews with writing which illustrated the editor's personality.

Suitably inspired, I began *Plane Truth* and ramped up my enthusiasm and gig-going to 11. The lengths I would go to see any halfway decent gig were absurd; one classic example involved Karren and I hitching from Manchester to London, only to find that The Janitors gig we were seeking was not happening. With nowhere to stay, we stumbled back to the garden of what may have been a Janitor's flat, but he was not at home so we slept fitfully on a cold lawn, fortified by slugs of whiskey. More worthwhile were our attempts to follow the Pixies, who were the sound of the summer of 1988, although again things finished horribly in London: trying to sleep in Victoria Station under the payphones while homeless people rummage in the coins-returned section for change is not recommended. It was a huge relief to establish contacts in the capital and gain places to stay.

Interviews for *Plane Truth* were very hit-and-miss initially. I was determined to avoid any of the clichéd questions about influences, and was trying to get at grand ideas about how music and lyrics might reflect a philosophy of life. When this worked, I had some inspiring conversations, but on other occasions I foundered, with interviewees who probably wondered "Who's this prat? He's not as clever as he thinks." A classic example of this was The Three Johns, who in early 1985 had taken the crown of My Favourite Band in the World, an accolade accorded to acts for only a few months in those dizzying times before I found something even more earth-shattering. If there are any aspiring fanzine editors out there, I would suggest that the way to arrange an interview is not to ask the band while they are on stage - although at least I did wait for the gap between songs. And when John Brennan announced to the audience, "No, we do not want to do an interview with *Plane Truth*," that ought to have closed the matter. Instead, Karren persuaded me that no meant yes (thanks Karren!), so we stormed their dressing room and started firing questions. When their first answer referenced *Death of the European* not getting airplay after the Heysel Stadium disaster, I interrupted to say that I had already heard that story, and moved on the next question. Even 23 years later, I feel my face flushing red with embarrassment at such rudeness; no wonder the interview stumbled into a hostile silence.

However, I was able to establish a rapport with some of my favourite bands around 1990. It was probably the last era where obscure bands were still able to book extensive tours so I would find myself seeing the likes of AC Temple, The Keatons, Levellers 5 and Dandelion Adventure up to 20 each times in a year. It was like being a fanatical supporter of four football teams simultaneously.

Dandelion Adventure were the finest band to emerge from Preston; the three of them (Fat Mark - vocals, Stan – guitar and Ajay – bass) had been familiar faces from Twang Clubbe days. After what seemed like an astonishing debut gig in 1986 with Mark ranting on about armadillos for hours before the promoters "persuaded" them to leave the stage (in retrospect, I suspect it was formless noise but I was impressionable at that stage), they re-emerged with greater focus in 1988, bussing in friends and families to help them get to the final of a Blackpool Battle of the Bands competition. However, it was with the addition of Jason as a second drummer to augment Jeff's sterling work, that they became a formidable proposition with Ajay flinging his bass around the dancefloor (I was among the fans who received war wounds from that), Stan enticing great sounds from his effects pedal, and Mark as an ever-compelling presence. I am sure there must be groups with two or more drummers that haven't worked well, but it does seem like a guarantee of a propulsive live set and a ludicrously crowded Transit van. Speaking of which, I had now been introduced to the joys of travelling with the band. The advantage of free travel to gigs outweighed the discomfort of sitting in the back of vans with no actual seats and being precariously wedged in among the drums and guitars. Around the time that *Jinx's Truck* was released, their later and finer record (theirs was not an extensive career), I was with the band as they experienced a freakish crash which not only damaged the front of the van but also messed with their psyches, as the registration number was similar to Mark's final line of the album, "You jinx". It was also highly flattering to be asked by the band to interview them for *Maximum Rock'n'Roll*; a sign that I was trusted to represent them fairly, which is surely the greatest accolade for any music writer. Recently Mark spoke to me about his contributing artwork for a Fall record with a modesty that he rarely showed as a performer, stating that he had come full circle from fronting a Fall tribute act. Despite borrowing a vocal style from Mark E Smith, the Dandelion Adventure were far more than copyists.

In contrast, if The Keatons were selecting their post-punk idols, it would presumably be Wire. Whilst never to be dismissed as a Wire tribute act, they did perform a one-off set consisting of covers of their songs. The Keatons had a great pop sensibility and wonderfully cryptic lyrics which, clueless as I was about public taste, I thought should have made them massive. Yet the elements of their gigs that I found so appealing could also be viewed as self-sabotage. The band operated what could be considered a squad system. Chief songwriter and lead singer, Neil Wilson, appeared live increasingly infrequently, especially after being punched in the face by a disgruntled audience member in Blackpool. Even when the same individuals were involved, they would swap around to keep things lively: on consecutive nights in Newcastle, Rhodri Marsden was vocalist and then drummer. And then there was Mo Bottomley. Membranes fans had shown that carrier bags full of torn-up paper could be thrown in the air to create a delirious feeling while dancing under showers of confetti. In Mo, The Keatons had their own mess artist. His first action with the band had been to explode a banana. On another occasion, he constructed a cardboard "love booth" at the side of the stage for the more affectionate and demonstrative audience members. In general, he specialised in mixing together inappropriate and messy food stuffs; I have particularly fond memories of dancing around in one of his discarded cardboard suits with melon pips streaming down my face. In the chaos of tuneful noise and mess, surely the only sane response is to dance manically and gleefully? Well, in Liverpool five of us did this whilst everyone else tried to melt into the walls at the sides and the back of the hall. It was after this gig that The Keatons were thrown off their support tour with a nascent Blur, for frightening their audience.

With hindsight, one of the strangest aspects of my gig-going odyssey was a passing and instantly dismissive contact with bands that would go on to be championed by the mainstream music press and become hugely popular. Throughout the *Plane Truth* years, if I had been an A&R man, I would have been the worst in the business. Here are some of my finest moments:

1987 – Walking out on a support band for the first time ever, during The Wonder Stuff's set at the ICA;

1988 - Turning up at the St Helens Citadel in 1988 to discover that the Dog Faced Hermans had pulled out of their support slot, and deciding that it was not worth paying £3 to see the headline act, The Stone Roses;

1990 – Joking with Norwich's finest, Basti, about the band sharing their bill at the Bull and Gate, who I laughingly dismissed after the first 30 seconds of their set, the Manic Street Preachers;

1991 – At tea time on Saturday at the Reading Festival, sitting in a tent and agreeing that it is not worth seeing Nirvana as they are a boring rock band. (This is about the only one in this list that I regret, albeit only slightly);

1994 – Seeing Oasis at a free festival in Preston Park and dismissively commenting that their best song is *I am the Walrus* which was hardly The Beatles' finest moment. Also being astonished that some otherwise sensible Mancunian friends are proudly stating they are local boys made good; what place has tribal, football-style loyalty got in music? Unfortunately, clearly more than it should have;

1995 – Watching Supergrass and The Bluetones do soundchecks, and wisely deciding there is no point wasting a couple of hours of my life watching their sets.

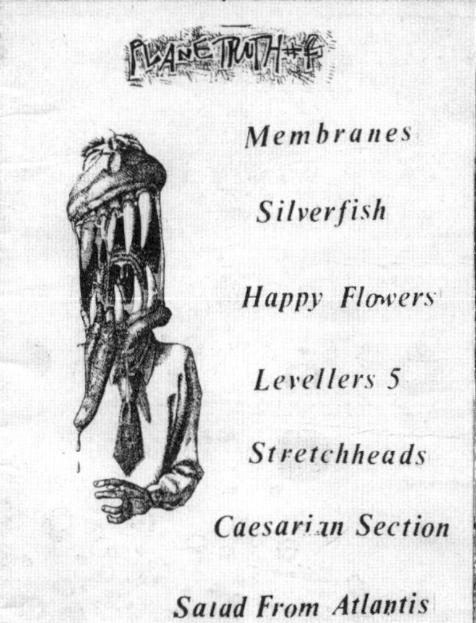

PLANE TRUTH
Membranes
Silverfish
Happy Flowers
Levellers 5
Stretchheads
Caesarian Section
Salad From Atlantis

Although I never saw Radiohead live, I did resist the blandishments of Hall or Nothing, the PR agents with the worst roster of bands, sending me *Creep* three times. It's no wonder, with this pitiful record of star spotting, that Steve Keaton was disappointed when I liked his new band, Hen, remarking, "We've no chance of being successful then!" I preferred to see it as a reflection of the reverse talent-to-popularity ratio (which I believe was Einstein's greatest discovery), and that it meant that *Plane Truth* had a purpose in voicing opinions and taste against the increasingly narrow types of sounds championed in the music press.

As some of my favourite English bands either split or found constantly loss-making touring a chore, I hitched my wagon to some of the prime American touring acts: Pavement, with Gary Young as a drink-addled Mo Bottomley, trying to make each show an event whilst technically being responsible for maintaining some sort of steady beat behind the drum kit; twisted guitar-noise merchants Trumans Water with a similarly wandering drummer; and Rodan, whose week touring the UK was the pinnacle of post-rock - as a live act they surpassed even Slint.

By 1995, edging towards 30 and maybe under the mistaken impression that it was time to grow up, I realised that the burning passion was dimming. After years of somehow managing to combine a permanent full-time job with ridiculous travelling (at one point, gig acquaintances in Leeds and London thought I lived in their cities, even though I was domiciled in Preston), I knew that I no longer had the overwhelming desire to ensure that I caught every brilliant gig and chronicle the thoughts of all those bands. Looking back, I am astonished at my energy in cramming so much in. There would be occasions where I did a full day at work, leapt onto a train to London for an 'unmissable' gig, then took what I egotistically called the Andrew Truth Gig Train home at midnight and would be back in the office the next morning after an unsustainably small amount of sleep. Any occasion when I was not at a gig or work, I would be writing fanzines or sending letters to gig/band-related friends. It is only possible to maintain that frenzied level of activity when possessed of the fervent belief that this is what makes life worth living.

After moments of falling out of love with music, I have returned to the belief that there is little to match the sense of elevation given by a sublime gig. Do I think that music was better between 1988 and 1995? Not necessarily, although it did mean more to me just because I was young and being introduced to sounds that were new to me at the time. Had I been born a bit later, I suspect I would have followed The Delgados with a similar devotion. If I were in my twenties now, I might be trailing up and down the country to leap around to Deerhunter, Times New Viking and Thee Oh Sees.

Times are different now, and whether paper-based fanzines are necessary when bands can promote their own music on the internet is debatable; the few recent examples I have seen are dreary. The mainstream is still rubbish but there seems little point in railing against it, I just accept that most people have chosen to prefer this type of music. I still get introduced to fine music through Marc Riley, Tom Ravenscroft - the Peel dynasty lives on - and The Freak Zone on 6 Music, although at least as much comes from recommendations by friends. Great moments still occur because people are performing or putting on gigs out of love for music rather than the anticipation of profit, as evidenced by the Tuff Life Boogie-promoted gigs taking place in Preston from 2011 which have meant that my enjoyment of living in the city has reached its highest level yet.

Tales from the Psychiatric Underground

The Simon Morris interview

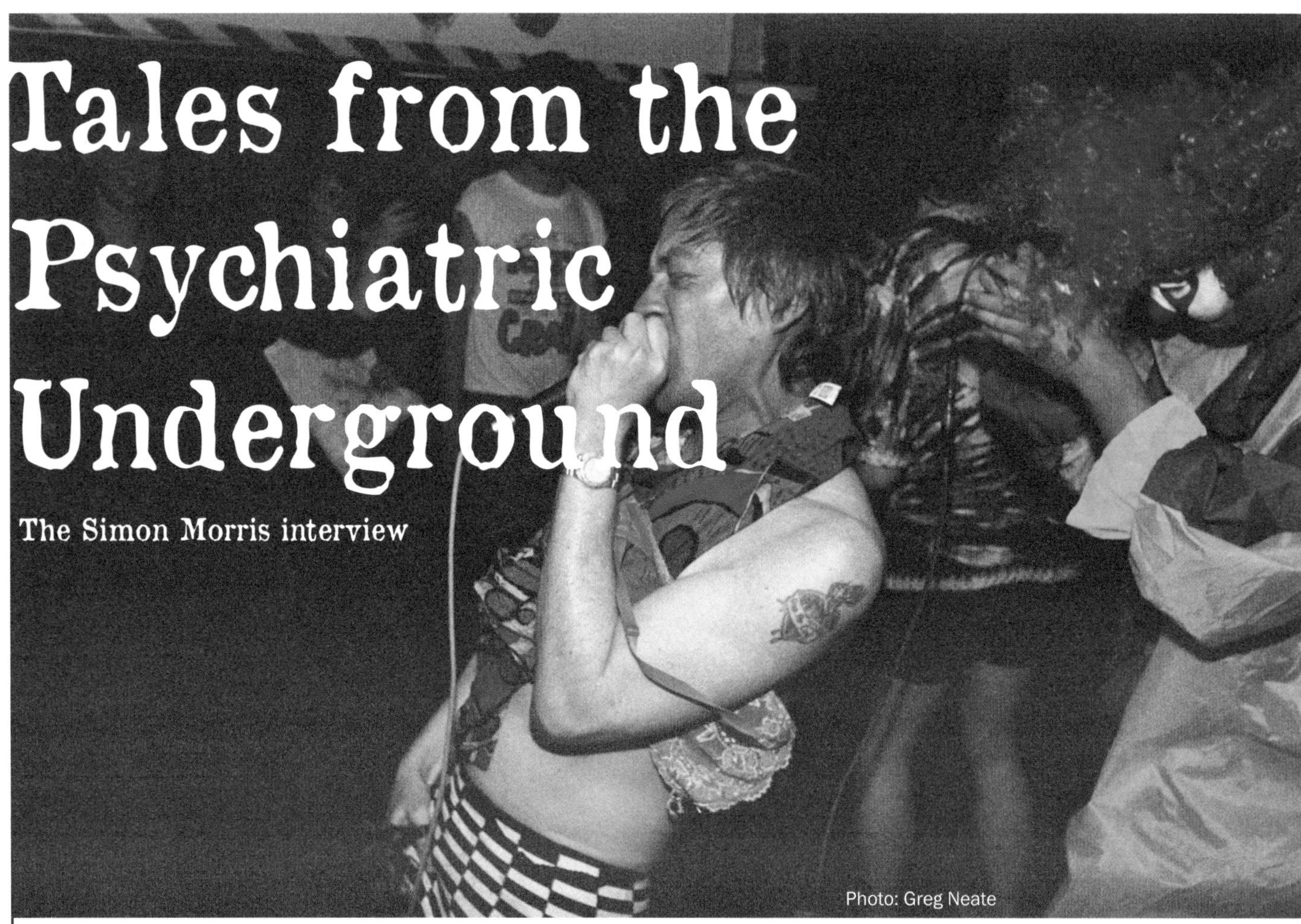

Photo: Greg Neate

Simon Morris was the second person I met through Ablaze!. We went out with each other for a year and a half in the early days of Ablaze!, and I was influenced by his fearless and off-kilter approach. Zine publisher and Ceramic Hobs singer since the mid-1980s, he's been in and out of mental hospitals, played an important part in the Mad Pride movement, and lives in Blackpool, a super-deprived, super-depraved British holiday destination.

How/why did you start Turnip Flag?

I'd seen zines like Andy Martin's *Scum* and John Robb's *Rox*, really enjoyed reading them and thought 'I could do that'. I was 16 and I guess had just started going out to gigs, although God knows there weren't many in Blackpool, so I had to travel. Had help from a couple of friends, including the all-important free stolen printing. We got a Ted Chippington interview for the first issue, I don't think anyone had asked him for an interview before, he was really nice. The intentions initially were simply to meet more like-minded people in other towns, and expand social horizons. Within six months of starting to publish I'd lost my virginity at the respectable age of 17 to an older hippy chick who liked Psychic TV and had bought the zine, so that ambition was taken care of quickly! After a while I realised I really didn't want to write about music but wanted to make the sort of magazine I wished existed, just for my own pleasure. Issue 7 with all the multicoloured printing, collage work and articles on Dada and Scientology was definitely something I was proud of - still looks good now. I guess *Vague* who did that kinda '60s-in-'80s *Oz/IT* influenced thing would have been an influence. It was a very unambitious magazine compared to yours, the maximum print runs were about 200 per issue if I recall and usually less, just distributed through the mail, word-of-mouth mostly. Same goes for the series of zines with ever-changing names I did during the '90s. Nowadays anything I do in print seems to get bootlegged online quite quickly, which is flattering in a way but annoying. I've tried to counter historification processes by, for instance, making websites without my name on them, where any connection is quite hard to prove. I guess I do much more internet work than real printed zines nowadays, the semi-anonymous stuff is always the most fun and mischievous.

What was your involvement with Ablaze!?

Sexual. Hur-hur. Well, we met after you sold me a very early issue at a Janitors gig and I guess you wrote little bits about my zines and bands in the early issues. I contributed very occasional pieces for yours: a somewhat confrontationally-phrased Walkingseeds review, an appreciation of Flipper, and a review of a Bernard Manning show! I remember you kindly helped me release a single on Stuffed Cat UK when the Hobs were really on our arses working in isolation as Orange Sunshine in the early '90s. The single wasn't too great and lost money but it was important for keeping the work going and meeting future contacts. I was more of an appreciative reader than actively involved in the magazine. I'm sure having read it from the beginning I was the first to moan when you featured a more conventional type of band such as The Wedding Present posing on a glossy colour cover. I can picture myself as a little intellectual snob back then saying "Why aren't you writing about Suckdog or Sun City Girls B sides?" or something. It really picked up and went out with a bang on the last issue - I thought all that Riot Grrrl and Nation of Ulysses stuff was great, especially as it annoyed certain people so much.

As a writer/artist/musician you have managed to continue doing what you do for an extended period of time without selling out. How's that?

This question is disingenuous. We all 'sell out' as soon as we buy a cup of coffee or use a computer or phone which includes coltan. There's no way of 'living differently' under Capital. It stinks of the most stupid form of lifestyle anarchism to imagine there is. I swore I'd never have a barcode on any Hobs release, swore I would never sign anything ever, swore I'd never be distributed by a major label, all of those happened in the early '00s, and hey, we had a MurdochSpace on more than one occasion - how the fuck is that 'not compromising'? I've sold out more than most especially as I've had the ignorance, vanity and hypocrisy to espouse 'principles'. I've taken easy options to avoid fights, been moulded by unseen corporate entities possessed by Capital escaped from human control and with a zombie lifeforce of its own. No escape. If it appears that I have not 'sold out', this is illusion. What I will say is that I've always been aware that making money diminishes the power of art - it simply seems like common sense to me from an aesthetic point of view. The best artists have day jobs and always will. I remain grossly uncomfortable at accepting money beyond costs for creative work as it cheapens and helps lower the standards of the work. An artist's primary audience should be their future self and a handful of select and fortunate specific others; everything I've done is for a very few. Elitism? Probably. Furthermore, intellectual property rights as used in the creative industries are hugely problematic; I want as little to do with propping up that edifice as possible. Putting a shop window through after drinking all day is more my level than networking upwards. I'm more likely to be found sleeping it off in a police cell than in the PRS, and I'm glad about that.

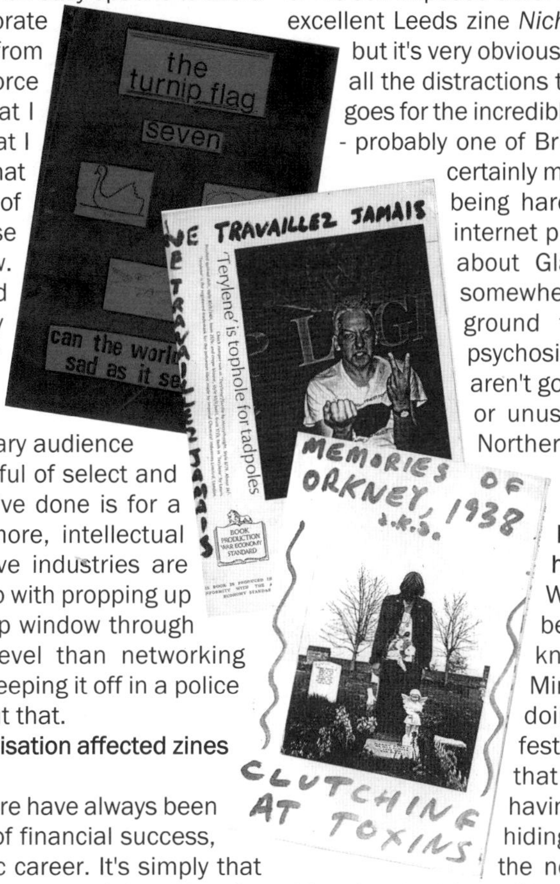

In your experience how has commercialisation affected zines and outsider art?

I don't think it has or ever did really. There have always been and still are zines done without hope of financial success, or as a stepping stone to a journalistic career. It's simply that some do use it as a 'starting point' towards a job writing for money. I remember Dave Simpson had a very kinda mainstream and respectable looking zine in Leeds [*Avanti*] long before he wrote for Melody Maker and The Guardian. Good luck to some of these people - his book on ex-Fall members was hugely entertaining, if very mean-spirited. I guess John Robb's zines weren't intended as moneyspinners but more of a cultural weapon. A lot of his focus changed after he started writing for the music press, presumably to pay for some of The Membranes' debts. I don't think you can 'infiltrate' the corporate world or work from within to any great success. The real underground is out there, it always has been. You're not gonna find out about it online or in a glossy ad-driven giveaway or in *Elle magazine*, which had a page on zines in its March 2012 issue - you have to do the work and digging to find the real stuff. The notion of 'outsider art' is more troubling, I have big problems with the intentions of curators of this material, even if in the case of someone like Nick Blinko, it's improved their real life. I hated that Daniel Johnston film and haven't listened to his records since. The cynicism of the marketing, not only by his supporters but by Daniel himself, stuck in my craw. Someone I really admire enormously (Philip Best) seems to include certain themes in his art deliberately as a kind of built-in boobytrap weapon to prevent co-opting, I think that's great. Obviously someone like Henri Darger or Adolf Wolfli would strike a very different and rather less savoury picture alive than after their unlikely posthumous canonisation by the art world.

Did you ever think of country, town and city zines as being particularly distinct?

Good question. I remember your zine being more city based than mine, had more stuff actually related to going out and seeing live bands, while I was often stuck rhapsodising about distant art movements or writing about books. I have known someone for many years who has worked on amazing self-published work in many different media while living an isolated life in a very isolated Welsh village (Mark of *OKOK Society* and other pseudonyms) - he's retreated almost entirely to the world of the imagination and his work is very distinctive as a result of his self-imposed exile. On the other hand I got a stash of the excellent Leeds zine *Niche Homo* the other day - great read, but it's very obvious they are living an urban lifestyle with all the distractions to creating art that can create. Same goes for the incredible *Hiroshima Yeah!* zine from Glasgow - probably one of Britain's longest running zines, almost certainly my favourite ever, and all the better for being hard to find out about and having no internet presence. The reviews in there are all about Glasgow nightlife. J G Ballard says somewhere that suburbia is the best breeding ground for extreme art (as well as for psychosis). It seems obvious to me that you aren't going to find anything really interesting or unusual in Shoreditch or Manchester's Northern Quarter, much as I'm happy to artfag it round those places with everyone else now and again.

Please can you give me a potted history of the Mad Pride movement?

We were involved right at the beginning of Mad Pride through knowing Robert Dellar of Southwark Mind, and have very happy memories of doing the early gigs and the 2000 festival in London. It seemed about time that people diagnosed or labelled as having mental health conditions stopped hiding away in shame and started to rub the normals' faces in it. It's a wonderful thing that the ideas of just a few individuals in London spread all over the world and have even influenced health and social policy. In 2011 we played the first Mad Pride shows in Lithuania, which were unbelievably chaotic fun - it's a wonderful country. I still have many contacts in radical anti-psychiatry. I can't really claim any great expertise in mental health, I've always been fixated on the art of the Hobs above all else, rather than political issues (and mental health is certainly a political issue). The philosophy is simply to provide an area for self-expression which challenges the unspoken rules of both entertainment/showbiz and mainstream 'art', allows for catharsis in band members and live audience and keep things FUN, even when the subject matter might be very dark and unsettling. We have had at least six full-time band members, including myself, with major psychiatric diagnoses such as schizophrenia. Steve Massey, our drummer from 1988 to 2000, was kidnapped by mental health services in 2000 and has now been detained in medium secure and high secure conditions for twelve years without trial. This has been very difficult for me to deal with personally, and if I'm honest, I'd still like to see certain people involved with his 'care' dead. No doubt some in the quack branch of medicine will say his imprisonment is all his own fault. There are liars in Lancashire Care with black hearts and bloated bank accounts from corrupt deals made behind closed doors with local councils, care home scams and the pharmaceutical industry.

The UK Mad Pride of 1999-2001 existed specifically "to put on gigs," and created quite wild and anarchic spaces where the most mental people in London could have fun and imagine a world where they were in charge. Reclaim Bedlam was the secretive and little known sabotage/direct action wing - destroying ECT suites and hospital CCTV, holding demos outside people's homes. The influx of social workers, politically-motivated people (Ben Watson, SWP) and grant-grabbers sadly followed a little later. Later still came the co-opting of our texts for academic discourse and training for those working within the psychiatric monolith. A case of 'know your enemy', maybe.

Do you think Blackpool is a place of extremes?

Yes I do, the extreme economic dependence on tourism means that the inhabitants don't have anything like the normal amount of community spirit which persists even today elsewhere in Lancashire. There's a harsh dog-eat-dog capitalist ethos, and coupled with that, the town attracts not only badly-behaved visitors but fuckups trying to 'start a new life' after prison or domestic disasters who then find their way to the real bottom of the barrel they thought they'd already hit due to the huge drug and alcohol culture. We're high in just about every bad league table - street violence, child prostitution, suicide, mental illness. My good friend from Russia, Phil Monopolka - the greatest living artist on the planet in my humble opinion - says it was the only place in the UK he felt at home! There's quite a nihilistic atmosphere on evenings out, among locals as well as tourists. The upside of this is that it's created some really unique art, from the well-known bands like The Membranes and Section 25 and the amazing dance music scene here through to mavericks like Dr Adolf Steg, Stan Batcow and Fes Parker, the director Patrick Keillor, great comedian The Divine David... I love it and hate it in equal measures.

Excerpts from post-interview emails

Would you consider changing the description of me in your book from 'schizophrenic' to 'psychotic'? Personally I find schizophrenia only works as a pejorative. [My girlfriend], in common with some Mad Pride elements, thinks it's a demonic word to be reclaimed, and the best shrink I've ever met thinks it's useful as a vague umbrella term, but said two years ago he wouldn't class me as schizo...but I think the word is bollocks, patronising and a calculated insult.

I don't really agree with your perception of shrinks as imperialist invaders, although it used to be true - over the last ten years, the Royal College of Psychiatrists has made some great statements against the use of psychiatry as a branch of politics/the criminal justice system and I'm actually friends with a number of the younger and much more free-thinking psychiatrists nowadays, one of whom, Greg Neate, took those Glasgow photos. Greg went to Ghana and interviewed witchdoctors from a psychiatrist's perspective, there's a blog about it which is bizarre reading. It is a fucked-up and brave profession, it's a pretty new thing that they are friends with us.

The stuff about the digital watch malfunctioning was a great analogy for how it must be for people around me when I go there, I have only been there full-time four times ('88, '89, '96 and '10) but I try to visit there briefly as often as I can and every piece of art/lyrics/sound sculpture I have put together since I learned how to do it in '95 comes from that place, it is the timeless place and the nearest I know to what is really there, away from this phoney dreamworld.

I saw with you how you went out of communication; meanings held in common here were no longer shared. I assumed the experience must be painful and fractured rather than peaceful?

Yes it can be painful and scary but it's like swimming in the deep end, ultimately more rewarding than paddling in the shallow end with everyone else, if you can get back and tell people about the strange fish down there. I am reading Philip K Dick's *Exegesis* (just published in full, about 1000 pages) and have so many similar experiences. Maybe, as one of the editors theorises, it is just undiagnosed temporal lobe epilepsy.

Ceramic Hobs at Grove House, Manchester, February 1988. Photographer unknown

Ablaze!
4

Ablaze! 4

Publication date: late 1988 or early 1989.
Offices: Hopewell Place, Leeds Six

I was like a baby fox on a mission - there was nothing I wouldn't take on. Having moved from the dullsville student flats to a friend's house on Hopewell Place (a secret corner of The Harolds, the cheap option estate for Leeds studes), I worked and lived without chair or bed, fridge or cooker. I had a typewriter and a little table to set it on, fierce fingers to stomp at the keys, and the most DIY attitude money couldn't buy. Living in an actual house that was not occupied by adults was very pleasing; my life was a nice blank canvas and I scrawled all over it with great purpose. William Potter, graphic artist and Cud bassist, resided a few streets away and took me under his wing, designing the new logo, and this issue's front cover. Nearby on Harold Avenue, The Pale Saints were posting out demos to anyone who would send them a blank tape and a stamp, and the Purple Eternal warmed our house by playing a raging gig in the cellar. I even got to sing with them; it was a good time to be in Leeds Six.

This issue has a refreshing air of egolessness. It must have been the drugs. It was energetically RAILING against everything, analysing musical politics and slagging off fanzine sell-outs. Was such a thing a possibility? James Brown moved from editing the thrill-packed *Attack on Bzag* zine in Leeds to spearheading lad culture with the launch of Loaded in London, and in the process did irreparable damage to our culture. But that hadn't happened yet - would that I had stopped him.

DUSTdevils Photo: Tony Woolgar

Printed by Hamish of Fat and Sweaty zine, the front cover lacks any band names. William had put them on an acetate which was meant to be placed over the front cover at the plate making stage but Hamish didn't see that or didn't know what to do with it, so I photocopied hundred of little fliers listing all the bands and the price, 30p, and stapled them to the front covers.

The DUSTdevils are everywhere. This interview documents one of my first meetings with Jaqi and Michael, progenitors of that strange and vortexy band. They lived in a dark, damp basement on Spring Road in Headingley, which seemed to suit their music. At this stage I had not met the other two members of the band, Keith Gregory and Tim Beckham, but they would both appear later as major players in this story. And of course I knew nothing of the bassist they would choose when they arrived in New York, a young man named Mark Ibold. In 2012 I was to become friends with their first bassist, Andy Johnson. Like I said, they're everywhere (see p.262!).

Long before Ebenezer Goode, Move Any Mountain and all that rubbish, The Shamen were a decent indie band plying psychedelic guitar pop with a political edge. This interview was tough. It took a lot for my teenage self to walk into the dressing room of men that I found intimidating, and argue with them until they capitulated and admitted their foolish ways.

The first section of this piece describes a show in Manchester, and the interview takes place at some subsequent gig. After this I saw them once more, at the Duchess in Leeds, and we must have made friends by then as they made plans to come round to my house afterwards. Sadly they got lost, mixing up landmark pubs Royal Park and Hyde Park, and I didn't get to hang out with them that night. Will wrote to me one time after that, and typically I failed to write back. This was all the more regretful when, in 1991, I heard about his tragic death. They had gone to the Canary Islands to shoot a video, and Will had drowned whilst swimming off the coast of La Gomera.

The Ablaze! Office.

ABLAZE!
I AM HOOKED

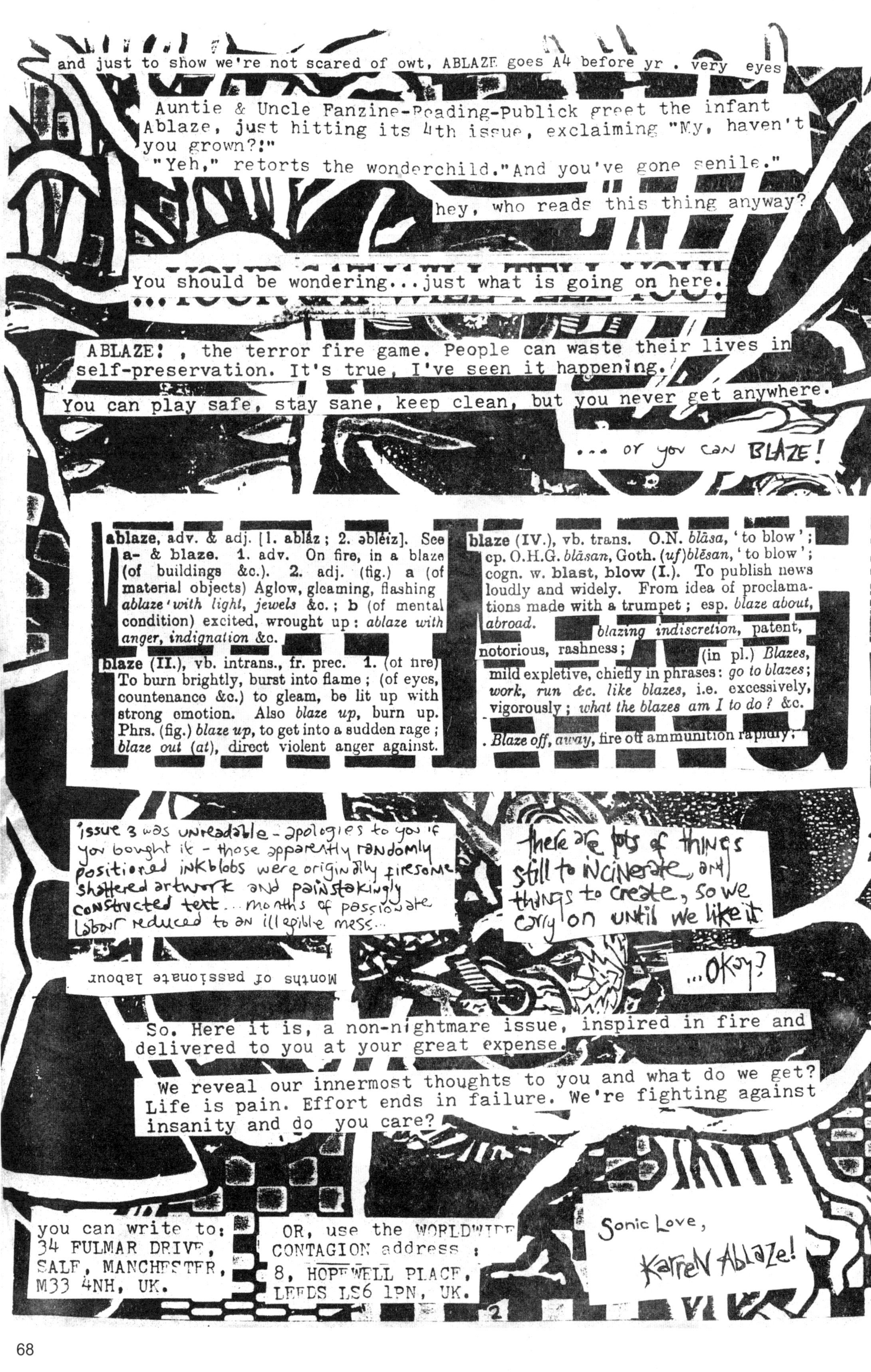
and just to show we're not scared of owt, ABLAZE goes A4 before yr . very eyes
Auntie & Uncle Fanzine-Reading-Publick greet the infant Ablaze, just hitting its 4th issue, exclaiming "My, haven't you grown?!"
"Yeh," retorts the wonderchild."And you've gone senile."
hey, who reads this thing anyway?
You should be wondering...just what is going on here.
ABLAZE! , the terror fire game. People can waste their lives in self-preservation. It's true, I've seen it happening.
You can play safe, stay sane, keep clean, but you never get anywhere.
... or you can BLAZE!
ablaze, adv. & adj. [1. abláz ; 2. əbléiz]. See a- & blaze. 1. adv. On fire, in a blaze (of buildings &c.). 2. adj. (fig.) a (of material objects) Aglow, gleaming, flashing ablaze with light, jewels &c. ; b (of mental condition) excited, wrought up : ablaze with anger, indignation &c.
blaze (II.), vb. intrans., fr. prec. 1. (of fire) To burn brightly, burst into flame ; (of eyes, countenance &c.) to gleam, be lit up with strong emotion. Also blaze up, burn up. Phrs. (fig.) blaze up, to get into a sudden rage ; blaze out (at), direct violent anger against.
blaze (IV.), vb. trans. O.N. blāsa, 'to blow'; cp. O.H.G. blāsan, Goth. (uf)blēsan, 'to blow'; cogn. w. blast, blow (I.). To publish news loudly and widely. From idea of proclamations made with a trumpet ; esp. blaze about, abroad.
blazing indiscretion, patent, notorious, rashness ;
(in pl.) Blazes, mild expletive, chiefly in phrases: go to blazes; work, run &c. like blazes, i.e. excessively, vigorously ; what the blazes am I to do? &c.
. Blaze off, away, fire off ammunition rapidly;
issue 3 was unreadable - apologies to you if you bought it - those apparently randomly positioned inkblobs were originally firesome shattered artwork and painstakingly constructed text... months of passionate labour reduced to an illegible mess...
there are lots of things still to incinerate, and things to create, so we carry on until we like it
Months of passionate labour
...Okay?
So. Here it is, a non-nightmare issue, inspired in fire and delivered to you at your great expense.
We reveal our innermost thoughts to you and what do we get? Life is pain. Effort ends in failure. We're fighting against insanity and do you care?
you can write to: 34 FULMAR DRIVE, SALE, MANCHESTER, M33 4NH, UK.
OR, use the WORLDWIDE CONTAGION address : 8, HOPEWELL PLACE, LEEDS LS6 1PN, UK.
Sonic Love,
Karren Ablaze!
2

'88 part one, a never-ending gig, int rspersed with unhealthy nightmare doses of paranoia and arrogance, ecstacy and torture.

What is there in me that made me do that?

THE GREATEST QUESTIONS

Will I never learn? Foolishly mounting the Preston train on a sunny summer Saturday morning knowing that its final destination is Blackpool. Entering a crush more stifling than the front at a Napalm Death gig - a pompous old 'lady' saying she wouldn't get on the train if she had to stand as if expecting 1000 people to instantaneously desert the train in sacrifice to her. Stood amongst all these people - without exception carrying The Sun but clearly incapable of reading the precise thought. I glimpsed the front and back headlines "THE KILLERS" ,"THIS FAT PIG . " ,"I HATE YOU" . A uniform deep smutty laugh rang out, even from the women and children. People whose idea of daring behaviour is smoking in non-smoking compartments. I had to escape, you understand. There was no way out but up so I had to jump through the flimsy roof and cling fearfully flat down to the roof, ducking further to get under the bridge skin scraped raw, leaping the electricity pylons before the relief of Preston station - a narrowing journey, but far less distressing than being inside smelling the odour of sweating, decaying unutilised braincells. I lept onto the platform to gasps from those in the vicinity and was rooted to the spot by a paralysing thought - why do I want to be in Preston? (Andrew)

The cyclist didn't look where he was going

another readers letter (+ our reply) -

I'm desperate to go out with a third year boy I met at a computer club in school, but I'd fallen for him too! It must be obvious to him because I act so really jealous of the girls in my class who have such nice friends and we'd meet after tea and go to the park every week. The big problem is that Steven doesn't trust me. with Rob. Now, whenever we're out at clubs or discos, strangely. Sometimes when we have a laugh or joke together I kind of latch on to other men and try to treat them like close friends. At a party recently, we got off with each aunt, and with teachers at school. I don't fancy them at all

Mark and I were always very depressed. It was his birthday yesterday and he asked Nikki to get off with him she'll bash me in. I was really scared and it really hurts. Sometimes, when I don't see him for a for a birthday kiss, but he didn't ask me. I just know that I'm 15 and have been going out with Steven for just over four hundred miles away.

I'm sorry you're feeling so down at the moment. I can see your problem here but think there are one or two things you should try to straighten out. Perhaps

You're going to have to wait and see. You may have lost a friend and gained a boyfriend!

Well all's fair in love and war as they say, but I think she's taking things a little too far here!

Although you're probably over the worst, it can take a long time to come to terms with your parents . Think carefully about all this and try to be honest with yourself — if you don't, you could have quite a few regrets later.

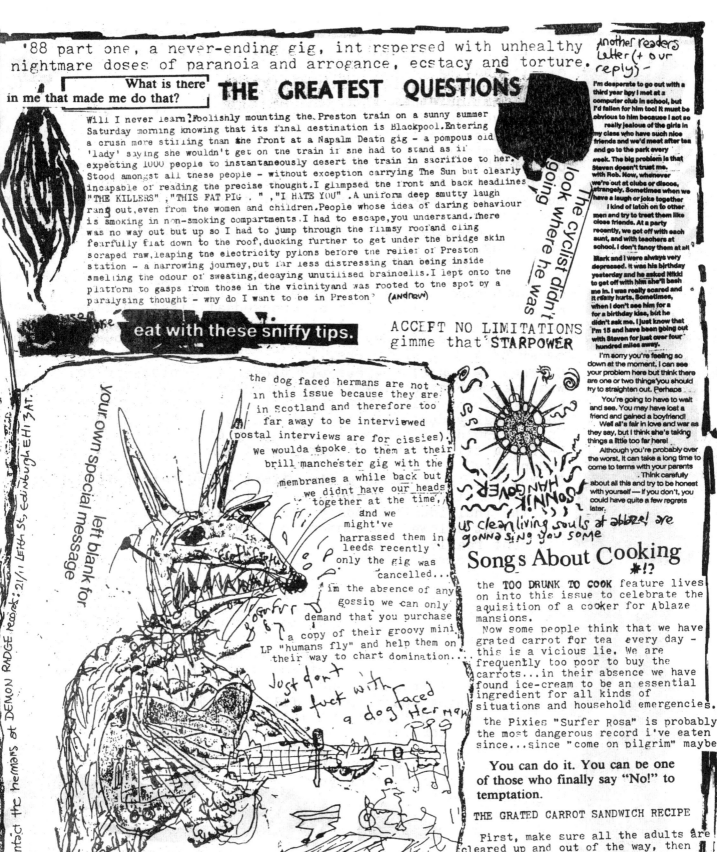

eat with these sniffy tips.

ACCEPT NO LIMITATIONS
gimme that STARPOWER

SONNIK HANGOVER

us clean living souls at ablaze! are gonna sing you some

Songs About Cooking *!?

the TOO DRUNK TO COOK feature lives on into this issue to celebrate the aquisition of a cooker for Ablaze mansions.

Now some people think that we have grated carrot for tea every day - this is a vicious lie. We are frequently too poor to buy the carrots...in their absence we have found ice-cream to be an essential ingredient for all kinds of situations and household emergencies.

the Pixies "Surfer Rosa" is probably the most dangerous record i've eaten since...since "come on pilgrim" maybe

You can do it. You can be one of those who finally say "No!" to temptation.

THE GRATED CARROT SANDWICH RECIPE

First, make sure all the adults are cleared up and out of the way, then follow these simple steps ;

1. Buy the carrot.
2. Find a carrot grater (you do not need to own one) but if you're stuck, a cheese grater will do.
3. Grate the carrot till it's really great.
4. Put it in a sandwich with some mayonnaise.
5. Eat the sandwich.

And there you had it. I bet it was dead nice as well.

If any readers have interesting grated carrot recipes maybe they'll send them in, for inclusion in a full length feature in issue 5. And we'll be giving prizes for the yummiest suggestions!

the dog faced hermans are not in this issue because they are in Scotland and therefore too far away to be interviewed (postal interviews are for cissies). We woulda spoke to them at their brill manchester gig with the membranes a while back but we didnt have our heads together at the time, and we might've harrassed them in leeds recently only the gig was cancelled...

im the absence of any gossip we can only demand that you purchase a copy of their groovy mini LP "humans fly" and help them on their way to chart domination...

Your own special message left blank for

Contact the hermans at DEMON RADGE records: 21/11 Leith St, Edinburgh EH1 3AT.

Just don't fuck with a dog faced Herman

ZANUSSI SPIN DRY

Ear death

Pic by Andy of DFH

King of the Slums, sparkling, screeching and grating, wicked-beautiful-like. They were featured in issue 3 a few months back,but that wasnt enough, wasnt good enough, we felt. Besides, a few things have happened since. But listen to this group's music,and you'll know that no further justification is necessary.

Did you hear their Peel session? It's very unlike them, we thought.Very produced, and 1988, breathtaking but lacking the "authenticity" of their earlier stuff. A new version of "Venerate me utterly", crystaline... Charley's voice has either improved or been brought out by this. But they sound like any other really good band, not that i can start to compare them with one.King of the Slums are too brilliant to get mixed into all the other music here, of BBC session producers, and fitted in, homogenized...they ought to stick out like a sore thumb.

Me & Julie cornered Sarah & Charley in the cramped dressing room of the International 1, where they were about to play supporting the Shamen.

K- Have you had the sort of coverage you would have hoped for, for your last EP ("England's finest hopes") ?
C- We're gettin' on the telly,on that Tony Wilson thing, "The Other Side of Midnight" it's called. We think they are going to do a film about us, which sounds quite interesting.
S- John isnt going to wear any clothes for it, is he?
K- You've got a reputation of being just a support band.
C- Yeh, well we're headlining in Norwich, and we headlined at the University of London.
K- Is it only in the South that anyone realizes?
C- Yeh, around here it doesnt matter how good a support band you are...unless you're top of the bill...
K- The sound at that gig you did in Wigan(at the Den) was pretty good wasnt it?
C- The sound on stage is always abysmal so i cant hear anything so i cant get into it.
At this point their record label boss Dave Haslam turned up to find out where their manager Nathan had got to and to hand out Boardwalk tickets.
K-I read that you wont go to see other bands.
C- No, I've never been to a gig in my life. I wont be going to this.
K-Why not?
C- Cos i fuckin' hate it, it's too bloody loud. It's okay on stage cos it's not too loud, but i much prefer to listen to records.No, i tell a lie - i went to see Roxy Music once, years ago, and that was pretty shit.
K- What records do you like listening to then?
C- Motorhead. They're the best band in the world, they're not so good now but they were really the business.
K- What about things that are happening now...more to the point, what d'you think of the Pixies?
J- You had to get that one in didnt you?!
C- I heard one or two o' theirs.Have they got a girl singer and a bloke singin'? I thought it was relatively interesting but it didnt take me 'ead off or anything.

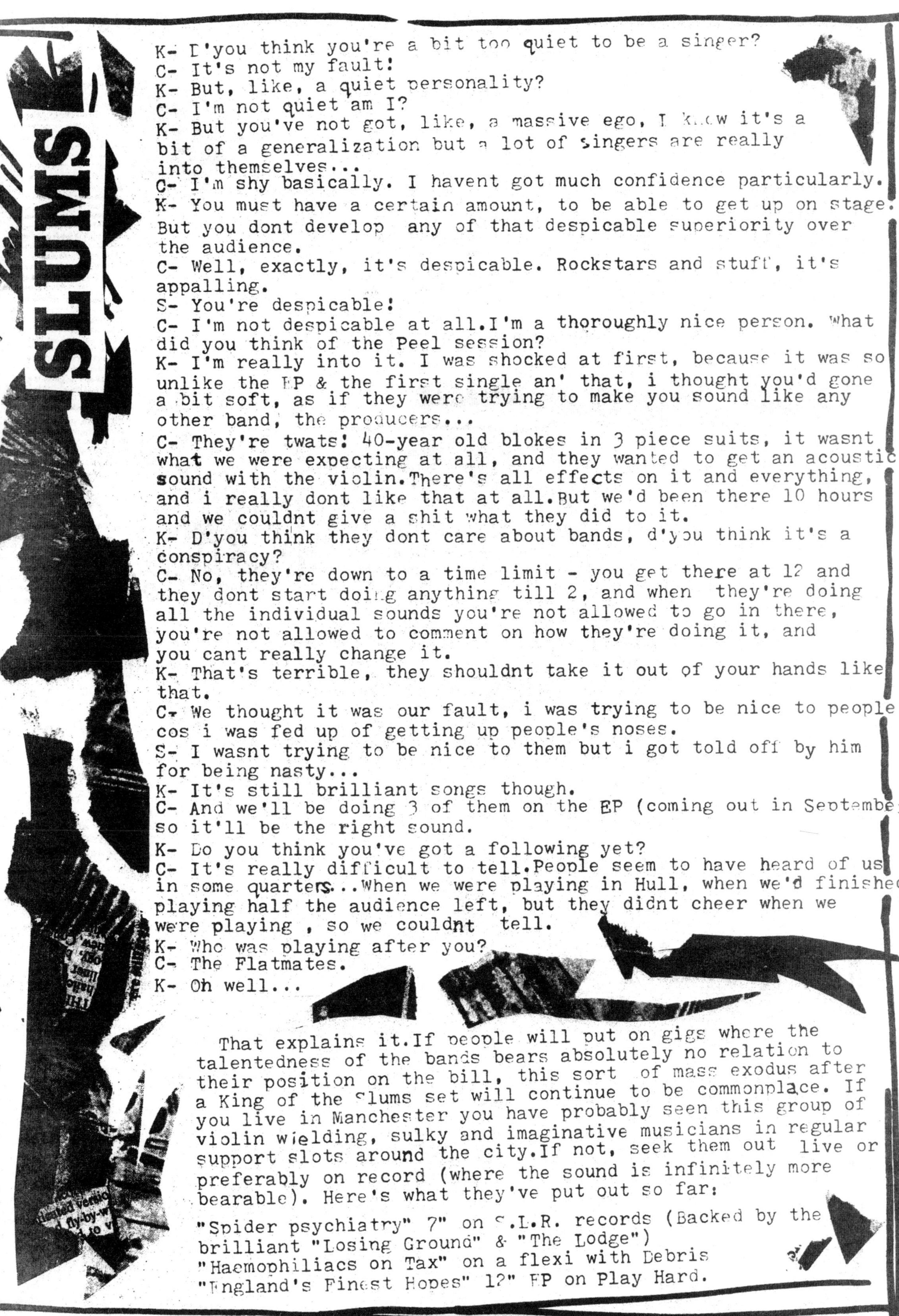

K- D'you think you're a bit too quiet to be a singer?
C- It's not my fault!
K- But, like, a quiet personality?
C- I'm not quiet am I?
K- But you've not got, like, a massive ego, I know it's a bit of a generalization but a lot of singers are really into themselves...
C- I'm shy basically. I havent got much confidence particularly.
K- You must have a certain amount, to be able to get up on stage. But you dont develop any of that despicable superiority over the audience.
C- Well, exactly, it's despicable. Rockstars and stuff, it's appalling.
S- You're despicable!
C- I'm not despicable at all.I'm a thoroughly nice person. What did you think of the Peel session?
K- I'm really into it. I was shocked at first, because it was so unlike the EP & the first single an' that, i thought you'd gone a bit soft, as if they were trying to make you sound like any other band, the producers...
C- They're twats! 40-year old blokes in 3 piece suits, it wasnt what we were expecting at all, and they wanted to get an acoustic sound with the violin.There's all effects on it and everything, and i really dont like that at all.But we'd been there 10 hours and we couldnt give a shit what they did to it.
K- D'you think they dont care about bands, d'you think it's a conspiracy?
C- No, they're down to a time limit - you get there at 12 and they dont start doing anything till 2, and when they're doing all the individual sounds you're not allowed to go in there, you're not allowed to comment on how they're doing it, and you cant really change it.
K- That's terrible, they shouldnt take it out of your hands like that.
C- We thought it was our fault, i was trying to be nice to people cos i was fed up of getting up people's noses.
S- I wasnt trying to be nice to them but i got told off by him for being nasty...
K- It's still brilliant songs though.
C- And we'll be doing 3 of them on the EP (coming out in September so it'll be the right sound.
K- Do you think you've got a following yet?
C- It's really difficult to tell.People seem to have heard of us in some quarters...When we were playing in Hull, when we'd finished playing half the audience left, but they didnt cheer when we were playing , so we couldnt tell.
K- Who was playing after you?
C- The Flatmates.
K- Oh well...

That explains it.If people will put on gigs where the talentedness of the bands bears absolutely no relation to their position on the bill, this sort of mass exodus after a King of the Slums set will continue to be commonplace. If you live in Manchester you have probably seen this group of violin wielding, sulky and imaginative musicians in regular support slots around the city.If not, seek them out live or preferably on record (where the sound is infinitely more bearable). Here's what they've put out so far:

"Spider psychiatry" 7" on S.L.R. records (Backed by the brilliant "Losing Ground" & "The Lodge")
"Haemophiliacs on Tax" on a flexi with Debris
"England's Finest Hopes" 12" EP on Play Hard.

its all fine and its all getting down ?

This is
MANCHESTER
city centre
The black blobs mark the sites of 18 city centre traffic 'spy' cameras.

Ab!aza! incandescentzine, living our daydreams... these days anything can happen so join in or go back to sleep. In a hurry, cos too muchtime's been wasted already. No space - trees died for this "style" is for those who've got nowt to say.

TAKE ALL YOU CAN GET / TAKE ALL YOU ARE GIVEN

it's too easy to be HAPPY about so much groovy music at the moment, when all around is corrupt, evil and very scary. it could be nothing more than a distraction, like flowers that cover chains. but bands reflect the extent to which they're aware of their political environment, and some hold genuinely arkward and challenging views which come across in music that's exiting and sometimes nearly exquisite...

and if you're into music you get into it cos of the music. there's no other way really...like, who goes to a gig becos they're into the band's politics?

it's all about communication, and how much a band want to say to their audience. it matters how they see the audience and whether they care if they are insulted, intelligence-wise or otherwise.

it's also about the reasons why people go to gigs and what their expectations are. if we're just after entertainment, we get upset if social comment isnt well-concealed enough to be safely ignored, but gigs can be events where ideas are shared and we get inspired, through encouraging or uncomfortable realisations.unfortunately these things tend to be one sided - bands preach and audiences listen, accept, consume...

and freedom of information.this is the stuff that's only available to those in power. if we had more facts about our lives we'd probably act differently, like the-way someone off a different planet would look at the non distribution of money, power, land, etc around here and they'd think we're all stupid.in a way they'd be right, cos we let our lives be controlled by dickheads becos we're ignorant of what's happening, and most of that is due to the habit of those who have the information of limiting people's access to it.

freedom of communication...why are we frightened to stop in the street? what's so scary about those little black and white cars? what's wromg with having cameras in the city centre streets? they only want to make sure we're being good. dont accept a single fuckin word they say. the newsreader may be called mrs neutrality but she's paid by mrs. thatcher. think about it - we should be using all the cannels we can to spread the ideas they want to suppress.

WHAT'S going on out there, *world?* Doesn't anyone have a happy, exciting, fulfilling, downright fun marriage anymore?

we reserve the right to laugh at you

● Hearing voices that no-one else can hear. Sometimes seeing, tasting, smelling or feeling things which aren't there.

And sometimes it can be a little embarrassing.

Tick

Are you doing enough for your underarms? Yes No

mike mean on behalf of Those Who Dont Agree. ever.

....proudly present, the fuckoff list

first installment

FLAMING THE SCENE FOR ALL IT ISNT WORTH

we accept yr challenge. broke, & knackered, but we persevere. noboby runs the "scene". if it's runnable than it's not worth running. some parasitic beings are living of the excess brilliance of some areas of creativity. such are band managers, music hacks. they like money, not music.perhaps the confusion arose because both words begin with the same letter, whatever, we shouldnt get these people mixed up with the ones who're actually doing something.

Nice friendly DJ egos, Police, record companies, tv presenters writers + misrepresenters It's all very sinister like a big swirling conspiracy, innit Mike?

Now is the time to DESTROY what exists Burn down those cities and build something better

Ms. Information, causing a storm of protest on the Shitty Life letters page, used to write "fanzines" (one of which was really quite good) and has now graduated to the big, mean and wellpaid world of the LOndon musicpress. Manchester's Champion defends herself; "But i dont get paid for writing for City Death"... I should bastard-well hope not.

'Nother NMF hack & traitor to the North, DJ dedd hedd attempts to operate a monopoly on happeningness from a city centre office.From here emerges an ironically titled + wellproduced studentzine...

you ought to know, Affleck's palace, the alternative kidz Lewis's, is spreading like apathy across piccadilly backstreets and seems to be controlled almost exclusively by the sinister IDENTITY in a desperate scheme to get everyone to look exactly the same, in stripes and pumps and casual anorakwear, kitted out and ready to be swallowed up by the monstrous HAIENDA culture......

Apologies to readers further afield for our concentration on Mancunian corruption, but Mike's a Manchester lad, and you'll find it's happening in YOUR town too.

DUST DEVILS

I MET UP WITH JACKIE, THE SINGER, AND MICHEAL, THE GUITARIST, OF THE DUST DEVILS, AND GOT THEM TO TELL ME A FEW OF THEIR THOUGHTS................

We had been discussing the sound of the set they'd just played at the International ? as support for the Swans. Typically for the supporting band it was poor, drums too loud & vocals not loud enough, but if it makes sense to describe their set as a highlight when the SWans were later on so impossibly brilliant, then that's what it was. Even their soundcheck was worth witnessing, if only to anticipate what was to come. People were DANCING to it, which says something in Manchester.

Karren- You said you started in America...
Jackie- Micheal & I first met in America.
Micheal- We've had 13 different line-ups, with various drummers & bass players. Me & Jack have been together all that time, & we've got a solid line up now. We started 3 years ago.
K- What made you move?
M- Fuck knows, it was a big mistake! I hate England.
K- Why dont you go back?
M- We are doing, in September.
K- Shit, I didnt mean it!
M- I despise England. I think England as a country sucks. It used to have a lot of charm, it used to be able to do things, but not anymore.

K- Did you come here with illusions that things were happening?
J- I did, I came from Australia, & the best thing about this place is the nature, the countryside. It's nice to be out of the city.
M- England's just falling apart. No-one's got any bottle anymore. Thatcher's ideal of England is just rubbing off on everyone. All the poor people are just out for what they can grab, and everyone plays safe, no-one makes any noise. All these fucking wimp bands are just playing along with the system, & I think it's despicable. For the first time in history, the trend in music has gone across to America, America's producing all the good bands. There's all the obvious ones & the small ones as well, like a band that Peel played last week that no-one's ever heard of, called Playhouse...

K- Dont you find any bands in this country at all inspiring?
J- Head of David.
K- Membranes...Walking Seeds.?
M- The Membranes are SO old, they were so good when they had Tills in the band. "Kiss Ass, Godhead" is like joke songs... Why didnt John Robb carry on playing bass, cos he was a genius! If the Membranes were the Membranes as they were, then he wouldnt be writing shit.
J- Something that's really annoying about England is "scenes", everything here is so trendy. In America they dont know the meaning of the word "goth", so a few kids wear black & have spiky black hair, they dont think twice about it,..
M- No-one's pocketed across there, it's just brilliant.
K- Yeh, i guess it happens all the time here, we're just so used to it.
M-There was this thing in Sounds the other week putting two bands together, Slab and another one..
K-Was that the Cyclic AMP thing?

→

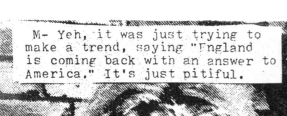

M- Yeh, it was just trying to make a trend, saying "England is coming back with an answer to America." It's just pitiful.

dust devils

K-They seem to get the same articles & just substitute a few words. Newspapers havent got enough to write about each week to fill a paper, there isnt enough happening.
M- Exactly- England is dead musically.
K- Oh, right.
J- We're gonna be on this Underground cassette, & we were talking to Dave Henderson & we said "there are a lot of wimp bands on this," all of them apart from us are these really wimp bands like the Chesterfields so we said "What about some good bands, like Sonic Youth and Big Black?" and he sais "Oh, people are scared of them."-It's really weird! That's what we're saying about English people, they've got no balls.

K- What do you think of things that people have been writing about you?
J-There was some guy in Melody Maker who was so pissed off with us, i mean really bitchy, it was brilliant!

K-What about people saying there's bits of gothiness in your sound?
J-That's just lazy.
K- I cant see it anyway.
M- It doesnt exist- It's because we come from Leeds & we've got a girl singer, since we came to England people have called us Goths. That never used to happen.
K- There were other comparisons - someone in Sounds mentioned the Cocteau Twins, something to do with the vocals being hidden- do you purposely try to conceal them?

M- The lyrics are brilliant & i think they're very important in the songs...
J-It's like a reaction to the way that vocals are always put out at the front.
M- I think it's more exciting to get snippets of the vocals, that's far more important than getting the whole picture. Who wants to know what we're saying? But if You can grab bits of the song that keep your interest, you can make your own mind up about what the song's about. You're given the title, which is well divorced from what the lyrics are about, we never use the title of the song in the lyrics, & that gives you a clue, and that makes you think. We're not just being arkward, We're just trying to make people think - rather than give them all this "nah-nah-nah" wimp band stuff.

K- You know a band from Manchester called the Slum Turkeys? Well they used to be called the Dust Devils until they found out that you were called the Dust Devils, so they had to change their name.
J- Ah! That's news. Apparently there's a band in America as well called the Dust Devils. It's funny how things go like that, words, like "gutter", that was around for a bit. Around the time when our LP ("Gutterlight") came out...
M- There was "In Gut's life" by Ut, and then Slab, they had an LP called "Gutterbusting". It's amazing how words go round, like Live Skull with "Dusted" & Head of David with "Dust Bowl".

Continues on next page →

K-Who was Edward Earl Johnson?
M-He was this guy in America who was put on death row for a crime he didnt commit, he was supposed to have killed a policeman, & he was actually killed. There was this BBC TV programme called "14 days in May" about the last 14 days of his life & all the appeals, it moved me quite a lot, so we did that song.("Losing Ground") That's his voice on the song, saying that he's got 12 days to live, and how the last time they gassed somebody it smelt so much like almonds, cos cyanide smells just like almonds.
J- It's a big issue, cos at the time they hadnt killed anyone since Gary Gilmour.
M- Yeh, it was 8 years since they had actually killed anyone... America's a great place for things like that, it really educates you.
J- You can just be so blasé about something like that, cos it goes on all over the world, all the time, every second of the day things like that go on...

And with this sobering thought we left the dressing room-kitchen to go and see the Swans.

What's goin' down in WALES?

Long gone have ye olde sullen days when Welsh rock meant a trip to Snowdon or a hideous night of 40-year old beerbelly white reggae muzos playing ten minute guitar solos to hordes of drunken schoolgirls and young farmers (yes I went to Corwen Pavillion as well!). There is a refreshing bout of young upstarts picking up guitars and doing something very worthwhile with them. What has brought on all this sudden change i in Welsh language music? you may well ask! Well I blame that wild upstart Rhys Mwyn from Anhrefn who for the last few years has singlehandedly shook the foundations of Welsh music till it came tumbling down in little pieces.....he started his own label and brought all the other weird little welsh dragons out of the woodwork with him. Now there's too many bands to mention going around playing gigs in local village halls and disused chapels...we even have our own hip music programme "Fideo 9" which every now and then comes up with the goods (trendy presenters and camera angles galore - hey what's going on?!)......
Things to look out for are ; Datblygu's new LP "Wyau" out in August and...and ...look there's too many things to mention, best if you write to the following addresses ;
Anhrefn, Rhys, Myddfai, Deniol Rd, Bangor, Gwynedd.
Datblygu, Y Dil Mel Lanol, Llan Gors, Powys, LD3 7uE.
PLant Bach Ofnus, Gorwel Owen, Y Fflat, Swyddfa Post, Rhosneigr, Gwynedd.
Fflaps, Alan Holmes, 6 Hill St, Menai Bridge, Gwynedd, LL59 5AG.
Mark Williams, Sprat & Mackerel Promotions, Bryn Tawel, Corwen, Clwyd LL21 OBD.
Article by Laura Lovechild.

ultimate music
80's acid rock'n'roll, swirl'n'fall,
the pixies...and live skull...are like happ'nin'
in my room at least.
this music says "fuck you, dead tv head"

Essential Radio Roundup:
DIY wed. 8-10pm 104.7 fm (Manchester)
On the Wire Sun. 2-5pm 103.9/95.5/104.5 fm (BBC Lancashire)
Meltdown Mon. 9-11pm 95.1 fm (BBC Manchester)
Hardstuff Sun. 7-8.30pm 88.6/104.1 fm (BBC Sheffield)

A PLAYLIST IS GENERALLY A NAFF THING TO PUT IN A ZINE, HOWEVER THIS ONE IS BRILLIANT, AWE-INSPIRING, MAGICKAL!

LIVE SKULL - the pusher man
A R KANE - Spermwhale trip over
JANITORS - Spin!
the Pixies - oh my golly/ Ed Is Dead/ Isla de Encanta/ Break My Body... (etc)
CUD - Punishment-Reward Relationship
SKIN - COME OUT
KING of the SLUMS - the Lodge
the SWANS - SEX GOD, SEX.

These sort of things and more different kind of things get spiralled out on DIY radio's BLAZE OR DIE, like the zine but with a lot less words and no pages. In fact it's nothing like the zine except that they're both done by the same person.

This man is responsible for DISSY (pg. 16 + front cover)...

William Potter!
COMICS ILLUSTRATOR!
RING: (0532) 742762 NOW!

the Shamen

Manchester International 1, 18,5.88 : holes in the sound, and in the atmosphere.I expected them to draw more people than this, does that matter though? those that were here formed in a polite semicircle around the stage, and dancing started but faded away with the increasing realization that these shamans are not fun people.their well documented slideshow was affecting my unslept body adversely - sickening images of war and a degraded pope were flashed side by side with images of women's bodies...anti-war, anti-religion,..anti-women?? it certainly began to look this way when the band (all men) started being abusive and patronizing to a (female) member of the audience,who had pointed out what she perceived as their sexism. caught in the whirl of sound and picture i looked around, certain that i was loosing my grip on reality...

I had considered the purpose of their slides was to induce mental delerium, confusion, which would either make you more susceptible to shamen doctrines, or make you think about the thing a bit more. In this situation though, i didnt want to accept the conclusions that seemed obvious, i.e. that this band are overtly sexist, because they were a band that i had trusted, musically and politically, to be fairly sound.

More information was needed - I decided to interview them.

Exploring the ambiguities in the way the Shamen present themselves is by no means an easy task. Things started off okay, but once i began to question their methods we were into a long and sometimes difficult discussion...

Karren- D'you think that people might come to your gigs expecting to see a fun pop band and find you serious and almost hostile?

Colin - I thought we <u>were</u> a fun pop band! Well, people who've heard stuff from the first LP, "Drop", might think we're doing a lot of different material, as you say, we're more serious now than we were then, so i think if your preconceptions of the group are based on that LP then certainly that would be true.

Will- Also, the LP, i wasnt in the band when it was made,but even at that time the live sound of the band was harder than the LP.

K- Who produced it?

C- Mike Hedges did a few of the tracks, Y'know he did the Cure, the Banshees, the Associates, stuff like that.

W- I think the tracks he did were the softest as well, he put some almost cliched psychedelic effects in them making them sound quite much more 60's like.

K- Is that not what you're into?

W- We dont really feel that psychedelia has anything to do with the 60's in particular. There's been the use of psychedelic drugs, and people have been making psychedelic music for a lot longer. Our attitude to the bands that are into reviving the 60's sound is that they're being revisionist and reactionary - it's putting the brakes on musical development, and psychedelia was always about innovation and comment, and most of the bands that are described as psychedelic cos they sound like 60's bands dont really fulfill much of those criteria.

K- D'you find that drugs help you come up with ideas for songs?

C- Psychedelic drugs are a vital part of your life - it's not something that you do just to get inspiration for songs or anything like that.

W- Because they reflect on lots of different aspects of your life, if you're into producing any kind of art at all, music or paintings or anything, then it's obviously gonna reflect in what you do.

K- Do you use nice melodies to get across your political message?

Colin- Well. i dont know how well it comes across at all - you've maybe heard about the scandal we were involved in with Mc Ewans lager up in Scotland - we were supposed to be doing a 90 second commercial for them using "Happy Days". and they had this song for 7 months, and you know "Happy Days" is about the Falklands war, it was quite critical of the government at the time, and Mc Ewans never realized this, they only found out 2 days before the advert was gonna be shown...

K- Would you've prefered it if they hadnt found out?

C- Yeh, of course. If they'd actually had the advert shown, cos it never got shown once, they spent about a million quid making it and booking broadcasting time...

K- Did they do you for that then?

C- Oh, they would've liked to but by that time they'd already paid us so it was too bad!...it was actually quite a good advert, the visuals were ripped off of a Czechoslovakian animator's work, have you ever seen a film called "dimensions of dialogue"? These two great big clay heads produce various things out of their mouths that interact, it's really quite a weird film, it was ripped lock, stock and barrel off of that.

K- Have you had a change of strategy with the slideshow?

C- Well we've organized the slideshow a lot better to fit in with the lyrics of the songs, it's definitely coming on, but we're actually gonna be taking some time off after this tour to make it even better, get more appropriate films and more slides and organize it a bit better, cos what we're doing is still very much in its beginning stages compared to how we'd like to do it when we get more time & resources.

K- The first time i saw you i found the slides made more sense in terms of what i knew of the music, the trippy patterns & that.

C- A lot of that was cos we didnt have the stuff together the way we wanted it. We dont want it to be a whole collection of psychedelic slides, just bright colourful effects and all that, we wanted other elements in it, photomontages... the idea of being called a psychedelic band has got certain connotations that we dont like, the 60's look that's in fashion and all that.

K- What sort of reaction have you had - has any one come up to you to speak to you about it?

C- Most of the people we've spoke to about it have liked what we're doing and the way we've developed it, but we've been getting a lot of flack about using a soft porn film with a couple of lassies playing about,and we've got some flack from that, from girls with, say, erm, strong feminist views, who reckon we're just showing porn for the sake of it.

K- I think there's something more than that... what's the actual idea behind using that piece of film?

C- Well the song we use it for is "Knature of a girl" but it depends who's operating the lights and how together they are. At the manchester gig we made a comment about how the film was in the wrong place, "dont pay any attention, I'm sure the boys would like to see it again anyway," we were trying to say that it was a mistake.

we used that film with a song that's about the darker side of sexual psyche and the exploitation of female sexuality, it's quite a twisted song about quite a twisted subject, and so we used a film and various slides to illustrate it. When we're singing about religious intolerance, with "Jesus loves Amerika", we're showing slides of the Ku Klux Klan and crossburnings and stuff like that which to me is just as obscene, just as offensive as pornography is. I dont see why feminism is such a sacred cow that you're not allowed to show that, when you can show anything else.

Will- One of the things that came across fairly strongly since we've been doing this tour, we've been working abroad most of the time for the last 6 months, & we've been showing these films plus some others, and we've not had that response anywhere in the continent - we reckon the whole thing goes back to the fact that the censorship laws in this country are twisted - so as soon as you show any kind of flesh at all, people say "that's wrong, you shouldnt be allowed to do that".

K- It wasnt any kind of flesh, it was exclusively female flesh. You showed pictures about war & religion that developed a sense of horror, in me anyway, and then pictures of the female body which seemed so scornful...i didnt know whether i was supposed to be offended or not...

C- But it's meant to be ambiguous - we spelt "knature" with a'k' which is ambiguous to start with, the lyrics are ambiguous - "she plays the strangest games, she aims to lose, and that's why i love her", right? The other thing we do with the slides, which nobody picked up on in this country, is that we've got a porn film on one side and we've got a whole list of erm, establishment figures on the other side, supposedly watching the film, and nobody has questioned us about that association, and the point of that was to show that these people are in an exploitative role. We were questioning censorship as well - if you're concerned about pornography think about this- when all the boundaries in Europe are done away with, the REAL stuff, none of this silly stuff y'get in this country, the real stuff is legal, and available in newsagents and stores, and is going to be coming over to Britain, and what's Britain gonna do, with our repressed attitudes towards censorship?

W- We understand feminist arguments about pornography, but take a country like Sweden, where all sorts of porn is readily available in newsagents and garages and all sorts of places, and they've got the lowest incidence of sexual abuse and sexual attack in Western Europe. Now I'm not saying there's no connection between the context of pornography in this country and the incidence of sexual abuse or attack, it's not as straightforward as everybody assumes. To show naked women does not mean that guys are going to run out & want to rape somebody.

K- Well I didnt say it was, and i didnt say it was the actual pornography that i was concerned about, i just want to know what you're trying to say to people using that kind of thing.

C- Basically what we want to do is ask questions The form those questions take very much relies on certain associations they have between what we project & what we sing & what was in people's heads to start with. You cant define what people are gonna think and what associations they're gonna have, what conclusions they're gonna come to about it.

K- Dont you think you're getting on dodgy ground trying to make it acceptable for women to be degraded at your gigs? like, you dont see naked men or anything...

C- Yes we do, y'see, that's where you're wrong again, obviously you werent watching the slideshow because we do have lots of what we call porno-political montages - if it's dicks you want to see we've got 100's of dicks, right, and they're all attached to like, James Anderton's body, or we've got the pope getting a blow job, and the royal family and all this kind of thing, we got lots of prominent political figures who we are humanizing in this way, because sex is like, the lowest common denominator after all, and so we attempt to knock these people off their pedestals and change public perception of them by using these montages, and we do exploit the male body particularly the male organs & things like that.

K- I dont think you were looking at your own slides, you had your backs to them...

C- I know what's in them, i can tell you which ones are used & where they come across, whether you miss them cos there's other things happening at the same time, i dont know.

W- You say are we not getting on dodgy ground and stuff like that, well basically we dont care very much if people think it's dodgy or not...

K- Even if people say you're a sexist band?

W- We care about that, but if people see us as a sexist band then they dont understand what we're doing.

K- How're you supposed to decide, when some hecklers in the audience accused you of being sexist, and you were patronizing & insulting to them?

C- That's all they deserved cos if they dont want to go into the band and investigate, at least listen to what we're singing...As far as we're concerned we can justify why we used that film, I dont see why i should have to stand up in the middle of a gig & say "look, woman, this is why we're doing it." There's just no need for it, and if she's too stupid to understand then that's too bad. We show swastikas as well - does that mean we want people to be nazis? As far as we can see, people just completely over-react to the feminism / sexism stuff. It's the same kind of mentality of people who would get offended over us using slides of the royal family or whatever, cos that's their thing, and they're totally against you degrading the royal family in any way. It's exactly the same frame of mind but just a different kick, their kick is sexism & we just cant be bothered with that kind of mentality.

W- People immediately assume that what we're doing is sexist...

K- You spoke in a sexist way to those people that were trying to talk to you.

C- They were NOT trying to talk to us, they were freakin' out.

au 10W sub-genius are floating through the other with a translucent vision

LY HERE Angus at the fu

The Shamen's g

W- If they wanna come up to us after the gig and say "what's going on there, what's that song about, what are you doing with that film?"...but the lassie came up and whipped the microphone away and toppled everything over on stage...

K- Dont you think women get enough, all the time, every day, and then to be confronted with that at a gig...you're looking at it from a very male point of view cos you're all men...

C- Well OK, that's one sin we cant really deny... we'll put it this way. the only time we got any of this hassle was when playing in this country, and basically the way we see the whole framework of the way sexuality is presented...the censorship laws, they create the context that makes people see things like that as sexist, not us. We dont feel we're presenting something that's got a sexist framework at all. The song is questioning traditional male sexuality and the exploitation of the traditional role of female sexuality, so we're trying to get people to think about these things. We're not just talking about exploitation as in Page 3, we're talking about the way that a man and a woman interact in a supposedly normal relationship, right. That's the sort of issues we're raising and trying to get people to think about.

K- What you're saying to me now comes across as more acceptable than what people at that gig thought you were trying to say, so i think maybe you ought to think about it a bit more...

C- No, what you're saying is we ought to think about it a bit more and then drop it from the set

K- No, i'm not saying that. You should get more control over what slides are being shown...

C- Our show isnt about balancing things...with each song we're attempting to present certain, at times strong, visual images which will in some way correspond to what we're doing, and they dont correspond exactly cos first of all, we're working on a limited budget, and second, the guy who usually generates the lightshow is the guy who drives the van for us, he's not a lightman and we've got to try and simplify things to make it possible for him to do it. We cant know for sure that everything's gonna go the way we want it to at every gig, but it's either that or we scrap the whole thing.

R THE BEER GIVE

THE SHAMEN 'Drop

after the tranq kick in – your basic hippy hop back beat. Jack your body, man.

pen a can of worms with a

Band banned —

"They also promised us

l for McEwan's Lager lots of beer, which we

orn about city

W- The way we perceive sexual relationships to some extent is just as governed by the context in which we grew up, and every step that a guy takes to combat his own personal sexism is something of a fight, so when we set up something like this it's a fair criticism to say that lassies might've presented the thing a bit differently.

K- It's a little bit unfair to show something that makes women feel horrified at their own bodies. People are a lot more used to political parodies and stuff.

W- Yeh, but i'll give you a comparison. I remember one gig in Italy and there was a bunch of lassies standing by the side of the stage and i was watching them when this film came up, and they were all laughing, turning to one another and making jokes and stuff like that, and one of the reasons we picked the part of the film that we used is because we reckon it's pretty funny - these two lassies doing excersizes, with daft captions like "coming up for breakfast", which we reckon to be pretty unerotic and quite amusing. It's just not serious porn at all and i dont see how women watching it can be offended, it's a pretty non-violent sort of representation.

C- To start with, the first thing you saw was during "Christopher Mayhew Said" which has fuck-all to do with sexuality so it's not hard to understand how people were getting the wrong idea that night, and the first time it happened i made some sort of joke about it which seemed to fall on deaf ears, and by the time the actual incident happened with the lassie coming up and hassling us we were just wanting to take the piss out of her cos there was no response at all in that audience and we were just into a wind-up.

Brewers ask for band to be dropped

W- They should never have let us get away with what we did to that girl.

K- I was going to talk to you afterwards but i couldnt be arsed hanging around, if i was going to get the same treatment.

W- As soon as i finished saying what i did i expected a couple of glasses to come flying towards me...

K- What did you say?

W- Something like, "Dont worry dear, the next time we come we'll throw in a few dicks for you," which was a bit out of hand...if a couple of glasses had come lobbing over that would've been fine, but...

K- Reasonable people might be more in favour of trying to discuss things, trying to find out what you're about, but you made it so difficult, and you're saying you expected beerglasses but you're complaining about somebody pulling at the microphone...

W- But nobody was bothered at all, even when we were horribly rude to that girl no-one said anything.

C- We were pretty blasé about things, pretty rude and scornful, and that's maybe just the way we are when we're on stage...

W- In interviews with the press we had made it clear that we wanted to be involved in some kind of discussion on these things and not take the traditional male supportive view to feminism which is "dont show any naked bodies", we're not prepared to do that.

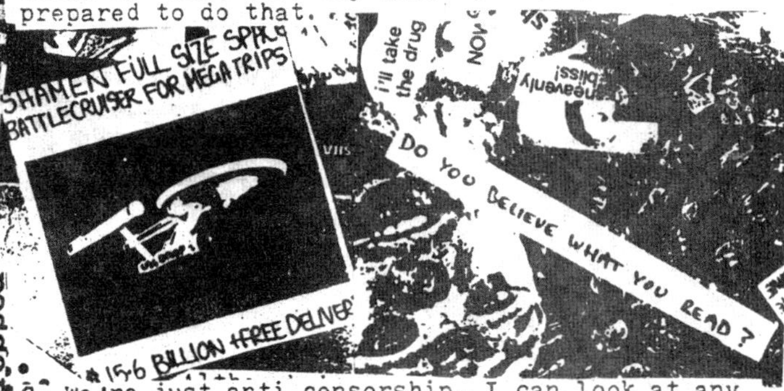
SHAMEN FULL SIZE SPAC
BATTLECRUISER FOR MEGATRIPS
i'll take the drug
DO YOU BELIEVE WHAT YOU READ?
BILLION + FREE DELIVER

C- We're just anti-censorship. I can look at any kind of porn - i practice self-censorship, there are certain things i dont wanna see so i dont go out of my way to look at them. What we're opposed to is being told what you can and cannot see.

W- The censorship laws in this country are such that if there's a film that's say 2 hours long, and it has one hour of sex and one hour of violence, you get all the sex cut out and all the violence left in. We dont agree with that, making murder seem to little kids like an everyday occurrence.

C- We're into the realms of a hypothetical debate about censorship which we have no control over- we arent part of the legislature where we are sitting down and writing out how things ought to be done, but certainly from my point of view the laws in this country are horrendous, they're all standing right on their head. If you go and buy a hardcore porn book and cut out a picture from it and lay it down on the table, and ask people "is that obscene?", anyone who says it is is saying that the sexual act between a man and a woman is obscene. Although i'm not denying that to place that picture in a magazine changes the context of the thing.

After so much discussion of sex and sexuality I asked if they consider there to be anything more to male/female relationships...

W- Undeniably there's an emotion which corresponds to what people call "love". Colin writes most of the love songs and most of his songs are bitter-sweet, a wee bit off the usual trodden track. Speaking for myself, love and emotional attachment in the present day society is always based on the roles that males and females play, conditioned and defined by society so everything is a bit twisted, and i think his songs reflect all these kinds of things.

By this time Colin was looking pissed off, the support band soundchecking had been making it difficult for us to talk comfortably inside and we'd been forced outside onto some fire escape steps

continues on page 82

CUD

CUD are a mine of information. Unfortunately, i only took a C60 cassette with me (most interviews last about 20 minutes) which wasnt adequately long, despite Carl and William talking simultaneously at close-on double speed."Half eight," they told me."The meeting should be over by then." When i arrived, the four band members and their manager were sat around a table in the corner of the pub, planning their strategy for indie-chart takeover with the eventual aim of offering themselves to a "silvernose" Cocaine Record company.

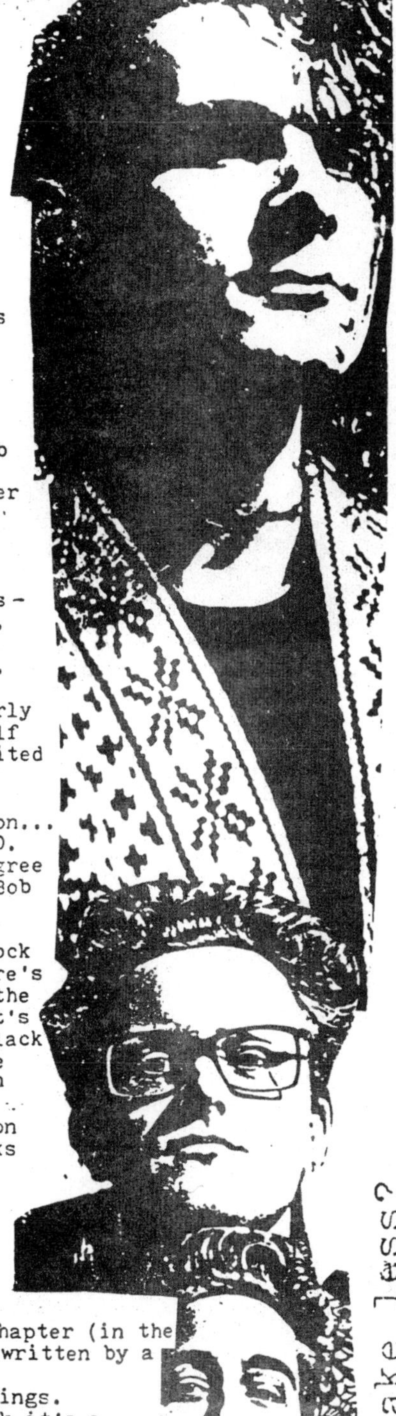

Carl, the singer, concerned that i might be getting bored whispered explanations of the proceedings.He's just finished a fine art course at Leeds Poly(a department that spawned many noted names in pop,such as Soft Cell. Fad Gadget, Scritti Politti and Zodiac Mindwarp) and he's got this curly orange hair that flops over his eyes a bit, shoes with enormous little zips on them and a vaguely absurd laugh that, once aroused seems to continue indefinitely.The others carried on conspiring, insisting on suffient preparation for long-winded hypothetical situations that may arise,in certain circumstances.They were arguing about whether to play live or mime for their appearrance on a new tv pop show (called "Pop it's not", supposedly an antithesis of TOTP, going out in 3 episodes- one of Andy Kershaw's music, one of Peel's , featuring Cud, and one of Tommy Vance's...like really useful categories, hey.)and what they'd need to do for a proposed set of European dates this November, including an expenses paid holiday for a music hack in their plans.I offered to go instead of James Brown, but was turned down presumably due to my lack of qualifications in the area of profuse tall storytelling, and, oh yeh, a job on the NME.

The meeting over, me, Carl and William (their brilliant bass player with a permanently bemused expression) gathered around the tape recorder, to the distaste of their friends who moved away in embarrassment, and i asked them about their involvement with the controversial youth cult, the church of the SubGenius.

William- No, i dont think we should tell you, cos it's very tenuous - only one of us is involved, apart from our manager, and that's him. And he knows nothing about it anyway.I'm the anti-church of the SubGenius person in the band, we've decided on this policy already.

Carl- In order of SubGenius involvement it's probably Martin (the manager), myself, Steve, Micheal and William,Steve's not particularly well up on the scriptures, he's like slack naturally. Whereas myself and Martin are learning slack, he was born with it, he's got unlimited slackness.

Karren- err,"slack"?

Martin- It's getting something for nothing, or a close approximation...

Carl- Martin sent off for an application form to join, it cost $20. I'm a member of the Leeds Clench, we're a rogue clench cos we disagree with some of the ideas...Bob doesnt exist on this planet anymore, Bob lives on Planet X now.

Karren- Is that where you're gonna go?

Carl- Hopefully, if we're slack enough.On July 5th 1998, at 7 o'clock in the morning,the Planet X-ists will arrive on earth...y'see, there's a conspiracy on Earth, and 66% of the population are fighting for the conspiracy, 33% are fighting the conspiracy,about 1% dont know what's going on at all, and something like 0.001% of the population are slack and the world will blow up when the planet X-ists take away all the followers of Bob to planet X.Come july 5th,Jesus with a machine gun will turn up, the fighting Jesus as he's known, clones of Elvis, clones of John F. Kennedy, there'll be thousands of them fighting on the side of Bob.And we'll all go to planet X where there's no clocks cos once you destroy all clocks time doesnt exist, and you live forever.That's why there's no clocks in my house at all. The only clock i've got in my house has got no batteries in it.

William- That's why he's always late.

Karren- If people live forever in a land where there's no clocks, what if one of them dies?How would you explain it?

Carl- But that wont happen on planet X.

William- Are you making it up? I never got to that chapter (in the SubGenius scriptures).It's a really funny book. It's written by a load of hippies in America.

Carl- it's not funny at all, it says lots of good things.

William- it's funnier than Fat Freddy's Cat...i think it's a yuppy religion.

Karren- are you into cattle mutilation?

Carl- no.Martin's heavily into that, but i've never been on a cattle mutilating expedition.

William- I think the saddest thing is that people can inject cells into eggs now and create pigs and cows that are fat enough to go to market within 2 weeks of birth, and have babies already bred with these extra cells.There'll be all these pigs that expand as soon as they come out of the belly.They're doing it already with mice.

Carl- We dont want to spend the whole interview talking about the subGenius.It's as important to the band as the fact that i play scrabble.

William- You could compare it to an interesting pair of trousers thet Carl wears.Or there are a lot of things you could say about Carls hat.

Karren- Or his shoes.But it's more dangerous than scrabble or stamp collecting, there are a lot of impressionable youths reading this zine. (And old fogeys too - we're not ageist!)

Karren- You take less?
William- I take less drugs than none. I get high on my own personality.

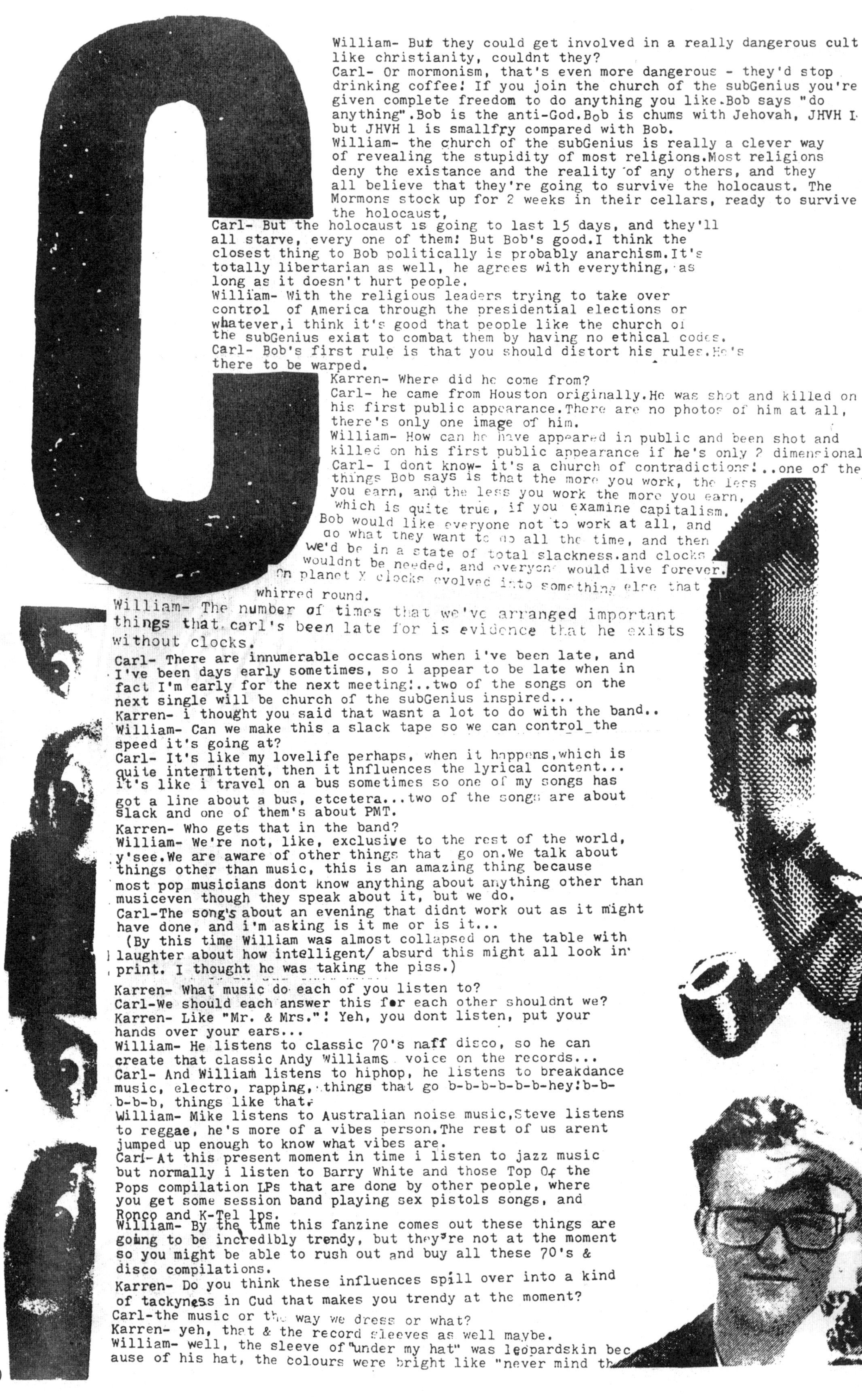

William- But they could get involved in a really dangerous cult like christianity, couldnt they?
Carl- Or mormonism, that's even more dangerous - they'd stop drinking coffee! If you join the church of the subGenius you're given complete freedom to do anything you like.Bob says "do anything".Bob is the anti-God.Bob is chums with Jehovah, JHVH I but JHVH 1 is smallfry compared with Bob.
William- the church of the subGenius is really a clever way of revealing the stupidity of most religions.Most religions deny the existance and the reality of any others, and they all believe that they're going to survive the holocaust. The Mormons stock up for 2 weeks in their cellars, ready to survive the holocaust,
Carl- But the holocaust is going to last 15 days, and they'll all starve, every one of them! But Bob's good.I think the closest thing to Bob politically is probably anarchism.It's totally libertarian as well, he agrees with everything, as long as it doesn't hurt people.
William- With the religious leaders trying to take over control of America through the presidential elections or whatever,i think it's good that people like the church of the subGenius exist to combat them by having no ethical codes.
Carl- Bob's first rule is that you should distort his rules.He's there to be warped.
Karren- Where did he come from?
Carl- he came from Houston originally.He was shot and killed on his first public appearance.There are no photos of him at all, there's only one image of him.
William- How can he have appeared in public and been shot and killed on his first public appearance if he's only 2 dimensional?
Carl- I dont know- it's a church of contradictions!..one of the things Bob says is that the more you work, the less you earn, and the less you work the more you earn, which is quite true, if you examine capitalism. Bob would like everyone not to work at all, and do what they want to do all the time, and then we'd be in a state of total slackness.and clocks wouldnt be needed, and everyone would live forever. On planet X clocks evolved into something else that whirred round.
William- The number of times that we've arranged important things that carl's been late for is evidence that he exists without clocks.
Carl- There are innumerable occasions when i've been late, and I've been days early sometimes, so i appear to be late when in fact I'm early for the next meeting!..two of the songs on the next single will be church of the subGenius inspired...
Karren- i thought you said that wasnt a lot to do with the band..
William- Can we make this a slack tape so we can control the speed it's going at?
Carl- It's like my lovelife perhaps, when it happens,which is quite intermittent, then it influences the lyrical content... it's like i travel on a bus sometimes so one of my songs has got a line about a bus, etcetera...two of the songs are about slack and one of them's about PMT.
Karren- Who gets that in the band?
William- We're not, like, exclusive to the rest of the world, y'see.We are aware of other things that go on.We talk about things other than music, this is an amazing thing because most pop musicians dont know anything about anything other than musiceven though they speak about it, but we do.
Carl-The song's about an evening that didnt work out as it might have done, and i'm asking is it me or is it...
(By this time William was almost collapsed on the table with laughter about how intelligent/ absurd this might all look in print. I thought he was taking the piss.)
Karren- What music do each of you listen to?
Carl-We should each answer this for each other shouldnt we?
Karren- Like "Mr. & Mrs."! Yeh, you dont listen, put your hands over your ears...
William- He listens to classic 70's naff disco, so he can create that classic Andy Williams voice on the records...
Carl- And William listens to hiphop, he listens to breakdance music, electro, rapping, things that go b-b-b-b-b-b-hey!b-b-b-b-b, things like that.
William- Mike listens to Australian noise music,Steve listens to reggae, he's more of a vibes person.The rest of us arent jumped up enough to know what vibes are.
Carl-At this present moment in time i listen to jazz music but normally i listen to Barry White and those Top Of the Pops compilation LPs that are done by other people, where you get some session band playing sex pistols songs, and Ronco and K-Tel lps.
William- By the time this fanzine comes out these things are going to be incredibly trendy, but they're not at the moment so you might be able to rush out and buy all these 70's & disco compilations.
Karren- Do you think these influences spill over into a kind of tackyness in Cud that makes you trendy at the moment?
Carl-the music or the way we dress or what?
Karren- yeh, that & the record sleeves as well maybe.
William- well, the sleeve of "under my hat" was leopardskin because of his hat, the colours were bright like "never mind th

bollocks" and sweet records, & it's also quite loud graphics cos of the 70's & 80's...it's an amalgamation of every single date in the history of mankind.
Carl- I had a very large hat made for me and the song says that when the rain starts we can both hide under it. I used to be really into Lovin Spoonfull, who wrote that sort of lyric quite often.
William- if people stick to taste then there'll only be about 3 things allowed, and that's what Terrence Conran decides on.
Karren- Who?
William- Terrence Conran, of Habitat.
Carl- We're very anti established ideas of taste, i think that's a bad thing, like the idea of Next, making clothes that are supposed to be in good taste...
William- Good taste is determined by the people who havent got very good taste.
Carl- It should be your own, knowing what you're into.

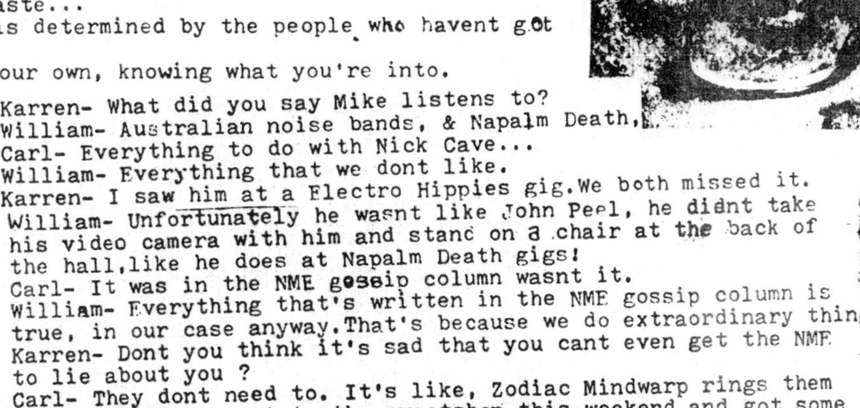

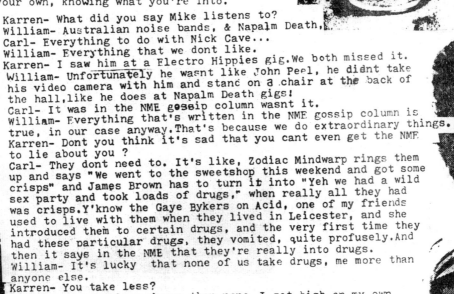

Karren- What did you say Mike listens to?
William- Australian noise bands, & Napalm Death.
Carl- Everything to do with Nick Cave...
William- Everything that we dont like.
Karren- I saw him at a Electro Hippies gig. We both missed it.
William- Unfortunately he wasnt like John Peel, he didnt take his video camera with him and stand on a chair at the back of the hall, like he does at Napalm Death gigs!
Carl- It was in the NME gossip column wasnt it.
William- Everything that's written in the NME gossip column is true, in our case anyway. That's because we do extraordinary things.
Karren- Dont you think it's sad that you cant even get the NME to lie about you ?
Carl- They dont need to. It's like, Zodiac Mindwarp rings them up and says "We went to the sweetshop this weekend and got some crisps" and James Brown has to turn it into "Yeh we had a wild sex party and took loads of drugs," when really all they had was crisps. Y'know the Gaye Bykers on Acid, one of my friends used to live with them when they lived in Leicester, and she introduced them to certain drugs, and the very first time they had these particular drugs, they vomited, quite profusely. And then it says in the NME that they're really into drugs.
William- It's lucky that none of us take drugs, me more than anyone else.
Karren- You take less?
William- I take less drugs than none. I get high on my own personality.

we had a namedropping session and got to talking about the Age of Chance...
William- It's harder to get along with them than most bands. I like their music sometimes...it's just that they beleive their own press releases too much. They try and impress us with their success and they underestimate us as well. They'd like us to flop. I liked the way they had the ambition to alter and be successful, it's just that they lost a lot of their humanity by trying to be a product.
Carl- They were quite willing to be seen as almost inhuman, werent they? they wanted to be really really famous, like, really a lot.
Karren- they may not have started out like that, they may have started out like you.
William- I think they always wanted to be really big, that's why all their singles had really crap B-sides.
Carl- The drummer went to college with my schoolteacher. They're all quite old.
William- The guitarist went to erm, they didnt have colleges in those days , he went to a primary school with my grandfather...

the evening was drawing on ...The conversation had drifted to the subject of "image"...
William- We were talking to this guy at the weekend who said we've got to have an image if we wanna get anywhere, and we dont think we've got one. We dont really wanna go and get one either particularly.
Carl- I dont think we present a very recognisable style that people could mimic, in the way that creation bands all seem to have big fringes and that..
William- He's not got a fringe, it's more of a middle parting. The fringe is over his ears.
William- We saw the Shamen cos we were playing a gig with them. I think their slideshow is just there to distract from the boringness of their stage personas, which dont exist really.
Carl- I think their slideshow's really juvenile, really 6th form politics. We had a slideshow when we played in London to compete with theirs, and it was like snapshots of our holidays and stuff and that was much more interesting than slides of the pope with no clothes on. It's that sloppy, very naive political content... they're making really strong political statements but they dont really know what they're saying, like with their interest in pornography...
Karren- It's piss-take pornography...
Carl- You cant do pisstake pornography, you cant have a picture of a woman with no clothes on & then say "it's a joke, i didnt mean it"..

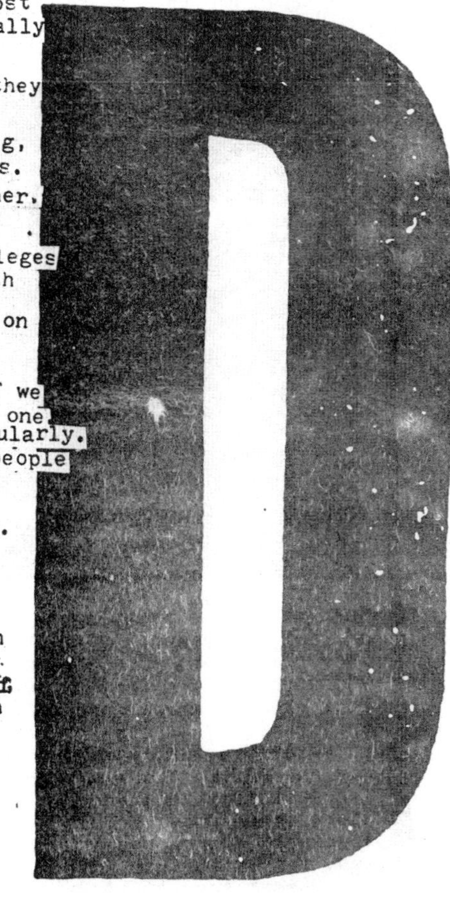

And some more showbiz gossip...

CUD's new single is "Slacktime" B/w "i've had it with blondes"/"Make No Bones" (Ediesta CALC. 002) 12"

Karren- The argument's got a lot of sides to it but you seem to avoid making any kind of political comment at all.
Carl-I think the bands that have made the strongest political comment havent been overtly politically motivated anyway, like the Rolling Stones, or the Sex Pistols...
Mike- Have you been saying luts of crap things about me and Steve?
Carl- We havent been talking about you at all.
Mike- Well i should be mentioned!
William- The Shamen are using a lot of that imagery cos it seems like a funny thing to do. They've got a very clever manager in terms of causing scams, they get lots of publicity but i think it's really tacky.
Karren- In a way they're going against that by saying things that people dont wanna hear...
Carl- But a lot of things people dont wanna hear, they dont wanna hear about for good reasons, like pornography...
William- When i saw them it seemed like "here's an interesting slideshow with some people in the way". But it's good that they're approaching the subject cos a lot of bands dont ever be political, and i'm trying to persuade Carl to be a bit more political in his lyrics.
Carl- The Shamen are too heavy handed...i would be more political if i thought i could make a comment in aparticular way...
Karren- It's just a matter af thinking realistically about what's happening in your life..
Carl- But it's difficult to put it in rhyme.
Karren- Rhyme..!
Carl- I'm working in a particular form. I'm not articulate enough and i admit i'm confused about politics
At this stage the tape ran out, while our critique of the Shamen and other subjects continued until chucking out time.

Brighten up yr mediochre life... with ABLAZE! noise information products

BACK ISSUES

Issue One with its blazing yellow cover, features PASTELS and INSPIRAL CARPETS interviews and stuff on Glastonbury, Sonic Youth, Cure, and an unbelievably useful free gift, all for 22½p

Issue 2, a gret rock special, contains in-depth interviews with the JANITORS, the GAYE BYKERS ON ACID and, erm, the HAPPY MONDAYS You can have it for our silly knock-down price of 20p, but be warned, it is printed in several loud fast colours which may damage yr already failing health.

Issue 3, now here's one to have, with a friendly lime green cover featuring the moon in profile, and inside you'll find interviews with the SHRUBS, the SLUMTURKEYS, and our first interview with KING OF THE SLUMS. The printing's a bit dodgy (a bit???) but it's only 15p so you cant complain really, can you? (NO!)

send the dosh along with a AS SAE (or 22p to cover postage + hassle) to the Ablaze! address or Worldwide Contagion if you want info on other zines

Ablaze! hasslement while you wait
we'll throw yr consumer durables in the fire
irresponsible lies and libelous accusations a speciality
available 24 hours a week

hey get me one o'them sonic spirular groovie thingies a) for tea
b) for xmas
c) for ever
a little competition aspacial created for any insomniac-head viewers up there

the Shamen, continued from pg. 78

The interview had been longer and more difficult than most, and perhaps would have continued indefinitely if it wasnt for other things they had to be doing, like a local radio interview and a gig. We'd tested each others patience with so many interruptions, and misconceptions on both sides. Obviously between me and the Shamen the issue has not yet been resolved, with our conflicting views on various matters. I still hold a degree of confusion about their attitude towards the use of pornographic material and i'm not sure how far they are concerned about issues they raise or how much they are simply trying to create controversy and interest in the band, by using the gossip- thirsty press. however this i have to say -

AS they themselves pointed out it is the context of pornography that is important, ie that in a society where sex is just another, very marketable, commodity, porn is big business. It is this aspect which is more worrying than the fact that we have access to pictures of naked people etc, but it is the latter that is the concern of censorship laws. Institutions in society would be threatened by people beginning to understand and control their own sexuality so they seek to limit experiences with prohibitive laws and the controlled hypocrisy of the media. The Shamen hail the spread of hardcore porn by showing bits of a mild and admittedly silly film at their gigs (sometimes in inappropriate places) Presumably they see the use of pornography (or the choice of whether to use it or not) as a way of increasing self-awareness, similarly they discuss their use of psychedelic drugs. However they choose to ignore the disadvantages of the continual misrepresentation of women as sex objects, which is what is necessary in order that pornography can be produced and sold. They, or their management, seem to think that people will be attract'd to their gigs for the "pornographic" content of the slideshow however the appearance of a few cut out dicks attached to James Anderton, the Pope or whoever is hardly stimulating viewing...if they want to effectively challenge censorship legislation and accompanying attitudes by promoting a more open-minded view of porn they should get their heads together and think of what might work better than poorly-organized and ambiguous collection of silly pictures, cos all this does at the moment is attract lots of nice publicity for them.

The Shamen are one of today's more interesting and thoughtful bands. I'll watch what they're up to but remain cynical about their motives... oh yeh, their music's not too bad either....

That night everything fell into place and the gig was one of the best I'd seen this year. The striking visuals and sound fuzed and provided an inspirational set. We left dazed by the Shamen's capacity for making groovy, dance-tempting music and severe, albeit slightly unsubtle, political statements.

THE PURPLE ETERNAL leeds' newest sonic delerium creators ambushed me outside their 4th gig, which they were about to make happen, at leeds uni.
the thing about the drummer is, he's into all about eve, and he's IN the mission fan club. But these are not predominant influences, fortunately, and apart from that purple eternal are a fine bunch of young enthusiastic flower-children, bursting with delicious sexy life and searching for the perfect non-working, all-reverberating drug-saturated lifestyle.

they seem to crave publicity. "mark is a goat" they tell me, 5, 6, 7 times, and mark is dutifully balancing on peter's shoulders imitating a stupid farm animal with horns.

the interview:

All- Our influences are... sonic youth!..big black!.. pussy galore!..loop!..and the birthday party!......
Karren-Where did you get your shirt?
Ross- From Shock.
Mark(possibly)-We've been going since 1962, we influenced the stones. we did our first demo 5 months ago. we've got the cliff richard syndrome...
Karren- What's that?
Mark-It's looking young and having bad acne, except... we're not virgins, honestly!
Someone- We like the Wombles.
Joe- And Foetus.
Ross- You should see my autographed nick cave book. It's really good.

purple eternal, "eternal" after a comic that they never read, and "purple" because it's a psychedelic colour, they reckon. a remarkable organization - their last song of their live set featured 2 extra percussionists and 2 vocalists, the whole fragmented demented unit working at it to create a beautiful, tantilizing sonic row. astounded, i asked sven about it. "it's the sort of music you have to put everything into" he gasped in utter exhaustion as he clamoured for more beer at the bar.

err, sure. Anyhow, other information that i managed to glean from this rather frantic conversation includes the fact that one of their songs is a political statement about Dallas, called either "Hot & Sweaty" or "Baby this bed's burning": "pay homage to the man who works on his oil well, hot and sweaty does it when the cash flows" is what they wrote on my bit of paper.

That's about it for tonight, except to quickly consult emma on the subject...
"it was so wild, one boy even danced to the soundcheck, his hair hidden in a baseball cap, his smile swallowed in a grimace.. when the band materialized, every thing happened..."
in fact when the band materialized we were lost for words and swirling spirals of light and sound.
OK, get this band, book them for gigs and corrupt them.....

the line up:
Karl-drums, record collection problem (Assumed) and brain power
Mark- guitar and farm animal problem (Definite)
Daren- guitar and arkward name spelling problem
Ross-"singing" and nick cave problem (Possibly dangerous)
Sven- guitar, no problem....

Write to: MARK ETERNAL?
1 MEANWOOD TOWERS
TOWERS WAY
LEEDS SIX.

Phil on bass and Stevie on drum programming. WARNING — don't mess around with the Hobs because we'll get you back, ...ns, knives and razor ...m, also among the Hobs posse are 2 trained black magicians plus a lethal black witch, we committed acts of sympathetick left-hand style voodoo magick against former guitarist A. Stratford with the result that he has made a loss of £60 of his own money, certain dark voodoo magick acts are soon to be carried out against former guitarist A. Pearson and against Karren Ablaze both of whom are down on the Hobs' shit list for various reasons, we have the dark forces on our side so all you humanoid weaklings and Wedding Present fans better fuckin watch out OK. The force of Satan and the face of death will plague you ever + always.

STOP PRESS - CERAMIC HOBS SPLIT

oh no, i cant go on, the CERAMIC HOBS have split up, and i dont know why, and simon has disappeared off of the face of the earth and has retired to work in a biscuit factory

The views expressed in this publication are not those of many of the British population so get lost fascists.

Does your swimwear reveal ugly hair?

Purple Eternal may have a single out in september, so peel your eyes (ugh) for that, or if you're too squeamish, just buy it.

The Dust Devils are leaving these detested shores shortly, their last British date is at Leeds' Duchess of York on Aug.23rd with A C Temple & Kilgore Trout. An LP in the Autumn too but we'll only be able to get it on import cos they're releasing it in America the bastards

WEATHER TERROR report

Manchester rain fast loud & hard delicious haze, summer sweat, dry throat, stale air all over the north

'Great sadness' at death of Harty

who gives a toss, people die every minute

ABLAZE TOP 3 SPELLING MISTAKES!

1. Delerium
2. Arkward
3. Micheal

We ought to tell you that some of the facts included among the pages of this desperate publication are actually lies, created purely out of "journalistic" licence...or was it the "off" licence, i really carnt remember...

ABLAZE HORRID PLACES IN THE WORLD THAT YOU REALLY WANT TO AVOID GOING ANYWHERE NEAR, PART 1

london.

(More in-depth geographical reports next issue)

the focus of intense interest.

Number of different words used 16

Average repetition per word 12

The following capital letters are used. They are listed in order of appearance—

J, P, I, A, H, T.

All the words used (except the two names) are Key Words.

FLIPPER

Last December Will Shatter, the driving force of the Californian hardcore band Flipper died of a heroin overdose. Flipper left behind some of the most intense & desperate music I've ever heard on their 2 studio LPs and a posthumous double live album; this was no ordinary hardcore band, most of their songs were played at the speed of dirges and instead of the usual simplistic politics, the lyrics chiefly dealt with depression, nihilism and self destruction. However coupled with this was a notably silly & twisted sense of humour. Take the single "Sex Bomb" (as covered by the Walkingseeds live), over a definitive punk 3 chord riff ridiculously inappropriate jazz horns are introduced while the vocals consist of grunts, screams and the line "Uh, sex bomb, ma baby, yeah!" Or some of the comments made to the audience on the brilliant live "Public Flipper Limited" : "If anybody needs drugs its you people..real bad" "Does anybody wanna see my left testicle? Its the only part of my organ I've got left....OK I know its not much, I know its not what you expected but I'm sorry. Are you satisfied, can we leave now?" Or the entire lyrics to the song "Flipper Blues":

"Two hundred and fifty dollars a month, I can't afford no speed, no job, it costs two dollars twenty five for a pack of cigarettes, and I gotta take my cat to the vet's".

However when the humour got darker, especially throughout their first LP Generic Flipper, the result was a frightening confrontation of damaged minds and everyday nihilism:

"Ever have to really cry, cry so much you want to die,
Ever sit in tormented silence that turns too loud, you start to scream,
Ever take control of a dream and play all the parts and set all the scenes,
Ever do nothing and gain nothing from it,
Ever feel stupid and then know you really are,
Ever think you're smart and find out that you aren't,
Ever play the fool and find out that you were,
Ever look at a flower and hate it,
Ever see a couple kissing and get sickened by it,
Ever wish the human race didn't exist, then realise you're one too.
Well have you....Ever... ? I have. So what." ("Ever")

Maybe its just me but Flipper seem more honest in their communication than almost any other band. Check out the same LP for a love song "I Saw You Shine" that would make the likes of the Wedding Present etc. wet themselves, because of the desperate & hopeless view of relationships as well as the cacophony. Flipper may not have been the most accomplished musicians ever to say the least. But they were genuine in their attempts at communication, certainly more than most bands. So give them a listen. (Simon Morriss)

PURE VERITE

Writers: Nik, Laura Lovechild, Andrew EM, Mike Mean, Simon, Karren.
Artists: William Potter, Rich Holden, Fatal Sneeze, Michael Dust Devil, Andy D. EM. — THANX Y'ALL!

thanks to Jeane for trying to teach me how to spell, + J.W. + Hamish for printing...

thanks to lots of groovy people who've helped + encouraged the progress of this issue into it's present state... including all the bands featured, not only for taking the time to speak to us but also for being brilliant + inspiring, all the contributors, and my friends. Apologies a millionfold to Vee VV for losing the interview tape, I do not expect to be forgiven...

* Ablaze! number 4 was brought to you by the letters W, R and J. (the letter Q is missing off of my typewriter). And the magick number 4. It was created despite meteorological adversity and conditions of domestick disharmony. We made it bigger, we made it better, we want it to beat the pulp out of surrounding non-happenings, to bring about a horrid end to laziness and careerism in local music (and writings about local music.) please communicate with us, if you are organizing gigs and trying to get things together, we'll be real interested to hear off you. Till Issue 5 — Keep Happening.

xx

Good Bands + Good Zines — Get in touch TODAY

the sky is the sea and this house is a flowerboat, sometimes yr mind goes so fast it's impossible to do anything...

New(ish) Manchester band (Worst) ★ BOUND FOR GLORY ★

I AM UNCLEAN! I AM UNCOUTH! I AM UNSPEAKABLE! YEAH

THE SLUM TURKEYS

One of the few bands in Manchester still making a lot of noise. They sent me their demo and it's real raw & rocking. Make sure you catch them live soon, before they grow up & calm down, cos sometimes they're great : vicious & powerful.
247 Bonsall St Hulme Manchester 1.

NON ROCKING

MANCHESTAR!

We wanted to put out a turkeys flexi, but it didnt happen. sorry

GRIM HUMOUR!

Richard Johnson, AKA Richo Grim, was the main man behind *Grim Humour* fanzine. He started the zine in 1983 at age 17, after seeing some fanzines in a local record shop and realising he could do it too. GH ran for 18 Issues and dominated the mid-late eighties UK fanzine scene from its base in Herne Bay, Kent.

For me it was like an older brother-type fanzine that I looked up to and was somewhat awed by. Richard now lives in Poland, but I tracked him down, via the world wide web, to find out the grim facts.

What were the early issues like?
They were great fun to produce but were held back by some appalling writing and grammar. I suppose many zines start that way, though? Beyond this, and looking back, they were very passionate, although this passion was always kept in check by some healthy cynicism. You know, the whole goth thing was going on at the time, so we [sidekick Andy P. joined at issue 4] took great pleasure in deriding these groups and the people who liked them, even though we probably resembled goths ourselves. I used to draw cartoons that kicked against them all, inspired by the cartoons one would see in *Vague* at the time. We also never cared about copyright and would savage comics and magazines to form part of our own artwork
Was *Vague* a big influence?
Vague was a huge inspiration, as, indeed, were *Panache* and *Kill Your Pet Puppy*. I didn't want GH to be the same as them, but I certainly wanted it to have a similar appeal.
I always remember *Panache* in the same context as *Vague*, how were they related to each other?
Well, Tom Vague and Mick Mercer of *Panache* used to be good friends. Mick was also editing *ZigZag* magazine around this time, and Tom was one of the main writers for it. Without doubt, their mutual respect carried over to their respective zines, too. They were incredible zines, although as I got older *Vague* resonated with me more as it took on more interesting subjects.
The youth culture that we were in at the time, it seemed like a post-punk/proto-goth thing that had no name, with haircuts inspired by The Cure...
Haha! Yes, and I have no qualms about The Cure or all that backcombed hair that was going on at the time. Even Nick Cave was at it! It was an interesting and extremely vibrant period to be a youth. Lots of interesting music around, many gigs, Peel, zines, small labels springing up; all very much part of the whole punk thing, really, but several years on.
You were impatient with the hippy elements of the scene... and do you remember this unnamed tribe having an enemy in the form of casuals?[1]
Yes, I always detested certain hippie sensibilities. However, again, I criticised much of what was going on around me at the time as well. I saw many lazy people around me everywhere, lazy in their thinking or general outlook. GH was always more about antagonising these people in an effort to get them out of their stupor. There were, of course, other youth factions as well at the time, and my two younger brothers often joined them (the second mod wave, then they became casuals, etc.), but these didn't really mean much to me in the context of the zine. I was more concerned with targeting those people who thought they were better or more sophisticated than the casuals!
Haha! The casuals were to prevail, in fashion terms anyway... Getting it back to you, were you doing other stuff at the same time like working or studying, or were you full time on the zine?
Yes, they were...! I worked at the University of Kent from February '83 in their repro department, which meant I had lots of access to paper and suchlike as well as my printing needs! I was sent on a part-time lithography course in London at the same time, for two years, but mostly went to record shops and gigs or to meet friends there rather than attend the course. Beyond English and Art, I'd hated school and could not wait to leave, and had no desire to go to college or whatever. I hated it all. I never liked the idea of getting a job much, either, but knew I wanted to feed my record buying habit and continue going to concerts, and had to make this compromise. This was far more important to me. The zine was produced as soon as I got home from work. I'd labour over it every day until late at night.
Did they mind you printing it at work?
Not at all. In fact, my first boss was a contributor to *The Guardian*. He started out as a jazz critic for them, then moved on to bowls. He actively encouraged me with my zine, even if he'd forever frown at my wearing black and having spiked hair and never understood the music I loved. I'd often print the zine after hours, so I'd save on the cost of the overheads. I just had to pay for materials.
Bowls?
Outdoor bowling.
Ah.
So I was pretty fortunate, it gave me leverage with all my decisions for the zine.
***GH* was very successful. How many were you printing?**
It was pretty popular, but I never realised fully quite how popular it was till much later on, when for instance a friend would introduce me to friends of his as, "The guy who did GH!" and they'd then regale me with stories about how they'd go in weekly to the record shop to see if a new one was out, or whatever! Beyond this, things got bigger when I started covering Big Black, Sonic Youth, Swans, Lydia Lunch et al in '85/'86. At this point, the circulation was about 1800, I think, but could have been twice as much but for my budget constraints on a zine which had, by this point, over 100 pages in it sometimes! Another high point was Savage Pencil/Edwyn introducing Sonic Youth at the Town and Country Club and brandishing a GH and telling the entire audience to buy a copy! There were 2000 people there and I was then besieged by so many that my then girlfriend, Andrea, got pissed off with me for not being able to talk to her for almost the entire show!

Oh wow, that must have been beautiful! Apart from pissing off Andrea I mean! What was it like being in a relationship with another zine wrier?
It was good being with Andrea [the editor of *Cloth Ears* fanzine] as she'd understand my compulsion to get back to the typewriter

once home from work. She had the same drive. However, there was more strain later on as I'd also started a record label [Fourth Dimension], got a group going [Splintered], ran a mail order service, etc. This was not so good once we started a family, either, as time was limited.

So DIY kind of took over your life?

Yes, DIY completely consumed me. But not the type of DIY I think Andrea would have liked me to have contributed to (but I was always useless at it and now dedicate the rest of my life to never doing it again!).

There are a few jokes about the appearance of a typical fanzine writer. Were there really so many about that they had a look? And was there a fanzine writer personality?

During the early to mid-'80s there'd be any number of zine writers often trying to sell their wares at the many gigs I went to in London. I think we at GH generally mocked the guys who produced them as resembling geeks or nerds. Many vaguely resembled Everett True, if I remember correctly. I have no idea where this placed us by comparison, but I'm suspecting we probably all thought we didn't look like such people ourselves. Ultimately, though, we ridiculed everybody from the bands to the fans, so it was probably only natural that fanzine writers got caught in the gunfire as well.

I've got a copy of GH 11 here, what year was this? You had a team assembled round you then, and Andy was second in command. You were printing up 3000, and boldly declared this on the intro page.

I think issue 11 was from '88 or '89 and, yes, by this time, there were people wanting to get involved or sending unsolicited work they wanted published in GH. Things were getting bigger and I had the full support of one of the indie distributors to help me, plus many bigger mail order outlets would also shift bundles of the mags. It was a healthy time, but the mags also had larger page counts by then and would take longer to produce. The claim of a 3000 circulation may have been a slight exaggeration, but I think the average print run was around 1800. Andy P. was also far more involved by this time too, but I mostly wanted to keep him as a writer contributing interviews and suchlike, whilst he became increasingly frustrated with this and wanted to do layout. I would very rarely let him, though, hence his starting *Fear 'n' Loathing* zine.

These things are hard to read! You must have been working for years with a shitty typewriter. Did you ever get into other technology?

Oh, we had a battered typewriter or two for years. Then, around issue 10, we progressed to a word processor, plus Andrea would do some typesetting at her work for me. It was only in perhaps the last 4 or 5 editions everything was put together using the help of a computer. We just never had the money for such things beforehand, even if the ideas to evolve in this manner were there and can be seen in the later issues. The battered typewriter was not some kind of stance. We just used whatever means we had access to.

By that time you were getting sent lots of promos by record labels. How did that affect things?

Yes, every day there'd be records and cassettes coming in, as well as orders for the zine and letters, starting around '85, when we were amongst the first to interview bands such as Sonic Youth. It only affected us in terms of our needing more time to review everything, and expanding not only the reviews section but also the amount of contributors prepared to get involved who we felt were good enough to do the task. It was enjoyable getting all these freebies, though, even if we did often end up slating them or would end up hassled by the promo companies if we wrote a good review. At one point, maybe around '89 or '90, I was pushed into interviewing Soundgarden. I went along with it, but then just never bothered to publish or even transcribe it. If there was a downside to it all, it was this.

GH had its fair share of imitators. What was the reach of GH's influence, do you think? How many people were inspired to start zines and such? Did you get a sense of that?

Of course I saw or would even get sent other zines clearly indebted to GH. It

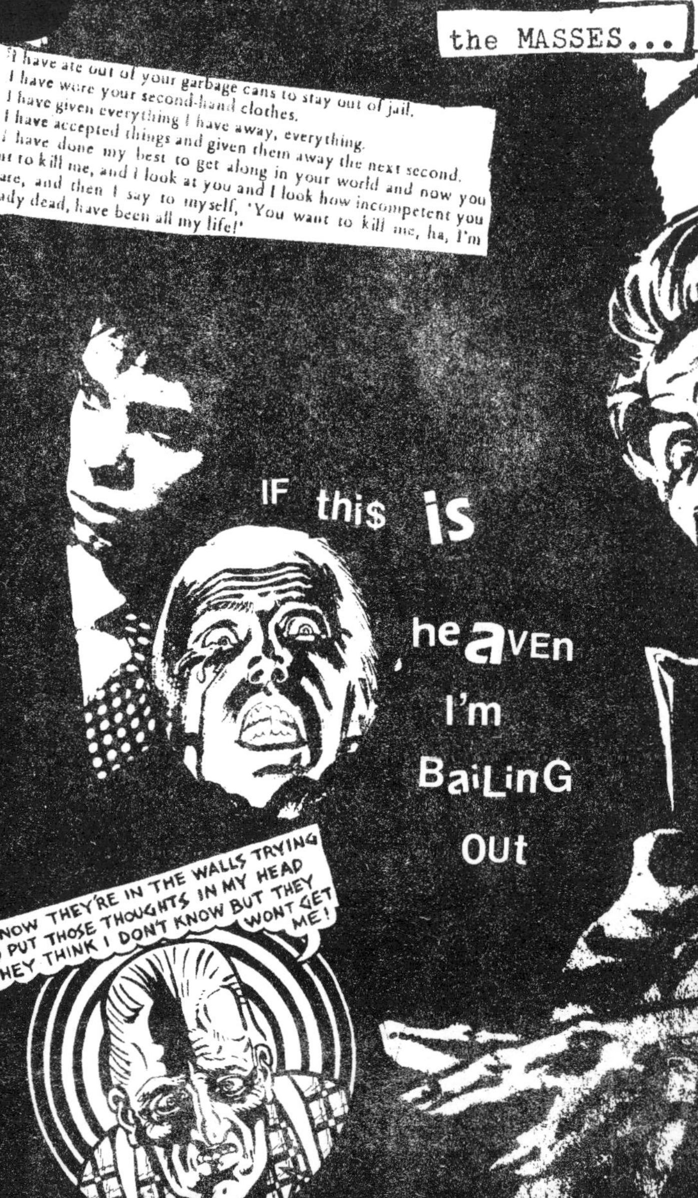

was flattering, on one hand, but also a little frustrating as I always preferred things with more originality in there. Having said this, the early *Grim Humour*s were themselves at least partly inspired by *Vague*, *Panache* and *Kill Your Pet Puppy*, so it's only natural that such cues have their role up to a certain point. I only had a problem if there was no personality inherent beyond this, really.

I was amused to read your review of *Ablaze!* 5 in GH14. Folded inside is a letter from you saying you hadn't totally slated it! Did you perceive a rivalry between our zines?

I can't recall a sense of rivalry between our zines or any competition with any other zines, but this was partly due to our own confidence. I felt we were producing a great zine, so I never felt threatened by the arrival of others. Of course, some others, including yours, were very good as well, but this respect might have been cunningly cloaked by a little healthy sparring in our reviews section.

We used to slate other zines really badly. Looking at it now, it seems horrific, but maybe that's because zines are an endangered species now whereas then they were everywhere. I think the truth did need to be told. If zine writers can't tell the truth as they see it, then who can?

Yes, things have changed now and, of course, there were loads of zines back then, and many were poorly produced, badly written or lacked personality. At the time I lambasted them for being such, but these days I can look back and appreciate that the people behind them all were at least trying to do something or validate this aspect of their lives somehow. I can't knock that, even if I could knock the results of it only too easily!

How often did GH come out, and why did you stop publishing them?

Towards the end, they appeared less and less frequently - maybe once every eight or nine months - simply because of all my other music activities, but I'd never planned to stop producing them. Another edition was waiting in the wings when Andrea and myself separated in early 1997, but then, quite simply, I could not afford to publish it. It took another few years for me to find the spare money to put into another mag, but by this time I'd grown bored of the GH moniker and changed the name to *Adverse Effect*. A few editions of this have surfaced so far, and another one is on the way as I write, but it'll be the first one since 2005. I intend to do two or three more of them for now.

You can read more about Richard's activities, buy *Adverse Effect*, and in the fullness of time purchase the *Grim Humour* book at www.fourth-dimension.net.

[1]In the 1980s, casuals were football fans who wore tracksuits and had their hair down flat, with a flicked over fringe, garnering the derogatory term *flick'ead*. They seemed to be more allied to the mainstream than punk kids, and at the same time also much more threatening. See the cartoon in *Karanoia '86* for a pictorial representation of one of these specimens. The sartorial element of this subculture later appeared in a watered-down and sanitised form with the onset of Britpop.

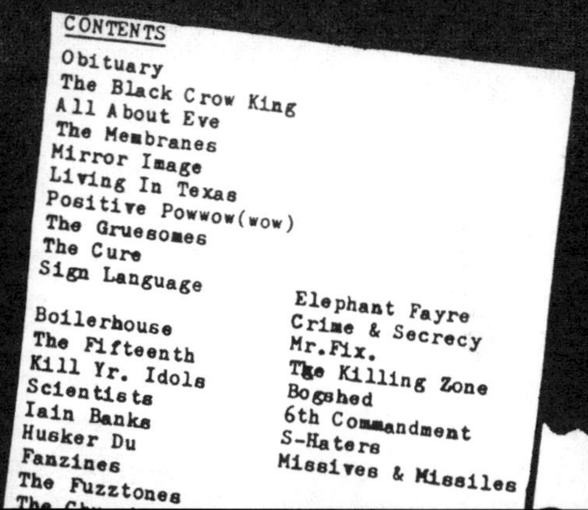

CONTENTS

Obituary
The Black Crow King
All About Eve
The Membranes
Mirror Image
Living In Texas
Positive Powwow(wow)
The Gruesomes
The Cure
Sign Language

Boilerhouse
The Fifteenth
Kill Yr. Idols
Scientists
Iain Banks
Husker Du
Fanzines
The Fuzztones

Elephant Fayre
Crime & Secrecy
Mr.Fix.
The Killing Zone
Bogshed
6th Commandment
S-Haters
Missives & Missiles

What was *that* all about?

Karren Ablaze! 'fesses up with **DAVE HASLAM**

If you know Manchester, you'll know Dave Haslam. Chances are you've danced to his choice of records at the Hacienda, read one of his books (one on the 1970s and one on Manchester, so far), attended his live in-conversation events, bought records on his Play Hard label or subscribed to his fanzine, *Debris*.

Debris operated from 1983 to 1989 and ran to 20 issues. Instead of slotting into the fanzine aesthetic of the time - the super-messy cut-and-paste style exemplified by *Rox* - *Debris* stood out with neat and orderly production. The content didn't conform either. Instead of interviewing the latest fanzine bands, Dave would be quizzing Raymond Carver.

DH: For me there weren't any rules, the main thing was that it was an extension of my interests. As you know, making a fanzine is a major task, so if I'm going to create one I might as well follow my own interests. The stuff I was writing about, whether it was music or books or whatever, wasn't written about in your average magazine, so the reason for interviewing a certain poet or writer was the same as interviewing a certain band: 'I want you to be interested in this because I think it's interesting and it seems to be an untold story.' When Raymond Carver came over to Britain in 1985 his publishers put him in a hotel in London, and as far as I know he was interviewed by no more than four people: *Time Out*, *The Times*, *Blitz* magazine and *Debris*. We were the only people in Britain who seemed interested. He died a few years later, and became a very celebrated writer, but for me he fulfilled the same category as Sonic Youth the same year, they were pretty much unknown and I had to trek over to Leeds to see them for the first time. It was about getting my voice heard and making a few things more conspicuous for whoever picked up the magazine.

I remember liking fanzines where you could get a sense of the personality behind them, obviously *Ablaze!* was an example of that, and that was an important part of it for me. I felt that the look of fanzines didn't have to fit a certain kind of category: there were some fanzine writers who thought that I was breaking the rules by presenting *Debris* that little bit cleaner and tidier. I didn't want it to have that throwaway element that some people, quite rightly, saw as part of the fanzine approach. I wanted to make it a cherishable object. I used to spend a long time doing it; I wanted people to hang onto it forever. And if I was going to change 40p, I had to make it look cared about – 40p was a lot of money to spend on a fanzine.

KA: Do you think that interview subjects were different back then?

DH: There were a lot of musicians at that time who were willing to see and talk about the big picture. I remember having a conversation with Pete Wylie, for him it wasn't just about the music, it was also about books and films, where you shopped and what you bought and your social attitude. He'd always found it hard to understand musicians who didn't see that all that was part of what they were articulating. So we benefitted from being able to talk to musicians who had made a choice about being on an independent label. If I was to carry the attitude I had then to music journalism now, I don't think I would end up with such interesting material because I'm not sure that musicians would want to engage with some of the subjects; Sonic Youth talking about the Manson family, or Mark E Smith talking about the Second World War. There was a bigger constituency of those sorts of musicians and that made our project as fanzine writers a little bit easier.

KA: I wondered if the differences between *Debris* and other zines at the time might be ascribed in part to the age you were when you wrote it. At 21, you'd already graduated from an English degree at Manchester University. Starting a zine as a teenager, you're very much driven by hormones and intensity and madness, but by the time you're 21, an element of maturity might be present. And you're very much a thinker anyway; you wouldn't put ideas out before properly processing them, but you'd also have had some breathing space to think about things by that time too.

DH: I don't think I changed that much between 17 and 21. There was a part of me that was very into the idea of writing, by the time I was 21 I enjoyed the process of trying to come to grips with something and finding the right words to talk about it. There were music journalists who had been around a couple of years before who were overly ambitious about how they wrote but I didn't want to go there, so that's another reason why I wrote about other things. It was partly a challenge to me. I remember at the time of the 1987 general election, thinking that I wanted to sit down and work out in my head what was going on politically and how that impacted on me. I read Oscar Wilde's *The Soul of Man under Socialism* as part of the research, and somehow I thought I was quite justified, being 25, living on Great Western Street in Moss Side and reading a load of theorists on the 21st century; I had the right to do that...

KA: If you are doing a fanzine, you give yourself the right.

DH: I think I did that partly for my own benefit. It wasn't an opinion piece, saying this is the right way to think about these things. It was partly an exercise in thinking and articulating; while people would pick up *Debris* cos they wanted to read another interview with Mark E Smith, they might pick up on that as well. There certainly weren't queues round the corner of Grass Roots bookshop, just to find out about what I thought about the 1987 general election.

KA: You must have known in yourself that it was worthwhile?

DH: I don't know if I felt like 'this is worth doing' or 'it's the only thing that I can do'. It was a mix of both. Quite a few of us got poached by the *NME* or *Melody Maker* or *Sounds*, and I remember - I think it was from the middle of '85 to the beginning of '88 - I wrote on and off for the *NME* and it was far less artistically and emotionally rewarding than doing *Debris*. I didn't like having to run my ideas past the editorial board, partly because I was in Manchester and they just wanted me to write about Manchester bands - they couldn't see why I would want to write about anything else. Every time I came up with any other idea they were suspicious of it and would always knock it back. There were a number of times when I did manage to persuade them to allow me to write something and then it would appear and a few times they'd butchered it in the editing process. But in almost every case, no-one was particularly bothered.

Whereas when *Debris* came out, John Peel would mention it on the radio and I'd have another slew of letters through my door. But writing for the *NME* it'd be like no-one cared, because people probably realised that the intensity and depth of communication wasn't there. That really put me off becoming involved more fully with mainstream music magazines. I also knew it would mean I'd have to move to London to really be in a situation where you could write about what you wanted in the style that you wanted to write in - you'd have to hang out with the people at the *NME*, go in the office and go drinking with them and all that kind of stuff. And that just wasn't something that interested me.

KA: Do you think that once you have the independence of doing a fanzine it's very hard to give that up?

DH: It is really hard. It isn't just a question of transferring from one format to another - it doesn't really work. I've done a fair amount of freelance writing since *Debris* but there's probably only a couple of magazines that I've had uniformly good relationships with. And, again, mostly it's to do with being in Manchester. In 2012 we're sort of conditioned into thinking of Manchester as one of the great musical and cultural capitals of the world, but no-one believed that in the mid-1980s and so being taken seriously was rare. That was an added reason not to get involved with the national music press.

KA: What was the overall project, for you?

DH: I genuinely felt that, not just *Debris* but all the other things I was doing around then, were part of an alternative. When I was in my early twenties, wondering whether I was politically sound or psychologically disturbed, I felt that there was a big mainstream, commercial, normal world, and an alternative was preferable to what that big wide world was doing. I actively sought out films, music, radio DJs - but I felt that a fanzine was probably the clearest expression of a sense of an alternative, because you had the means of production and distribution and you had the content all in your control. My whole problem with the big wide world was that I didn't have any sense of power in the midst of all this mainstream shite.

There was a political dimension to it too. Although I was living in a big city, I didn't particularly feel part of it. There were a few little groups

The *Debris* office, 1987

of people that I felt an affinity towards, people putting on alternative nights or running alternative bookshops... I also felt that the good thing about a fanzine was that it involved you having to communicate with people outside your immediate sphere. It was quite endearing communicating with people who wanted to buy copies of *Debris*, and we were sent letters from people all over Britain, as well as a few from abroad, written by people who seemed to think that what I was doing had some kind of value for them in their lives, so I would assiduously keep all those letters. While it was a primitive form of social networking - it wasn't instant - I felt that network, those connections, was a really important part of why I was doing what I was doing. I didn't want to do it in a black hole. The fact that there was somebody somewhere in Middlesex, or wherever it was, who would write me a four-page letter about how they hated school, and wasn't John Peel great, and the normal things that were in those letters, was quite rewarding.

KA: I used to get some really intense letters...

DH: There was an intensity about a lot of those letters. Why were fanzine editors seen as being people to whom you could write intense letters? That's what I mean about that communication being quite important. A lot of things go back to John Peel; I bet he used to get letters like that. That depth of feeling was a really important part of it. In the mid '80s there was a particularly alienating real world that lots of us wanted to keep our distance from, or to challenge in some way. Partly we wanted to create an alternative and partly we wanted to challenge what was already out there, hence the anger in quite a lot of fanzines. There was that sense of oppositional culture.

KA: The mainstream in the eighties seemed particularly brash and unyielding. It was horrible and glaring and bright and soulless.

DH: Also it was quite keen to demonise anyone who didn't fit in. It wasn't that we created an alternative; it was that we were shut out of the mainstream. We were passive recipients of the mainstream disdain. But we turned that situation into a positive by articulating and defining who we were.

KA: I want to trace back some things that happened. I remember coming to see you in your office and now I'm kinda curious: how come you had an office? Was it for the record label, or the fanzine?

DH: I first got an office for the fanzine because the space was cheap and I was at that point in my life when I'd move every few months, and every time I had to carry all my records and possessions around, and one or two places I stayed in got burgled quite a lot, so I thought 'well, if I get a central office and kinda move a load of stuff into that...' The first office I got was in that building on Princess Street. I had 90% of my worldly goods in the office, all my records and posters and magazines and a few clothes; I used to sleep in there sometimes.

KA: Back in '87, I came to see you and you helped me out. I had the artwork of *Ablaze!* and I asked you a technical question, whether there would be shadow lines when it was printed. You said you weren't sure but maybe Tipp-Ex would help, and I remember you kneeling on the floor in your office, Tipp-Exing the *Ablaze!* artwork with me watching on protectively. And it just really sticks in my mind because... people helped in different ways but that was just, y'know, that was particularly tender. You were helping another fanzine. And also I remember the day I went into your office and you'd just got *Sister* by Sonic Youth and you were like 'have you heard this?' and I'm like 'no', and you were like 'you've not got a copy of this?' The look in your eyes was sheer compassion, and you gave me your own copy.

DH: Wow, I don't remember that.

KA: I think I used to hang around town on a Saturday afternoon and sometimes made your office part of my route. But at some stage later than that I started to perceive you as part of the establishment.

DH: Right, Okay.

KA: Maybe because of you DJing at the Hacienda... I slagged you off in my fanzines under a pseudonym. I felt that you were part of a conspiracy, and I'm wondering if there was any basis for that?

DH: A conspiracy against...?

KA: (reading from *Ablaze!* 4): "NME hack and traitor to the North, DJ DeddHedd attempts to operate a monopoly on happeningness from a city centre office. From here emerges an ironically titled and well-produced studentzine..."

DH: Well, when I started putting on gigs it was because nobody else in Manchester was putting on the bands I wanted to put on. I started at the Boardwalk, usually along with Nathan McGough. He'd come over from Liverpool, he was Roger Eagle's nephew and a big mate of Tony Wilson's. In 1986 we put on Primal Scream, it was £75 and we had to pay for half the cost of the van for them to come down from Glasgow. The first time Sonic Youth played in Manchester they slept on my floor - it was all like that. Nobody had any money, everyone was doing it because their videos aren't on MTV and the *NME* is interviewing Bruce Springsteen, so it was 'how are we gonna get word out about Primal Scream?' You do that for almost self-sacrificing reasons really. But then you begin, if you've got good ears for what you're doing, to put on bands that become a little bit profitable, so you put them on again and maybe next time you make a little bit of money and then you start thinking 'well maybe I should start a regular night?'

The DJing started off with the guys in Big Flame saying 'we need someone to play the music before and after the bands come on - do you fancy doing it?' and I'd do it. And then one time we didn't book the bands and they said 'can you DJ the whole night, Dave?' and I remember I didn't even think I was a DJ; they put out a flyer saying: *Next week, no bands - disco featuring DJ Miserable Dave.*

So you fall into these things; you start doing it more and you suddenly think, 'Oh OK, I'm a DJ', and then the Hacienda come along and say, 'do you fancy doing a Thursday night?' so people who you originally thought weren't opening any doors for you begin to open doors, and you go through some of them. But that then means you start associating yourself with people who you'd started by not associating yourself with. I don't know how much I rationalised it at the time - I remember just thinking 'OK, so I enjoy DJing, and if this club, owned by New Order - who are one of my favourite bands ever - and Tony Wilson - who's just discovered what my name is - are saying "Come and play music for five hours every Thursday - we'll give you £40. Play what you like," then you do it.' Obviously there's a whole load of other ways of looking at that.

What happens in a city like Manchester, like any other city, is that actually a small number of people do a large number of things. I remember being in a room and I turned to Bruce Mitchell, the drummer from Durutti Column, who does a lot of other things, and I said 'if a bomb dropped on this room now the Manchester music scene would be really fucked,' and I didn't mean it in a kind of big-headed way; I was just aware that there weren't many of us who really made things happen.

We weren't necessarily working together, just working to make the city come alive. That's what gives you hope if you're in a dead, neutered, valueless, cultural desert. It only takes a few people to turn out something wonderful and I think that's great. But from the outside it could look like a conspiracy. 'They've got it all sewn up'. And maybe there's a little bit of truth in that, in the sense that when you're all in that group, somebody starts doing something else and you're eyeing them suspiciously, thinking, 'well where have they come from?'

KA: Who were the people in that room?

DH: Oh, I guess at that point, 1986-ish, I was thinking about Tony Wilson, Alan Wise, Paul Cons, Roger Eagle, Eliot Rashman, Nathan, Paula Greenwood, Bruce Mitchell and a few others. It wasn't so much who, it was more that I was struck how few people it took to make things seem busy and make things seem possible.

KA: So you think that there was a bit of a clique there?

DH: It wasn't so much a clique as a... I don't know what you would call it.

I think Factory was quite cliquey, which I didn't realise at the time, but that idea that 'you're either one of us or you're one of them, you're either in or you're out' was quite a Factory thing, both for Factory and for people who didn't like Factory. People had very strong views about the Hacienda, about whether it was a sell-out or whether it was pioneering. There was that kind of thing where we were all in it together - it's like a project for Manchester. You're asking people to feel engaged in the Factory thing but at the same time you don't want anyone to criticise it. I was working at the Hacienda and I was on Tony Wilson's TV show *The Other Side of Midnight* and that said which team I belonged in.

KA: And so to miserable little alienated teenagers, that was selling out. It doesn't take much...

DH: Yeah, it doesn't take much. Even just going on the telly; and the first thing I went on to talk about was cultural/critical - Raymond Williams - I didn't even go on to talk about music. I don't think just alienated teenagers feel like that, I think lots of people are like that, asking 'why have you got an opinion?' If you do whatever you do, what I would call putting your head above the parapet, there are going to be some people who are going to cheer you on and other people who are going to take a pot-shot.

KA: You already said people had a problem with how you designed your fanzine differently and the way they were supposed to be designed, so you'd already stepped out, you'd already gone into the firing line.

DH: In a way. I remember being quite innocent about it. I remember going in the toilet of club called the Venue and somebody had written on the wall something like "Debris = pretentious shit" and it took me aback... I've seen that mindset operating a million times now, but it was my first experience of it. Maybe we're a bit more used to that now on the internet, people having randomly passionate negative opinions about everything, and yeah I'm kind of used to people having anonymous randomly horrible things to say, but back then I wasn't used to it. It didn't put me off.

KA: I'm sorry for my part in that. It was only much later that I thought: he was really kind then I slagged him off, so I just wanted to come and talk to you about it face to face...

DH: Yeah it's great, it's good.

KA: How did *Debris* end?

DH: I finished it because I got too busy. Part of the reason for doing the fanzine was to spread the word about bands, and that led into flexis, and flexis led into the record label - so running the record label took over some of the function of getting the music out there. And by '89 I was DJing twice a week at the Hacienda, and my son had been born the year before. I think there was a change in the culture, especially in Manchester, between '86 and '89 where we just started listening to different kinds of music than we had previously. A lot of the music we were listening to was made in America, and a lot of that was Detroit techno. You could write about it, but you couldn't interview people...

KA: You just had to dance to it.

DH: Yeah, you consumed it in a totally different way. So whereas at one point it might have been interesting to me to write about why Morrissey is a vegetarian or what Mark E. Smith thought about the regeneration of Salford Docks, the records I was listening to weren't made by those people; they were made by people who were living in Detroit who I wouldn't have any access to. Some of them might have been interested in talking to me about post-industrialisation because they lived in Detroit, so they'd know all about it, but the opportunity for me to talk to them about it wasn't coming up. So the point of doing the magazine kind of drifted away really.

is without a contract?
So all you A&R men out there- get
busy, you're missing out!
3x7 is 26 and I have proof

John Robb

There are many ways in which you might know John Robb. You've probably watched him talking on the TV about culture and punk rock, or maybe you've seen him propping up the bar at a gig doing much the same thing. You might have been to one of his lectures, seen his band, Goldblade, or if you are of the correct vintage, The Membranes, where you could have danced under a moving canopy created by crazy kids who would immerse you in swirling newspaper confetti. You might have read his books on music, his articles in *Sounds*, or his webzine, *Louder Than War*. Or you might have seen his fanzine, the glorious *Rox*, which enjoyed a 30-issue reign as the UK's Noise Bible from 1977 to 1989.

So I want to ask you all about *Rox*. How old were you when you started it?

I started *Rox* when I was 16, in 1977. Someone brought a *Sniffin' Glue* to school and it was amazing to see something so simple and inspiring. My mate Mark Tilton's dad was a printer and knew about photocopiers so we put the first issue together. We also did a one-off sheet called *Broadsnide* in which we critiqued the school we were at and got into loads of trouble. When I got asked to leave the school, it was still inside my report.

What were you like at school/what was school like - I'm guessing it was shit and they didn't let you express yourself?

When I think of school now, which is rarely, it seems all in monochrome. It was a big school, lots of pupils, and everyone disappeared into this scrum. It had been a boys' grammar school, and still tried to continue in that tradition, even though it was now a mixed comprehensive - they even had caps for the first years, which was a great cause of bullying! We were into glam rock and The Beatles and Stones, whilst the cool kids liked smoking and Northern Soul. Everyone tried to wear flares and had their ties in big knots. When punk arrived, we were in the sixth form and suddenly everything went into colour, a small bunch of us became your archetypal teenage rebels. We pushed the boundaries, we tried everything. That was a great time, and the band and fanzine came out of that.

JOHN ROBB

Oh wow, that's a beautiful description. Which came first, the zine or the band?

They came together. The great thing about punk for us was the DIY thing. Before that music seemed something distant that only glam rock alien droogs did on Top Of The Pops, and that was great but we wanted to be involved because our heads were full of ideas. *Spiral Scratch* by Buzzcocks showed you that anyone could make a record, and we formed The Membranes and we made a record. We didn't have a clue what we were doing! Our first gig was at a Northern Soul disco in Kirkham, we had never used amps before or a real drum kit, and we thought tuning up was putting all the machine heads in a row - we must have sounded mental - the Northern Soulies wanted to beat the punks up but our drummer knew a couple of them and calmed it all down. Our second gig was in Cleveleys, at a crappy talent show - we played and so did Zyklon B, the best local punk band. We came last and a nine-year-old girl reading a poem won - the local press was shocked by these punk bands playing the

Ah's a diggin' man!

DIG THOSE CWAZEE RIDDUMS DADDIO

tappety tappety tap

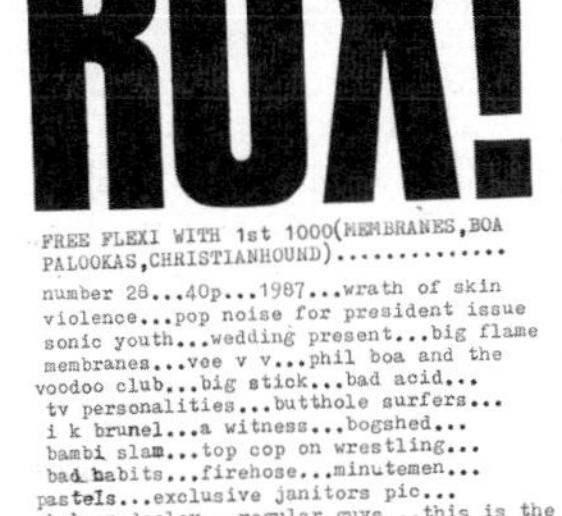

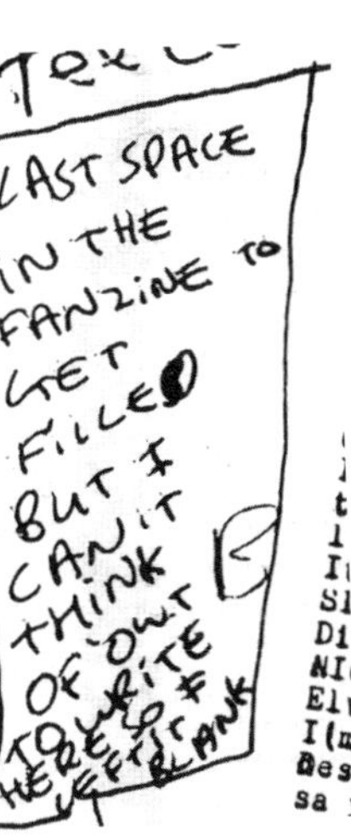

gig. I don't think the organisers knew what was coming. When you grow up in a town there is so little space to make music - in a city there are always people who will help you or find you gigs to play - we had none of that!

How long did The Membranes survive in Blackpool before escaping to Manchester?
We were there from the start of the band till 1984. I went to North Staffordshire Poly in the middle of all that and hitched up and down the country - to Blackpool to rehearse, to London to hang out. At one point we really had it happening in Blackpool, we used to run our own label Vinyl Drip and put on weekly gigs at an old club called JR's. We put on local nights as the Vinyl Drip Club, we had the fanzine and the band was taking off, getting written about in the press, getting played on Peel and playing gigs round the UK, but we wanted to live in the city and we were getting sick of not being allowed in pubs because of the way we looked, or getting attacked for having funny hair. London or Manchester was the choice, a whole bunch of us moved at the same time - some to London and some to Manchester.

It sounds so exciting, such a powerful energy at the time, only marred by knobheads beating up punks. What were those early *Roxes* like?
The late seventies were full of chaotic energy, but also with a great soundtrack and when I read books about post-punk now, they don't capture the fallout of post-punk as I remember it - it was far more mixed up than people like to make out - Southern Death Cult and The Fall and Killing Joke and tribal drums were all around, and John Peel was the best guide. We would document the local scene and the other stuff we loved, but we also made the zine like an explosion - full of cartoons and collages out of old encyclopaedias - our heads were full of ideas. As the recent Goldblade song says, 'my mind is like an atom bomb' and the music and the zine reflected this. We lived right in the middle of a cut-and-paste DIY culture: our clothes were cut and paste from Oxfam, creating our own Dickensian look, our music was cut and paste and so was the zine...

How many issues of *Rox* were there?
I think there were about 30.

How many copies did you used to sell, and did you enjoy going round gigs selling them to people?
We used to print 3/4000 depending on how much money we hadn't lost on our travels round the country. I had no problems going round selling them, it was a great way to meet people – I am still friends to this day with people I met doing this. We also used to post them off to people to sell round the country and also sell them at our own gigs with The Membranes and give them to people to sell at those gigs and get the money back another time. The fanzines were crucial to the Death To Trad Rock scene of bands at the time - they would promote the bands and the gigs, put the gigs on or put you up in their damp and mouldy flats!

Doing a zine was a great way to get to know people quickly, but then again I think things were quite open back then and you could just start talking to someone at a gig and ask to stay at their house. I think people might be a bit more uptight now... When you started to work for *Sounds*, were you daunted about moving into proper mainstream music journalism?
I was not daunted really. Punk taught me that you can never have any fear. We were empowered by the music and we tried to pass that empowerment on and still do. We learned that the people running the culture can be ignored and we can make our own culture. That was the whole point of the fanzines.

***Rox* was ace because it was so messy, it took down another barrier to zine production. But it was really nicely done as well - the pages are great cos there are loads of bits to read and really interesting graphics. Do you think a lot of zines were influenced by it? Mine certainly was.**
There was a definite plan to what we were doing, I hated that hip graphic [design] at the time that was about space - really dull fanzines would have the title then loads of white and a really earnest paragraph about some music they were trying to really like at the bottom. We were the opposite. The whole thing was 3D: the music, the clothes, the graphics were all an avalanche of ideas. I wish I could make the *Louder Than War* website look a bit like that! I loved drawing all the cartoons and cutting things up. A lot of fanzines certainly started to look like *Rox* at this time - it's not my place to claim

influence, but the editors have always told me they were really into our whole style and ethic and I think you could say the mid-period of fanzine culture was something that we were a key influence on...

Definitely, *Rox* embodied the fanzine aesthetic of that time, it was the god of fanzines! Did you coin the phrase 'Noise Bible'? That was a great description of what you did.

Noise Bible was one of my phrases - this was another thing I got really into - planting phrases everywhere and seeing if they stuck. When I was writing for *Sounds* I got quite a few of these off the ground like Britpop and acid casuals and loads of others - we were even using grunge before grunge ever existed!

To be honest I found your fanzine really inspiring and it was great to see not just another bloke making a fanzine - [the scene] was quite male-orientated at the time.

How do you manage to do all the stuff you do? It seems like you think really, really fast, Also you seem to have a really good memory, how do you manage that?

I don't like getting bored and my mind is always racing - there's so much stuff to get engaged in! I have a photographic memory. I can remember whole things that happened over the years. Luckily I got bored of the rock 'n' roll lifestyle years ago so there are no clouds in there - I don't drink or do drugs - not a straight edge thing, it was making my own mind up and I don't join clubs! All that side of punk was very inspirational to me, that thinking for yourself and questioning everything, Crass made me think about being vegetarian and how to have a consciousness but still make a great racket!

What do you do at Salford University? Do you do lectures? What are they like?

I do lectures in lots of places. I just go in there and tell people that you can make music without permission and the value of DIY. I tell the girls they don't have to be X Factor singers.They should empower themselves by playing musical instruments and making their own music and they don't have to be pin-ups to be creative. I tell the boys that they don't have to wait to be told they are any good. The youth still have great music but X Factor has clouded the process and the anti-rock bias of the music industry makes it tricky for young bands who are nearly always rock bands.

Don't you ever get nervous, talking on the TV?

I'm never nervous on TV, it seems perfectly natural!

Are you really 50?

No.

Ha, sorry, I thought you said you were in some article!

I'm 51. I look after myself. The body is the vehicle and the weapon for the mind - don't want to encourage a breakdown! I got things to do! ... You're a Buddhist now which I find intriguing.

Yeah, since like 1999. It helped me make sense of things like suffering from a long-term illness and not being able to play anymore - how not to be so pissed-off about that as to get lost in depression and self-pity. Very helpful for strengthening the mind

It seems like a logical conclusion to being passionate about music... maybe a search for some kind of spirituality or a search for wisdom... I like the Jains.

Could that be in the future for you - meditation and enlightenment?

I've looked at it... I'm interested in everything and picked little bits up as I've gone along, I've met holy men in India and read stuff. And I visited the Buddha's tree in India!

It's good to know that those options are there, and not just for people in the East. It's another aspect of the possibilities of being human, that we can turn inwards and find new worlds that way... In what ways do you think people can DIY now?

DIY is all over the internet now. Like punk, it's a spirit and a state of mind - you can make your own culture and you don't have to obey alien orders, as Joe Strummer once said! The ideal applies worldwide. We are linked to so many similarly motivated musicians and culture types everywhere.

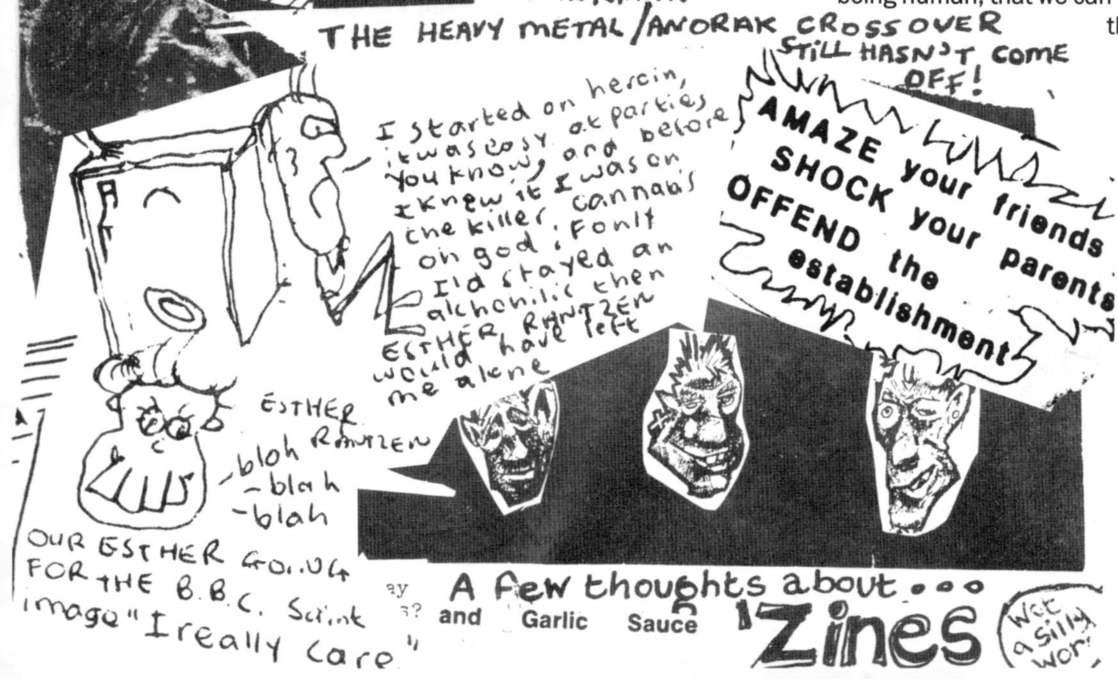

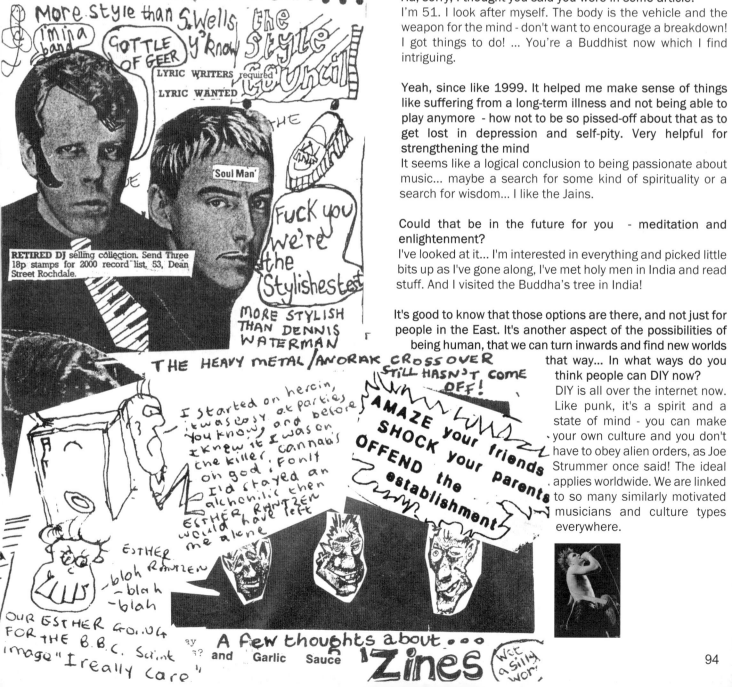

Ablaze!
5

Ablaze! 5

Publication date: April 1989

Ablaze! 5 was all about new things. American bands! Glossy cover! Proper design! A flexidisc! Free stuff from record labels! Throwing Muses! Micheal Walsh! Arrogance! And... an electric typewriter!

And then there were American bands.
The moment Pik played me *Surfer Rosa* in 1989, the USA became a desirable destination. I wasn't gonna get there for a few years yet so it was fortunate that most of the bands I wanted to see came over here. At the time there was a healthy tour economy whereby foreign bands could easily play a dozen or so venues across the UK, instead of the London-and-maybe-one-other half-assed meanderings that happen now. In order to attend as many of these shows as possible, all one needed was a piece of cardboard and a marker pen. Droves of youths would transport themselves freely and carbon-neutrally across the land, with accommodation assured by a network of floors. Most of these band followers were, in truth, goths, and since by this time there were no decent goth bands left in existence, I declared band-following to be evil and in need of stamping out. Yet it worked for me, as I trailed round the country with a bag of zines on my back. The practice was stamped out of my world by dodgy drivers scaring me with requests for sexual favours. I wanted to know why it disappeared for everyone else, so have asked resident roadside sociologist Ross Holloway to examine the phenomenon – see page 129.
Ablaze! 5 was the first to have a glossy cover - and that's how I learned that, some of the time, people only really look at the surface. Readers began to perceive *Ablaze!* as a colour, glossy publication regardless of how the inner pages were printed, so now I was equipped with the knowledge of how to wow everyone on the cheap. Another plus was that William Potter totally got on board and designed the entire thing. At this point *Ablaze!* stopped looking like a *Rox*-wannabe and took on its own identity.
This issue also boasted a giveaway flexidisc, the one that the Slum Turkeys had been grooming me for, with The Purple Eternal on the flipside. I made believe that my flexis were the products of a label called Keep Britain Noisy, which in my imagination was following in the footsteps of Blast First Records. When Liz Naylor phoned me from Blast First's London headquarters and said they wanted to advertise in my zine, and that they would send me some *Nothing Short of Total War* box sets, it felt like the very most exciting moment of my life. I worshipped that label, and here they were, phoning me and sending me free stuff!!
While the zine was zooming ahead, the editor was lagging behind when it came to understanding what was going on. I was trying to understand how music and politics related; a rather '80s project, and one for which I was unequipped. In the epilogue I confess to "a mind stretched to breaking point". These bands were my teachers. I was meeting people from other cultures, people older than me who'd had time to think about stuff, and they were challenging me more than the blokes in the philosophy department I was *supposed* to be learning stuff off of.
Ablaze! 5 is infused with a fierce arrogance. By this time I was getting plenty of positive feedback about the zine and, being a stranger to that kind of thing, didn't really know what to do with it. Who knew about the simplicity of a polite "thank you"? I must have decided I was bloody brilliant. I felt fine about going round to The Edsel Auctioneer's house and declaring myself to be their new bassist. After my tryout revealed that I could barely play a note, I changed tack and insisted on interviewing them. It's no wonder they "treated me with a certain suspicion", though we did end up becoming friends.
This issue marked the start of my love affair with Throwing Muses. I was lucky to speak with Tanya, Kristin's effervescent sister, whose generous heart and bright intelligence gives this piece its fizzling energy. At one point she mentions a new band she's formed with Kim Deal, called The Breeders...
This interview also heralds the arrival of Micheal Walsh. Micheal became a central figure in *Ablaze!* world. He was a dandy; a black, Yorkshire dandy, with a copy of *The Importance of Being Earnest* in his jacket pocket. An eloquent and erudite musicologist, he nevertheless barely wrote a word for us. But he hung around, being annoying and inspiring, until his eventual disappearance. He was to leave town a few years later amidst tales of gangster threats, and we were never to see him again. One of my hopes for the publication of this work is that it will somehow recall him from the ether. Walshie – *phone home.*
The major event of this issue was the Dinosaur Jr., Rapeman and Band of Susans gig at Leeds Polytechnic on 14th October 1988. A group of *Ablaze!* correspondents defied the pickets and interviewed all three bands. I didn't take part in any of these conversations, perhaps in order to co-ordinate them all, though apparently I was kicking around while Patrick questioned Lou Barlow. Vee quietly got on with grilling the Susans (printed in the following issue), and I was careful to keep out of the way while Doug interrogated Steve Albini. He was (and still is) such an icon, and back then I was scared of him. He had a reputation for being mean and cutting and I didn't trust him on the Rapeman thing at all. Five years later I was to work at his record label and he showed me how to play guitar ("You have to make it look really difficult, put your fingers like this", i.e. as contorted as possible), and a few years after that my name turned up on the Friends of Shellac record.[1] Yet I still don't think I would have fared very well at that interview, where my angry British feminism would have clashed with their nonchalant aggression, and am grateful to Doug and Sean for upholding Leeds' radical feminist heritage for me. Doug later wrote a song for his band Nerve Rack that went "Buttfuck Albini / see how he likes it."[2] They might have considered that somewhat unnecessary, but it was the way we felt in Leeds.
I was also too nervous to meet Sonic Youth, but wrote it up from the chaotic tape that Ross brought back, after he and Mark hitched two hundred miles down to the Blast First offices to meet them.
Re-reading *Ablaze!* 5 in the twenty-first century took me a long time. Its youthful naivety pained me out. But it describes a moment when everything was changing and opening up; I was meeting people who were explaining things to me about music, politics, and how easy it is to DIY. And there's a real sense of demystification. Sonic Youth, The Sundays, Dog Faced Hermans, Dinosaur Jr., The Pixies and folk from the 1 in 12 Club are all here saying it was easy (or hard work, but), it was cheap(-ish), and (okay, often implicitly) - do it!

What we've left out: Pretty much nothing.

---

1 Otherwise known as 'Futurist', a 12" of instrumentals recorded for Montreal dance troupe La La La Human Steps and given away to the 800 or so people named on the front cover (the recipients' name circled in silver marker to add a personal touch and, more importantly, to deter sneaky re-selling!)

2 The song appears on *Ablaze!* 6's flexi.

Opposite: Idea for the cover of Ablaze! 5 by William Potter

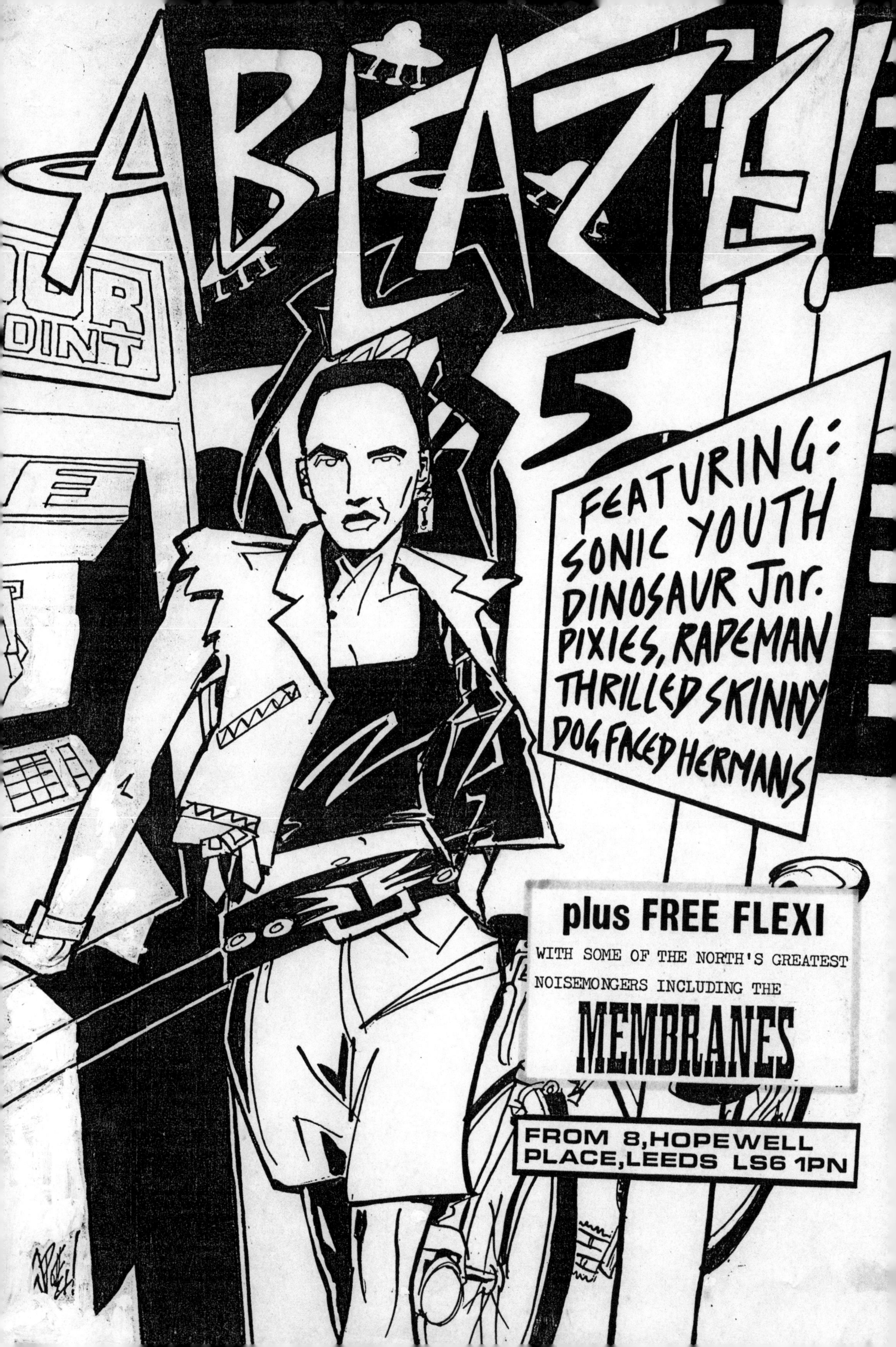
ABLAZE!
5
FEATURING:
SONIC YOUTH
DINOSAUR Jnr.
PIXIES, RAPEMAN
THRILLED SKINNY
DOG FACED HERMANS
plus FREE FLEXI
WITH SOME OF THE NORTH'S GREATEST
NOISEMONGERS INCLUDING THE
MEMBRANES
FROM 8,HOPEWELL
PLACE,LEEDS LS6 1PN

ABLAZE!

FREE FLEXI
SONIC YOUTH
DINOSAUR Jr
PIXIES
THROWING MUSES
SUNDAYS
THRILLED SKINNY **UT**
RAPEMAN

5 *85p*

ABLAZE!

SONIC YOUTH
DINOSAUR Jr
PIXIES
THROWING MUSES
SUNDAYS
THRILLED SKINNY
UT
RAPEMAN
FREE FLEXI
5 ***85p***

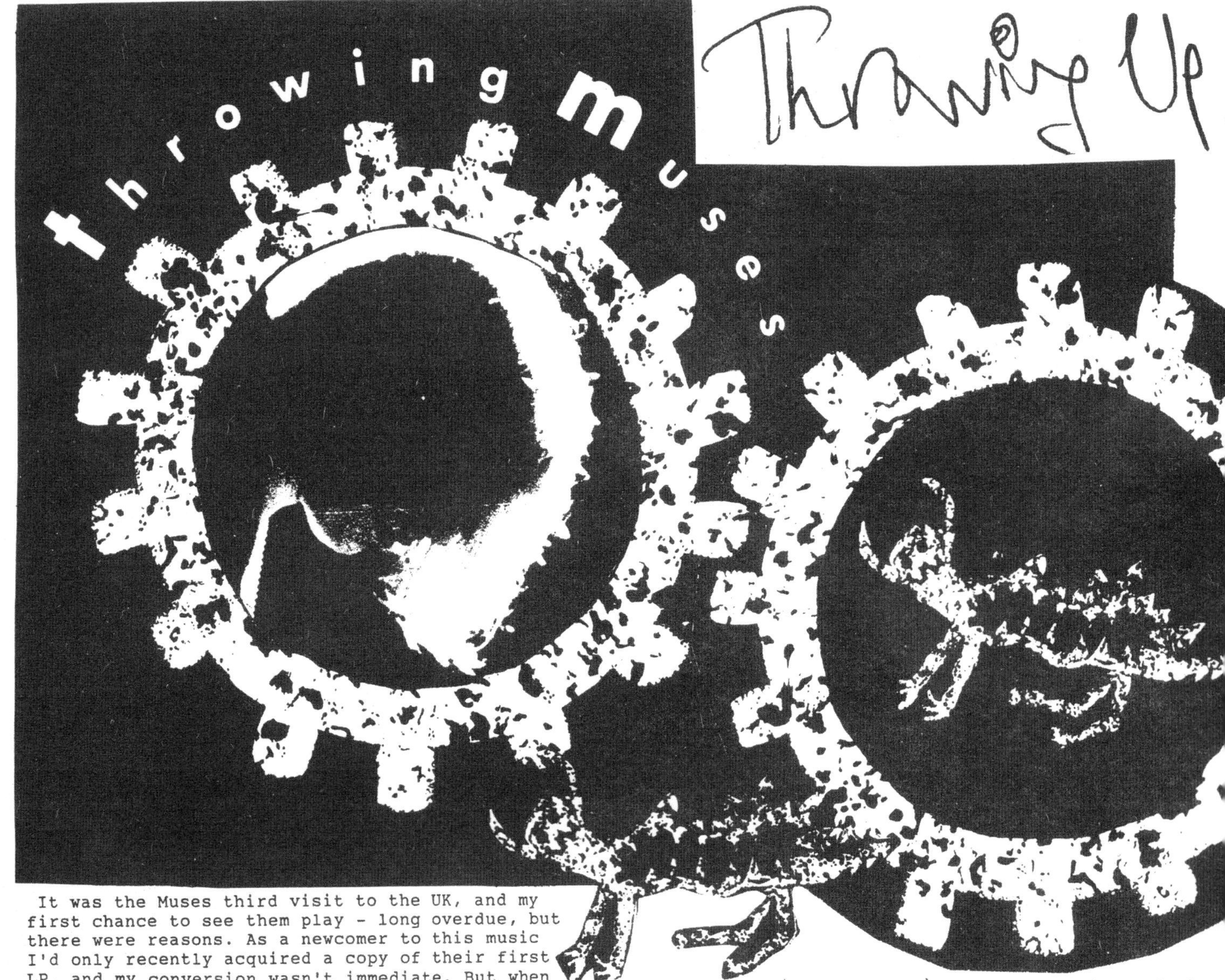

It was the Muses third visit to the UK, and my first chance to see them play - long overdue, but there were reasons. As a newcomer to this music I'd only recently acquired a copy of their first LP, and my conversion wasn't immediate. But when it occured...well, I guess it was fairly total. A friend gave me a whirlwind introduction to their subsequent works, which was like watching a much speeded up film of a wild flower growing and bursting into bloom. And another confession, while we're at it: I thought the Throwing Muses were scary. In my mind they didn't fit, they were odd shapes moving unpredictably; crazy women.

Now, of course, I realise that nothing could be further from the truth. In their way they threaten only staid, useless music, but what they offer is so natural, and real, it is growth...joyful generation.

At Sheffield's Leadmill, before their gig there, I was fortunate enough to spend some time with Tanya Donelly, guitarist, vocalist and sometime songwriter with this amazing, amusing Boston four piece group. I'd seen her moving around the building, singing happily to herself and chatting with people. This was the penultimate date of the British tour, and they've made various TV and radio appearances. Several other papers were interviewing them that evening; it must get tiring, or at least feel really strange, talking to these strangers who act as if they have a right to probe into your work, your life.

"Really, I don't mind," Tanya assures me."We put ourselves in that position."

But don't you feel shy? I'm nervous and I've only travelled 40 miles; you've come considerably further.

"I have been known to be shy..." at this point I first notice her ridiculous, charming laugh which seems to rise from nowhere and disappear back there straightaway. They've never been to Sheffield before, she says, which lead me to ask the question I'd been suppressing for several minutes...

Although with all the travelling the Muses have been doing, it seems fairly natural that one of them should be wearing a large compass around her neck. Do you get confused about where you are?

"Oh no!" she smiles, "It's an REM promotional device. Warner Brothers were handing them out. It's completely non-functional!" I suspect that was a question she'd answered many times that day.

Micheal, my aforementioned friend, arrives having missed his train earlier. He sits down and immediately begins to laugh. "Why are you wearing a compass around your neck?!" he wants to know. Tanya explains again.

Micheal also wants to know how important dancing is to the appreciation of Muses' music.

"I would hope the music would affect people's bodies before their heads. That seems to be a natural progression, music-wise, it is for me, so when I hear something I'm impassioned by, it goes through that. I want people to move to it; definitely there's a charge there."

Do your American audiences react differently to those over here?

"People move more here," she says, surprising us. "They're definitely more physical, in The States they kinda watch more. It depends where you are: in bigger cities, LA, New York, San Francisco, they'll be dancing. Still, even when people're watching it's a good reaction."

Throwing Muses songs have become much more hummable, haven't they?

"Yeah, the last one ("Hunkpapa") is more hummable, I don't think that's a bad thing."

Neither do we! It was possible to sing along to material like "America..." but only with the greatest of effort; you'd have to spend an hour concentrating on just one line. Have you had to tone things down so that people could understand you?

"It wasn't a conscious effort, I don't think we could have done it if we'd tried to, it was really spontaneous. I want people to listen to the music, I don't wanna alienate anybody, we're not being elitist, like, just a band for musical scholars!

I want it to get into people's heads and ips, and not be an effort.
"I love our earlier stuff, and I'm really lad we did that, it was definitely genuine t the time. It would be different if I hought we were compromising something to o it but I don't think we have. If we'd ried really hard and crafted the songs hen I would think that, but we didn't - t just happened! People seem grateful to s, they can listen to it now."
Such answers may have been prepared or ust repeatedly required in the previous nterviews since "Hunkpapa" was released, nd are good to hear but not strictly ecessary - someone, somewhere must have been accusing them of 'selling out', but we can't even think in such terms.

Is it a difficult thing, I wondered, to go into a studio and make records?

" 'House Tornado' was a really difficult one, 'Hunkpapa' was GREAT though, it was just fun the entire time!" It's that delirious laugh again."But yeah, it's like trying to make a record in a hospital, basically - it's really hard to feel passionate in a studio."

Next came an idea that there really wasn't time to go into; with all this talk of feminine psychology, yin and yang etc, I've been wondering whether there really is a difference between male and female minds. If there is a difference, surely it's due to conditioning and nothing intrinsic in people? As I'm attempting to get the the question out, her friend Patch enters the room and says hello.

"This is Patch!" Tanya exclaims. "Do you think we're coming from a female angle? I think we are. We're women and we're women singing, I wouldn't say that we're a 'women's project', I think it's a people's project, definitely. Men have the luxury of being able to represent the human race when they sing, while women represent women. I think we're successfully overcoming that, and I think Kristen's songs definitely come from a human perspective, though she's a woman and they're coming from her body so they're female songs."

I guess in Western society certain qualities are taken for granted as feminine, others as masculine, and the Muses are bringing out, from their bodies as they will constantly tell us, this sort of music which seems to have been so supressed or ignored.

I'd heard that Kristen had been in hospital recently, to have a tumour taken out - is that true?
"It was actually a tumour in her sinus,yeah she's OK now. It might be a chronic condition or something..." her voice lowers , very serious for a short while."It was removed a few months ago. They've no idea what caused it, it was benign and because of that they had no clue what it was or where it came from. There's always something coming out of your body...babies! tumours!"
Hasn't it affected her singing?
"They said it would but it hasn't.they don't know if the condition was aggravated by her singing style..."
If it was, it'd be too sad, too ironic...
"People are saying you're the new Talking Heads" admits Micheal, to our general mirth mixed with horror.
"I don't know what that means, I don't." she says, a degree of concern showing through her voice.
"Is there something inherent in American bands that makes the struggle to express things?" he inquires.
"You mean the cathartic thing, that throwing up thing? That seems to be something a lot of your people people think is an American thing, TV shows, it's all therapy. I dunno if it's because it's so easy to feel like you're not being watched there at all. I'm told that Americans are really ready to give all that up, that they're more willing to talk about their childhood than anyone else in the world."

I'm completely lost now, being sat right next to this woman but sensing the oceanic gulf between us. The expanse is bridged by her friendliness, and the music...
"We come from the East coast though, which is very tight-lipped. If you go down to California you're gonna find that kind of garrulous nature...basically I don't know!"
Do people think you're mad?
"I think people think Kristen's mad, you mean crazy-mad? Yeah, they think she's crazy, sometimes, but as soon as you meet us you realise there's nothing unusual, ha ha! on a personal level..."

You toured with the Pixies last time just as they were getting loads of attention, and now with the Sundays...
"We wouldn't wanna tour with a band that wasn't pre-energizing the audience, and when we go out half our job's already been done, they're already in that frame of mind, so it's really important. It helps me play too, it definitely inspires us..."
The Sundays have just walked in, because it's their dressingroom we'd hijacked for some peace & quiet. Tanya feigns fury:
"I'm trying to do an interview! I hate the Sundays! ...No, no, this is YOUR dressingroom,.."
As she implores them to stay, their guitarist is taunting us. "Don't ask her about that story!" he warns me.
"Don't even start."
What? I wanna know...
"He's making it up!"
"Making WHAT up?" he enquires slyly.
"Making nothing up."
The Sundays leave us, with a final "Don't feel guilty. It's nice and cold out here," and Tanya is still sat beside me, giggling. The two bands adore each other, but seem to be tired of telling the press this. The situation resembles that on the last tour; are you chums with the Pixies?
"Yeah, pretty much best. Kim's my best friend. We live in the same area of town. Kim and I are actually doing music together with Dave, their (our?) drummer. We go into the studio the day after we get back, to do a demo. It's her songs; when we started out it was gonna be both of our songs but Sire/ Warner Bros. wont let me do my songs, it's all sorta weird publishing crap."
But this sounds like it's gonna be great - what are you calling yourselves?
"The Breeders."
Brilliant! And an excuse for further giggling...
What do you and Kim do for amusement?
"Ah, it's normal stuff, we go out drinking, we go dancing to this club called Access (Axis?), it's the only place I can dance cos it's real dark. They play French and Italian disco, weird stuff...we do the limbo..."
What's that?
"Don't you know, you have a pole between two people...it's just something that always ends up happening at the end of the evening, in one of our apartments!!!"
Micheal notices my bewilderment:"She's far too serious," he explains to her. Oh, it's a joke? Well you never can tell with these Americans...
if you'll only dance in the darkest of nightclubs it must be difficult to stand in front of hundreds of people and sing and play guitar...
"It's easier for me now than it used to be. it feels more natural to me now, at first it was like, 'this is crazy! This is the stupidest job in the world!' It just felt completely insane to me, to be watched, to be TV,or whatever. I have a hard time making eye-contact; if it's just a crowd I can deal with it, but if I see a personality I think 'Oh god! They're human beings! Every single one of them has a personality!' Ha Ha!"

Do you and Kristen write from completely different perspectives?
"We're semi-similar I guess, cos we grew up together and we're sisters 'n' stuff, but we're completely different, I don't know what inspires the music so I don't know how that shows itself!"
Seeing the Muses play that evening, from within a mass of uncontrollably joyful human bodies, I had a sense of their ultimate, complete SANITY. Their dynamic songs took on an incredible life that showed itself spiritually and physically, intellectually and sexually. Kristen sang songs for her man and her child with such intense passion that the feeling spread to the edges of the room and probably much further. It was irresistable - no degree of exhaustion could keep people from dancing. Elated and energized, I left behind so much cynicism, taking instead a headful of light...I guess this is my way of saying they were very good. Listening again to Hunkpapa all their power and wonderful sense of order was apparent, but only as a faint reminder of their live capabilities...
How could I ever have been scared of these people?

We'd wanted a serious chat with these energetic Scottish glee merchants for quite a bit of a while, but circumstances kept getting in the way. Eventually Andrew, Sven and I met up with Andy (dynamic guitar), Colin (pounding bass) and Wilf (wild drums & saxaphone sometimes), and we climbed into their van outside Leeds' Duchess of York. Unfortunately Marion (vocals & lyrics, trumpet, cowbell and anything she can lay her hands on) remained in the pub, where they were about to play with the Ex and Jackdaw With Crowbar.

Since their magnificent debut EP "Unbend" appeared on their own Demon Radge label, bursting with dancemaking joy and weird scrapey noises and trumpets all over the place, people all over Britain have been muttering about this great new band from Edinburgh with the funny name. With the release of "Humans Fly", a mini LP, the press seemed to catch on, and the band were asked to appear on Def II's Fsd music show. They've since provided a sprinkling of gigs around the place and a second 7", featuring their wonderful version of the Italian folk resistance song, "Bela Ciao"

Part of what sets them apart from so many other bands is their unwillingness to keep to a certain style of music. "I couldn't do that because my interests are too wide," one of them explained:"there are so many different types of music, and in each kind there's really good stuff and really bad stuff. Some people seem to think there's only one good sort of music and that all the bands that play that sort of music are alright. Hopefully we'll never fall into a trend, altough journalists always try to pigeonhole us, calling us 'indie-thrash' or whatever. That's just laziness."

No-one can really summarise a band's music in one line, so is it best not to try?

"We quite like playing music that makes people dance. It's really good to see a load of folk getting into it, it makes you want to play better. You get carried away by the whole thing and hopefully it builds into something really exciting . You can't do that without an audience, they're as much a part of it as we are."

They'd just seen the Ex for the first time and were enthusing about them with new found admiration: "I know that over the next few months it's going to affect us, cos when I see something I really like, you don't try and copy it, but it creeps in slowly. They were great, the way they jump about...and they seem to have a really good attitude."

"When we started we'd just seen Big Flame and Bogshed playing and I think it really influenced the way we approached what we were doing. We had gradually been getting faster and faster anyway, but seeing Big Flame we thought "shit, they're playing THAT fast, I'd quite like to try doing that.'(I hope they never get to see Napalm Death!-ed) It was more the spirit of what they were doing than actually trying to copy their music, although everyone copies from everyone...Big Flame stole lots from the Minutemen."

When asked if they'd like to recommend any Scottish bands of note they went straight for The Stretch Heads, a fast thrashy original combo with an LP out now on Moksha records ("Five fingers, four thingers, a thumb, a facelift and a new identity", produced, incidentally, by Colin Herman). They also informed us of the "totally amazing" Nyah Fearties ('Fearties', apparently, is Scottish for 'afraid'), a duo playing acoustic bass & guitar, and Fini Tribe who they admire despite the enormous musical gulf that lies between them.Fini Tribe write all their songs on a computer and have been doing well in the acid house charts, we're told.

"We find a lot of bands that we've got a lot in common with, just odd bands around the country that we've played with and that we get on with, like the Membranes, Jackdaw, Death by Milkfloat, Shrug..." Via a discussion of the Ex's obvious political stance, we began to consider how overtly political Dog Faced Hermans lyrics are."They are political but not very flag-waving and obvious. It depends on how you want to defineit.For me it encompasses pretty much everything, how people relate and how power structures operate, how they are used to manipulate and control things. That permeates everything, in just about everything you do you can find evidence of that. The way a band works, to me, can be a much stronger political statement than what they say. There are loads of bands that preach really heavy politics but don't necessarily act like that. I just think that the way we work and treat other people when we're working with them is as political as any sort of lyrics."

This brought to mind their habit of swapping positions on the bill with bands they tour with, so that there's no headliner/support distinction."I assumed other bands did that too. It's quite normal to us cos we feel we're on the same level as the bands we play with." Sometimes it can be a drag to be first on the bill if there's no-one in the place and it fills up later, but we wouldn't say 'we're not gonna play cos it's beneath us',I don't see it as 'top' and 'bottom' and the money gets split depending on how far people have come rather than how many times they've been on the cover of the NME."

Dog Faced Hermans seem to be known, if not always through their music, rather through the 'strength' of being stuck with one of those wacky indierock names. Where the hell did they get it from?

"It's from an old Hollywood film, in which this woman was having a bad dream and came in saying 'Oh I've just seen a dog-faced herman in the garden!' and we thought 'what an amazing name...'"

Amazing by name, amazing by nature, the Dog Faced Hermans sound may not be pretty but it's certainly pretty good. There's no need to tell you, surely, to venture forth to see them play live so I'm not going to bother. See you there.

The 1in12 club is a relatively new venue in Bradford which opened last summer. It was started by some people who had been putting bands on at various places in the city for several years, and they managed to get some grants from the council to enable them to convert a derelict building into a decent place for young and unemployed people to go and see bands at non-rip off prices. For 2 years the building was converted, the members themselves replacing floors and walls and doing painting and plastering work, while one guy did all the plumbing and another did all the electrical work. This summer'll see the opening of a café, library and bookshop on the top floor.

The club is run collectively, by groups of members working on things like band booking, the bar, the PA etc. They use the bar profits to cover running costs and door takings go mostly to the bands, and i've seen them split all the money made on the door between two bands playing there one evening.

Other activities include raising money for Leeds Abortion fund and putting on benefit gigs for various causes. At the time we spoke to them they'd been giving moral support and whisky to striking post office workers (shows you how long ago we did this interview!). The club was named as a reaction to a government report in '81 that claimed one in twelve people on the dole were defrauding the social security, implying that unemployed people are scroungers and ommitting the fact that they're in really bad shit.

A similar thing has been set up in Belfast, in the shape of Warzone, and apparently there's a project in Norwich currently underway. Their message to anyone attempting this sort of thing is that although it takes a long time, and requires loads of commitment, it can be done. There are empty buildings in every city, as well as people with time and ideas, and there aren't many good venues anywhere (because club managers only wanna make profit so they put on discos), and there are loads of bands wanting to play, and people wanting to see them play...add it all up!

Groups that have done gigs at the 1in12 so far include the Ex, the Three Johns, Thrilled Skinny, Anrefn, Chumba wamba, Joyce McKinney Experience, The Instigators, and Nerve Rack...If you'd like to play there, phone Bradford 734 160. If you've not been there yet, you'll find it on Albion Street which is off Sunbridge Road. It's dead cheap to get in, and you can join for a couple of quid to get in even cheaper (and get involved in running it if you want).

Good news for Manchester in the form of a new night at the PSV. MELTDOWN TO ZERO will occur each Weds. night from here onwards, and if you've got a quid you can go and dance your ass off to what promises to be the broadest selection of sounds ever experienced in one building, courtesy of GMR's Meltdown team.

If you're thinking of recording a demo, check out THE DUNGEON a professional 8 track studio with the lowest rates in Yorkshire. For £5 an hour you get the benefit of lots of complicated equipment (don't ask me what it all is), a friendly atmosphere and free drinks! (well, tea/coffee...)

Martin Dungeon can also help you out by getting your demo heard by the right people, due to his contacts in The Biz.

Recent clients include The Shrubs, Len Liggins, Blitzkrieg, Coma and The Pale Saints. Phone Martin on 0532 715886.

SONIC YOUTH

"Just another scuzz rock band"

WHEN SONIC YOUTH WERE IN BRITAIN FOR THEIR TWO DATES AT THE ASTORIA IN LONDON, ABLAZE! WAS OFFERED AN INTERVIEW SO ROSS & SVEN FIGURED THEY MIGHT AS WELL HAVE A DAY OUT IN THE SOUTH AND MEET THE BAND OF THE 1990's.

The hitch from Leeds to the Blast First HQ meant we, as usual, turned up an hour late. Fortunately Sonic Youth's timing was similar so we didn't miss much. Our partners in this escapade were Hit The North 'zine, from Manchester.

This was the first of a particular round of interviews, and typically most of the quotes they threw at us were later repeated, word-for-word, in some big music papers. Just remember, Ablaze! heard it first (and printed it last).

All four of them were present, & these are, in case you don't already know, Thurston Moore (guitar & vocals), Kim Gordon (bass & vocals), Lee Ranaldo (guitar) and Steve Shelley (drums). Let's go.

What's the greatest misconception about Sonic Youth?

Kim: "That we exist."

Steve: "I guess that we're evil."

"WHA THE !?!?..."

Why did you include a text with "Master=Dik"?

Lee:"It was culled from a fanzine..."
Thurston:"...Maximumrock'n'roll.We were reading that this kid was so put out that bands like us had destroyed punk rock, or something like that, it was the most ridiculous argument in the world. It sort of fitted the nature of the record, which was like the worst record ever made. He was such a lame brain, he really had nothing to stand on. He was like saying 'fuck Sonic Youth and Hüsker Dü, or Journey and Reo Speedwagon.' So we printed that on the sleeve because that record..."
Lee:"Held up all his arguments."
Thurston:"It was such a lame brain sort of record."
Lee:"He actually wants Thurston to produce his record, he's in this band and he wants Thurston to produce them. Also we had a lot of problems releasing that record because people here (Blast First) thought it sucked and we made a sort of intuitive connection."

When we asked why "Master=Dik" was released at a lower price,Thurston said it was always going to be put out at a lower price and Lee said it was a condition of release because it "sucked too much."

Do you think you're gonna be legendary and pioneering like the Velvet Underground, or just another punk group? (Shite question - Ed.)
Thurston:"It's too absurd for us to think about."
Kim:"Just another scuzz rock band from East Village."
But you've left underground cult status behind and are in the gap between that ...
Lee:"And being a real band."

Do you like other bands on Blast First?
Kim:"We like most of them; most of them we at one time we suggested to Paul Smith that he put out."
Thurston:"All the successful bands."
Kim:"Except Head of David, we didn't know them, and Band of Susans..."
Thurston:"The worst band in the world."
Kim:"That was totally Paul's doing, we had no responsibility for them."

What do you think of the Rapeman name then?
Thurston:"We love the name 'Rapeman", we just hate Steve Albini."
Kim:"Yeah, Steve Albini's a really bad name."
Lee:(about Rapeman)"It's the best name of the year."
Steve:"He chose the name, we're not going to go up in arms about it."
Kim:"It's just I think it's a bad name."
Lee:"It's just not a very good name."
Kim:"It's not a very cool rock'n'roll name."
Thurston:"We'd have called it 'Big Black'."
Lee:"We wanted to change it to 'Grapeman'."
Thurston:"Yeah we're making Grapeman t-shirts."
Lee:"There's this character called Goofy Grape, a soft drinks guy, we want to change it and have Steve Albini's face on the Goofy Grape face."
Thurston:"We're not going to play the Astoria the night Rapeman play."
Steve:"Yeah, we're boycotting."
Thurston:"If Albini leaves the band we might play."
Kim:"Until Albini plays naked - then everyone will leave."

Did you have anything to do with the Swanic Youth record?
Thurston:"No, not at all, that was some dickweed."
Steve:"It's somebody we know, he's like a joker and a funster."
Thurston:"It's like a calypso, it's like not a funny funny record. It's a piece of crap."

Cool Rock Ciccs & Moby Diks

Kim, have you any plans for a Harry Crews record?
Kim:"No...I think it would be a mistake. Because it was a short term thing it was seen as another of Lydia's projects, which is unfortunate. It just sort of ended up helping her with her career. I suppose I got out of it what I wanted to get out of it,so from my point of view there's no point in me working on a record. It'd just be like an extension of her career."

Unrelated, do you know why Head of David didn't turn up to support you?

Kim:"I think they're afraid of Lydia!"
Liz Naylor:"That's right, Lydia has designs on Eric of Head of David."

Is that why they never turn up?
Liz:"Oh yeah, Lydia's there all the time."
Kim:"It's true, if she's arriving or not,you never wanna think of sex again."
Thurston:"Yeah, five minutes with Lydia will put you off sex forever."

Would you be as big in England if you weren't American?
Thurston:"We'd be bigger."
Thurston:"Probably not."
Kim:"I think we'd be bigger."
Steve:"We wouldn't dress like this either. The possibilities would be limitless."
Thurston:"Here you're in a different situation, with bands getting on the covers of magazines when they've only been going for six months, it's not a healthy situation. In America you're touring and nobody knows who you are. Here if you last a year then you've really done something."
Kim:"Bands don't get time to develop ."
Thurston:"When we first came here it seemed like people thought we were a brand new band, they couldn't understand the fact that we'd been doing this and refining it, working on it for years..."

Lee:"It's like people are picking up on Die Kreuzen now, and they've been going as long as we as we have, or longer...and the Buttholes..."
Thurston:"Bands over there have a more working relationship, they're not there to get their faces on the cover of a magazine..."

(They didn't seem interested in commenting on various comparisons that've been made by the press, between them and certain British bands, except to say that most of those comparisons are a load of crap. However they did want to talk about the Jesus and Mary Chain. Pay attention, cos this is quite relevant.)

Thurston:"We like the Mary Chain, they're good people."

You actually like them? What about that track on the Master=Dik b-side where you seem to be making sarcastic comments about them?
Thurston:"We'd seen a great interview with them, where there were a couple of things that Jim said in a Scottish way that we picked up on and then we were using that on the record. And there's this Minutemen song called 'Under the influence of Meat Puppets' (Ya mean Firehose? - smartass ed.) and we just stole the title and changed it..."
Kim:"Whenever it was that the Mary Chain first came out people were asking us if we were influenced by them, and we'd been around for 3 years before that. It was just an example of how the press here creates the world for everyone that lives here - it's like believing what you see on TV."

"I remember before..." "I remember after before."
"I remember before before." "That's now."

This seems like a good point at which to leave Liz, Sven, Ross and the other noise kids muttering and opinionating away in that sacred office, and engage in some mutterings of our own.

Master=Dik 12", a beautiful mess of a lament about, presumably, Ms Ciccone's (late) marriage. Someone in the NME heralded it as the way ahead for music in 1988, an inappropriate judgement perhaps, on a severe joke of a record - a Ciccone Youth single if ever I heard one. And if you heard the b-side, well that just serves you right for listening to it. My immediate impression was that too many drugs had gone into the making of it. The fact they actually got it released seems to say so much about them, suggesting an increasing disregard of critical opinion. And the way their untidy records have been taken so seriously speaks volumes about the press.

Similarly with Sonic Death, a livetape compiled from Thurston's collection and put together in the most profoundly (almost carefully) couldn't careless manner. It's made up of tracks that may cut off at any moment and usually do, with 'The World Looks Red' at what must be at least double the speed it was recorded at, and countless other scraps that you might have taped over were they yours & not Moore's.. Yeh you guessed, I was one of the suckers who bought the thing, and at the time I took it's lack of tracklist and coherent form as a personal insult. You'd have to really love the band to view it otherwise...and now, well I think it's OK.

When they were hanging around London late last summer being everyone's favourite dudes, a Peel session got recorded. We listened with hope, dreaming back to times of Evol, squalid guitar trips ...intense, fascinating seduction & all that bullshit(I'm getting lazy now),uh, so what did we get?

Fall covers, FOUR of them, as if we haven't had quite enough of the likes of 'Psycho maffia' and 'Rowche rumble' in the last decade to keep us humming dementedly for ever without them being brought out of cold storage & given the sonick treatment, attempted Manc accents and all. While we've been gazing idly across the Atlantic for sound-merchants to revere, our idols've been staring back attentively - eyeing the place up for stuff they can nick. It's ironic so it's probably cool.

What, we wondered, would these wayward young whippersnappers come up with next? A 13 single boxset tribute to Rick Astley? Acid house parties in outer space? A 12" of Madonna songs? (Hang on, this is getting a bit ridiculous...)

Almost predictably, the answer to these questions is an enourmous ear ringing 'no'. Instead they created a stunning double album, with mystical symbols on it's four vinyl faces and some rocking sounds arising out of them. Parts of it are vey irritating, but then, it's a long LP. I guess 'Total trash' speaks for itselfand something like 'Providence' takes a lot of getting used to, or a bit of visual elaboration, being a disturbing concoction of Mike Watt's amp crackling away to itself and some messages he left on an answerphone. This is the least intelligible, least songlike 'song' on the entire unwieldy LP - clearly a must for single release. They're talking A-side. Financial genius or...

Ah, but you know Daydream Nation when it hits you full-power, unfurling from the sweet beginnings of 'Teen Age Riot' and swallowing you whol before you've experienced 'The Sprawl'. 'Hyperstation' is very dangerously blissful and surely the daydream capital of this comatose pleasant land.

After enduring their exposure in the grey pages of those weekly things, and our first sight of them on TV thanks to Snub, where they argued about how they fit in relation to 'punk-rock', the yoof metamorphosized again to their other schizo guise, the ones with the Madonna fixation, and put out an album to confirm their position as the simultaneously most awkward and best-loved band of noisicians in the entire cosmos.

At a point in time called now, they've just been united with big new Seattle rave band Mudhoney on the joint single, and the two are embarking on a proper UK tour. About time ...I knew we'd get here in the end.

THE EDSEL AUCTIONEER

I encountered them through a 'bassplayer wanted' notice snatched from the wall of a Leeds clothes shop. Examining the crumpled piece of paper, from which the picture of a young, dungaree-clad woman stared resentfully back, my mind was filled with one overwhelming question - WHO or WHAT is this Edsel Auctioneer? - something, it seems, a lot of people have been asking recently.

Visiting their home I was greeted by two well spoken young men, who offered me some beautiful soup and an even more wholesome demo tape - physical and spiritual sustenance indeed. As we spoke it emerged that John Peel, champion of good music worldwide, got quite carried away on hearing the cassette and insisted that the boys visit the South and record a session, an offer rarely extended to bands without some form of vinyl product to present. "Theirs was the best demo I'd heard in quite a long time" Peel admitted on air, unarguably a great compliment, in view of the vast number of tapes the man is bombarded with.

Happily the appreciation is mutual - they commented on John's bravery in supporting them publicly, before he'd even heard the session. "We look up to him as a surrogate father" they confided.

However they didn't find the BBC producers as sympathetic to their sound. "If you're in a band and you've never done anything like that before, don't expect them to be open minded about throwing a guitar across a room, cos they're not." They recalled some choice quotes from the day:
"Is your guitar meant to sound like that, or is your amp fucked?", "How many hit records have YOU had, sonny?" and "Come back in half an hour lads," giving you some idea of the problems involved in having your songs taken over by Mott The Hoople's drummer.

Aidan and Ashley form the nucleus of the group, and it seems that a stable line up hasn't yet emerged. The two of them treat me with a certain suspicion, showing a fear of cameras, tape recorders and psychoanalytic interview techniques

Aidan is dark haired, wide eyed, enthusiastic and possesses a tendency to mutter strange things. Ashley is blond, reserved and the more level headed of the pair. I'm sure they'll think no one wants to know these things, so I'll go no further.

Quizzing them on their conscious reasons for being in a band and making music brought out a degree of confusion; I guess a lot of musically inclined kids end up getting groups together as it's an easy and common thing to do."If you ask yourself why, it doesn't add up, it's not something you rationalize," explained Aiden."Writing a song about the things that you do, the things that happen to you, is the most stupid thing in the world. It's well naive."

On the general usefulness of songs:"Other people should get something out of songs, and learn from them. It's therapy, entertainment, all those things. Something like Dylan's 'Positively Fourth Street', that got me totally, it summed up how I felt at one point...songs like that appease you, otherwise you'd be writing it down yourself."

They object to anyone's attempts to compare their music with that of other mighty names. All bands have starting points and they openly admit to theirs: The Byrds, Slade (!) and the Mary Chain. "Those things should free you, but too many people playing in bands are just playing reference games. Some do it consciously, all the time, making references to the bands they really love, and they'll never get beyond making demos."

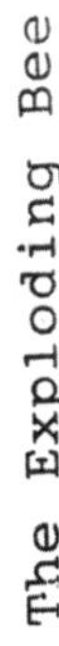

The Edsel Auctioneer

17, Harold Ave.
LEEDS 6
LS6 IJR

SONIC FOLK

If you heard their demo you'd understand the hysteria surrounding this band. It features a raging set of 'sonic folk'rock melodies, in which layers of acoustic and electric guitar sounds are combined to wondrous, powerful effect, and topped with Aidan's wistful vocal musings. The ensuing session revealed an even mightier, fuller sound, promising great thi things if further recordings should take place. Response to the session included, among bewildering fan mail and general praise, a couple of offers from indie labels, while some majors have been "snooping".

The Edsel Auctioneer are probably the best known group of Leeds' fast growing Harold Avenue scene. Their street currently houses the best part of two other great noise bands, The Pale Saints and Sonic Hangover. I suggested that this quaint, terraced musical enclave seems to have produced bands with a vaguely similar sound. "That's cos we share the same effects pedal!" they revealed.

They were visited recently by burglars who kicked down the door and disappeared with their two Sonic Youth guitars, ironically ignoring the TV set and record-player nearby. "Ragin'," said Aidan for some odd reason "They'd obviously heard us practicing and thought 'these are the instruments they make that God Unholy Row with, so if we nick them, they wont have anything to make that row with.'"

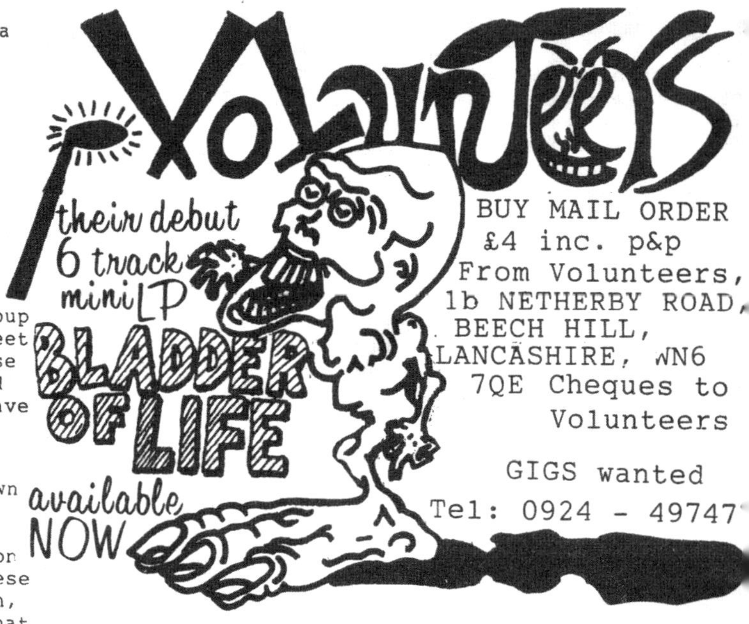

Volunteers
their debut 6 track mini LP
BLADDER OF LIFE
available NOW
BUY MAIL ORDER
£4 inc. p&p
From Volunteers,
1b NETHERBY ROAD,
BEECH HILL,
LANCASHIRE, WN6
7QE Cheques to
Volunteers
GIGS wanted
Tel: 0924 - 49747

"Ash you twat, did you have to drop the keys down the grid?"
"Aw shut it - me mam'll be home soon..."

Maybe there'll be a new generation of bands starting up using your nicked equipment. "They might be very good bands," Ashley warned, "But they'll probably get electrocuted." Hey people, take them scuzzy stringed things back to Nº 17, I'm sure the lads'll be glad to help you fix them, or somet...

"The Edsel Auctioneer" is certainly a name to conjour with. The band were reluctant to discuss it's origins, except to say that it was chosen when in a self-pitying frame of mind. The Edsel was an American car created in the 50's, notorious for it's failure to sell. They were visibly shocked when I pointed out that the letters of edsel can be rearranged to form the name of our fair city, an odd coincidence which takes on further meaning as we witness the town centre being torn down and replaced by some plastic yuppie paradise. Peel also found it a bit of a tongue-twister.

There's so much more to say about The Edsel Auctioneer but I think I should leave them in peace now, for fear that my clumsy style will misrepresent and hurt those subtle emotions they hide beneath a roaring, glorious (bu... no way overblown) sun-beat mountain ra...e of sound. Does that sound pompous? ... meant to be. As with all these things, you can only find them out for yourself.

Double issue: Dec/Mar.
OUT MARCH, £1·60 INC. P&P
FROM SONIC LIFE / BLAST FIRST, 429 HARROW RD, LONDON, W10 4RE
WITH BYRON COLEY, STEVE ALBINI, FRUISH, C. CARROL, LIZ NAYLOR
RUEBEN BURROUGHS, JASPER, WILLIAMSON, SMITH - MANY FEATURES
KILLDOZER, ARSENAL, GLEN BRANCA, LYDIA LUNCH, PAT NAYLOR
ALL BLAST FIRST MERCHANDISE, WRITE FOR CATALOGUE

The SUNDAYS

This article is difficult to write without sounding like a shite-for-brains NME journalist. Unless you're really dead bored we'd like to advise you not to read it. Go & listen to their single instead.

Watching The much-muttered-on-about Sundays as they played at the Leadmill, supporting the Throwing Muses, I suddenly realised I'd do anything for these four sweet pop musicians.

Not having read similar rantings about them in the music papers, I was blissfully unaware of the degree of fuss being made over them. I didn't even possess a copy of their stunning debut single, "Can't Be Sure", released on Rough Trade recently. My introduction to them in fact took place in their dressing room that evening - I'd been talking to Tanya Muse in there, and she'd gone off to soundcheck for a while...this guy came in and we started talking, and it wasn't long before my curiosity prevailed and I asked him who he was."One of the Sundays," came his reply, yeah that makes sense, and then Harriet came in and commented that the whole place smelt of sick.

My head was still in interview mode, so when you you're in the same room as 2 of the 4 that can transform a Throwing Muses audience into a bunch of Smiths t-shirt wearing dorks, you don't miss the opportunity...

Everyone's gone Sunday mad.

"Yeah, we don't understand why though."

It's just that incredible song...

"We hate it now. We've had to listen to it so many times, and we recorded it ages ago.'

Well I just heard it on the radio and I thought it was dead good. Why are you called the Sundays? Everyone thinks Sundays are really boring.

"We wanted to chose something that didn't sound really wacky. There's no particular reason for it, we began by thinking that all band names are crap, so we just chose one that didn't really mean anything."

Apparently they played at a church hall recently but the vicar was concerned about what aspect of Sunday they were reflecting...I think he said it was okay, for them to play in the end.

I heard you're refusing to do interviews on this tour.

"It's just because we've only just started and we're just the support band. People are going to be so sick of hearing about us...we thought the tour was going to be a real hard slog as well, and we wanted to concentrate on playing."

How's it been?

"Great, it's really good touring with the Muses, we get along with them really well."

When I'd introduced myself, David told me off for saying I was "Just from a fanzine," while he lets himself get away with calling the Sundays "Just the support band." Should there be that differentiation anyway, between supports and headliners?

"At the end of our set we tell people not to stay for the Muses," Harriet tells me.

When I ask if anyone takes any notice and leaves, they laugh...ah, a joke. Fortunately the rest of the audience aren't quite as credulous.

Why did you sign to Rough Trade then?

"We wanted to avoid going on a label where we'd be compared to another band currently on it. If we went with One Little Indian they'd say we're another Sugarcubes, or if we signed to 4AD we'd get called Cocteau Twins rip-offs. We're not likely to be lumped along with anyone currently on Rough Trade...we like them as people as well. It's going to sound like we keep saying we like people, but it's true."

While we're going for all the obvious questions, I ask Harriet about her wonderful voice. Predictably, she doesn't think it's anything special. "It's just bedroom singing, like anyone can do." She's trying to stop the process of mystification, but maybe it's too late in her case. The Sundays are constantly on their guard against the superficial judgements of critics, but the press have courted them and caught them...

I told them the lyrics of "Can't be sure" sounded as if they were written from the point of view of an outsider, a foreigner. They hadn't thought of it in this way, but said there isn't any one interpretation of the words "without meaning to sound pretentious," David adds. No, they couldn't sound pretentious if they tried. In retrospect I decided it didn't really matter...in retrospect I bought their single and gave it a good listen, finding in it more than I'd anticipated. "Can't be sure" pales into insignificance beside "Don't tell your mother", a Smithesque journey into mid-teen social-life restrictions. I'm sorry, but it's beautiful.

When not being very reluctant pop stars, they pursue their careers on the dole..."Every day is a Sunday for us!", ah, a quotable quote.

Harriet doesn't like talking into tape recorders, so when mine broke down and reduced the rest of the conversation to a whirring jumble of high-pitched exclamations, I figured it served me right for even attempting to capture them, to turn these pleasant, very modest people into media objects. This intervention of fate got me wondering about the whole machinery of hype and misrepresentation. We're all dragged into it, and it seems to perpetuate itself in a rather scary manner.The Sundays' recitence and reluctance to join in the sordid games of the 'music' industry is a positive statement against this sort of bullshit, but no way are they going to convince anyone that they're musically as mediocre as they believe themselves to be.

EVERY DAY IS LIKE SUNDAY....

NERVE RACK

Nerve Rack - tall young men from Leeds with a handful of axes to grind, right next to your delicate ears. Since late '87 the three racketeers, individually known as Mark, Doug and Ste have been creating a forceful uproar together of such gnawing intensity, you'll be kicking yourself (and everyone else) for having missed out on the experience of their live performances.

You might know of their existence through the remaining evidence of a spray-paint campaign last summer. Attractively coloured Nerve Rack logos now adorn various brick walls in the Leeds Six area including the odd butcher's shop. When the window of one of these simultaneously, but unrelatedly, received a well-aimed brick, it was rumoured that these innocent locals were to blame..

Doug (mean guitar & occasional yelling) admitted: "I did consider going round and leaving a note saying 'Nerve Rack wish to deny responsibility for any damage done to this window.However we sympathise with and support whoever did do it.'"

Fair enough. Do you think you're basically a political band?

"Yes, but only in so far as I'd feel a right twat singing about something that means nothing to me.I have to sing about something that gets me going in some way, so that could be political like say 'Miracle of dead baby', or some other personal feeling that gets me aggravated."

'Miracle' is one of the tracks featured on their hard hitting debut release, the 'Fish Struck By Virus' cassette.What's that song about?

"Profits before people - the low value placed on life in favour of big profits. Initially it was inspired by babies dying due to cuts in the NHS but it grew to cover a broader issue, the myth of the 'economic growth' culture."

"Most of the songs express what you could call political views, but they're not aligned to any particular '-ism'."

"I used to write quite political songs but in a very straightforward way, very black & white, but that's because I listened to too many Crass albums," Doug confessed."The problem is trying to write things in a fairly oblique way, rather than making it so that people don't have to think about it."

Someone suggested that taking political stances might hold them back musically...

"It depends how you do it. Sonic Youth express political views in some of their songs but in such a way that it's not always obvious. On the other hand, the Ex are an extremely political band but they make good powerful music, same goes for Chumbawamba. I don't think it has to hold you back."

When listening to "Fish struck by virus" I have never been struck by any particular band that I'd like to compare, musically, to Nerve Rack. However, as we sat discussing this in Doug's kitchen, his housemate, friend and band critic Sean suggested (probably not for the first time) that they might be compared to that great, late US rocking unit, Big Black. Doug's reaction seemed inevitably rehearsed but heartfelt:

"Get lost!" And turning to me for a second opinion, asked"Did it make you think of B** B**** at any point?"

Not at all . What's the problem?

"It's the Purple Eternal, they've been spreading rumours..."

Not MORE rumours... let's get this straight. D'you sound like ANY band?

Sean, ever obliging: "D'you want a list?"

"If you're good enough you should be able to transcend leather trousers & long hair."

Mark (brief introduction - provides vocals & neat bass sounds. Very tall.):"There's been so many names of bands that people reckon we sound like that I can't believe we sound like any one band."
Doug:"Tony Woolgar (Leeds' Other Paper) is convinced we sound like a cross between the Fall & Dead Kennedys but I found it hard not to laugh in his face."
Those sort of things are physically impossible anyway. Perhaps you sound like a mixture of what each of you listens to - is Nerve Rack a product of your influences?
Doug:"If it was a hybrid of what we listen to it would be extremely strange ...I listen to a lot of hardcore and he listens to a lot of..."
Mark:"Hip hop, and Slab, and Tackhead, and that doesn't come out at all in what we do."
But maybe there is something of that, the way you don't sound messy at all...
Mark:"We do spend quite a while getting songs together, fiddling around with different bits and throwing bits out, so maybe that's why, because it's more carefully thought out rather than counting to four and thrashing as fast as we can."
I wondered whether they felt conscious of how people view the band, and whether they're receiving press attention or not.
Mark:"It's a good thing not to get loads of people flocking to your first few gigs to see you."
Doug:"It's given us a chance to get our..."
Mark:"..act together?"
Doug:"I was trying to avoid that...to get used to playing in front of audiences without the added pressure of getting used to playing in front of very big audiences. We've built it up and gained experience without being in the spotlight from the very beginning, which might be the Purple Eternal's downfall - cos they've had so much attention early on they're going to do a lot of growing up in public I think."
Yeh, you seem to have a more sober attitude.
Mark:"We haven't hyped it, we haven't written to people and said 'come and see us.'"
Doug:"The first thing on our minds wasn't to get a demo out and send it round to all the record companies. We're not really interested in that way of doing things, we want to achieve some sort of stature before we go bringing records out."

Do you think being based in the "Gothic heart of the world" is a disadvantage?
Doug:"I'd like to see a stop put to it for sure."
Mark:"It shouldn't matter. If you're good enough you should be able to transcend leather trousers and long hair."
Doug:"I think Leeds is quite healthy in that there seems to be plenty of places to play and a potential audience and there's also a vague history of fairly good [non-goth] bands, so in a way I think it's good, I cant see a place that would be better..."
Mark:"But there's still that terrible legacy..."
There's not going to be another generation of people like that.
Doug:"But a lot of people come to Leeds because it's the 'Goth capital', and there's Salvation, and I'm sure there'll be bands coming in their wake who'll keep the flag flying..." he sighs.

Those sort of bands are popular because a lot of people who go to see them aren't local...band following is a fairly evil thing and it ought to be stamped out.
Doug:"Yeah, STAMPED out."
Sean:(some smartarse comment I can't make out about fans being stamped out.)

When asked whether they see Nerve Rack as being potentially successful now that louder & harder bands are getting more attention, Doug pointed out the disparity between the treatment of bands here and those from the other States:"British bands aren't getting any attention, partly because these American bands are just a lot hipper, more credible. There are loads of English bands playing good stuff, but people seem blind to it. It could prove to be a problem for us but I think it's more of a problem for people who're so closed-minded, they think all the good things are coming from America, for whatever reason. They're wrong."

"Fish Struck By Virus", the 6 track dead-head wakening cassette-only release, can be obtained by sending £2 ($5 US), to 43 Elsham Terrace, Leeds, LS4 2RB. Two tempestuous tracks also appear on "Crime in your neighbourhood" Vol. 2, out on Inward Collapse records. Invite them into your neighbourhood to take it by storm - phone Doug 0532 741 747.

NERVE RACK

GO SKATE TO
CRASH!
OR GO HOME
RECORDS
TAPES
& CD$
AND OCCASIONAL SKATE GEAR
35 THE HEADROW
LEEDS 436743
192 WOODHOUSE LANE
LEEDS 465823
AND WE'RE FUCKING CHEAP TOO!
ACCORDING TO RECENT VIRGIN POLL

THRILLED SKINNY

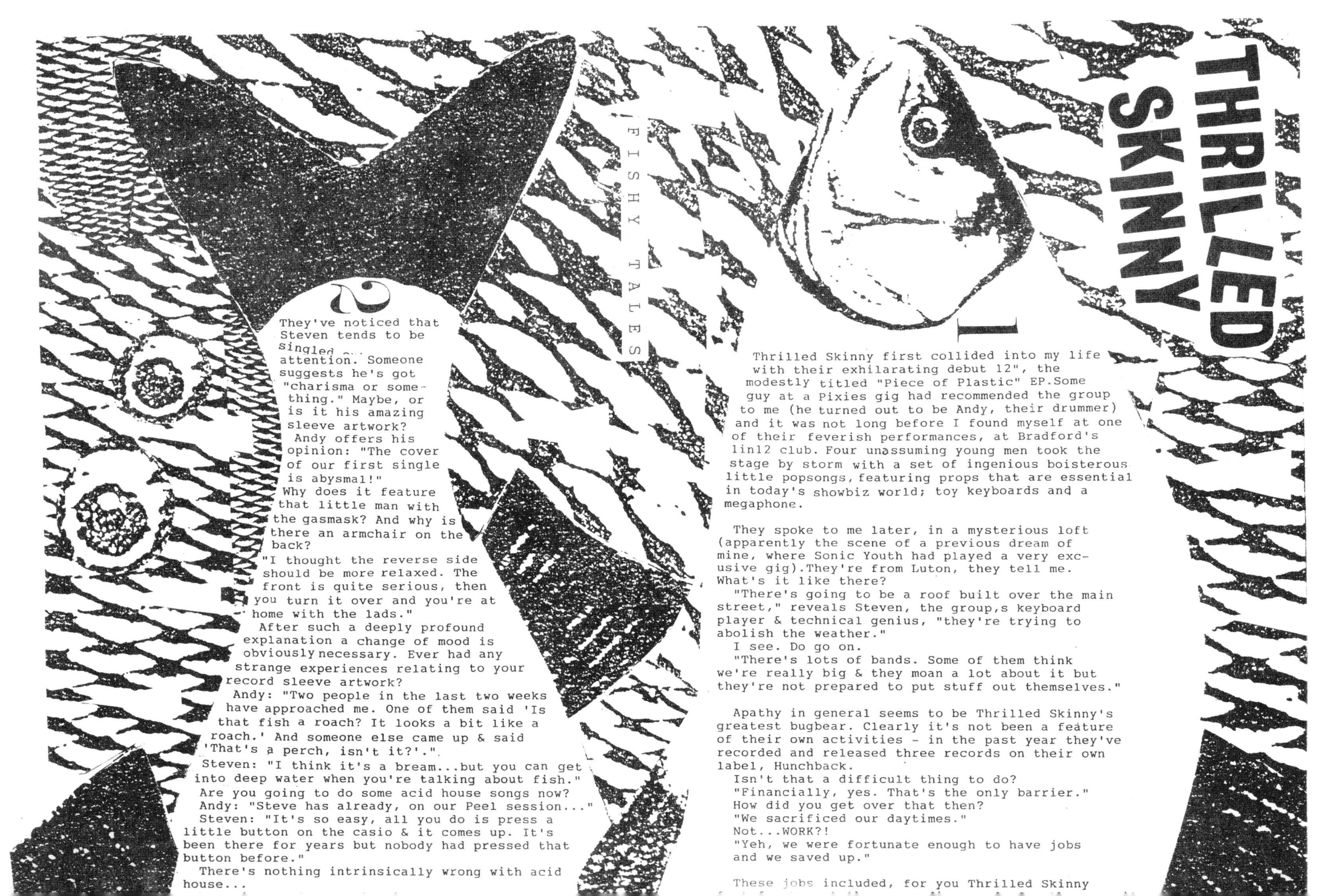

1

Thrilled Skinny first collided into my life with their exhilarating debut 12", the modestly titled "Piece of Plastic" EP. Some guy at a Pixies gig had recommended the group to me (he turned out to be Andy, their drummer) and it was not long before I found myself at one of their feverish performances, at Bradford's 1in12 club. Four unassuming young men took the stage by storm with a set of ingenious boisterous little popsongs, featuring props that are essential in today's showbiz world; toy keyboards and a megaphone.

They spoke to me later, in a mysterious loft (apparently the scene of a previous dream of mine, where Sonic Youth had played a very exc-usive gig). They're from Luton, they tell me. What's it like there?

"There's going to be a roof built over the main street," reveals Steven, the group,s keyboard player & technical genius, "they're trying to abolish the weather."

I see. Do go on.

"There's lots of bands. Some of them think we're really big & they moan a lot about it but they're not prepared to put stuff out themselves."

Apathy in general seems to be Thrilled Skinny's greatest bugbear. Clearly it's not been a feature of their own activities - in the past year they've recorded and released three records on their own label, Hunchback.

Isn't that a difficult thing to do?

"Financially, yes. That's the only barrier."

How did you get over that then?

"We sacrificed our daytimes."

Not...WORK?!

"Yeh, we were fortunate enough to have jobs and we saved up."

These jobs included, for you Thrilled Skinny

FISHY TALES

2

They've noticed that Steven tends to be singled [illegible] attention. Someone suggests he's got "charisma or some-thing." Maybe, or is it his amazing sleeve artwork?

Andy offers his opinion: "The cover of our first single is abysmal!"

Why does it feature that little man with the gasmask? And why is there an armchair on the back?

"I thought the reverse side should be more relaxed. The front is quite serious, then you turn it over and you're at home with the lads."

After such a deeply profound explanation a change of mood is obviously necessary. Ever had any strange experiences relating to your record sleeve artwork?

Andy: "Two people in the last two weeks have approached me. One of them said 'Is that fish a roach? It looks a bit like a roach.' And someone else came up & said 'That's a perch, isn't it?'."

Steven: "I think it's a bream...but you can get into deep water when you're talking about fish."

Are you going to do some acid house songs now?

Andy: "Steve has already, on our Peel session..."

Steven: "It's so easy, all you do is press a little button on the casio & it comes up. It's been there for years but nobody had pressed that button before."

There's nothing intrinsically wrong with acid house...

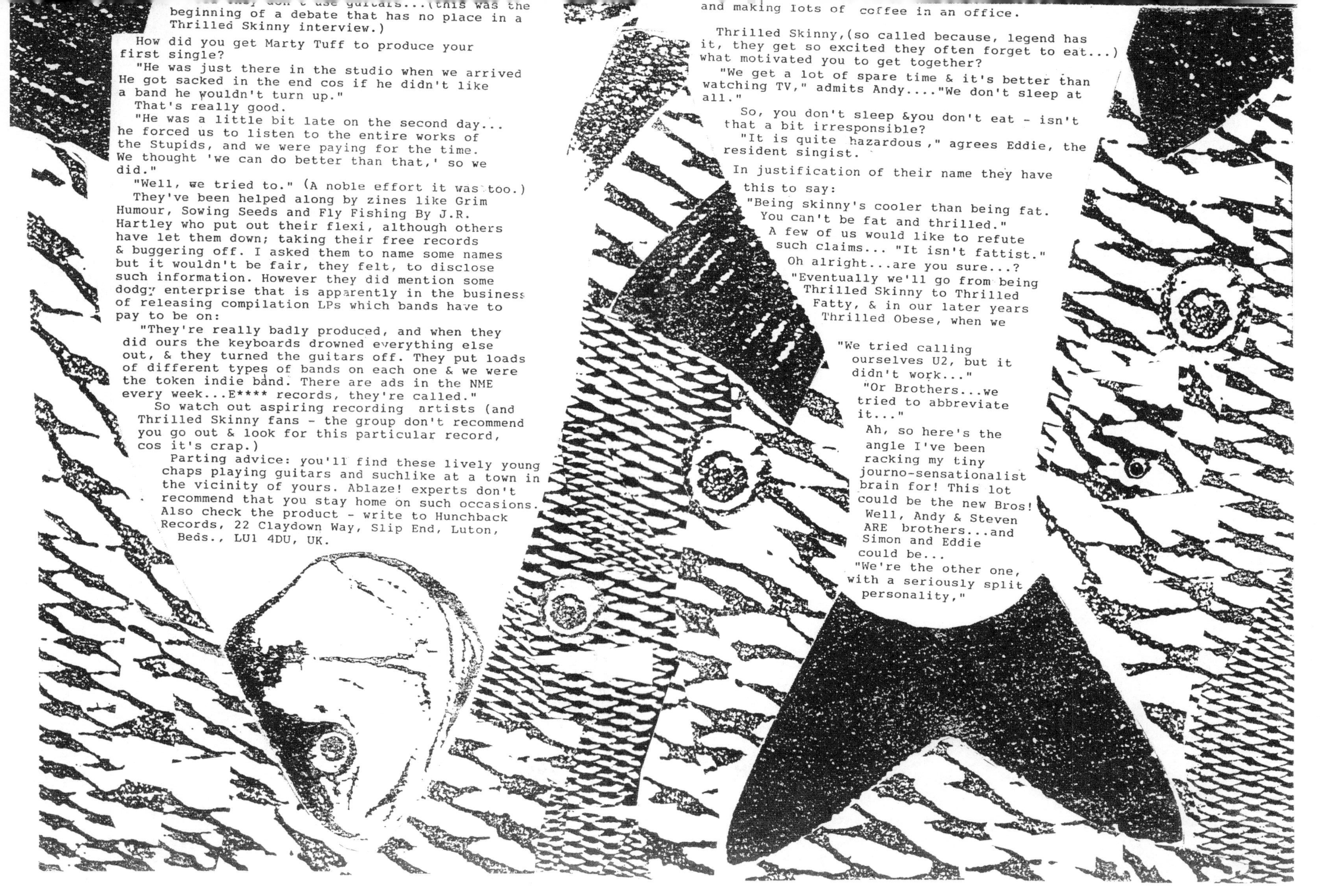

and making lots of coffee in an office.

Thrilled Skinny,(so called because, legend has it, they get so excited they often forget to eat...) what motivated you to get together?

"We get a lot of spare time & it's better than watching TV," admits Andy...."We don't sleep at all."

So, you don't sleep &you don't eat - isn't that a bit irresponsible?

"It is quite hazardous," agrees Eddie, the resident singist.

In justification of their name they have this to say:

"Being skinny's cooler than being fat. You can't be fat and thrilled."

A few of us would like to refute such claims... "It isn't fattist."

Oh alright...are you sure...?

"Eventually we'll go from being Thrilled Skinny to Thrilled Fatty, & in our later years Thrilled Obese, when we

"We tried calling ourselves U2, but it didn't work..."

"Or Brothers...we tried to abbreviate it..."

Ah, so here's the angle I've been racking my tiny journo-sensationalist brain for! This lot could be the new Bros! Well, Andy & Steven ARE brothers...and Simon and Eddie could be...

"We're the other one, with a seriously split personality,"

...y don't use guitars...(this was the beginning of a debate that has no place in a Thrilled Skinny interview.)

How did you get Marty Tuff to produce your first single?

"He was just there in the studio when we arrived He got sacked in the end cos if he didn't like a band he wouldn't turn up."

That's really good.

"He was a little bit late on the second day... he forced us to listen to the entire works of the Stupids, and we were paying for the time. We thought 'we can do better than that,' so we did."

"Well, we tried to." (A noble effort it was too.)

They've been helped along by zines like Grim Humour, Sowing Seeds and Fly Fishing By J.R. Hartley who put out their flexi, although others have let them down; taking their free records & buggering off. I asked them to name some names but it wouldn't be fair, they felt, to disclose such information. However they did mention some dodgy enterprise that is apparently in the business of releasing compilation LPs which bands have to pay to be on:

"They're really badly produced, and when they did ours the keyboards drowned everything else out, & they turned the guitars off. They put loads of different types of bands on each one & we were the token indie band. There are ads in the NME every week...E**** records, they're called."

So watch out aspiring recording artists (and Thrilled Skinny fans - the group don't recommend you go out & look for this particular record, cos it's crap.)

Parting advice: you'll find these lively young chaps playing guitars and suchlike at a town in the vicinity of yours. Ablaze! experts don't recommend that you stay home on such occasions. Also check the product - write to Hunchback Records, 22 Claydown Way, Slip End, Luton, Beds., LU1 4DU, UK.

DINOSAUR Jr

You might've read the Dinosaur interviews in the music press where they try to coax the singer and guitarist, J.Mascis, away from the TV. Having failed, the writer has to make up the bulk of the article.
We caught up with Lou Barlow, the bassist in the band, at the Rapeman/Dinosaur/Band of Susans gig at Leeds Poly in October. He proved to be, like, a bit more coherent, you know...

A:What did you think of it [the gig tonight], was it better than Chester ?
D:Yeah...No! This was not better than Chester, Chester was a lot of fun
A:You look like were enjoying yourselves
D:Well, I was...kinda...
A:You looked like you was totally fucked as well
D:I wasn't. I only drank like, a beer, before I played. That kind of gives you the alcoholic edge, you know. I don't drink very much but when I do it makes me fell a little bit more... strange...
A:Like diving into the audience ?
D:Yeah...well...no By the end of the set I was just so frustrated that I felt like I wanted to do something I could remember the show by rather than it be just feel like another stupid show that I played.

I felt I should dive into the audience and then...

A:So you don't always do that ?
D:I did at our last show in the United States before we came here I did and that was a lot of fun
A:We didn't know if you were out to hit someone because they'd touched your bass or...
D:Oh no. I don't give a shit. Someone can fucking take my bass and bash it on the stage into a million pieces and like I'd give them money..I don't know. It's no big deal for me you know.
A:How about breaking the mike stand ?
D:Ahh...I didn't..I just
A:You just walked into it
D:No I kicked it but I mean I don't do that very often. I was being a baby. We fucked up a song and we were all like out of tune and I was just like this is stupid so I kicked my mike stand. It was dumb but I did it, and they were mad and they took my mike stand away so I couldn't sing any more.
A:Or couldn't yell between songs.
D:No I couldn't yell between song and abuse..try to blow their monitors
A:Were you saying anything or were you just screaming ?
D:I was just screaming. I like to just say nonsense so people say "uh what's he saying ?" It just like makes me more energetic or something. It makes it more interesting.
A:Is this your first tour of the UK ?
D:No...well we played two shows in London about a year ago. So that was kinda weird.
A:Did you have to be dragged kicking and screaming to the NORTH of England like most american bands ?
D:No fuck man I love England now. I mean we just played Holland like. In Holland like they're really nice to you you know and you get like hotel rooms and food and shit. And you come here you know and you sleep on people's floors and get treated like shit by bouncers and it's like America and I love it, you know it's like...it's great. I actually really like England a lot. [missed the subtlety of the question I think - ed]
A:I hear a story that SST bands come over over to Europe, play a load of dates in Holland and Germany and maybe one in London and that's it.
D:We did that last time but, you know, this time, you know, like since we're on Blast First, you know, they're starting to put us up here.

A:Since when have you been called Dinosaur Jnr. rather than just Dinosaur ?
D:Well, we had to have our name changed. There's a band called the Dinosaurs in San Fransisco.

A:Did you see the hassle outside with all the demonstrators ?
D:Oh yeah, it was a lot, like, more mellow than I thought it would be, you know. I thought there'd be people throwing things at us while we were playing and stuff.
A:When you got turned of, somebody said to me ah, probably the demonstrators cut the power or something.
D:No, I bent the mike stand when I kicked it so they were, like, "fuck you, your going to fuck with our shit we're not going to let you use our PA". So they shut us off. They were pissed at me for smashing the mike stand.
A:How did you get them to turn it back on ?
D:Well, just our guitarist was, like, "what the fuck is your problem", you know, "turn on the PA. Just our bass player is kind of being difficult". They just took the mike away from me so I couldn't sing. That's cool because I didn't have anymore songs to sing anyway.

A:Did you think of jumping into the audience with your guitar ? D:No cos I only have one bass right now and if I break the bass then I'm going to really be bummed [?]. If I had a couple of basses I'd surely smash the shit out of that cos I'm getting really sick of it. It would be such a drag to spend, like, 200 pounds on a new bass.
A:You could buy one for 30 quid.
D:I got a really good bass now, you know, like, mine cost $600 so it's like...I wouldn't want to smash Although if I had another one I would. Cos, you know, you get bored and you want to just like do something exciting.
A:Have you been playing chords on your bass for a long time ?
D:Ah, cos I played guitar before, like, in a thrash band, so, like, when you're in a thrash band you try to play as many notes as possible, like, fucking just move...
so when I started playing bass I started going: dthoo dthoo, it's just to, like, make it sound like a guitarist...you just play, like, as many notes as possible to make it sound as powerful, you know.
A:You've got a very full sound for a three piece.
D:Yeah. Yeah. It's something we kind of worked on. If we've worked on anything at all it's so that we sound powerful, so we don't sound like idiots when we're up there.
A:How did you get signed on Blast First ?
D:Cos Sonic youth played Dinosaur records to Paul Smith; who runs Blast First; a million times and he hated us at first because you know we're the stupid American rock band and he generally likes the new wave sort of things I guess but he kind of got into Dinosaur so he signed us.
A:Have you ever paid a gig as big as the Sonic youth one you're going to do ?
D:I don't know...Oh yeah yeah yeah ! We played this festival in um...Belgium, last year. And there was fucking tons of people there, like thousands.
A:???
D:Futurama ? We played Furutama last year and now it's huge. And, like, we played with the Young Gods and guess eventually like Pop Will Eat Itself and all those bands played...when they were hip, that was a while ago it was a year ago people like that shit ! But there was like tons of people there, that was the biggest gig we've done. I don't know if Sonic Youth will be bigger than that. I doubt it.

A:What do you think of the LP, has it come out the way you wanted it to ?
D:I don't care ! You know, I don't care. It's OK. I like it. I liked the last one better but that's..this one's more accessible, I don't know...
A:The tapes in between songs are a good.
D:Oh yeah, it's just an idea. Like, you know, you've seen Sonic youth do it and all that shit. But it's just like, you know, I've always been into, like, doing tapes since I was little, so...
A:On some of the tapes, is it actually you doing it ?
D:Yeah yeah a lot of them. You can't actually...
[drowned out by J.Mascis drumming]
D:That's our guitarist !

They were, like, one of my favourite bands. We weren't nearly as good as Rudimentry Peni. They were the best actually. Or pretty damn close anyway.
A:Did you all go to school together or how did you meet up ?
D:We met up cos me and this friend of mine wanted to be in really fast speed-thrash band. When we were in high school, like, when we were 14, 15 years old. So we put an ad, like, in the record store and said we want someone who's really into like The Exploited and Minor Threat and the Circle Jerk and Black Flag so...um...he called us and we started a band. And then when we got older we just decided to switch over and play different musics.

A:ARE YOU REALLY THE LAID BACK AMERICANS YOU'RE MADE OUT TO BE IN THE INTERVIEWS ?

D:YES, IN A WAY WE ARE

A:You're not. You're a bit more active than that.

D:Yeah he's a drummer too.
A:What else does he play ?
D:Whatever he wants to.
A:Have any of you been in bands before ?
D:Oh yeah. He played drums and I played guitar in this thrash band called Deep Wound. We put out a 7" record with 9 songs on it.
A:Like Rudimentary Peni - put as many songs on as you can.
D:Oh yeah we were like that yeah. We had the Rudimentry Peni record, they were the greatest.

A:What do you do in America apart from this. Have you got jobs or anything ?
D:I work. J doesn't work. Murph works sometimes. J's a student.
A:Has he actually got a name or is he just J ?
D:Just J. Well it's supposed to be Joseph but, like, I guess he figured a long while ago he'd change it to just J. Cos that's cool. It's not J-A-Y it's just J.
A:So what job to you do ?
D:I'm an orderly, like, a nurses aid.
A:Have you heard of the importance of John Peel in America ?
D:Oh, you know, all the records are in the stores, in the alternative stores, all the Peel

sessions from Sid Barrett to like whatever...
A:Extreme noise terror...Because he's just about the only person who plays any indie music on the radio.
D:Yeah see he played our thrash band on the radio once, Deep Wound, he played Deep Wound. If he put that an his record, we're psyched [?].
[is John Peel the Record label now more important/Well-known than John Peel the Radio Show ?]
A:Basically if you get on the right side of John Peel you've sort of made it on the indie scene in Britain.
D:I hear if you get on the right side of a lot of people you'll make it.
A:John Peel is THE influential person.
D:As I hear it there are a lot of influential people in the UK. If you do this and do that. I guess we've been on the right side of enough people to make it or at least we'll be the flavour of the month.
A:Do you think you're getting a harder sound as you go along ?
D:Yeah, in a way. Well, I don't know, we've always just totally thrashed out when we've played, you know. Cos playing live is really weird, you know...everyone can hear what we're doing. We get up on stage and we feel like we want to make as much noise as possible. The coolest thing to us, is just, like, really noisy shit. So we just like noise more than we like mellow stuff. Live anyway. What we listen to and what we sound like are something entirely different. But when we play live we just want to make a lot of noise. Or just be powerful. Cos that's fun and it doesn't sound pathetic.
A:So what do you listen to then ?
D:I like Skin, Swans. I kinda get, like, locked on, like, these times when all I do is I listen to the Swans. Then I like this band from the States called Mud Honey, and I like Head of David, and I like Rapeman a lot. Sonic youth, of course...
A:What about Foetus ?
D:I really haven't gotten into Foetus before. Maybe I haven't listened to it enough, you know, cos I hated the Swans when I first heard them but I just kept listening to them then I really liked them. Maybe if I listen to Foetus a lot I'd like that but I haven't done that yet.
A:What about English stuff ?
D:I really like Jesus and Mary Chain for a long time. I didn't get into, what's it called ?
A:April skies ?
D:I kinda liked April Skies a little bit but then I didn't like the album. But, like, Psychocandy I used to listen to that everyday. The first single, I was just totally blown away by that. I was really into that for a long time.
A:That's interesting cos when I first heard a Dutch bootleg [of yours] it sort of reminded me a bit of J&MC, sort of pop songs with feedback in a way. More melodies than you get in a lot of these sort of noise bands.
D:Yeah in a way, like, when I first heard the first J&MC single it was, like, it was before we started geting really noisy. I heard...well, it was while we were getting really noisy...like, I heard J&MC and, like, this is it ! Right, you know, like, I want to be something like this you know. And we all really liked them a lot. So I think it probably did have a lot to do with us just, like, piling noise onto our songs cos we like noise anyway. We were into hardcore which is just complete noise, you know, and we were at a point where we just wanted to find the middle ground and J&MC they sort of found it first, you know, like. Cos when I heard Upside Down I was just, like, fuck man, this is the coolest thing I've ever heard.

D:So the J&MC definitely, you know.
A:The last time I saw a mike stand kicked off stage was at the J&MC.

You can get your mind blown dead or you can get your mind blown alive. Prepare to meet UT, and have their living daylight blasted into your cerebral cortex.

For me, the more I discovered about this group, the more I found myself enticed. I knew nothing until "In Gut's House", their last LP, was sending bright coloured sound-waves around my living room, while my first glimpse of UT live had me SEEING all that. Speaking with them was another experience altogether.

UT interviews may be a little like their music, with so much going on at once, thin things can get a little difficult to follow. Arriving late, after a space-age horror tubetrain journey, didn't help. They were a little impatient to set up and settle down for an evening's practice, and we were getting psyched up for a Harry Crews experience later on, but this was a conversation so enthralling and refreshing I found it hard to tear myself out of it. Enough i: oduction; here's some of what went on before our tapes ran out or broke down.

My first rem was at the appearance of another pe. in the group - a drummer called Charlie an addition they seem really pleased with:

"He's the first person we've brought in, he totally involves himself and instigates things, it's been ideal."

Did you bring him in because there wasn't enough of you to go round the instruments?

"No, we've been together ten years and we've been really happy with three. When we started we had a fourth member for a year, so we had been easily moving between three and four, but this is the first point that we've been really keen to have a fourth member. We've used drummers before, as visitors, as it's real and we want it real, and it's worked out, it's just been magical."

"It's given us more freedom which is the idea of it, and also a bigger sound. What he brings to the band is just perfect for what we wanted, largely cos he's the right person, the right element."

I asked Charlie if he was in a band before this. "Yes," came the reply: "The Hars."

Who?

"Every time he says that I can't understand what he's saying," remarks Sally. "Whores."

In the end he has to spell it out: "W-h-o-r-e-s."

Unsurprisingly the name leads to a discussion of permitted band names, in the light of the Rapeman fiasco. people wouldn't have as much problem, like a black band calling themselves Beatnigs - as long as you're the victim the world can deal with it. It's really hard for them to take that simple step."

When asked how they feel about the Rapeman concept Jacqui's response is unusually positive:

"To us it's beautiful ..r, provocation."

Charlie thinks she ought to rephrase that.

"No no no, 'beautiful provocation', that's my language," she insists, but faced with various protests some explanation's clearly required: "If a girl band called themselves Whore people'd think 'Wow, this is great, this is right on', cos they're saying what society makes them, that can be taken in, and to me calling your band Rapeman while you're men is the sa me thing. Men are trained often in this society to be rapemen. The concept, the word 'rape' is so heavy to people...the actual thing... there's so much in television..." she's

speaking like notebook sketches of some complicated ideas, you can fill in the rest,"and there's such a fine line between what is and what is not rape, and people can't deal with it, they can't even admit that that could be. All they can see, if some band calls themselves Rapeman they're glorifying rape, which is like..."

"No, no, it's like...if we called ourselves that people would immediately think we're anti-rape cos we're girls..."

A chorous of discordant voices rises out of abbreviated sentences. It's not easy to untangle, and without a way of expressing intonation there's less for you to go on, but bear with us...

"There's a very big difference between language here and in America. There the language and images are much more violent all the time..." so people there have fewer problems with that "very black humour" of Albini & co.

"To us the feminist thing is, like, 15 years behind here...the dialogue going on now is closer to what they did in America in the early 70's."

Nina agrees, and adds that"It seems that people've just caught up with the idea that you should, even if you're a man, be a feminist in certain ways, so when someone calls themselves Rapeman that JARS COMPLETELY against the whole rethinking that all these men have been trying to do."

Personally taking a less favourable view of the issue,I wondered why Rapeman were doing something that's so reactionary. They felt that that was what he was trying to send up rather than promote, being "Obsessed with the whole terrain of how sexually violent images have saturated our modern society" and therefore not acting outof character just to get attention, as had been heavily suspected.

"With Rapeman he goes right for the jugular.He has a comicstrip mentality where everything is exaggerated and extreme, you're either the good guy or the bad guy, that's his vision and he goes for the black."

And here's a strong UT characteristic starting to show up. Briefly summarized: "Just about everything's fuckin' easy to be misinterpreted - why make it easy for people?"

Because a lot of people aren't going to get it. A lot don't understand Rapeman and they're not gonna appreciate UT. So if you have something to say, isn't it more effective to say it in as few clear words as possible, to get your meaning over?

"Things aren't learnt just cos they're spelt out. People shouldn't demand a literal justification.There is this thing, art...you can say things in one sentence, but why? Why did Shakespeare write a whole play when he could've said 'He goes out, she comes in, she goes away and he goes mad and she gets killed.'?"

You're right, that wouldn't have been nearly as much fun. With this music there are no attempts to be awkward, but that's often the way it seems to turn out:"We just try and move ourselves, and if that's difficult then it's just difficult. We have an aesthetic away from what seems too easy, too false, too surfacey."

"Some of our music has got more simple in certain ways, whereas most bands do the opposite."

Being unable to place their monstrous hysterical sound amidst those produced by the bands that have so far dictated my musical experience, I enquire whether they feel themselves to be unique, or are there any similar groups in rheir view. In answer they describe "the scene prior to us and prior to Sonic Youth, Swans, Live Skull etc." in terms of Mars. Neubauten, DNA and Teenage Jesus & the Jerks, who were apparently happening in '77 & '78.

"We were attracted to these sounds, the combination of the electric, raw, hard feel and these incredible merges of notes ...that's maybe what it's all about, the attraction of sounds within the dirt."

"We're also attracted to the unpredictable, and the things that're beyond what you expect to do.It's not that we don't love pop and aren't influenced by the Beatles and all that, we're attracted to other things going on and are bringing them together."

"We started after Mars and DNA and all that, but before Sonic Youth.Everything we'd ever been into - jazz, rock, classical, blues, came through us." The list of bands that they come up with, apparently their influences, features Television, Stooges, Velvets, Led Zeppelin,

UT -- Laying on the hands.

oBITCHary- RAPEMAN

When Rapeman played their much publicized gig with Band of Susans and Dinosaur Jr at Leeds Poly late last year, Ablaze! newshounds were on the scene to bring you this report on what was one of the Hottest, and most controversial, New Acts to emerge from the US in Recent Times.

Rapeman formed from the shattered remains of the mighty Big Black and Scratch Acid. They were: Rey Washam (drums), David Wm Sims (bass), Steve Albini (guitar & vocals). The band's name was taken from the name of a hero in a Japanese comic book that they like. "The name has a connotation we appreciate - this comic book and the complete bewilderment you feel after reading it." More 'defence' of the name later.

They released one 12" live EP and a dynamic LP, on Blast First. Their initial attempt at recording the EP wasn't up to scratch:"So we said, 'this current batch of songs we're working on suck, let's forget about them, go on tour and write some more when we get back.'" The final result proved to be worthwhile but still disappointing; Albini admitted:"The EP is a bit of a downer, I can't see anybody listening to it and thinking 'this is the most exciting thing I've heard in my life'.It's not the kind of record you put out to start some incredible kind of hype."

Nevertheless, they seemed fairly happy with the way things were going for Rapeman. Sims explained: "It's a lot easier than being in Scratch Acid, things get done a lot more quickly and efficiently".

Albini:"Rapeman is a lot more work for me, in that we play every day...but we're not gonna burn out."

An obvious Albini sideline has been his production work for other bands. Is this something he does for money, or because he likes the bands?

"I produce people I like for money. I do a lot of stuff for nothing, for people whose music I like, people that just haven't got any hope - people that are such total fuck-ups they haven't got a prayer outside."

Further explanation was required:

"A fuck-up is someone who can't tie their own shoelaces, someone who has to take acid when they get up in the morning to feel normal. So about half of what I do is what you might call charity work, for my friends or people who need help, and then I do stuff with people who I have some degree of affinity with as far as their music or personalities go, who pay. The ideal producer, in my opinion, is someone who can make the band sound like they want to sound."

It seems, then, that Rapeman turned out to be a fairly blissful marriage, despite this dis disappointment with their first offspring. However, they've had some adverse reactions, particularly in this country, to their chosen name. Wasn't choosing the name a little dumb in view of a lot of people's idea of Big Black and Scratch Acid being misogynist bands?

Sims:"I'm not gonna lose sleep over what people put on me, or the band."

But if it stops you getting gigs, like it nearly did here?

Albini:"So much the worse."

Sims:"We just would've played somewhere else if we hadn't played here."

Albini:"The name Rapeman was just chosen as the name of a band with no agenda in mind. We knew it was gonna cause some shit but we figured it would die down fairly quickly. We never really took into account English people."

Sims:"There hasn't really been any problem to speak of in the states."

Don't you think the objections are justified - if you were a woman wouldn't you feel offended?

Albini:"No. I'm not capable of being offended."

Seeing the word 'Rapeman' on a poster in the middle of the street, completely out of context, is offensive.

"But there's no way of looking at the name that tells you it implies any particular perspective. It's just two syllables. If you removed the first and put any other verb in there the argument fall falls to shit."

But the verb in question is 'rape'.

"Exactly. That first syllable really bugs people." The thing with rape is that it's about men's power over women, and using 'rape' & 'man' really brings that home.

"But if we'd used 'rape' &'women' it would be read as a command. If we had just used the word 'rape' you wouldn't have used that either. There's a political touchiness about the word 'rape' in England."

"I'm firmly convinced that there is no morally correct or incorrect name you can give a rock band. We could have picked just about any other name that in abstract, in root, would have been just as horrifying but if we didn't use the word 'rape', no-one would have been offended."

Perhaps there are reasons for that. Many women have a gut reaction to the word. Fear is a powerful emotion and isn't easy to express on an intellectual level. For Albini, Sims and Washam the name Rapeman may signify this frightening character they've been fascinated by. Maybe they also wanna take a stab at feminism, a conviction that tends to be ill-represented by those who feel threatened by it. Rarely are bands required to qualify their names - after all, rock music is trivial & unimportant, I'm sure it's never influenced you or me, and you never see band names taken further out of context, scrawled on walls, do you?

Rapeman served to highlight our uncoolness & hypocrisy in wanting to live in an environment free of constant mental & physical threat. It may seem naive to attack cultural symptoms and not their causes, which we have less access to, and I guess while sexism is so all-pervasive it's a futile, unrewarding struggle. Anyhow, Albini & co get my grudging respect for being further examples of the male species' unrelenting arrogance and stupidity.

To finish then, a few more words from the man himself, and some late news:

"...all the fuss being made about our name...we picked it so we don't care what anyone else thinks about it. Odd as it may seem, we just don't give a damn. They can't affact us at all, we're certainly not gonna change the name..." (Albini, talking to Grim Humour).

"Actually, I wish we'd never called ourselves Rapeman." (Albini, to some fans in Amsterdam).

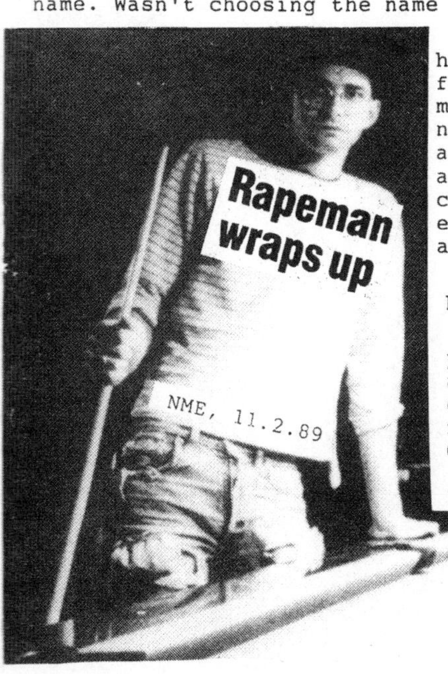

Rapeman wraps up

NME, 11.2.89

● **RAPEMAN** led by Steve Albini (left) have split following months of controversy over the band's name.

The group who faced a barrage of criticism on their visit to the UK last year, including the picketing of their gigs, had previously denied rumours of a split.

But their record label Blast First have confirmed that the group, who took their monicker from a Japanese comic, have disbanded. There is no news yet of leader Albini's future plans.

THE PIXIES - DYNAMIC DEMONS

PIXIES

A Pixies interview wasn't what we'd had in mind, to be
honest. Our arrival at Birmingham's Irish
centre was somewhat premature so I
guess we had time to kill, and
lusions to shatter. And there
they were in the bar, and I
found myself talking
to Kim, and she said
did i want to
interview
Charles,
and i
said
yeh.

So here we are, face to face with the embodiment of vocal perfection.What can you say to that? We go for the straight-from-the-heart approach, cos with these Pixies that's just where it comes from. OK maybe not exactly, but "it" really is something physical, not cerebral....Doesn't it freak you out Charles, people approaching you back-stage?

"Not really, it's just people coming over saying(adopts some insane warped english accent):'Good show, we liked it!!',real low key. We're not handsome popstars, at least I'm not."

True enough, although this is the most gorgeous ROCK band ever to've bludgeoned it's wicked way into my record collection, the individuals comprising it aren't exactly works of art, unlike their songs... Oh, Kim's lovely, but somehow i've forgotten the proposal i'd dreamed up for this fat little American fellow in his plain blue sweatshirt & baggy trousers, because I'm captivated now, because he's talking to us about "Cactus":

"I dunno if you've ever smelled cloth that smells like another person,a boy-friend's shirt or something...like i found a handkerchief that smelled like my old girlfriend from highschool...and it's just about being able to smell some-one, those kind of memories...the song is about a guy in prison asking his girlfriend, this woman, to send him her dress with her blood & her sweat & her food that she ate..."

And now we're miles away, in a Pixy state of being where verbal meanings become insignificant and all is sensual and intuitive, and all we really want to know is; How d'you do this, how d'you translate these feelings into those songs?

"I dunno.I know e, I know f, I know g, I know a, b, c, d, e sharp, e, f sharp,, now the minors: e minor, g minor..."

He's hitting the strings of the guitar on his lap as if to show us that this is really nothing special.

"I have some songs, ahh, and I like records, and I wanna make records, and it's the same with those guys [the other 3 Pixies], except these are more like my songs, but they're into it cos they have an interest , playing e minor, g minor, singing loud, playing loud, ya know what I mean? That's all it is."

I know that, say , the songs of Surfer Rosa is reducible to a load of notes and singing, but knowing is different from feeling, and that record feels infinitely greater than that - it feels cataclysmic. So you can't really tell a Pixies fan otherwise.

"If other people say it's good that's because I've done enough of the right combinations of things to make it interesting. Lots of people can do that, y'know? A lot of people're just boring because they're so aware of other records and things instead of being totally inspired...if more people just go 'f'kin' brillyant!, I wanna be like that!', ..arghh, just be more instinctive..."

The sentence breaks and fades but we seem to understand...except, where does this inspiration come from?

"Listening to records, listening to Beatles records when you're 8 years old...'gee, I wanna do that, I wanna scream like that '"

So it is from other songs really, but the Beatles, that's our mums & dads music - are you telling us this wonderful noise is in any way close to all that groan-ups' stuff? What about the things that happened since, the bands we know about?

I actually wanted to marry the guy,
or at least the guy's voice.

The Moon & the Melody

"I got one Sonic Youth record, I haven't heard it in awhile.I'm not a cool person, i don't buy a lot of records.I listen to old stuff, new stuff, whatever.I'm ten years behind everything, I listened to the Birthday Party for the first time this year.'

Isn't "Pixy" a funny name?

"I guess so, kinda cute."

Where did you get it from?

"From Joey, he didn't know what it meant. He still doesn't. Sometimes he comes across words he doesn't understand,but he likes the sound of them, and"Pixy", he just liked that word."

With such a growing appreciation of the group over here, almost amounting to unanimity, we wondered how they're treated at home, in the States. With less rapturous attention than in foreign land it seems, they're "just another college underground indie band."

"I think they like us over here because we're sort of humorous, a little bit silly, and British people GET IT. American's don't, they're too serious."

Who's this guy you've got producing your next LP, Gill Norton?

"He produced the single we just did, and he's done Throwing Muses, Wet Wet Wet, Echo & the Bunnymen, all them hard-rockin' bands."

Was this your idea, or 4AD's?

"It's never our idea. We didn't even know who Steve Albini was."

What d'you reckon now that you do know?

"He's alright, smart guy, knows his stuff, arrogant in a very entertaining sort of way.He's just a college graduate liberal like all the rest."

What did you do before you became "Black-Francis-of-the-Pixies"?

"I was a student...of anthropology."

What does that involve?

"Ah, going to class if you wake up on time, going to lots of movies...I don't know how intense it is over here, but there, if you can get together some student loans or if you have money already,you just go & have a 4 year party."

Nice if you can afford it, but most are gonna wake up with a megahangover & without an advance from 4AD to see them through...

I read something where you were saying that you thought everything in the world had already been done.Isn't that a bit fatalistic? There's always gonna be stuff we don't know about.

"I meant more in terms of a physical place I think, like goin' to California! Aint nobody been there before!..'cept Indians, y'know.Things don't seem to exist until people discover them, and now California does exist and for the people in California, Europe exists. Everything exists for everybody. There's maps everywhere in the world, there's a telephone everywhere in the world,You can take a boat way up to the farthest river in New Guinea and you'll find a drum of Royal Dutch Oil at the end, a filling station... Everything's been touched, except deep beneath the sea maybe, and in space, but I'll be dead by the time they start having shuttles to the moon, man."

In expressing this capricious desire for novelty his voice is really working, amusing us with various weird accents, and magical crescendoes from whispers to yells. Hovever, we're fearful about losing our hero to the enormous scary void out there...C'mon, you don't really wanna go up in one of those shuttle things?

"Why not?! I think it'd be GLORIOUS to go to the moon. Can you imagine what they must've felt like, what a TRIP,they must have been hyperventilating, their hearts must've been racing..."

"I'm not saying there's no excitement here, I'm not saying it's a dull place, but I mean, something entirely virgin like the fuckin' moon, they thought they were gonna have to deal with a mile of dust, they had mis-calculated how old the moon was and there was only really about five or six inches of it I think, but they don't know,they might land in a CLOUD of DUST, and just like stepping out...'oh my god, there's earth!'... and you know how SACRED the moon is, to cultures, religions, and philosophy and art - the moon, that's up there with the sun, and the clouds!!!... And then, they've been there man, it's like it's gone...oh, it's gone..."

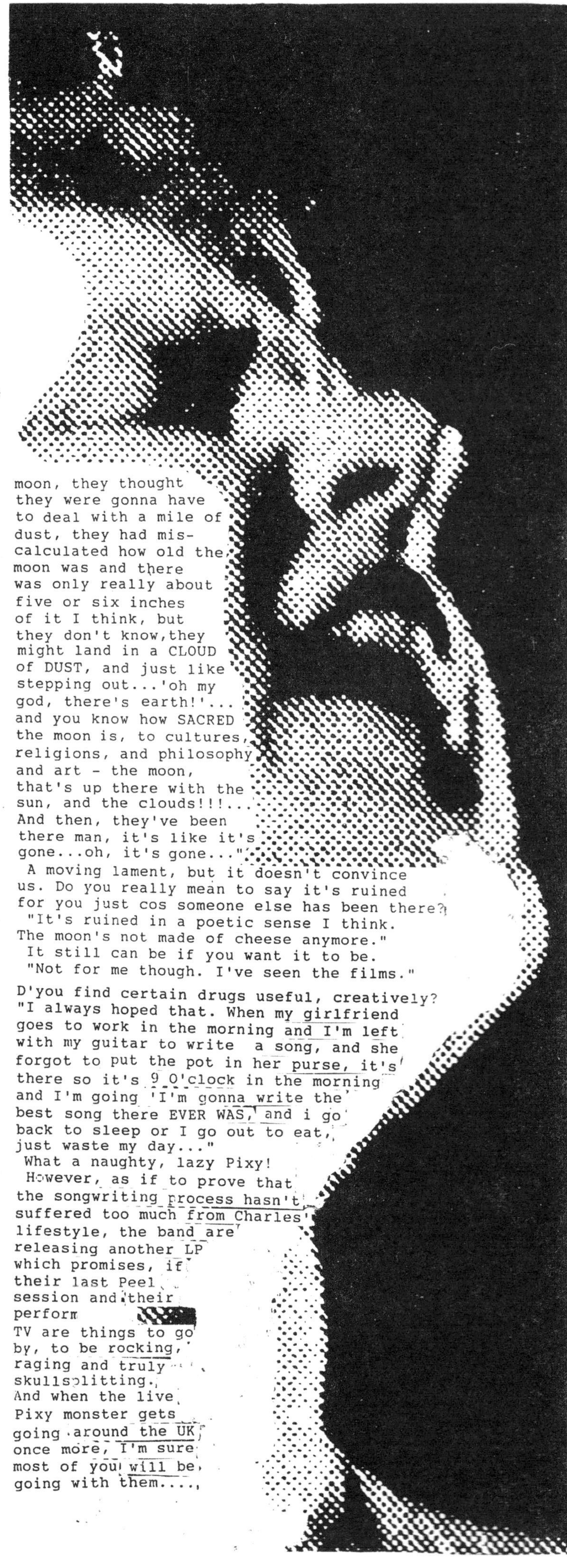

A moving lament, but it doesn't convince us. Do you really mean to say it's ruined for you just cos someone else has been there?

"It's ruined in a poetic sense I think. The moon's not made of cheese anymore."

It still can be if you want it to be.

"Not for me though. I've seen the films."

D'you find certain drugs useful, creatively?

"I always hoped that. When my girlfriend goes to work in the morning and I'm left with my guitar to write a song, and she forgot to put the pot in her purse, it's there so it's 9 O'clock in the morning and I'm going 'I'm gonna write the best song there EVER WAS,' and i go back to sleep or I go out to eat, just waste my day..."

What a naughty, lazy Pixy!

However, as if to prove that the songwriting process hasn't suffered too much from Charles' lifestyle, the band are releasing another LP which promises, if their last Peel session and their perform[illegible] TV are things to go by, to be rocking, raging and truly skullsplitting. And when the live Pixy monster gets going around the UK once more, I'm sure most of you will be going with them....

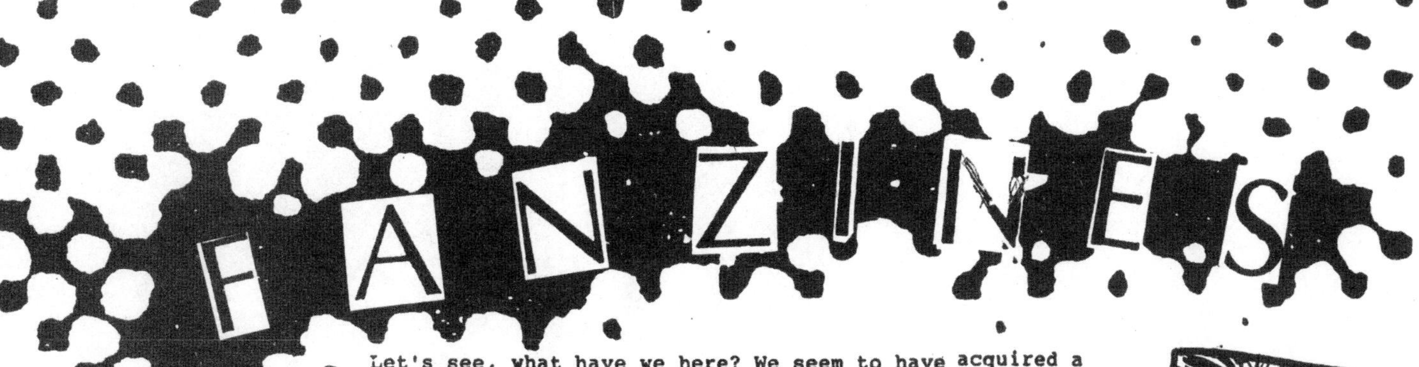

Let's see, what have we here? We seem to have acquired a great many fanzines recently, so I'm going to guide you through this (fairly arbitrary) shortlist collection that decorate the floor, in no particular order at all. People do zines for different reasons. SLICED EYE has no contact address and features no groups. A lesson in necessary perversity, it features words and pictures dragged out of any conventional context so that the most innocent notions become incredibly sinister. There's one clear message here though, from GMT, a band that doesn't exist (post- Ceramic Hobs, pre- Satan, the Jesus infected needles and blood).It reads:"We will wage our war with any tools we have available. Just so long as we make you realise that we hate you, the consumer, with every bone in our bodies, every cell in our brains.We will not cease till every consumer is diseased with the final cancerous monochrome cells, dripping with pus, blood and vile discharge." With that warning in mind you'll probably be too scared to buy anything again so you had better forget it and read on...

Circus of Life is a nice quality, thoughtfully written zine that's worth reading even if you hate the shit bands that are in it (Godfathers, Batfish Boys, Dawn after Dark, Salvation etc in iss. 5, which costs ya 50p & A4 SAE to: 9 Coppice Close, Chase Terrace, Walsall,Staffs. WS7 8BJ).

SOMETHING SPLENDIFEROUS is an entusiastic A5 zine, 40 pages packed with jangle music like the Pastels, Primal Scream, McCarthy, The Motorcycle Boy etc, plus a free 4 track flexi.It's 50p & SAE from Andy, 33 Findhorn Place, Fintry, Dundee DD4 9PE.

ISMO 2 is a A5 publication with an odd combination of articles. It includes interviews with Roy Harper & some guy that used to be in Status Quo (!!)as well as stuff on the Pixies, Shamen, My Bloody Valentine etc. £1 from 15 Holne Court, Exwick, Exeter, Devonshire. MILE OF BAD ROAD no. 1 came out ages ago, full of Dog Faced Hermans, Hagar The Womb, Shrug and the like, from 74 Egerton Rd, Middlesbrough, Cleveland, TS1 3LS. I tell you this mainly bacause there'll be an iss. 2 out soon which promises to be EVEN BETTER than the first. Similarly with THE great & mighty PLAIN TRUTH, which firstly brought us Goat People, AC Temple, Kilgore Trout, NOMEANSNO, Cyclic Amp and Llwybr Llaethog all for 10p & SAE, and secondly is gonna bring us The 3 Johns, Volunteers, Shrug, Eugene Chadbourne, a Japanese group called Yximalloo, and info on some new Italian bands and Shimmy Discs, all for 15p, from Andrew Truth, 18 Golf view, Ingol, Preston.

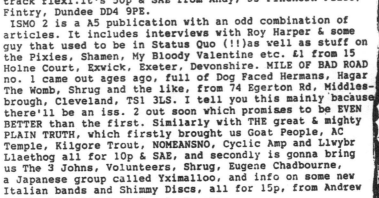

Alphabetically now, 7 more A5 size things: ANARCHY, PEAS CHIPS no. 1 is a lovely red and yellow affair, raising money for the Preston Music Collective and being real informative. Features Chumbawamba, Feed Your Head, articles on squatting, pirate radio, Poll Tax etc and costs just 25p. P.O.Box 172, Preston, Lancs. BLACK SCHOOL BUS is a late adolescent acid-trip of a zine, quite charming, trundling along with a sound track by the Walking Seeds, Loop, Spacemen 3, Pussy Galore, My Bloody Valentine, Bomb Party,Suicide, Magic Roundabout and Inspiral Carpets. Send yr 40p to Simon, 10 Ashfield Rd, Longsight, Manchester 13. CRIME PAYS is a real punk rocker, making minimal use of a typewriter, prefering lots of scrawly pens and tippex. For exclusive interviews with Echo & The Bunnymen (!), Revolutionary Army of the Infant Jesus, Gone To Earth and Plague Dogs, plus lots of raw humour, it's 25p (I don't need to say '& SAE' every time now, do I?) off Pete F, 58 Huskisson St, Toxteth, Liverpool 8. CAGED IN no. 666 is a non-music comic-zine creature, 48 grotesque pages full of gooey tales drawn by those ever-famous Various Artists (not the same ones, actually) for just 50p from Rich, 14 Woodlands Dr, Hawarden, Deeside, Clwyd, CH5 3LA. I'm warning you, it's freaky stuff. Next up, we have a footy zine, HULL, HELL & HAPPINESS.Being ill-qualified to comment on the sport content I'll just mention that it also features Hull music and various other zines...the issue I've got is the first one which sold millions of copies so there are now none to be had, but buy subsequent ones from 119 North Road, Withernsea, E. Yorks, NU19 2AX. THE IDEA part 5 was inspired by Dog Faced Hermans, Stump, Thrilled Skinny and Strawberry Switchblade amongst others and costs 35p.

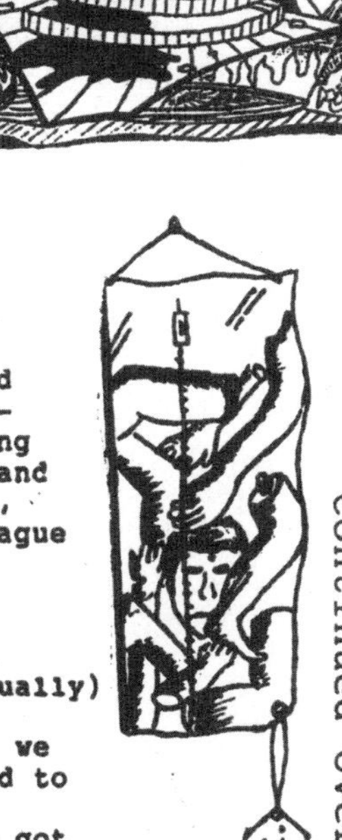

Continued over...

and the Rolling Stones, but not the Raincoats, a group often cited by music-writer folk as having something greatly to do with these with these guys' sonic row."We didn't know the Raincoats and we certainly don't relate to their music." So there.

Among their contemporaries they admit to being quite partial to the Jesus and Mary Chain, Nick Cave, the Buttholes and "pretty much everyone" on Blast First, their label.

It's somehow strange to think of you lot supporting those beastly Butties. D'you have an affinity with them?

"Oh yeh, they have this sort of psychedelic dirt blues band thing that we have also.We like playing with certain American bands with that kind of over-the-top-ness and that looseness. They're more contrived than us though, more vaudeville.That's where we're different from them: we're like the inside, the inverse, the eye of the hurricane."

UT, a beautiful idea fearsomely executed, misunderstood, but they don't care - it's a vital part of the game.Bursting out of the space given to them, as a all female trio from New York...they don't wear raincoats & they're too old to be sonic youths...a (unintentionally) awkward concept that defies classification - just utterly wonderful and inspiring.

THE IDEA part 6 is a video zine, showing DFH, SS, Shrug, Dan,Ghost Dance, Joolz, New Model Army, Magic Bastards, Into A Circle etc. and costs considerably more. I haven't yet seen this so I can't give an opinion,but it's available from 8 St. Paul's Road, Thornaby, Cleveland, TS17 6LH for £7.50 incl. p&p. And...THE MELODY HAUNTS MY REVERIE is "all about hope" and janglepop, written with passion by Alistair, and available from him at 64 Lugar Place, Troon, Strathclyde, KA10 7EA. A moving tale, and only 50p...

Back to the big (A4) bastards, BEYOND THE GUTTER concentrates more on writers and artists than bands - issue 1 features Ivor the Anarchist, Hooligan Press, an interview with Paul Problem Child and stuff on Employment training and an essential discussion about the scarcity of women actively involved in the 'punk' movement. Just 25p - 4/7 Gunnet Court, Muirhouse View, Edinburgh. GET OUT and never come back 5's got Happy Mondays, Dave Howard Singers, King of the Slums, Nort, DFH and plenty more to amuse you, 50p from 41b Hallgate,Wigan, Lancs, WN1 1LR. BOLLOCKS FROM UNCLE JEFFREY is the raving maniac of the pack. I've got a copy with the original 'shocking' cover which you probably can't get cos it appears to've been censored. Full of healthy fun & depravity with the Buttholes, Sonic Youth, Henry Rollins, Pat Mills, Playground & Rapeman, all for 50p. 21 Houghton Rd, St. Ives, Cambs, PE17 4RQ. GRUNT is a ace new magazine for Leeds, but i expect you can read it wherever you live. No.1 is 50p and includes interviews with Rapeman, Cud, Crow People and Purple Eternal.Contact Mr Gobshite c/o Box Grunt!, 52 Call Lane, Leeds LS1 6DT. Another non-music rebel is TRAVELS IN NIHILON, 20p from Clive, Church Wicket, Wembdon, Bridgewater, Somerset TA6 7RR. It's a fairly personal collection of stories, cartoons and opinions...

OUT OF DARKNESS 2 features interviews with The Beloved, Balaam and the Angel, THe Crows etc, plus essential info on many things and a free 4 track flexi. Chris who writes it also runs SUNSHINE DISTRIBUTION, a convenient way to get hold of various zines, booklets and anarchist literature. Write for his zine (30p) or just a list (SAE), c/o Raven Press, 75 Piccadilly, Manchester M1 2BU.

Such a fine and varied selection of fanzines as this makes any generalization extremely difficult, since they're all so obviously produced by people with diverse inspirations and aims. However, these energetic, imaginative folk seem less concerned with making money than with making available information and ideas to anyone who's interested, often at a cost to themselves (if not in terms of cash, then certainly in time & effort.) There's no such thing as yr 'average zine, although the development of various groups & styles is detectable. A national network of zines made possible by distributio points in lots of cities might provide an exciting, if not financially successful, challenge to the big weeklies and their attempted cultural monopoly.

WORLDWIDE CONTAGION is the Ablaze-run distribution service. We buy/sell small quantities of zines, records and tapes to make the process of obtaining the things a bit easier. Send a small SAE to

8, Hopewell Place, Leeds, LS6 IPN, UK

for a copy of the current list. (If you'd like us to stock yr zine etc. please send sample copy & SAE.)

Caught in the YES SMOKING (compulsory cancer) truck of a trans pennine train, escaping bad goth & worse acid...as good a non -place as any in which to tell you the truth about those items of plastic delivered unto the cracked house by approval seeking manipulatory bodies...let's call this the RECORD REVIEW section.

CLINT RUIN & LYDIA LUNCH - STINKFIST
(Un)dressed in a cover that has caused considerable interest and uproar among unruly guests, this 3 track LP (or wrong-speed EP, formats have got so confusing) seems to divide into two parts, side one and side two. One contains the heaving, groaning "Stinkfist", a very Foetal slime -instrumental, which we tend to overlook in favour of Two's enthralling "Meltdown Oratorio". Here Lydia quits panting like she's auditioning for a dubious Swedish film role and grits her teeth and rails at everything ever, particularly herself, with such passion, such poetry, that you can understand just how she feels (Psycho! -ed). We're then left with the inevitable (sic) "Son of Stink". Uh, you can almost smell this vivid, intense production. Not for Wedding Present fans.

SCREECHING WEASEL lp (W,G.O)
Here'a a proper singalong punk-rock record, 27 neat tracks, some so naff and bland that they're really quite funny. Ben Weasel's voice changes so much from track to track it's difficult to believe there's only one of him, fortunately it's true. Coolest tracks are "Work", "California Sucks", "OMW" and "Clean cut asshole"...a lot of the time here seems to be spent being verbally vindictive to their highschool pals ("You're nothing but a dirty, smelly cumbag hippie"), bawling out well-considered political comments ("Society makes me wanna puke all over you"), or telling pleasant little stories, like in "Wavin' gerbs", an invaluable insight into the mind of someone who cooks small furry animals for the fun of watching them burst. But really, the whole thing rocks. I'll bet they're OK live too.

MASTERS OF THE OBVIOUS - Hammeroid EP.
An intensely irritating little record. Four tracks of awful music with hilarious lyrics that'll make you wanna chuck up, fro: two sad people in Massachusetts. You may've heard Peel playing the dismal "Rot Rot Rot! and wondered what the hell was going on. I wonder why he never gave us the benefit of such gentle melodies as "It's so big it's fluorescent" and "The turd that came to life"? I think we should be told. This record is one you gotta have, if only to amuse your relatives at xmas.
Write: M.O.T.O., P.O. Box 411360, West Somerville, Mass, 02144.

EMBER DAYS - "Listen to the liars"/"Still Life" flexi.
Three people on piano, guitar and synth playing in a parlour. Presumably they had to keep very quiet so's not to disturb the neighbours. Whispered male vocals are almost detectable...if there is any life here it certainly hasn't woken up yet. Could be shy English pop - somebody's sure to like it. (Write: Wroxeter records, P.O.Box 35, Dudley, DY3 3NG).

SAD SOCIETY - Contaminate b/w Ambition
A 2 track 7" from Edinburgh's Sad Society, plainly packaged, with 'punkrock' written all over it, but actually quite poppy & lively. "Ambition", my favourite, has a nice message: "I'll tell you something, ambition's all you need/There aint nothing, no nothing that you can't be." Get it for £1.20 incl. p&p, from 29 Durar Dr, Clermiston, Edinburgh, EH4 7HW.

THE STRETCH HEADS - 'Bros are pish' EP. (Moksha).
From the same label and land as the Shamen, the Stretch Heads emerged, chucking this frantic one-sided piece of vinyl our way, nearly slicing a few heads off en route.
It comprises of 5 fast tracks off their 1st LP, though I can only count 4, one of which is a degenerate version of SAW's "I should be so lucky" ("...sucky fucky mucky..."), the others being degenerate versions of their own taut, trebleful and manic songs. One of these is called "headache", and I think I can guess why. This is hardly music for pleasure if you are on the listening end, but I'm sure it makes them feel better.
"Worry", the last track, seems to involve an introduction to someone's family and social worker. It's a shambles from start to finish, except that...it gets worse as it goes along. The drummer dies, the bass falls to bits, and screech vocals give way to distorted moans.
Ends with an innovative never-ending groove with an irritating jump. These people are obviously casualties of a shitty chart culture and they should be hospitalized, no I mean recognized as the genius souls they surely are.

SHRUG - "NEVIL WANLESS" EP (Our Mam's)
The first thing which attracted me to this record was the picture of Mike Neville on the front - a familiar face from the past. Here comes an educated band from the North, with 3 drummers, down to earth musically, even verging on crappy, but with something really attractive about them. They've obviously got a lot of humour which shows through in the lyrics as well as in the music, a social conscience ("Anti -violence, anti-work, anti-lots-of-things, except chocolate"), and some intense preoccupation with roads. It's like a whole load of things which remind me of being a kid, right down to the "Van with quare wheels" (yeah, I know, and round windows too), which is the best track on this brilliant, innovative EP.Get this record or die in ignorance.
(Jeene)

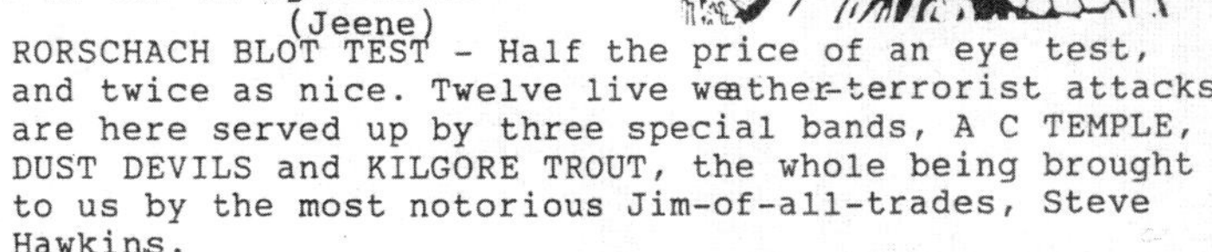

RORSCHACH BLOT TEST - Half the price of an eye test, and twice as nice. Twelve live weather-terrorist attacks are here served up by three special bands, A C TEMPLE, DUST DEVILS and KILGORE TROUT, the whole being brought to us by the most notorious Jim-of-all-trades, Steve Hawkins.
A C Temple are so dangerously different from all other bands, but are caught in a sad comparison trap, from which few help them escape. This record does help them though, it plainly reveals them as having little in common with a NY sound, their noise chaos being far too disciplined, too tidied-up, to get thrown out with that trash. The guitar wails stray but that's all,they're closer to the Trouts than the Devils, who suffered similar treatment and enjoyed it so much they went to live it. Enough journo-filth, you you can't talk these sounds of perspiration-seeped panic, racing through the blackness, Dust Devil tantric whirls take you right out and shake you, stop! Here Jackie's singing manages to remain a little above the meshing guitars. Kilgore Trout bring serious pounding and racing urgency to the party, this whole thing took place in one room, on one night, can you imagine?

A secret celebration of gods know what, clawing at some glorious hights, conjouring heavy black, bright sights...Buy this LP and go blind happy.

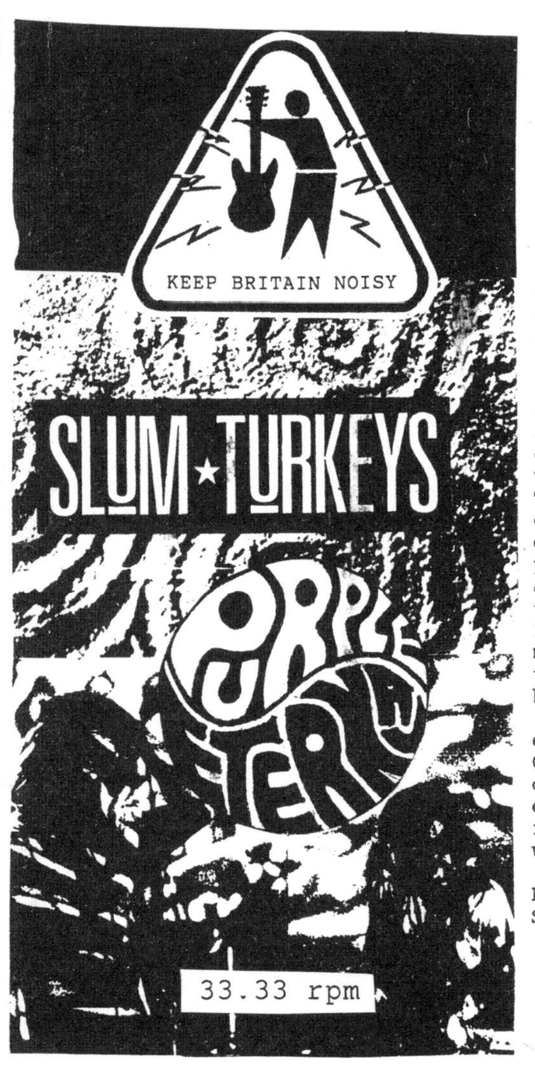

KEEP BRITAIN NOISY
SLUM★TURKEYS
PURPLE ETERNAL
33.33 rpm

KEEP BRITAIN NOISY records, in conjunction with ABLAZE!, are deliriously proud to present this free gift of a limited edition record, one for each of our wise readership, filled with churning great noise from the middle North.

This may be yr first introduction to these particular bands so I'll make it good and quick.Put the floppy plastic between a hard record you already possessed and a playing needle on your music machine.Flick the ON switch.

SLUM TURKEYS dwell in Manchester. Not the Manchester you know, of acidhouses and studey janglebands (keep London in the South) but a real dreamcity of serious excitement and raging sonic power activity.Someone round here(UK)'s gotta make a nasty glorious row, and I guess the Turkeys figured they'd set to it right now, God bless 'em.

"No Axe To Grind" was recorded ages ago, now available in matching shades during LIVE occurences, and recounts the day when the lads received a significant burglary visit resulting in the loss of their essential geetar collection. NB the 2nd half of that last sentence was made up, I don't know what it's about & Paul wasn't saying. Tell-it-straight time (like Daily Mirror) * Drummer (Tony) on this track quit recently & replaced by machine. * Singer/ guitarman also gets to play bass with The revered Membranes in place of Wallis Tadpole (in place of M.S Batcow in place of John being bass player & Tilton on guitargenius work, it's weird the trivial & possible incorrect scraps of nonsense you carry round in your head isn't it, I can recite the Lord's Prayer if you give me a line to start off with). Where were we...ah, * and I've forgot the 3rd bit but never mind, "No Axe To Grind" will knock your tiny head off, get into it kid or go to the Hacienda.

PURPLE ETERNAL, Leeds' finest children, produce some disturbingly excellent volumes of psycho-grunge, music for your trip to heaven. Currently a quintet in the business of performing gigantic gigs in only the luckiest of towns. "Going Down" is on the flexi cos it's extra fucking GOOD (not an opinion but an unquestionable truth, you incredulous freak),engineered by Steve Hawkins because only the best will suffice in conditions such as these.

Remember the name for future heard-it-first reference.Purple Eternal Let's hope it stays that colour for ever & evermore................ SUCK IT TILL IT BLEEDS.thank you.

WRITE: SLUM TURKEYS c/o Paul, 521 Charles Barry Crescent, Hulme, Manchester, M15 5DL.

PURPLE ETERNAL c/o Mark, 1 Meanwood Towers, Towers Way, Leeds LS6 4PL.

DIGESTIVE SYSTEM hail from Sale in S. Manchester, home of James Anderton and a massive branch of Tesco. Their cassette, "The Smoking beagles are dead", contains 6 tracks of rocka-punk-metal fusion, with titles like "De-Hulme-anization" & "Life up the bosses arse". Write to them c/o 43 Oak Rd, Sale, M33 2FD.

PRONG / GODFLESH - Leeds Duchess.

And God was made flesh and dwelt among us, packed as we were a bit like squirmy fishes in an inadequate sized box,for the start of a divine torture ritual.Godflesh are a sublime combination of a Head of David, a Napalm Death and an evil drum machine spitting out the whipcrack backbone on which the two guitar creatures create their body of holy menacing noise.Prong's cruel-looking 3 pointed logo suited Godflesh more than those it was meant for. The crowd, gathered seemingly from most corners of this sad land, reacted coolly when they should have been twisting and thrusting their mortal frames in all the directions demanded by this gorgeous nightmare sonic scape. They were pretty good.

A Prong is a sharp piece of metal. Prong are a BIG sharp piece of metal, the sort to be avoided if you can't cope with the sounds and (unsightly) sights of people performing, and getting into, this dead-braincell music. Prong took the knee-high stage along with a few of their demented devotees who insisted on flinging themselves off it into the fat faces of their friends, a pathetic sight, a bit like seeing lots of people tripping over the same paving-stone. Despite my prejudices about this sort of thing, it has to be said that Prong were apocalyptic. Like adrenalin-charged muppets they constructed some mean, massive sounds. i liked it best when they went fast, but these Prong songs are weird beasts that keep changing speed all over the place. Less like prongs than huge telegraph poles being inserted 3 by 3 into your delicate auditory apparatus. Avoid.

Pages, lines for you to follow, cross-referenced for your inconvenience. A big life sketch of growing ideas, thrown at you as they appear to us. Add it up & suss it out. Answers on a postcard single (pref. Fire Engines), before we all go old & watch Neighbours, to get off yr ass And BLAZE zine, Leeds Six, N.England.

A tired "editor" writes, with a mind stretched to breaking point, fingers barely scaling the keyboard that glares night and day, beckoning schizophrenia...

So much that we wanted to tell you there hasn't been time and space to include. As this is being written, the Muses are the biggest force imaginable, but just so many people and groups have inspired & helped, whether they knew it or not. So, we haven't told you anything of My Bloody Valentine's dream-sex-delirium records and gigs, Fugazi's great mind blast MLP & roof-raising performances, or Loop, Rollins, Crane, Walking Seeds, Membranes ...or how we went to Holland to see Gun Club in a field, and Union Carbide Productions in a park in Rotterdam, and the big-city trip to London to see Foetus, Harry Crews, The Fall & Micheal Clarke, and the Butthole Surfers in the space of four days...

Sad things have been happening too. The Dust Devils left Leeds for it's US equivalent, New York; we tried to set up some radio thing but totally fucked it up; man's assault on life continues and British poor can't afford to vote... but we just bury our heads in the sound and carry on as if it isn't happening. I don't know what to do.

No, I've tried and I can't list all the good people that've helped & encouraged us without going right off the page and under the table. Thanks, I think you know who you are. Also no-thanks to those who've got in our way, ripped us off & messed us about, you know that we don't need you at all.

If you like/hate this zine thing, or need/have any further info, or if you are just feeling a little bit l o n e l y   o r   b o r e d , feel free to write to us
love, Karren

Ross's hitching sign with messages scratched into it by Sonic Youth - 'Hitchhiker Murder - Lee', 'Please, please, please - S' (Steve) and 'HIT THE NORTH - Kim'

Ross Holloway on *HITCHHIKING*

So, back in the dark days of Thatcher's Britain, before neoliberalism had inculcated itself deeply into the everyday consciousness of the nation, not having the bus or train fare to visit another part of the UK was not generally considered to be either a moral crime or a threat to our social fabric.

The first time I ever hitched was to Waterstones bookshop in Manchester where Nick Cave was doing a reading from his forthcoming novel *And the Ass Saw the Angel*, as well as signing copies of his collection of lyrics and jottings, *King Ink*. I was still at school, in sixth form, and for many music fans at school and university age - and for musicians and general hipsters claiming benefits - hitchhiking was the default way you crossed the country. A particular subset of the hitchhiking community even had its own name: 'kitbaggers' were distinguished by the army surplus kitbags they carried as they followed bands like The Mission around on tour. In the late '80s, there was scarcely a good hitching spot to be found that didn't have 'Stoko the Eskimo' ('Eskimos' being fanatical followers of The Mission) scrawled somewhere in thick black marker pen.

One of the best hitching spots in the country had to be the slip road about a mile south of Leeds city centre that leads onto both the M1 south via Sheffield, Nottingham, Leicester and terminates in London, and west to Manchester and Liverpool. Technically this slip road was prohibited to pedestrians, but there was a grass verge roughly 100 feet long, which potential lifts could safely pull into. And pull in they did. Back in those days, you would go not only prepared with a cardboard sign clearly stating your intended destination, but also prepared to queue as you could anticipate at least two or three pairs of hitchhikers to be waiting. On the M1 slip road north at Brent Cross in London, it wasn't unusual to arrive to find up to another dozen pairs of hitchers.

Hitchhiking was a gateway to adventures, to gigs and clubs and people in other cities you wouldn't otherwise have been able to afford to visit, and also to meeting people you probably wouldn't have met in the run of everyday life. There were two types of people who typically offered me lifts. The first wanted someone to skin up spliffs for them on the motorway, and could range from scary Hell's Angels types to travelling salesman in suits. The other group, who would overlap with the first if I were describing this using a Venn diagram, were those that had hitchhiked themselves. There were the random ones: the chief designer for Bentley who, on seeing our leather jackets thought we might be able to chat about motorbikes, the black girl in the hire van who played us this new band she was involved with called Soul II Soul, and the folkie on his way down to London from Barnsley in a battered old Lada with a guitar on the back seat. When I asked him where he was playing, he replied 'the Royal Albert Hall.' It turned out he was in the Dubliners (but preferred to live in Barnsley). Other times it was just ordinary people doing you a favour. Whoever it was, I always came away with a reaffirmed faith in the general goodness and kindness of humanity, and a reminder that you couldn't judge people by appearances. I had trusted people and they'd trusted me.

In addition, there was a community of hitchers you'd either meet randomly in service stations in the middle of the night or at gigs, with whom you felt an unspoken solidarity, who you would put up for the night when they were in your city and who would help you out in the same way. We were co-operative, we were reciprocal, we had a community. Aren't these the kind of positive values that politicians then and now bang on about?

I've scanned the internet for reasons for the huge decline in hitchhiking in the last 20 years and in the few sources I can find, the reasons given are a general sense that hitchhiking is seen as risky, that people don't have the trust in others they once had, and that hitchhiking may have just been a particular isolated phenomenon associated with the counter-culture of the sixties that slowly faded until the point that it died when we became fearful of the kind of people who gave lifts, following the murders of several female hitchers in the mid-nineties. In North America, hitching is illegal in some places and seems considered an 'outlaw' practise. In Europe it is universally legal, but now uncommon.[1] In Japan, however, maybe because of low crime rates, it is reportedly still quite common.

These are all compelling reasons, but I think here in the UK there is a missing factor from these analyses. I think the government decided to stop it. I recall two occasions in the early nineties, once in Leeds, once in London, where the police rocked up and moved everyone back behind the motorway sign. These signs were always just before the slip road began, and before the point where vehicles could pull in safely to pick people up. Those hard shoulder or waste ground strips where lifts could pull in were technically on the motorway (and thus it was illegal to stop there unless in an emergency), but were the only spots where drivers could safely stop. Proponents of this change would, of course, argue the police were merely enforcing the letter of the law. I think the powers that be were just being mean. This meanness was just part of the mindset of Thatcher and her ilk, who disliked the idea of people being given a 'free ride'. Perhaps they were also wary of the culture it represented, a culture that had values in which commerce was not so important. I firmly believe it was for similar reasons that the Tories began the process by which maintenance grants for students were rescinded – too much time for free thinking and not enough time worrying about getting a job.

Since I've learnt to drive I always look out for hitchers, but in three years I've only encountered them on one occasion, and I did of course pick them up. When I drive up the M1, I notice that where once you could have pulled in to pick up hitchers, barriers have been installed. These aren't for safety – you're not up to speed as you enter the motorway on a slip road – but I doubt anyone questions why they are there.

Maybe people don't believe in trust anymore, and maybe people are more averse to risk than they once were, and just maybe the case of Fred West and others who murdered hitchhikers did end the phenomenon. And maybe cars are just extensions of our personal space now, and not just machines for getting us from A to B. Or could it simply be that we have been denied the opportunity that hitching once gave us to get out of our safety zones and discover that there are lots of caring, sharing, wonderful people in the world, who we've never met before?

Graham Sutton, pre-Bark Psychosis, resting at a service station between hitches. Note the carrier bag of *Ablaze!s* that he has to lug home.

[1] This may not be true right across Europe. We know that students often hitchhike short distances in France, for instance, using established routes between town and campus.

WILLIAM, it was really something

William Potter contributed his design skills to three issues of *Ablaze!*, starting with the cover of issue 4. Creator of *Groin* fanzine and lots of comics, he's also the bendy bass player of Cud. When I first met him, William had just finished studying art at Leeds Poly in the wake of Scritti Politti, Fad Gadget and Soft Cell[1]. We met up more recently in London, where he now lives and works as a writer/editor for kids' magazines and books. I wondered whether he had offered to help *Ablaze!* because he felt sorry for my poorly-designed zine?

Cud at Kirkgate Market 1986

CUD INFORMATION

April, is it still April?

Dear Karen,

Thanks for the zine. Really, you'll have to sort out the printing. I don't mind sending you stuff, but it really is a dreadful blurr. It's no good cutting out and enlarging 'Bob' now, because his so mucky! Tell me when you're doing another and I'll send you Part 2, as long as you promise to fix the duplicator.

It was interesting to read the Shouts int[illegible]

William contributed a cartoon to *Ablaze!* 4, and placed its hero, Dissy, on the front cover.

WP: Did you ask me to do it? I don't think I volunteered.
KA: I don't think I would have had the confidence to ask, or the nous.
WP: This was '87, or '88, the first year of Enterprise Allowance[2]. You got an extra tenner a fortnight or something, you had to have a business plan, and mine was comics.
KA: Ajay from Dandelion Adventure set up a badge-making business, and that during his year on Enterprise Alllowance he allegedly made six badges.[3]
WP: The best one I know was Steve from Cud, his was a drum repair business. He had some cymbals, he had the guy from Enterprise Allowance come round and showed him some cymbals he had smashed in the van and convinced the guy that he could fix them. It was a good system.
KA: Tell me more about your zine, *Groin*.
WP: I can't remember the spark that made me do my fanzine. It was less about bands, it was more a silly shouty arty thing. It was only later that I realised that if I did a fanzine I could get into gigs for free and talk bullshit to the bands backstage. *Groin* predates Cud; I put Cud in the third issue. The first two issues were crap, the third one was good and then I had to stop cos it was too expensive and time consuming. Then I did the Cud fanzine. Instead of doing a fanzine featuring other bands and a little bit of Cud, I just did a fanzine all about Cud. I don't think it was as radical in design. I sold out – to my own band!
KA: Did you design the Cud sleeves?
WP: The first few, yeah. The first sleeve had a big zoomed in picture of the Merrion Centre – we're from Leeds! Brutalist Leeds. Big bold stripes – I was influenced by bands like Age of Chance and their shouty sleeves, so I was doing big American football style fonts. Then I did a really tacky letter print on it in green on red, it was garish. It was meant to look striking. Then we got some designers and never looked back. I created the Cud logo and then we got some designers to make us a better one and we stuck with that for the rest of our career.

KA: Were you designing stuff for us to promote your emerging freelance comic art career?
WP: I didn't think it was about publicising myself, more of an ego thing. Whereas I paid to do my own zine, it was great if someone else was willing to go to all the expense of printing one up with my stuff in it. [Looking at *Ablaze!* 4] The cover doesn't represent the contents at all, it's like a ghetto kid and it's got the Rotunda in Birmingham there. I could've put the names of bands in logos in there, King of the Slums in Coca Cola lettering... What people would have made of that zine, looking at the cover?
KA: A hip hop zine?
WP: Not many people were buying hip hop zines. It didn't fit in.

William then decided to devote great swathes of his time to making the entirety of issue 5 look totally brilliant.

WP: The thing I remember most is working on issue 5 and spending most of the weekend sticking photocopies together, and missing the opportunity to see the Happy Mondays for free at The Warehouse. Martin Baker, Cud's manager at the time [the Reverend Martin Baker], had managed to book them, and all the band were going, and it was all set up, and I said 'No, I can't go, I'm working on this fanzine.' And now I'm like, 'I should've gone! It would've been brilliant!'
KA: People liked the cover. Mudhoney made a joke about it in the next issue, saying the next one should be made up of half of Mark's butt and half of Dan's butt.

WP: That would be good. I'm not sure I would have wanted to work on that, trying to merge two buttcracks together... I know the printing didn't work very well, I wasn't using Letratone, I was using acetates stuck together. This was the point where fanzines became so much more professional with writers like James Brown on the verge of becoming professional journalists. He quit it [fanzining] quite early. I interviewed him for *Groin* and he recorded it in case I misquoted him, in which case he would sue me. So I included every 'umm' and 'err', every repetition. He loved it apparently, and offered me some writing for the NME.
KA: Did you do it?
WP: I did... I went to see Butthole Surfers and was supposed to write about the support band, I wrote it up in a fanzine way, in a ranting poet kind of way. James could keep an attitude and write like a proper journalist. It's taken me many years to go from fanzine writing to editorial writing. [Looking at the *Ablaze!* 5 artwork] This is an independent handmade zine but we're competing with everything else on the racks, it's quite distinct...
KA: The cover design was so audacious. I saw you matching these images up, resizing them on the photocopier. I'd never see anything like it.
WP: It is a monster. I used really low-quality images and printed them really high. This was how my artwork was, I would get photocopies and make them bigger and bigger until they became really distorted and then I'd paint them and then shrink them back down again. Imagine getting a tiny stamp-sized image blown up until it was really distorted; I loved that kind of image work. Instead of going for a really good quality 300 dpi we've got something printed in a newspaper, a mixture of high-tech imagery and best quality printing.
KA: You designed the entire thing for me... It was the best one, design-wise.
WP: I loved distorted images and really horrific images. It's all kind of stretching, like slightly moving things, putting them back together, photocopying them, moving the paper. And working with these exploded dots, taking the image and blowing it up and up and up... I spent hours at the University photocopiers doing this cos it was really cheap. They got to know me in there. It totally reminds me of my degree stuff, and my own fanzine, and you know I did a thesis on fanzines as well, a short history of fanzines from *Sniffin' Glue*, including *Ablaze!*, and including my own fanzine. I designed the whole thesis in a similar style to this. It was fun. It's great to see all these again.
KS: You spent ages on this Thrilled Skinny piece didn't you? This is probably why you missed the Happy Mondays.
WP: I did a comic a couple of years later when I worked for *Deadline* magazine, I didn't have the money to pay for Letratone, so I'd buy one sheet of Letratone and photocopy it and cut it out with scissors and knives and glue it on letter by letter. It's funny to look back on it, even cutting and pasting all the words. People don't do that now, they do a blog.

By this point William had trained me well in the art of the photocopier, and went back to just designing the cover. Or so he claims.

WP: The cover's a horrible colour.
KA: You prescribed a stronger pink. I didn't believe you that the two-colour design was going to work. But it's my fault for getting it printed at Salem Church by YTS employees - they used the wrong pink.
WP: You've got a flexi – are they rare tracks?
KA: I dunno. I paid for a double-sided flexi. I could have said to the bands, you send me five tracks and I'll choose one, I didn't even know that I had choice, that I had any power in the process. They might have sent me out-takes, and that might have been the best publicity they ever had. I had no confidence at all, it was a massive process to build that up. You and I have the same birthday and we should have the same kind of personality, but you always seemed loads more confident than me.
WP: That's cos astrology's a load of nonsense. By the time this was out you were Karren Ablaze!, people knew who you were, you made an impression.
KA: I did learn to march into wherever I wanted. Look, I used the *Ablaze!* font you designed!
WP: I'm glad you used it sparingly.
KA: How much of this did you do?
WP: I did the cover - you did all the rest.
KA: No! This is so Wiliam Potter! No, like how, how did I manage to do that?! I'd always fill all the space with text. I didn't have a sense of style!
WP: I would've done that... (looks through pages)... I wouldn't have done that. I recognise these stylings I put on everything, that was my signature.
KA: You must have given me the old photocopies. Did I really design this?
WP: Yeah, you were creative.
You and I, when we did our fanzines, we weren't real designers, we were people who wanted to put a message out. I was more artistic and I did comics and things. I used to pretend to be an editor when I had comics. I imagined I had a 32-page Marvel comic. Now I'm working with designers and I and see that it's a total skill that I don't understand at all. I can spot mistakes. There's always a fight between editorial and designers , who put all the facts out of order.
KA: Like hairdressers - they've got their own ideas.

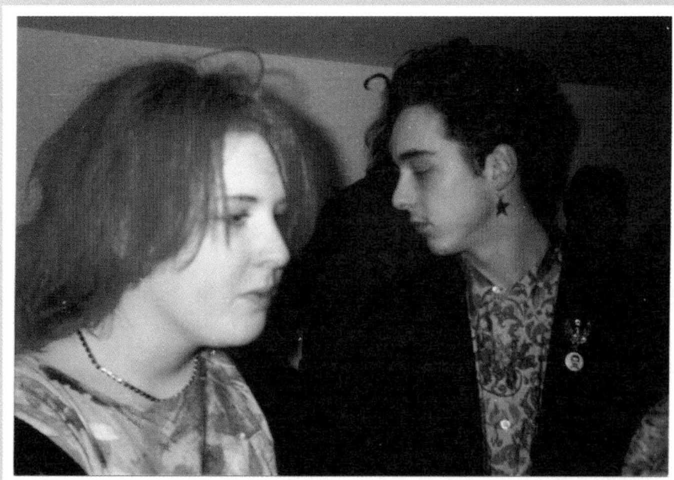

Karren Ablaze! and William Potter at a party in the basement of Hopewell Place, having lots of fun. Photographer unknown.

Ablaze!
6

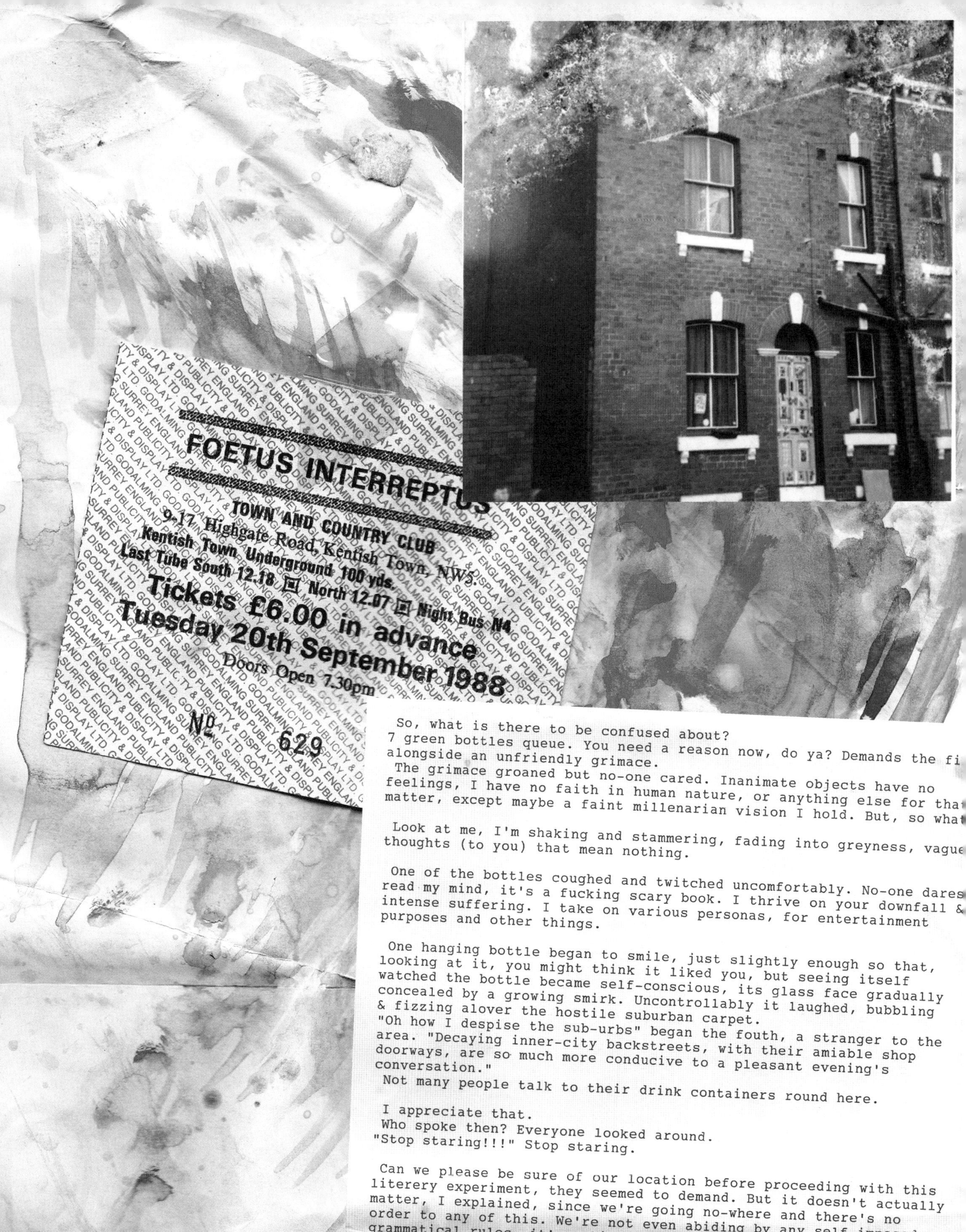

FOETUS INTERREPTUS
TOWN AND COUNTRY CLUB
9-17 Highgate Road, Kentish Town, NW5.
Kentish Town Underground 100 yds.
Last Tube South 12.18 North 12.07 Night Bus N4
Tickets £6.00 in advance
Tuesday 20th September 1988
Doors Open 7.30pm
№ 629

So, what is there to be confused about?
7 green bottles queue. You need a reason now, do ya? Demands the fi alongside an unfriendly grimace.
The grimace groaned but no-one cared. Inanimate objects have no feelings, I have no faith in human nature, or anything else for tha matter, except maybe a faint millenarian vision I hold. But, so what

Look at me, I'm shaking and stammering, fading into greyness, vague thoughts (to you) that mean nothing.

One of the bottles coughed and twitched uncomfortably. No-one dares read my mind, it's a fucking scary book. I thrive on your downfall & intense suffering. I take on various personas, for entertainment purposes and other things.

One hanging bottle began to smile, just slightly enough so that, looking at it, you might think it liked you, but seeing itself watched the bottle became self-conscious, its glass face gradually concealed by a growing smirk. Uncontrollably it laughed, bubbling & fizzing alover the hostile suburban carpet.
"Oh how I despise the sub-urbs" began the fouth, a stranger to the area. "Decaying inner-city backstreets, with their amiable shop doorways, are so much more conducive to a pleasant evening's conversation."
Not many people talk to their drink containers round here.

I appreciate that.
Who spoke then? Everyone looked around.
"Stop staring!!!" Stop staring.

Can we please be sure of our location before proceeding with this literery experiment, they seemed to demand. But it doesn't actually matter, I explained, since we're going no-where and there's no order to any of this. We're not even abiding by any self imposed grammatical rules, it's entirely inconsistent.
You could start by spelling the words right, suggested one arrogant and quite outspoken git of a Skol Special Strength...You've fuckin' had it MATE i calmly whispered, grabbing it's thin neck & thenceforth watching the opaque green coloured material of which it was composed take off in a thousand little directions starting from the wall, my arm jolting back as the blow occured and we saw how dead it now was or is, how much more space it can cover when it no longer contains liquid, and rules.

Violence. They all shuddered at the thought.One or two began small and insignificant conversations and a couple actually left the room. Some party this has turned out to be, I thought,

Ablaze! 6

Publication date: Early 1990

"*Ablaze!* is a huge scary creature, a living story, created in spite of the severe hazards of life."
Somehow we had reached 1990.

At a Stretchheads and Dandelion Adventure gig in Edinburgh in the late summer of 1989, things got really strange. Simon Morris, still my boyfriend, started to malfunction. Like when a digital watch that used to tell the time suddenly switches to a readout of random figures and non-figures, he flipped in an instant from my closest friend to someone I didn't know at all, whose language I couldn't understand. I sat with him in Karen (Archbishop) Kebab's flat, looked at him and held his hand, but didn't know what to do.

Simon was ill. I knew he had suffered at least one severe psychotic episode in the past; naively, I hadn't thought it would recur. After eight months of apparent stability he just... disappeared. It was as if he had died, while leaving someone else in a body that looked kind of like him. The replacement Simon walked and talked but it was all broken-up, weird shit. While his body adjusted to the internal torture of medication, his mind found ways to resist the imperialist invasion of psychiatrists. It was a long time before they let him out of the hospital.

The night Simon went mad, we travelled back to the North West in the back of the Dandelion Adventure van. A traumatic couple of hospital visits ensued. I felt too stressed to carry on with my course so took a year out from university, went a little bit crazy myself, and then got back on the Ablazey horse.

The swirly cover was designed by William Potter, who claims, somewhat improbably, that I designed the rest. He had certainly empowered me with the knowledge that nothing looks better than dot-screened photos enlarged on a photocopier.

What you probably can't tell is that the cover features images of personnel from each featured band and was meant to be in a much deeper pink, rendering the images visible. But there had been something of a print liaison fail: I'd told them the colour we wanted, and they used a different one. It serves me right though; I'd elected to have it printed at Salem Church, a sinister-sounding organisation in Leeds that used Youth Training Scheme labour – essentially, sullen and unwilling lads with no other option but to work for really low pay. One or two people pulled me up for this at the time and they were right to do so. I should have thought on. But printing costs had gone up, and I was pretty defensive about the cover price increase to £1.50, a lot of cash in fanzine land.

Me: "Want to buy a fanzine? It's got interviews with Mudhoney, Rollins, fIREHOSE and..."
Yorkshire bloke, spluttering into his beer: "ONE POUND FIFTY? I could get a pint and two packets o'crisps and still have change out of one pound fifty!"

Issue 6 rolls open with a very charming interview with Mike Watt. I can remember neither this interview nor the associated gigs; all that remains is an impression of the warm glow of his powerful wattage.

Band of Susans had been slated by Sonic Youth as the worst band ever, but they were a powerful force of multiple guitars drifting towards pop structures. On reading their interview I was pretty impressed at how, suddenly somehow, I was able to write coherently about music. On the second reading I realised that this was not my work at all, just another victim of the missing writer credits. A young man called Vaughn Allen, here using the name Vee, was responsible for introducing the first signs of polish and professionalism to *Ablaze!*, with his confident, emotionally-engaged writing, although his subjects just weren't playing the game. He asks the Susans if they were "taking guitars along new avenues"; perversely they claimed to be simple rock'n'rollers and not experimentalists at all. Masquerading thusly as dumb yanks, they use their platform to bitch about the temperature of British beer.

Sheffield scordaturists A.C. Temple were at the height of their powers. They had just produced a perfect third album, *Sourpuss*, and were sending the indie cognoscenti into ecstasies with their heavenly shows. This piece summarised everything I felt about them, except that I had a thing for their bassist. They really were that glorious, and I still recommend you experience that particular album if you can bear their brisk English energy and the dazzling reflection of sun on guitar strings.

Before I re-read the The Sun and the Moon interview, or even realised that it was there, I had a dream about The Chameleons. I found them playing a show in a Buddhist Centre, as you do. They were really, really, nice and they invited me to tour Europe with them. Happy dream! The waking reality is that I never saw Mark Burgess in either of these bands, and was immensely grateful to Phil Throd (now of Cath and Phil Tyler fame) for this snippety interview. What became of them? What became of Mark? I need to know. Wikipedia tells me that he is still alive and has formed an array of bands, often with rather grandiose names, including a Chameleons rerun which I am gutted to have missed out on. Someone will probably now tell me that I have already seen The Chameleons, but my memory's hazy. They were a mythical band, and I suspect they were overlooked by the media as simply a northern phenomenon. Dreamlike and passionate and a little bit gothy, they made deeply evocative songs that refuse to be forgotten.

Sd played his drums like a well trained gorilla

Running Order:
7.00 pm : The Doors.
7.15pm - 7.40pm: Records by Tony the greek.
7.40pm - 7.50pm: Frank Sidebottom.
7.55pm - 8.30pm: The Membranes
8.35pm - 9.10pm: Alternative T.V.
9.10pm - 9.25pm: Interval
9.25pm - 10.45pm: The Chameleons.

Henry Rollins, on the other hand, was memorable for being a jerk. He rounded on me and my sweet friend Emma for our correct use of the word awe. We were paying him a compliment, which doubtlessly arose from a sense that we needed to appease this violent egomaniac, bragging about the weights he can lift and the teeth he knocked out. It's an encounter I've retold sometimes to impress the boys, but from the evidence we have here, he was a frightful bore.

Hopefully Henry has grown up and moved beyond baring his teeth at little girls. He is well-remembered in Leeds, where there is an abiding legend of his having once lived in a house on the Harolds. Leodians are keen to speculate about which house it might have been, or even to declare gleefully that they reside in the Rollins house. Should one contest such a view, declaring that he merely stayed at his guitarist's place occasionally, uproarious protest is guaranteed.

My account of the Mudhoney debacle given here is patchy. Ross remained conscious a lot longer than I, so his account earlier on in the book adds a few salient points.

A.C. Temple bassist Chris Trout also had his own band. It's obvious now, looking back on the Kilgore Trout interview, that he was chatting me up. "You should see my bedroom" was an invitation that I did decide to take up, having a massive crush on this prolific and magical songwriter. We began a relationship which lasted seven years, and during the first three he became a mainstay of the good ship *Ablaze!*, under the nom de plume Lucy Nation.

(In case you think that my praise for the Trout back catalogue was fuelled by other motivations, I can assure you that, even now, that stuff stands up, especially if you like intense-to-the-point-of-panic, melodic mid-eighties post-punk.)

My journalistic approach was pretty superficial: I was straight up there on the surface of things, asking how the soundcheck went. Bands might have been waiting for more probing questions, but most of the time, analysis was not on the menu. Then I'd go home, transcribe the conversation and add a bit at the end about how ace they were - honest fanzine fare.

Live Skull, though, were one of my most beloved bands, and this interview gets nowhere near their essence. I wish I'd got to talk to guitarists Mark C and Tom Paine, original members and originators of the Live Skull sound. On the positive side, Thalia Zedek has some interesting things to say about their lives in Manhattan, and you get to learn about Mr Snuffer. And at least I saw them before they split up, which happened shortly after this tour.

There were a couple of anomalies in the record review section. I'm not sure why I was dissing Paul Smith (Blast First Records head honcho), but this was another case of biting the hand that feeds. And I don't think David Gedge and Satan actually reviewed anything, unless they did and I didn't credit them.

I tended to address the readership of this issue in derogatory terms, like the raddled captain of a pirate ship. In fact my own attempt at piracy – the launch of a Leeds radio station called Fervour FM - was foiled around this time due to shipmates not showing up as agreed. So when one of my tutors suggested that it might not be such a great idea to run a zine, launch a radio station *and* do a degree and all at the same time, it was Fervour that got the elbow.

After 18 months at the lovely Hopewell Place, I was evicted. My friend and landlady Jean had evidently become sick of me and decided to tell me straight. It's true that I was not the most thoughtful housemate; I'd had Mudhoney round for an all-night drinking session, played music stupidly loud, and didn't do the washing up. Yet I hadn't seen this coming - it was a massive shock.

One day shortly after receiving this news, I wandered into town, burdened by thoughts of impending homelessness. I was going to have to find somewhere to live, all by myself, and I'd never done that before, and the eviction experience was not making me feel confident about sorting out a new tenancy.

But there was something in the air. It was... summer! I was traipsing past Leeds University's landmark Parkinson steps when it came in on the breeze, and caused my heart to leap with the promise of brighter times.

And the very next moment, Ross Holloway appeared. Right on the back of the first sign of the best time of year, his arrival was portentous. I told him of my predicament.

"Come and live at ours," he said, "We've got a spare room."

And so I moved into the Purple Eternal residence, 6 Ebberston Terrace in Hyde Park. I took up the spare room[1] rent-free, and marvelled at how these young men could survive on a diet of booze and drugs, alongside an exercise regime that consisted of kicking in walls, smashing stuff, yelling at each other and occasionally playing a gig. It was impossible to cook, due not only to the permanence of grime – nobody was doing any cleaning here – but also the way that Karl would ceremonially destroy one piece of crockery every day.

In return they had to put up with my constant playing of Throwing Muses tapes - filled with emotionally-charged female voices, anathema to their boyrock way of being - and with my fighting with Chris Trout, whom the Eternals quite admired for his intrepid drug consumption. It was a perfect experience of landing on my feet, and I'm purple-eternally grateful for their kindness. But after six chaotic and hungry weeks, and with their landlord due to visit, it was time to get out.

What we've left out:
Interviews with Nomeansno, Shrug and God, Swans tour diary, record reviews, demo reviews, fanzine reviews, flexidisc stuff.

[1] In 2009, this same room became the scene of a murder, when a fine art student was killed by a burglar who had thought that no-one was home.

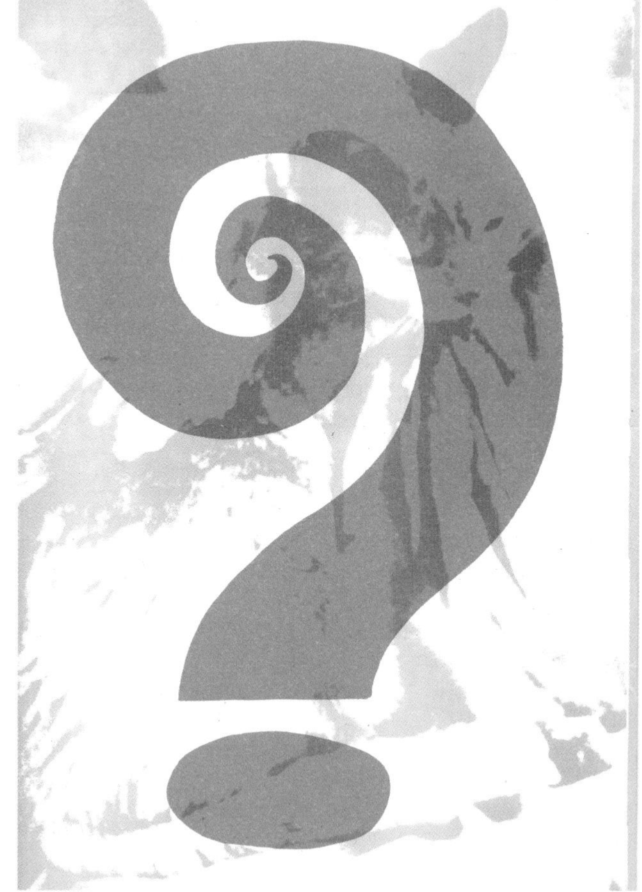

ABLAZE!

SWANS
MUDHONEY
ACTEMPLE
FIREHOSE
BAND OF SUSANS
HENRY ROLLINS LIVE
SKULL
KILGORE TROUT
NOMEANSNO

£1.50

with EDSEL AUCTIONEER, NERVE RACK, NITRO PUPPY and SANITY PLEXUS

ABLAZE! OF KITTENS
CRACKED HOUSE
8 HOPEWELL PLACE
LEEDS LS6 1PN

Solemnly we hereby equip you with your noise-bible for the 90's, the 6th incarnation of the north's blazey monster.

A few points to note:

CENSORSHIP! of your favourite scumzine has occured, out of respect for our printers at Salem Church. So you'll find that all F-words herein are sprinkled with asterisks - now we're just like the NME, ho ho.

A PRICE INCREASE! has indeed taken place, due to increased production costs. Don't like it? Well, you didn't HAVE to buy it. The response to issue 5 was so favourable that we feel our readership is intelligent enough to appreciate the value of this publication, so...

THANK YOU! to everyone who has given support and inspiration. You may or may not know who you are (we attract all kinds of identity-crisis types!).

ABLAZE! is a huge scary creature, a living story, created in spite of the severe hazards of life...Untie your dreams and head for the ultimate...

burning love,

Karren Ablaze!

Karren A.

WHAT YOU GET:

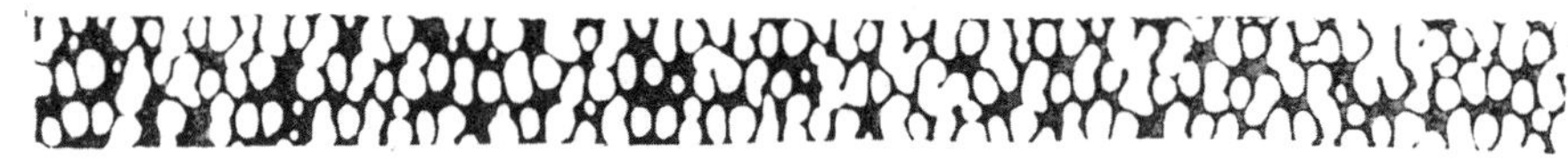

HASSLE MERCHANT:

Karren Ablaze!

CONTRIBUTORS - WORDS:

Andrew Truth
Anthony T.
Ashley Horner
Doug Aikman
Jeane Moffat
Mike Mean
Old Trout
Phil Throd
Shaun Tackhead
Simon Morris
Steve Hawkins
Tony Armpit
Vee
Bob Z.

PICTURES: LAYOUT

David Slade
Neil Dainty
William Potter (cover)

PHOTOGRAPHS

Paul Greco
Tony Woolgar
Wosia

THANKS TO:

All contributors
Good bands everywhere
Liz & Pat Naylor
Colin at RT Dist.
Gerard Cosloy
Dave Simpson
John Keenan
My friends
My family.

To celebrate Sonic Youth's leaving Blast First and signing to some major label for lots of money, here is an exclusive interview, conducted by Tony Armpit.

"I don't care about all the hype. We're a world class band at this point, it's that time now." Lee Ranaldo.

Tony Armpit:"Do you like the sound of vacuum cleaners?"
Kim Gordon:"Oh! I just bought a really expensive vacuum cleaner. I forget what it's called now but it's some kinda luxurious one. When we first started we had a drill which we put through a wah-wah pedal, but the drill broke and we couldn't find another one with the same kind of tone so we stopped using it."
T:"You've moved on from using screwdrivers and other appliances..."
K:"Well the tunings are more involved now, we don't need screwdrivers."
T:"Lee, with the sounds being so abrasive on your solo LP 'From here - infinity' , complete with grooved picture in the vinyl, it could be dangerous for record players - had you considered this?"
Lee Ranaldo:" I never looked at it that way. I really thought people would pick a track and leave it on all day, at least an hour. All the tracks are chance. I don't think it's damaging, it's just the sounds are so harsh...unless you try play the drawing, which some people seem to have. Then your needle's gone."
T:"Hendrix still excites me & this evening (Manch uni) it felt similar..."
L:Well at one point I actually felt the ghost of Jimi Hendrix fluttering over the stage."
T:"I was asking Kim before about the various sounds of vacuum cleaners."
L:"I definitely like the sounds of vacuum cleaners. In fact some friends of mine in New York did a rock piece which was a transcription of a Rhys Chatham song called 'Guitar trio for wind instruments'. It involved 4 vacuum cleaners through amps, I swear to god this happened, it was great."
T:"How about other household items, like hairdryers? "
L:"I really like the sound of a new metal fan being switched on, it goes through a complete overtone thing.
T:"I believe you've used drills before - how did it work out?"
L:"We didn't find it overly but on the Ciccone LP the track 'Needle gun has the sound of jack hammers mixed into it. Unfortunately they're too identifiable and there are better things but I can't think of one right now.
Was Mark E Smith here tonight?"
T:"I didn't notice him, why?"
L:"Well we have this sort of dialogue happening.
T:"Can you tell me?"
L:"No not really, it's very personal."
T:"Oh go on."
L:"Well it might have something to do with him being obnoxious."
T:"Kim, have you any future desires, in music maybe?"
K:"I'd like to see acid house music die very quickly and also I'd like to see all the english weekly papers go bankrupt."
T:"I see. Were you an insubordinate at school?"
K:"Yeh I was part of the Chicago Five. I went under the name of Bernadene & played in the Weathermen. In fact this guy Raymond Pettibone has documented what happened & it's coming out soon."
T:"Oh yeh. Thanks. See ya."

sonic Yout
York live p
'rock' inst
nd, Sonic Y
red a collab
nation wit
anson, app
s. Moore,
of Glenn,
ous melod
by occasio
lets. In this
classified
lly placing

GIMME THAT STARPOWER

fIREHOSE

Mike Watt was sat in a Mexican restaurant trying to eat his tea. He'd called us over to do an interview so I bolted my beer and braced myself. He looked like a loony. I had been on the verge of cancelling this meeting when I first met the guy, but couldn't get the words out of my head. "Don't be scared," he'd warned me.

I had to do it though. A few nights before, fIREHOSE had appeared at the Boardwalk in Manchester like the sun appearing on the Eastern horizon when you've not been to sleep all night. They did some awesome rock'n'roll and were set to do the same for the kids piling into the Duchess of York tonight.

I gave him a copy of issue 5 and as he saw Kim Gordon's image on the cover, he began talking about his friends, another racing flow of words in his totally music, bass voice:

"Kim, Thurston, Lee, Steve Shelley - Ciccone Youth!"

Did you inspire them to start doing Madonna cover versions?

"Well, that was my way of gettin' back into the music scene after D. Boon [Mike's musical partner in the Minutemen] was killed. I flew to New York, and I stopped by their house and I said, y'know cos I was into Madonna before that, 'I'm gonna make a Madonna record,' and Thurston says 'I wanna be on the other side!', and that's how Ciccone Youth was made. Then there was this LP, I only have one song on that, I made it in my house first...I never imagined it'd be on a CD!"

"What's on your mind, about fIREHOSE?" he asked me, a question that startled me with it's bluntness, but it soon became clear that 'Superficial talkin' ' doesn't go down well with Watt.

OK then - I want to know how you do it.

"In a way I come from a tradition, I was in power trios since I was 11, with D. Boon...In them days y'didn't have to worry about why y'did it, you just did it, and then punk came along and y'could play in front of people...We've been doing that same thing but with a different band..."

It seems like playing comes so naturally to you.

"But we're boys! Actually his [D. Boon's] mum got me onto bass, I was guitar for 4 months, so it was kinda natural, we learned together that's all. It's different with fIREHOSE cos I didn't learn with them."

I heard a nice story about how fIREHOSE started.

"Ed just came to my house...in America you have to pay to unlist your phone number, so my phone number was in the book, and he called me and came over, literally. I didn't put ads out or anything. That's the way bands should be, they should be organic, they shouldn't be collections of superstars, I think.Then, what do I know? I've only been in 2 of 'em...3 of 'em...4 of 'em!

What were the bands before the Minutemen?

"Just me and D. Boon. We played with other people, but before punk rock you cou'dn't do your own gigs. It was a much different world, you just played in your room, copied records, it was real stupid! It was the stupidest thing I ever did in my life."

It's good practice.

"No, I think as soon as you get a guitar you should be writing songs, but that was the mentality of the 70's, it had to be destroyed. I hope there's not bands sitting in their rooms copying fIREHOSE. That was the neat thing about punk rock - these guys didn't know how to play but they're doing it anyway! That was righteous. It sounds naive now...after a couple of years they'll learn, but they'll learn their way, not...they've got these things now, video tapes that show you how, it lays it out for ya, it destroys songwriting. Songwriting comes from here [thumps chest]. Copying records, I guess that's a little more individualistic cos at least you gotta use your ear to do it, not some video tape! I saw it in a music store in London, this guy showing you how to do this bass solo in 'My Generation', and the song 'My Generation' was all about, y'know, destroying that! It's the snake eating itself, probably it'll go on like that forever.

Is there anyone you'd like to collaborate with?

"Madonna!"

Is that your ambition?

"Well, my ambitions are the songs. They're my wars."

Does she know you want to work with her?

"No!! I haven't told anyone that, you're the only person I've told. I think a lot of that stuff's chance, I mean the Sonics, that was out of the blue, honestly. Well, me and Thurston met years ago in a club in Hollywood, I wrote a song about it, and we talked

about Richard Hell. There's a song on 'If'n', called 'Me and you rememberin'', and it's about that. I had a lot of bad memories back then, and sadness, and I was trying to figure what it is when you remember."

Oh right.

"I had a lot of bad memories right then, and sadness, and I was trying to figure **what is it** when you remember..."

You don't get that context, hearing the record.

"I'm tellin' ya, it was just something that really happened, so I just take things and make them songs...See that's my real battle, somehow workin' the specialness of everyday life and makin' it..." He searched a moment for the right word, then made a fist at the tape recorder. "There, for the tape recorder! Make it like that!"

For some reason he started talking about beards.

"I only do beards on tour cos I shave and get rashes; hate beards, hate beards! Whatever, touring aint real in a way, the whole day spent devoted to one event..."

Band followers do that too - do you know Steve, and Mat? (Two legendary liggers - if you aint met them you aint been to a gig.)

"Ha ha them dudes who come to all them gigs!!?"

Yup.

"But y'know, in a way that's kinda neat & special. But in another way, man, see, my life is a **full** day...It takes a lot of colours to make a rainbow, truly, so."

"I dig playing for the different dudes. One thing: if I can work a town I get to see it - y'understand, if I didn't do this for a living, I couldn't see anyone; I live in a one room apartment, we're not rich. So, in a way I will make the sacrifice of doing one thing, make the sacrifice in order to check out your pad. It's neat! They lie to you in the media over there about Europe..."

Do you get time to look around cities?

"I wake up at 8 every morning, I can't help it. At home I wake up at 6 - I'm a different kind of rock'n'roller, I'm a kind of...dude! But I walk around the whole town, check it out, every tour. So in a way, if I sound negative I aint."

fIREHOSE

HOSE

Go to pg.144

THE BEST BAND IN THE WORLD

The first phaze took place in the Duchess of York pub, Leeds, during the afternoon of Thursday 18th of May, 1989. Those present included the entire personel of Sheffield art noise band A C Temple, Mr Gob-shite and myself. Tony Woolgar went off to buy a can of coke and was not seen for hours.

For some god-weird reason the members and entourage of Birdland, crap blond-boy jangle rock band, were arriving and playing Pixies songs very loudly.

"They've got a cat with them," remarked Jane, A C singist.

"Is it bleached?" asked Chris the bass creature.

AC temple

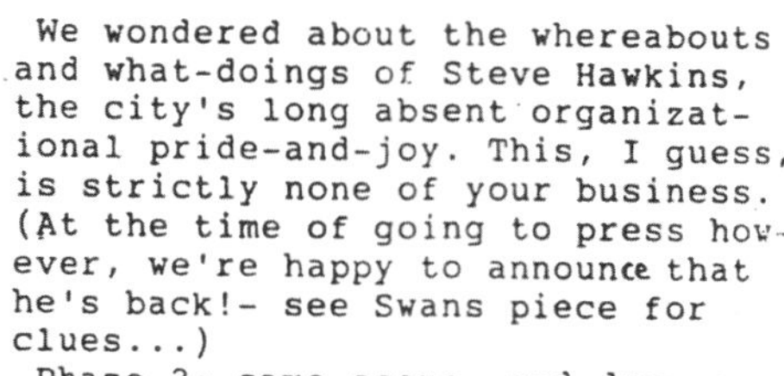

We wondered about the whereabouts and what-doings of Steve Hawkins, the city's long absent organizat-ional pride-and-joy. This, I guess, is strictly none of your business. (At the time of going to press how-ever, we're happy to announce that he's back!- see Swans piece for clues...)

Phaze 2: same scene, and drummer Matty is drumming with beermats on the table right next to my tape-recorder. People are shuffling. "Questions questions" mutters someone, impatiently. I'm cowering in the corner awaiting inspiration.

"Tell us the whole story of A C Temple, right from the beginning," I suggest, in order to give myself a bit of time.

Jane begins:"A long time ago, in a little market town in England, a boy was born called Noel Kilbride, at the same time as a whole load of other musical people, and he went to college and he met these people and they started a band, the band moved house and some other people came along, and the new A C Temple was formed in June 1988."

There have been various line-ups then, the group having had about 10 different members so far, according to Noel's estimate. The current A C Temple is a wonderful 5-piece thing.

Jane:"Noel's the only original member, and I've been with them for 2½ years."

Noel:"Chris plays in Kilgore Trout, Tim does weird things, he used to drum in the Dust Devils. We're a Yorkshire supergroup now, a combin-ation of Kilgore Trout, Midnight Choir, Dust Devils, Beserker Joe, Absolute and A C Temple."

Jane:"We're the least successful band on a successful English label, there's a huge music paper conspiracy against us...we're the best kept secret in rock!"

Obviously A C Temple reside just a few too many miles past Manchester for our dear British journos to be able to appreciate them. Unsurpris-ingly, this is a very sore point; as Jane sadly recounts:

"It's like maybe two of them came to see us 3 years ago and they didn't like us so that's it; there's no idea that the band might have developed or matured at all."

Jane Bromley

Noel Kilbride

Despite my complete lack of faith in most things musicpress-like, I'm certain that this state of affairs will gradually alter - no-one can be so utterly stupid and deaf...At least European writers seem to know what they're doing.

As the band also suffer from the negative side of the inverse talent: audience size ratio, a little moaning is justified.

Jane:"We're enjoying a revival at the moment, which makes me think we've had our peak cos no-one came to our gig in Rotherham the other week."

Noel:"8 people came to see us in Sheffield last week."

Tim:"No it was 11, 11 paid."

Chris Trout

Heavy interrogation time is here - why, I want to know, did the band fall to bits after "Blowtorch", their 2nd LP? Noel's "Serious ideological differences amongst other things" is not accepted, Sean Gobshite has a dramatic story of a row occuring in the face of industrial action at a British seaport...

Noel:"The truth you mean? The truth is a many sided story with certain reducible facts which will always go down in history as whether to cross a picketline, or whether not to cross a picketline.

"We'd just recorded the LP and had certain disagreements over the original mix of it, and there'd been a build-up of pressure...basically the people in the group didn't like each other..."

Jane:"The thing came to a head just before the LP came out, over the proposed trip to Europe. Some people decided they didn't want to do it anymore.

"It was such a desperate time, it was very urgent that we found new people, and because of that, the whole atmosphere led to a good band being formed quickly. It was quite an exciting period and since then it's just got better and better."

Noel:"Which band was this?"

Tim Beckham

Photos: Wosia

Matt Silcox

Phaze three and things were dissolving in the Duchess so Jane and I retired outside to the pavement, where the Birdland soundcheck wasn't so audible, and we talked about interesting things. It emerged that she is a student teacher.

"What do you teach?" I asked.

"Infants."

The idea certainly appealed to my imagination; mad Jane rolling her eyes around, controlling her naughty pupils with a fearsome roar, stood at the front of the class like she's swaying onstage. The kids don't know about A C Temple, it's probably the sort of thing that would give them nightmares, and she hadn't yet had the chance to teach them musical-type things; these are two quite separate parts of her life, but when I listen to her singing "Crayola" this is always brought to mind.

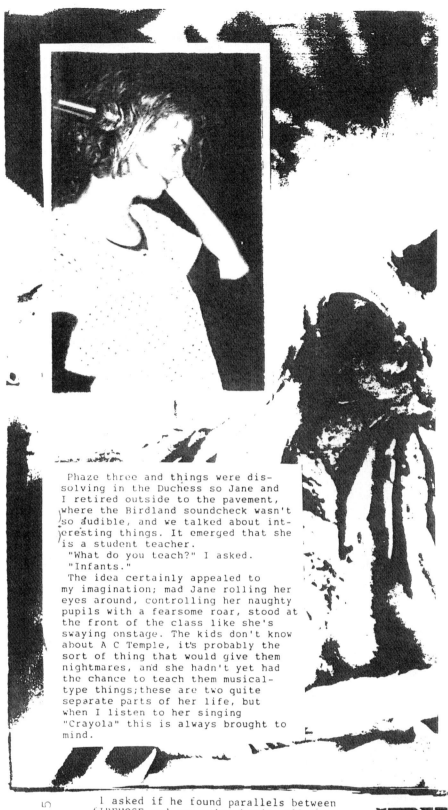

Phaze four sees me stood with lots of other people gazing at a stage on which 5 people are doing amazing things with musical instruments. We're starting to sway about uncontrollably as the newest A C Temple sound issues from the speakers. They have come such a long way since "Blowtorch"; from something fine to these incredible new songs that are sparkly as hell. They said that these would be on their next LP and I knew it was really going to be an intensely splendid record.

A few months later, as if to prove me right, "Sourpuss"was released on Blast First. "Sundown Pet Corner", the first song, is the most joyful thing I've ever heard, showing their newfound confidence and even featuring wild HM-style guitar solos. Except maybe for the second track, "Miss Sky", with delightful poppy words delivered in breathless wonder. Chris and Jane duet on "Stymied", bringing in a mournful note, sorry tales, but with that iceskating engine band battering at everything everywhere...Once when I was little and it was coming up to xmas, my dad phoned santa to check that the presents were coming along OK. I spoke with santa on the phone, and he let me hear the elves and the fairies working away in the workshop at the North Pole. This is what the beginning of "Horsetrading" is exactly like - do not doubt my words. This LP captures them building icecube towers that drip and melt in the brilliant sunshine. You will never have heard anything like this because it's stronger, stranger, braver and more intricate than any other warped mechanical icemirror dreamworld you have previously known...I swear.

"Sourpuss" is the ultimate refutation of every word ever printed in the music press. A record to wake up to if you're ever scared of the day, and to carry round screaming in your head all day...it's pretty good.

On the basis of this, and mind-shattering gigs that have since occurred all over the land (& beyond, of which I've only seen video'd evidence) it's fair to say that A C Temple is the chief contender for the Best Band in the Known Universe Award. Their only challenge comes from...ah, I'm not allowed to say. Just get yourself to that Kilgore Trout article as soon as I've told you about...

Phaze 5, the future: A UK tour, a new LP, and inevitable world domination for A C Temple. Don't try and tell me it's just a phaze...

From pg. 5

f

I asked if he found parallels between fIREHOSE and any other bands. All I could think of was Nomeansno with their stoppy-starty songs.

"Yeh, I met those guys, 2 of them are brothers, they're good guys. They're kinda more in the Minutemen tradition, with the little songs! Well it's an older band, with D. BOON, this guy I keep talking about, see almost all my music was with him, so when I tell you about the past that's why I tell ya. Nomeansno is from there more. Y'see, Ed don't come from that, Ed is from the more straight, like, REM...Nomeansno is real angular, kinda European in a way."

"That's what fIREHOSE is like in a lot of ways: different things meeting, it's difficult to classify, but the tensions inside the band are different - like, some guy coming from pop & melodic meeting angular guys. It's hard for me to classify cos **I'm against it**, so I try to destroy that...

THE SUN AND THE MOON

If you ever had any sense in your head you will have been into the Chameleons. For this reason, you may also have appreciated the work of the Sun and the Moon. Oh, we don't need to justify the inclusion of this Mark Burgess interview, conducted ages ago in Newcastle by Phil of top Middlesbrough combo Celestial Orgy...yes all the stars are here...stick with it & you'll get the latest Sun and the Moon info too, at the end...

Phil: What did you think of it (Riverside gig)?
MB: I thought it was good, those that came were really sound.
- Why did you play the Chameleons song at the end? Didn't think you were going to do any.
MB: No, we weren't. We did in the Shetlands, they were so heavy up there that if we didn't they'd have skinned us alive, and tonight this lad kept going on about it, and Andy Whit, he was in the corner going 'Shall I or shaln't I?', and I thought he was talking about 'Faith' which is the Abbo's song that we do, so I said 'yes' and he started 'Don't Fall' and caught me on the hop. Y'know, I didn't expect it...but we don't mind.

- Why did you leave the Chameleons?
MB: Mmmmm it was boring really...never did anything, couldn't get 'em out of bed...I left in August '87, and we (the Sun & the Moon) started in September...
- What's the difference between the two?
MB: Well, I think the line-up's better looking, and I think...ummmm...we write different kinds of songs...more concentrated on songwriting rather than jam outs.
- All this ecology stuff...
MB: Well that's just down to the lyrics which is what I do. It would've gone in that direction anyway...
- Does it bother you that everyone wants to hear Chameleons songs?
MB: No, no it doesn't bother me, cos it's going to take us a while to sort of...carve our niche.
- Do you feel there's a kind of "macho element", like, lads on stage, fists in the air kind of...
MB: Well no, none of the girls ever get up, well a girl got up with us at the Astoria, but I mean it's an open invitation...the lads must have more bottle.
- Do you think it's got anything to do with the sort of music you play?
MB: Mmmmm I wouldn't know, I hope not. Can't answer that really, Freud might be able to help you. If he wasn't dead.

- Is this like a fulltime job?
MB: We're not making a living yet.
- Are you working?
MB: I do some work when I need it, fixing cars, labouring, anything, rather than sign on...
- Who was your favourite Doctor Who?
MB: Patrick Troughton.

We hope you enjoyed that little piece, now here is the news: the Sun and the Moon have kind of split up, but this isn't as bad as it sounds. Mark is keeping the name and is getting a band together for recording and live things this year, and in the meantime, apparently, he's gonna be doing some solo acoustic gigs. Also, Andy Whitaker, Andy Clegg, Aky and John Lever (an ex-Chameleon) are getting together under the name of Weaveworld, so it seems like a positive and productive kind of split, with no animosity or personalities clashing or anything like that.

"What I wanna do is: whatever style I play, y'could tell it's me, that's my goal: y'could go 'Oh I can tell that's Watt', even though I'd be playing reggae, or funky..."
D'you listen to lots of different things?
"I like Erik B & Rakim right now, Thurston turned me onto them...he's really observant, his eyeballs are like windows, he takes in everything he sees and then has a way of reorganizing it and telling ya about it that's really neat."
Can you tell me what the phone message you left, that's used on 'Providence', is about?
"Thurston came to see us play in NYC. We go to a store to buy some cassettes, he buys some cords, maybe $90 worth of stuff, and we go into the van and smoke a little bit of the ol' marijuana, so Thurston lost his memory, and I gave him some trash to throw out, and when he threw out the trash he threw out everything he bought, so the next day we played in Providence, Rhode Island, I called him up and said 'hey Thurston, I think I know where your shit is! It's in the Trashcan!' and that's what that's all about."
Last question: Did you call yourselves fIREHOSE so you'd have your name written in all public buildings?
"No, I got it from a Bobby Dylan song, 'Subterranean Homesick Blues'; 'Keep away from those that play around with firehose/ you don't need a weatherman to know which way the wind blows.' He did a video to it way back in the 60's, and he's holdin' up all these little cards, and one of them said 'firehose', it looks so funny. I chose the name, I didn't do it for publicity!"
Right! Thanks a lot!
"Thanks!"

It was really ace talking to Mike Watt, he is a dude and an inspiring one at that. The fIREHOSE LPs I know are 'Ragin' Full On', 'If'n' and 'FromOhio'. They're on SST. There's a brilliant Peel session that I really like, I've got it on tape if you want it. Right, that's it.

ROLLINS

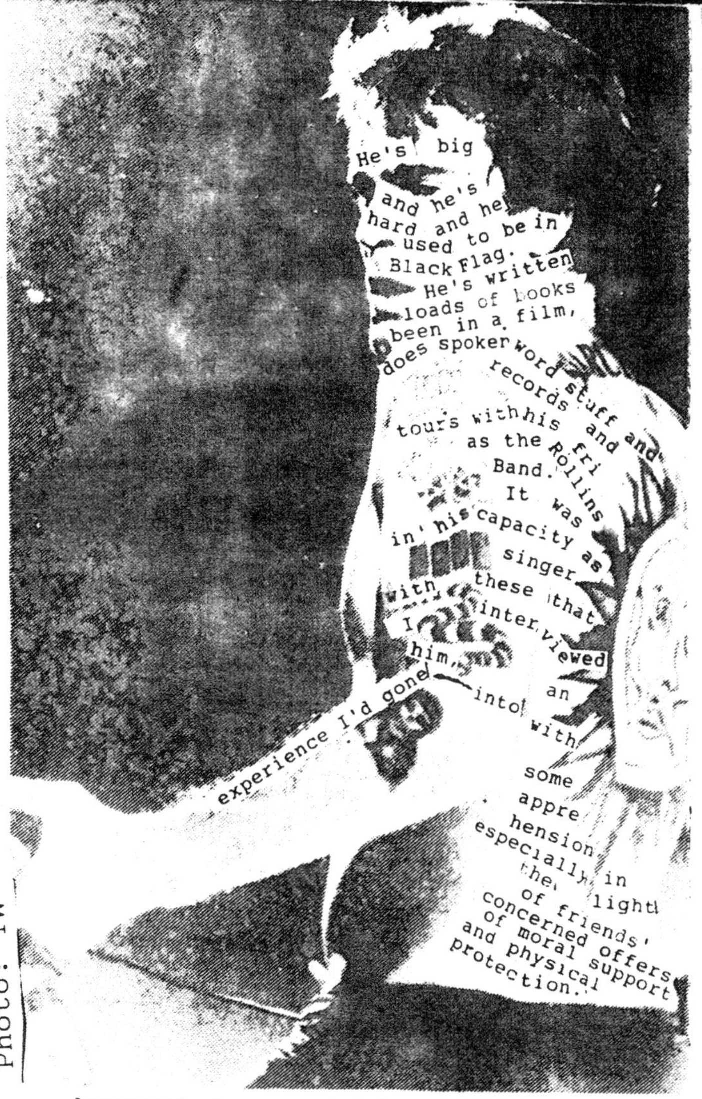

He's big and he's hard and he used to be in Black Flag. He's written loads of books been in a film, does spoken word stuff and records and tours with his friends as the Rollins Band. It was in his capacity as singer with these that I interviewed him, an experience I'd gone into with some apprehension especially in the light of friends' concerned offers of moral support and physical protection.

Photo: TW

Apparently he can make short work of interviewers who don't know what he's about. All I know is I saw this band play last year at Leeds Uni and they ******' rocked like hell.

I arrived at Leeds Poly in time to see a lengthy Rollins band soundcheck. As Simeon (drums), Chris (guitar) and Andrew (bass) were limbering up onstage, a dark haired, mean looking guy was doing push-ups and waving dumbells around in the centre of the hall. When he joined the others I heard a mighty bellowing sound fill the room. He claimed he didn't need a microphone, and proved it too.

Em and I slowly wandered over to him afterwards, and introduced ourselves. His greeting was so gentle that I thought we'd got the wrong guy. We all agreed we'd like to get the interview over with, and settled down to do so, beginning with some smalltalk:

I commented that they'd taken a long time doing the soundcheck, like the best part of 1½ hours. Henry reckoned that if you're the first band to soundcheck the sound people use that time to work out any problems with the PA, "so it makes everyone else's soundcheck go nice and easy."

"I hope so," I told him.(As it turned out, Nerve Rack, the first band on, barely got a chance to soundcheck and when they did it was in front of the audience. Because of all the delays their exciting set had to be cut short.)

The band have spent some time in Leeds in the past, recording LPs, doing shows and just "hangin' out". "I know a few people here and I've always had a good time playing here, people have always been really friendly."

Strange that people from so far across the sea should end up here. We wondered what attracted them to this wonder town.

"Err nothing. It's where the guitar player was living at the time, he went to school here."

The university?

"Yeh."

What did he do?

"He majored in philosophy. Heavy dude."

Weird. I'm doing that.

"Oh. Anyway, in '86 when Chris & I wanted to record he said "Why don't ya come over here because there's a good studio in town, a good engineer, and I know a good drummer in London.' So that's how it worked out..."

Where do you live?

"When I'm not on tour I live in Los Angeles. When the band practices we're in New Jersey, so we spend a lot of time on the East coast." They don't spend much time there though. "My usual cycle runs 10 or 11 weeks on the road, 3 weeks home. This time it's gonna be about 3 months on the road, one week home, 2 months on the road, 10 minutes home, I dunno..."

Doesn't all that work ever get you down?

"It keeps me charged up. It's what I like to do."

The name 'Rollins Band' struck me as somewhat egotistical; at best it sounds as though they were stuck for something better to call themselves. We asked him why they chose it.

"Because." He paused goodnaturedly (I think). "I'm Rollins, and they're the band."

But they're not just your backing band.

"No. I'm one-fifth of the band. Our band is 'guitar bass drums vocals sound. I'm only 20% of the band. When Black Flag split up I wanted to get another band together, but not another 'name' band, because I wanted to give myself the freedom to do 2 tours with the band and then never do it again without it being this thing where these guys would be 'Well I was in this band and the singer quit,' y'know? I wanna do exactly what I want - if I don't wanna play music anymore and just write books or go drive a milktruck, then I'm gonna do it.

Which brings us kinda neatly to the Rollins cover of a Pink Fairies song, a raging inspiring version of "Do it".

"Their version is really psychedelic and laid back. It was a song that always used to be on a tape in the van with Black Flag...we just made it more kind of hammered down..."

As the words go "Don't think about it...don't talk about it...don't write about it...don't sing about it - do it!" the song appears to criticize those activities that Rollins spends so much time doing; writing, talking, singing. But at the same time it seems to express his impatience at inactivity & self-deceit. We asked him if it lyrically summarizes his attitude.

"Somewhat," he answered with a friendly smile."Sometimes when I don't think and just do I fuc* up real bad. When you say 'don't think about it - do it,'yeh that's cool but sometimes taking one second out to think about something does the world of good. I learnt some serious lessons the hard way...I nearly killed a guy a few weeks ago and it really blew me away."

What happened?

"It's no big deal, just me being an asshole. I was in Australia and we were doing a photosession for this magazine against this cliff and y'know, 30 million metres down is the shore, it's like this beautiful mountain we're on, and the guy's setting up his photo stuff, and we're milling around and I'm taking big rocks and throwing them off the cliff just for something to do...I can't hear them hit the ground cos they're so far down, so I'm like 'OK, f**k, I'm gonna take this big ass rock and throw it off,' so I run up to this cliff," words run into each other now, a racing whirlpool of verbs "I go 'eurrrghh' and I throw it and I watch it go and see it falling and falling and falling and it hits the ground and explodes into a million pieces......... about this far away from a fisherman."

Photo: PG

He gestured to us in horror, and went on to spell out the implications of having a big rock dropped on your head from a great height, but I'm sure you can imagine that for youself...

"So I was like, god damn, shit, I nearly puked, the sheer stupidity of it...If I killed someone who was gonna kill me I wouldn't think twice about it..."

And he went on to tell us about someone he met at a show who happened to spit some beer at him:

"Three nights later I punched all his teeth out...I nearly lost my hand, they had to pull teeth out of my knuckles at the hospital..."

Was he alright?

"I dunno. I got his teeth at home...where I come from, you spit beer at someone, they stab you."

Sounds tough. You're very aggressive aren't you.

"Yeh, I'm aggressive. I'm male, yeh, but I don't go for the, like," he flexed his biceps a bit."I enjoy weightlifting, I enjoy working out, I'm a physical person. That was just dumbells," refering to his activity earlier on, " you oughtta see me when I get the real thing out, I'm working out like a motherf***er."

We didn't really understand why, and he began to sound annoyed.

"I'm workin' the muscles in my body. I prefer not to be fat, I prefer to be solid. I'm doing 52 shows in 56 days. I play extremely hard. If I wasn't in top physical condition I'd get destroyed by my own music, OK?"

OK. We don't mind. Your appearance ia somewhat awe-inspiring...

"If the idea of someone keeping their body in good shape is awe inspiring I'd hate to think of the lifestyle in which such a thing would bring them awe. You know what brings me awe?"

No. What?

NO MESSIN' BABY - DO IT!

"Teenagers that smoke and drink and shoot drugs and sit around and destroy their bodies. That puts me in awe, that blows me away. These kids are shit-faced out of their heads."

Maybe we were using the word "awe" in a slightly different sense here, but...do you despise them?

"I don't despise them. I despise the destruction done to their bodies. I like [illegible]ng people y'know, and I hate to see good young bodies get destroyed while the man gets richer. Where I come from in America, young black kids are shooting each other over crack, and who gets rich? Y'know, Bush. And the police love it, cos it's blacks killing blacks, it's the best thing that's ever happened to the LAPD. All they wanna do is contain it so that they're not shooting each other on Barbera Streisand's property."

"I'm 28 years old, I'm not 21, I'm not young, and I know a lot of people my age who I grew up with,& they're just fried man, f'k'n destroyed. I've seen what happens when you grow up doing that shit to your body."

He's alright, is Henry. A mite screwed up maybe, but who isn't? This becomes increasingly apparent if you take a look at some of his pubiished writings; we read "Body Bag', a collection of stuff, available from Creation books. The Rollins Band's new wreckoid, "Hard Volume", is intense and mighty as you might expect, but also has it's subtler moments. "Do it", the previous LP, is essential rock to wake your house up with. Both are on World Service records. As for talking to the guy, our brief encounter has shown us that he's fiercely into personal space and demands a lot of respect, no bad thing unless you fear your face being taken apart for accidentally stepping inside his void.

ROCKSHACK

GUITARS AND AMPS

ONE OF THE LARGEST STOCKS OF GUITARS IN YORKSHIRE

47 QUEENS ROAD, LEEDS 6
AND
MERRION SUPER STORE, MERRION CENTRE, LEEDS 2
TEL. 753175

The day broke without a sound to warn us, pure rising light as we lay in the silence of a creaking house and then our sounds, those of inane conversation and laughter, started to fill the world. But it is time for you to go and the world to end. Whispering your name I drifted outwards and dreams filled the vacuum, the absense of my favourite drug.

Events collide with one another in different realms, crossing across, and a ringing sound pulled my sleeping form from the bed, shattering it...I was grunting into the red receiver...Emma's voice was penetrating the clouds.

"Hello Karren?" it enquired. "Sorry, have i got you out of..."

What time...day...are you reminding me of something? "Emma, oh my god, Mudhoney were here...Jean's not speaking to me...there was a party, weird people in the cellar...Simon left at 6...the vodka...SubPop..."

She caught snatches of enfevered memories with wearied amazement, but asked "Have you been doing any work?"

Cancel the reality daze awhile , this is what happened (as far as the facts can congregate in my tiny brain): Yesterday waking was so irrelevant we saved it for the afternoon...we made our way to the city inadvertantly avoiding those cornershops conducive to providing beer anytime on a sunday in return for your cash, custom and extreme gratitude. Outside the venue two scruffy kids were seated on the pavement, in the cool air & faint summer atmosphere. It was Mark and Karl of the Purple Eternal. We sat with them.

Having been in and out of the venue we returned to the pavement, a crowd of us this time, centred by Simon who held the taperecorder. Ross, Mark and Karl were allowed to speak in loud voices about the trials and pleasures involved in being fairly young, fairly foolish and being in a fairly unknown trip rock band. I sat at the edge and observed who I now know as Mark,the singer/guitarer of Mudhoney, the main band set to play Leeds Warehouse that night. He walked into the street and inquired to the world in general, in impressive drawl, "Where's Karren Ablaze! ?", a pertinent question if I ever heard one.

I greeted him, asking about the availability of alcohol "Y'mean vodka?" he suggested. "Yeh, anything..."

And here the fun began, as Mark with the superbly sculpted nose reached into the van, picked up a 70cl bottle of clear liquid and handed it to me, much to the horror of his friends and much to my great delight. He grinned under his streaked blond hair veil and me and Simon went to macdonalds to get pissed.

The rest is a bit blurry. I think the Purples played a great set but were largely ignored, and Mudhoney rocked and I clinged onto Jeannie to stay afloat, and then they decided to do the interview at my house, the word went round, a crowd went back and I was supposed to navigate the van.

Well.

It takes 20 minutes or so to walk from the venue to our house, but the best part of an hour later the van pulled up at the front door, full of impatient Seattle-ites singing "You're no good, you're no good baby you're no good" at me. And you wonder why I'm paranoid.

Down in the cellar I sorted out my best journo voice and tried to ask the weirdos what they thought about the accusation that they blew Sonic Youth off the stage on the last tour, not an Ablaze! line I have to admit, but something to get the disaster started.

"I don't know if that's really possible," offers Mark, "cos what we're doing is so different from what they're doing, it's like saying that a lemon's better than a lime, or a pickle! It's like they're totally unsimilar, and if you like pickles better than lemons, then..."

I think we get the idea. Some comparing activity is bound to occur though, not only because of their support slots with da Youth, but the twin 12" heralding it, on which the 2 acts swapped songs. These worldly-wise creatures are too cynical however to get flattered by such whispered nothings:"Oh, they're just trying to get in on the guestlist anyway."

The question "How do you react to your fans?" was a pretty dumb one, in view of their seeming desperate search for groupies on tour, but they told us:

"Well, we let them ride in our vans and get them in on the guestlist, and sometimes we let them stay in our hotels...hahaha...we're hoping to be as big as the Mission someday."

And we wish them the very best of luck.

Then Hawkwind and Lemmy and GG Allin and then I got to ask a serious question (thanks to Emma of the IllogicalTortoises) : How come when you're onstage your beads don't hit you in the face?

Mark:"I've seen pictures with both me & Steve with out beads hooked round our noses...It's kinda like an engagement ring, or wearing your boyfriend's sweater or underwear, it's like saying to the world 'He's mine and I'm his,' and at night we sleep like this..." at which point, to our collective horror, they hooked their neclaces over one anothers heads.

Considering their uniform hairlength, I asked just how important they consider long hair to be.

"It's not important at all, except it looks good on video!"

"If god didn't want us to have long hair he wouldn't have made hair grow."

They did a version of Spaceman 3's "Revolution" that night so I asked them about it cos I could think of nothing better to say.

"Don't know them."

Oh god...

"'Revulsion', that's our song. Mark wrote that about the oppression of drug addicts."

Ross:"Yeh, you never have enough money."

Simon asked them if they'd seen the film Streetwise, this was the interesting bit, when they talked about their freak friends:

"My friend Slam's in it, Slam Hate, selling bis butt, he got hit by a car & his head smashed the windscreen, he's got the thickest skull in the world..."

"Pete from Dakota, he had the coolest Micheal Jackson fake leather suit, that guy was so awesome, once he turned up for the show wearing nothing but these blue spandex pants, he's the ultimate groupie..."

"There was a rumour going round Seattle for a while that Slam's dad was Richard Peterson, he was another addled person, he could tell you exactly how tall the top 20 buildings in the USA are, to the very inch, seriously.He's like this tall Johnny Mathis fan who's about 50 years old, he plays trumpet & piano simultaneously, keeps time with the chains that he rattles, & like he talks to himself, like one of these wandering crazy people...he has 2 albums out...he opens up for punk rock shows...Y'must have some characters like that in Leeds, like the Sisters of Mercy?"

"He used to do this '25¢ to answer any philosophical question'."

"Print this word for word...we wanna be the cover stars next issue..."

"Yeh, half of Mark's butt & half of Dan's butt."

Has anyone ever said Mudhoney is a dumb name for a band?

"I said that," said Mark.

"I don't like the name at all," said Steve. "I wanted to call it Steve, kind of short for Steve Is Really Cool And Neat And Goodlooking And Very Smart, but they thought that would be too long so we compromised on Mudhoney."

"I wanted to call it the Mervyns."

"Steve Mervyn And Two Other Guys..."

The tape machine continued to record drunken inanities while I went and crashed out somewhere. And that's what I'm gonna do now. This was the worst Mudhoney interview ever.

I hope everyone gets what they deserve.

THE KILGORE TROUT INTERVIEW

IN TWO PARTS
part 1, which isn't about music,
part 2, which is...
CHOOSE WHICH BIT YOU READ
and don't hassle me about it
(I left it mostly unparaphrased,
I liked it just the way it was.)

"Kilgore Trout"'s the name of a character in a book isn't it?

"Yeh, the character is in quite a few books by Kurt Vonnegut, including 'Breakfast of Champions', that's the best one. All the bits of it are written in short paragraphs that are really easy to read, and there's little pencil drawings in between...it's really funny. The character is an alter-ego for the author almost, which is something I didn't realize when I took it. Having called the band Kilgore Trout it occured to me that if we ever sold any records and got noticed by anyone and Kurt Vonnegut found out, he'd think 'That's someone really trading off my livelihood there,' cos it's a major feature of his work really."

You like books that are easy to read then?

"I like reading science fiction cos it's dead easy to read and says all kinds of dead meaningful things as well, but not in a way that books that have their meaningful ness writ large all over them do."

Isn't science fiction really trashy?

"It is, cos authors write SF cos they like the freedom to be able to do whatever they want, and go off on stupid ideas and be able to invent things so that their characters can go off and do whatever they want them to do. They'll more often than not go off and write really stupid stories...do you know what this is?" He stopped and pointed over to an enclosed area lit by floodlights. "It's not a football ground but occasionally there's talking from it."

It looks very sinister.

"Maybe it's dogs."

What???

"Greyhounds!"

Ah...(no need to be paranoid about dogs with megaphones holding floodlit meetings in Sheffield suburbs then)...What sort of person is Kilgore Trout?

"He's a SF writer himself, which Vonnegut is, and he writes millions of brilliant short stories....and lives on dogfood and cant sell any of themeven though he's really brilliant, and that's a kind of parallel with Kilgore Trout the group, possibly."

I can see that. This led to a discussion of band names during which I accused him of having chosen one which sounds whimsical, and he slagged off some other bands for their names, and we ended up talking about fish.

"You should see my bedroom. It's got so many fish in it, they cant all be human(?!)."

Live ones?

"Yeh, some live ones but they're so obscured by all this algae that grows in the summer that y'cant see them. No dead fish, although i' ve got no objection to having dead ones. I've got china ones and soft fuzzy ones & glass ones..."

Did you see that ladybird?

"No."

I disturbed it. It probably flew away.

"It will've done. There were loads of bees here earlier doing the clover.I've been here for hours, I've got better ideas of things to do than watch bands soundcheck when I've got to listen to their gig later."

Are you a rampant carnivore?

"Yeh, I mean no, err, I just don't like vegetables. This is like Smash Hits, you

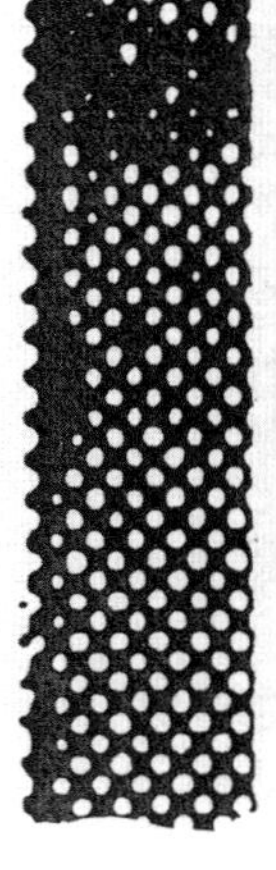

L G O R E
R O U T

asking me what kind of food I like." (Hardcore zines like to talk about whether people eat animals or vegetables too - ed.)

Well, it's more interesting than stuff about music anyway.

"Yes. I don't mind. Yeh, vegetables. I hate onions."

I think people who hate onions are really strange.

"Why? They're not bland, like, people who hate potatoes might be strange cos they're really just harmless things..."

Perhaps you're not strange mentally, perhaps you've just got strange tastebuds.

"D'you like meat?"

The taste of it? Yeh I could handle it when I was eating it, I thought it was nice.

"They're such an obvious - there's the ladybird, it's back- such an obvious thing to dislike cos they taste so strong, such a characteristic taste, I just wanna throw up when i taste them, when you get one on a sandwich by surprize."

You never liked them?

"No, cos when I was little I was at boarding school and for years and years and years you used to get given all this food and you had to eat it all. So I had to eat brussel sprouts and cabbage that had been cooked for 200 people by a couple of people so they'd been cooked in a big pot so they weren't even properly cooked and if I hadn't finished, cos I was a rarity there, by the pudding I'd be sat with it pushing the brussel sprouts round my plate, and afterwards if the master on duty was particularly sadistic, after lunch everyone would sit for half an hour and read a book to let their food settle, and I had to sit at the back of them with my still uneaten brussel sprouts and ONCE, this is dead interesting for your fanzine as well, once I had to have it brought out again at teatime...so that's why I don't like them."

Go to pg. 23

Live Skull did some dates in the U.K. last year and I caught up with them halfway through this mini tour, at the Barrel Organ in Birmingham. The first time you see a band is when the songs start to come alive, the photographs become people. The first time I met Thalia Zedek she was approaching all the strangers in the near empty pub, making discreet enquiries about the availability of amphetamines.

I watched the band soundcheck like a kid being introduced to the cast of Neighbours. Five mysterious Americans went on fusslessly and retraced the sounds of dreams, the real mirror of iceworld stuff.

Thalia is one of those people I describe as really **music**, a living song, one of those people who always seem to be singing or playing imaginary instruments, & they talk tunefully too. She's something untamed, a screaming bitch from the nasty side of New York City (you may have sensed something of this if you listened to the last couple of LPs, or if you witnessed her request for tequila during their set that night).

We did an interview a few nights later, when they played Leeds' Duchess Of York. The tape of this lengthy meeting that I didn't lose turned out to feature the new two-thirds of Live Skull; Sonda Andersson, Richard Hutchins and Thalia Zedek. Tom Paine and Mark C, the tall, serious looking guitarists, are the only original members remaining.

Too many people seem not to know or care about Live Skull. The band get nothing like the sort of press adulation that their peers Sonic Youth have been receiving for their similarly timed tour. Some people seem to think Live Skull are a sad gothgloom band... they're wrong, of course.

"We can't understand where that awful rumour started," muses Richard (drumplayer). "Like, I like some Joy Division and a couple of songs by the Sisters of Mercy but we don't sound like that. Maybe people think we're gloomy and we look like we don't eat...we're not that skinny...I dye my hair black...that's about it!"

"We get categorized into places we don't fit, so people who're into hardcore say we're dreadful cos we're supposed to be a hardcore band but we don't play it right, and people into gothic think we're noisy..." He continues:"We go from a couple of different styles, you could label one song this and one song that; it hurts us a lot to get pigeonholed."

Journohead attempts to do so can be quite amusing though.

"Yeh. 'New York art noise terrorists' is my favourite."

Like you go round hitting people with guitars.

"We do hit people with mikestands...in Paris."

"Crazy people," remembers Thalia.

Are you a violent person?

"Depends," is her enigmatic reply.

"She's mad," offers Richard helpfully.

"They were jumping on me, jumping on stage."

"They were like into it."

I asked Richard whether he agreed with my opinion that stagediving is an entirely pointless and stupid activity.

"No, I only stagedived once in my life though."

The language of Live Skull is often unintelligible and intriguing. Song titles rarely correspond to lyrics. 'Live Skull'- what does it mean? 'Bringing home the bait'- what's it all about?

"It's all arbitrary, to sound really cool.The songs are all love songs, except four."

They sound like they're about relationships that got a bit f--ked up.

Thalia: "A lot of the songs we do now were written during a period of my life when I was having a really hard time so they reflect that. The newer songs are like a little less angry.My favourite song [on 'Positraction'] is 'Amputease', but it didn't really come out that well on the LP. It's about letting someone put you to sleep and operate on you, and slice you up..."

Uh, did that happen to you?

"Well, not literally. Kind of like figuratively."

The bands' many line up changes are probably best illustrated diagrammatically. However I can't be bothered drawing one. The most recent incarnation seemed fairly stable (we thought...)

"We've been this way for about a year and if we keep touring this way there'll be another line up change! Musically I hope we're tighter, we got to know each other as people better, but if you're like with someone 24 hours a day, I mean sleeping with them, sitting with them, playing with them, eating with them...if you people see us arguing **we're not** breaking up, **we're not** kicking members out, we're just irritable cos we've seen too much of each other."

Thalia and Rich proceed to quarrel about some fight that occurred...

"I didn't hit you! You hit me!"

o you forgive each other quickly like brothers d sisters?
No."
h dear.
Sonda's like...once I fell into her...I was like lking to her today and she just walked off for d sentence," Thalia recalls, astounded." She tes me for something. Sonda can kick some ass n."

t was pizza time and everyone was munching. chard offered me some and I accepted, half refully avoiding bits of animals and worms erein. "I'll be eating beefburgers tomorrow cause of you," I told him.
'And stagediving."

I have to ask about the big blue god on the cover of 'Snuffer'...
"Well, it's a statue that Mark happened to pass on his vacation, and he's a photographer so he had his camera. It's in front of a travel agency."
"Someone was running for sheriff named Mr. Snuffer, who had big sideburns. Me and Tom, since we don't like to shave a lot on the road cos it takes a lot of fuss and cos if you get sores it cuts them open, got called after him.So first of all I was Mr. Snuffer, and then Tom was..."
(I hope you're following all this).
Where's the photo on the cover of 'Dusted' from?
"That's in New York City, it's now torn down but it used to be a pick up place for grown men. Mark, being the photographer, thought that with all those weird textures of everything crumbling, and the light, it'd be a great place to take pictures, so he took all these pictures and we liked them, the same as with 'Snuffer', we just liked the picture so we said 'how'bout we use them for the cover?' "
I got that kind of impression, like with the painting on the cover of the 'Pusherman' EP, it was just there so you used it.
"Yeh, that was right before I joined. I don't like that picture!" he admits.
It's kinda spazzy but it's good for that reason.
"I actually prefer all the covers since I've joined! Like the 'Positraction' cover, even though my hair's bleached on that photo - we **have not** changed drummers again!"
You all look so mean on that picture.
"Well, that's New York for ya," explains Thalia.
"I was really drunk during that session," Rich continues."It was in a great park out in Brooklyn. He's a great photographer, Michael Lavine. He used all this colour distortion and he put vaseline on the lens..."

You lot seem to put over a very serious, thoughtful image.
"Yeh, we got our serious sides," agrees Thalia, "but we're not serious people."
"We f--k up a lot," Richard admits.
"Our songs are serious doesn't mean we're like that all the time, or that we want to be. We have some stupid songs...a lot of stupid songs."
"I think individually though, our personalities are pretty intense," says Sonda,"Not so much hyperactive, but just the kind of people who live in Manhattan, under all the other stress."
"Yeh," joins Thalia,"living in Manhattan is like living in the warzone. It's like, you have to see all this gross shit every day -you go out of your house and there's someone dead lying in front of you."
"Our sense of humour's probably triggered by that," Sonda considers, her psychologist hat on, "because you have both sides, the dark and the light, and it's like you're living under the dark all the time, you have to get that emotion out somehow, and once you get it out you can lighten it a bit."
D'you think it damages you, living in a city?
Thalia:"It definitely makes you more f--ked up."
Sonda:"I think a lot of people there are damaged to begin with...otherwise we wouldn't be living there. There has to be something wrong if you chose to live where we live. I would say 99% of people who live on the lower East side , the East Village, are dysfunctional in some way or another."
Richard:"We're hooked on heroin!"
Sonda:"Also, it's nice to go to a place where you're not the only one like that...no it's true! It's really great to see someone who's more f--ked up than you are."
Thalia:"And the drugs are great! There are incredible people in New York you know. People are really together in a way cos everyone there is going through the same shit. It's definitely duller over here, New York's insane.
"I liked London - we were there for 24 hours so I can say. There's other places I haven't really been to, pulling up at 6 o'clock in the night, setting up the equipment, doing the soundcheck, having a few beers..."

Sonda:"I liked the tube."
!!?!
"Never never, no wait, never never never in Manhattan would you find a subway train with posters, padded chairs..."
Thalia:"No-one begging on the subways!(In a slow, mechanical voice:) 'I-am-not-a-bum,I-would-like-to find-a-job,'."
Sonda:"You'll find these fake amputees coming on, they'll wrap their legs up and put themselves on a little platform with wheels, and fake it! They'll go 'I-am-a-Vietnam-Vet,-I don't-do-drugs,-I-don't-wanna-shoot-up,-and,like,steal-from-you-so-I'm-begging-you-for-your-money,'and after a while you're like, 'please gimme a break!'
Thalia:"There's people like dying on the streets of New York..."
Richard:"Without exaggeration, we've hardly seen any here..."
T:"No-one's asked us for money since we've been here. It happens every single corner in New York."
S:"I give 'em money but I don't really have any to give. You have your favourite bums..."
R:"The crazy woman with the hat who's afraid to ask you, she's usually on 1st Avenue..."
T:"I was on the corner of East 4th Street, there's one who really looks like she's about to die...it's really weird, it sticks in your mind a lot."
S:"This is the new thing in Manhattan, instead of asking you for money they just go (Rasping, screaming:) 'HELP!!HELP!!!'"
T:"You get angry, you get angry with yourself and you get angry with everyone."
S:"So music is definitely an outlet. Everything is an outlet, drugs is an outlet...sex is out."
Why?
S:"Cos New York is like the AIDS centre of the universe. Only the animals are safe! It used to be guys, gals and goats...now it's only goats."
T:"But it's a fun place to visit."
S:"It really is."

If you're in a band it seems sadly clear that an important way into people's hearts and sheeplike minds is through the music press. This is something Live Skull were hoping to utilize. At this point, though, it wasn't working. They'd just had a hopelessly unperceptive review of their ill-fated London gig printed in Sounds. I was gonna quote some of it for you but I wont, it's that worthless. All I can say: Sam King, get in touch with me sometime.

Since the time of this interview it has come to my attention that Live Skull have ceased to exist. This is such tragic news. On a personal level it means no more exquisite records and gigs to fuel my addiction, but it's pretty sad for you, too, especially if you never got to see them...oh...
I don't think they split cos they hated each other. The word is that they just gave up.
In their five or so years of existence, Live Skull released the following records:
'Live Skull' 12" EP, Massive records, 1984.
'Bringing home the bait' LP, Homestead records, '85.
'Cloud One' LP, Homestead, '86.
'Pusherman' 12" EP, Homestead, '86.
'Don't get any on you' LP, Homestead, '87.
'Dusted' LP, Homestead, '87.
'Snuffer' mini LP, What Goes On records, '88.
'Positraction' LP, What Goes On, '89.
(Tracks also appeared on 'Speed Trials', 'Wailing Ultimate', 'Human Music', 'Beautiful Happiness' and 'Like a girl I want you to keep coming' compilation LPs.)

'Cloud One' features the great Swanic 'Great Slave Lake'...'Pusherman' has the ultimate good vibe house destruction 'Raise the manifestation' as one of the flipside tracks (a fun party tip: play this record at 33rpm)...'Dusted' and 'Positraction' should be found in the record collection of every musically sane human being...
This is such a distressing loss. They had even more ace things happening, like 'Tri Power' (track on 'Like a girl...' comp. LP) and 'Alive again' (from 'Human music'), but they're not now...Oh I just don't wanna talk about it.

KILGORE TROUT

part two

Did Kilgore Trout exist and split up and then get together again?

"No, it's split up again. It's done this loads of times really.. There were 3 of us originally and then the bassist split up - yes - he had a really weird thing, he met this Iranian woman," he goes on to tell a dubious tale about an angry husband and a scared James who ended up leaving the country,"but he was leaving anyway cos he wasn't having a good time, and then Andy (guitar) and Julian (bass) joined and that lasted a year. This year I wasn't going to do anything at all but Graham (Sinclair, Thunderball records) came along and said 'here's the money to record a single' so I recorded it myself and I felt obliged to get a band together to do gigs,"

Huh - you did it (Bad Puddings EP) all yourself?? That's brilliant!

"I thought it was loads easier to do it myself cos when you've got no money and a crap studio it's really hard to record a live band well, and just doing it myself with a drum machine and stuff, and knowing in advance where I wanted all the pieces to go...I think that's a really good record, still, several weeks after recording it."

(This is a dead dumb question but it provoked an interesting reply, so:) What do you think are the differences between A C Temple's & Kilgore Trout's sound?

"The new A C Temple stuff, I think, but then I'm totally biased, is completely different from the old stuff and it's really audience-friendly, a good number of the songs are really catchy and immediate, and people like that. I dunno, there's less and less difference, I mean Kilgore Trout is kind of my songs, and the more input I have into A C Temple there's going to be less and less difference between the two. Before, with the old A C Temple, I'd have said that Kilgore Trout was songs trying to fit into a vaguely traditional popsong structure and be quite listenable, whereas A C Temple stuff was more to do with the sounds of guitars, harmonies between guitars, a musical thing ...but then I'm talking a load of shit because most of Kilgore Teout stuff is kind of one chord dirges, although I always think of them as being songs."

"It always seems to me that it takes people loads and loads of listens to get what there is in Kilgore Trout out of it. There's a song (on the new record) that Andy used to play guitar on, and it took him several weeks before he came back and said 'I like this song' and he'd heard it millions of times..."

"I was thinking it's similar to what the Band of Susans do, they have really simple tunes, and the way the song's written is with the rythm of the vocals over that...Music, the actual putting together of it, is probably what musicians are best at talking about, which is why they make such ace company..."

For me, Kilgore Trout represents the pinnacle of human musical achievement. There have been a pitifully small number of releases documenting the band's 5 years of existance (if it can be called a band). 1986 saw the appearance of "Stick it in the bank man", a furious 4 track 12", cluttered and intriguing, on Hits $ Corruption records. Chris thinks this is not very good. I think he is very wrong. (Available from Noel, 767 Abbeydale Rd, Sheffield S7 2BG). Four racing glorious tracks appeared on the brilliant Rorshach Blot Test LP. You may also be interested in the Dust Devils and A C Temple material that makes up the rest of the space; I don't think anyone would object to you killing your parents to get ahold of this record - essential isn't the word.(Jim Crow records, 7 Beulah Mount, Leeds LS6 2JZ). "Bad Puddings" EP sees the Trout sound soothed down yet complexified, a heartful of sadness turned into 4 rattling crashing classic tirades for any time. (Thunderball records, 7 Quarry Springs, Harlow, Essex,CM20 3HR). Precious things can also be found on the Imminent 5 and Take 5 compilation LPs, ask your stockist about those.

Gods and dogs, thumbscrews and cheeses...in a sense these songs are just THERE, existing for their own beauty alone, to unfold as you can handle it. Supremely superficial, they wont stand anyone telling you what they are about. This is what music is like, and if you don't like it that is because you are old and stupid.

Contact Chris, 664 Abbeydale Rd, Sheffield 7.

DOES THE BRITISH INDIE SCENE WORRY YOU?

DEVIL'S JUKEBOX JURY

Gettin' judgemental: Kaz A, Mike M, Anthony T, Old Trout, Simon M, Jeane M, David Gedge and Satan.

SLUM TURKEYS _ Ugly as sin (Crack)

Is this about me? They do seem to choose nasty subjects to sing about. When I first heard this on the radio I wondered who this latest Big Black ripoff group was. They do have a problem with that. But these, along with Houndgod & the mightiest Membranes, are doing very good work irritating the places most Manchester bands don't know exist.
The posher version of "No Axe to grind" featured on the B-side is a fine thing to listen to...I'm still fond of that song.

BOMB DISNEYLAND "Nail Mary" 7" (Vinyl Solution)

Horrible heavy metal. The worst band in the world?

SINK "Don't burn the hook" 7" (Vinyl Solution)

As my mum might say, "I wish they would", and never surface. This is just boring.

MEMBRANES "To slay the rock pig"

The Mems latest vinyl outpouring makes perfect sense when considered from the viewpoint of a psychiatric detention centre. "Space hopper ignites" is a prime example of utterly mindblown lunacy. The hit single "Autoflesh" is an obvious standout, but the final track "Growling people" truly captures the mood of England as a fascist state for the 90's. The beerguts, tattoos, Victorian singsongs of the new national brotherhood is translated via an early Swans grindcore epic. They hit the nail on the head once more. (SM)

MEAT PUPPETS "Monsters" (SST)

This sounds like 3 squeaky-clean college kids impersonating the Meat Puppets impersonating Bon Jovi. Don't be fooled by the silly lyrics and titles - this is rock music, and crap rock music at that. (AT)

POOL "Aphonia" (Fundamental)

...nd me of Coil circa

BUTTHOLE SURFERS "Widowmaker" EP (Blast !st)

"Bon song" is cute like poison ants devouring your flesh as you squirm in total terror because every movement is echoed 7 times in the filth mirror life-is-more-dodgy-even-than-a-really-sick-joke scene. "1401" has a lovely butties guitar melody. "Booze tobacco" is a youth anthem for our times, not suitable for all you straight edge things though. "Helicopter" is very long, I can't be bothered listening all the way through. This is a 10" but you can also get it on CD, and guess what, it sounds exactly the same. This is for yuppies. (KA)

VOMIT LAUNCH "Exiled Sandwich" (Rat Box)

This is an excellent 13 track LP from a nice Californian group, apparently their first. Don't be scared by the name, they may sing about sticking your head in a toilet but they play some really lovely tunes and there is spacey guitar and cool female vocals AND YOU'D SURELY BE INTO IT IF YOU KNEW ABOUT IT, that's why I'm telling you. A mega green & purple cover too. (P.O. Box 4527, Chico, California 95927.)

THE PASTELS "Sittin' Pretty" (Chapter22)

"Zooom", the last track on side one of this LP, is the most ultimate good vibe song that I have ever ever heard. It has someone playing a harp on it and it is quite orgasmic. Well done the Pastels: it's always nice to see Ablaze! readers doing well for themselves.

HAPPY FLOWERS "BB Gun" (Homestead 7")

Worth buying mainly for B-side track "I ate something out of the medicine cabinet" in which Messrs Anus and Horribly Charred Infant eat something out of the medicine cabinet while Mom is out and send themselves stark screaming insane. Not for the squeamish and morally-incensed.

FUDGE TUNNEL "Sex mammoth" (Vinyl Solution)

The worst band in the world! Music for sad boys.

EDWARD BARTON INTERVIEW

An excerpt from Karren Ablaze's diary, 16.3.89: "I just met Edward Barton, he's on this 261 bus [probably a common enough occurence in Manchester, but I'm not there that often these days], he's just got off in a long orange beard. I was too scared, respectful, to approach him at his gig [at the Boardwalk ages ago, supporting Stump]. He carries a small battered black suitcase and a grimey green shoppingbag from which a lone guitarhead peers. He said 'It's broken'. I commented that he tends to maltreat them. 'I have to get up early on Sundays and go to carboot sales,' he explained.

'That's where I get them all from.' He's writing a new book of words and his old one is [was] still available from 'that recordshop in town, err,' [Piccadilly Records.]

JELLO BIAFRA "high priest of harmful matter" (Alternative Tentacles)

This is a spoken word double LP, the second on the subject of the censorship of rock music things by grown ups and christians and government people that goes on all the time but you don't find out about it. And other stuff.(No! I know I'm not very eloquent, but neither would you be if you had to run around screaming like a maniac all day. Which is what I have to do to bring this to you. Um...) so you ought to hear this record at least once - prepare to be shocked and enlightened.

MARC ALMOND "Jacques" (Some Bizarre)

Songs about sweating cabbages and chrysanthemums with supposedly heartfelt observations on life. The inimitable Marc Almond sings, and very well too, the stirring songs of Belgian/Parisian Jacques Brel. (Jeane)

FEEDTIME "Suction" (Decoy)

One of those damn LPs that sounds more like a compilation than the work of one group. They're into "smashing pigeonholes." Tut tut, young people. I don't know.

HONOR ROLE "Rictus"(Homestead)

These sound like a mildly groovey group...it's that 4 boy line up doing the vocal/guitar/bass/drums thing, but it's a sound that swings around in the speakers with metallic tunes and gruff Albini-esque singing about dead everyday things that I don't understand. I really like the one about a boy called Skippy, it's called "Skippy". It's good that one.

WALKING SEEDS news: Frank Martin, sexy Seeds' singer, was gunna design this horrid mag for us but didn't have the time, cos his band were too busy SUPPORTING THE HOUSE OF LOVE on tour. Yes it's true (unless he was lying): does this mean that our best-loved psyche-ROCK act is going for a wimp-out phaze? Or have Creation records, their new label, finally getting theirselves sorted out? We hungrily await developments, and a new LP...

ALTERNATIVES "Buzz" (SST)

It's fun this, doing a zine & making friends & going to gigs & getting records sent to ya, & you certainly should try it, but it gets real diff icult sometimes when all kinds of stuff is expected of you & you're only this dumb kid having a mental breakdown. So I don't know about this record, the 1st track has no singing and no noise. They are happy smiling Americans if the cover is anything to go by. (KA)

LES THUGS "Still hangry" (Decoy)

Here Les and friends demonstrate their near-grasp of the English language. But it sounds so good, with nice soaring vocal harmonies that recall long-ago Cure-y/goth-punky things...well done Mr Thugs!

LUSH "Scar" (4AD)

Lush must be wary of the press attention heaped upon them.While Miki certainly looks striking,a photo every time they change a tour date must get wearing:it certainly has on me.Not that this is a bad debut mini LP; at least Scarlet and Thought-forms are fine songs,but as the Future Of Rock'n'Roll or even London's Answer To Throwing Muses, Lush have a few bob short of a pound at the moment,as they would probably be among the first to admit.When they get themselves sorted out properly in the songwriting and production departments,they'll really be good as opposed to just over-exposed. (Old Trout)

"Nothing short of total war" various 'artists'

Just when you thought it was safe to ignore it, a crumbling Blastfirst (like, Mekons???!) hits us with this wonder. Lots of fun for the media here - the LP has a sister package of singles with big holes in the middle & extra tracks, plus its limited edition to get all the sad collector dudes going. There's also a CD, undoubtably with even more trax, but they dont send that sort of thing to the likes of us.(We wouldn't know what to do with a CD. We'd probably attempt to ingest it in some manner.)
Within the snazzy b&w gatefold sleeve a perceptive observer will discover a piece of plastic coated in unceasing spirally grooves. Between silly, sexy, shit unreleased sonix stuff fom '85, live bigblack, ut, HoD, an unreleased Rapeman song, ciccone out-take, new Ranaldo & Big Stick monsters etc,you'll find mindfuc*ing voices you'll remember from all over the past. Like that bloke talking about the censorship of the 'Flower' sleeve on the SY live 'bootleg' double thang...i dunno if you recall that but it did my head in. And the hole thing ends with a lovely live Butthole Surfers snog.
If ya only buy one LP all year, make it this one. (No. This is a lie - make it "Sourpuss" instead.)

RHYS CHATHAM "Die Donnergötter" (Homestead)

"Waterloo No. 2" is total brass band stuff but dead haunting and I like it. "Guitar Trio" is played with 3 guitars, one of which is played by Nina of UT, and it's ace Band of Susany kind of stuff, in fact Karen Haglof & Robert Poss play on "Die Donnergötter", and it's mixed by Martin Bisi. Rhys Chatham is one of these totally cool musical people and there are involved sleevenotes here with lots of long words in them. Micheal and Gavin didn't like this but that's cos they are wimps. (KA)

KITCHENS OF DISTINCTION
Love is Hell (One Little Indian)

This is really very good.From their striking (not to mention hideous but in a nice kind of way) sleeves to their relaxed and considered music,this group seem to know exactly what they want to do and how to do it.The L.P. kicks off with "In a cave", a gorgeous melodic piece which employs the common Kitchens device of havi · a brilliant chorus which is repeated a couple of times to lull you into a false sense of security before they hit you with an even more brilliant chorus you just weren't expecting. This song wins them my undying affection anyway because a:it borrows a substantial chunk of the vocal melody of R.E.M's mighty "Time After Time" and b:it has some intangible relationship with the first Associates L.P.I have yet to put my finger on.Other highlights include the bit in "The Third Time We Opened the Capsule" where the guitar effloresces in after the second chorus,"Courage, Mother" and "Mainly Mornings"with its list:"television...radio... telephone,it all helps,the car... the sex...the love...the alcohol, it all helps".A quality group who know where their towel is as you can see.

BOB MOULD "Work ok" (Virgin?)

Husker Dudes take note:this is an ace and bitching L.P.and equal to anything recorded by that group:proof as if it were needed that Mould was the genius force behind them all along.O.K. so there are one or two fine Hart songs in the Dü canon,but sit "Intolerance" alongside this and what you have is no comparison at all.From the opener "Wishing Well" (not counting acoustic hors d'oeuvres "Sunspots") the Mould of old is well in evidence with his eminently hummable songs;honest,humble, lyrics and that voice that tears through you like it was carrying all the pain of the world in its fragile crystal tones.Other moments to cherish are the single "See a little light" with a chorus so poppy they had to buy a licence for it,the sprawling 3/4 epic "Brasilia crossed with Trenton" and "Compositions for young and old", as Mould,a brilliant and ever-improving writer,sets about creating a blueprint for '90s American mainstream rock in much the same way as he did for a large sector of '80s "post-hardcore". (Old Trout)

ABLAZE! POLL RESULTS

Since no-one was psychic enought to send us any votes we were forced, as other publications apparently are, to completely fabricate the results. Here they are:

CRAZIEST GIGS
1. Satan The Jesus Infekt'd Needles And Blood, Liverpool Jacaranda, last summer.
2. Walking Seeds, M/cr Green room, October.
3. Dandelion Adventure, Preston Carribean club, Dec.
4. Radio Mongolia, Swinging Sporran, M/cr, April.

AWESOMEST EVENTS
1. A C Temple live, anywhere.
2. Hearing Celestial Orgy's space guitar echoing through the sunset golden magic forest, Treworgy Tree Fair, Cornwall, July approx.
3. Bits of Futurama days 2 & 3, Bradford, October.

STUPIDEST THINGS Y'COULD DO
1. Fall in love.
2. Like the Stone Roses.

SNAZZIEST VENUES
1. Duchess, Leeds.
2. Barrel Organ, Birmingham.
3. Green Room (Die Happy nights only) M/cr.
4. Take two, Sheffield.

Argh this is getting boring. I hereby award prizes to anyone who assasinates a popstar this year and to the agents who bring about the downfall of the Manch. fash. cospiracy flare dept (& all the other components too, please.) Something for you to do on a rainy day.....................

LILLIAN AXE "Love & War" (MCA)

Hahahahahahahahahahahaha... nice of MCA to send us this, it's right up our street: the soft focus picture of a naked woman clutching her breasts on the cover lead me naively to imagine that Lillian Axe is a solo artist...closer inspection revealed a back-cover pic of 5 well made up long haired bare chested white boys in leather trousers etc, with names like "Stevie Blaze" (no!!!)...to think I have contaminated my stylus with such fridayrockshow material & lyrics like this:"She was 19...legs up to here/ I had no idea/I'm not the kind of man/ who lets a woman tell me/ just what I can & cannot do..." Not exactly an anthem for female liberation, hmm? It surely gets worse, but I could not make it as far as track 2,"She likes it on top"...This is one of the hazards of record companies knowing your address.

MY FAVOURITE LPs By Karren A.

I like Positraction and Sourpuss and Love Agenda and The Sensual World andRorschach Blot Test and some of Human Music...that's a double LP so you can do anything that you want with it, you can play all the sides in 16 different permutations (I counted them) but if you go to side 1, the 3rd track will stand out & beat you up a bit: "Alive again" is the start of your new life, as the light pours out & drowns you in involuntary dance delirium. Get over that to side 2 and you'll meet Salem 66, with a slow-growing wallflower song, just before the American Music Club (no, I'd never heard of them either), and "I'm in heaven now", with a truly delicate drum scheme fluttering, ghosted behind the staircase of melancholy strings and a thought-story you can cope with...Oh what was I...Oh, I like Rembrant Pussy horse and the Dougal & the Blue Cat film soundtrack LP. The end.

(Those records are on these labels: What Goes On, Blast First, probably EMI, Jim Crow, Homestead, Red Rhino I think, and Music For Pleasure.)

FRUIT FREEDOM F

Fax: **0274 542235**

"BRITAIN'S TASTIEST CRISPS"

Telephones: **0274 546405/6 496468 490449**

Registered Number
472391 England

Seabrook Potato Crisps Ltd.

Directors: C. BROOK R. C. BROOK Mrs. J. C. BROOK-CHRISPIN Secretary: Mrs. B. RAMSDEN

Registered Office

SEABROOK HOUSE - ALLERTON - BRADFORD - West Yorkshire
BD15 7QU

Recommended for Quality - The family favourite for Salads, Grills, Picnics, etc.

Factories: ALLERTON & PRINCEVILLE, BRADFORD *Deliveries: COAST TO COAST*

Our Ref. RCB/VMD *Your Ref.*

11 July 1989

Ablaze Magazine
8 Hopewell Place
LEEDS
LS6 1PN

Dear Ms Ablaze

We acknowledge receipt of your letter together with issue 5 of Ablaze magazine.

Our advertising budget is fully committed and we have no interest in placing an advert in either issue 6 or any subsequent issues.

Yours sincerely
SEABROOK POTATO CRISPS LTD

R C Brook

R C Brook
Managing Director

Shard: Ablaze! and Me

Chris Trout

In an ideal world, Chris Trout would need no introduction. Songwriter, multi-instrumentalist and mentalist, he has perved, and purveyed noise, in a great number of seminal (eek!) acts: Kilgore Trout, A. C. Temple, Spoonfed Hybrid, Coping Saw and Smokers Die Younger, to name just five. Trout began writing for *Ablaze!* from issue 7 onwards, under the moniker Lucy Nation, and subsequently went on to commit further acts of music journalism and bloggism[1] in the world. Here he presents his peculiarly Troutian recollections of Ablazeworld, complete with a selection of wild inaccuracies, which I've corrected in the footnotes. That'll be the drugs then.

I first became aware of *Ablaze!* after finding a copy of #3 in Rare And Racy in Sheffield. I bought it because it had King of the Slums in it. This must have been 1988. The Salford turn were notable mainly for the dangerous violin of Sarah Curtis, a player so individual – for which read LOUD – that twenty-five years later I've still heard nothing like her. I digress. Already. But if you'd prefer to short-circuit the vain and possibly superfluous reminiscences that follow, you could do worse than 'Fanciable Headcase' and 'Leery Bleeder'. We could all do worse. Many of us have. My particular #3 was so badly photocopied that much of it was illegible. But I was able to establish that the zine's creator was a mardy Manchester schoolgirl who styled herself Karren Ablaze! and was clever, music-obsessed, funny and slightly mental in roughly equal measure.

Those are the best kind. She had me from the start, although I hadn't twigged this just yet and she didn't yet know I existed. Later, at some gig or other in the medium-sized venue at Manchester University, I had a bag of badges I'd made intending to hand them out at shows to "advertise" my band, Kilgore Trout. Quite how I thought this was going to work is not clear, as the badges simply read DRUGS NOT JOBS, which wasn't even the title of one of the band's records but a parody of the earnest mid-eighties lefty slogan JOBS NOT BOMBS. I'd still – cautiously – stand behind either sentiment, but DRUGS NOT JOBS – actually the creation of Duncan McTaggart – was more clever, funny and slightly mental than JOBS NOT BOMBS, as well as being a considerably more accurate reflection of most of our lives at the time.

Being a boy – that's a bit like a cross between a puppy and a poltergeist, kind of awkwardly beautiful but it's definitely not pretty – not even having about my person a supply of entertaining trinkets of popular culture to give to people for no cash outlay was enough to lend me the courage to schmooze at strangers. I'd be exactly the same now, as it goes, which is maybe one reason why that elusive career in telesales never materialised. So when I spotted the impossibly cute bleach-headed girl with the bag of zines – and knew without having to ask that this must be Karren Ablaze! – I simply waited for her to get to where I was sitting and then asked her to hand out the badges for me on her rounds. I also bought a copy of #5, whose cover (Sonic Youth, Dinosaur Jr., Pixies, Throwing Muses, Ut, Rapeman) read like a roll-call of most of my favourite acts of the time. It was fucking impeccable, really. Still is.

Some other stuff happened. I remember watching Throwing Muses at Liverpool Royal Court. This would have been mid-1989. I'd been in Liverpool the night before, "doing the sound" – cluelessly – for an Edinburgh band called Archbishop Kebab. Most of the touring party had eaten acid and stayed up all night playing at weekend schizophrenics. I hadn't eaten any acid (which was uncharacteristic – perhaps somewhere in the dim recesses of my 23 year-old unconscious I'd noticed that I was a tad fragile) but I'd had so little sleep that by the next evening I might as well have done. Throughout the Muses show, my fucked brain kept transmuting the distant, bleach-headed figure of Tanya Donnelly into Karren. I wouldn't have put it like this at the time, but it looked very much as if I was in love. Fuck's sake. Not again. (I wouldn't have put it like that at the time, either.) Anyway, in December of that year I headed off around Europe for a couple of weeks, playing bass with A.C. Temple, and was slightly mental, although probably neither funny nor clever, throughout. More or less immediately upon returning, I took a train to Leeds and bombarded Karren with posh cider until the rest was history. When the time is right, somehow you know. Except for all those times you get it hopelessly wrong and end up looking like a twat, obviously.

We spent much of the following seven years screaming at each other. We were in our twenties. That's what you do. Isn't it? One way or another, neither of us had yet come within sight of being Right In The Head. I hope we never do. And we loved each other fiercely. Episodic memory is a wonderful and merciful thing. I'll offer you three or four good ones. New Year 1990, climbing the steep, wooded banks of Whirlow Brook, up, up and away at right angles to the beaten path, emerging through a break in the barbed wire fence into a high, sunlit, snowy field somewhere near Ringinglow where we held each other, swinging round and round together in laughing wonderment like a pair of characters in some sentimental Hollywood rom-com. But it wasn't sentimental, it was as real and as delicious and as mad and terrifying as the spinning Earth upon which we danced. Accompanying Pavement to Chatsworth[2] on their day off (Gary wanted to see a "castle"), then introducing them to the concept of hot knives (don't ask) and forcing the poor buggers to review a carrier bag's worth – that's an acceptable unit of measurement, in case anybody asks – of questionable demo tapes. Seeing the immortal Shudder To Think twice in one day in Manchester in 1993. It was my birthday, and the first time I heard them play the one that starts "Happy birthday baby, yeah..."

I could go on. And I will, don't fucking doubt it for a moment, but let's try to talk about the zine now, eh? ("Zine" is good. It's ambidextrous. It refuses the prefix. It could go either way.) The first *Ablaze!* I had any useful involvement with was #7, mostly assembled in the large Headingley bedsit Karren – still a student – was renting from an affable but slightly sinister Rachmanite called Mr Singh. The bathroom was in the cellar. It was tiled and cavernous, like something out of a Victorian asylum, and it had spiders the size of Frisbees. In the final weeks Karren was the only tenant, and it seemed as if the builders Mr Singh had brought in were hammering on all six surfaces of our box at once. It was summer, too, and it was hot. By some miracle, we survived both each other and the tasks at hand: degree and zine were both successfully completed.[3]

Gentle reader, I'm using "we" a lot here, because for me that's how the story goes, but don't be misled into thinking that *Ablaze!* was at any point in its existence anything other than Karren's baby. As with Coping Saw later, I was happy and lucky to be in a position to put my abilities, such as they are, into the service of her vision. Fortunately, these noble acts of self-sacrifice didn't preclude me carrying on being precious, opinionated and obstinate, or I'd have been back on the chain gang within weeks. But somehow – just about – everything held together, and "we" went on to produce #8 and #9 (they're The Ones, I think) and – eventually – #10, in collaboration with our long-suffering Wetherby Grove housemate Gavin Bradbury, a lovely man – I haven't actually seen him since about '93, because for some reason, probably both watery and domestic, we fell out horribly, but I'll confidently assert this in the present tense – who, with his ridiculous long hair and Olympian tea intake, was integral to *Ablaze!* from #8 onwards.

Your twenties are underrated as a time of growth. Yes, the rate of change slows – it would have to, really, when you consider what's gone before – but still we leave our third decade a very different beast from the one that entered it. By the time #10 was ready to fly the nest, Karren had had enough of both me and the zine (there were afterlives – there always are – never trust a Catholic) and it was all over bar yet more shouting. *Sic transit gloria mundi.* But #10 was and is a perfect swansong. Quit while you're ahead, innit. Hurts more at the time but history will still respect you in the morning. The print run was 5000 (previous maximum had been 2000) and for the first time *Ablaze!* Was using a real live grown-up magazine distributor, stepping out of the international tweecore record shop underground shadows and onto the racks of the dayjobnation's newsagents. And it contains an extended Party Political Broadcast on behalf of the Nation of Ulysses, and sentences like "Men wish to die because of their suppressed need to be female." I'm not sure I really understand this one now, and I'm quite sure that I didn't understand it then, and I'm even surer that it only tells one part of one story, but I'm surest of all that it's a Thing Worth Saying, whatever the fuck one of those is, and I'm stating without fear of contradiction that for a woman – a mere woman – under 25 – a mere child – to have snuck this kind of thing – whatever kind of thing it is – into your local branch of WH Smith[4] alongside the humdrum, dumb-dumb likes of *Select* magazine and *Total Guitar Frottage* is a fucking huge achievement, a practical, subversive, effective act of popular culture frequency-jamming. And trying to write about it turned me into Emily Dickinson for a moment back there, which is always a bonus.

It's time to shut the fuck up. It usually is. I'm older and heavier now, so like one of those rust-streaked leviathan oil tankers you'll have to allow me plenty of time to slow down and stop. I'm still a writer, and I'm slowly getting better at being a writer, which makes me happy, and for which in this particular parallel universe I have mainly Karren to thank. A while ago, somebody sent me a link to a blog post entitled "The Top Ten Most Scathing Things Anybody Has Ever Said in Print About a Band", or words to that effect. Somewhere in there was one from Ablaze! 10 concerning the deservedly-forgotten "shoegazers" Chapterhouse, a C-list act from a C-list genre if ever there was one. "This band's label offered us thousands of flexis for nothing, which would have helped the magazine's permanently tottering financial situation no end," it reads, "but, fuck it, we'd rather eat out of dustbins for the rest of our lives than put out a Chapterhouse flexi."

It's funny cos it's true.

1 Trout's collected adventures can be discovered at the misterchristrout.com website.

2 I wasn't there.

3 My degree was completed a year later.

4 I applied to WH Smith but was turned down. They said that there was too much in it, that the content of one issue should be spread over six.

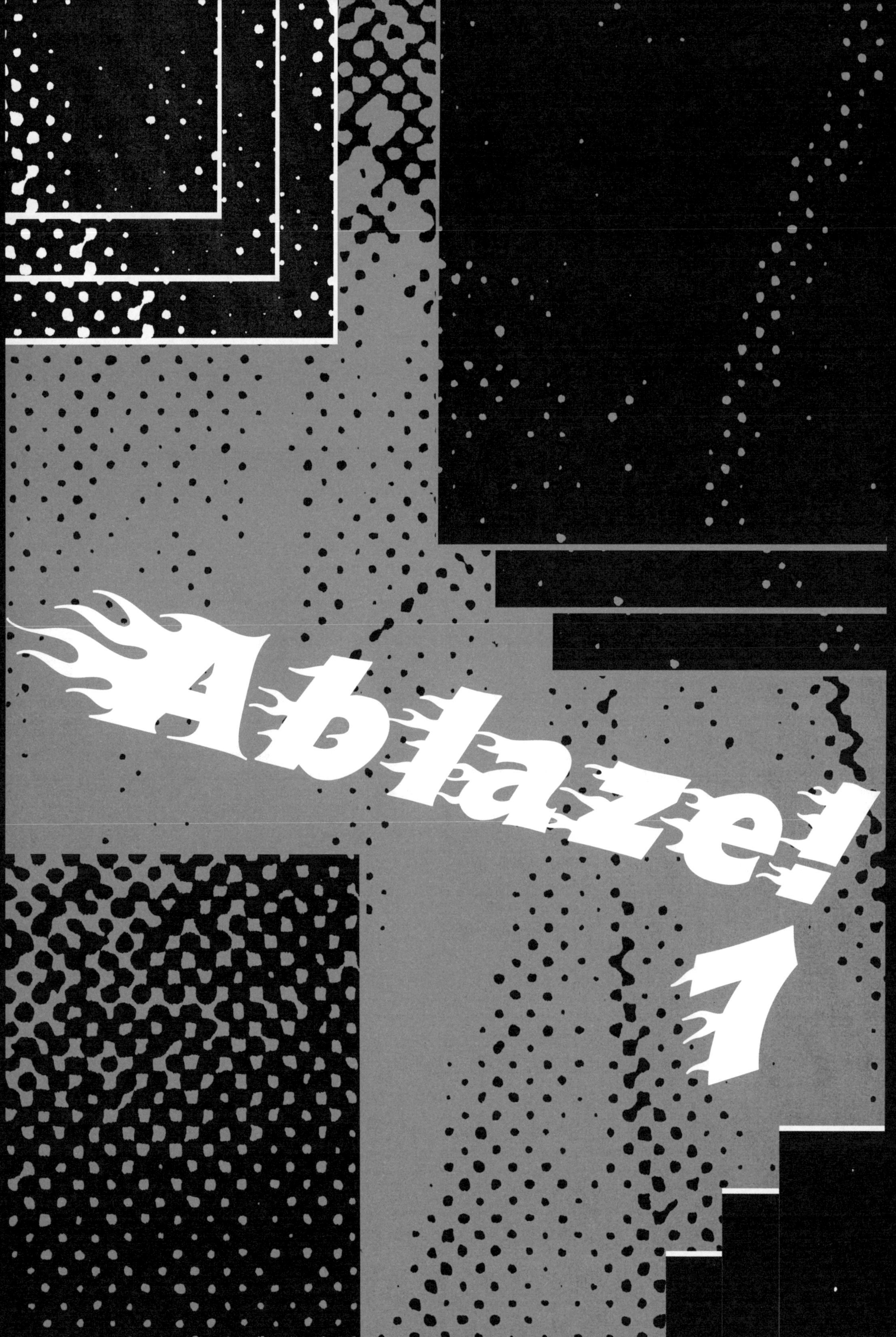
Ablaze!
1

Ablaze! 7

Publication date: Late summer 1990

I wasn't sure where to go after the Purples' palace, so I got drunk and randomly selected a large bed-sitting room in Headingley. It was fairly gross - as these things tend to be - with a bed in one corner and a kitchen in the other, and a landlord who liked to let himself into girls' rooms to read their diaries. My neighbour changed her locks; a move I judged unnecessary till I came home one day to see that a pile of clothes had been moved in order to access the journal underneath. Maybe I should have sold him my zine to sate his thirst for details about my life. I did make a friend there, an ex-corporal called Frank who lived in the flat downstairs. You can read about him in the Band of Holy Joy record review.

Ablaze! 7 opens with a flagship piece on rock'n'roll, punk rock, gender and sexuality by Terry Downe. This chap is a mystery – real name Terry Bloomfield, at the time he lived on the Isle of Harris and authored some amazing works which are now as scarce as he is.

Ablaze! had attracted many contributors by this stage, yet I enjoyed pretending that the staff was comprised entirely of stuffed animals, possibly to justify the snazzy photo session I'd commissioned with prodigious music photographer Ian Tilton. It was an easy one for him – all he had to do was capture the personality of a variety of inanimate toys. I was too shy to be photographed.

I should not have cashed in my electric typewriter and got a Commodore 64 and a dot matrix printer. The results, in terms of readability, are quite nasty. This set up did, however, provide the facility to print 'reversed' white on black text - just as unreadable but appealingly kooky.

What an intro. What was going on there - I'd nearly given the zine up? Maybe breaking up with Simon, taking a year out of university and being kicked out of Hopewell Place had taken their toll. I'd decided to put bigger bands in it – like who? The Stone Roses? Why did I want to increase the circulation beyond 2000 anyway, except for an unthinking sense, like so many bands, that more sales equals success?

If you ignore this strange intro, it flows from Terry's beautifully argued piece about proto-grrrl pop to Archbishop Kebab telling me to form a band, and my suggesting it might be time for girls to reclaim guitars.

Fluff was a beautiful three-piece that played without cliché. They were snippety-snip economical in their aesthetic. They were among the first to do the stoppy-starty thing and I loved that – so exciting in 1990. Yet, at the time of writing, and apart from in this zine, the only remaining evidence that this band ever existed is in the minds and hearts of their other love-struck fans. An unassuming trio, they hid out in Hyde Park and ultimately deprived the world of their songs.

Steve 'the Weave' Hawkins wanted to be their manager, and stopped me from putting them on the flexi for this issue. I told it how I saw it. The slight friendship I had with their brilliant drummer Tim Beckham was destroyed when he concurred with Steve to stop the flexi release going ahead. It was as though they were being oh-so-careful about how they wanted to launch the band that they carefulled it into nothing. I was bitterly disappointed that they opted for obscurity, and then broke up. Tse Tse Fly arose from their ashes, but that was a different band...

Happy Flowers were fun. We would frequently hear criticisms of what went on at Maida Vale and now I wonder if examples like this opening paragraph are why Peel never quite called my band in for the session that we so craved.

It is strange but I cannot now remember a thing about Cranes. I do not recall even liking them, although clearly for a time they were a big deal to me. They must have rapidly become uncool in my mind in the light of subsequent wonders (hold onto your hats for those to come, Mr/Ms Reader). What is clear now is that dear Alison had very little to say for herself, as opposed to lady Rose of early '90s glossy popsters Heart Throbs, who oozed confidence and useful opinions. Yet I wholeheartedly supported Alison in her shy, idea-free utterances, and sought ruthlessly to trip up Rose. What was I playing at? Was it her confidence I found offensive? I didn't like her band enough - but then why did I interview them? *Dreamtime* is a memorable pop song alright, and Rose was working hard to break taboos and speak the unspoken, but I was suspicious of the money around them and what I believed to be their imminent success. Was I so cynical as to interview them simply because I thought they were about to be successful? And I wonder how much this interview might have depressed them. I only hope that they were made of tougher stuff and able to withstand one girl's delusions. This is my apology to the Heart Throbs.

The Keatons were an important band. Rhodri (of *Glottal Stop* fanzine) was very amusing, and still is. He now plays in Scritti Politti and writes for proper newspapers. The quote I would like to have pulled out of this piece is "the theory that all of our songs are about war is... disputed territory."

It seems that Kim Deal and I had been to the wedding party of The Stone Roses' tour managers, and the following day I travelled to the Britannia hotel at Piccadilly to meet her. I was nervous as hell, but also a chancer, creeping upstairs and knocking at her hotel room door rather than ringing from reception, just in case she wanted to whisk me inside and make out with me. I should have known - she's a breeder; all was platonic. She bought me drinks and explained lots of stuff to me. I didn't know much at all; I didn't even understand all her language. I was so in awe of Ms Deal that most of my comments appeared in brackets. Highlights include her description of the drinking habits of vampire bats and how much she fancied Ian Brown: "I wonder if he'll call..."

All along I'd been resisting Manchester's move from post-punk to baggy, its desire to let it all hang out and dance all night. Keith Gregory once noted how I never went over to the dark side, and my move to Leeds was thusly well-timed; it was and still remains a bastion of post-punk. But I wasn't above a cynical cash-in to sell more zines. The Stone Roses interview was lifted from *Made in Manchester*, I reprinted my account of the Happy Mondays debacle from issue 2, and, perhaps most cynically of all, the Inspiral Carpets interview from issue 1. By this time, due to their association with the Madchester epidemic, they too needed to be denounced despite how lovely, and rather skilled at songwriting, they had been.

Mayomberos Alive! called the payphone in the hallway outside my bedsit from the Dublin petrol station where they worked and insisted that I interview them. I believe that such antics did get them the sack in time, and would dearly love to know what happened to them. The Silverfish piece starts off well but for no reason at all I start writing about Ut, a band quite unrelated.

In case anyone ever thought otherwise, what we were doing was the opposite of visionary. When writing, we were heads-down, into the music, lost in the moment (often very brief moments by the look of these record reviews), absolutely making up every aspect of everything as we went along, and making predictions that pretty much never came true. There was one band that we'd be right about... but that's a story for another issue.

My stay in bedsit-land was brief. Change was heralded by Justine Wolfenden, co-author of the letter that incited Morrissey to such ire. Both of us had migrated over the Pennines at different times and for different reasons. University was my excuse, rock and roll was hers, though in the fullness of time she was to ride the academic rodeo all the way to the top. Back then, she was going out with Keith Gregory, first of the DUSTdevils and then of The Wedding Present. Justine managed their merchandising operation and then started a record label, Hemiola, and a band, Hem. We're jumping ahead though – she was still in full-on drop-out mode at the time that she paid me a visit.

Her reaction to my pad was a bit extreme. "You can't live here!" she declared, "Our kitchen is bigger than this! Come and live in our house, we have two spare rooms, you can have them both." I could not refuse such a kind offer, and was glad to give Mr Singh my notice.

But then Mr Singh came to see me. He said that he was going to knock the room next door into mine. I was about a week from completing this issue, and requested that he wait till I'd finished, at which point I wanted to move out anyway. He agreed, and in a state of considerable house-moving and zine-finishing stress I went to Sheffield to get the thing printed.

I returned from the printers to find a man poised, hammer in one hand and chisel in the other, to knock down one of my walls. I begged him to wait another day, and he kindly took this as an opportunity for an early knock-off, saving my computer equipment from building dust destruction, and me from asthma death. I got my stuff together sharpish, and decamped to Wetherby Grove.

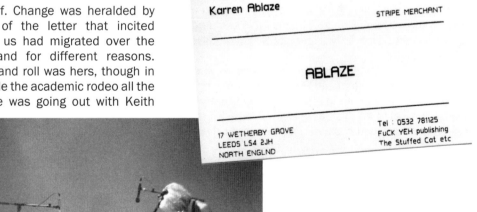

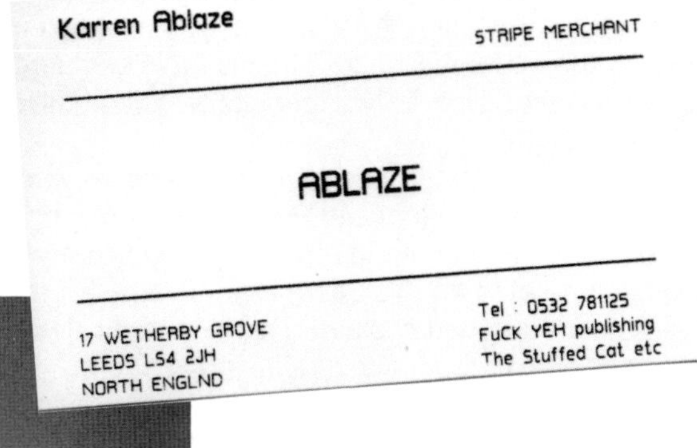

Karren Ablaze
STRIPE MERCHANT
ABLAZE
17 WETHERBY GROVE
LEEDS LS4 2JH
NORTH ENGLND
Tel : 0532 781125
FuCK YEH publishing
The Stuffed Cat etc

Fluff live in Leeds

Photographer unknown

Heart on the Staves

Notes from Ablaze! 7, pertaining to 1987's Stone Roses interview in Made In Manchester,

After I left the Salisbury that night I rushed to Little Jo's house to tell her what a bad time I'd just had trying to interview this local band who were already acting like rock stars. It was with Jo that I'd shared most of my Stone Roses experiences - we both used to make quite a fuss over them. One time (too far past to give it a date) we followed the buzz of excitement along the dark city centre streets at 3am, and post-club crowds were trailing along behind Piccadilly train station, to a dodgy building where the Roses were due to play. Publicity was totally grapevined, I can't remember what we thought about it as my head was certainly swollen with amyl nitrate, except that there were no toilets so you had to piss on the floor outside, and we stood around in small groups for hours, feeling cold and miserable, till they eventually decided to play. Most people seemed to have gone home by this time, but it was worth the wait, in my tiny fascinated head, to see them do such classics as "So Young", with lyrics altered to suit the situation- "In a misery dictionary, there is no monitors, there's no mo-o-o-o-o-o-nitors, I can't hear myself"... They only sustained 20 minutes of crashing rock enervation before Reni had some kind of fit and started to smash the windows behind his drumkit. Disorganised murmurs about what was going on circulated, and the only explanation we got from Ian was "our drummer's a bit temperamental."

Another time we saw an ad saying they were going to play at Dingwalls, so Jo and I hitched down to London and stood at the front with a Japanese girl who quite liked them too, while the other 15 members of the audience stood at the bar. I stayed on in London while Jo got a lift back to Manchester with the band. All she remembers about that is them stopping at a service station in the early hours, for a game of football in the car park.

So it was a bit of a surprise when the world started warbling about them. Ian, Johnny, Reni and Mani started opening their mouths for every photograph in a manner in which my mum had advised me not to do at an early age. "Close it - it makes you look stupid," she had scolded. However, their dream of adoration was coming true, much to my displeasure.

Yet when they came to Leeds last year I decided to go over, for old times' and curiosity's sake. They sold the Poly out and it was crawling with young Manc-o-philes. I had arranged to interview them again - we clearly had a lot of catching up to do, so I turned up early. Ian was having fun humiliating a member of security who had questioned his right to be in the building, and when he swaggered over I greeted him. "Fuck off" was his charming reply. "What's up?" I asked, somewhat bemused. "You slagged us off in your fanzine. I'll give you the time of day but not an interview."

At home later I was wondering what he meant when he said I'd slagged them off. Looking through back-issues I found, in the badly printed issue 3, this paragraph:

"...the audience at Stone Roses gigs seem to me to include a significant proportion of big idiot men who like to kick up lots of havoc at the front so that fragile creatures like myself (oh yeh!) get pushed over when we try to dance... The Roses still emit the same arrogance that attracted me to them, yet I can't cope with their tragic decision to learn to play their instruments and make (completely spineless, very commercially viable) pop music. I love songs like 'So Young', 'I Wanna be Adored', 'Heart on the Staves' etc, but 'Sally Cinnamon', everyone's favourite happy sicky love song has always made me want to eject the contents of my stomach through my mouth. . . "

So that's the passage he had noted down and harboured ever since. Paranoid? I'd say so, but then so many of these creative types are.

The night had been something of a depressing one. The sight of so many kids indulging in blind worship of a shit rock band really did my head in. I felt that the use of incredibly bright lights to dazzle/blind us was unethical, a bit like the sort of thing people do to rats in laboratories. And when some kid's inflatable banana hit the stage, Ian's act of bursting it for him seemed somehow spiteful, although I don't believe such items are in any way useful. The realisation that this is what most people enjoy struck me so deeply that I toyed with the idea of giving up the fanzine as a hopeless task. Oh, Manchester...

tape because you told me you thought we'd gone poppy and pretty weak. I think that's because the demo's you've heard which were weak were done on 8 Track. 'Heart on the Staves' etc. were on 24 Track. Check out this version of 'So Young' which is really different to the single version. I've also put on the tape

MISSION IMPOSSIBLE

which was what we used to start the set off with when we first started. Please don't let anyone anywhere have a copy of the song Mission Impossible!

Enjoy the tape

IAN X

P.S.

... was really

ABLAZE!

KIM DEAL
(PIXIES / BREEDERS)
CRANES
HAPPY FLOWERS
LUSH
KITCHENS OF DISTINCTION
DANDELION ADVENTURE
SILVERFISH
HEART THROBS
THE KEATONS
STONE ROSES
HAPPY MONDAYS
INSPIRAL CARPETS
Manchester cash-in special

7

plus Stretch Heads / Kilgore Trout flexi

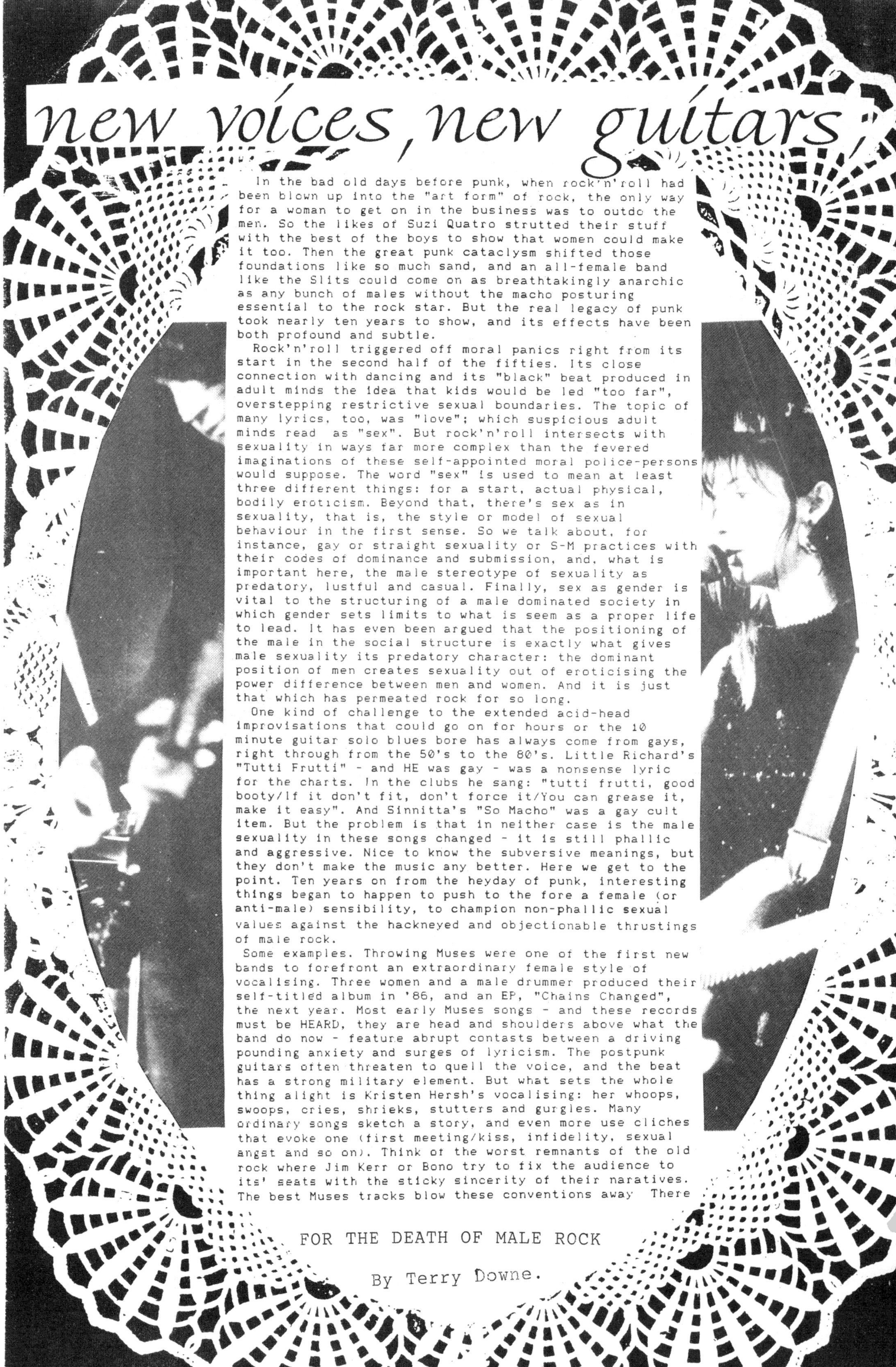

new voices, new guitars;

In the bad old days before punk, when rock'n'roll had been blown up into the "art form" of rock, the only way for a woman to get on in the business was to outdo the men. So the likes of Suzi Quatro strutted their stuff with the best of the boys to show that women could make it too. Then the great punk cataclysm shifted those foundations like so much sand, and an all-female band like the Slits could come on as breathtakingly anarchic as any bunch of males without the macho posturing essential to the rock star. But the real legacy of punk took nearly ten years to show, and its effects have been both profound and subtle.

Rock'n'roll triggered off moral panics right from its start in the second half of the fifties. Its close connection with dancing and its "black" beat produced in adult minds the idea that kids would be led "too far", overstepping restrictive sexual boundaries. The topic of many lyrics, too, was "love"; which suspicious adult minds read as "sex". But rock'n'roll intersects with sexuality in ways far more complex than the fevered imaginations of these self-appointed moral police-persons would suppose. The word "sex" is used to mean at least three different things: for a start, actual physical, bodily eroticism. Beyond that, there's sex as in sexuality, that is, the style or model of sexual behaviour in the first sense. So we talk about, for instance, gay or straight sexuality or S-M practices with their codes of dominance and submission, and, what is important here, the male stereotype of sexuality as predatory, lustful and casual. Finally, sex as gender is vital to the structuring of a male dominated society in which gender sets limits to what is seem as a proper life to lead. It has even been argued that the positioning of the male in the social structure is exactly what gives male sexuality its predatory character: the dominant position of men creates sexuality out of eroticising the power difference between men and women. And it is just that which has permeated rock for so long.

One kind of challenge to the extended acid-head improvisations that could go on for hours or the 10 minute guitar solo blues bore has always come from gays, right through from the 50's to the 80's. Little Richard's "Tutti Frutti" - and HE was gay - was a nonsense lyric for the charts. In the clubs he sang: "tutti frutti, good booty/If it don't fit, don't force it/You can grease it, make it easy". And Sinnitta's "So Macho" was a gay cult item. But the problem is that in neither case is the male sexuality in these songs changed - it is still phallic and aggressive. Nice to know the subversive meanings, but they don't make the music any better. Here we get to the point. Ten years on from the heyday of punk, interesting things began to happen to push to the fore a female (or anti-male) sensibility, to champion non-phallic sexual values against the hackneyed and objectionable thrustings of male rock.

Some examples. Throwing Muses were one of the first new bands to forefront an extraordinary female style of vocalising. Three women and a male drummer produced their self-titled album in '86, and an EP, "Chains Changed", the next year. Most early Muses songs - and these records must be HEARD, they are head and shoulders above what the band do now - feature abrupt contasts between a driving pounding anxiety and surges of lyricism. The postpunk guitars often threaten to quell the voice, and the beat has a strong military element. But what sets the whole thing alight is Kristen Hersh's vocalising: her whoops, swoops, cries, shrieks, stutters and gurgles. Many ordinary songs sketch a story, and even more use cliches that evoke one (first meeting/kiss, infidelity, sexual angst and so on). Think of the worst remnants of the old rock where Jim Kerr or Bono try to fix the audience to its' seats with the sticky sincerity of their naratives. The best Muses tracks blow these conventions away There

FOR THE DEATH OF MALE ROCK

By Terry Downe.

are no tired steroetypes of love and loss here; instead before our eyes (our ears, anyway) a subjectivity in anguish is conjured up as if in its actual creation.

Those guitars, with their repeating figures, are always interesting, but it is the voice that draws the ear. We need My Bloody Valentine to show what you can do to demolish rockist guitars if you really put your mind to it. We would probably think better of their earlier stuff if they hadn't crashed through the looking glass in '87 with "You Made Me Realise" followed by the LP "Isn't Anything" and the current EP "Glider". The LP's title says it all: the idea is to play rock'n'roll as loud and raucous as any, but make it sound as though IT'S NOT REALLY THERE. The guitars are de-gutted, turned into straw figures then enveloped in feedback like a shrieking wind. The old macho rock guitar is deconstructed - its noises broken up and put back together against the grain of the instrument. In the half buried vocals, too, Bilinda sings with a kind of rapt vacancy, and Kevin Shields sounds so ungendered that the contempt for standard male posturing is all the more strongly felt. On the first side of "Glider" the Valentines have retreated (or advanced) so far from a track like "Strawberry Wine" that against the sounds of a gigantic mechanism slowly turning we hear wordless sighs, the merest hint of a song.

Lush's "Scar" and their "Mad Love" EP take on board the same themes, combining eviscerated sonic holocaust guitars with Miki Bereyeni's fragile vocals. Or again, Cranes' "Self-non-Self" mini LP pushes the boundaries of the new music in a slightly different direction. The song "Beach Mover" is swallowed up in drum detonations and shards of spiky guitar while an indecipherable female voice wanders through the ruins. It is not only not a pushy male sound, it is scarcely ADULT, not really formed into that of an articulate being. Which is precisely the point. The hard edged articulate (or aggressively inarticulate) vocal of the rockstar is negated by an abstracted incoherent immaturity.

It is the style or mode of being of these voices that provides opposition to the old rock, not the fact in itself that they are women's voices. Male singers, too, can oppose the the Jaggerisms that still cling on to life: by cranking up the hysteria as Husker Du's Bob Mould did, or, more interestingly, by writing lyrics that while not necessarily impenetrable do not tell a story or invoke the same old threadbare scenarios of lurve. Kilgore Trout's songs are gems of that kind. But the female voice is particularly suitable for anti-rock manoevres because it embodies a subjectivity oppositional at root to the social order whose structure supports the male psyche: one that is constituted by words, concepts, codes. The French analyst Jacques Lacan called this basis of social reality the Symbolic order. Because women cannot be fully socialised into the dominant structures of patriarchy, they remain more closely connected to the order of the Imaginary: the realm of image and identification rather than concept and categorisation. So male desire is expressed as DEMAND, while female desire, deprived of a conceptual language to state itself in, is peculiarly ready to give inarticulate voice. The Imaginary quality of female vocalising is a weapon against male-centred rock music. Male voices (generally) address or hector the listener from their position in the dominant social order (whether they are "rebels" or not doesn't matter, they still inhabit the Symbolic order). But the female voice in flight doesn't narrate: it delivers a vocalese, an incantation. Think of AC Marias' "One of our girls has gone missing" or Hugo Largo's "Drum". Better still, think of the Cocteau Twins whose string of albums over the past 7 years has Liz Fraser's voice incomprehensibly swooping and whirling above dense textures of keyboards and guitars. And, of course, My Bloody Valentine: inarticulate (anti-Symbolic) voices enmeshed in the very centre of their deconstructed guitars. It is this fight on two fronts that will kill off the old rock: the combination of a female vocal subjectivity with weirded out guitars. And of that there is no better example than in AC Temple's "Sourpuss" LP. The intersection of Jane Bromley's vocals and the detuned guitars in songs like "Sundown Pet Corner" or "Miss Sky" led the last issue of Ablaze! to name them contenders for the title of "best band in the known universe". This is white guitar pop that has at last cast off the fake authenticity that black forms were thought to provide in the sixties.

The last five years have been the years of new voices and new guitars, making music that celebrates a non phallic sexuality. As the Valentines in particular show, the deep eroticism possible in this combination has the power to wipe out the predatory sexuality of pop "soul" tracking down its' mate, or the tired old blues rock stutting. Love and hold onto the new music through the Manchester nonsense - it will pass - and the ever more deadening b.p.m.'s. We can conquer the (male dominated) world yet.

the ABLAZE! DISORGANISATION

has a new address:

17,Wetherby Grove
Leeds
LS4 2JH
U.K.

CON-TENTS

Printed by Juma Print of Sheffield

Flexi pressed by Flexi Records of London.

Cover photo by Ian T. Tilton.

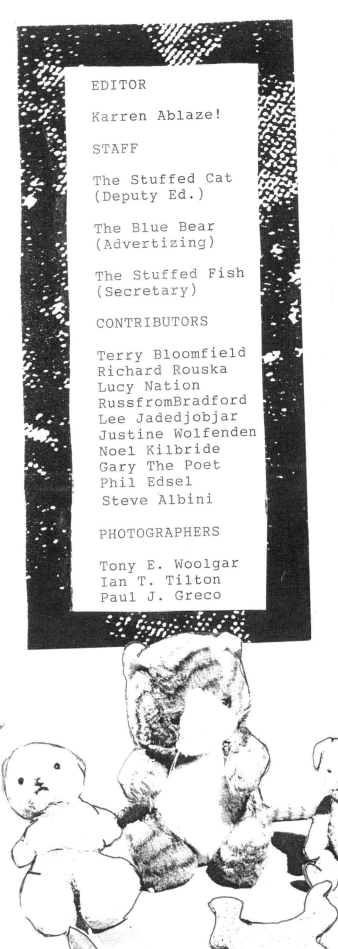

EDITOR

Karren Ablaze!

STAFF

The Stuffed Cat
(Deputy Ed.)

The Blue Bear
(Advertizing)

The Stuffed Fish
(Secretary)

CONTRIBUTORS

Terry Bloomfield
Richard Rouska
Lucy Nation
RussfromBradford
Lee Jadedjobjar
Justine Wolfenden
Noel Kilbride
Gary The Poet
Phil Edsel
Steve Albini

PHOTOGRAPHERS

Tony E. Woolgar
Ian T. Tilton
Paul J. Greco

A TYPICAL ABLAZE! EDITORIAL MEETING

To the "scene", I give this: the Seventh Ablaze!, the return of the kids' best-loved pop zine. And, to go with it, a few words of explanation.*
Ablaze! is a creation out of anyone's control that ceaselessly fights for its' right to survive and grow. People often ask me what it's like to look after, and I explain to them, in exasperated tones, about the cost, the time, the hassle... but these things inevitably come with any worthwhile project. What really gets me, though, are stupid people that have to be dealt with: unwitting misogynists who can't quite believe that this is the work of a woman, and various rip-off merchants and leeches (pseudo zine distributors), and idiots like Ian Brown...************
There was an evening, before the publication of issue 6, when I really felt like giving it up. It was when I saw the Stone Roses play at Leeds Poly, and realised that this is what most of the kids are really into. Herd behaviour that gives the Press its influence, fuelling unthinking faith, is what bands like that are about. And that's what Ablaze! is up against... A million people versus one beast of a fanzine.**************
And who gives a fuck about fanzines? I don't, on the whole; those that are proclaimed to be the best are generally those that have been going for the longest time and have become quite formularised along the way. Ablaze! makes massive leaps each issue, and if you've been left behind already, that's not my problem. Along this monsterous journey I've encountered many brilliant people, and it's the knowledge that there are these dudes around who are prepared to use their hands, and their heads, to step across pre-set boundaries and actually DO things, that makes it worth continuing.********************
However it feels about time to try and break out of the cosy indie network that has incubated Ablaze! thus far. The size of the scene, being miniscule though geographically wide, has prevented the circulation of this thing getting beyond 2,000. Maybe hardcore fanzine-ists will grumble when we adjust the focus to include more mainstream acts, but the scope of each issue has always been determined by my tastes, so if I chose, through a lack of favourite bands to praise, to draw in some more popular acts to revile, it's the same viewpoint that's gonna come through.*
Anyhow, I've told you enough for now. This has been an Ian Cheek-esque rant. Fierce things and love,*******

Karren Ablaze!

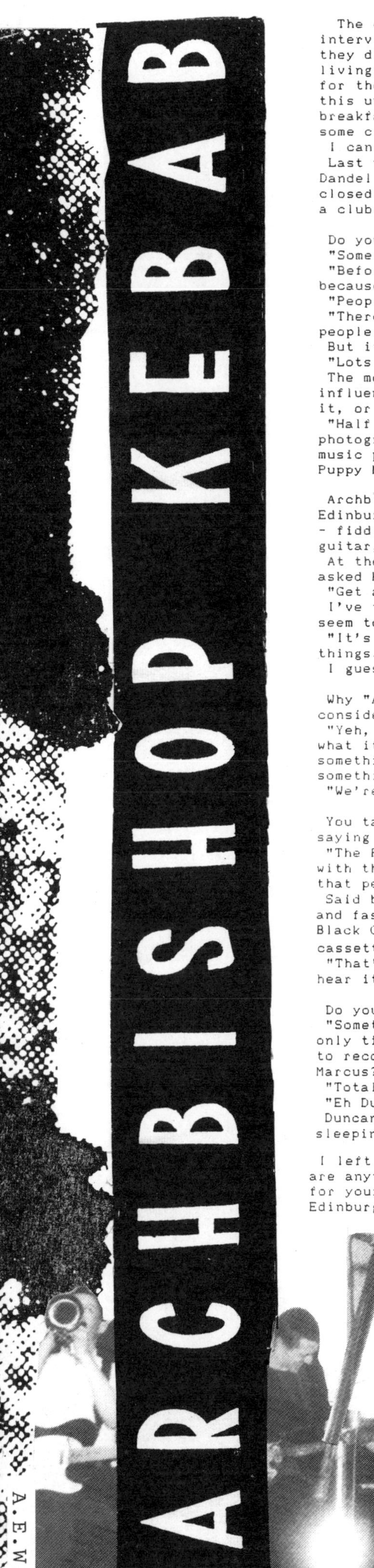

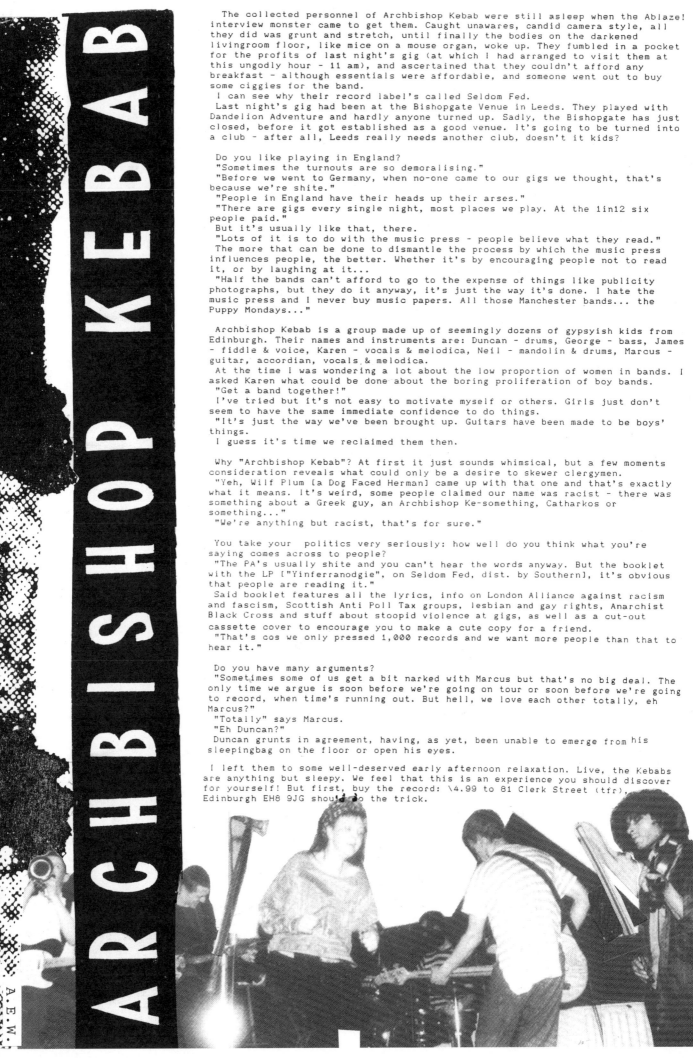

The collected personnel of Archbishop Kebab were still asleep when the Ablaze! interview monster came to get them. Caught unawares, candid camera style, all they did was grunt and stretch, until finally the bodies on the darkened livingroom floor, like mice on a mouse organ, woke up. They fumbled in a pocket for the profits of last night's gig (at which I had arranged to visit them at this ungodly hour - 11 am), and ascertained that they couldn't afford any breakfast - although essentials were affordable, and someone went out to buy some ciggies for the band.

I can see why their record label's called Seldom Fed.

Last night's gig had been at the Bishopgate Venue in Leeds. They played with Dandelion Adventure and hardly anyone turned up. Sadly, the Bishopgate has just closed, before it got established as a good venue. It's going to be turned into a club - after all, Leeds really needs another club, doesn't it kids?

Do you like playing in England?

"Sometimes the turnouts are so demoralising."

"Before we went to Germany, when no-one came to our gigs we thought, that's because we're shite."

"People in England have their heads up their arses."

"There are gigs every single night, most places we play. At the 1in12 six people paid."

But it's usually like that, there.

"Lots of it is to do with the music press - people believe what they read."

The more that can be done to dismantle the process by which the music press influences people, the better. Whether it's by encouraging people not to read it, or by laughing at it...

"Half the bands can't afford to go to the expense of things like publicity photographs, but they do it anyway, it's just the way it's done. I hate the music press and I never buy music papers. All those Manchester bands... the Puppy Mondays..."

Archbishop Kebab is a group made up of seemingly dozens of gypsyish kids from Edinburgh. Their names and instruments are: Duncan - drums, George - bass, James - fiddle & voice, Karen - vocals & melodica, Neil - mandolin & drums, Marcus - guitar, accordian, vocals & melodica.

At the time I was wondering a lot about the low proportion of women in bands. I asked Karen what could be done about the boring proliferation of boy bands.

"Get a band together!"

I've tried but it's not easy to motivate myself or others. Girls just don't seem to have the same immediate confidence to do things.

"It's just the way we've been brought up. Guitars have been made to be boys' things.

I guess it's time we reclaimed them then.

Why "Archbishop Kebab"? At first it just sounds whimsical, but a few moments consideration reveals what could only be a desire to skewer clergymen.

"Yeh, Wilf Plum [a Dog Faced Herman] came up with that one and that's exactly what it means. It's weird, some people claimed our name was racist - there was something about a Greek guy, an Archbishop Ke-something, Catharkos or something..."

"We're anything but racist, that's for sure."

You take your politics very seriously: how well do you think what you're saying comes across to people?

"The PA's usually shite and you can't hear the words anyway. But the booklet with the LP ["Yinferranodgie", on Seldom Fed, dist. by Southern], it's obvious that people are reading it."

Said booklet features all the lyrics, info on London Alliance against racism and fascism, Scottish Anti Poll Tax groups, lesbian and gay rights, Anarchist Black Cross and stuff about stoopid violence at gigs, as well as a cut-out cassette cover to encourage you to make a cute copy for a friend.

"That's cos we only pressed 1,000 records and we want more people than that to hear it."

Do you have many arguments?

"Sometimes some of us get a bit narked with Marcus but that's no big deal. The only time we argue is soon before we're going on tour or soon before we're going to record, when time's running out. But hell, we love each other totally, eh Marcus?"

"Totally" says Marcus.

"Eh Duncan?"

Duncan grunts in agreement, having, as yet, been unable to emerge from his sleepingbag on the floor or open his eyes.

I left them to some well-deserved early afternoon relaxation. Live, the Kebabs are anything but sleepy. We feel that this is an experience you should discover for yourself! But first, buy the record: \4.99 to 81 Clerk Street (tfr), Edinburgh EH8 9JG should do the trick.

flu

Leeds' excellent FLUFF interviewed by the Stuffed Cat

Could I write not just between the lines but all over them as well, three times or more? Otherwise, you see, I'm gonna have a tough time telling you about this band. Anything I say about them, no matter how many weekends I spend ineffectually hassling the typewriter keys, is just going to be bullshit. Because of the nature of music - it doesn't translate, (maybe if it did there would be no point in having it at all.) And because it's not a sound that's ever been previously described (so that you might understand it by association) it's something I've never heard happen before.

No dead things happen in their songs but their faded out memories, laughter at slaughtered teddybears, dogs and tropical bird mix. It's to do with plurality and with ignoring the rock treadmill churning round. Their stopstart song changes are almost comical when you first hear them; I mean, amusing in their unpredictability. They're refreshing cos they're reaching just beyond, which is the coolest thing in any, erm, art. Praise seems stupid - how can they comprehend your awe? Fluff are incapable of stooping to average depths, they don't sniff around money/gigs/deals/press - as you'll see. They wait till these things come to them (and sometimes send them away). If Fluff continue to accelerate as they have been doing they will go way into orbit, defying any definition... So, I can only offer clues.

I wanted to have a Fluff track on this flexi - it was the plan for ages and the band were into it, till Steve Hawkins (these long stories are necessarily abridged) came back from America and started throwing his slight weight around cos he wanted to be their manager. Suddenly, his intentions for Fluff were announced and these included the prevention of our putting a track by them on the flexi. The band had agreed to do it, but he told me that, in the (tragic) event of him becoming their manager I would no longer be dealing with a group of people, but one person only, i.e. him. Fluff hadn't even begun discussions about his proposed management, and at the time of going to press they haven't signed anything, yet the appearance of the Fluff track (the brilliant "Ash") has been prevented... "Why?" you shriek inconsolably. Strangely enough, one of the band had a dramatic turnaround of opinion following a series of cosy nights drinking with a certain would be manager, and now refuses to allow the track to go out. We are heartbroken to be unable to show you any of their music. Maybe you could write to them with bribes for tapes. Anyhow I'm grateful to Simon and Jayne for their reasonably reasonable attitude all along although I'm disappointed that they couldn't sort themselves, and Hawkins, out over the simple issue of someone offering to release their unsigned band's material. I don't want them to be hurt by my telling you this, though I know Steve Hawkins will object to being portrayed as a silly jerk. It's just that since the scales have fallen I thought I should share this insight with you.

Lament over. Here's an interview with a band you've probably never heard.

Why have you got such a crap name? It doesn't have anything to do with your music and the way the band is.

"We continually fluff things up! It says lots of things about the band," Jayne, bassist, disagreed.

"All our songs have one syllable titles," offered Simon, guitarist.

It has 3 'f's in it.

"And 'f' is the 6th letter of the alphabet," added Chris, co-interviewist, significantly (or perhaps not.)

Later, when I went off to seek the toilet in this gross building that held us, the tape recorder was left running...

"That Karren Ablaze! is a dead loss," said Tim, drummist. "I don't think our name's crap."

"Let's reanswer the question," suggested Jayne.

"It takes a long time, choosing a name, cos you have to live with it. I like names to sound good, not just for their meanings, and I think Fluff sounds good AND means something."

Fluff, for our purposes, means the combined musical output of three individuals: Jayne Lockey, who laughs a lot in a Birmingham accent, Simon Cleave, who says the most but very quietly, and Tim Beckham, who frequently utters cryptic comments that are usually unrewarding to follow up. It had taken what seems like years of pursuit to get this band to give me an interview, but now we had them in this concrete boat of a cafe. We sat on some sort of pyramid thing.

Why are you so elusive? You seem to shy away from publicity - what's your attitude to the music press?

"When you see bands like Ride," Simon began, and I braced myself for a scathing attack on media hype mechanisms and crap bands, only to be astonished by his pragmatism:"they've got all this new stuff [equipment], so it's worth doing it."

But!!! (My theories shattered) what about the weird side effects y'get from press attention?

"You read the music press, that's a side effect," Tim offered. Nothing more sinister than that.

(Later: "You can't go after sympathetic press. You have to deny its importance outwardly and accept it when it comes along.")

"We've never gone out on a flyposting session. I don't like seeing our name around, especially Leeds," admitted Simon.

Why don't you play more gigs?

"We wait till people ask, we don't like hassling for gigs. naively thought that if we practiced for long enough we'd ge to the point where people would ask us to play."

That this has actually started to happen is exemplified by the Pale Saints requesting Fluff's presence for their Leeds show.

"The whole process is frustratingly slow. But we don't begrudge any other bands doing what they want to do.

Jayne, are you an undiscovered bass hero?

"Oh yes! No."

"I think," thought Simon, "that people are still surprized that Jayne's a woman and that she plays bass."

Jayne, are you an undiscovered bass hero?

"Oh yes! No."

"I think," thought Simon, "that people are still surprized that Jayne's a woman and that she plays bass."

"I think that surprizes everyone, that I'm a woman!"

Chris reckoned they used to be a "real woman's band" in their previous incarnation, Moth Moth.

"There were only two women - we kept it even. It seems odd that there's still not many women involved [in this type of music?] There's quite a few good role models though, like t Muses" mused Simon.

"A C Temple's a classic example of the sexist group where the woman's "just the singer"..." Chris commented.

"Well, you can't argue with tradition." smart-assed Tim.

I can argue with YOU though, worm.

What's the idea behind setting out to have even numbers of men and women in the band?
"At the time," Simon told us, "we didn't want it to be a traditional thing, we were all non musicians and it made sense to have some idea drawn up before we even started. For effect... that's why it didn't last. We did a photosession before we even got a name! We were students, having fun. It wasn't very well thought out - it's very different now."

"So," grinned Chris,"you use weird tunings do you?"
"We're ripping off A C Temple."
"All references to A C Temple will be deleted from this interview forthwith."
That's what you think.

Tim, isn't your drumming strange? I believe you're in another band...
"No, my drumming is natural, it's not strange."
It's a bit arty.
"There's a lot of experimentation. It suits the songs, they're written with that in mind. That's why they're all so short - they're just ideas. Most are about two minutes, some less."
Does that tie in with the weird titles they've got?
"No, but that ties in with the timing. When we get to the end of the song we're so tired we can only utter one syllable."

Your songs seem really awkward when you first hear them. They go in a different direction from (Trad pop/rock) expectations, they sound really unpredictable. (Here follows Simon's substantial and very interesting bit so pay attention.)
"We realised that people come round to it when they've heard more than one set. They say "Oh I saw more in the same songs than the first time round." That's good, that's encouraging. The reason is that if we got bored... we couldn't practice 5 minute droning songs more than once a day. It'd be so boring. At least with these song structures there's more to engage your attention when you're playing. But it does mean that it tends to go over people's heads sometimes at gigs, especially cos you're at the mercy of sound people."
"It does make sense to have the songs that length, it goes along with not having trad tunings, not having trad song structures, not having 4 bars and 8 bars and a bridge and a chorus. I've got no proper knowledge of music but everyone has, if you've got records, it's what you hear all the time, so when you hear a band doing that it does sound awkward. I don't like repetition either..."
So you wont be making any house records then?

Are you embarrassed to sing and play in front of people?
"Yeh, I get really nervous. It's easier when there's loads of them, then you start performing."
"What do you think," asked Chris, "when you get psyched up a bit, do you think MEAN?"
"Ha ha ha ha!" Jayne doubled over.
"No," said Simon. "I have to concentrate so much singing and playing and being in time, trying to make sure nothing's an afterthought. Like vocals, that often happens."

A note on Fluff vocals: they are executed by Simon and Jayne, and have conquered past shyness to become impressive, weird and truly wonderful.
"Have you ever thought," questioned Chris, "of getting another member, to relieve you of your guitar duties while you sing?"
"No, I like the way it pushes my ability to play it every time we do a song... [He claims to write guitar parts that he can't quite play]. We had 2 guitars in MothMoth, but if you strip one guitar away you've got so much more space to play around with. That space is what I think makes it sound so good."
Apparently, Fluff songs played on guitar alone are unrecognisable because it's all carried by the bass.
"We could have more drums carrying things... that might upset the rhythm section... I keep looking for ways to make it more interesting for us.
(I think Tim should sing as well, that'd be fucking mega, like Nomeansno - their best bits live are when the drummer sings too.)
Another person would ruin the 3-piecefulness of it, wouldn't they?
"Mmm yeh no, I like power trios. Firehose, Minutemen, The Jam,"
Tim: "Cream."
What are your lyrics about?
"I write mine and he writes his, they're about two completely different things in the same songs," said Jayne.
"They're about wnat everyone else sings about," Simon claimed, somewhat unconvincingly.
"They're not about love."
(Later: "They come from god... the garden."
"They have nothing to do with the titles. They're stories about things that interest me, whittled down to their essences.")
I can testify (tsetsefly?) that Fluff lyrics are strange affairs. Do I love them? You guess. My rough transcript notes (therefore, apologies for any inaccuracies/sheer flights of fancy herein - I can't be arsed to play the interview back again after all this time, I think I've lost the tape anyway) feature lines such as "lies dead on a teaspoon," and "why do crows have so much fun... when we don't?". A letter given to me with their heart achingly delightful tape featured cryptic notes/red herrings for each track. The entry for "Joey" reads: "Good fun at school maybe, but that's what comes of swimming in a sea of chrome. Steps should be taken except they're too hard to climb."

(So much of this is tied up with numbers, though I can't grasp why. Tim admitted to abhoring even numbers, but when I asked for an explanation he said "It's all to do with the reverse side of the tree," and would elaborate no further.)

What a band. They've got a brillant drummer and a total basketcase seeking to control them. They're capable of outgrowing themselves each week. Listen out - you'll never have heard anything like this in your life.

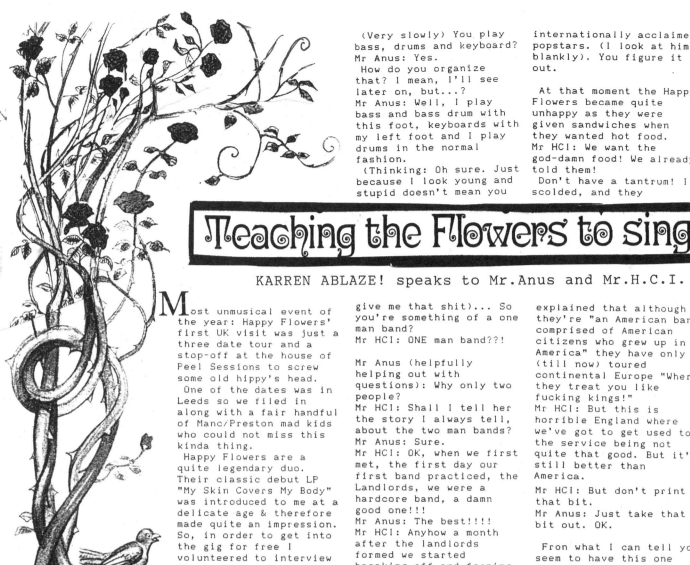

(Very slowly) You play bass, drums and keyboard?
Mr Anus: Yes.
How do you organize that? I mean, I'll see later on, but...?
Mr Anus: Well, I play bass and bass drum with this foot, keyboards with my left foot and I play drums in the normal fashion.
(Thinking: Oh sure. Just because I look young and stupid doesn't mean you give me that shit)... So you're something of a one man band?
Mr HCI: ONE man band??!

Mr Anus (helpfully helping out with questions): Why only two people?
Mr HCI: Shall I tell her the story I always tell, about the two man bands?
Mr Anus: Sure.
Mr HCI: OK, when we first met, the first day our first band practiced, the Landlords, we were a hardcore band, a damn good one!!!
Mr Anus: The best!!!!
Mr HCI: Anyhow a month after the landlords formed we started breaking off and forming all these little two man bands so there was like Big Foot...
How d'you get by, being called Mr Anus?
Mr Anus: How d'you mean, "get by"?
Like, when you have to sign a cheque or something...
Mr Anus: Well it's not on my passport you know, it's not what my mother calls me...
Mr HCI: Not usually. So we formed all these other two man sub bands: Big Foot, which was the bass player and myself, The Rock'n'roll Brothers which was the bass player and him, the Mel Cooly (?) Fusion Project which was the bass player and the drummer, and Happy Flowers which was us. We were the only one that ever made a decent sounding tape, well Big Foot made some pretty hot tapes and the Rock'n'roll Brothers made a good one but they lost it, but we were the only ones that put out a single and played live, and it just sort of exploded into this stupidity.
Mr Anus: The strange thing is that we are arguably the worst of those two man bands and yet we've become internationally acclaimed popstars. (I look at him blankly). You figure it out.

At that moment the Happy Flowers became quite unhappy as they were given sandwiches when they wanted hot food.
Mr HCI: We want the god-damn food! We already told them!
Don't have a tantrum! I scolded, and they explained that although they're "an American band comprised of American citizens who grew up in America" they have only (till now) toured continental Europe "Where they treat you like fucking kings!"
Mr HCI: But this is horrible England where we've got to get used to the service being not quite that good. But it's still better than America.
Mr HCI: But don't print that bit.
Mr Anus: Just take that bit out. OK.

Fron what I can tell you seem to have this one joke that you're kids going though terrible traumas.
Mr Anus : Hahaha, It's art! It's art! It's art! No you're right it is a one joke band. But that's OK cos many bands don't even have one joke
Mr HCI: Like... ?
Mr Anus: Oh we wont name anyone.
But some bands have very many and you seem to get away with...
Mr HCI: Well, we approach it from so many angles.
Mr Anus: When we can't get away with it anymore we'll think of another one I guess.
Mr HCI: There's not so much of that on our new album anyway.

Where does your interest in the terrors of childhood stem from? Is it memories - was it so bad for you that you cant get over it?
Mr Anus: Well...
Mr HCI: I...
Mr Anus: Go ahead.
Mr HCI: No you go ahead.
Mr Anus: After you.
Mr HCI: No.
Mr Anus: I insist.
Mr HCI: You go first.
Mr Anus: You started first, you fuck.
Mr HCI: You started first and I...
Mr Anus: I'm gonna vomit

Teaching the Flowers to sing

KARREN ABLAZE! speaks to Mr.Anus and Mr.H.C.I.

Most unmusical event of the year: Happy Flowers' first UK visit was just a three date tour and a stop-off at the house of Peel Sessions to screw some old hippy's head.
One of the dates was in Leeds so we filed in along with a fair handful of Manc/Preston mad kids who could not miss this kinda thing.
Happy Flowers are a quite legendary duo. Their classic debut LP "My Skin Covers My Body" was introduced to me at a delicate age & therefore made quite an impression. So, in order to get into the gig for free I volunteered to interview the terible twins Mr Anus & Mr Horribly Charred Infant. The following discussion took place in the Duchess' rather spacious dressingroom type thing, beginning with a few tentative probings (i.e. no planned strategy at all, employing the typical Ablaze! interview method of stumbling in late not knowing what the band look or sound like, and proceeding to insult them on various levels):
How old are you?
Mr HCI: I'll be 27 in a month and he'll be 27 thirteen weeks after that.
You're not brothers or anything are you?
Mr Anus: Yes.
Mr HCI: We get asked that a lot - No, it'd be tough to be thirteen weeks apart if we were brothers.
Mr Anus: We could be fraternal twins (Mr HCI gasps) No I guess we couldn't. I was never very good at biology.

So there's just two of you? What does each of you do?
Mr Anus: Generally, he plays guitar and sings, and I play bass, drums and keyboard, and sing.

all over the place if you don't speak right now.
Mr HCI: I had an awful childhood and I can remember it quite vividly. Your turn.
Mr Anus: I had a fine childhood, I think. We sort of started the childhood trauma thing by accident, cos we did one song that was kinda like a childhood trauma deal and that seemed to go over prettty good so we figured well, being Americans we should exploit this to its fullest, which we have done quite profitably, yek yek yek. How's that?
Mr HCI: There's a charge for the interview, by the way, £5...
Mr Anus: We take American Express. That's not all we do but it's most of what we do, people seem to get off on it so, we being ruthlessly exploitative and capitalistic, we do what people want.

Erm, d'you think you've been quite influential, d'you think there have been kids around trying to be Happy Flowers?
Mr Anus: I hope so cos it's quite easy to do actually.
Mr HCI: Some kids we know in Austria are planning on putting out a Happy Flowers tribute record, sorta like the Byrds and Jimi Hendrix and all those tribute records, they're gonna do one of those, just a 5 song 7" though. Apparently someone's gonna do "Stop touching my food" on a 5 string acoustic guitar. So that'll be nice.
Mr Anus: It's hard to tell sometimes if bands are consciously ripping us off or if they just can't play.

D'you want to tell me how you got to be called Happy Flowers which is such a lovely name?
Mr Anus: Well that sounds all pretty factual to me so I'll let you handle this one.
Mr HCI: Well "Happy Flowers" came from an interview with another band in Maximumrock'n'roll back in '83, one of the questions was why do hardcore bands have such self-deprecating names, and they, whoever answered it, said "Well, if you called yourselves something like Happy Flowers nobody would go see you, they'd all think you were a bunch of queers." So naturally I chose that name. Well it was just before the Landlords formed and I knew I wanted to be in a band called Happy Flowers. I was pushing for that name for the Landlords but we ditched it, luckily, because Happy Flowers would be a lot less interesting if they were called the Landlords, I think.

Landlords is a scary name.
Mr HCI: We picked that name because we had to play somewhere that night and the landlord lived downstairs from where we practiced and was always giving us shit. Although my current landlord, my friend Brian's mother, is very nice.

So (I slurred, as the batteries were running down) yeh, and why are you called Mr Anus and Mr Horribly Charred Infantthen?
Mr HCI: He was over at my apartment, I called him an asshole, he said "that's Mr Asshole to you!" and it just sort of degenerated into Mr Anus. So he had to make up a pseudonym for me, and we were walking down the street and he said how about Mr Horribly Charred Infant and I laughed so hard I nearly fell down and hit myself, so we picked that.

It's a bit sick isn't it?
Mr Anus: Well, no not really yes. The idea actually came from a book, it had this picture of a horribly charred infant, so I was thinking of this picture I had in my mind which was really awful, and I thought that would be a nice name...
Mr HCI: UT broke up?
Mr Anus: Have they? (Switches to narrator's voice) Currently reading the fanzine, Mr HCI ignores the interview entirely.
Mr HCI: Sorry, you were answering a question...
Mr Anus: (Snatching the copy of Ablaze! from HCI's hands) Now I can read it.
Mr HCI: Don't mess up the flexi man!
Mr Anus: It's MY flexi.
Mr HCI: IT'S MY FLEXI!

What are your songs REALLY about?
Mr Anus: Pick a song and I'll tell you.

"Jenny tried to kiss me at recess."
Mr HCI: That's true, except she never actually caught me and her name wasn't Jenny. I couldn't remember her name when we were in the studio, but her name was Amanda, and she used to chase me all over the playground at recess in second grade.

At that poignant moment I left them to their sulking fits and yelling attacks, and went to hang out with the Kids downstairs. After pondering in disbelief what Mr Anus had told me about playing so many instruments in such irreverent ways, I was quite freaked out to watch him placing a keyboard and a bass guitar on the floor by his drumkit and proceed to stamp on them. Their set turned out to be a highly dramatic affair, in which the ridiculous tumult of screaming, bad guitar playing, very bad bass playing and TERRIBLE keyboard playing, not to mention Anus's infantile drumming techniques (like trying to play the inside of his nostrils) seemed perfectly reasonable. Their contrived pre-pubescent anarchy should go down well with right-on fools everywhere - perhaps it's time they expanded their market from its hardcore-scene limitations and launch their inventive, fake child's-eye view on the masses.

the End

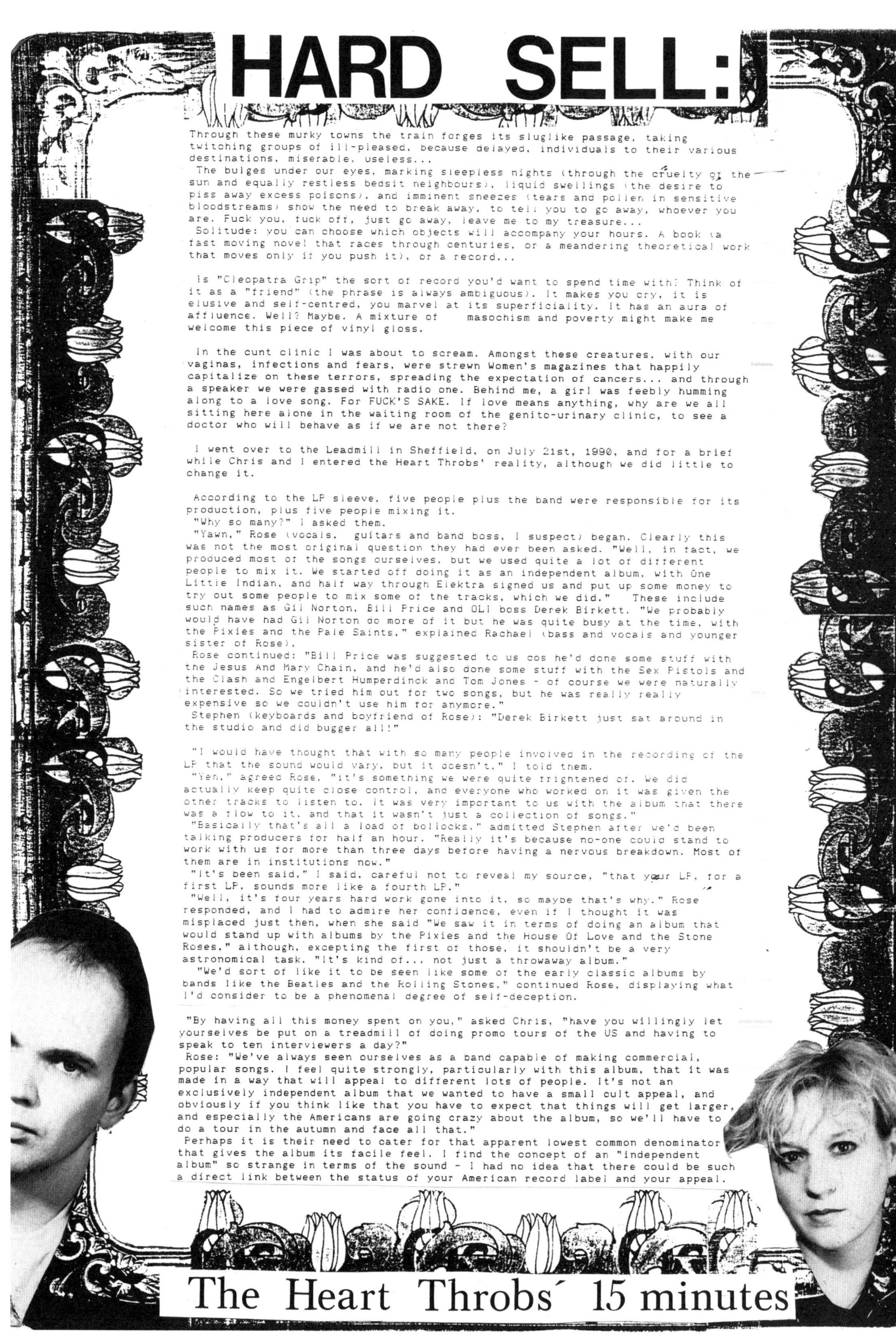

HARD SELL:

Through these murky towns the train forges its sluglike passage, taking twitching groups of ill-pleased, because delayed, individuals to their various destinations, miserable, useless...

The bulges under our eyes, marking sleepless nights (through the cruelty of the sun and equally restless bedsit neighbours), liquid swellings (the desire to piss away excess poisons), and imminent sneezes (tears and pollen in sensitive bloodstreams) show the need to break away, to tell you to go away, whoever you are. Fuck you, fuck off, just go away, leave me to my treasure...

Solitude: you can choose which objects will accompany your hours. A book (a fast moving novel that races through centuries, or a meandering theoretical work that moves only if you push it), or a record...

Is "Cleopatra Grip" the sort of record you'd want to spend time with? Think of it as a "friend" (the phrase is always ambiguous). It makes you cry, it is elusive and self-centred, you marvel at its superficiality. It has an aura of affluence. Well? Maybe. A mixture of masochism and poverty might make me welcome this piece of vinyl gloss.

In the cunt clinic I was about to scream. Amongst these creatures, with our vaginas, infections and fears, were strewn Women's magazines that happily capitalize on these terrors, spreading the expectation of cancers... and through a speaker we were gassed with radio one. Behind me, a girl was feebly humming along to a love song. For FUCK'S SAKE. If love means anything, why are we all sitting here alone in the waiting room of the genito-urinary clinic, to see a doctor who will behave as if we are not there?

I went over to the Leadmill in Sheffield, on July 21st, 1990, and for a brief while Chris and I entered the Heart Throbs' reality, although we did little to change it.

According to the LP sleeve, five people plus the band were responsible for its production, plus five people mixing it.

"Why so many?" I asked them.

"Yawn," Rose (vocals, guitars and band boss, I suspect) began. Clearly this was not the most original question they had ever been asked. "Well, in fact, we produced most of the songs ourselves, but we used quite a lot of different people to mix it. We started off doing it as an independent album, with One Little Indian, and half way through Elektra signed us and put up some money to try out some people to mix some of the tracks, which we did." These include such names as Gil Norton, Bill Price and OLI boss Derek Birkett. "We probably would have had Gil Norton do more of it but he was quite busy at the time, with the Pixies and the Pale Saints," explained Rachael (bass and vocals and younger sister of Rose).

Rose continued: "Bill Price was suggested to us cos he'd done some stuff with the Jesus And Mary Chain, and he'd also done some stuff with the Sex Pistols and the Clash and Engelbert Humperdinck and Tom Jones - of course we were naturally interested. So we tried him out for two songs, but he was really really expensive so we couldn't use him for anymore."

Stephen (keyboards and boyfriend of Rose): "Derek Birkett just sat around in the studio and did bugger all!"

"I would have thought that with so many people involved in the recording of the LP that the sound would vary, but it doesn't," I told them.

"Yeh," agreed Rose, "it's something we were quite frightened of. We did actually keep quite close control, and everyone who worked on it was given the other tracks to listen to. It was very important to us with the album that there was a flow to it, and that it wasn't just a collection of songs."

"Basically that's all a load of bollocks," admitted Stephen after we'd been talking producers for half an hour. "Really it's because no-one could stand to work with us for more than three days before having a nervous breakdown. Most of them are in institutions now."

"It's been said," I said, careful not to reveal my source, "that your LP, for a first LP, sounds more like a fourth LP."

"Well, it's four years hard work gone into it, so maybe that's why," Rose responded, and I had to admire her confidence, even if I thought it was misplaced just then, when she said "We saw it in terms of doing an album that would stand up with albums by the Pixies and the House Of Love and the Stone Roses," although, excepting the first of those, it shouldn't be a very astronomical task. "It's kind of... not just a throwaway album."

"We'd sort of like it to be seen like some of the early classic albums by bands like the Beatles and the Rolling Stones," continued Rose, displaying what I'd consider to be a phenomenal degree of self-deception.

"By having all this money spent on you," asked Chris, "have you willingly let yourselves be put on a treadmill of doing promo tours of the US and having to speak to ten interviewers a day?"

Rose: "We've always seen ourselves as a band capable of making commercial, popular songs. I feel quite strongly, particularly with this album, that it was made in a way that will appeal to different lots of people. It's not an exclusively independent album that we wanted to have a small cult appeal, and obviously if you think like that you have to expect that things will get larger, and especially the Americans are going crazy about the album, so we'll have to do a tour in the autumn and face all that."

Perhaps it is their need to cater for that apparent lowest common denominator that gives the album its facile feel. I find the concept of an "independent album" so strange in terms of the sound - I had no idea that there could be such a direct link between the status of your American record label and your appeal.

The Heart Throbs´ 15 minutes

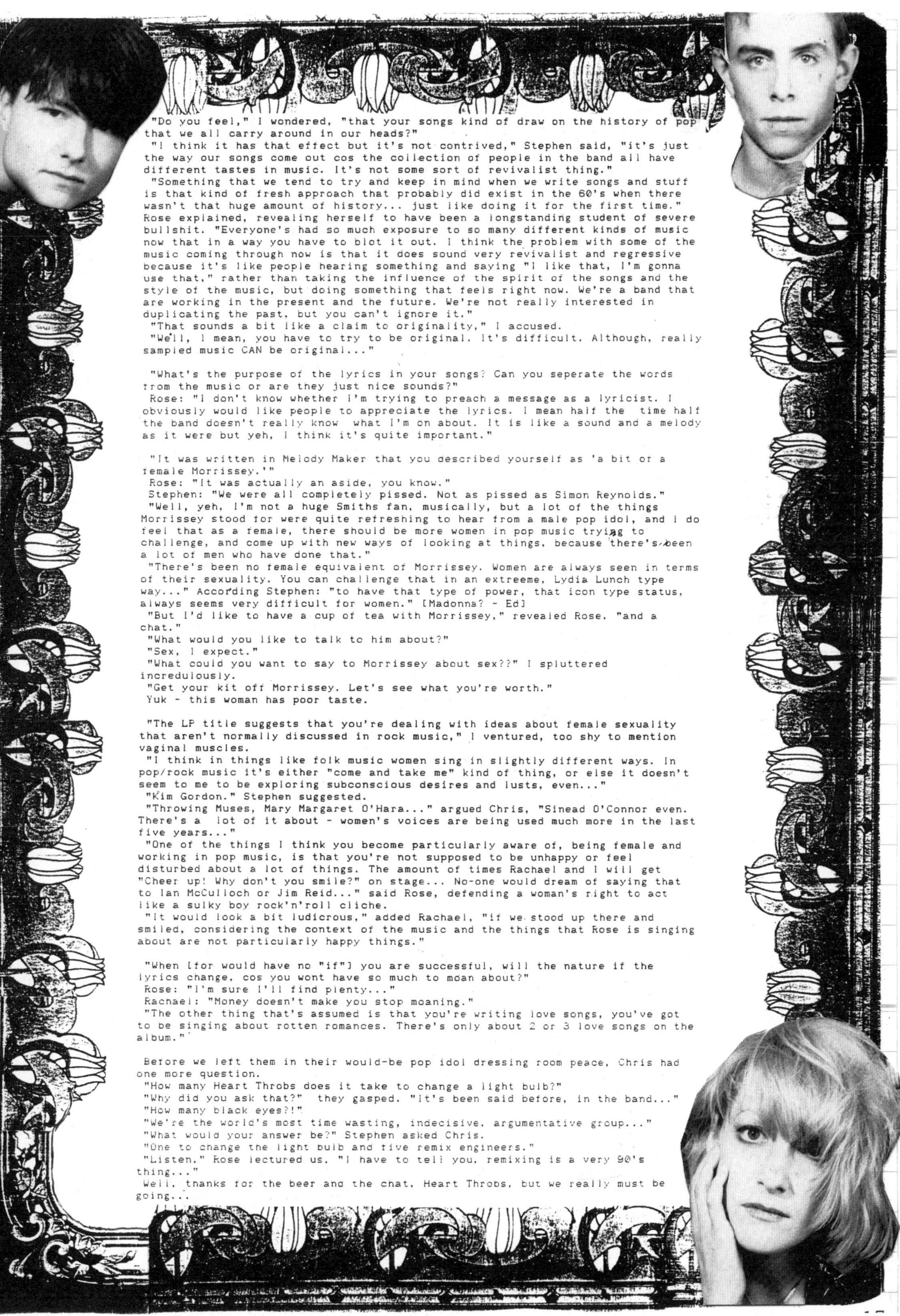

"Do you feel," I wondered, "that your songs kind of draw on the history of pop that we all carry around in our heads?"

"I think it has that effect but it's not contrived," Stephen said, "it's just the way our songs come out cos the collection of people in the band all have different tastes in music. It's not some sort of revivalist thing."

"Something that we tend to try and keep in mind when we write songs and stuff is that kind of fresh approach that probably did exist in the 60's when there wasn't that huge amount of history... just like doing it for the first time." Rose explained, revealing herself to have been a longstanding student of severe bullshit. "Everyone's had so much exposure to so many different kinds of music now that in a way you have to blot it out. I think the problem with some of the music coming through now is that it does sound very revivalist and regressive because it's like people hearing something and saying "I like that, I'm gonna use that," rather than taking the influence of the spirit of the songs and the style of the music, but doing something that feels right now. We're a band that are working in the present and the future. We're not really interested in duplicating the past, but you can't ignore it."

"That sounds a bit like a claim to originality," I accused.

"Well, I mean, you have to try to be original. It's difficult. Although, really sampled music CAN be original..."

"What's the purpose of the lyrics in your songs? Can you seperate the words from the music or are they just nice sounds?"

Rose: "I don't know whether I'm trying to preach a message as a lyricist. I obviously would like people to appreciate the lyrics. I mean half the time half the band doesn't really know what I'm on about. It is like a sound and a melody as it were but yeh, I think it's quite important."

"It was written in Melody Maker that you described yourself as 'a bit of a female Morrissey.'"

Rose: "It was actually an aside, you know."

Stephen: "We were all completely pissed. Not as pissed as Simon Reynolds."

"Well, yeh, I'm not a huge Smiths fan, musically, but a lot of the things Morrissey stood for were quite refreshing to hear from a male pop idol, and I do feel that as a female, there should be more women in pop music trying to challenge, and come up with new ways of looking at things, because there's been a lot of men who have done that."

"There's been no female equivalent of Morrissey. Women are always seen in terms of their sexuality. You can challenge that in an extreeme, Lydia Lunch type way..." According Stephen: "to have that type of power, that icon type status, always seems very difficult for women." [Madonna? - Ed]

"But I'd like to have a cup of tea with Morrissey," revealed Rose, "and a chat."

"What would you like to talk to him about?"

"Sex, I expect."

"What could you want to say to Morrissey about sex??" I spluttered incredulously.

"Get your kit off Morrissey. Let's see what you're worth."

Yuk - this woman has poor taste.

"The LP title suggests that you're dealing with ideas about female sexuality that aren't normally discussed in rock music," I ventured, too shy to mention vaginal muscles.

"I think in things like folk music women sing in slightly different ways. In pop/rock music it's either "come and take me" kind of thing, or else it doesn't seem to me to be exploring subconscious desires and lusts, even..."

"Kim Gordon." Stephen suggested.

"Throwing Muses, Mary Margaret O'Hara..." argued Chris, "Sinead O'Connor even. There's a lot of it about - women's voices are being used much more in the last five years..."

"One of the things I think you become particularly aware of, being female and working in pop music, is that you're not supposed to be unhappy or feel disturbed about a lot of things. The amount of times Rachael and I will get "Cheer up! Why don't you smile?" on stage... No-one would dream of saying that to Ian McCulloch or Jim Reid..." said Rose, defending a woman's right to act like a sulky boy rock'n'roll cliche.

"It would look a bit ludicrous," added Rachael, "if we stood up there and smiled, considering the context of the music and the things that Rose is singing about are not particularly happy things."

"When [for would have no "if"] you are successful, will the nature if the lyrics change, cos you wont have so much to moan about?"

Rose: "I'm sure I'll find plenty..."

Rachael: "Money doesn't make you stop moaning."

"The other thing that's assumed is that you're writing love songs, you've got to be singing about rotten romances. There's only about 2 or 3 love songs on the album."

Before we left them in their would-be pop idol dressing room peace, Chris had one more question.

"How many Heart Throbs does it take to change a light bulb?"

"Why did you ask that?" they gasped. "It's been said before, in the band..."

"How many black eyes?!"

"We're the world's most time wasting, indecisive, argumentative group..."

"What would your answer be?" Stephen asked Chris.

"One to change the light bulb and five remix engineers."

"Listen," Rose lectured us, "I have to tell you, remixing is a very 90's thing..."

Well, thanks for the beer and the chat, Heart Throbs, but we really must be going...

the

Scene: Preston Ribdale club, closing time after another Martin-created night of mayhem from The General Havoc, Kilgore Trout, Dandelion Adventure and these rather queer Southern people.

"Hello!" "Hello!" they said.

All the Keatons present introduced themselves:"Warren, Steve, Neil, Alison, Mo, Rhodri."

Rhodri:"I'm the fattest one but I'm not fattist."

We spoke quickly, all huddled together, lest the angry man with the vacuum who had been trying to kick us out should instead resort to sucking us into his hoover bag.

So what's all this I've heard about dramatic line up alterations?

R: "It's through circumstance not musical differences."

Steve: Cos people have got appalling jobs like in Nabisco and stuff and they can't get away so we just do gigs with whoever is available. There's a supergroup of 3 and a feeble group of about 12."

R: "Except we dont do 8 at a time."

What's been the smallest number of Keatons ever?"

S: "4."

And the biggest?

"6."

Ah, that's not a very vast variation.

S: "No, but the 4 and 6 are different, if you counted up all the groups together it'd be about 12. We've done a gig with 10 guest singers and gigs with 10 guest guitarists so we've done gigs where there's been a band of 16."

(Durrrr...) Does this like vary your sound quite a lot?

S: "Yes. And for the benefit definitely. Because we do loads of gigs in London to basically the same people we try and do something different everytime but when we play Preston we just do the same old rubbish!"

What's the significance of the number 7?

Neil: "That's cos the beat goes 1234567.

R:123456!7!"

So is that weird?

S: "There's 'the 7 shades of colours'..."

Neil: "That came later."

R: "So when you hear the song you gotta remember: 12345,7!"

S: "Rhodri knows about music."

7 isn't your favourite number is it?

S: "Any diabolist connections?"

N: mumble (prob. not)

R: "Intriguingly I ate 7 slices of toast this morning."

Weird. Very very strange.

R: "In fact I only ever do things in sevens since releasing the record. Just in case."

Like 7 pints.

S:"7 PIES, more like."

R: "With copious chips."

Mo: "And 70 inches round the waist!"

Would you like to tell me about your approach to lyric writing please?

N: "Yeh, I do it quickly. Thrash a tune out first and write the words over it."

Do you use strange dictionaries and things?

N: "No, it all comes out of my head."

R: "Almost immediate isn't it? You could make one up on the spot. In fact you do..."

N: "There's only 2 or 3 songs where I've spent time, actually thought of it beforehand and added music to it."

R: "They're all about war as well... tanks and war."

N: "There was a phase...of 3 or 4 songs...but the theory that all of them are about war is... disputed territory."

S: "All the songs are about tanks and relationships."

Are they anti-war songs or do you believe in killing barmen?

All: "Yeh, yeh."

M: "No, we're about taking them to bed."

S: "Bedding barmen."

So is that what being a Keaton is all about then? You're just after groupies?

S: "The bigger and hairier the better.

R: "We're all about having sex. We're a very sexual band."

keatons

How do you cope with being a sex symbol?
R: "I can cope with it. Most of the girls seem to go for Dave but he's not here at the moment."
S: "They go for his David Gedge-like hair."
R: Steve's got the rugged charm y'see, I've got the baby eyes and Mo's got the come to bed arms, Warren's got the sexist moustache and Neil's got everything really. One luscious lump!"
Barman: "Oi!" etc. "Clear the premises!" etc.
R: "In fact we deny our involvement with any form of bream."
What are your favourite books?
R: "Delia Smith's book of cakes! That's not a witty off-the-cuff remark, it's true."
Yeh, recipe books are food pornography, they're wonderful
R: "I love seeing naked cakes."
S: "John Wyndham or Willard Price."
R: "You pretentious bastard."
S: "Willard Price wrote 'Gorilla Adventure', it's very good."
R: "The Dalek Pocketbook, which in fact states that 'j' is the forbidden letter of the dalek language."

Erm, I'm told you play the bassoon, Rhodri.
R: "No, Mo plays the bassoon."
M (in a correcting tone):"No, I play the clarinet."
R: "Oh yeh, he plays the clarinet, I play the bassoon, that's right."
What's a bassoon?
R: "It was invented in 1842."
M: "By Alf Bassoon."
S: "It's furry."
R: "Warren likes to have sex with it. It's a wood instrument, it's a rock posturing instument. When you play the bassoon it just means 'Suck on this then make my tea'."
Generally: "Yek yek yek."
R: "The next single's gonna be called 'Spread 'em, bitch.'"
S: "This is IRONY, everyone. Heavy, heavy irony."

I believe you're fans of Brain Fag.
S: "Yes, Harlow's biggest and most splendid band."
What do you see in them?
R: "I see a few people who are very nice."
S: "Young people who're very enthusiastic."
R: "Sexy."
S: "Marvellous."
W: "Are they a band?"
S: "Yes Warren they're a band. They're a type of toilet tissue."

This is a deep important question - what are your favourite plants, planets and words?
N? W? (without hesitation, whoever it was): "Cannabis plant cos it's got really nice leaves."
S: "Mercury, tremble..."
R: "Lozenge, xenophobe 9, and..."
S: "Cactuses are very good."
M: "Vegetables, the moon, and..."
R: "Gorrila hat."

Then we had to move as the hoovering up was getting really serious. I announced that I wanted to talk to Mo, sexy Keatons dancer, puppet-show host and toothpaste dispenser (truly) about art...

So, art: What is it? How is it spelt? Tell me about puppets and things like that.
M: "What you do with your interveiwing is art... I do various things as well as this, paint pictures & write as well. The puppets came from when I worked with children on a playscheme, they gave me all the best ideas and I 've stolen them."

continued on p. 37.

Silverfish ain't no goldfish (except in their drinking habits). The ace thing about going to see them is that everyone gets sweaty and wild while Lesley throws back her thick black hair and brays at the hot air like a demented ass (or should I say "AAAAAAAAAASS"), and mad Fuzz fuses with his guitar and Chris plays with basely neandearthal nerve and the drums get a damn good hiding at the hands of Stuart, and the whole thing is dead dead messy and loud as shit. They just scream and jump about, like rock'n'roll reborn with a knife it its gut and a big fucked grin on its face.

I was thrilled to bump into Lesley at an A C Temple gig in London early in the year. I told her that I'd like to do a Silverfish interview and that I felt funny in my head. She laughed and suggested I should get really pissed.

But getting pissed can be a writer's downfall, especially at gigs by bands you could do with speaking to. Silverfish first played Leeds supporting Fire Party. I can recall nothing of the gig itself but I've since spent a while ascertaining which one of them I slurred to in the van on the way home (we got a brief lift cos they were kidnapping Andrew Ruth, Preston's fanzine king.) (For the record, it was Stuart, not Chris). And now Fire Party are far far away and too inactive for even a postal interview (they're doing other things for a bit.) So there are some morals in that story, but not very many.

Down to the real blathering: the Silver Fishes came back to the Duchess, and me and Ken snuck into their dressingroom. Charlie, ex-UT, was there, so I began by asking this drummer boy what Sally, Nina and Jacqui are going to do now that their band has unformed.

"Nina's gone to America for a while, and Jacqui might be doing some writing. We might be doing another LP though - our last gig was yesterday but we've got about 5 or 6 really cool songs that someone wants to record, so we're negotiating now to do that."
At least there's something left to look forward to UT-wise... at least it will afford some consolation to bereaved fans.

After various Silverfish stopped moaning about the performance of their lighting man that evening, I hassled them about why their last scheduled Leeds gig was cancelled. They'd been due to support the Lunachicks in the winter, but the NY cookie monsters had their UK thang postponed (Why does this keep happening? I just wanna snog them all! But not at the same time probably.) and it turned out that the venues just didn't want the 'Fish without the 'Chicks.

We went on to establish that Lesley had lived in London for six and a half years, Fuzz for twentysix and a half, and that Fuzz, Stu and Chris had been pals for years and years. For what that's worth. And before we knew it, we were slagging off God. But no-one's interested in this, except maybe them, so instead here's a 'Fish's eye view on some stuff:

"We've only been going for just over a year, but we've worked... The way we are live, most of the bands that are classed with us, Terminal Cheesecake, God, just tend to stand on the spot and do their job. We jump around and generate a lot of excitement. We're not dead tight; it's the attitude rather than the professional playing that matters."

Does it bug you to see people dancing in herds?

"If I saw a fight I'd just stop playing and stop it," insists Fuzz.

Robbie from Loop band Spin Out was there too, and told us this tale: "Chris here stopped a guy getting chucked out at the Sheffield gig... the bouncers were gonna chuck him out and he [Chris] got off the stage, ran up to the door and grabbed hold of him, yelled at the bouncers "f'k'n' leave him alone!"... and he was still playing the bass the whole time. That was brilliant."
A round of applause was given for Chris's cool dexterity.
"I was playing with my knuckles the other day," the hero admitted.
"Chris is the missing link," Lesley decided.

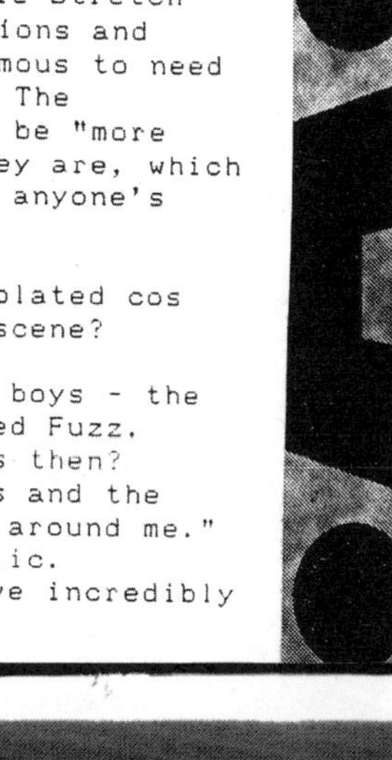

On the subject of who they admire in other bands, the names Richie Stretch Head and Ajay of the Dandelions and Houndgod, who is far too famous to need a surname, were brought up. The Stretchies they consider to be "more energy over content"than they are, which is a notable achievement in anyone's book.

Lesley, d'you ever feel isolated cos there's mostly boys on the scene?
"Naaah!"
"Lesley doesn't get enough boys - the bigger the better!" commented Fuzz.
Do you get lots of groupies then?
"No, I just get the weirdos and the chronically strange hanging around me."
You should eat lots of garlic.
"I just fart wildly and have incredibly bad breath."

A.E.W.

Silverfish were asked to put stuff out on God's label, Pathological, and got hassle off them for going with Wiiija instead.
"They wouldn't even put their own stuff out on Pathological so that says it all really. They signed to Situation 2, part of Beggars Banquet.
"It's not worth talking about," they agreed.
"We're getting stuff together for an LP (this may have all happened when you read this) hopefully with Steve Albini and maybe in Chicago.* Depends how far we can twist their [Wiiija's] arms."
"It was quite strange getting a phone call from Steve Alibini."
"I thought it was someone taking the piss trying to get our address."

What are the important things about Silverfish?
"We've all got big nobs," Lesley declared proudly, "especially me."

*AS WE GO TO PRINT, SILVERFISH ARE RECORDING WITH ALBINI AT SHEFFIELD'S AXIS STUDIO...

"I don't like having my toes sucked, she added. "It's like standing on a slug with bare feet! But I'd pay somebody to tickle my feet all night - my eyes fall back in my head and I float off in a cloud of ecstacy."
There's a fine occupation for one of you yobs in reader-land!

The last word?
"We say DO IT YOURSELF by actually doing it."

It's true! For example, when Silverfish get pissed, they get really paralytic. Charlie and Fuzz stayed at my house, and Fuzz insisted he'd never been there before. (I could recall, through a haze, demanding to know why him and his girlfriend were spending so long in our bathroom after the Fire Party gig. I later assumed that they'd been indulging in some pre-longjourneyhome copulation, but when I quizzed him about it this time he denied it: "Nah, we got all that over with at the Duchess.") So I had to show him where the bathoom was again. Then, after an hour or so of animation and opinionation on the state of music today etc, he asked me where the bathroom was. Fuzz truly merits the "Memory-span of a goldfish" prize of a golden bowl to wear over his dreads.
Next afternoon, the rest of the 'Fish entourage turned up (I think) and Lesley made some tea and Chris (London fanzine king, author of the sadly missed Irreversible Neural Damage, one of the coolest and straight-uppest zines about) helped me fold some fanzines. Verdict: Yeh, I quite like these people so buy their records: so far, there's 2 12"s from '89: Dolly Parton/On the Motorway/Weird shit & Don't fuck (Wiiijit 4) and the TFA EP, Total Fucking Asshole b/w Die & Driller (Wij 5), so visit your local Wiiija dealer now and get that braying vibe.

Mayomberos ALIVE!

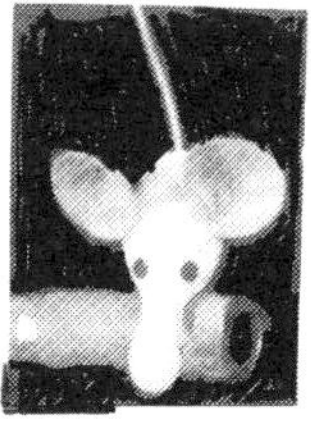

One thirty AM, in August blackness, I was sitting in my room contemplating strange shaped birds, sea birds and the nature of the human psyche when the telephone rang. A man in an Irish accent addressed me as "chuck" and suggested that I fetch a pen and paper. I did so, bringing with me a lamp, and crouched in the hall to note down what they had to say.

"We're phoning from a petrol station in Dublin. Can you hear the cars going in and out?" said the man who identified himself as Mr Say. "Me and Iz work here at night, it enables us to make international phone calls to people we don't know. The telephone can be an art form and a means of mind control - listen -"

His voice ceased and I heard a series of bleeps which slowly blended into another humanoid voice, also Irish male type.

"Pick up your Hamlyn Guide To Astronomy and turn to page 61."

Oddly enough, I realised the said volume was lying on the grubby carpet before me. Opening it at that page I saw a purple diagram. At the centre was a small circle, surrounded by another, much larger, circle. Three white arrows emerged from the right hand side of the page; the lowest one hit the centre point of the circle, the middle one joined with the outer circle, and the highest one went way, way out and seemed as if it would continue to do so for an undeterminable period. This final arrow, I knew, depicted the course of the individuals on the other end of my phone line. I told them so.

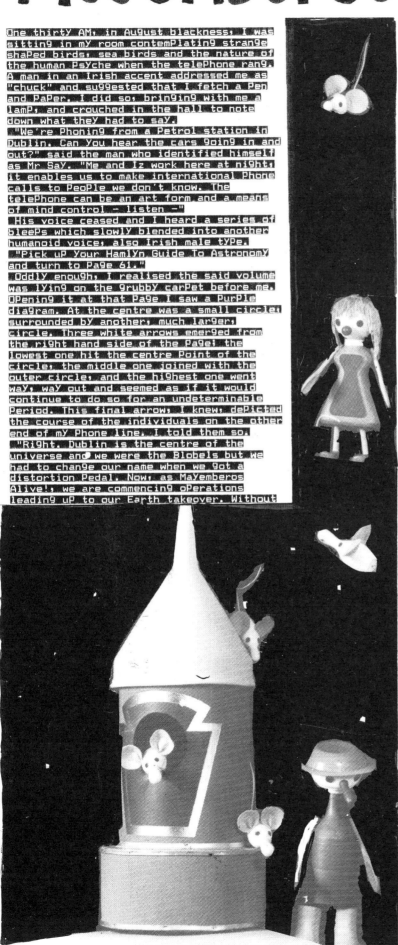

"Right. Dublin is the centre of the universe and we were the Blobels but we had to change our name when we got a distortion pedal. Now, as Mayemberos Alive!, we are commencing operations leading up to our Earth takeover. Without your knowledge we have already gained control of your body, and while you sleep, those things you think of as dreams are in fact real live nocturnal actions that advance our cause."

"But... no!!" I exclaimed, quickly remembering. "I really did those things? That's... disgusting!"

"Don't worry about inappropriate sexual partners and mindless slaughter of friends, after all this is just the beginning. We've already tackled the indie network and successfully infiltrated several fanzines... Swedish Nurse, Jaded Job Jar, Planet Ruth..."

friends could also be implicated in this dreadful cannibalistic conspiracy.

Mr Say came back on the line. "I like snakes, I put them in a box and give them to someone but it's difficult to know if they're male or female," he explained. I nodded. "We sound very innocent but we're actually incredibly evil. We get high on tea, we come from Planet X, we have green eyes too. Soon we'll be as big as Genesis. Do you know, we can hear Genesis on our planet?"

The voices were swapping over now. I felt confused. Was it Mr Say, or was it really Iz?

"Bunny and Tiger," Say said reassuringly. "They started us in the music business. It was Bunny that told us about you and the Stuffed Cat. Stuffed Bunny said to call you and tell you to write about us in Ablaze!"

"Right! Where are they now, Bunny and Tiger?" I enquired, in near frantic tones of concern.

"Oh they're gone, gone far away. There are a lot of customers here now, will you send Lizzy over to us soon?" Say asked, and it sounded quite urgent. But why should I send them my friend?

"Look, I know you're in a spaceship so forget the customer nonsense. If you were really in a petrol station you'd have sold 10 bags of Tayto (cheese & onion flavour) by now, and I would have heard them rattle." This was as logical and assertive as I could be under these stressful conditions at 2 AM.

"No!" shouted Iz. Had things really got out of Mayomberos' control? Was I THAT smart? "Tell the kids that we are a two piece hippy hop power drill combo with cassette only releases and a begging letter system of self-publicity. Do not go to the police or you will be destroyed."

Hmm. Obviously not that smart. I mean, I don't see what use the police would be anyway, when they can't even protect you from landlords that rummage through your clothes when you are out. But this indicates that I'm under some very close surveillance from these guys. Probably Mr Sing is their agent - it makes sense, Mr Sing and Mr Say... indie music and property exploitation - do they have a finger in every damn pie?

"Tell them we play golf. Tell them about Nostradamus! Tell them our address is 20 Stamer Street, SCRD, Dublin 8, Eire, and tell them that our new tape is available for \1.20 including postage. Tell them..."

Okay, okay. I'd had enough. Slamming the phone down, I felt something soft brushing my face. A large black moth fluttered in front of my eyes, and another, and another...

Muttering "bloody cranks," I brushed off the swarming beasts and entered my room, locking the door behind me.

THE

It took them weeks to get a copy of "Bossanova" to me, which was plenty enough time to doubt, and in that period I interviewed Kim. She must have thought me very dim to have no word of praise for it.

So I ended up a bad case of Pixy fever, yet again, and I'd only just recovered from a dose of the Breeders. They swelled my room with joy in the form of a Peel session that was nothing like enough to prepare me for the glory that is "Pod." "Iris" remains an integral part of my shrieking mental structure, but how was I to imagine "Limehouse"? "Glorious"? Or the heart-shredding "Oh"... which is about my bathroom with has crushed spiders in the plughole... it's just in the 3rd bit where her lament slips up and grates like the violin - is that real? It doesn't matter. The deeper you listen into it, the deeper you get, "lost in the moss"...

And yeh it did sound sparse when the sleeve first got pulled off, but this is the record that has revealed Kim's massive, brash, tender, bright, intense, fun genius that "Gigantic" only hinted at.

Still, the pixies track me down sooner or later, even if I pretend not to care. They had pursued me into Virgin records where the plastic flowers hung, and as I rummaged through bargain racks a slither of whitebright feedback clawed into my ears. "What's this? " I wondered, but the world is a strange place and once he kids have got into the Stone Roses it's no real wonder to hear feedback in Virgin. But it was fast followed by a groovy guitar bit, which thrilled me as I flicked those discs, and then...Oh. Ridiculous heavymetal shrieking. And then!!! Then it turns into the Pixies, unmistakably, and I realise what is going on, or......ten minutes later recover from aimless psycho-style staggering round the aisles, face opening and closing like a fully functioning fish.

It's just...

"ROCK MUSIC!!!!!!!!"

And little bleeding pixies follow me down into my dreams, oh leave me alone. I will not go to Reading, I told them, even though you have a massive glorious fresh and incredibly long set to play out there in the sunshine to the thousands of jumping squelching roaring pixy people. So I won, I lost...

"Rock Music" is convulsive. It mashes my head, it is...it. Makes me, makes... arghhhh!!!!!! Which is what Pixies records should do. I had this abolish Gil Norton theory for a while but now I'm not so sure. I'm not so young, maybe I'll go with the merciless flow awhile, and find out...

"IS SHE WEIRD?????????"

I'm just enchanted, you've got me, and I guess it's all sealed. I'm with ya, "every morning & every day..."

For those bolts of sheer excitement, and despite those bits, such as "Allison", "Stormy Weather", that are too facile, too common, for me to feed off.

But here's where I tell you about my Kim Deal interview, officially on the subject of her own band... "Breeders" are heterosexuals, she told me. Jo isn't one. presumably Kim and Tanya are. I expect Brit is too.

INTERVIEW

We sat in a bar in the Brittania hotel, all blue gold luxury and obscene finery, "It's like, come on in! It's my home!" she squealed, having finally emerged from her room, mischievious princess in her palace, with a walkman and a Dread Zepellin tape. "I just went into Our Price and asked if they had any good tapes. They were telling me about all this dance stuff..." but she had plumped for the rock'n'roll gone hideously wrong. Passing it to me she said "listen to it for as long as you can." I made it through about a minute, the twilight zone noises being too much those surroundings. There was a wedding party going on and best dressed children were scampering around obnoxious respectable old types in this place where I didn't feel right at all. But it was impossible not to get into the spirit of the thing: the Pixies are here! So Manchester became, for a little while, frame-trembling Rock Music City.

Kim Deal is unafraid and younger than youth. I like her a lot but I know it's not cool to make such a fuss over someone cos they're partly behind "Pod", or even mainly, but... she played me a tape of a new Breeders thing they'd done over here, her and Jo with Spiritualized's drummer, a song optimistic and wondrously exciting to hear, even though it lacked Tanya who was on holiday:

"So it seems like, what the plan was, whenever we have time to go into a 24 track, we'd do some stuff. Tanya's coming over here soon though..."

So d'you think you'll be recording over here?

"Probably, yeh,"

Any plans for who's gonna produce it?

"No, uh-uh, dont know, don't want Steve Albini to do it again, and I don't want Gil Norton... What are some good albums, and then we can figure out who produced them?"

I sat there dumbly, refraining from saying something totaly unproductive, like "Surfer Rosa"...

"Who does the Sisters of Mercy?

You're kidding!!!!!???? (But she wasn't...).

Who chose who was gonna produce "Bossanova"?

"Charles did: "Let's choose Gil again," "Ok," (She shrugs and smiles to show the carefree way in which the decision was taken). That's about it, that's fine. He, Gil, works really hard. Albini comes in, he doesnt give s shit about your career, your success, he doesn't get any points off the album so he doesnt care how well that album does, he gets a flat fee, he's really cheap."

It's kinda too obvious to mention the incredible difference in sound since "Surfer Rosa"; from that rawness you're definitely going in a more commercial direction...

"It's mainly since we got a little bit of popularity since "Surfer Rosa", we've been able to spend more money and go into that little factory thing, money producing... everything sounds the same once you've been through that big machine, I don't know why, I don't know what piece of equipment it is in the studio, is it this sampler that they use? They've got like one common denominator and every studio sounds the same..."

"it seems alright, I would've like to've done it weirder, more keenly commercial, so it sounds like jingles, really really... this way it was kinda like, the songs are basically good songs, we did it weird though: this time we just went to a studio and learned the songs and played them, I was recording my bass & I was thinking, 'how does this song go?' It was weird, we'd never done it like that before."

Were you short of time?

"No we weren't, we just put that time limit on ourselves, for some reason - I don't know why... 4ad would've been happy not to release anything off us this year, but it would've been boring."

How much say d'you have about what goes on with the Pixies? Is it basically Charles's group?

"Mainly is, yeh."

I'd imagine the freedom to have your own group is really good.

"Yeh. And it's not only 'This is what were gonna do,' cos there's 3 girls, I go (leans forward intently) 'D'you think its a good idea?', 'Well what d'you think about it?', and we'll like talk about it for a half hour! So there no way I'll go like 'This is what we're gonna do,' cos they'll go like: 'No we're not! Shut up!!!' So that's good."

Did you see the Simon Reynolds review of the LP? He seemed to think it wasn't like that.

"He hated it, he hated it! It would really have made me nervous if they were kinda all iffy and he really hated it, but they were all really good and he HATED IT, DESPISED it, he nailed the album completely, the group, the songs..."

(Her dramatic voice, slowed down and emphasised so gets almost scary sometimes.)

Has he got something personally against you?

"It sounded like it, didn't it?"

He was a bit bitchy about Jo.

"Yeh, he was... I think he's a really big Throwing Muses fan & then he's also a Pixies fan, and I just don't think he liked us fucking with those two things, y'know?..."

Maybe he would've liked it to have been more Muses-like?

"Yeh, he was saying like I was leading the band with iron clenched...rule (trying to quote a piece of the review that actually refered to Kristen's hold on the Muses), and we'd been begging Tanya to show her songs to us but and she can't, it was weird, it's Sire, there are these contractual obligations that she has to fulfill, that she can't do solo things or duets, she can only be on a music accompaniment so it was a big thing about trying to get her involved as much as she could possibly be involved and we had to sneak her in things..."

Without it saying they were her songs...

"Exactly, or sing... she only ended up singing a little bit, we wanted to make sure that there weren't any obvious duets on it and things like that. We didn't know that at first, I remember first practicing at my house and it was like 'you write half, I'll write the other half,' but this next one's gonna be more hers cos Sire's gonna be out of the way then..."

It's like she hasn't had a chance to develop on the Muses albums.

"She hasn't! And the songs she sings are always some of my favourites, it's always like two of Kristen's and then one of Tanya's songs but then that's easy if she only has two on the album! So she can but her best on, but still... So that did seem weird didn't it, Simon Reynolds? What's his problem? But he didn't like one single thing. We should have died! We should have been executed!"

I'm surprized you take much notice of reviews.

"Yeh, but we had to, that one, cos it did seem so personal. If he didn't like the songs cos it'd be like, 'fine, don't buy it.'"

I'm told, and gather, that these Pixy people talk about the same sort of things, about bits of records and stuff, as we do and journos do, but to REALLY HATE something...she explained by an example.

"I listened to the worst thing in the world, the Wilson Philips, their album, you know who I mean? With the three girls? It's the daughters of the Beach Boys and The Mamas & The Papas. It just really sucks. And for Simon Reynolds to make out like we're doing this really shitty music..."

Did you set out wanting to make the Breeders an all-girl band?

"Not really, uh-uh. Guys wont play with me so I had to get dumb girls! No, Tanya & me wanted to do something and I knew Josephine, I'd met her when the Perfect Disaster opened for the Pixies in London for two nights, and I didn't remember the band that much but we met again when she was on vacation in Frankfurt with her girlfriend and we were playing and they came to the gig and afterwards we spent the entire night together, the three uf us at this trainstation, it was really fun, and I just remembered that and I knew she played bass and we needed a bass player... I couldn't even remember if she could play good bass or not! So it was good that she could play."

I heard she's got a degree in philosophy...

"Mmm, she's got a masters in philosophy. I do have to bring a dictionary with me, I dont understand half the words that she says, her and Tanya both, it's real girls' tedious tedious TEDIOUS analysing, it's fun!"

(At this point I begin to wonder just what she means by "fun")

Who was teasing Jo about her hair on the LP?

"The drummer, he's from Kentucky, cos she's goin' bald. You know on the LP sleeve, those snippets of hair? Each of us had instructions, it was something Vaughan wanted to do, like "cut some of yur hair off," "OK," and he actually mailed Jo's hair back to her cos she was going bald!!!"

(I don't wanna hear any Wiggs jokes from out of you, OK?)

Where did you get your drummer?

"It was Steve Albini's suggestion, yeh I was thinking about it today and I figured it must have been because he's really into the Mekons, and there were girls in that band and there was a violinist in that band and I thought maybe that's why Steve Albini thought he would be good in our band... they

actually have one of their songs that I really like (she tries to explain it to me & I don't get it.)
Y'don't have any Mekons tapes on ya do ya?"

Nope. Is Britt the one from Slint?

"Yeh, yeh, 19 years old from Louiseville, Kentucky. Picks his nose, burps, it's like we're ready to play, & he's picking his nose! We're like 'ready? ready??!'"

How old are you?

"I don't want to tell."

OK

"Good!"

I just thought I'd ask cos you've got such a young drummer...

"Yeh right, I mean like 23 would be old to be round a 19 year old guy..."

(She still doesnt reveal that dreaded age!)

I kind of couldn't remember too much why I wrote down this question, but are you scared of world overpopulation?

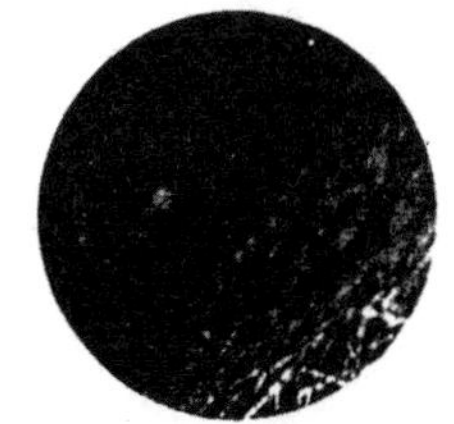

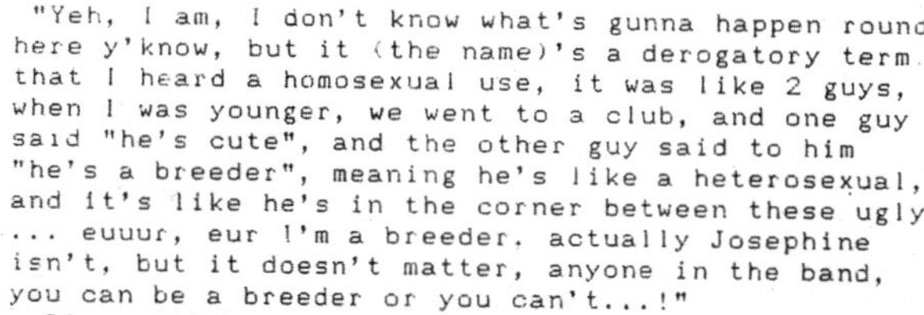

"Yeh, I am, I don't know what's gunna happen round here y'know, but it (the name)'s a derogatory term that I heard a homosexual use, it was like 2 guys, when I was younger, we went to a club, and one guy said "he's cute", and the other guy said to him "he's a breeder", meaning he's like a heterosexual, and it's like he's in the corner between these ugly ... euuur, eur I'm a breeder. actually Josephine isn't, but it doesn't matter, anyone in the band, you can be a breeder or you can't...!"

D'you think you and Tanya might breed, cos Kristen has, and she's still in a band?

"Yeh, we're real breeders!! Yeh."

What's your favourite animal?

"That'd a good question... I dunno... the baby ones are really cute. The vampire bats are good, I saw them drinking blood in Cincinatti, in the zoo, it really was!! They had a nocturnal cave display, and you went in, and there was this long statue with a little bowl, it looked like a birdbath, and it was filled with this RED LIQUID! (she descibes this with a mixture of delight & horror, typical Kim: torture can be fun , terror can be beautiful, as long as its new and strange enough...) and I just looked at it, it's like they drink, they're all around like little, ugly little creature birds, and they're drinkin' blood. (Leans forward, widens eyes, makes little creaturely sipping noise tp tp tp) It was so weird, really gross, in the dark, some of them're hangin' upside down, they wrap their wings around themselves, it's really good."

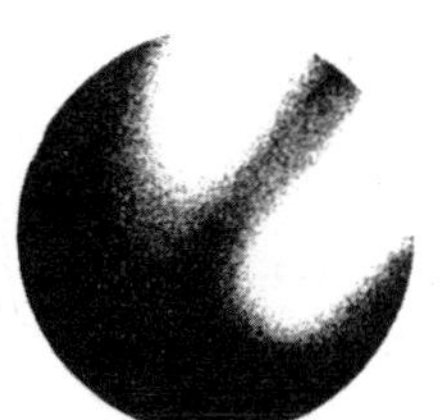

How long have you been in Manchester?

"3 weeks, we practice Monday through Friday, regular kinda hours, then we go to Reading, I don't know what we do after that, then we tour, I know we're touring somewhere, we tour in England and in Europe, and the Pale Saints are gonna open up for us in Europe, and Barf Market, sorry Bark Market! is opening up for us here, I think they're an American band."

What've you been doing with your spare time here?

"Just walkin' around, looking at tape shops... Went to the hacienda one night, it wasnt that great: it's really hot, theres people around looking at ya,if you do any drugs at all or anything, y'cant do anything, it's like 'you'd better behave' kind of thing, really kind of pressured."

"We stayed in Brighton for a week with Josephine & that was nice, and the guy who played on... do ya like the new song by the way? (I said I liked it very much) anyway the drummer is that Spiritualized guy, John, he's really cute, (this, I believe, is Kim language for 'I fancy the arse off him') he's really good but don't tell Britt!"

Did you see Ian Brown last night? (We were at the birthday/wedding party of their tour managers Chas and Shirley Banks

"Yep. He talked to me for about five minutes. But y'know I was SO nervous I can't remember what he said. All the time I was thinkin', 'boy, he's really cute, he's really cute, he's even cute in person too!' So I was thinking so much about talking to him that I think I was a really bad conversationalist. He was talking about these five bright lights, this mystical or spiritual thing, and I must have seemed like a really dumb chick, cos I just went 'oh, yeh,' and I wish I could do it over again and then I could really listen to him. I was just so nervous."

(I told her I thought Ian has some sort of messiah problem that is either scary or, more probably, extremely laughable.)

Did you stay out late last night?

"No, not really, after He left, cos I was a bad conversationalist....ah, maybe he'll call, I don't know, he probably wont, he was pobably loaded too right?

(Where I come from loaded means having lots of money, though I suspect Kim means something else.)

I can't believe you fancy Ian Brown.

"Oh yeh, he reminds me of some people I used to chase around at school, like in 3rd grade, Timmy and Jimmy. Me & my sister used to chase the boys..."

She gobbles up Stone Roses anecdotes and then tells me an ace Kim one in return.

"I used to go to a school, it was this 7th Day Adventist college in a hospital, and we had a dorm there and we had to follow all their rules: y'couldnt eat any meat, hoofed animals, y'couldn't drink caffeine or anything like that, but they had a lot of affairs, a lot of divorces and stuff, really sexually risque, and I remember one seminar we had on the evils of rock music and they played these songs backwards and stuff, it was weird, it was dumb..."

It didn't do you any good

"Naah (squeals), it was so stoopid, I mean you're bound to find one in a million records that says exactly backwards "I want you to have my devil baby." you know what I mean? It's bound to happen just by chance, the combination of words together are bound to create something weird if you listen to enough of 'em backwards. You could do the same thing with gospel records backwards, they've definitely got messages in there, and just throw it in their faces like, 'Here, dummy!' "

→

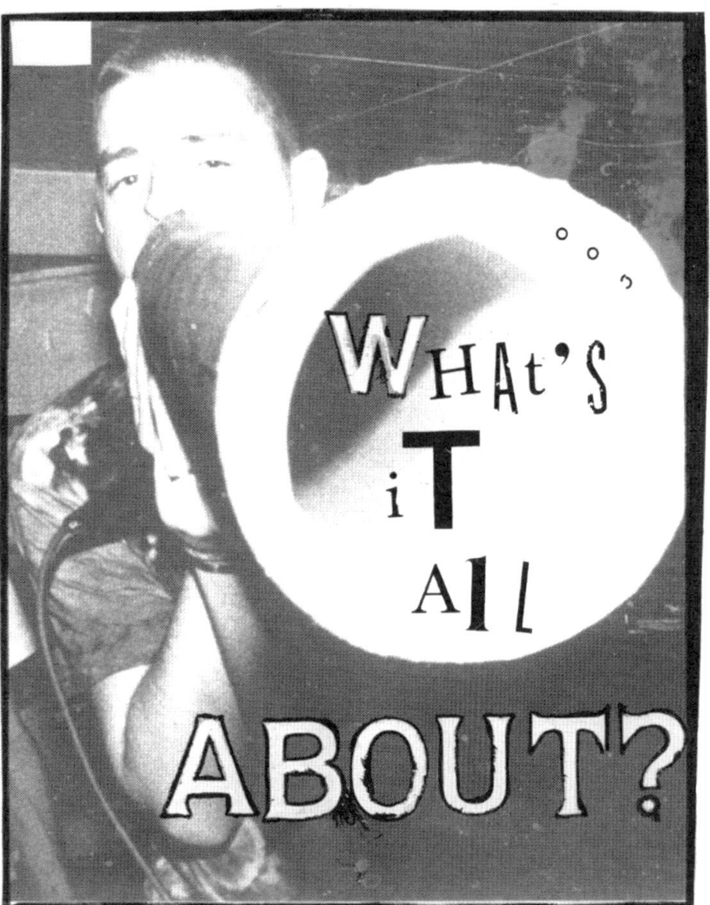

A voyage into unknown lands with THE STRETCH HEADS, top Scots trendsters and inventors of Acid Arse music. Karren Ablaze! retorts.

Basically, the Stretch Heads are fucked up. Not in a lame kind of way, more in a ninja warrior housewife up yr arse kind of way. They did a few dates of the A C Temple UK roadshow thing so for a while Chris and Noel's house was populated by lots of strange little Scottish people jumping about and shouting "WASHAH!" a lot. So I took my chance and got the tape recorder out, on one of those nights when you just sit around in someone's room and only garbled nonsense can survive in the thick, smoke-filled air. An extract of the proceedings can be found on this issue's beautiful flecksy-disk.

Next day I decided to take a more direct approach. Rather than trying to interview them without any questions, I decided to push them all into a stolen car and put a gun to the driver's head shouting "take us to Manchester! We're going to see the BeeGees."

"JUST WHO THE HELL DO YOU THINK YOU ARE?" I demanded, in the meanest and most down-to-business tone imaginable.

"Yeh, ah'm Richie an'(chomp, chomp) ah'm really glad to be here, ah wanna win all the money, all the money..."

"Where the fuck did ma hat go?" Must've lost it in the struggle. "I only want to know cos I had some prawn cocktail crisps in it." P6 explained, true crisp monster style. "We're the wee confused boys from Scotland, we're called the Stretch Heads and we're a really wee and confused and mixed up bunch."

"What's the question?" some degenerate asked me.

"WHO ARE YOUR PARENTS?"

"They're really good," confessed Richie. "Big Flame fans, into the Thistle, what more can ya ask for?"

Noel (what's he doing here?): "You've got parents who are into Big Flame??"

"My dad thinks they sound like Captain Beefheart though."

"We're the children of the gen-er-a-shun," sang Phil.

Addressing Mac, I demanded: "Have you got a mum and dad or was you found under a bush?"

"My father was a fish, my mother was an apricot. That didn't bother me though, I came out fine." As we could clearly see.

"Ma daddy was a doctor," said Noel pretending to be Andy.

"Gawd bless the queen muvver, gawd blesh the queen muvver, gawd bless 'er wooden teeth..."

"SO. WHAT DO YOU PEOPLE DO FOR YOUR LIVINGS?"

Mac: "Eat food. And, err, model a Starsky."

P6: "I fix heads."

Noel: "I fix guitars."

P6: "What do you fix Karren?"

Karren: "I just break things."

Mac: "I fix ma face... ma hair..."

"Aye, fuckin' Mac should fix his hair man. He hasn't washed it for AGES. He secretly wants to grow all these dreadlocks and kid on he's in Bad Brains, but it's gunna take about a year of fuckin' big fuzzy Starsky hairstyle and I don't think I can cope," lamented Phil. "We're gunna invest in loads of hats for his christmas."

"I CAN SEE THAT IMAGE IS REALLY IMPORTANT TO YOU. DO YOU SPEND A LOT OF TIME SHOPPING FOR CLOTHES AND HAVING HAIRCUTS?" I asked, really getting down to the nitty gritty of this rock'n'roll interview lark.

"Aye," answered Phil. "Mac's starting to verge on smell-o-vision as well. I definitely think the audience should start scratching his longjohns and start having a good sniff. 'Ave a bang o' this namba man."

At this point I lost control of the tape recorder and these alien beasts began to reverse my dictatorial position.

"We want to make some noise. Spong'e didn't influence us." "Spong'e?"

"That was a band we all used to be in. Spong'e is gaelic for Sponge. Stretch Heads is gaelic for Up your fuckin' Arse music."

****%23£23£$23**z&&\7(%)****

"Psssshoww!! And the Stretch Heads were no more. What's Karren after? What's she want? She wants into our SOULS. Wants to know what makes us tick. What makes us JACK. We're jackin' right now. Jack it. Richie got his jackin' hat on. WASHAH! Spirit of ninja, spirit of ninja, jujitsu, wahshah! Number 37 please."

"So, Karren, do you think that the word Stretch-Heads indicates an expanding consciousness and an overall awareness of the sleaze on the planet?" they demanded.

"No," I replied. "Not really."

We were nearly in Manc-land by this time. "If people in Manchester started wearing plates in their lips that made them look like weird African warriors, then everyone in Glasgow would start doing it six months later."

After threatening to tear off their facial features like plasticine, they gave me back the power machine and I again became journo-headed.

"ARE THE STRETCH HEADS TRYING TO BREAK DOWN INHIBITIONS AND ENCOURAGE PEOPLE TO DO WHAT THEY REALLY WANT TO DO?"
"At our gigs?" they asked.
"Yes. People might want to do cartwheels and stuff."
"Well hopefully the frustration they feel cos they can't do what they want will teach them something about their own inhibitions, about what their parents taught them, basically. Taught them not to be strange, cos strange is different." P6 is, incidentally, a psychiatric nurse in his spare time. And tells us, in mock yank tones, "STRANGE IS SEXY. STRANGE IS FUN."

"Gigs should be psychic orgies, cathartic experiences. Everyone should feel at one with the scene and start throwing themselves around and crying and biting each other and acting it all out. Cos they're all we've got - gigs are all we've got for letting go of the tension."

"People," I explained, "don't wanna cross that spectator/spectacle line. Can you take it away please?!"
"From day one we never really felt that it was a matter of entertaining and impressing people. It's just been a matter of making people react. Richie's had the odd glass thrown at him but he doesn't mind, I'm sure he'd rather do that than work in a newsagents or something. Mmmm, want some crisps anyone?" he offered as we smashed into some weird bodies in the city centre street and bumped over the heads of Barry and Andy and Maurice Gibb.

End of Kim Deal Interview

(Having heard strange coded messages in an Altered Images song later that day I sensed the extent to which spooky weirdness can be seen to go on in supposedly innocent records.)
How old were you when they were telling you this?
"23."
What would they say if they knew what you're doing now?
"They'd hate it, you're not allowed to smoke in that religion, drink beer... The girl that I was dorming with, she was a 7th Day Adventist, I wasn't, and she followed all the rules and was really strict, but I remember one day her boyfriend was coming over and she had these hickies on her boobs from a few nights ago, she met a guy, and it's like 'You're so religious, and you've got hickies! On your boobs!! And your boyfriend is coming down to visit you!!!'"
Hang on... hickies?
(She makes explanatory slurping noises...)
Love bites?
"Yeh! (still squealing)"
Well, you've gotta do something.
"Exactly, it's gotta come out somewhere."

You used to be married?
"Yeh."
Did you get out of it cos you joined the Pixies?
"No not at all. It started to dissolve like the first year afterwards and I was already in the band then. He helped us out a lot, we're still really good friends. He's in a band now, Mente, in Boston."
What are they like?
"Kinda like Gwar, I think."
Oh god.
"They hold up dead fish and a crucifix or somthing, I dunno, they wear wigs, I've never seen 'em... I did once, David drummed for 'em... It seemed like it didn't it, that when the band got popular I divorced the guy? But it wasn't like that."

What star sign are you?
"Gemini. What are you?"
Sagittarius.
"My mum's saggitarius."
Erm, I think I've run out of questions.
"Oh really? Want another beer?"
No thanks.
"OK, I'm gonna get another half, OK?"
OK.
We talked on awhile, about whether American women have got their heads together more than British ones (Conclusion: possibly) and I saw her later, we listened to Buzzcocks and Altered Images, after her and Paula (of Playtime records) played banjos to the Rolling Stones. That night I slept in the light of the moon and dreamed of worm monsters crawling out of my skin.

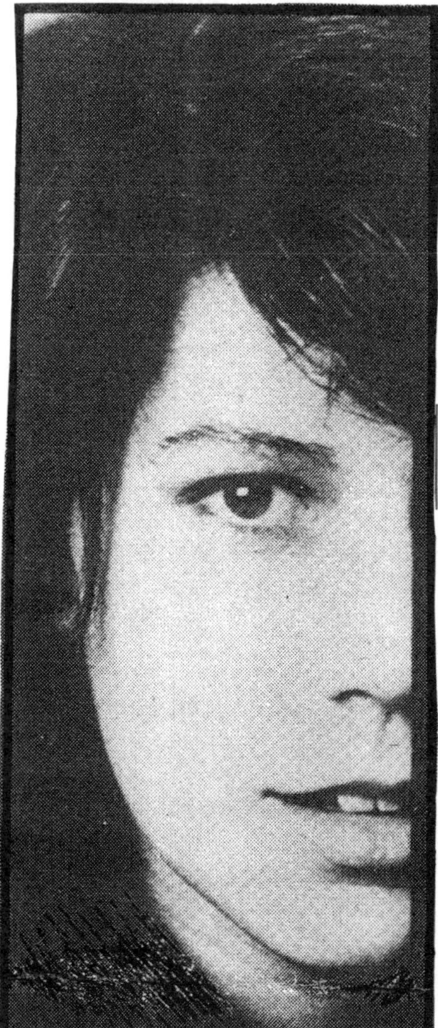

BORED IN THE NORTH

archive interviews

Here's the bit where we tell you the bitter truth... about Manchester. Because, as usual, Ablaze! was there first............

As this title was being born in the spring of 1987 we released a compilation tape of local nonentities, among them the Stone Roses. The interview from the accompanying magazine, Made In Manchester, is reproduced here so you can see what arrogant creatures they were even then................

That summer, Ablaze! 1 featured a centre page interview with a cheesey-organ infested little pop group from Oldham. The Inspirals appealed to me with their whimsical niceness and their "Garage Full of Flowers" flexi which seemed to be aping the pompous closing line of "Tell me", the flipside of The Stone Roses' debut single.........

And the spring of '88 had me descending to the bowels of the Boardwalk where a scruffy bunch of casuals lurked, unwillingly mumbling away from the tape recorder, behind a door marked "Crappy mundanes". The dress sense suspicions were mutual............

At around that time Ablaze! relocated to Leeds, wisely abandoning the fashion industry (did you know Happy Mondays then-manager also ran a jeans company?)/ Debris clique conspiracy scene.........................

Yet now we've decided to cash it in (anyone with problems about this should contact us immediately) and f'k'n well stamp out the tiresome manch myth once and for all. We didn't bother to do this earlier cos it all seemed so boring and we didn't really think it would last. Instead it escalated ridiculuosly, showing our faith in humanity to be once again misplaced, and being another sad reminder of the herd mentality that operates on a mass level, inducing conformism of musical consumption, and worse still, production. Now we're based in the same town as the Bridewell Taxis... it just gets worse!!!*****

HAPPY MONDAYS by Karren Ablaze! (age 4½)

It's painful to play back my dreary mondaze interview. The text in Ablaze! the second goes something like... this:
Into the boardwalk again, through a ringing door that shatters my nerves, dowm the stairs past the pool table and in through a door marked "crappy mundanes": There they are, smoking, uninviting, in their crumbling basement rehearsal room. The brickwork and plaster is painted brown, happy monday pictures are drawn on bits of wall where the stuffing is falling out and shredded cig boxes lie on the floor.

"I don't like doing interviews here," I had told them
"How d'you think we feel? We have to rehearse here."

I asked if they actually wanted to do the interview, arranged through their manager. They said yeh, why, does it look like they don't?
A bit. All my questions fall flat [Cos they're shite - Older, wiser Ed] and I can't find why it is that their records sound so warped and twisted, all pulling in different directions and good.

HAPPY MONDAYS

Shaun Ryder on Inspiral Carpets

'They're just knobheads man, clueless knobheads. Who wants to be a pop star anyway. We were more clued up when we were 13'

"Who are the people in the band & what dc you play?"
"Paul, keyboards; Mark, guitar; Paul, bass; Shaun, singin' & Gaz, drums."
"And Bez!" Shaun added, irritated at his exclusion.
"Bez plays percussion but he's not here."
"Who writes the words?"
No reply was forthcoming as if no-one was going to own up until, reluctantly, one spat "Singer," like it was the most self-evident thing in the world.
"What sort of things d'you write about?" I enquired dimly.
"Anythin'," revealed Shaun. "Don't really write 'em, don't really write anythin'. Just say it, whatever happens."
"D'you think some of the things you sing about are depressing?"
"No. Don't know. Some of 'em's funny, it's not meant to be serious or owt, y'know what I mean?"
"You've got a strange singing style haven't you?"
"Yeh I can't sing, I shout. I cant rap so I shout. I don't like singin' really."
"You don't?" I asked, startled.
"It's gettin alright now, it's not too bad."
What does each of you listen to?"
"Anythin', anythin' an' everythin', no particular bands."
"D'you feel like you're part of the Manchester scene?"
"Wheres the scene?"
As I laughed nervously someone lit up another fag and I reminded myself to stop gazing into that bloody crystal ball.

"Do you all get on then?" I said, feeling safer ground under my feet.
"Yeh we all get on. Cow's a twat, apart from that we're alright."

What d'you get out of being the Happy Mondays?
"48 cans of lager!!"
"Its just alright."
"What d'you want to get out of it?"
"Future, money, enjoyment, a laugh..."
"Fame?" I guessed, and was treated to their utmost muttering, sniggering ridicule.
"Yeh."
"D'you think you're going to?" I continued probing, and they started to give me the FUCKING TERRORS!!!!!
"Dunno."
"It's like sayin' "What's gonna happen tomorrow?" innit?"

"What sort of people like your music?"
"Loonies!"
"Definitely."
"Leeds people."
"What sort of gigs d'you prefer doing?"
"Far way ones." says Paul. I hate goin' up north, its all down and... (blows a rasberry)... Newcastle!!"
"It's North here," I told him.
"No, this is as North as I'll go. I like goin' down but I don't like goin' up."
"So, what's nice abut going to the South?"
"Cos it's more near Europe!", a comment met by unanimous spluttering.

"Why d'you hate your manager?" I said, looking at the dodgy wall drawings and asking to fall into the trap of their dubious humour.
"Cos he's a Jew."

I decide to end this experience which, apart from time spent in the headmistress's office, probably constituted the worst 20 minutes of my life.
"Interviews are better in the pub," they told me. I don't think they could really be any worse.

BREEDERS "POD" LP (4AD)

If you listen closely in the right speaker when the Breeders play "Happinness Is A Warm Gun", you'll hear the sound of my cigarette lighter openning and lighting. That, and the fact that the drummer finished the sessions completely covered in soot after a meeting of the Anglers' Club in the pub across the road are the most interesting things about this album. (S.A.)

COWS "EFFETTE AND IMPUDENT SNOBS" LP (Glitterhouse)

This almost made me shit blood when I first put it on; it's ugly, DAMN ugly. Cows produce a kind of distorted, slow, horrible type noise which is strangely compelling, like the way you get crowds of people round an accident. This is the kind of record you have to play loud so it sounds like some kind of blast furnace thing. Excellent. Bet they're all built like pipecleaner people though. (Russ)

FOETUS INC: "SINK" LP (Self-immolation/Some Bizarre)

This is a retrospective double LP covering the multifarious incarnations of Foetus (aka Jim Thirlwell). It incorporates unreleased material, out-takes and alternative versions of some of Thirlwell's top tunes. He is at his best in the guise of "Eruptus" where he achieves his greatest intensity or flaunts his unique sense of humour, e.g."A wo-man's place is on my face" ("Bedrock"). Having seen photographs of young foetusface, I can only assume that he must be joking.

For those not acquainted with his music, this is a good starting point which allows the listener to find their favourite "Foetus" without having to wade through the flim-flam of nearly a decade's worth of Thirlwell. (JW)

VARIOUS "WORLD DOMINATION OR DEATH" LP (One Little Indian)

I'll say this here and I'll say it now: I HATE THE SUGARCUBES! Always have done, always will (Unlike some journos at the "big" music papers; witness MM squirming when the last album turned out to be a load of steaming turd and trying to pin the blame on "bloody Einar") Anyway, this is a compilation of Icelandic bands who surely want to be seen as artists in their own rights and not another novelty item for trendy people's record collections (like the Sugarcubes) and so appear on an album with the Sugarcubes and with a big picture of Iceland on the front. Actually after the previous vitriol the Sugarcubes track isn't that bad, it's just that it sounds like something the Slits used to do, only they used to do it a whole lot better. Reptile sound very much like the Dog Faced Hermans, especially on "Gun Fun". Bless are obviously the sort of fey, shy creatures whose parents don't understand them and as such should be scorned by all persons of sound mind. (Does this mean that all cultures throw up such types and that even in the Braziliam rainforest there are thin, spotty youths who would rather stay at home and write poems than go out hunting with their fathers?) Bootlegs are your standard punx and do a couple of undistinguished punk!thrash!metal! things. Oxtor seem to be a rockabilly band - why anyone would want to be a rockabilly band is totally beyond me, but I'm sure it's not bad if you like that sort of thing. Ham are by far the best thing on the album. If this record was a party then Ham would be the gatecrashers in the kitchen who've drunk all the beer and eaten all the peanuts and are just trying to annoy people. They're worth going to see (if they ever get through immigration) [they did last year and yeh, they was good!- Ed] Almost good enough to make buying this worthwhile. Almost. (Russ)

VARIOUS "THROUGH THE LOOKING GLASS; 1967" LP (Imaginary)

Having spent a good proportion of my formative years in spaceage catsuits yearning to be an extra in "U.F.O" and wigging out to anything with a cheesey organ and "trippy" lyrics, I was really looking forward to this record. Unfortunately, a fair amount does NOT make me lie back and think of Shrimpton...so much of it is vacuous, limp and flaccid in comparison with the originals.

What? Noise make a Cream song sound like the Mary Chain, and the Shamen make their particular track sound like everything they've ever done. I am informed by the press release that Colin's Hermits (who cover "Strawberry Fields") are XTC's Dave Gregory and Andy Partridge... what can I say, except that this effort certainly didn't get my senses working overtime... In fact I used to have five, but one by one they fled, leaving me clamouring for the return of Candy Flip.

It isn't all bad though. Styler and Baldwin of Green On Red cover Cream's "Sunshine Of Your Love" in fine style. Mind you, with regression merchants like them it was always going to sound authentic; although not as authentic as Bevis Frond, who no doubt still believes it to be 1967. Mark Burgess' reading of "You only live twice" is very caberet, all soft and gaspy, and, oooh, it's lovely. The Thunderbirds deliver some good bongs and aahs in "My White Bicycle", but overall it's a mundane version - same for the Bomb Party withy "For What It's Worth", who try REALLY HARD but are onto a bit of a non starter compared to the definitive version by The Muppets.

All this goes to show really, is that you can't keep a good song down; that is unless, of course, you're Spiral Jetty, who defile Love's "7 and 7 is". You see, I've always had a bit of a thing about Arthur Lee and Love, and it was bad enough having to listen to this patchy piece of vinyl to begin with, but when I heard how the aforementioned shitehawks had desecrated a song that is the embodiment of my existence so far, I was filled with righteous ire, and therefore, before I take my leave, I want it to be noted publicly that if e'er I chance upon a member of "The Jetty" I shall happily suggest they take up self-immolation as a hobby; otherwise I'll set the fuckers aflame meself. (JW)

LEATHERFACE "FILL YOUR BOOTS" (Roughneck)

The cover really put me off. "Oh no, a Sunderland band who obviously wish they came from Chicago and got produced by Steve Albini." The horrible picture, the band's name and some of the song titles ("New York State" and "Razor Blades and Asprins" are the standouts) seem to suggest an unhealthy interest in the dark side of the good ol' USA. Then I put it on: "Oh my god, it's the Wedding Present with a collective case of laryngitis!". Once I got over this, it didn't seem half bad at all. (Russ)

THE BAND OF HOLY JOY "REAL BEAUTY PASSED THROUGH" LP (Rough Trade)

Well bugger me. My mate Frank, who has just educated me in the values of war, capital punishment, competitive sports and Real Music ("Not like this rubbish your lot listen to today! I've seen it on Top Of The Pops, leaves your head empty it does. You never hear anyone whistling those tunes in the street... and that dancing! Well they might call it dancing but in my day...") might just like this. BOHJ don't play noisy horrible guitars, they don't scream and bang their heads or rock in any way. Rather, I can hear violins and quiet keyboards and a light unobtrusive percussion with cissy boy vocals producing something ultimately dead wimpy and sad that doesn't jar too much with Songs of Praise on a Sunday night. Any pale frail soft-spoken waif-kids who wanna borrow this so they can have something to feel all serious about are going to have Frank to contend with, and I'm telling ya, he don't take no shit off no-one. (KA)

ANASTASIA SCREAMED "SAMANTHA BLACK" 7" (Roughneck).

Anastasia Screamed,did she? I'm not really surprised, if she had to deal with these twits. What is going on? Is my record player broken or is this band playing in a collapsing crazy house or did someone sit at the mixing desk randomly sliding their knobs up and down really fast? Maybe I'm coming down with 'flu. But I'm certain this boy would benefit from a few years of intensive singing lessons. A few Husker Du-isms during the MegaCityFour-esque flipside render it slightly less objectionable. "Ah lo-lo-lo-lo-lost ma head" he sings. Well for god's sake go and have a look around where you last remember having it.(KA)

JUDGE MENTAL AND THE HEAVY DREAD BEAT "TALBOT ROAD" Tape (Pumf)

At last, the complete collection of the legendary Judge Mental sessions that took place in Blackpool last winter, many of which recorded while Simon (formerly the brain behind Satan he Jesus Infekt'd Needles And Blood), vocalist, was on weekend leave from the acid casualty/amphetamine psychosis ward of Victoria hospital. Hear tales of eccentrics on the Manc scene, slices of a dozen different realities and too many personalities in one brain that got scrambled. Only 2 of the 34 tracks are songs and they're covers anyway, and 31 are Simon's wraps that seemed to come easier than conventional speech. The music provided by Stan is mostly on keyboards with lots of out of step, not quite recognisable samples, and some of it's dead funny. Features such classics as "A Rolling Hulme Speed Freak Gathers No Moss Side Acid Off Stratty" and the very scarey "Double Of Dutch"...

erm... lost a few lines...

"Teaching the kids to learn how to skip/ Here we go for another bad trip"? The last track is a thoughtful medley of bits of other raps that tells a tale with a definite moral. Roll out the cats... (Available from 130 Common Edge Rd, Blackpool FY4 5AZ for £1.37 plus some postage.)

HARRY CREWS "NAKED IN GARDEN HILLS" LP (Big Cat)

From gigs that Lydia, Kim and the Wrestler did in the interests of education, and I can't think of a nicer way to learn; though I've still not checked any of the guy's books out - that'd be a bit too much like doing as you're told.

Well, it's pretty tuneless, sloppy, rowdy and dumb, i.e. a whole lot of fun, with "musical" adaptations of Crews' material plus a Teenage Jesus and Sonic Youth classic each. The cover's gorgeous too. A triple goddess record.(KA)

KAGE ENGINEERING "FLIGHT" 12" (Ascension)

have charmed me with their bold optimism and pop competence, although their pseudo-German stuff's a bit giggle worthy. "Flight" is big and bright; Glenis incites joy with her clear voice, and I love the other kid's loudhailering, and it's skilfully keyboarded together. "Whistling" is just excellent too. The flipside has a drum machine solo version of the title track with German vocals ("For intensity," they explained), and yet another version that's even more minimal. They are from Skipton and are this issue's hot tip for children's TV appearances and wild fame.(KA)

WREVIEWED BY: LUCY NATION, KARREN ABLAZE!, NOEL KILBRIDE, JUSTINE WOLFENDEN, RUSS FROM BRADFORD, VARIOUS INCARNATIONS OF RICHARD ROUSKA.......... AND THE STUFFED CAT. & Steve Albini

GREENHOUSE have released two 7" singles on their own Firebomb Radio One (through Southern). "World's Turn"/"Always Something Wrong" is worthy jangle with good tunes and "Tigers"/ "Risking your life for your accent" is my favourite and I totally recommend it for this song, "Tigers", forces you to imagine a forseeable event - the extinction of tigers. There aren't words for it really, but this song, with its' knowledge of capitalistic life, suggests such a tragedy would be treated superficially : "The news reader looks sad... the shops didn't close... and next month's fashion is stripey clothes," while the vocalist's crying out the name "tiger" fills your heart with grief. I ruin it by trying to explain it but that's what I'm supposed to do. Greenhouse are a seriously sussed band and they're about to release another record on Native records. I have no details, I'll leave it to you to check it out.

NERVE RACK "GNAW" LP (Meantime) Genius! Top Leeds power trio releases its debut LP and it's a raving axe murderer! "Blow To The Head", the opening track (if you play side two first, as I tend to do) descends dead-beatfully in with so much promise that you're instantly hooked. The wailing identity crisis chorous is, third time round, followed by a highlight of highlights strawberry-flavoured bit that never fails to make me happy. And "Blood Beats" very intensely, and the boy on the back of the sleeve can see himself reflected ever onwards down a trail of decreasing mirrors. Terror! They have that guitar in their command, no question. And "Mudhead" has an extended introduction on my copy where it is already scratched, rather fortuitously, and when budged the needle sinks down into the heaving sea of mud from which the monstrous cool vocal of Mark rises. There, I've reviewed a quarter of it, don't let me ruin the rest for you! It's in a bright yellow sleeve - now - BUY!!! (KA)

TEENAGE FAN CLUB: The other Teenage Fanclub and not the type that played tonight at the Leadmill in Sheffield. The original teenage fanclubs of the early 70s, the days of David Cassidy and Donny Osmond fanclubs that would give you value for money. You see in those days popstars cared about their fans. I remember in ther spring of 1973, outside the Vallance nighclub in Bradford (gone, demolished to make way for a Tesco superchain). Such a brilliant place it was. Sure Slade got their major break there. Well my kid sister was a big fan of David Cassidy. I asked the guy could I have his autograph, he was a total gentleman about it all. He said "Sure," in his American accent and even invited me for a cup of coffee. He gave me a special David Cassidy package, my sister was over the moon. We chatted about the Partridge family and I even got to find out that he liked Donny Osmond, that was the rival. Then we parted on a rather hazy night. You got so much for your money in the fanclubs then especialluy the Cassidy one. Now all that the bands give you is a photocopied photo of themselves outside some obscure country park and a dumb newsletter. The teenage fanclubs don't give a shit nowadays. My sister still goes to the odd Cassidy concert whenever he tours Britain. She's now 28 and expecting her fourth child. In those days bands cared. And now I rest in peace, yours, Gary.

MAZZY STAR "SHE HANGS BRIGHTLY" LP (Rough Trade)

The cat was neither male or female but it was very fat. It lived in a forest with blackberries strawberries and cherries. It hung out with the squirrels and stupid birds but it was well aware that real communication is a myth. Sometimes it sat around picking its' toenails contemplating this ultimate aloneness and sometimes it cried. But it was much better to be an 'it' than a 'he' or a 'she', cos being these things clearly brought terrible problems. Just being was enough, and being furry, specially, was more than enough. Erm, it listened to the Mazzy Star album a couple of times but wasn't sure whether it liked it or not. (KA)

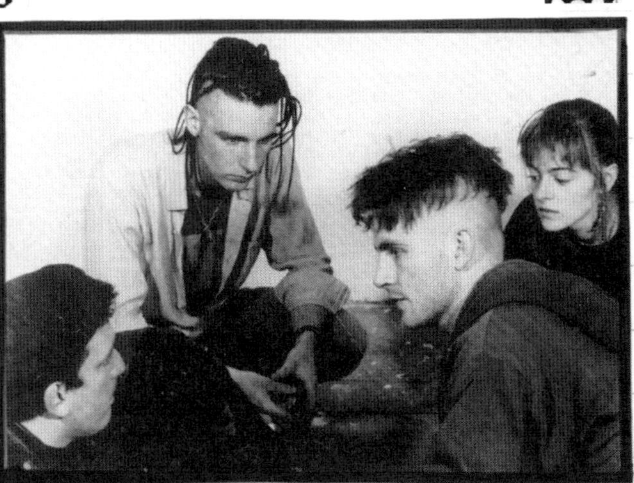

WREVIEWED BY: LUCY NATION, KARREN ABLAZE!, NOEL KILBRIDE, JUSTINE WOLFENDEN, RUSS FROM BRADFORD, VARIOUS INCARNATIONS OF RICHARD ROUSKA... AND THE STUFFED CAT. & Steve Albini

GREENHOUSE have released two 7" singles on their own Firebomb Radio One (through Southern). "World's Turn"/"Always Something Wrong" is worthy jangle with good tunes and "Tigers"/ "Risking your life for your accent" is my favourite and I totally recommend it for this song, "Tigers", forces you to imagine a forseeable event - the extinction of tigers. There aren't words for it really, but this song, with its' knowledge of capitalistic life, suggests such a tragedy would be treated superficially : "The news reader looks sad... the shops didn't close... and next month's fashion is stripey clothes," while the vocalist's crying out the name "tiger" fills your heart with grief. I ruin it by trying to explain it but that's what I'm supposed to do. Greenhouse are a seriously sussed band and they're about to release another record on Native records. I have no details, I'll leave it to you to check it out.

NERVE RACK "GNAW" LP (Meantime) Genius! Top Leeds power trio releases its debut LP and it's a raving axe murderer! "Blow To The Head", the opening track (if you play side two first, as I tend to do) descends dead-beatfully in with so much promise that you're instantly hooked. The wailing identity crisis chorous is, third time round, followed by a highlight of highlights strawberry-flavoured bit that never fails to make me happy. And "Blood Beats" very intensely, and the boy on the back of the sleeve can see himself reflected ever onwards down a trail of decreasing mirrors. Terror! They have that guitar in their command, no question. And "Mudhead" has an extended introduction on my copy where it is already scratched, rather fortuitously, and when budged the needle sinks down into the heaving sea of mud from which the monstrous cool vocal of Mark rises. There, I've reviewed a quarter of it, don't let me ruin the rest for you! It's in a bright yellow sleeve - now - BUY!!! (KA)

TEENAGE FAN CLUB: The other Teenage Fanclub and not the type that played tonight at the Leadmill in Sheffield. The original teenage fanclubs of the early 70s, the days of David Cassidy and Donny Osmond fanclubs that would give you value for money. You see in those days popstars cared about their fans. I remember in ther spring of 1973, outside the Vallance nighclub in Bradford (gone, demolished to make way for a Tesco superchain). Such a brilliant place it was. Sure Slade got their major break there. Well my kid sister was a big fan of David Cassidy. I asked the guy could I have his autograph, he was a total gentleman about it all. He said "Sure," in his American accent and even invited me for a cup of coffee. He gave me a special David Cassidy package, my sister was over the moon. We chatted about the Partridge family and I even got to find out that he liked Donny Osmond, that was the rival. Then we parted on a rather hazy night. You got so much for your money in the fanclubs then especialluy the Cassidy one. Now all that the bands give you is a photocopied photo of themselves outside some obscure country park and a dumb newsletter. The teenage fanclubs don't give a shit nowadays. My sister still goes to the odd Cassidy concert whenever he tours Britain. She's now 28 and expecting her fourth child. In those days bands cared. And now I rest in peace, yours, Gary.

MAZZY STAR "SHE HANGS BRIGHTLY" LP (Rough Trade)
The cat was neither male or female but it was very fat. It lived in a forest with blackberries strawberries and cherries. It hung out with the squirrels and stupid birds but it was well aware that real communication is a myth. Sometimes it sat around picking its' toenails contemplating this ultimate aloneness and sometimes it cried. But it was much better to be an 'it' than a 'he' or a 'she', cos being these things clearly brought terrible problems. Just being was enough, and being furry, specially, was more than enough. Erm, it listened to the Mazzy Star album a couple of times but wasn't sure whether it liked it or not. (KA)

PAUL DORRINGTON AT THE READING FESTIVAL 1990
I would have reviewed the Tse Tse Fly demo tape, but I haven't got one, so I'll review their bass player Paul Dorrington instead. Day One of the festival saw Paul get off to a quiet start, just the twenty odd cans, and he was spotted chasing Blixa Bargeld round the hostility tent shouting "Who won the war anyway?" (Good question - Observer reading proof ed). Fortunately, Blixa's mind was on higher things, allowing Paul to escape being used on the next Neubaten LP as something to bang metal with. By the time I'd arrived at Reading it was Day Two,but Paul had lost all conception of "time". He was after "Guy" Chadwick yelling "Who's the fucking ugly cunt in the stripey T-shirt?" (Guy did nothing - he couldn't exactly sue for slander,could he?). After fortunately failing to notice Genesis P.Orridge, Mick Jagger and Candy Flip, Paul swayed back into the Beer Tent. By Day Three the strain was beginning to show. It was then that Paul decided to use Reading's on-tap press and media facilities and pursue a bit of career. He espied famous octogenarian Mr John Peel talking to some people nearby. "Oy John,don't talk to them, come here and look at my belly!" Mr Peel declined. Not to be discouraged, Paul decided that he'd like to give him a Tse Tse Fly demo tape. Unfortunately he didn't have one, so he gave Mr John Peel a potato with the Tse Tse Fly logo on it instead. John didn't laugh, but I did. Shortly after this, one of Paul's friends tried to swap him for a woolly hat, at which point he decided to go home.
Paul Dorrington is now in Leeds living as a recluse. (JW)

FUCK IT. FUCK IT LIKE A STUFFED CAT, LIKE A CAKE MACHINE. BEAST! OH BEAST.

you wanna know what we think of the new sonic youth lp, huh? is that why you buy Ablaze!? well screw you kiddo, cuz there's only one good track on it and that's lee's song, and there's one king and that's kim, and there's one dripping silk essence of sssexxx, and that's thurston with his heaven hair. so just don't ask, just don't ask us.

winter falls before shut eyes, i am the stupid, the ugly sign. when i say the biggest spider i've ever seen without glass before it is crawling around my desk looking sharp, evil and immense, i am not joking. it's my friend and it listens to the rattling keys. its stalk machine monster limbs are hairy.
spider is going to build a web as big as the room. i steel myself for the inner cold, the attack. i guess avoidance doesn't work. oh machine. i know how it goes.

A RANDOM PLAYLIST
last track on "Swagger", Blue Aeroplanes.
"Pod"
"Gnaw"
Buzcocks' "Time's up" "A ripping spin" Salem 66, esp "Prima Vera", as well as everything I ever hear by 'em.
"I've been waiting for you" by Kim D. and Neil Y.
"The Clash"
"Tigers" by Greenhouse
"Double of Dutch", Judge Mental & the Heavy Dread Beat
"the Dreaming" LP, Kate Bush
"ROCK MUSIC!!!!!!!", "Diggin' fo' fire", "the Happenning" (non-cissy Happenning bit only), "IS SHE WEIRD???" or what, and "DOWWWWWWN to tha well" by the Pixies.

PEOPLE WHO WERE SUPPOSED TO BE IN THIS FANZINE: Lydia Lunch (I didn't make it to the interview & she ain't wrote), Fire Party (currently they're not up to enough for an interview to be worthwhile), Salem 66 (they split up - hopefully a beyond the grave feature next ish), My Bloody Interview (a long story: the interview occurred but - maybe next time?). We still haven't interviewed the Walkingseeds, or the Butthole Surfers, or the Cure, or Kate Bush...

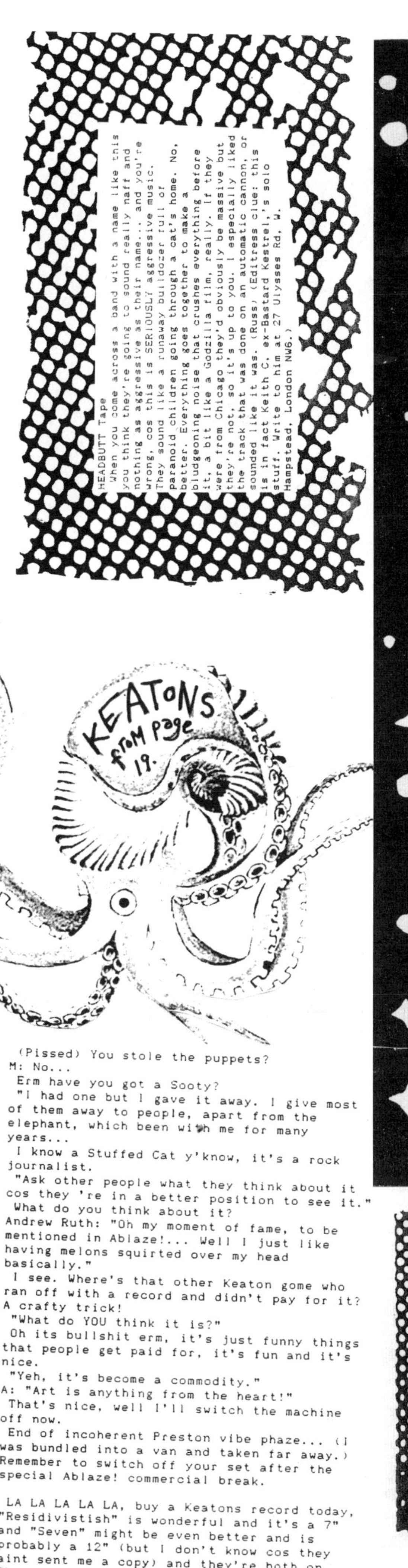

HEADBUTT Tape
When you come across a band with a name like this you think they're going to sound really naff and nothing as aggressive as their name... and you're wrong, cos this is SERIOUSLY aggressive music. They sound like a runaway bulldozer full of paranoid children going through a cat's home. No, better. Everything goes together to make a bludgeoning noise that crushes everything before it, a bit like a Godzilla film, really. If they were from Chicago they'd obviously be massive but they're not, so it's up to you. I especially liked the track that was done on an automatic cannon, or sounded like it was. (Russ) (Editress clue: this is in fact Keith C, ex-Bastard Kestrel,'s solo stuff. Write to him at 27 Ulysses Rd, W. Hampstead, London NW6.)

(Pissed) You stole the puppets?
M: No...
Erm have you got a Sooty?
"I had one but I gave it away. I give most of them away to people, apart from the elephant, which been with me for many years...
I know a Stuffed Cat y'know, it's a rock journalist.
"Ask other people what they think about it cos they 're in a better position to see it."
What do you think about it?
Andrew Ruth: "Oh my moment of fame, to be mentioned in Ablaze!... Well I just like having melons squirted over my head basically."
I see. Where's that other Keaton gome who ran off with a record and didn't pay for it? A crafty trick!
"What do YOU think it is?"
Oh its bullshit erm, it's just funny things that people get paid for, it's fun and it's nice.
"Yeh, it's become a commodity."
A: "Art is anything from the heart!"
That's nice, well I'll switch the machine off now.
End of incoherent Preston vibe phaze... (I was bundled into a van and taken far away.) Remember to switch off your set after the special Ablaze! commercial break.

LA LA LA LA LA, buy a Keatons record today, "Residivistish" is wonderful and it's a 7" and "Seven" might be even better and is probably a 12" (but I don't know cos they aint sent me a copy) and they're both on Chewey records which is at 8 Matson House, Bradstock Rd, Hackney E9. Beeeeeeep.

So yo***STOP fuckin' PRESS***

Did you really read this far? Or just turn to this page? Whatever, You've been instantly initiated into the secret inner core of Ablaze! readers. We go to the printers in two hours and it never feels complete. Hope you ignored the dubious sentiments of the official introduction to this issue - that's just the curtain behind which lies a frantic, obsessional reality of Ablaze!. Seven was meant to be a raging work that would scream of punk rock, girl-style, but these things don't ever grow up like you expect them to. Instead you got this humble journal of in(die)cision, patched up, thrown out...

A lot of things have happenned, but... All I can remember are these snippets: Ritchie has left the Stretch Heads and is now a fulltime Dawson, with Jason Dandelion taking his place on that manic drum stool. There is a Stretch Heads LP which may be called "Eyeball*Origami Wit Vegetarian Leg" but it might not be. A C Temple are going to record an LP at the end of this year which might be called "Belinda Backwards" or it might be called something else as well. (Insert word "aftermath" instead of *). The Edsel Auctioneer are in limboland currently - Chris has gone off to be a Pale-Saint all the time and they've been auditioning new drummists. And they're all at college anyway. There are rumours that Rough Trade is going to be bought out by an American major label but don't say I said so. I mean there were also rumours that the General Havoc had signed to Factory so there you go. Never trust anyone from Preston. The bits of this zine that I lost/missed out will hopefully appear in the next Plane-Truth so please buy that. And... I'm going back to school hopefully so expect the next issue in the summertime. Thank-you everyone who has been nice to me. Read Ursula Le Guin books and look after yourselves and your friends and parents and pets and e veryone else (I'm feeling slighly senti-mental as this issue reaches its shuddering climax...)
love & kittens,
Karren & the Stuffed Cat xx

THANKS TO; THE PURPLE ETERNAL for accommodation when I needed it, A C TEMPLE for showing me some new bits of the world and giving me a job, PLANE TRUTH fanzine for doing half of Ablaze!'s work. FLUFF, for sounding so wonderful, STRETCH HEADS for all the culture they've brought into my life, and... all contributors, advertizers Jumbo records, Leeds (best shop in town), Colin Simmons, Anton, Liz Naylor, everyone who's sent stuff, given advice & helped... Thanks Jusine & Keith, Patrick, Simon, Anthony... Southern & Caroline for distribution... the people who are going to pay me the money they owe... those who will not rip me (& others) off in future... the promoters who will continue to hold open the doors of venues to me (plus one), and the record shops who will continue to give this beast pride of place on their counters... the many wonderful bands who not give up. And Chris, who does not believe in thanks. BUT IS RESPONSIBLE FOR MANY OF THE STRAIGHT LINES (& INDIRECTLY FOR A FEW SHAKY ONES) IN THIS FANZINE.

a useful thing

A TROUT

A HEAD

RECORD OF THE WINTER:

SIDE A (non-label side):

1. KILGORE TROUT
"Shoes"
"Forget the "indie-dance crossover", here's this. Kilgore Trout wouldn't know the "Soul II Soul rhythm" if they woke up in bed with it. "Shoes" is the Pet Shop Boys without the irony."
Write: 664 Abbeydale Rd, Sheffield, S7 2BB for that information you crave.

2. P6/SNKHNGVR
"Crisps"
Mmm want some crisps anyone? An advert for the British SackofPotatoes Marketing Bored.

3. STRETCH HEADS
"Manic Depression", live as a bucketful of maggots. Wrote by Jimi. Their favourite animals are kangaroos, anteater aardvark things and flying anteaters.
Write: Mr P. 6. Eaglesham, 27 Argyl St, Paisley, Scotland

4. THE SAD DRAGONS
A lament for the Stone Roses fans.

SIDE B (label side):

1. Anonymous grimy noise that may damage your stylus. Switch it off!!!

N.B. PLAY THIS RECORD AT 33 R.P.M.

Ablaze!
8

Ablaze! 8

Publication date: Autumn 1991

Really.
Why don't you find
your appropriate
postions in life?
Toilet attendants.....
NME journalists......
Better still. Why not
go fucking
hang yourselves?

Wetherby Grove is a street of typically tall and narrow through-terraces that emerges from the steep banks of Burley Hill and hangs almost diagonally over the semi-industrial Kirkstall Valley. From this point one can breathe in the swirling exhaust fumes of the car-choked Kirkstall Road whilst enjoying the charms of Burley, an urban "village" then in the process of becoming a new feeding ground for landlords, offering an overflow site for cheap student housing outside the central bohemias of Hyde Park and Headingley. With the original communities of families and old folks slowly fleeing to quieter realms, the best thing about the place was that the corner shop stocked copies of a local history zine entitled *Early Burley*.

The house itself was perfectly suitable. Unrenovated since the '60s and lacking central heating, warmth was supplied to its six rooms via three gas fires. But we cared nothing of such niceties, for our time at 17 Wetherby Grove signified a golden era for *Ablaze!*. It was now part of a dedicated rock'n'roll household. Keith was playing with The Wedding Present, and Justine had just launched Hemiola Records.[1] I was the least rock'n' roll resident as I had yet to finish my degree, which involved spending several months up in the attic composing a dissertation on feminist epistemology with the aid of a Commodore 64, a process so tedious that only my dreams made up for it; in them I would climb out of the skylight and fly above the rooftops.

That tiresome time did bring one other benefit. Occasionally I'd leave my academic lair and wander into the living room to get something or other, and observe that Keith would be listening to a certain band's cassette tape. They sounded pretty good. "Who's this?" I'd ask him, and he'd tell me some entirely forgettable name. The next day I'd come in again, same tape, same question. Eventually I learned to remember the band's name, which was Pavement.

After a while Justine and Keith moved out to a place round the corner. They probably fled to avoid the horrendous shouting matches I was regularly holding with Chris Trout,[2] but did not make a big deal of it at the time. I always thought that was overly kind of them.

Justine and Keith also possessed a couple of seven inches and a ten inch by that Pavement band, and when they left they took those vinyls, but bequeathed me (or forgot to take) a copy of that cassette. I installed Gavin Bradbury and Barry Millington in the house, and suddenly *Ablaze!* had a three-strong team of Gavin, Trout and myself, and the sounds of this cassette became our daily fare. Most of the songs on it were to appear publicly some 18 months later, albeit in a very different order, as *Slanted and Enchanted*.

Barry, though an *Ablaze!* non-participant, had a kid's keyboard which he let us borrow. We had to find out more about Pavement and, since they were resident in the United States, we figured that a postal interview would be the best way to interrogate them. Reluctant to conduct our enquiries telephonically, we sought to reify the experience (kids: read 'keep it real') by putting our questions on tape, so at least real voices could be exchanged. (We also inserted a burst of cheesy cheap keyboard auto-fanfare – using Barry's keyboard - between each question asked, in order to underline the momentousness of the occasion).

We sent off our cassette and a few weeks later (this was fast!), a FedEx package arrived at our house. Inside the magical and strange envelope there was a new cassette, along with a colour photocopy of some Polaroids, underlined by the members' names in Dymo tape.

The reply-cassette was glorious. We were gratified to hear the fanfares coming back at us, where they'd copied our questions, and in between there were wondrous speeches, fragments of conversations; Mark Ibold describing his favourite train journey, from New York to Pennsylvania. Spiral talking about Echo and the Bunnymen, Stereo Master taking us aside in the kitchen to murmuringly take control of the situation while he grabbed a beer. A mock hospital visit (at least I think it was faked – it's ever so hard to tell). And a song, a two-track version of 'Secret Knowledge of Backroads', which is these days credited to The Silver Jews, but David Berman was there and perhaps he and SM had written it together.

We were, for a while, a relatively happy household. I didn't partake of the hotknife sessions, but the giggling was infectious. We had a lot of input from the postman who brought promos by the sackload, and from Micheal Walsh, who annoyed and delighted us by turns.

Andrew Truth lent me £760 and I bought a Canon StarWriter, a machine much more elaborate than an electric typewriter but much less so than a PC. At the front end there was a keyboard and a tiny screen that displayed 12 lines of text, at the back there was a black inkjet printer, and somewhere in the middle was a floppy disc drive. The whole thing folded into a box shape; it was dinky and represented a huge leap in technology for us. I mean, it had five different fonts, and bold, and italics! Also it did backgrounds: horizontal or vertical lines, or dots even! I squandered these rudimentary typography tools like a post-communist Russian in a Disney store, proudly displaying all five fonts at once on the front cover and littering the rest of the zine with some really tacky effects. We were thrilled with our little piece of the cutting edge.

1991's Reading Festival was something of a focal point for this issue. It brought Mercury Rev, Babes In Toyland and American Music Club over to us, although all three had to wait till later on in their UK visits to be interviewed by us. It was a time when Dinosaur Jr. produced no more thrill. I dissed Sonic Youth - and they didn't even notice - and I address De La Soul as "lads". Gavin and I did a survey of most popular band merchwear; imagine a festival with no Nirvana t-shirts.

It must have been the phone interview format that made me feel comfortable enough to ask Mercury Rev about their sexual fantasies (whilst in the middle of painting the living room with a very argumentative Trout). My subsequent meetings with Dave Baker would always involve him asking if I'd got rid of "that jerk". We couldn't afford to buy a Chinese meal with Babes in Restaurant, but it was a memorable event just the same. Mark Eitzel charmed me by being both humble and interesting.

Chris Trout interviews the Pale Saints, and it turns out the boy knows about music and can write and everything. Gavin throws himself in at the deep end with Hole and comes out of it very well. The Muses interview is very nice, and we get to read about the birth of Belly at the end.

The fanzine reviews suggest an unspoken manifesto of honesty *űber alles*. It would have been so easy to keep opinion to ourselves, maybe just list the contents of each, and promote the zine network in its entirety. That I didn't even think of this shows how locked into the moment I was, probably being all arrogant and stuff. We also come over as ambitious and almost imperialist, trying to poach writers from our favourite zines. In other areas our honesty policy was more fruitful. The truth is we hated nicey-nice zines that regurgitated press releases and claimed to like every record they were sent. We were very clear about what we loved or hated and saw no reason to couch our passions in tactful phrasing, so we told it as we saw it and made enemies as we went. We must have caused hurt, and to this day we don't know which fan/musician/fanzine writer sent back a copy of this issue cut into tiny little pieces along with a letter suggesting that we should all die or write for the NME. They kept hold of the Pavement flexi though.

The demo reviews were such hard work that we decided to kill the pain and share the burden. Two-thirds of us were stoned, and we were all happy to disagree.

Trout got busy with the record review section and treated most of the vinyls in his own particular, erudite manner (with notable exceptions, like not having heard The Stooges, but

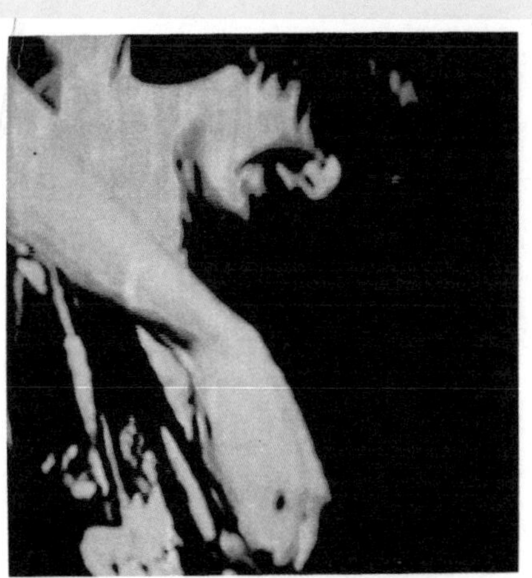

STEREO MASTER

M. IBOLD

SPIRAL S.

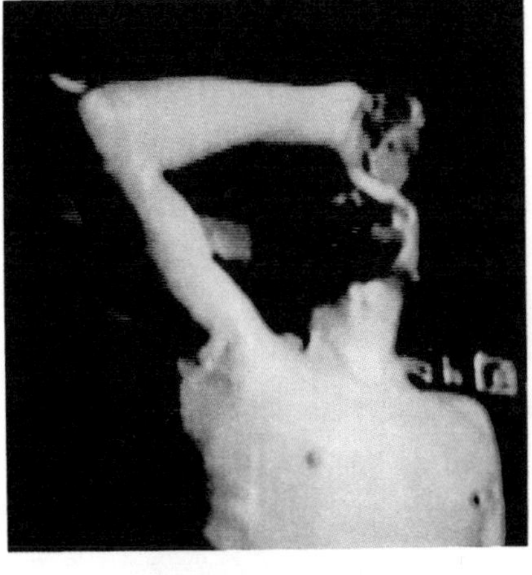

G. YOUNG

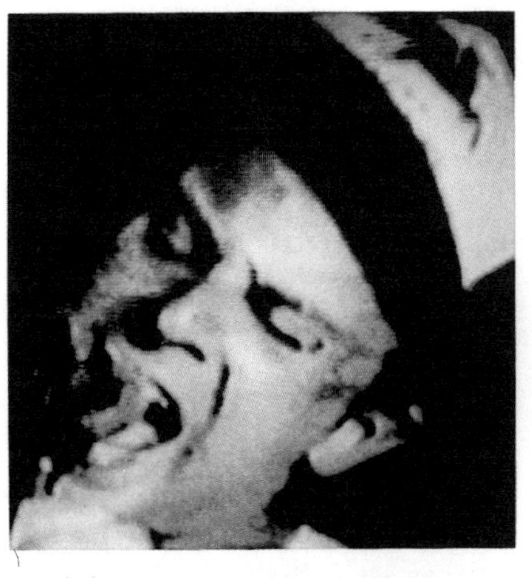

BELMONT N.

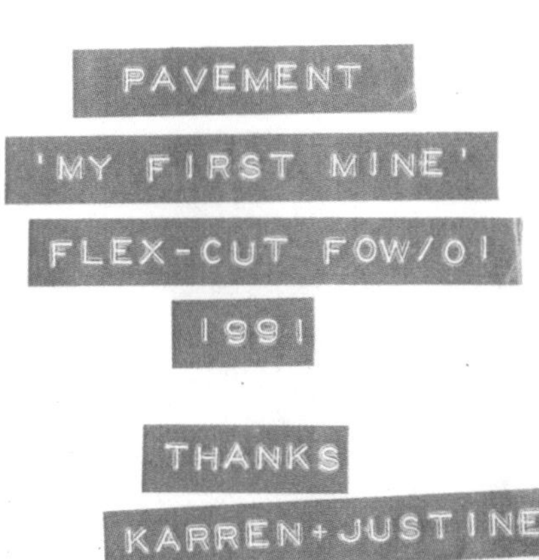

PAVEMENT
'MY FIRST MINE'
FLEX-CUT FOW/01
1991

THANKS
KARREN + JUSTINE

10/16/91

Hi Karen,

I'm in the P.O. right now. I've been coming here everyday hoping that the Pavement song would just get here already. Not today. I did receive your letter today, though. So I'll try to answer your questions. FLEXI is happening but I'm not sure you'll get the tape in time for upcoming issue of ABLAZE! MANAGEMENT SITUATION well, that's us. We manage. We Lazy. We live in CALIFORNIA + NEW YORK + NEW JERSEY. That causes problems in situations like this. My phone bills are way up. I'll call you or Justine when I get the tape for further instructions. I'm using a shitty P.O. pen and they're yellin for it back. BYE!

MARK

then neither had I, you *didn't*, in those days). He went about likening most everything to Big Black, doubtless with good reason, and slating The Wedding Present whilst driving the bassist from his home. Our review of the monumental *Spiderland* is a testament to the 'many records:little time' ratio we were dealing with. We needed a little more time to fall so deeply in love.

Compact discs had started to arrive in the post; they were piling up silently on the mantelpiece. When the collection got tall enough, I took them to Gerol's Records and raised enough cash to buy a CD player so we could find out what they sounded like... Oops.

The issue ends with news of three deaths, but two of them were only bands. I didn't understand about death back then, and was young and out of my depth when writing about the passing of Lee from Pregnant Neck, a fellow zinester and correspondent. When he had written to me of his desire to kill himself, I had taken it as a mere overflowing of the teenage angst that I presumed we all felt. If I'd thought he was actually going to do it... Only just into my twenties, being fucked up was our way of life, a condition of existence. It was hard to spot who needed more than records, zines, beer and friends to keep going through those times. It seemed particularly sad and pointless as there were so many bands, so many shows he would have loved - like Huggy Bear, who later emerged from his barrio - but I guess he just couldn't stay.

And in the midst of death, we announced the advent of Pavement's first UK release, in the form of a beautiful flexi-disc. Lee really should have stuck around.

1 Hemiola Records released vinyl by the likes of Unrest, Eggs, Thinking Fellers Union Local 282. Offered a Pavement single, Justine turned them down in order to focus on bands that really needed a small label like hers.

2 He has quite a set of lungs on him, and those lungs were usually full of drugs that he put in there with his hash pipe.

ABLAZE!

8

BONG-WATER

THROWING MUSES

Pale SAINTS

MERCURY REV

BABES in TOYLAND

AMERICAN MUSIC CLUB

BLEACH ♥ HOLE

BAND OF SUSANS

FOREHEADS in a FISHTANK

LANGFIELD CRANE

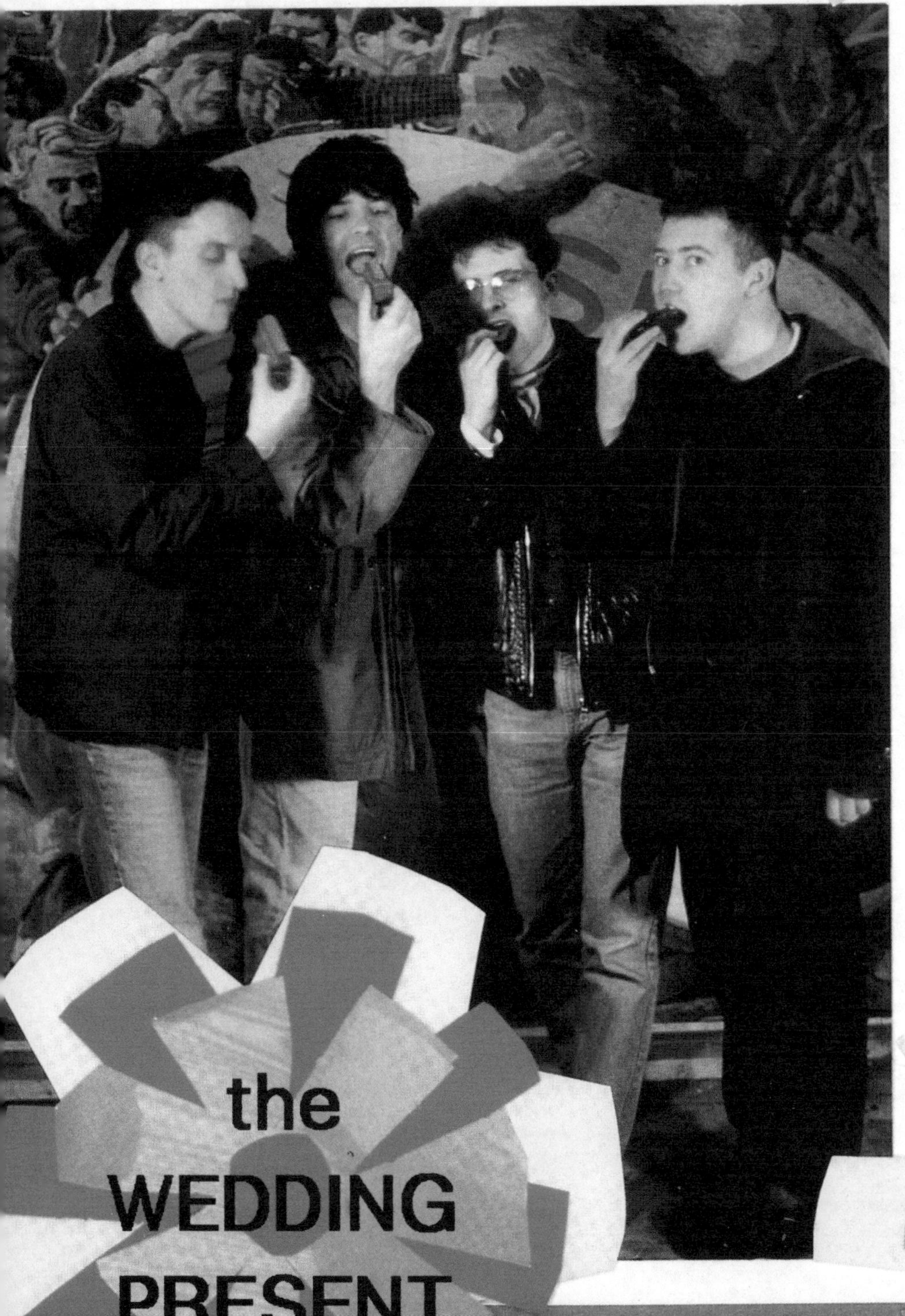

the WEDDING PRESENT

ONE POUND FIFTY

and on flexidisc: PAVEMENT & FLUFF

UMBRELLA TALES

THE LIGHTS, THE SOUND, THE RHYTHM... THE RAIN. READING '91... edited highlights.

9.30 Friday morning - feels like I've been in this tent forever. Last night our arrival was greeted by a euphoric bombardment of the senses, a kid city of tents and smells and battery-powered cassette players, burning fire and punk rock, indie pop and damp earth. I love everybody despite the treacherous rain that clings to my skin... and so it ceases.

Just in time for **BABES IN TOYLAND** to redeem themselves. I think they symbolise something important for most, something along the lines of "dresses don't mean y'can't rock", but I knew this anyway; so they need to be something *more,* and so far they just haven't been... but today it sounds good, and Lori's sticks move good (they are the first things I see, rushing into the arena) and Kat's scary madness comes and dwells amongst us, the guitar sound blows in the wind and **THAT DRUMMER** sings her sad song. Well.

SILVERFISH are a bit too sexy for me. Les enters utterly jubilant, raising her arms and striding the front of the stage in greeting, feeding off all the vibes. Later she peels off her shirt to reveal a snazzy summer dress, while Chris dons his cowboy suit, Fuzz is kitted out in full evening dress and from the second row Stu is invisible (ace trick!). Grinding pelvises behind me, long hair in my face, my ribs resisting snapping - the bemused security weren't to know whether we were screaming in agony or bliss.

I spend a while hanging out with top rock stars and journalists, and am on the verge of depression by the time **DINOSAUR JR** lumber onstage. They are Dinosaur Jr, they sound like nothing out of the ordinary and provide excellent background tunes for me to talk over...

SONIC YOUTH and the sun goes down. Thurston tells us there is a full moon but he is wrong, there is a bite taken out of it. I look to this band for the answer to life's mysteries but they tell me nothing. Their trick of providing incidental music between songs ("Have you heard the new Primal Scream single?") while they adjust their guitars is cute. But I don't like their new stuff too well and even when they play "Expressway..." I am bored. Oh Sonic Youth, go make your money. It's just a different world...

But who cares about all that, when **AMERICAN MUSIC CLUB** are about to play in the Mean Fiddler tent? The feeling is scary: I've never seen them before, what if they're crap? Just hold on... I watch as several old-type people move about in front of me, the stage crew, surely. Except, they're picking up the instruments and starting to play them! What is this? All these kids gathered to pay homage to five thirtysomething beings playing music that is COUNTRY-derived, of all things? Yet their music, unlike their clothes, is quite possibly timeless.

Singer Mark Eitzel is a star. He is balding and bearded and too nice and too too sad. A tent full of hardened Big Black fans are nearly moved to tears by classics like "Blue And Grey Shirt" and "Mom's TV". If I was surprised that he stopped a song to ask what someone had just shouted to him, I was perfectly freaked when he stopped another, said "I got the lyrics mixed up", told a few jokes, pissed around with the guitarist, played a bit of a different tune and then rejoined the song at the point at which he left it. Completely cool. The guy who plays the the knitting machine type contraption deserves a mention too: apart from Mark's creamy voice, that's where a lot of the beautiful sounds come from.

Saturday morning and things are somewhat spaced. I don't know how. Just grass and mud, blue sky and clouds, thousands of the meek waiting, just waiting, and **MERCURY REV** are playing. A beautiful Galaxie experience but infinitely weirder. Sitting on the ground I see nothing of their stage antics, I don't know them or their songs, but it all sounds drifty. Later someone tells me they're from the North East coast and I think "Oh, Newcastle."

[Well, what do you expect after 40 hours in a field?]

DE LA SOUL are ridiculous. Their juvenile attempt to pit one half of the crowd against the other (by instructing half to drawl "aaaasshole!" and the rest "kiss ma aaaass!" turns out to be the biggest bit of bullshit the weekend has to offer. For some reason, I had expected these to be good. If you're reading, lads, don't tear this up just yet - check the Mercury Rev interview first, could be some work in it for you.

THE FALL? Egoful, half-hearted, depressingly unadventurous. Though I'm told that everyone has to get old.

I'm sure that **JAMES** are superb: I hate their records greatly, but they can be very special indeed live. If only I had been able to keep still long enough. So many paths to walk along! Things to do, people to see!

Gavin witnessed the **EDWYN COLLINS** riot, and I was distressed to hear that

TOUTS were seen selling their wares

shite

T-SHIRTS 100% COTTON XL
£8·00 EACH INC. P&P
GREY ON WHITE / PURPLE ON BL

What We Did At The Weekend (essay plan): checking out the T-shirt scene / trying to blag one off silverfish / speculating about crop circles / avoiding the backstage area / hanging out with cool rock kids (hello Andrew, Kim, Davi Lesley, Martin, Gary, Angie, Declan, Karen...) / pacing the planet / breathin in airborne plastic bottles / deferring to the swans / basking in the sun / cringing in the rain / swimming in the holy water... and not getting too ruffle

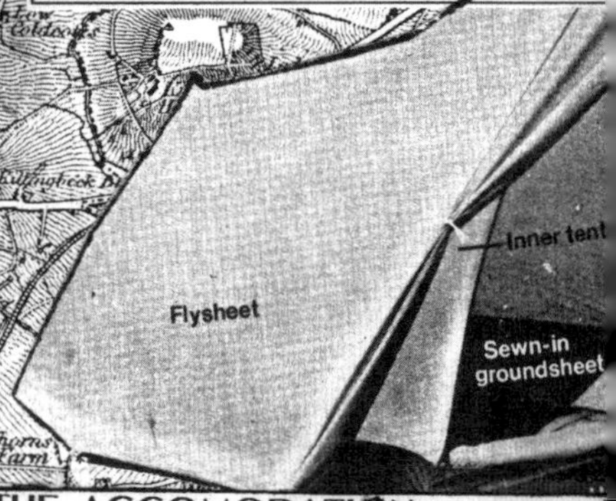

THE ACCOMODATION was superb

the poor man shed frustrated tears at the premature cessation of his set. Those nasty people in charge should be ashamed of themselves. Seriously.

Well, all you suckers thought that was the end and went back to your tents to take drugs, but my cool friends and I knew better. Gathered round a tiny homemade stage in some faraway field we witnessed **HEADCLEANER** (the London one) making longdrawnout, nondescript noises with serious male vocals. However, dismissal is not yet warranted, as they weren't all there at the time. No, really - their drummer had broken a thumb and so had to alternate with a stand-in person, and their bassist had wandered off home and so was replaced by the delicious Gary Chapman (ex-**BRAINFAG**, now of Harlow rock gods **PLUG**) who performed "marvellous"-ly considering he'd only had one and a half minutes to learn the songs.

Sunday, and things are getting a bit much on this here planet of sound. I jump up on a satellite, which happens to be full of water, so I go for a swim. Checking out space for unexhausted possibilities is... pretty exhausting. But **KITCHENS OF DISTINCTION** provide some constancy in that they sound like they always do, and so anchor us. The between-song humour ensures their continued place in my heart, for now.

Reliable informants tell me that **BLUR** were something very special. (Their LP is especially *awful*. Was that it? LN)

Multitudes gathered to experience the **DR. PHIBES AND THE HOUSE OF WAX EQUATIONS** thang, so it was quite an effort to take my eyes off the backs of the heads in front of me, such is my need for a focal point whilst hearing a band. They were wondrous, swirly, beautiful and highly appreciated. To snarling anti-prog rock criticists I say fluffy cats, because this is a band I intend to pursue at least those 70 miles down the M62. A summer sound you can wear all year round.

The **NEDS'** "Be Silent / Consume / Die" backdrop was certainly a poignant message for the pizza (etc) and Sisters (etc) digesting masses present. But so what, since we're all here for as much entertainment as we can cram in. I've really nothing against little Ned and his strange wastepaper basket friends, they do what they do and people like it and it's all good clean fun as far as I can tell. Sadly I was too hyperactive to be capable of actually watching their set (you noticed?), so...

FREE T-SHIRT OFFER!

If you despise James, or just despair at the sight of hordes of spotty young virgins wandering around in James gear giving the band unnecessary publicity, then you probably already own one of these snazzy items. If you don't, read on.

Ablaze! has got together with part-time telephonist / failed pop star Paddy to bring to you a once-in-a-lifetime chance to rectify the situation and simultaneously give your street cred a much needed kick up the arse. 5 limited edition T-Shites, plus 25 surprise gifts (badges or sweets, who knows?) are on offer to the people who send a strange, amusing or just correctly addressed postcard to Ablaze! / Paddywack Offer, BOX T114, 52, CALL LANE, LEEDS, LS1 6DT as soon as you like.

Gavin was esp. good at this).

A town in the south invaded by the music-obsessed kids of Britain may not be heaven... but why not? This year I was surprised to find enough goodwill to go round, helped by the fact that there were few police, doing only moderate damage. Even a vastly commercial event such as this holds the possibility of makingssome holes in our thick mantle of alienation.... But then, festivals always make me feel like this!

READING '91 T-SHIRT SURVEY

1. Carter The Unstoppable Sex Machine
2. Pop Will Eat Itself
3. The Wonder Stuff
4. Ned's Atomic Dustbin
5. Sonic Youth / Mudhoney / James
6. Silverfish / Pixies / Nirvana
7. Sisters Of Mercy
8. Kingmaker / Senseless Things
9. REM / The Fall / New Model Army / The Cure
10. Bleach / Fields Of The Nephilim / Mega City Four / Teenage Fanclub / Wedding Present
11. Babes In Toyland / Hole / Pale Saints / Ride / Jesus And Mary Chain / Iggy Pop / World Party / Chapterhouse / Happy Mondays / Bauhaus
12. Johnny Mathis / A.C. Temple / Th' Faith Healers / Perspex White Out / Gallon Drunk / Rollins Band / My Bloody Valentine / Blue Aeroplanes / Bob Dylan / Black Flag / Dinosaur Jr / Inspiral Carpets / Throwing Muses / Revolting Cocks / Motorhead / Pere Ubu / Jane's Addiction / Tad / Slowdive / Lemonheads / Popguns / Cinderella / Field Mice / Bob / New Order / Bolt Thrower / Manic Street Preachers / The Beautiful South / Dead Kennedys / Buffalo Tom / The Cult / Big Black / The La's / The Cramps / Blyth Power / Dan Dare's Dog / The Smiths / The Pogues / Cocteau Twins / Poison Idea / Ramones / Godflesh / The Damned / Fudge Tunnel / Leatherface / Morrissey / Metallica / Lard / Loop / Fugazi / Head Of David / Fatima Mansions / Gaye Bykers On Acid / The Fat Lady Sings / Terminal Cheesecake / Fishbone / Husker Du / Stone Roses

With the massive technology available to us we were able to monitor the T-shirt wearing behaviour of EVERYONE at the festival this year. We sent our higly-trained team of T-shirt inspectors out among the crowd to interview thousands of young men about why they buy shirts and which are their favourite ones. Here is a selection of their responses:

ANDY REDDITCH from **BIRMINGHAM**
Fave shirt: Spandau Ballet ("the ultimate band").
Most important thing about a band **T**-shirt: Gold and tinsel.

PETE SLUNK from **HACKNEY**
Fave ones: Headcleaner and the first Silverfish one.
The thing: Swear words and wit.

DOUGAL from **BRIGHTON**
Best one: Death To The Pixies.
Why: Cos available at gig.

JASON DUCKERS from **OXFORD**
Fave one in the world: Carter.
Depends on: The band and the quality.

ADAM WILLIAMSON from **MACCLESFIELD**
Bestest: M.B.V. "eye" one.
The thing: Band more important than design or quality.

ALISTAIR from **SOUTHEND**
Fave shirt: The Family Cat.
The thing: "Whether you get to do it with the band."

PLEASE NOTE: High positions in this chart do not imply that the bands concerned are in any way musically good or interesting.

MERCURY REV

i would like to protect you from the frightening fact that my mercury rev interview was less than perfectly executed. however... the uniform lack of competence that i choose to display in all such circumstances was combined with the facts that i was in leeds and they in london, i was covered in white paint and they were late, i was engaged in damaging justine and keith's answering machine and they couldn't get their conference call function to work, my stoopid boyfriend had been arguing at me and they kept putting me on hold (a thing which i was on for 70% of the interview), i wasn't used to talking to such sexy american men and they weren't used to talking to such a sexy english woman... and so on. not worth printing then, you quality conscious lambs murmur. naaaaaaaah, chuck it in with the rest we cackle. and so.

are you david?
"this is too much technology for us."
where do you live?
"i live in a different place than he does."
what sort of place?
"in a city..."
sean?
"ah we're all from, uh yeah, we're all from around different places. we kinda all met in buffalo new york and now we're all kind of spread out. i guess the most people live there."
are there 6 of you?
"yeah."
sometimes it seems like more doesn't it?
"there are too many people."
do you all hate each other?
"we don't. a lot of times we don't get along, we fight."
why?
"it could be anything from stepping on my shoe to stealing my guitar... david stealing my gum... when it's in my mouth..."

"Lady Di looks pretty attractive, but I know I'll never be able to touch her"

are they bastards?
"we're all bastards yeah. i'm probably the biggest."
this isn't happening is it?
"no. like everything else."
(confusion. mutual embarassment.)
"hello?!!" (this is david)
hello.
"this is awful!"
"so what am i supposed to ask you?"
i'm supposed to ask you, how can you have a band under such circumstances?
"it's like a boyfriend and a girlfriend. sometimes, it doesn't have to be that way, but sometimes boyfriends and girlfriends fight, and makin' up's the best part. d'you know what I'm talking about?"
i know exactly what you're talking about. that's why i don't have any questions for you, cos my boyfriend's been arguing at me...
"being in a band is like having sex. our relationship is based on fighting and making up, so when we play live it's like making up."
is it stressful?
"sex can be stressful, but then it's supposed to be stress relieving so, that's what it's like, you play and then you're done, you're exhausted and you're dripping wet and then you smoke a cigarette."
why is sex stressful?
"it's stressful getting to the point, like dating... we have to keep romancing each other, giving each other flowers and stuff. occasionally it's kinda beautiful y'know? if we hung out with each other all day and didn't go out, we'd get used to each other and that's when we fight. if we don't see each other and then we get together, then everything's kinda like a surprise to us as well as the people that come to see us and it's all great. or not... you having a bad time with your boyfriend?"
it's just that he's a bit mad.
"crazy?"
yeah, kind of weird, he yells a lot.
"i wouldn't put up with that shit."
well he's an artistic genius y'see.
"oh yeah."
and i love him.
"i still wouldn't put up with people yelling at me."
it's stressful, but sometimes it's beautiful.
"you put it right back in my face!"
is there a danger of you splitting up?
"well even if we split up... it's hard to know. everything you're doing is a danger. it's like somebody saying 'are you gonna die?', y'know? - 'well i'm sure, someday'. 'is the band gonna break up?' - 'yeh, i'm sure'. the only difference is, once you break up y'can get back together, once you die you can't."
did you like sonic youth at reading?
"i've seen 'em when i liked them more, like when they played with neil young they were kind of young'n'taut'n'ready to rock. sometimes they're out there and wild and just jammin', and sometimes if they've had a bad day or if they're sick or something then they might have a bad show but then again the bad shows are the ones i like and the good shows are what everyone else likes. at this they had too much time to hang out and the sound wasn't so hot... for sonic youth, you're supposed to be in a small club and freakin' your brains out. de la soul were the band that came off best."
they were hilarious.
"that's what they do, they're hilarious but they're really cool. we're hoping to do a record with them. maybe if you print that they'll read it and say yeah. we wanna do a split single with them so if you could sort that out for us..."
i'll try. was it scarey playing in front of all those kids at reading?
"no it was amazingly relaxed. playing in front of two people is a lot harder. well we haven't played in front of two people but it would be awful, especially if it was two people we knew and cared about. if you have less people in the crowd than you have on the stage, that's got to be a lot harder. so what bands do you like? the bloody valentine people?
yeah and... american music club and live skull...
"live skull were pretty awesome. the guitarist from the swans and the drummer from live skull have a band called sugartime..."
if you see them, get them to send me a tape! so where exactly do you live?
"i live in baltimore, i live in rap central, kids rap all over the streets and stuff. everything is 'potholes in my lawn'."
got any good presents to take home to your mothers?
"well, hopefully i'll be alive. cos i think she'd be pretty bummed if i died. did you like our show in leeds?"
i was tired and uncomfortable and melting in the heat so i felt that your songs were meandering too much for me... but i liked your reading thing better.
"yeah, being out in the air and stuff. i was so relaxed i almost went to sleep. i think it would be the ultimate thing, to get up on stage and go to sleep. tell me who's done that before."
that would be novel wouldn't it, you could go down in the rock'n'roll history books.
"and you could dream on stage. i think jonathon dreams onstage."
when he's awake?
"yeh."
that's clever.
"he knows how to dream. he dreams when he writes letters. he's dreamy."

"I think Jonathan dreams on stage... he really knows how to dream"

"sean y'gonna get back on here and fill in the gaps?
there's a lot of them... i haven't answered anything."
"hey." (this is sean)
has england freaked you out?
"some things, like the corn and chicken sandwiches."
are they good?
"no."
are they crap?
"yeah. cheese and pickle sandwiches. we don't have things like that."
have you got a present for your mother?
"i got my mom a whole bunch of postcards from tenby. i'm supposed to call her today. david said he got his mom a box of candy and some bitters... what's that? oh some cans of bitters."
what are you doing today?
"we're going to portobello road. we're trying to make friends. we're not doing very well."
what's 13 x 7?
"let's see... 107? 21 x 7? ahm, 91."
what does death need time for?
"aaah, love."
right. have you got any sexual fantasies? (thanks to dregs for some inspiration.)
"oh yeah, lots."
tell me one of them.
"oh jesus. when we went to tenby there were these sheep... it would be cool to meet a nice sheep."
animals are nice. if rabbits were bigger...
"that would be cool. pull those long ears back."
ask david what his is
"i don't know if i want to answer this phone." (this is david.) "i have so many of them, it's all that's on my mind. what did he say? did he tell you, let me guess, about his fantasies of animals?"
sheep.
"oh my god! he wouldn't do that, but he sure does think about it all the time. when he eats food he looks at it and goes, 'this used to be an animal, gosh, i wonder if it was sexy?'... lady di looks pretty attractive, but i know i'll never be able to touch her."
what would you like to do?
"pretty boring, just boring sex. just something about it that's unobtainable. i'm not into that crazy stuff."
what label are you on in america?
"rough trade but it folded. we were doing really well but now all the records that were put out there are all bought, we're never gonna see anything from it. except for the fact that people have the music, and that's the whole reason for anything."
what's your address so i can send you a copy of this?
"box 66426, baltimore, maryland, 21239, usa. people sending stuff in the mail is really good, we wanna recreate the communication lines between bands and fans but we don't want them to be fans, just people. that would be really good. they could send their sexual fantasies and maybe if i get time i could send my sexual fantasies back. they could send us music, cos that's the only way we hear new music. maybe we could exchange sexual fantasies when you get sick of that creep."
maybe.
"i could screen 'em for ya, if i could find some females with no inhibitions, and then send 'em your way."

with that thought on my mind i bid sean and david farewell. only afterwards did i recall the incompatibility between american and british videotape. well i'm gonna send them things to make up for such a lame interview, and if you do as well, that would be even better. get yerself a copy of their weird lp while you're at the shop.

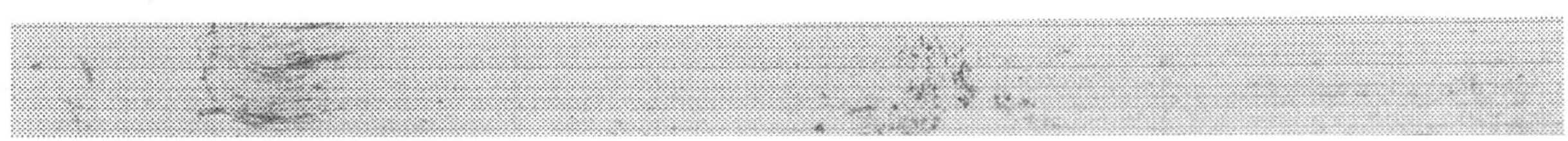

THEIR LIVES REVOLVE AROUND PLACES OF REFRESHMENT!
THEIR LANDLORD FEARED THE HOUSE WOULD CAVE IN!!
THEY COME FROM MINNEAPOLIS & PLAY PUNK ROCK, COOL STYLE!!!

THEY ARE BABES IN TOYLAND

Lori, Michelle, Kat. Onstage we see three scary women, grinding and screaming out weird rock music (the sort to have kittens by). Offstage they're pleasant, friendly people who frequent restaurants and who don't bite (except when tucking into their dinners). We gathered in a Cantonese hot food establishment near Leeds' Duchess, before a gig to break all fire regulations.

"Oh! I left my vitamins in my socks"

Approaching my information gathering mission the lazy way, I requested an account of the Toyland story so far. Obligingly they began, with the intention of telling me a paragraph each. Weird talkin', scraggly haired guitarist/ vocalist Kat first:

"From the beginning: I moved from San Francisco to Minneapolis to try and be in a band, and I met Lori initially at a barbecue and then at a tea party, and we started jamming together and Lori thought of the name and then we met Michelle and that's all for my paragraph."

Quiet spoken, intense bassist Michelle next:

"And then, we didn't really know how to play so we started to learn. Both me and Lori had only been playing for about six months but Kat had been in a lot of bands on the West Coast. We practiced in Lori's basement but the landlord said we'd have to stop or the house would cave in."

Kat: "He came down and Lori hid behind her drumset and we were just sitting there: 'Oh, a drummer? No!!! We didn't hear a drummer!'"

Big brash drummer/vocalist Lori takes her turn:

"And so, since we've started we've done, oh, eight or nine tours consecutively. This is our second time here [in the UK and at the Duchess]. We left last October after we recorded 'To Mother'."

Kat, in a special goofy voice:

"Hey Lori, why don't you tell 'em about the single?"

Lori: "Oh, it's on Insipid Records, it's an Australian single. It's gonna be pretty hard to get hold of here. But just in case, for record collector fanatics: it's on pink vinyl, there's 500 in leather covers stamped in silver and then the other covers that are limited are little accidents that Kat and I had with ourselves."

"Blood!!!" pronounces Kat, with obvious relish.

Lori: "Our blood phase." Their enthusiasm for this gory artwork suggests that the Babes' creative juices flow in more than one direction.

Kat and Lori bring the story up to date (I should point out here that although Michelle does talk as much as these two, her voice is quieter and so tends to get drowned out):

"We were on Twin Tone, and 'To Mother' is on Twin Tone, and we've signed with Warner Brothers recently."

Wow.

"And after we go back we'll probably not tour for a while, and work on a new record for Warners."

The frequency with which these people tour caused me to ask whether they were getting all of their essential nutrients?

Michelle: "We eat pretty good."

Kat: "I take my vitamins with my beer so I always swallow them. Oh! I left my vitamins in my socks!"

Oh dear - minus four points for multiple vitamin abuse.

Several things about my experience of these here Babes In Toyland suggest that they can't keep themselves away from, erm, "places of refreshment". They appear uncannily at home in this restaurant environment, not made in the least bit neurotic by waiters, menus, knives and forks etc. Other factors suggest that this is actually their natural habitat - Lori worked in a high class restaurant for many years, Michelle has been a waitress, and Kat describes her past occupation as "bar attender". I ask them about Minneapolis and they tell me there are "some nice barbecues".

Are these people food monsters...?

Lori: "Seriously you guys, I think we should order the Steam Drunken Giant King Prawns In Garlic."

...Or beer monsters?

The waiter dude arrives and they order drinks. Everett True is the worst offender (No, he hasn't joined the band, but was merely hanging around in order to polish up his interview technique under my guidance.) He orders a pint and a vodka with his tea.

A friend described you as like UT reincarnated as a rock band.

Michelle: "That's flattering, I like that."

Lori: "I think that people think that because we're girls they have to use that [i.e. comparisons with other female artists.]"

You must get really tired of people coming at you from a women-in-rock angle. Like the way you were lumped in with that offensive trend Sounds tried to start up, "foxcore".

> "I Can't believe what what my tea f'k'n leaves say!!"

Kat: "That was really bad."

Lori: "That was Thurston's fault, he thought of that word."

Kat: "But he didn't know the press was gonna grasp it like a diamond ring!"

I asked the wonderful Lori whether being a drummer and a vocalist simultaneously causes practical problems.

"It's pretty cool... I think it's because if you're drumming you don't really write melodies - you don't end up banging on your drums and just singing without any other instruments around. But guitar and bass you can kind of sing along to, that's why there aren't many [drummer/ vocalists]."

Kat: "Sometimes she hits the mike with the sticks!"

If you all sang it would be dead good, like Nomeansno.

Michelle: "I used to sing but it didn't sound that great. I like to put all my energy into one thing, playing really hard."

Kat: "It sounded good, it sounded really cracky/snappy."

Michelle: "Well, when we get another microphone..."

We took a brief excursion into superstition land. I asked about their star signs.

Michelle: "I'm Aquarius."

Kat & Lori: "Sagittarius."

Everret: "I was born on April 21st, that's the Queen's birthday."

And Robert Smith's.

Kat: "That's why they're both good writers."

Robert Smith and the Queen? You sure?

And Chinese horoscopes.

Lori: "I was born in the year of the rat."

Michelle: "I was born in the year of the rooster."

Kat: "I'm a rabbit."

And... tea leaf reading.

Lori: "Oh my god. I can't believe what my tea f'k'n leaves say!"

Kat: "What??"

Lori: "I can't tell you!"

You can really read tea leaves?

"Oh yeah," she replied gravely.

Kat gazes into her cup and announces, "Looks like tonight's my night!"

"What do mine say?" asks Everett.

Lori peers in. "HA HA HA HA." A laugh to spook anyone out, but Everett is looking especially worried.

D'you really beleive in all this stuff?

"Not really."

Because, you know, Sagittarians are supposed to be good at sport.

Kat: "Oh, is craning neck a sport?"

Lori: "Is sucking face a sport?"

Possibly not. At this point I decided to leave them to it.

AMERICAN MUSIC CLUB'S MARK EITZEL

KARREN ABLAZE! SPEAKS WITH THE MAN HIMSELF ... ON THE PHONE!

Having been suitably astounded by AMC's performance at Reading, I approached the charismatic Mark Eitzel (the band's singer, songwriter and occasional guitarist) to ask for an interview. To my surprise he considered my request (he spoke to me! he spoke to me!) and suggested we talk on the phone as they had planned an immediate escape from the festival. Ten a.m. I was to call him, a dreadful hour for conversation, but he was awake and friendly. I asked him,

How come you always write sad songs? Is it because they're what you're good at, or because you only write when you're sad, or because you're sad all the time?

"Pretty much yes to the first two and, uh, it's because that's pretty much what I see - if you look at people's eyes you don't see joy very often."

Do you agree that your lyrics could be construed as sexist?

"Well no, I never thought of that. Why?

Because you sing a lot about your relationships with women and refer to them as "beautiful", "pretty", that sort of dimension, and about how they should stay with you rather than doing other things... I just hear things like that.

"Well, um, no, um... it's not conscious if it's sexist. I guess I should use the *Spinal Tap* reply, "Sexy? What's wrong with being sexy?", but no. I didn't think there was anything sexist in what I'm doing, but if you think there is then I guess there is... I don't sentimentalise anybody, especially because I'm writing about people who, or one person who gets f*cked up a lot and does a lot of drugs. It's hard for me to be sentimental about people who do that. Or maybe I'm being *too* sentimental, maybe the sentimentalism is in its way a little bit of a lie because it's kinda f*cked, it's not real."

But if it's something that you feel, how can it be anything but real?

"Well, it can be, pretty easily. A lot of what you think is just phoney anyway. It's always pretty hard to find out what is really going on."

Well, I met someone yesterday who argued that mathematics is the ultimate reality. Things exist on so many different levels that you can't really say any of them isn't real.

"That's true, even though he's right or she's right, because mathematics is pretty much it, but I don't know, I don't agree; I have this social side to me so I can't go that far."

Where do you live?

"I live in California, in San Francisco."

You refer to your house a lot in songs.

"I've lived in some houses and I always have trouble living with people. I spend a lot of time at home, so maybe that's why."

Ah, wherever anyone lives, whether it's with your best friends or people you don't know, you always have problems. It's a metaphor for life. Have a lot of your songs been written in the same house?

"Mostly the ones on the early records are about living in the North Beach neighbourhood, and recently they're about living in the Mission so they've all kinda got a more violent turn to 'em."

What do you listen to?

"I'm a big Replacements fan, and I've been listening to Smokey Robinson a lot recently. That's about it, I don't listen to much. There's a band I like in San Francisco called the Red House Painters, sometimes they really suck but they play really slow really quiet really long songs and I like that, because most bands aren't brave enough to do things that crowds will get bored with..."

I can think of a few over here.

"Yeah, but to do it well and to really believe in themselves, there's very few people that'll do that. They're a little too ambitious for me, but just because I'm not doesn't mean they can't be."

You're really not ambitious? You don't push the band?

"I do, but when I deal with other people I'm not a prick. Well, I *am* a prick; but, like with soundmen, I don't tell soundmen what to do."

Steve Hawkins is doing your sound right now, isn't he?

"Yeah"

Well, he manages Fluff [he did at the time of the interview, before their tragic demise] they're the opposite of that group, they take one really brilliant idea and just use it once rather than over and over again.

"Which is what my big problem is! I'm just not really imaginative."

Really? Musically?

"I'm not. I just have my few chords and I stick to them pretty much. I try and grow out of that, but it's hard to do."

Aren't you more of a lyrics man anyway?

"Pretty much I guess, but even then I'm sure I'm rewriting the same song over and over..."

Well some bands really do hasve only one song and do it again and again, but I've not heard any of that in AMC.

"Not yet!"

How do you account for your band's appeal to The Kids? Isn't it old people's music? It's not exactly punk rock.

"No, it's not exactly punk rock... there's all kinds of music that I like, and I guess it *is* old people's music cos it's pretty smooth and it's not very challenging, it's not loud and there's no odd noises, but after a while you get to the point where you can't make weird sounds because it gets in the way of the song. But a band like Sonic Youth, they're brilliant, they can do it because it doesn't get in the way of the song; but if they tried to sing about the things I'm singing about they'd probably have to quiet down and slow down. I think what I'm doing is a lot harder - here I am bragging - but it's hard to sing about things of the heart without it being incredibly corny. So, I dunno, I'm always surprised to see anybody at our shows. We do get all kinds of people and it's weird. Okay, the young people are there maybe because they saw us in the British press... but I won't put down young people. When I was 18 and 19 my favourite performers were Joan Armatrading, Joni Mitchell... it's just that now it's got to the point where everything is classified so strictly, you're not supposed to cross boundaries..."

Something that struck me as strange when I saw you, although it's quite superficial as well, is the way you all look: you look nothing like the rest of the bands people were going to see at Reading, you look kind of old.

"We *are* old, we're all in our early thirties and we don't care about looking young. I don't care about fashion that much."

That's not the important thing anyway. It's just that so many people do the fashion thing, it shocks you to see someone who doesn't.

"I mean f*ck, it would really destroy us to have to spend a lot of time thinking about that stuff."

Do you get on all right with the rest of the band?

"Yeah, it's great. I've known Danny and Vudi for about eight years and we're just really good friends. And I play in another band with Tim the drummer, called the Toiling Midgets (?), it's kind of a grunge band, everybody plays really slowly and there's lots of feedback. They're an old S.F. punk band, and we've got a record coming out soon on Matador."

What are your audiences like in America, are they different from those in Europe?

"They're about the same... engineering majors! We have good fans, we really do."

You appreciate them.

"I'm intimidated by them!"

I noticed you stopping a song just to find out what somebody had shouted at you. I wondered if that was because you couldn't concentrate or because you're really concerned about what anybody might say.

"Both. I don't make any bones about the fact that performing is a pretty artificial thing, and if somebody says something I get really distracted, and it's more interesting really to know what they're saying, cos it's more of a kick, because it's more of the moment, y'know? And if somebody's saying "f*ck off and die", then I can tell *them* to f*ck off and die, and then I'm happy. Or if somebody's saying "do another song" then it's like, okay, we will."

It was really cool the way you got the lyrics muddled up in "Western Sky" and stopped, and told everybody you'd got them muddled up, and pissed about for five minutes,and then went back to the song.

"There's people there who know the lyrics better than I do, and I fell kind of embarrassed - AMC fans ask me "why did you change the lyrics? Fuck you" as if... well shit, I wrote the song! So why be phoney about it?"

For the sake of looking really professional. A lot of people will carry on - really big bands that have billions of fans who know the lyrics by heart and recite them in their sleep. You seem really sensitive about what other people want, which is nice.

"Well it's because it's really uncomfortable to be in a crowd watching a band, I hate it, I don't like crowds much. I mean, I'm not going to tell you that I'm a great person or anything, it really is part of the show, you're in it with this group of people and you're trying to make it good. Basically, I'm trying to win people over. I'm not a saint or anything, but I'm aware of how shitty it is to go see a band."

But most people just love it, they don't mind about crowds and they'll take anything from the artists.

"Yeah, but I don't. When I'm in an audience I'm really respectful, I'm quiet and I'm sensitive about the people around me. Most people aren't like that, but so what? If a performer's TOO nice usually I will hate it, I think "who's he trying to suck up to?" so I'm willing for people to accuse me of that, but on the other hand we're not really precious, if people wanna talk all the way through or tell us to f*ck off that's fine too. Frankly we're just entertainers. You're being nice and I'm trying to undermine that!"

AMC (l-r): Mike Simms, Dan Pearson, Mark Eitzel, Vudi, Bruce Kaphan.

People who're performing in other ways tend to establish more of a rapport with their audience, whereas many musicians limit themselves to one role and ignore that side of things.

"I never understood why - why are musicians special? They're not."

I think it's throwing away an opportunity really, if you have all these people around you and you're not listening or taking anything from them, it all goes one way.

"I mean yeah, where's the fun in that? If we had a set that we had to go through relly quickly from one song to the other we would fall on our faces. If we had to try to be Sonic Youth or something we couldn't do it, we couldn't imitate any other band, and there's this wall between you and the crowd if you follow the set list really closely and then go home. What's the point of that? Why not just make records and never tour? And also there's this thing through the '80s, this really crass, really commercial thing with crowds, like "oh yeah, f*ck 'em, lets show them how evil

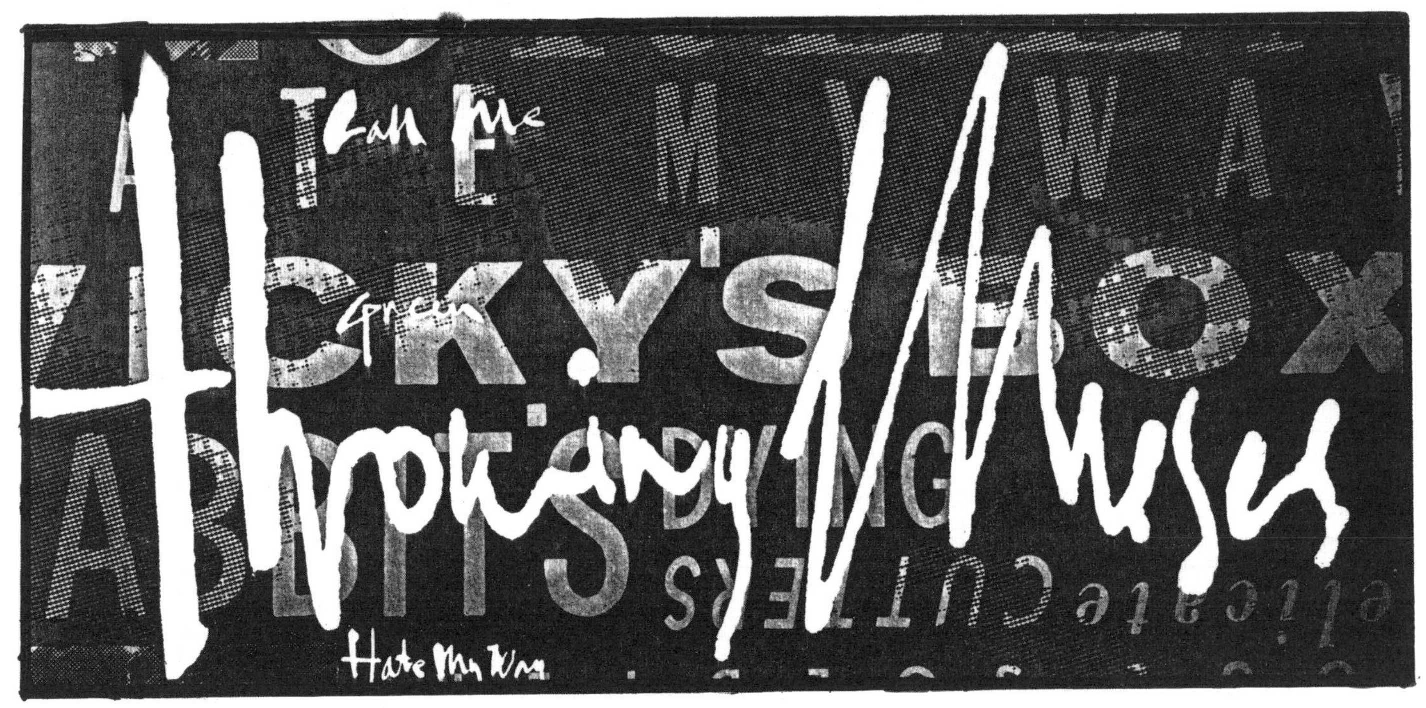

KARREN ABLAZE! DISCUSSES DRUMS, DREAMS, STUFFED ANIMALS & THE REAL RAMONA WITH TANYA DONELLY.

Springtime 1991. I took a bus out of dreary winter Schoolwork City and found myself in lovely leafy (dark damp stone town) Edinburgh. Calton Studios is possibly the most unfriendly, inhuman venue in which to see a band – bare breeze block walls, no chairs, just the bar at one end and the stage at the other. I sought sanctuary in the toilets but found none – no mirror greeted me with any comforting affirmation of my existence. Entering kids reflexively gathered in front of the empty stage, and before long the place was packed, but the uncomfortable wait ended with such a stirring, exciting set that all my heavy wintertime miseries fell away. Greg of the mighty Quality Time zine was there, and we teamed up with Alan, Phil and Craig (cool Muses followers) for the next two gigs, in Glasgow and Newcastle. At the latter Tanya agreed to give me an interview, so we sought a quiet place, pre-soundcheck time. Although we ended up in a dark draughty stairway with plenty of intrusive noise, she was undeterred, talking in many expressive tones and laughing a lot, as usual.

My first question concerned the tape they had been playing before the set, a collection of Ennio Morricone's Western theme tunes, which I somehow felt was telling us something specific about the new Muse sound. The drums were weird on it, I told her, because they behaved more like the other instruments, they weren't *just* keeping time.

"I love drums, drums are my favourite instrument."

They're pretty predominant on this LP.

"They're pretty loud live aren't they? You can hear them!"

I tell her that I don't see the point of them, when as if to confound me, the drum soundcheck begins, shattering our shortlived peace. What about the two minute long drum solos at the beginning of each song that you play live?

"Just giving David space!" she grins.

How did it feel, recording *"The Real Ramona"*?

"This one was a bit strange," she sighs, preparing to pack a great deal of feelings and events into a small number of words. "There was a lot going on, within the band microcosm, a lot of not so good things, so it was kinda tense at times, and there was friction between the producer [Dennis Herring] and certain people, y'know, it was just stupid shit. Plus we were in Hollywood which is an interesting place, because it doesn't have a *real* personality of its own, so you can kind of project whatever you want onto it. And once you've learned how to do that you can enjoy yourself, but there is definitely... after a while you're just ***'Get me out of here!'***"

I try to imagine the goings-on that have thrown stumbling blocks in the band's path, and ask whether Kristen has been having a bad time, as I knew she was having problems with her son (along the lines of her ex-husband trying to force her to choose between Dylan and her band).

"Yeah, that's kind of been a constant thing, y'know, that's not new. Ever since they've split up there've been problems. It's really bad that that has to happen to people."

Do you think she will end up having to choose one part of her life or the other?

"Hopefully not. And that's the kind of choice that she wouldn't... up to now she has kind of chosen the band, which is incredibly hard, and hopefully it won't come to that. She's pregnant again so," she ponders, laughing highly, "there's gonna be a certain amount of settling down at some point, when the baby comes."

One obvious thing to me about the LP is that sense of things being held back, of passion contained and blunted. The most telling sign is the brightness-and-fullness-and-up-thereness differential between "Red Shoes" as played live on the previous tour and the vinyl version.

"Yeah, that was our problem on that one, we remixed it twice, three times. We went back two months after the record was finished, and basically it wasn't a mixing problem at all, it was just that we didn't play it really well! And you can't go back and fix that, and that's my only real performance regret on the record. It's just that when you're in a studio, and I don't wanna sound prima-donna-ish, but if you don't feel inspired on the day, you just don't, and it's really easy once you're in there and you've been in there for four months just to go, [in dismissive tone]'ugh, sounds fine.'"

How long??

"It took four months to make. Well, really it took three and a half months, then there were all these weeks after when we mixed it."

But that's *a quarter of a year*, I announce, flabbergasted by the notion.

"It was, it was kind of horrible, although we all kind of went through stages. The thing that's just horrible about it with us is that the songs start to suffer after a while because we've got really short attention spans, y'know, and it makes me really

scared... cos we're definitely not the sort of band that goes in and slams 'em out, either. There's a middle ground that we haven't yet found."

The Muses' musical career is considered in some quarters to have suffered the process of a gradual blanding-out, although my opinion is that you make stuff that a lot of people can like, and that you do it well. Any comments?

"In some ways I can understand it, like with *"Hunkpapa"*, there are definitely things that we did... I mean, I love that record, but we *thought* about it for the first time, we thought about a way to do something, and that's not the way to go into a studio to make a record. You can't think about anything besides the four people in that room, really. With *"Ramona"* we didn't care anymore, by this record we just did't give a shit about *how* we were supposed to do things and what we were supposed to have in it, it was just "this is how we've written this record". And another thing as well is that we were so distracted, there was so much shit going on, we weren't thinking about the music so much, it was like "I've gotta do my guitar part", but I wasn't as neurotic about it or worried about it or paying too much attention to it, it took me not as many takes to get done as it has in the past, cos we were just like [screaming manically] "Aarrgh!" all the time, just completely emotionally raw. Real articulate sentence, he he he!"

You know, this tour has improved the quality of my life. And it's springtime.
"Is is springtime? [surprised] Ha ha ha."
How do you feel about setting out on tour?
"Oh I love touring, that's my favourite part of this job. I love hotel rooms, I love clubs, I like playing... Really, touring is my very favourite thing to do."
It must feel good being in this band unit with people that you're close to.
"Yeah, and the people we bring with us as well. It's nice."

Sometimes in the press the idea of you and Kristen competing with each other is suggested.
"It's definitely there at times when I play... this is very shifty ground... there's a healthy sexual exchange, I think, that goes on if there's one at all; there's nobody taking anything off anybody, nobody's taking anything away from me, nobody's putting any shit on me either, there's nothing where I go away feeling in the least bit compromised. It's more appreciative. The people that we attract... we're not babes or anything! We don't have a babe crowd."
The issue of competition between you and Kristen was probably brought about by the fact that you've been doing stuff with The Breeders, perhaps in the way that Kim was - cos it was stuff she couldn't, for whatever reason, do with The Pixies.
"Yeah, to a certain extent. Although a lot of that stuff was Kim's, we'd always wanted to do something together. Initially it was gonna be half her, half me; but I had record company problems so it ended up being all her stuff."
What's your schedule for The Breeders? Have you got any recording plans?
"Not as yet, just because she's so busy and I'm so busy. Hopefully this summer. We've gotta play it by ear. We call each other and make these big plans that change on a weekly basis."
D'you think you'll be recording in this country again?
"Yeah."
Because of Jo? (She's based in Brighton.)
"And because it's like a big vacation here for us! Ha ha ha! Plus they [The Pixies]'ll be coming off a tour that ends up here in England. Plus my boyfriend lives here most of the time anyway - my lover!"

Old news now, I know, but Leslie Langston's replacement with Fred Abong caused press squelchings anout "The new sexual symmetry within the band." I just thought, "So what?"... What did *you* think, Tanya?

"When you know somebody really well, the way David and Kristen and I know each other, when you're with somebody to that extent, you stop thinking of them as having a maleness or a femaleness, you know what I mean? It didn't even occur to me when people, this sounds really unbelievable, they talk about 'the shifting sexual power of the band,'... I'm like, '*What??!*' Fred and Leslie are like... Fred and Leslie!"
You get a lot of bullshit journalism written about you, it must be quite amusing.
"Well it's just mainly stuff that never occurs to us, we don't really know how to respond to it, we just go [in deadpan tone] 'Yeah, he's a guy.' Heh heh heh. That stuff could be very true, it's just that we haven't put ourselves in a position to think about it that way. Probably, objectively, they know more about what our effect is, but... I don't think about Fred's pants too much!!"
I see that Everett True was there last night (at the Glasgow gig). He was so impressed by your set, he could hardly speak!
"Yeah he was! He was so funny! He's really sweet actually. It was really funny though because he was supposed to interview us right afterwards, so we went back to the hotel and he didn't have anything to ask!!! It was just completely, tape recorder on, he wasn't saying anything, we weren't saying anything...!"

PHOTO: GN.

Have you been dreaming any good dreams lately?
"Last night I dreamt there was a funeral procession walking through a park near my house in the States... I dunno what that's supposed to mean. Yeah I actually have really good dreams lately, really technicolour. They have a beginning, a plot, a cast of characters and an ending - that's really strange cos I've never dreamed like that before, where it's like an action adventure!"
Have you got any Stuffed Animals?
"Mmm no. I had a teddy bear that I was given when I was born that I still keep."
Do you bring it on tour?
"No! Ha ha ha ha! Along with my rainbows and my unicorn!... My family used to move a lot, and when I was twelve, finally by that time I was so *pissed off* with it, you know the way →

that twelve year olds are pissed off about things going on in their lives, that I refused to unpack at one house, so all my stuff was in boxes for like a year, this was my stand you see, and all of my animals got mould, and mildew, and then *maggots*."

Eeeyeuch!

"I know. So I went to open the box when we were moving again, and it was just this teeming mass of shit! I ended up having to throw all my stuff away. I've done that three times in my life too, I've thrown everything I own away. I mean that was for sanitary reasons, but I'm really lazy about sorting through things and deciding what's important to me and what's not; so I just have this stuff around all the time, and there'll be one day when I'm just like "Chh! Everything goes!" and I don't look at it at all cos I'd end up in one box for four hours: 'This tiny little piece of plastic! I found this when we played in....'"

My solution is to have an extra room to put it all in, and just shut the door. At least it's still there.

"I definitely wanna be the kind of person that travels light - Leslie's like that, it's amazing, like all she'll own is a bunch of books and a futon, and it's so *ideal*, her world is so uncluttered. I used to marvel at her when I walked into her apartment."

As everyone now knows, since this tour the band has undergone a radical line up alteration. Fred has left, putting Lesley back in the bass playing shoes, and Tanya has also left in order to have more Breeders time and to do solo stuff with the help of Fred and two kids called Christopher and Thomas Gorman. Whether propelled by record company restrictions or musical ones, the split is said to be amicable. I hope that this parting will provide the space in which Tanya can spread her creative wings, without depriving the remaining Muses of their essential heterogeneity. With a new LP in the new year, I guess we'll soon find out.

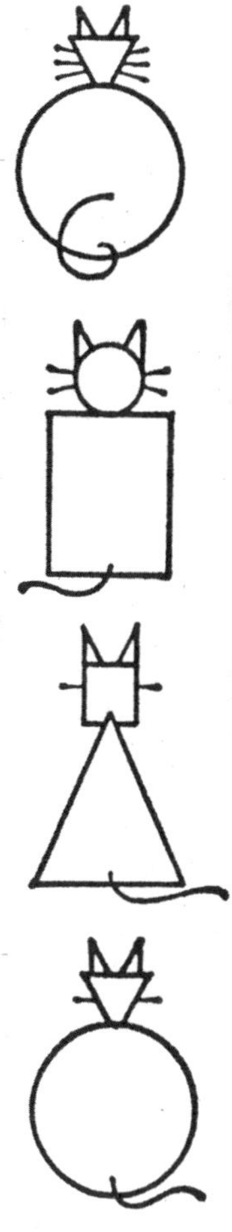

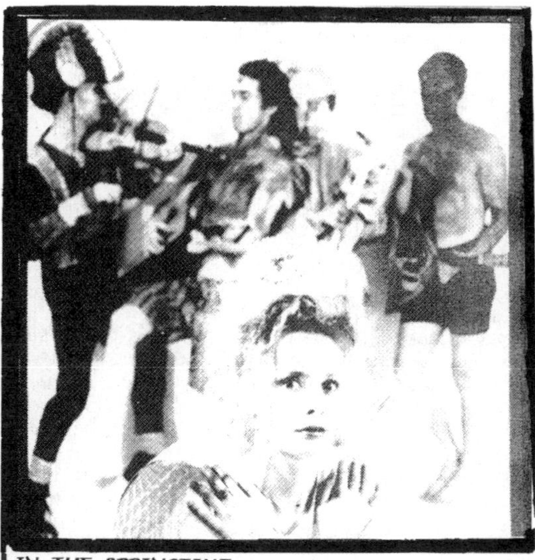

IN THE SPRINGTIME Guitar deities AC Temple mini-toured Ireland. They gained the adoration of the kids in Derry, Dublin and Cork (due to typically useless organisation, two other dates in Kill and Belfast did not occur) and saw lots of things out of the van windows. From Derry to Dublin there was a dead sheep, the Giant's Causeway, police with guns, soldiers with guns, heavily barricaded police stations with video cameras, barbed wire, loudhailers etc., very spooky business at the border, hags-head trees and hedges, and a fellow driving the wrong way down the motorway in a wheelchair. From Dublin to Cork there was a "flowers ahead" sign, Cashel Rock, a dead badger curled up like a sleeping dog and lots of hitch hikers. The countryside is very very beautiful, utterly fairytale, and the people equally pleasant, so if you're in a band an Irish holiday is recommended. The kids are rocking and it isn't far away.

the world is by being evil ourselves", and I hate that, I hate being in a crowd and having the band just completely hate me."

But also all those people are cooperating because you've got a whole load of people staring at one point, taking everything - the band wouldn't have that sort of power if they didn't give it to them in the first place.

"The whole theory now is that a band tours in order to sell more records, and a band tours in order to sell more T-shirts, and I hate that, I really do. I think a band tours because that's what the job of a band is to do, it's to play in front of people. I hate the fact that the crowd is just something to be shooken down now. I mean, you go to a discotheque and it's like, OK, you pay at the door, and you show your20 pieces of I.D. to get in, and you get in and you have the people with the little headsets walking around looking at you, making sure that you're not going to become a problem for them, which is more of an expense, then you go to the bar and everything costs about three times as much as you usually get it, and you dance to this robotic music which is just, you know, an extension of the engine of a 747, it's not fun! You're there to be shaken down, cos all you're good for is as something to give money. People that come to see AMC, I may just do a set and hate them and tell them to f*ck off, or just leave the stage without any communication at all, I've done that many times, but definitely they are not there to be shaken down, they're there to be given an experience, cos that's what a musician's job is to do. You perform, you give people a good time for a night. I think that's a really f*ckin' good thing to do. I think that's probably why we've been as unsuccessful as we've been, cos we're not assholes; we try our hardest to avoid the whole career rock thing, because it's soul-destroying."

Presumably you see success in different terms.

"No, I don't have a house, I don't have a car, I'd love those things! Of course it matters, we are playing the game and we're going to continue playing the game as long as they'll let us."

You're having fun doing it, though?

"Not really! It's work, it's not that much fun. Like at Reading the other day, we sat around and watched all these bands, we all got headaches, we waited to play..."

Did you hate the festival?

"I don't know, it was OK, it was kind of weird, I guess it was great. I mean, I like all the bands that were playing, I like Dinosaur Jr - I didn't get it, I never get that music too much, it just seems pretty rote to me - I'm an old punk rocker and all that stuff seems old hat. But I liked Sonic Youth and I liked Iggy and I walked around the crowd and saw people get progressively more wasted and thought "gee, it would be good..." I saw people have their first beer and I saw people take their first drugs and it's touching, it really is! It's fine that they can all do it in a safe environment - I saw lots of people face down in the mud and nobody was f*cking with them."

The first AMC LP isn't available, is that right?

"Yeah, and it's shit. As far as I'm concerned I hope it *never* becomes available. It's absolute shit."

OK. Where did you rip the name off from? It sounds like some tacky cassette mail order company.

"We didn't rip the name off, and that's what I wanted it to sound like. When I thought of the name - it's a shit name, with the worst three words ever in any band name - I wanted it to sound like the most generic thing possible. And it was in '81/'82 and all the bands who made it in America were from New Zealand, Australia or England, and I wanted to say "no, let's do *American* music" even though it's not American music... We do play country but that's because we like George Jones. There's a lot of soul in country music y'know, and it's pretty much the last American songwriters left that write real songs. Everybody in the band except me has a pretty good country background... but if you take country music and put cool words to it, it's really nice. I really like country music."

Finally, my boyfriend suggested this question, which I'm a bit embarrassed about, but... what does death need time for?

"Well... death takes time just like everything else... it needs a lot of time. I dunno! What a dumb question!! Oh, your poor boyfriend."

"And if we sit here / and drink enough beer / we'll be two inflatable dolls in a hooker's bad dream" - "Gary's Song"

THE MOST BORING BAND IN THE GALAXY?

Ladies and gentlemen, The Wedding Present! Or should we call them The David Gedge Band? Justine Wolfenden speaks to *all* of them, and brings us The Truth. Snazz photos: Jayne Lockey.

There's no polite way of putting this, so I might as well just come out with it: the first time I ever saw the Wedding Present play live I fell asleep. Stallones, 1987. My cousin Johnny was wearing his cap back to front like Ben Volpelierre-Pierrot. We sat down. I hadn't been drinking. I wasn't even all that tired. They came on stage and within moments I was in a state of hypersomnia.

Well, I've changed, time's moved on and nobody knows who Ben Volpelierre-Pierrot is any more; but they probably know who the Wedding Present are. Everybody holds an opinion on them. Alan Moore's a fan. David Bowie included *"George Best"* in his top ten favourite albums *(this speaks for itself! Ed.)* and it's rumoured that the Fugazi tour bus contains their tapes. The likes of *Maximum Rock'n'Roll* use them as a reference point; and the somewhat *zaftig* David Lewis Gedge can get recognized even in the smallest Sub-Post Office on the outskirts of Leeds.

The sloppy minds of the King's Reach Tower neocracy fit the Wedding Present up with easy adjectives such as "shambling", "parochial" and "earthbound". They could be describing themselves. Ask anyone who's ever actually *worked* with the band to describe them, be it producer or press officer or whatever, and they'll probably say "professional, very professional".

So, who would *you* believe? The people who spend days and weeks living and working with them; or the poor sod who spends £60 travelling up to Leeds to sit for two hours in a room with them, trying to persuade them that it's not really an artificial situation, and of *course* 12,000 people are interested in what they think about "the scene that regurgitates its own shit©"?

This is where I come in, for not so long ago I was that "poor sod", and Rule One would be "hide the tape recorder" because as soon as they see it they start to shrink away. Keith becomes inaudible, Simon practically invisible. Paul gurgles into his beer, but if you ask a question often enough he'll most probably answer. His girlfriend told me that he thinks he's autistic... yes, well... but I consider this as good a point as any to start, hence we begin:

"I saw Gedge... and he said 'I hear you've thrown your cap into the ring, then?"

So, Paul Dorrington, who are you and where did you come from?

P: "I'm a boy racer from Billericay, me!"

And?

P: "And I was in Umlaut, they were a fantastic band, a German synth duo, but we weren't German and there were three of us, and we had these synthesizer things and it was all very technical and outdated. My first band was the Blue Meanies, an excellent group; and then it was Andrew; and then Moth Moth, who supported the Swans, and that was me and Ruth Dorrington and Simon and Jayne from Fluff; and then there was A.C. Temple and Tse Tse Fly."

Paul, surprisingly, is a very talented performance artiste and is notorious for his role in the *Candy & Andy Roadshow*. There was a review of "Paul Dorrington at the Reading Festival" in the last issue of *Ablaze!* I asked him if he had any comments to make on his performance.

P: "Well, I'm proud of it. I'm glad someone was there to witness it because I can't remember *any* of it."

Describe your behaviour in a few words for those who missed the review.

P: "Boyish"

Are you sure? Drunk and obnoxious perhaps?

P: "No, no, no, no, no. I just copy my friends and do what they do."

Hmmm. Tell the readers about how you joined the band then.

P: "Well there was all this going on, and they asked all my friends to try out, and I was probably drinking at the time, and I ran up and said, 'oy, what about me?', and they *(Keith and Simon)* said 'we didn't know you played guitar.' I asked twice - I didn't think it was getting through - I pestered a bit and the first time I realised that anybody had actually heard me was when I saw Gedge in the Duchess and he said 'I hear you've thrown your cap into the ring, then?' and I went, er, yeah."

So what did you think about that?

P: "I thought, that's the first time he's ever spoken to me."

So did you want to join the band?

P: "Well, I did at the time."

So, it's been six months, what do you think of them all now?

P: *(on Keith)* "Thorough. Keith's an organisational person, but it's good to work quite hard really. Oh, and he likes coming up to me and saying 'What's the nastiest thing we've done to you so far?' and 'I'm glad we're horrible to you', that sort of thing."

K: *(laughing)* "I only said that because I'd heard about you being really horrible to somebody else."

P: "That was when I was little, I'm reformed now. *You* can't bear a grudge, I didn't even know you then."

Simon?

P: "Well, he's only the drummer, inne?"

Charming! How about David?

P: "He's all right. He's a flexible sort of chap, basically."

What do you mean? That he'll accept any sort of rubbish you care to play?

P: "Er, well, yeah."

Now, for those of you who find the Wedding Present wearisome, we have an Information Interlude. Did you know that an octopus has three hearts, sunglasses were invented long before any other sort of spectacles, spiders can't chew, nine out of ten science fiction readers in the U.S. are male and flies can get athlete's foot too?

But enough! We now move on to Mr.Showbiz himself, the ever-charming David Lewis Gedge, of whom I've become inordinately fond, and do you know why? Because he *communicates*, and also because I suspect he's the kind of person who knows that Spock from *Star Trek*'s family name is "xtmprsqzntwlfb".

So, David, about Paul...
D: "That's good that the first thing I ever said to Paul was 'I see you've thrown your cap into the ring'. Y'know, he's the nicest bloke I've ever been in a group with, but it's hard because it's early yet and he's not really buckled down to the ins and outs of being in the group. At the moment he's like the new boy, so he's like happy and carefree, he doesn't seem to have the worries that we've acquired over the years. I think that maybe as time goes on, I hope I'm wrong on this, but I think he might get dragged into it more, and then we'll probably start saying, 'oh god, I hate that bloke, when are we going to kick him out?' or something. At the moment, though, he's really nice to be in a group with."

What about Peter and *that* interview? *(Peter Solowka's first post-Wedding Present interview was partly spent talking about David's lack of friends and Keith's taking the humour from the group)*
D: "The funny thing, I think, is that it was a complete waste of time for him, because he's got a new group, and there's loads of interesting things going on in the Ukraine; so he spends three-quarters of an interview in the biggest music paper in the world talking about the Wedding Present, which is brilliant publicity for us, but doesn't do much for his own group. I thought that was a bit daft."

What about the lack of humour jibe, Keith?
K: "All I said was look at your guitar more, so you don't make mistakes!"

This leads us on to a(nother) very interesting moment; for as any long-suffering journalist or avid Wedding Present watcher will know, the chances of capturing the words of Simon. P. Smith on tape are roughly the same as your chances of being killed by terrorists overseas **[1 in 650,000. Fact!]** so, I know it's been a long wait, but here it comes:

☆SIMON SPEAKS☆

S: "I know I was annoyed with Peter for saying things in the Ukrainians interview, slagging us off; so I don't really think we should do that, I don't think it's a fair thing to do. I wouldn't like to say 'we sacked him because he did this and we hated this and he was really horrible', I mean, I know I feel like there were things he did; but I don't think you should say them in an interview."

(I shan't ask you whether it was worth the wait, because I'm sure it will have been.)
D: "Peter Solowka's done more Peel sessions than me now, you know."

Oh.
D: "I've almost forgotten what it was like having him in the group, which is a bit strange."

Not as strange, however, as Keith's "Normal Bloke" story, which he told me when the tape recorder was off, so I can't quote him literally. You see, years and years ago there was this lad who used to promote the gigs that the Wedding Present played in Scotland. He was an affable chap and they all got on well with him. They nicknamed him "Normal Bloke", and each time they drove to Scotland they would say, 'oh, I wonder if "Normal Bloke" will be putting us on tonight?' and then, in the years that followed, occasionally someone would say 'oh, I wonder what happened to "Normal Bloke"?'

What point to this longeur, you may ask. Well, "Normal Bloke" was a particularly witty monicker because it was a pun on said fellow's real name: he was, and indeed *is* Norma*n* Bl*a*ke! Yes, teenage fannies abound... and speaking of fannies; teenage, pre-pubescent and even middle-aged; Keith also told me that he'd read an article which stated that a high proportion of trainspotters are autistic, which would tie in very nicely with Paul Dorrington, but this isn't *NME*s "That Perpetual Motion", so moving swiftly on:

Information Interlude #2
Did you know that in the last year alone the off-tour careers of the Wedding Present's road crew have included: gig promoter, Greenhouse prime mover, *Vox* picture researcher, Hemiola Records label boss, computer genius and Rough Trade Distribution National Sales Manager. Wooh! The crew consists almost entirely of friends and they usually employ at least 3-5 women.

"Les, the barber, asked him what The Mission were like, and he said 'f*ckin' Whitesnake'."

Why so many friends, David?

D: "Because it means you can pay 'em low wages and they don't mind because they're your friends."

And the women?

D: "Because you get the chance to see them undressing on the tour bus!"

Ahem. Talk then turned to the forthcoming European tour, which starts on October 21st in Germany and should end on November 26th in Finland, unless they get snowed in. I asked for past tales of tour bus debauchery.

P: "I saw David naked."

K: "First one to bed, me!"

S: "Well, Joe drank beer and gaffa-taped people into their bunks... so he got locked in the boot."

Yes, well sound engineer Joe "little brother d'y'wanna hear me burp bollocks or barbados?" Hickey is *not* the sort of person you include in a family fanzine, so once again we move on.

Being on tour for so long means they'll miss the big winter tours of many other bands. I asked who they'll be sorry to miss, and names like Nirvana and Shudder To Think came up, which led me onto 'the greatest band you never saw':

S: "Big Black."

P: "I'd have liked to have seen Bauhaus when I was younger."

K: "Pitchfork."

D: "The Wombles."

At this point Keith rescues David from further shame by enquiring:

K: "Aren't you going to ask us about Steve Albini? Everybody else does."

NO!

Simon then amazes us all by speaking voluntarily again:

S: "Don't you think that Steve Shelley (Sonic Youth) is getting to look more and more like Curley Watts (*Coronation Street*)?"

Keith imparts the information that he shares a barber with one of The Mission.

K: "Les, the barber, asked him what The Mission were like, and he said 'fuckin' Whitesnake'."

We also discover that he's distantly related by marriage to Rowan Atkinson, which might explain his predilection for face-pulling. You know, considering one of them looks like Dave Hill from Slade and the other has an overwhelming fondness for garlic, Keith and Simon are an amazing double-act - if only you can persuade them to talk. Paul Dorrington is bloody great, and David Lewis Gedge is the world's second most charismatic ergo-maniac after Paul Robinson from *Neighbours*, which is why I'll return to him one last time. His regaling me with tales of the big Wedding Present Family and their merry times on the road led me to ask him about the oft-levelled accusation that he has no friends, only business acquaintances.

D: "I've got friends, but no-one knows about 'em, you see."

Don't they?

D: "No, they're secret. Yeah, they're like, err, in me head; they come and visit in me room, and I talk to 'em sometimes. My girlfriend's not there, though."

IS ANYBODY THERE?

D: "No."

Aah...

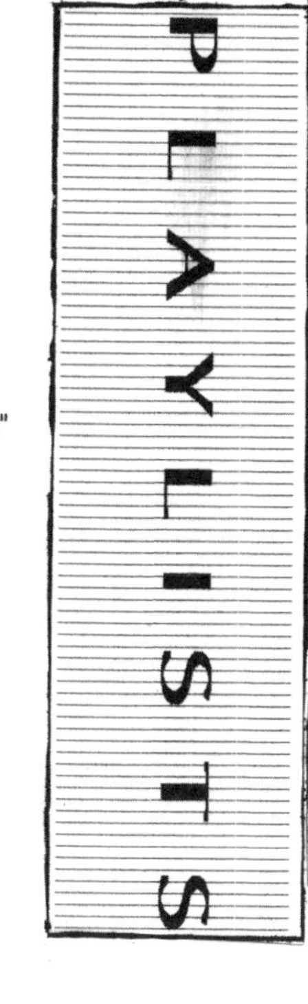

KARREN ABLAZE!

MASS - on off! "Terminal"
WHEN PEOPLE... - "It Ain't Necessarily So"
PAVEMENT - *"Lies and betrayals, fruit covered nails..."* (esp. the end)
NERVE RACK - "Dream About Nixon"
B.E.F. feat. GREEN GARTSIDE - "I Don't Know Why I Fuckin' Love You"
PIXIES - "Alec Eiffel"
NATION OF ULYSSES - "Aspirin Kid"
FLUFF - everything
NIRVANA - "Smells Like Teen Spirit"
HENRY ROLLINS BAND - "Do It" baby

LUCY NATION

LEATHERFACE - "Bowl Of Flies"
R.E.M. - "Country Feedback"
COCTEAU TWINS - "Fotzepolitic"
JOHN TRUBEE - "What Are You Trying To Do?"
CAN - "Thief"
DRILL - "Compressed Head"
MERCURY REV - "Frittering" / "Coney Island Cyclone"
THROWING MUSES - "Two Step"
POSTER CHILDREN - "Love"
BLUE AEROPLANES - "Pony Boy"

GAVIN BURNBLACK

MERCURY REV - "Car Wash Hair"
HOLE - "Teenage Whore"
PAVEMENT - *"She's got the radio active..."*
THE JESUS LIZARD - "Nub"
A.C. TEMPLE - "Lifesize"
LET'S ACTIVE - "Horizon"
AMERICAN MUSIC CLUB - "Jesus' Hands"
HIS NAME IS ALIVE - "Chances Are We Are Mad"
SLINT - "Good Morning, Captain"
RAILROAD JERK - "Talking RR Jerk Blues"

HOLE IS WHERE THE HEART IS.

Her motivation is selfish, in a totally positive way. In spite of the essence of what Hole do, or perhaps because of it, she doesn't falter. It's her thrill as much as ours; she's in control; by her catharsis, even in the midst of such torment, she controls us.

"I'm presenting myself in this way where I'm really vulnerable, saying things that are really pure to me and it makes me get into this Jesus thing or something where I just do it. That's the big thrill isn't it? What would be more boring than being in Intastella? 'Hi! I'm gonna be adored.' I wanna get under their skin for myself."

Hole *is* a group. Courtney Love is an unwilling interviewee and focal point, albeit a very charismatic one. When the interview began she said she was going to stop doing them because nobody else in the band spoke; a genuine gripe if not a serious one. When asked about the emphasis being on Courtney it is left, predictably, to Courtney to reply, perhaps half-seriously:

"They're on a train to hell with me. I know sometimes they wanna get off."

As Courtney departs to get another light, conversation falters for the first time in twenty minutes. Courtney returns to deliver her parting shot.

"We are a pop band and it's not a joke. Some of it does get lost, but it's there."

INTERVIEW BY GAVIN BURNBLACK. Holy imagery: Tony Woolgar. Thanks to Tracey and Eugene.

Question: When does an interview with Hole become an interview with Courtney Love?
Answer: Sooner rather than later.

Hole are Eric (guitar), Jill (bass), Caroline (drums) and Courtney (vocals and guitars); come from Los Angeles and have an album (*"Pretty On The Inside")* produced by Kim Gordon and Don Fleming. As we start to ask questions Courtney storms around, looking for a light, while Caroline tells us her hero(in)es are Karen Carpenter and Rat Scabies. Only when Courtney has found a fellow nicotine addict does the interview really start. Caroline speaks for all the rest of the group when she says, "My horizon's not as wide as hers. I don't see the big picture as well as she does."

Everybody seems to love Hole; indeed, a certain *Melody Maker* hack seemed deliberately and cynically to dismiss rock music as "dead" and proclaim dance music as the only viable music form left just so that when he reviewed Hole a couple of weeks later he could take credit for discovering the saviours of the (w)hole genre.

"I think that's really perceptive of you. Yeah, he was just our warm-up."

The reaction of the rest of the press, both here and in the United States, cannot be dismissed as easily; already they have cottoned on to the fact that (wait for it) three-quarters of Hole are women.

"We're getting completely excellent press. It's certainly not, 'They're beautiful, ethereal, wispy, post-Ride; I cried, I wept'; but we're getting a really positive, provoked reaction."

Reservations do persist however.

"American journalism is just skimming the surface, and the English journalism is just overanalysing the whole thing; they have a morbid fascination with this, like... it's so *eighties* to dwell on the girl thing. It's *over!* Stop talking about it! There is nothing kooky, or cute, or funny: it's just we took back the night and that's the end of the story."

Hole's songs are scary. I remember vividly the first time I heard them, lying in bed listening to John Peel, minding my own business and suddenly being confronted by Courtney, screaming about abuse and pain in a way that even someone as jaded as I am found frightening. In spite of myself I was totally convinced. Forget what every other group says: these records *had* to be made. Hole should be listened to with all the doors and windows locked, and certainly not at night. I struggled for the word to describe the way I felt the first time I heard "Dicknail". I tried "threatened" and "intimidated" but just settled for "very uncomfortable".

"It's new to you, because it's women expressing rage and working real hard at a musician level, transcending; and it's not like we're Dickless or something, other people write our songs and aren't we cute; all of us, we're so beyond that. Women are far more interesting at this point. You've got thirty years of rock history with the white male perspective; that was the problem with the evolution process, that women would form bands and attempt to masculinise themselves rather than play what they intuitively know how to play."

Jill adds, "I know a lot of girls might feel the way you feel, heterosexual or homosexual women, they might feel the same threat or whatever."

What would be more boring than being in Intastella? 'Hi! I'm gonna be adored.' I wanna get under their skin for myself."

So why Hole? Whether rock music is dead or not you can discuss when you've finished your homework. If you conclude that it is, Hole are obviously not its resurrection; that's True journalistic hyperbole, nothing else. So why are this band so special?

"I like the provocation aspect of doing this. It's not as if we're pioneering it, we're just *there*; it's something that has evolved to this point. At the same time we are real admirers of songwriting and we attempt to put a lot of thought into what we are doing. It's very articulate, it's very thought-out; the dynamics in the songs, the song structures; we're all musicians. The only part of it that bothers me is that people think it's just because anger or some sort of rage is being expressed, hostility, but then it's got this real negative vibe to it. I think it creates value where there once was a void; it's something coming back to me, personally from it. I think that a lot of really nihilistic bands like The Birthday Party and Flipper left something behind, but at the same time do give a lot to human dignity; that's the trip that I'm on. If I'm gonna go out every night on this tour and sing these songs about hate, about wretchedness, I've got to justify it some way, that it creates positivity."

Pale SAINTS

INTERVIEW BY LUCY NATION

"We have a lot of gender problems in our group. It's something we think about more than the music."

"If you think," I fulminated in a letter to *"Melody Maker"* a couple of years back, *"that the very tepid Pale Saints LP is the last word in slightly wigged-out janglepop, then you are a banana."* Harsh words indeed. Well, since then Harold Avenue's finest (sorry, Edsels) have released the fine, if over-produced, *"Half-life, Remembered"* EP and the truly excellent *"Flesh Balloon"* EP, featuring the superlative-inducing vocal debut of new(ish) guitarist Meriel Barham; and suddenly they're up there with my favourites. I don't eat words lightly, either. Not my own, anyway.

We spoke to Ian (singer/ bassist) and Meriel on a scorching afternoon at the end of summer. Unable to conduct the grilling in the Royal Park beergarden owing to the landlord's alleged propensity for feeding live cats to his rottweilers (it makes such a *noise* on the interview tape) we were forced to adjourn to a dingy indoor hostelry. This suited Ian, anyway, who was clad in black from head to foot and had expressed a wish to avoid "melanomas". Pale by name...

They were about to go into the studio with producer Hugh Jones (who did such a good job on *"Flesh Balloon"*) to record their second LP for 4AD, though at the time we spoke they still hadn't finished writing the material for it. I asked Ian if he felt under pressure:

"I think that hard work can only account for a small amount of what goes into it. If the raw materials aren't in your head in the first place, no amount of trying hard is going to make any difference.... the songs usually just write themselves and present themselves, they just appear and I don't really feel as though I've written them, they just present themselves when they're ready."

This reminded me of Barney from New Order's theory about being an aerial that picks up ideas floating around in the collective unconscious, though later Ian would (wrongly!) dismiss the entire New Order oeuvre as "money music". I enquired further into the Pale Saints' writing process, and particularly their use of unusual time signatures, one of the features which constantly distinguishes their music from the ordinary.

"I've always been attracted to that sort of thing. I can't just sit around all day and hack away at a really boring rhythm. I find that if you begin with an interesting rhythm, you're off to a good start. I think Chris (Cooper, drummer) used to find that quite annoying, because he could never work out what the time signatures were, but he's getting more used to it now. It's healthy, isn't it, for listeners to get something other than what they're used to hearing all the time?"

I'm glad he's got the health of his audience at heart. Talk moved on to "Kinky Love", the Nancy Sinatra cover featured as the A side of the *"Flesh Balloon"* 7", and the one with Meriel's fab vocal. Why did you cover that?

"Partly because we didn't want to waste songs from the (new) LP on a single. My conception of it was to make it more different than it was, but it ended up being about the most commercial thing we've done.... I thought it was a really really lovely song, and the lyric was just so hilarious, just to shove it in people's faces, to have it played on Radio One.... it's nice to wind people up if you can do it successfully; I mean, it would be nice to have done it a bit more successfully."

So you thought it would disturb people?

"Not really disturb them, just kind of.... especially with Meriel singing it, because originally I thought I'd have to sing it, I didn't think she'd have anything to do with it.... there's some quite amusing lyrics in it, like *"I understand you're a man and you've got to have your kinky love"*, so that would have brought a different dimension to it."

Meriel took up the baton:

"It was quite funny, Bill Wyman on *"Roundtable"*, he's well into cricket, and he was saying, I can imagine listening to this watching the cricket, which was quite weird: I mean, obviously to him that's all it was, just sort of background music."

Ian: "It was obvious when *"Roundtable"* gave their verdict that, although it wasn't universally despised by them, it wasn't going to do very well. I think it sold one more copy than the previous EP. I like to think that might have been Bill Wyman, sitting on his lawn, sipping away at his gin and cocaine cocktail."

Who else was on *"Roundtable"* ?

Meriel: "Rick Astley"

What did he think about it?

"Didn't like it. I think he said, oh it sounds like The Sundays. Probably the only indie band with a girl singer he's heard of, you know."

Ian: "I don't know if *I* like it ("Kinky Love") any more."

In a dastardly effort to circumvent the absence of an interesting muso technology page in this organ, I asked how the glorious guitar sounds on "Kinky Love" were achieved.

"Roland GP 16," averred Ian, "it's great, you programme the ingredients off cereal packets in and it gives you this amazing cornflakey sound."

What about Meriel?

"I leave that to Graham (Naysmith, other guitarist). I like to use simple things where you press it and it says On, and you press it again and it says Off."

"You can't afford one," this is Ian, "that's why you don't use one, isn't it?"

"Well, to be honest, yes."

"Or is it like, complicated things are for boys?" (Withering look)

"Did you see that film last night, *"Prejudices"* ?"

So is it difficult, working with boys?

"That's what they are, let's face it.... er, it just pisses me off. If someone wants to take a picture of the band, automatically they ask you to stand at the front, and that really winds me up."

"I thought," interjected Ian, "you used to get upset because they usually shove you to the back?"

"It's so dangerous," ignoring him, "all these kids

are growing up with these images. Every time a girl is in a band, she's like a focus, 99 or probably 100 percent of the time."

"I'm the only girl in our band, aren't I?"

Well, Ian, it's funny because, listening to "Hair Shoes" (on the 12" after "Kinky Love") you're used to hearing a woman singing on the previous track; then when your vocal comes in, it still sounds like one.

Meriel: "It's that pink dressing gown you wear, isn't it?"

"It's all those pink babyclothes my mother put me in. I have her to thank and she'll never let me forget it. She's on a cut of all our records because she's responsible for our success."

"I get confused for a bloke," rejoined Meriel, "When we were in Sweden it wasn't until I informed the customs guy that something about so long and white was a Tampax that he suddenly realised: Oh right, you're a woman then. I think he was quite shocked. That made my day, really."

Ian: "We have a lot of gender problems in our group. It's something we think about more than the music."

Discussion of Meriel's past incarnation as the singer with an early line-up of Lush led to further speculation on the differences between working with men and women.

"I think girls can be more ruthless," decided Meriel, "and that's all I want to say about the subject.... no, it's about personalities, not whether a person's male or female. When I was in Lush, it wasn't the same band it is now, anyway; just a bit of a laugh, a thrashy sort of thing that didn't really seem to be going anywhere, well not to me anyway; but I think Emma in particular was quite ambitious about wanting to be in a band, and she's stuck at it, and that's why they're where they are."

So how did you meet the Pale Saints?

"It's back to that Lush connection. Miki the matchmaker agency."

Ian: "She runs this little musicians' agency from her bedsit."

"I still owe her some commission, actually."

"Now she's in a famous band, she gets all her mates into other famous bands, just to completely fuck them up as well.... of course, what we really wanted was a glamorous busty singer. I don't know how we ended up with Meriel."

"I like to think that might have been Bill Wyman, sitting on his lawn, sipping away at his gin and cocaine cocktail."

Don't you think the name Pale Saints is asking for it a bit, what with the nature of the music? Is it supposed to be funny?

"No, it was just that it seemed like we were wasting a lot of sleeping time thinking of names. We thought we might as well pick one. I suppose it was asking for it a bit, it's an easy name to take the piss out of. Maybe we got a bit of press out of that, maybe it was a good thing, but I don't really think about it."

What about a song title like "Half-life, Remembered" ?!

"Yeah, probably. I think it was just an accurate representation of my state of mind after trying to think of a title.... I think song titles are really important - what's the point of recording something that's good and then giving it a shit title - so I spend a lot of time trying to think of a title which actually makes people want to listen to it, and I think that one was probably a case of my head getting into too much of a tangle after thinking too much."

It certainly made me want to listen to it. He's a dab hand with a title, actually, is Ian: witness "A Deep Sleep For Steven", "Language Of Flowers" and "Two Sick Sisters" for starters.

"Serious" questions duly dispensed with, we moved on to the silly part of the interview, with apologies to Rosanna Greenstreet, who compiles the questionnaire in the Weekend Guardian, but probably isn't reading this anyway (if you'd like to speak to the *Ablaze!* solicitors, Rosanna, the Stuffed Cat is available at this address anytime).

Who do you most admire?

Ian: "This is really fanzine territory isn't it? People who can think really clearly, generally. David Axelrod, who was involved with the Electric Prunes after they started to flounder, and he wrote these kind of rock operas which are just full of, like, thirty-minute guitar solos. I'd quite like to be able to write one of those; I mean, I really detest guitar solos, but..."

Aren't there a number of guitar solos in your own music?

"Yeah, I don't know how they manage to slip through the net really. I think guitar solos are a waste of time, generally."

"It's that pink dressing gown you wear, isn't it?"

Isn't a guitar solo just the same as a vocal, part of the melody line?

"No, I think it's just an excuse for a guitarist to show off the things he's been practising in his bedroom. I prefer the *sounds* you get out of a guitar rather than.... honestly, it just seems like a display of technique to me, a lot of the time. Sometimes it just makes me see so red that I almost.... they (solos) have had me on the border of leaving the band so many times, you know, just a guitar solo, they wind me up so much sometimes.... but, you know, if you're in a band which tries to operate in a way where everybody brings something to it, you can only fight so hard without doing the ultimate and saying, right, I'm off."

Weird! Do you argue with each other a lot?

"We don't really talk that much about music at all. I live with Graham and we see very little of each other: that's possibly a good thing for the band, there's no point getting embroiled in domestic things or those things end up getting discussed at rehearsal, you know, why haven't you done the washing-up? Have you seen that casserole dish? It's in a fucking disgraceful state."

So, Meriel, who do *you* most admire?

"I never have these things in the front of my mind.... I think Edwyn Collins and Teenage Fanclub have a sort of wit that appeals to me.... admire is such a huge word, I don't really like using it. It makes you feel like you're the size of an ant."

Ian's off again:

"People who invent really simple things. I admire people who design bathrooms in hotels, where you pull a shower attachment out of the sink and you put it up and you can stand in the bath - it serves two functions. Just things like that, I think "that's brilliant" and I have to take a couple of pictures of it. You know, beautiful things, because it's an ugly world, isn't it?"

The next question, "What objects do you always carry with you?", prompted Ian to stand up and empty his pockets onto the pub table with the resentful air of one wrongfully searched by police. The contents of Ian's pockets were as follows: keys, wallet, handkerchief, sunglasses, red and green plastic digital watch (no strap), 0.88mm Jim Dunlop nylon plectrum and two saftey pins, open.

Meriel: "A comfortable bra, though that's not always the case.... nothing in particular, a few elastic

bands..."

Ian: "What about your paper pellets to flick at people and your codeine tablets? Don't you carry those around with you all the time?"

"Not any more."

What single thing would improve the quality of your life?

Ian: "*"Halliwell's Film Companion"*. It's the one that lists all the directors' names and all the films they've ever done, and all the actors and stuff, because I've got such a bad memory."

Meriel: "I can't answer questions like that."

Ian: "Wouldn't a big bag of money improve the quality of your life?"

"Probably."

"You see Meriel's materialistic like that. I can exist on pieces of cardboard spread thinly with margarine."

"I think," this is Meriel, "an Access bill that never arrived would be the best thing, actually, at the moment."

What does death need time for?

Cue much laughter.

Ian (tasting the words) "What does death need time for? Is that two questions rolled into one?"

No, that's one question.

"Oh dear."

Meriel: "I have no idea."

"Oh dearie dear. I think you'll have to buy me about twenty pints of beer before I can answer that one. Before I'm even interested in thinking about it. I think it's the same as the, er, four enemies of a man of knowledge, something like that. Along a similar line. I'm not interested in going along that one either."

Oh well. What's your favourite record this week?

Meriel: "What's that Brian Eno track?"

Ian: ""Hollow.""

"I've only heard that recently, and that's affected me more than any music has for a long time."

Ian?

"Gene Pitney, "A Town Without Pity", is rarely off my personal Wurlitzer, and Michael Nyman; there's a bit on the *"Zed And Two Noughts"* soundtrack which is really good, and the Sea Urchins' last single."

"Have you seen that casserole dish? It's in a f**ing disgraceful state."**

How do you feel about being godparents to the shoegazing thing?

Ian (adopting shaky old person voice): "We're very pleased they're all doing well." (Normal voice): "No.... I like some songs that Chapterhouse have done. I like some of the stuff that Slowdive have done, usually the last song on the EP, which is presumably the one they knock together in the last forty minutes. I don't like their LP."

Meriel: "It's a bit of a yawn really, isn't it?"

"It's sad, because I think they've got potential, and they've realised it in some of the EP tracks, yet they've chosen to put out an LP that's probably more accessible, but it's going nowhere."

Long silence.

"I can see we've exhausted the interest value on that one."

BERNARD MANNING!

We sent Simon Morris to a recent Bernard gig at Blackpool's Sandcastle to suss out the (extremely dubious) scene.

Unfortunately Bernard Manning wasn't wearing his usual nightclub bouncer's gear; instead it was a voluminous white shirt and jeans. However references to "pakis", "niggers" and "queers" proved that this was indeed Britain's most offensive entertainer in the extensive flesh.

"Give us a light son," he kept repeating, as a series of fags were smoked. "I like a drink, I like a smoke, I like a f***... I do a lot of f***in' drinking and smoking." No-one is immune from the fat twat's scathing tongue: Lenny Henry and "his f***ing fat wife", John Lennon ("he wanted peace... he f***in' got it"), even George Formby ("what a c*nt"). Mr. Manning is not averse to giving us some philosophical insight into world problems ("I don't know what they're fighting for in Ireland... I mean, they're all white, aren't they?"). Such charming homilies are received with rapturous applause by the packed out audience of holidaymakers.

Well, I was pissed, having called at my uncle's working men's club on the way there, so I was soon laughing like a drain, whatever that means, but then I'm a white male so I'm all right with Bernard aren't I? The sheer scatology of some of the jokes, together with the lowest common denominator racism and sexism produced a kind of numbing effect; it was so offensive that you really couldn't take offence, if that makes any sense. The only really obscene bits were when he attempted to sing; then he came across as the small-minded pompous cabaret act that he undoubtedly is.

DEMO TAPE REVIEWS

REVIEWED BY G. BURNBLACK, K. ABLAZE! AND L. NATION.
YOUR HOST: THE STUFFED CAT!!!!

SUGARDRIVE "Fireworks" (93, Hunter House Road, Sheffield.)
You can spot the old goths in here, but they write a nice tune and it's much better produced than most demos.
K: It's kind of half-good isn't it?
G: The (male) vocalist sounds like Simon from Fluff.
L: Reminds me of "Teenage Riot" type Sonic Youth.
G: It's all a race against death isn't it? It sounds like two different groups.

BLIND JUSTICE "Self Injustice" (Gus, 60 Lupin Close, Gurnos, Merthyr Tydfil, CF47 9DW)
Eggy, Gus, Grant and Gavin from Gurnos.
K: Oh my god. Can we say anything nice about this?
G: Hee hee, ho ho ho, hurr hurr.
L: Dyslexics play Pin The Tail On The Donkey with their Thesaurus
; *"She don't notice me as I glance then stare/ I don't exist, I'm not there/ Sends me into katagenisis*/ She don't notice me, no."*
K: I think we should put that they're from Wales and they sound like something horrible.
(* catagenesis = the backward evolution of a species.)

SLUNK "Only Available On CD"
G: Sounds like everyone on Amphetamine Reptile.
K: This person gave me the tape at Reading when I was doing the T-shirt survey; he was wearing a Headcleaner T-shirt.
L: Cup of coffee anyone?

FRANTIC SPIDERS "Seven Shocking Hours" (51 Priory Road, Exeter, Devon, EX4 7AP. £2.50)
"She Fell Down A Bank" is really nice. Lyrics sound good. Definite presence of ideas and individuality.
K: I think they'll do well in the future, capture the Lush/Muses crossover market, once they get rid of the biscuit tins.
G: I imagine them drinking lots of cider.
L: I like them - much more interesting musically than Lush. It sometimes strays into what I imagine Sarah territory to be, but generally it's too weird for that.
G: I'm having my female vocals problem again.
K: That means you're a misogynist.
G: No it doesn't. I hope they haven't got a following because then it would be too late for them to change their name.
K: "Spiders" is good.
G: "Frantic" isn't.
K: No, "frantic" isn't. "Hysterical" maybe?
L: The bit with all the Smiths' titles in the lyrics is really bizarre.
K: If they were in Leeds, I'd be going to their gigs and interviewing them and stuff, but they're not. Tell them to move to Leeds.

BONE "Tooth And Nail Cuts" (PO Box 45, Skelmersdale, Lancs., WN8 6XY.)
This isn't a demo, apparently, it's two songs from a forthcoming LP. Second track, "If I Had No Lips Would Ya Still Kiss Me", is better, less buffalo (as in 'bellowing like a').
K: I saw these live and I left the venue about three minutes after they came on. They were the second Fugazi band in a row but here they don't sound like Fugazi at all.
L: That's true actually.
G: More like a very bad version of Codeine.
K: No, Adam And The Ants... if I was the singer it would be really good.
G: I'm getting to like this. Perhaps that's why the track is about twenty minutes long.

TWICE VIOLET "A Cupful Of Sun" (David Moore, 1206 W.Franklin #8, Richmond, VA 23220-3761)
Anglophile pop-rock from Virginia.
K: Dreamy.
G: It makes a change from English people trying to be American.
K: It sounds a bit like The Chills.
L: No it doesn't.
G: Not only does he want to be English; he wants it to be 1982.

BABY ABATTOIR CASUALTY "Bush Needs Cutting" (40 Dale Crescent, Patcham, Brighton, BN1 8NU)
Pure jazz on a Casio and distorted guitar. Karren would like to point out that the name is in bad taste.
K: This is brilliant. This is worse than Sonic Hangover.
G: Barry on acid.
K: A sub-Barry keyboard. Worse than The Ceramic Hobs as well.
G: I'd like to turn this off now.
K: No, there might be a ballad at the end.
(There wasn't.)

IDIOT GODS "Slow Drag" (111 Hetton Road, Leeds, LS8 3AF)
G: Plodding's a good word.
K: Pathetic's another good word.
G: What's the vocalist about?
K: He's about Happy Mondays isn't he?

KOCHMAN "Every Day's A Weekend"
After The Idiot Gods Karren, Lucy *and* the Stuffed Cat all felt unable to remain in the room, leaving Gavin alone to pass judgement on Kochman until Ann Magnuson popped by for a cup of tea and a chat.
G: Definitely one for the ladies. Kochman *is* sex personified. Eight songs to *live* to. Any thoughts Ann?
A: They have Toby Savage dolls now? I *want* one!

SPECTRAL ALICE "Chops" (Rob Julian, 12 Welburn Ave., West Park, Leeds.)
Ann has to leave just before we return. None of us believe that Ann has been here but we soon turn our attention to Spectral Alice. Karren's supposed to be putting out a record with these and Purple Eternal.
K: Oh dear me.
L: It's garbage, isn't it?
K: Like, sub-slug species. I keep meeting one of them in town. He grins at me and asks if I've played the tape.
L: The bit with the harmonics on the second song was OK until it went grungy again.
K: The cover's good.
L: The vocals aren't.
K: Have you ever tried to sing on acid?.
L: No.
K: Well, it's a bit like that. It sounds really good at the time, but then in the cold light of day...
G: It becomes a demo tape.

HOWL IN THE TYPEWRITER "Dog Turd In Shrewsbury" (130 Common Edge Road, Blackpool, FY4 5AZ.)
A red C90, a grey C60, a badge, a booklet, seven posters all in a "lovely, clippy, sealy plastic bag". Features "Water Yr Plants" and "Melt". Value for them that digs such.
G: (Taking the tape out of the bag) I feel like Quincy.
K: Who's Quincy?
G: Bad television pathologist.
K: Stan's my friend. Don't write that down. No, this is great. It's a great pop tune. No, honestly. It's basically one man.
G: There's no-one there to tell him to shut up.
L: There is here though. Bring back National Service. He should get his hair cut.

B.P.M. CITY *"Home"* 12" (Happy Valley)
This one sounds best when you wobble it between your hands. The accompanying postcard says they're *"not knobheads"* though. So that's OK. (LN) (21 Runswick Ave, Whitby, N.Yorks.)

SOFA HEAD *"Twat! EP"* 12" (Workers' Playtime)
Side One is an utterly redundant cover of "Feel A Whole Lot Better" coupled with one of their own, a sub-metal riff workout. I thought these were punk rockers, too. Everybody's looking backwards. The other side is live and plays at 33 and probably sounds awful and goes on for ages; but we'll never know because we're not going to listen to it. (LN)

H.P.ZINKER *"Hovering"* LP (Roughneck)
Progressive rock. Or, more accurately, since that term is twenty years old; rock which would have been progressive in 1971. (LN)

HIS NAME IS ALIVE *"Livonia"* LP (4AD); *"Home Is In Your Head"* LP (4AD)
Last year's excellent *"Livonia"* LP reached us just after we went to print with #7, and it's seldom been far from the turntable since. A stranger record you'd be hard put to find: hymnal female voices recite oft-impenetrable lyrics over fragile acoustic guitars, fire-belching fuzz guitars, backwards metal percussion and what sounds like samples of Hawaiian music. Now there's a new LP out, and yup, it's even stranger. Perhaps this is a partial result of the band's bizarre working process: mastermind Warren Defever records a load of stuff at his home studio in Livonia, Michigan, and sends the master tapes over to 4AD's Ivo Watts-Russell to mix. The music is then put back together in a different form, skeletal and atmospheric; indeed, reminiscent of Ivo's own This Mortal Coil project. For *"Livonia"* the band sent Ivo eight songs; the finished record featured twelve. Less a band, then, than a transatlantic collaboration.
Anyway, *"Home Is In Your Head"* is another fine record: 24 (one uncredited) tracks ranging from fairly accessible ("There's Something Between Us And He's Changing My Words") to downright obscure ("Put Your Finger In Your Eye"). Highlights include the country-tinged "Why People Disappear" and the scalpel noise interludes on "Chances Are We Are Mad", though my favourite is the lovely vocal and acoustic guitar of "The Well". There's a His Name Is Alive first, too: on "Hope Called In Sick" (titles!) they actually sound like a clumsy rock band for about a minute.
Only two beefs: no Angie Carozzo on the new record ("How Ghosts Affect Relationships" is great) and, since "Darkest Dreams" is still my top His Name Is Alive song, and the only one actually mixed by Defever himself, is my impeccable aesthetic trying to tell me something? Ivo, Ivo, how much more of that beautiful chaos have you left unheard on the multitrack? A shame. Bring them over on tour to make up for it. (LN)

RAILROAD JERK *"Railroad Jerk"* LP (Matador)
I thought this was boring the first time I played it. I'm up to play number fifteen now and I love it. Big, angular, arrogant swagger of an LP which frequently threatens to explode but just about holds itself together. Disjointed but somehow still connected, like a contortionist in a dustbin. Manages to poke fun at both The Who and The Rolling Stones as well as rhyming vase with face. *"You can put me to sleep but you can't make me dream"*. Awesome. (GB)

SILVERFISH

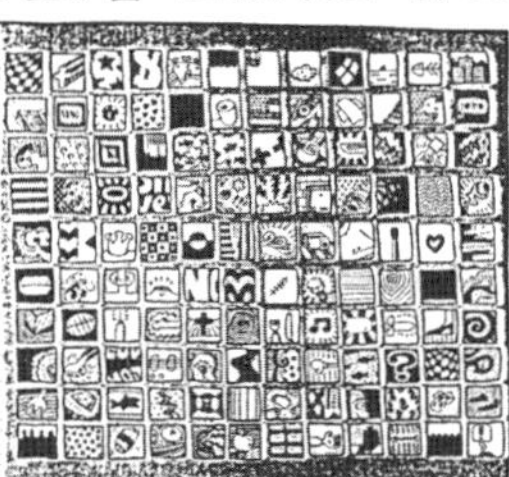

FAT AXL

SILVERFISH *"Fat Axl"* LP (Wiiija)
I met **Silverfish** when they were recording this in Sheffield cos they stayed at **Chris Trout** and **Noel Kilbride**'s house and were too busy playing **Othello** with **Steve Albini** to speak to me. When I first heard this, at **Jack Nitro Puppy**'s house, I wasn't too sure about it: it didn't kick me in the face as quickly as the singles did... [why don't you drop a few more names instead of reviewing the record Karren? - everyone else in the world] Oh, OK. This LP is named after **Barbara Ellen's** description of singer **Lesley Firth** as a "fat Axl Rose" and it features a brill cover of **Grandmaster Flash & Melle Mel**'s "White Lines" plus loadsa sexy stuff like "Baby Baby Baby". **Jesus Christ** - this is a rocking record! **A. J. P. Taylor**! **Marilyn Monroe**! **Elvis Presley**! **Ursula K. Le Guin**!(etc. etc.) (KA)

SPACEMEN 3 *"Recurring"* LP (Fire)
I'm confused. People who previously loved each other so much that they didn't sleep together are now sworn enemies having been forced to take opposite sides in the Sonic Boom / Jason conflict. Such misguided passion is alarming - both sides of this LP sound *exactly the same*. One side and five songs each, every song spacey and laid back with minimal, repetitive lyrics conjuring up images of smoke-filled rooms and rolled-up pieces of cardboard. Nothing to get your knickers in a twist about. (GB)

MERCURY REV *"Yerself Is Steam"* LP (Jungle)

For once, as the cliché goes, the press hyperbole is justified: this is a *luminous* record. Honestly, I was completely disillusioned with American stuff for a while; it seemed to be reverting to smelly old rock; but in the wake of *"Yerself Is Steam"* and brilliant LPs by Pavement and Poster Children I'm excited again. Mercury Rev have made a sprawling beast of a record:it's probably about 50 minutes long, but when you're somewhere in the middle of it you can't see the horizon on any side; the thing seems to stretch out forever in every direction. "Sweet Oddyssee Of A Cancer Cell To The Center Of Yer Heart" has been unflatteringly compared to Marillion in the *Ablaze!* offices (I've never heard Marillion, me) but it's the prog rock sense of anything-could-happen-in-the-next-five-minutes that makes this record so special. Their aesthetic judgement is spot-on anyway: the indulgences are strictly of the sumptuous blizzard variety - no wanking egos loose here. (LN)

THE PIXIES *"Trompe Le Monde"* LP (4AD)
Though my close acquaintances shun me and the people I live with do not allow me near the turntable with it, I **love** this record. It was made for me and my kind! It was made with Stuffed Cats in mind!
Though no record will ever have the same emotional and physical effect as *"Surfer Rosa"* (ahhhh); this is a record to make us all feel five years younger. I don't know why, and I don't know why these Pixies aren't hip anymore...
Even though I am a lone bag of rags amongst the well dressed at Pixy gigs these days (where have they all come from? The white collar workers of this country are all wearing Pixies T-shirts!) I still proclaim them the best rock and roll band in the world.
Do you care? Do you want to know this? You know **John Peel** played the whole LP right through one night, interspersing the madness with his faltering interview with Charles! Black! whatever ye call him? I heard bits of it and glumly announced my disgust at what sounded like the most crass, clichéd and overblown rawk excrement I'd heard in days. First impressions, huh?
This happens every time. Right now I'd say "Space (I Believe In)" is my best track, though I prefer to call it "Jefrey With One 'F'". Wouldn't you? Then I like "Motorway To Roswell." These are two tracks that turn such **seemingly** mundane things into ultra glamour happenings. That fat boy sure has read a lot of books. I can only assume that the band has achieved technical and conceptual perfection and that they are now reaping the benefits of working with the same damned producer for three albums, although something certainly has come amiss in terms of intra-band politics if rumours about Mr Thompson's tyrannical rule are to be believed.
Oh, but! Hear "Alec Eiffel"!!! Make this band god. Make that double god. Jesus, even the sleeve is gorgeous. There are fifteen songs on this record, each of which is hot and happening and emanating funny fields full of weird joke animals. Too much? You said it. (KA)

NIKKI SUDDEN (featuring members of REM) *"I Belong To You"* 12" (UFO)
I'm very glad he doesn't belong to *me*. (KA)

NERVE RACK *"Experiments With Facial Hair"* LP (Meantime)
Second album by this fab Leeds power trio, and a fitting sequel to *"Gnaw"*. On this one, Cliff, Frank and Tommy discuss their various personal experiences of beards, moustaches and sideburns, and still find time to include a musical tribute to late great nihilist rockers Flipper. [Really? - Nerve Rack.] On "Dream About Nixon", the track Meantime should take for the chart topping single, Mr. Guitarist really masters beautiful punkrockness. "Rottweilers" is scary, specially when the same Rackist snarls *"I've got two dogs... I've got two dogs... Two dogs and a sawn off shotgun!"* really loud. "Eye And Socket" features Mr. Bassist's very serious policeman vocals and plenty o' cool sounds too. Fifteen years of listening to punk rock 7"s shows; but more recent digestion of US musical milestone types is also evident. Cute *Ablaze!* style noise made by lovely people - worth investigation.(KA) (£5 vinyl, £8 CD, from Meantime, 11 Salutation Rd, Darlington.)

NATION OF ULYSSES *"13-Point Programme To Destroy America"* (Dischord)
Boys in donkey jackets from Washington DC, punk-rocking to lead The Kids in a massive revolt against The Grown Ups, using methods like the extension of trick-or-treating (getting what you want using violent threats), not sleeping (thus gaining extra time and space), not cleaning your teeth, and wearing pyjamas (*"a bold new uniform for the army fighting against the nauseous prospect of the ethical workday, and also as a salute to madness and possibility."*) One of the most fascinating things about this record is the difficulty it presents for the listener attempting to discern whether they are actually serious or not. All we know is, if they *are* serious, they are very serious indeed, which is beautiful, despite their tiresome pseudo-militarism. And you know what; they do sound good, kinda walking the tightrope between Dead Kennedys-esque mania and Fugazi control but with even more elastic bands. Oh, I know you don't know what I mean, and since this is a record that I recommend you should go search for, I can excuse myself from describing it cos you're gonna hear it for yourself, aren't you, if you've any cleverness in your bones. (KA)

OZRIC TENTACLES *"Strangeitude"* LP (Dovetail)
To the press release's *"Gong without the inane lyrics, reggae without the prejudice, Hawkwind without the aggression,"* I'd like to add "Pink Floyd without the songs" and "Mike Oldfield without the 1970s". Dungeons and dragons? *No thanks, hippy.* (LN)

GODSEYE *"Love's A Bargain"* LP (Twenty 20)
"Lamerock", Justine calls it, and that's as good a summary as any. Godseye are sub-Dinosaurs from Boston doing that guitar pop thing, rarely getting too worked up about anything much. The final, and title, track is my fave, kinda Lemonheadsy. Gavin still insists that we can't waste time on stuff like this in our desperate "race against death"; I say listen to it anyway. (KA)

THE POETS eponymous LP (BMG)
Do they know what year it is? Do people call each other "baby" in Denmark? Do people call each other "baby" anywhere? Most of this is tosh, but the chorus of "Death Angels Of Israel" is a cracker worthy of Boney M, ideal for those first-thing-in-the-morning moments. Worst track: the one that goes *"You're only nineteen/ do you want to bleed?/ do you want my seed?"* No thank YOU. (LN)

POSTER CHILDREN *"Daisychain Reaction"* LP (Twin/Tone)
I thought this was going to be standard grungecore when it started up, but as soon as the muezzin wail vocal of "Dee" kicks in, all such doubts are dispelled. Brilliant guitars, brilliant songs; lots of time changes and unexpected tuneful bits. Kind of a poppier Bitch Magnet, but better, and much more diverse. The riff on "Love" is a gem. Even their take on a standard rock blueprint, "Chain Reaction", works by dint of a perfect melody and the meatiest tom sound ever. The lyric of "Water" (*"One, one, two, one, two, two..."* etc) is a piece of genius. If only "Where We Live" didn't keep threatening to turn into "You Just Might Be The One". Come to Blighty and make your fortune, Poster Children. (LN)

RADICAL DANCE FACTION *"Wasteland"* LP (Earth Zone)
Whenever I'm lurking on the outskirts of a festival clutching a hot cup of tea wondering where my friends might be, I hear this music pulsing away in the distance. Chris describes RDF as *"Crass on E"*, and Gavin says all sorts of derogatory things about them, but I say these are fine young people with their hearts in the right places. And it keeps them off the streets. (Whispers of "What does it sound like?" fill the nation. You mean, uh, the music? Echoey, druggy, dog-on-a-string white reggae. OK?) (KA)

EDITH STRATEGY *"Going Up" / "Ton Beau Paradis"* 12" (Big Cat)
The family has gathered for Granny's eightieth. Imagine Uncle Terry after ten pints impersonating Billy Mackenzie accompanied by Auntie Marge on Bontempi Organ.
Congratulations, you've successfully imagined Edith Strategy. (GB)

NAUTICAL WILLIAM *"Love"* 12" (Mojo Filter)
"You gotta do what you wanna do... you gotta go where you're going to... love love love love love." Oh, do FUCK OFF. (LN)

PRAM *"Gash"* MLP (Howl)
A *great* record. It's brilliant that there are always people prepared to say "fuck you" to current trends and make something so determinedly claustrophobic and insular. The rhythmic repetition on "Dead Piano" and "Inmate's Clothes", combined with the beautiful toy instruments and Rosie's disconsolate vocals, makes for compulsive listening, as do the haywire time signatures on "Flesh" and the killer melodica riff on "Pram" itself. Hurrah for self-expression and rulebook-burning excellence. (LN)
(£4.50 to P.O.Box 2055, Birmingham B13 9NB)

PLEASURE THIEVES *"Chasing The Runaway"* 7" (Minta)
Music journalists long past their sell-by date love this kind of stuff because it reminds them of the good old days when a song was something you knocked together with some bits of wood and a ball of string. We have machines nowadays, and noisy mental fucked-up guitars: we don't need any more po-faced songwriters "saying" things at us. (LN)

Insular English pancakes

MR.PECULIAR *"Loonyverse"* 7" (Lust)
Choppy wah-wah guitar and badly-played baggy drumbeat. Now, where have I heard that before? Oh yes, that's right. Everywhere. (LN)

THE YOUNG FRESH FELLOWS *"Electric Bird Digest"* LP (Frontier)
Music for wankers; and by that I don't mean it has a good beat. (GB)

SLINT *"Spiderland"* LP (Touch And Go)
Not what I'd come to expect from Touch And Go; long, hypnotic songs which build so slowly that you don't notice until you're trapped, and a guitar sound The Breeders would kill for. Possibly the soundtrack to your favourite Western or a thriller starring Harry Dean Stanton. (GB)

SENSELESS THINGS *"Is It Too Late?"* 12" (Decoy)
Unfeasibly awful. People have been making bad punk rock records for about sixteen years now. Tape The Damned's *"Machine Gun Etiquette"* off your big brother and you need never bother yourself with the likes of Senseless Things again. (LN)

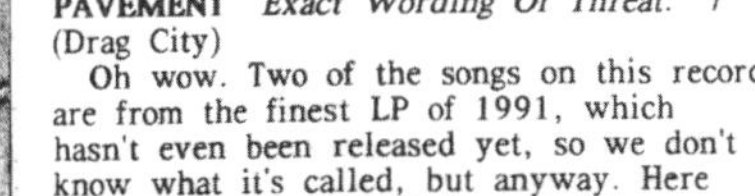

PAVEMENT *"Exact Wording Of Threat:"* 7" (Drag City)
Oh wow. Two of the songs on this record are from the finest LP of 1991, which hasn't even been released yet, so we don't know what it's called, but anyway. Here you get "Summer Babe" (beautiful bass-driven pop song), the very odd "Mercy Snack" and the awesome "Baptiss Blacktick", which contains the very best five seconds in the history of rock and roll: the bit where the music stops and the singer goes *"I'm just waiting/ waiting for the Baptist/ that fucker/ AAARRRRGGGHHHH!"*
Total cool genius. (LN) (Drag City, P.O.Box 476867, Chicago IL 60647....$5, cheques Dan Koretsky)

CRAZYHEAD *"Everything's Alright"* 12" (FM Revolver)
MTV-friendly pop/rock. Why send it to *us* ? (LN)

VELVET MONKEYS *"Rake"* LP (Rough Trade)
A bedroom in studentland.
"Hey, this album features Thurston Moore and J Mascis."
"But it's just tedious, self-indulgent garbage which only gets put out because of who's on it; and people are too scared to see it for what it is in case they appear not to be trendy. It's supposed to be fun but it isn't, it's embarassing and shouldn't be encouraged."
"Yeah... well I'm going to buy it anyway."
(GB)

A.C. TEMPLE *"Belinda Backwards"* LP (Blast First)
Listen up you kids, do you have a place in your heart for a *great* pop band? (If not, see me afterwards.) Then look no further.
"Belinda Backwards" might be on Blast First and it might be produced by Kramer; but expect neither heads-down sub-Dinosaur grunge workouts nor weird New Yorkers taking strange drugs and performing rock operas on cutlery.
No, A.C. Temple have thrown off all previous (mostly erroneous) comparisons and presented us with a big, fresh LP chock full of most of the classiest songs you'll hear all year.
For the first time, the vocals stand out, demanding to be heard, Jane Bromley's incredibly powerful and emotive voice (and I'm the one with the female vocals problem, remember) grabbing your throat and refusing to relax its grip for ten songs from the first line of "Glitterhall" (*"I had a fine time looking for the edge of the world"*) to "P2", a song Abba would reform to cover if they ever heard it. In between you get "Come Sunrise (*"You steal the sun from my eyes/you drive the pleasure away"*), "Lifesize" (*"Wanna get fucked up thoroughly?"*) and "Space Bore" (*"Jesus was an Englishman and this is why they picked on you"*) songs to fly like an angel or sit and weep in the dark to, depending on your frame of mind. A.C. Temple have always been a majestic live band, and Kramer is to be commended, his notorious speed in the studio perhaps helping to capture that live power.
What else? I could tell you about the time A.C. Temple supported Band Of Susans and not only blew them off stage but blew them back to the early seventies; or the time I was really depressed and this record helped me a lot, but these are bits of me (pretty sizeable bits too, what do you want, blood?). No, some things you have to do on your own; make this LP a part of you. (GB)

A cool salad

WHEN PEOPLE WERE SHORTER AND LIVED NEAR THE WATER *"Porgy"* LP (Shimmydisc)
What about when people were shorter and lived near the water? Tell us about it, boys.
The band appear to comprise seven old and ugly gentlemen from New York City who have, under the guidance of Shimmy guru Kramer, recorded their own versions of the entire score of the Gershwins' *Porgy and Bess* musical. Apparently they have a history of amusing themselves with concept LPs like this one, which features lots of squealing and tumbling around. "My Man's Gone Now" is pretty commercial and has a sweet yellow sound with aah aah backing vocals. The best best track however is "It Ain't Necessarily So" which is wonderful because it has a very good extra tune and a single note on a keyboard that plays throughout, and it all sounds like the Membranes or something. The track after that sounds like the Dead Kennedys. It's *more* than Gershwin. It's When People Were Shorter And [We get the idea - The Stuffed Cats]. (KA)

MERCURY REV *"Car Wash Hair"* 12" (Jungle/Mint Films)
If you don't already love *"Yerself Is Steam"*, try trepanning. This is more of the same: genius without frontiers, in a nutshell. Flip it over to find what sounds like Swell Maps and a violinist covering "Coney Island Cyclone" accompanied by a version of "Chasing A Bee" which was probably recorded in intergalactic space. Mercury Rev play marbles with the asteroids. (LN)

LUL *"Hail The Frisians Free"* LP (Schemer)
Post-hardcore meets rambling prog rock with some appealing tunes. I saw these live in Ghent a couple of years ago where they completely blew the dreadful All away with their all-singing power trio routine. Some baffling lyrics, though: *"He's got at least six fries on his pair of pants/ he virtually carries the red lantern/ six fries on his trousers!/ why must we watch this man?"* Why indeed? (LN)

TEENAGE FANCLUB *"Everybody's Fool"* 7" (Matador)
Dinosaur Jr. as performed by the Barron Knights. The bit where the rhythm guitar breaks into Status Quo is particularly laughable. Rot in hell you dire combo. (LN)

LANGFIELD CRANE *"Stevenson EP"* 12" (Astragarda)
Oh god you strange band. It took me about 120 listens before I could reconcile myself to the, er, psychedelic funk of the title track, but finally something clicked, and yes it is rather good, though there's still this nagging feeling that one day I'll wish I hadn't written that. Still, the Aesthetics Police don't seem to be hammering down the door right at this moment, so what the hell. "Oh Softhead" is sort of fluffy and inconsequential *(What? -* The Fluffy Cat), but "Sweet Wire" on the other side provides another fine example of the kind of folky (yes! sorry! I know!) rock this lot do best. (LN)

SMASHING PUMPKINS *"Gish"* LP (Hut)
Gish as in Lillian, smashing as in 'to smash'. I really tried to like this. Mike The Bike loves it and we normally see trouser to trouser, but I can't grasp it; too lazy for its own good perhaps? Extremely well-crafted but lacking any sort of spark. "Rhinoceros" sounds like the sort of song others might hail as classic but just reminds me of Blur; "Bury Me" also recalls Pink Floyd's *"Relics"*. The last track, and my favourite, sung by bassist D'Arcy (the rest handled by songwriter and guitarist Billy Corgan) is reminiscent of His Name Is Alive but *just* too straightforward. File under disappointing. (GB)

SCRITTI POLITTI *"Cupid And Psyche'85"* LP (Virgin)
Karren, I think you've put this in the wrong pile. (GB)

'F' FOR FANZINES

In this section our mad team of reviewers goes through a batch of underground publications separating the wheat from the chaff, the snaz from the cack, the fanzines from the nafzines, and **is** really nice about the good ones and incredibly nasty about the shite ones - just for the hell of it, beloved reader! Remember - when sending off for zines, (except in the case of *Tongue In Cheek* and *Fist*, which are heavy, and *Alarm Clock* which is foreign) failure to enclose the correct sized SAE (or enough dosh to cover post) will entitle the people concerned to spend your money on much-needed baked beans or drugs and not send you anything. So.

THE SNAZ-O-METER® - Described by its manufacturers as 'a device with which to make enemies in the fanzine community' - This is how it works:
We put the fanzine type object on the tray on top, and the wonderful electronic cogs and mice assess its quality on a scale of cack to snazz according to the following criteria:

No numbers on pages.......................................Minus 3 points.
Begins with the word "Hello."........................Minus 10 points.
Begins "Hello And Welcome To..."...................Minus 15 points.
Features Dance Naked......................................Minus 15 points.
Features Splintered..Minus 20 points.
Features Fluff...Plus 150 points.
Features Pavement..Plus 100 points.
Title has initials PT, SN or TIC.......................Plus 50 points.
Is called either *Dregs, Quality Time or Perturbed*.Plus 50 points.
Features a Sonic-On-A-Stick..............................Plus 25 points.
Features pic of Ken Barlow on cover..................Plus 35 points.
Has "charm"...Plus 15 points.

THE BEST

QUALITY TIME # 1. This fanzine's stunning graphics make it the most appropriately titled journal. Greg expresses himself through images rather than words, and in these manic collages he has found the perfect medium. Sample the classic unpredictability of the Keatons, the pizazz-injected Stretchheads, the true story of Betty Boo and the Dandelion Adventure split (with excellent verbal documentation by *Plane Truth*'s Katie Kat). *Quality Time* stands out from the indifferent stapled masses by virtue of its visual *aliveness*, and implicitly poses the question "Why bother producing a zine that looks like a lowlife version of a f***ing parish newsletter?" (16 pages A4. 50p from 55 Evington Valley Rd, Evington, Leicester, LE1. **47 points.**)

PLANE TRUTH #6 & #7. Cute bastards for those in the know. Ish 6: Mayomberos Alive update, Inside Out, Faith Healers, Levellers 5 and Badgewearer interviews and a marvellous ½ of an in-depth Chills interview (the estranged partner of which is in *Swedish Nurse #* 2). #7 has way improved graphics and more gorgeous text (with bonus typing errors), courtesy of Harlow's action merchant Anthony Chapman. Basti and Bleach, Dawson and Datblygu, the wonderful Pram and the awesome A.C. Temple (with pin up!) plus cool art and all sortsa bits. Andrew's motivation stems from the way that certain bands do something to make life just that bit more worth living, along with the presence of others sharing similar tastes and decent values, as opposed to the inhumanity of the majority. (*"...the threat of violence virtually vanishes at gigs. Only in a deserted park can I feel equally at ease."*) Start your *Planetruth* collection now. (24 & 32 pages, A5, 30p each from 18 Golf View, Ingol, Preston, PR2 7EH. **65 points.**)

DREGS # 4. Totally horsef*** fanzine. In past issues Duncan has been investigating such important questions as why time keeps changing speed and why the weather is so damn weird. In this one he turns his attention to the sexual fantasies of the stars (including Babes In Toyland, Chumbawamba, Boo Radleys and Mayomberos Alive). Plus interviews with Fugazi, Subhumanz and Carcass, and much other stuff. Intelligent & well laid out. Check the back issues too. (48 pages, A5, 40p? from P.O. Box 110, Liverpool, L69 8DP. **62 points.**)

RECOIL # 4. Another favourite, this one features **well written** interviews with the gorgeous Dr. Phibes, poor ol' Grant Hart, Keith Le Blanc, and the Doo Badleys (as our Gav calls 'em.) Also incredible poems by John Toshack, stuff about Gerry Anderson and David Lynch, and an excellent assessment of the chocolate scene in Britain today. More than a music fanzine. And the cover photo of Ken Barlow, tragically supping whisky, picture of Deirdre in hand, is worth a million quid. (32 pages, A4, £1 from 39 Nicholas Rd, Chorlton, Manchester M21 1LG. **50 points.**)

PERTURBED # 6. A collection of piss takes of your favourite and not so favourite pop stars. Very very funny. Especially good is "Alvin Stardust - the pop star who's into God and shit like that." Oh yeah, and a Lilac Time interview as well. [Any Perturbed kids reading - come and write for us, OK? - Ed.] (48 pages, A5, 50p from Peter Perturbed, SDUC, Lampeter, Dyfed, Wales, SA48 7ED. **62 points.**)

TONGUE IN CHEEK # 10. Massive and packed with stuff. A zillion trillion reviews of records, tapes, literature - including many useful addresses - and interviews with NoMeansNo, Jesus Lizard, Morrissey, Buffalo Tom, Shudder To Think, Lemonheads, Mass etc. It has to be said that Ian hasn't exactly been *attending* very many of his interviews lately; but I know life isn't always easy. Perversely enough, this issue's front cover is on the back... Obscure! (62 pages, A4, cover price is £1 but he's losing money on that so why not send £1.50, plus 50p to cover postage cos it's a heavy bastard. 55 Albion St, Otley, LS21 1BZ. **65 points.**)

SWEDISH NURSE #2 & #3. Martin's Thwedish Nurth is certainly one of the most intelligent publications on show here: excellent writing (do something for *A!*) and brilliant taste in music, plus an increasingly militant gay stance make this one a must. #2 has interviews with Wire, The Chills, A.C. Temple, Therapy? and Nomeansno amongst others; #3 the remarkable Pram plus Vagtazo Halottkemek (try saying *that* after a few shandies), Fflaps, Headbutt and some of Martin's beloved NZ bands. (44 and 32 pages, A4, 60p and 40p from P.O.Box 148, Belfast 1, N.Ireland. **65 points**)

THE REST

KILL YR GIRLFRIEND (Or She'll Kill You First). Not very weighty despite vast number of pages. Three tiny band interviews (Keatons, Belltower, Teenage Fanclub), plus lots of reviews of gigs (by surreal people who're on some sorta weird drugs) and even a record fair. Enjoyed "How To Be An Indie Kid Part One" and "Goths vs. Baggies" but most was uninteresting, and too much space is wasted. (80 pages, A5, £1? from Tim, 26a Judges St, Loughborough, Leics. **13 points.**)

YOU FLEXI THING!

FLUFF

FLUFF, a virtually unknown three piece from Leeds, split up on September 2nd, 1991. I had severely wanted to put out a song of theirs, "Ash", with issue 7. The interview in that issue explains it, I guess, and this is the next part of the story.

Fluff accepted Steve Hawkins as their manager. Alternative Tentacles, one of the labels to express an interest in the band, held a meeting with them to arrange a deal, and at this meeting it was suggested to them that they drop their manager as the label didn't wish to work with him. They did so, and within a week the band had split. Tim Beckham, Fluff's uniquely gifted drummer, parted from Jayne Lockey (bass/vocals) and Simon Cleave (guitar/vocals). The reasons why this happened are not entirely clear to me, as different parties have wildly various accounts of these events, but it is possible that Tim's friendship with Steve may have influenced his decision to leave; though Tim maintains that it was Simon who split the band. Tim will carry on playing guitar with A.C. Temple, and Simon has moved from bass to guitar in Tse Tse Fly, making room for Jayne to come in as the new bassist.

Many people have expressed regret over the demise of a band so amazing. It is therefore unnecessary to describe my own disappointment. However, Jayne and Simon are optimistic and looking forward to infiltrating the Fly.

This track, "Us", is taken from a live (i.e. rough) pre-production recording for what was to be Fluff's debut EP. In the year since "Ash" was recorded they wrote a vast number of songs (few of which have actually been recorded) in the course of which their sound blossomed into something far more rich and strong than before. Now that the band no longer exists there's nothing to stop me releasing something of theirs. I want everyone to hear it. So put the needle onto the disc, and close your eyes...

Last minute **COMPETITION** for the beady eyed among you. Tell us how many stuffed cats are concealed within the magazine, & the randomly-selected winner gets a bag of records. *Fun* all the way.

PAVEMENT

STEREO MASTER

M. IBOLD

SPIRAL S.

S YOUNG

BELMONT N.

PAVEMENT
MY FIRST MINE
FLEX-CUT FOW/01
1991

THANKS
KARREN + JUSTINE

PAVEMENT. What's it mean to you? Yanks call it **"SIDEWALK"** anyway, saving this term for the actual *surface*, as in "Is it pavement or asphalt?" Apparently. It sounds like a **name for a *hardcore*** band... but it isn't. Mark Ibold is their newly acquired bassplayer - previously they didn't use bass and were a bit unsure as to whether they wanted any at all. I called him in New York (no expenses are spared, y'see, when it comes to getting the facts for **you**, our reader) and asked questions. Steve and Scott both sing and play guitar, Gary is the "really great" drummer, and Bob is the second drummer and he sings and drives as well. Their gigs in the states have gone down well, they've had 2 7"s ("Demolition Plot J-7" & "Exact Wording Of Threat") and a 10" ("Perfect Sound Forever") out on Drag City, available here only as expensive imports. They recorded their debut LP (the best thing since *"Surfer Rosa"*), the perversely named *"Slanted And Enchanted"*, a year ago but for some godweird reason it wont be coming out till at least January (on Matador there, and they've not sorted out a label for European releases yet). So this is Pavement's **first UK release**... Are we proud? You bet your clockwork christmas trees we are! It's called **"MY FIRST MINE" and it goes like this...**

Andrew Johnson

WORK EXPERIENCE

At 16 years old, Leeds was the centre of my musical universe.

Not only was I head over heels for city big-hitters The Wedding Present, I was also equally drawn to the oddities and noiseniks bubbling on the underscene - you know the ones, the sound of the Harolds and all that. And lately I'd been picking up 7"s in plastic bags and compilation tapes from a little label called Fluff records.... Apparently there was a scene below the micro scene in Leeds and at its epicentre were the bands Boyracer and Hood. I was enamoured, to put it mildly, with Hood. Very much enamoured with Hood.

Leeds was my Seattle or Manchester or Detroit, or that place where Ned's Atomic Dustbin came from and, even better, it was only a tenner return on the train, or even less if my dad could give me a lift to Todmorden.

My Trans-Pennine contact came in the form of my girlfriend's sister, Nicola. She'd escaped over the border and was forging a brave new life as a student at Leeds Uni. And she was in a band. Yeah, a band. And they'd played the hallowed ground of the Leeds Duchess of York. Supporting Bleach. Yeah you heard. Bleach.

Me, my girlfriend Lynsey and my friend Craig would arrange weekend visits to Nicola's Headingley boutique terraced shithole. I think that it was in that very shithole that I caught a glimpse of my first copy of *Ablaze!*... Probably glimmering on top of a bass amp and underneath an empty Pot Noodle tub (directly below the Field Mice setlist). I stuck it in my bag and had it away.

For the next month I proceeded to pick over every review and article within. It looked proper. A cross between some superior tweezine and the Melody Maker. It had a surprisingly wide-angled view on music as well, and of course it based itself in some shiny office block in Leeds city centre. Seeing as my mum wouldn't let me go to London (on account of the bombs), a job at the NME was off the cards. But *Ablaze!* was very much on the cards. They'd reviewed a Hood demo. I wanted in. I wanted to work in that shiny, plush office with a computer and free records. I wanted that Hood demo.

So as the other losers on my college media course planned their work experience around making adverts for hospital radio, I fired off my letter to the hip priest who sat at the helm of the *Ablaze!* empire. I wanted a job. For a week. And only my mum could stop me.

My plea for work experience was met with an unexpected positive response from Karren. I can't even remember if there was any health and safety employee insurance shit to blag with college. But I managed to convince them that it would be beneficial to me, rather than being clapperboard on the steam train documentary. My mum was satisfied that I had a safe enough base at Nicola's gaff. And I suppose that was it really. My first job in the music industry.

Of course I know now that the magazine came straight outta a mid-row terrace somewhere in dark, autumnal Leeds. At the time it was a shock. I had to be there on my first morning at 9am sharp. For a free thinking, left-leaning spirit, Karren didn't half take her responsibilities as my employer seriously. Truthfully, I think I did a nine-to-five shift for the full working week. And we never fraternised after that cut off point.[1]

I think the bloke who also lived at *Ablaze!* smoked a lot of weed. It was cigarettes like I'd never smelt before. Let's be honest, he probably wondered what a 16-year-old was doing in his front room. I wondered what I was doing in his front room. In fact I'm 36 now and I can't remember what I did in his front room.

We probably listened to loads of records I didn't like. I read the press releases that came with 12" singles. One day we went to the Merrion centre and I helped interview Louisiana popsters Hula Hoop. Can't remember what questions I asked, probably Hood related. I went to the place that printed the magazine, was it on Call Lane? I did a review of a record (which didn't make the cut).

And at the end of the week I finally got to see my Leeds poster boys Hood. At the Royal Park. No-one was there. Including their drummer. Karren had a word and I joined the band. It was the defining night of my whole life. Really.[2]

They were incredibly positive times. Before blogs and myfacepage and limited 3" drone CDs. It was proper. People got on Top of the Pops. Boys got banned from gigs. Nirvana played the Duchess of York.

I've got a lot to thank Karren for. Thanks. x

Karren's disputational footnotes:

---

1 Neither are true – Ablaze! staff didn't get up till 11 (unless we let him in and went back to bed), and Andrew and I went to a gig together at least once that week.

2 I remember it thuswise: Chris Adams announced that they needed a drummer for the gig and I jumped up, sat behind the kit and quickly demonstrated my inability to hit things with sticks. At the same time Andrew wistfully whispered "I know these songs. I know how the drums go." I mentioned that pertinent fact to Chris, and Andrew then joined the band, destined for interglobal ultrastardom.

Ablaze!
9

Ablaze! 9

Publication date: Spring 1992

I may have introduced myself as Snow White, but there were more than seven dwarves. The ranks of contributors had swelled to 17 or so by this issue. Tall in their achievements, they were dwarfishly helpful in constructing this issue. Hitch, Wedding Present record sleeve designer, created the front cover. It was a relief to work with someone who knew when to just use one font.

Reading the My Bloody Valentine interview, I wonder at how the uber-cute Kevin turned into scary old Lord Shieldsy. What he told us made sense, but I didn't believe him then and I believe him even less now.

We weren't so bothered about Nirvana but they just kind of jizzed in our faces. We did go to see them at Bradford University though, and that's when it all went mental. The band had a meltdown and scored all guest-listed press people from the list. Not that there was many of us – mainly Ablaze!rs there to have a quiet word. We stood outside the grey concrete blocks of the university, having been denied entry to the sold out show, feeling a bit pissed off. Inside Nirvana's people were freaking out. Things cooled down after a while and we did get in. Sensitive to their predicament, I couldn't face talking to a band that didn't want to be talked to, so decided just to enjoy the show. Our photographer Tony Woolgar was more intrepid and attended an interview arranged for fanzines only, where he was joined by Tracey and Eugene from *Sleep* fanzine. *Sleep* didn't go past its debut issue, and they kindly passed the tape to us. Patrick and Jeremy also handed their interviews over, and that's why we ended up with three. We weren't being greedy, it was just the way it happened.

I think it's obvious how much we loved Shudder To Think. Live, they could never be as pure as their crystalline recordings - someone would destroy the moment with their elbows and cigarettes in those grim pre-smoking-ban days, back when breathing was a privilege - but no-one could take away the blessed moments of eye contact that Craig bestowed upon us as he sang. This band brought us early tidings of post-rock. Everything they did was exquisite, up to and including *Pony Express Record*.

Nirvana's appearance on Top of the Pops was broadcast whilst I was interviewing STT at the Duchess and it caused quite a stir. Even more excitingly, Pik was watching the show in the company of Kris Novoselic, Dave Grohl and Kurt Cobain backstage at their Sheffield gig.

KA: I dumped that Nirvana thing on you....
P: That was pretty heavyweight.
KA: I wanted to watch Shudder To Think that night.
P: You just delegated your minor tasks away. I got a call asking what are you doing – you did give me two days' notice. No, it was fine, I'd got used to it by that point. You'd given me these instructions and got me on the guestlist plus one. Usually I prefer to pay for my own ticket but on that occasion I agreed. So I tried to get someone to come with me, but couldn't because none of my friends knew who the hell these were. They regretted it later. I got to interview Chris N. on a very squeaky tape recorder. I think the BBC Radio Sheffield people had tried to interview Dave and Kurt. Dave is very eloquent and Kurt somewhat less so. We did the interview before the gig, and all of a sudden everybody in the backstage area went crazy because Top of the Pops was starting. They'd recorded it two days earlier. You remember the sequence, where they're not playing at all, and they're just making fun of the whole thing in the great tradition of miming, and they're just cracking up. So you've got this band monkeying around on the screen and the same band monkeying around in front of the TV. I was like, hang on a minute, this doesn't happen very often. I tell people and they don't believe me.
KA: How did you find them?
P: Chris is a very solid guy, Dave is a very solid guy, I'd seen Dave's band before, Scream, but Kurt... it didn't seem that it was the same kind of setup. Kurt was just behaving very oddly. Once you've met a lot of people you can see who knows what they're doing and who doesn't know what they are doing, drugs or no drugs. Some say star quality isn't having something extra, it's having something missing. But it's easy to say after the fact. I'd rather have a beer with Dave Grohl than Kurt Cobain. Great gig by the way.

Nirvana were interesting to us because we'd never seen an indie band – i.e. people like us – go through this process. Well, there had been The Stone Roses, but the sound they made was so hideous I could only tune it out. Nirvana were tolerable, a little repetitious, but exciting and occasionally adventurous. And what was happening to them was so sudden and dramatic and seemingly unwanted too.

In the first two interviews they attempted to dodge expectations and bullshit in whatever way they could: angrily, sarcastically, seeing themselves about to be swallowed up by the media machine. When asked about the future Chris said "we left our crystal ball at home and we can't read tarot cards." Maybe that was a blessing for those poor young things, squirming angrily in the spotlight.

In the third piece, interviewers Tracey and Eugene were into the same bands as Kurt, and got on well with him. Kurt expressed the concept of an independent band as a band that were capable of making a choice about which (indie or major) label to sign to, citing how Sonic Youth signed to Geffen, arguing that Geffen proved they could deal with them. His justification for signing with them was that fans were approaching them after shows to complain that they couldn't get their records. Could they have not have organised a little merch stall? They wouldn't have sold five million that way, but they might all still be alive.

When I was given the tape I was frustrated at Trace and Eugene's whimsical interview style, yet it turns out that what really adheres to one's memory are not the deep and meaningful moments but the exceedingly odd ones, particularly Trace's description of the cat she'd like to have.

Alright, I said that we weren't being greedy just now, but I think there is evidence to suggest that maybe we were. I've since shrugged off accusations that we were trying to be "a proper magazine" as bullshit. It was a fanzine, duh! But if that's true, why were we interviewing Nirvana and putting them on the cover? Kurt had his excuse - record distribution for the kids – but where was ours? We were just having fun, and it was an unexamined assumption on my part that selling more copies was a good thing, that our increasing notoriety was necessarily beneficial. I was being driven by a version of the justification of existence theme – only none of it was enough: it was that old low self-esteem/arrogance axis, alchemised by a slight measure of success. Does anyone realise they're doing this when they're doing it? I doubt it, otherwise it might not work. But through all of this, and I'm guessing it was the same for Nirvana, we just wanted to carry on doing what we were doing. There was no grand plan - just interview more bands! Sell more records! Because that somehow meant that you were good - that what you were doing was worthwhile.

Oh and the elephant layout was shit, I'm sorry about that.

There were still no images of Pavement available in the UK other than the colour-photocopied Polaroids that we'd reproduced (in black and white) on the inner back page of the previous issue. I sought to enhance these monochrome splodges using Tipp-Ex, and the dubious hip priests theme spoke of the intensity of our ardour.

One time my band played with The Pastels and I badly annoyed Aggi by sticking my used chewing gum to the mic stand. It went all over her fingers and her guitar strings and she was like that for the whole set, getting stuck and not being able to play properly.

I have yet to come to terms with the fact that when I passed articles and reviews to Trout for proof reading, he styled himself as the editor and inserted comments as and when he saw fit. One part negligence and two parts trust is all it takes to lose that glorious experience of control over your own project.

There are some extremely passionate record reviews here, at a point when music got out of hand - it got too good. Gavin had the honour of reviewing *Slanted and Enchanted* from Justine and Keith's pre-release tape where all the songs had different titles and were in a totally different order. When it actually came out we were rather disturbed by the new running order - this record had become the soundtrack of our lives. This review ends with the only prediction we ever got right.

All three of us took a crack at The Wedding Present. I hope that Keith didn't mind. Maria's there in full effect, reading you your rights regarding Pussy Galore. Simon Morris comes back after a few issues' absence in a mental hospital. Gavin is spot on once more, this time about Pearl Jam. Justine's review of the Leaving Trains is similarly perfect, as are all her reviews here. Even Micheal Walsh wrote something; the first of his reviews is incredible, and so unappreciated at the time. We gave it a patronising response, but he was way ahead of us. I could not dig the Beat Happening! They were in a different register, an alien breed I could only get when mediated by other bands' covers. Trout's "the awful Green Gartside" is an oxymoronic phrase never uttered before or since. We were going nuts over the Pale Saints LP – is this what caused Trout and Ian to collaborate in the form of Spoonfed Hybrid? And J. Germiceter, in case you hadn't guessed, is Ian Masters.

In the fanzine reviews section I discuss the previous issue's policy. It turns out I really meant it. Yet our guiltiest moment can be found amongst the demo reviews. One single band had complied with our capricious demands for yellow stickers and bribes: SIDEways sent us a big bar of Galaxy and said they wanted to move to Leeds because of us. Were we kind to them? Did we appreciate the compliment? Did we reciprocate their love? We did not. We scoffed down the chocolate, laughed at their demo and slated the fuck out of it in review. Holding truth-telling above all, we were careless with dreams. There was no subtlety, no thought of toning it down. I now find it unbearable to contemplate how they might have felt when they eagerly bought their copy of *Ablaze!* and flicked to the back pages. I hereby call the youths of the *Ablaze!* team to account; somewhere along the way we had become a nasty and arrogant clique.

8 October 1991

Editor
ABLAZE!
17 Wetherby Grove
Leeds
LS4 2JH

Dear Karen,

Thank you for sending me a sample copy of ABLAZE!

There is no way that the major newstrade buyers would accept the title without a major upgrade in the production quality. I also have doubts as to how appealing the editorial would be to the "mainstream" retail outlets, like W H Smith, who we would rely on heavily to develop an economic sale.

Thanks for your approach. If you have any questions, then do contact me.

Yours sincerely,

JAMES BILTON
Managing Director

JB/TC.178

MAGNUM DISTRIBUTION LIMITED
Caverswall House, 44 Clerkenwell Close, London EC1R 0AT
Telephone: 0787 880505 Fax: 071-608 0646
Operations at:
Sulby House, North Street, Sudbury, Suffolk, CO10 6RE
Telephone: 0787 880505 Fax: 0787 313344 or 0787 313302
Registered Office: 7 Pilgrim Street, London EC4V 6DR
Registered in England No. 2529276

ABLAZE!

No9/£1.90

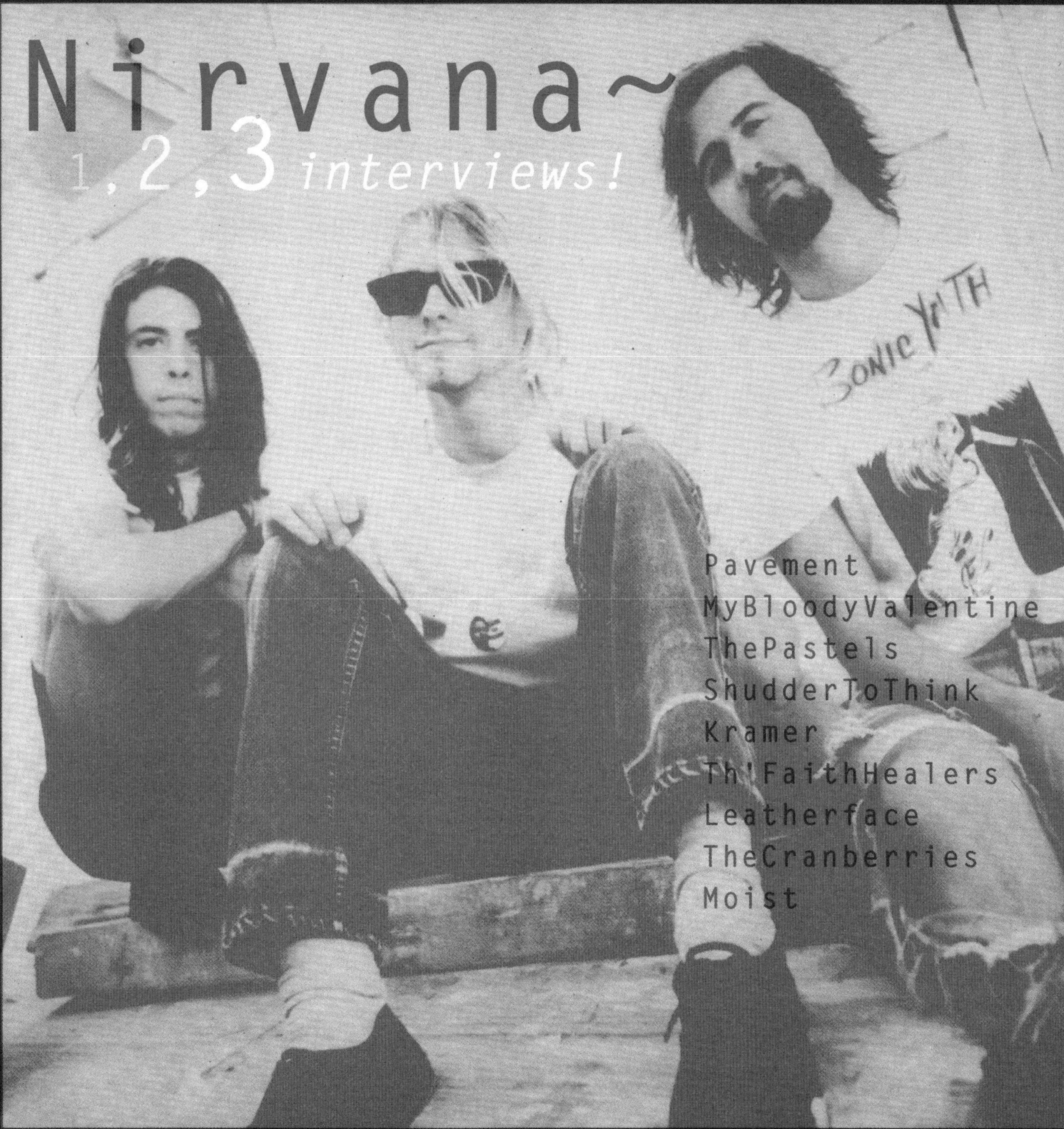

Nirvana~

1,2,3 interviews!

Pavement
MyBloodyValentine
ThePastels
ShudderToThink
Kramer
Th'FaithHealers
Leatherface
TheCranberries
Moist

Exclusive Wedding Present Flexi!

In the world, there is Pavement. Scott (or Spiral Stairs to his friends) a person of guitar, is not present at the interview although he did leave a message on Mark's phone for us. Steve, or Stereo Master, a thing of vocals, *is* here. So is Mark Ibold, bass child, and Bob, the drum kit hit man. Gary Young, another drum being, is also not present.

Because it was, at-the-time-of-going-to-press, too early to get Pavement in the flesh in the UK, and as god did not give us the airfare, and because postal interv ews are for losers, we did what we could: a tape of questions was swapped, thanks to Federal Express, for a tape of answers. This was the closest to physical we could get.

I actually think it is my duty to you to explain some things: i) On the cassette I sent them, each of my questions is preceded by an awful fanfare noise from Barry's keyboard. ii) The tape begins with Pavement songs sung onto our answering machine, by members of the *Ablaze!* problem solving team. iii) Since I cannot be bothered to figure out which voice belongs to whom, such knowledge is probably permanently denied to you. iv) Then, *this,* I told them, *is the first question: Is the all-pervading hiss on your records an excuse or a joke? It is because the sounds you make are greater in your head, and you can't get things to go like that in reality, so you have to sabotage it? Or is it an MBV like attempt to cause a generation of kids to throw their hi-fi systems away in disgust?*

Take it away, boys.

- I think we should do it in the most fucked up way possible. [Whether this refers to their music or to this interview I cannot tell. It seems to make sense, either way.]
- The hiss just comes from Louder Than You Think Studios in Stockton, it's only available there, and it's not intended to make anyone feel that their stereo is shoddy.
- I think we're afraid to admit that we're connoisseurs of static. Each static tune has been specifically chosen for each track.
- We're trying to reify the sound of fresh socks out of the drying machine.

How unfair do you think "a band with a big Fall problem" is as a description of Pavement?
- I don't think Pavement has a Fall problem..
- HOW I WROTE ELASTIC MAN, HOW I WROTE ELASTIC MAN...
[someone is singing, in a most amazing Southern English accent. You'd have to hear it.]
- There's a lot bigger problems in this world.
- No bigger than Spanish television has an American television problem.
- HIT IT IN THE HEAD, WITH A TWO BY FOUR...
[Hur hur hur hur hur hur hur... that accent's killing me.]

Why do your record sleeves look like Swell Maps ones, like things on Rough Trade in 1980?
- Karren's secret darts, Karren's secret darts/ we heard the one about the Fall, but we found out it was just the start/ it was one of Karren's secret darts, your secret darts Karren they hurt, ouch.

Tell us some Pavement mythology.
- Whenever we practice, flocks of birds congregate on the roof above us.
- The big Pavemenmt myth that bothers Scott especially is that Pavement is a New York band.
- That we share the driving on our tours equally.

Tell us about angels.
[Angels? *they say.*]

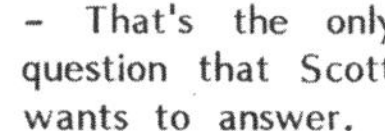

- That's the only question that Scott wants to answer.
- Angels are the only epistemological being that doesnt have sex organs. E-P-I-S-T-E-M-O-L-O-G-I-C-A-L. [How dare you patronise me so? I've written that word more times than you've played your Fall LPs.]
- We're gonna move onto question number 6, the band's having a little discussion about how they should answer, if they wanna write down the questions or do it this way because you're *rattling* them with that music between the questions, it's throwing Bob off, and Bob is a storyteller. So, I'm in the kitchen right now, hiding from the band, on the pre-tense of getting another beer from the... not that that really needs to be mentioned, also my friend David's here, he's the secret like spiritual omen [¿] of the band, he's never been thanked on the record but he's part of our concept. Scott's in California along with Gary, so you won't hear from Gary.
- Steve!
[The machine goes off. Then it goes back on again. There's noise, and indecipherable talking, and I know it's... a test for me, a recognition thing, I've got to try and figure out the whole thing. I fail.]

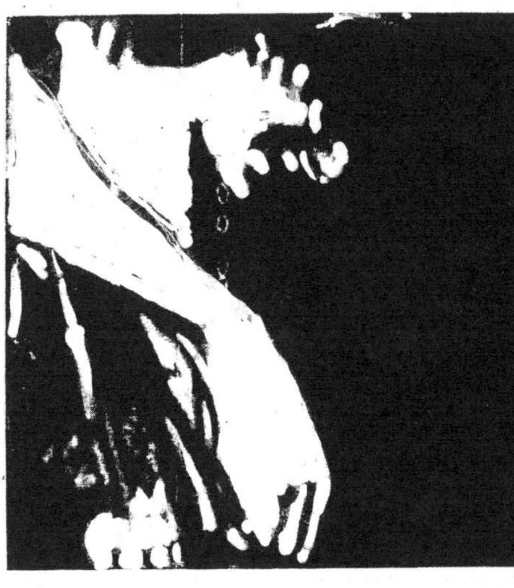

STEREO MASTER

PERFECT SOUND NORMAL DESIRES

PAVEMENT

interview by Karren A

- Moving onto question number 6, y'got Mark, y'got Barb [Bob] Spiral... here's Mark.
- Mark.
- Yes?
- How long have you been in this band?
- What, August, September...
- Remember the evil way you got into this band?
- Oh, gard [god].
- Remember the brutal...
- That was very subversive...
- Remember Bob, you were gonna be the only drummer?
- Yeah that's right. But then I obviously wasn't gonna be enough...
- Because that one arm of yours just wouldn't do.

- Here's a future, unreleased Pavement song, it's called "Secre Knowledge Of Back Roads". [Unhappily only I have this tape, and i can't be transferred onto paper, There are occasional hiss bursts, it' recorded in a house, not a studio, on tape decks not a prope machine with some lame vocals and laughing and some passable ones just guitar and drums, makes me feel like it's only my delight holdin the whole thing together.] It's the first thing we did at a little track recording studio at Hoboken NJ where we like to flesh thing out.

Describe the characters in Pavement.
- You know that it's impossible to talk about yourself, so that's wh you start bands.

Tell us what your best day would be if you could do anything in the world with anyone, anyhow.
- The lamest question in history.
- Bob would be in Louisville.
- Two members would go to that big rock concert with that band on 4AD, the Breeders.
- I would hold hands with Tanya Donnely.
- I myself would like to visit my friend who's very sick, he's in the hospital right now.
- In fact let's go over there now, maybe we can get him on tape.
- Fuck, man. Excuse me, miss.
- We're in St Mary's hospital.

[They're pretending that, in between two tape recorder clicks, they have travelled to St. Mary's hospital and that they are surrounded by doctorey and nursey type things.]
- What room is this?
- 242.
- Dr Conlan, Dr Howard!
- There he is man.
- David! How're you doin'?
- You look good, man.

[Seems to describe an accident on a journey to a country club in which his larynx is destroyed, through some kinda vocoder thing.]
[I hope you can transcribe his response, they say. I can't.]

Describe the place you come from, and/or the place where you live.
- I'm from Stockton. The only way to describe it, unfortunately... you *can't* describe it. I'm trying to think of the words, it's hard to. It's flat, and it's sort of like Devon-shire, except there's less grass and more dirt.
- California. Everyone knows California is going to its grave in the ocean.
- I just wanna say before David goes in you might remember a great song be Youth Brigade called "We're Gonna Sink With California When It Falls Into The Sea". Well, in fact some of us have a different view, we're not necessarily gonna sink, we're gonna make the best of it...
- The city planners and architects have designed Stockton with a double purpose. It's a practically beautiful city but it's also gonna make a beautiful reef.
- We have a few skyscrapers there and every one of them is ready to be its own island. Palm trees and lighthouses. We have some oil wells, even, ready to be set up when geological time takes its course

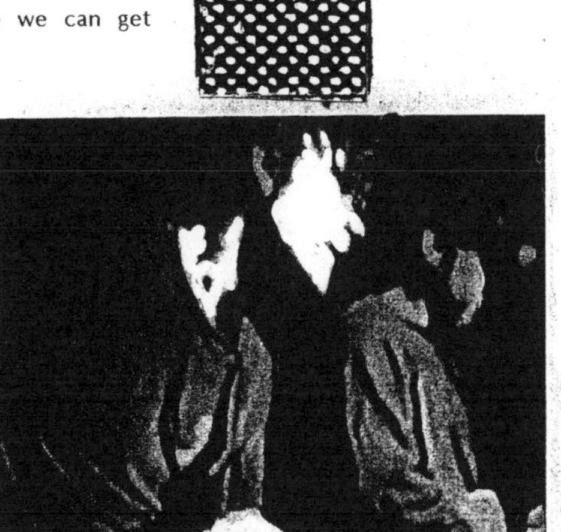

M. IBOLD

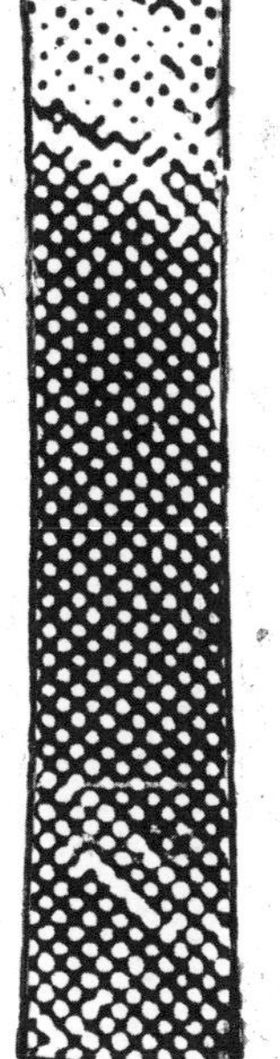
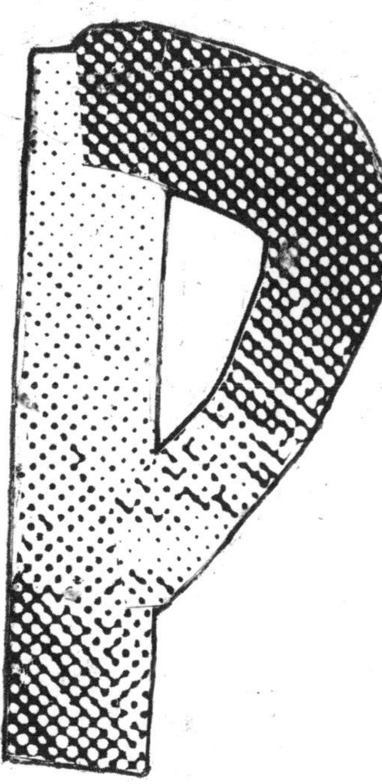

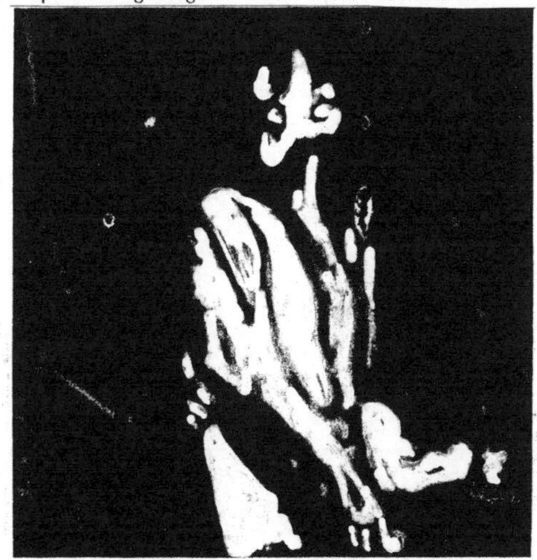

SPIRAL S.

- The moral is, turn your fears to your advantage.
- I think that's something that people in Stockton really feel, even when you walk down the street, and people are wearing scuba equipment in the post office...
- The strange thing is, even if you go into the simplest... I mean, you have Harrods, I know that's a big thing in London, I know you're from Leeds or whatever, if you go out to any department store, we have an inordinate amount of swimming wear. Cos, Stockton is completely inland, I know you know that , or maybe you do know that, because Europeans generally have a better idea of world geography. We are literally 90 miles inland, nonetheless giant, and I don't think it's one of those displacement theories of Los Angeles culture dripping into us, which everyones always saying that we get everything secondhand from LA as if were like fuckin' people from Germany or something. We want two states.
- I know people say that the parking lots surrounding the stadiums are an improper use of space but Californians continue to import glass from other countries and turn it into their advantage.
- They always have,
- And they always will.
- It's something that might even relate to the music and the larger world, like artful, internalising them so much to yourself that they're not anyone else's, but you spit it back out and no-one else'll notice that it's erm, it's like going through, when you eat it and you spit it back out in a way because of where you're from, it doesn't sound like it's from anywhere else even though it is.
- When it sticks to the wall like a Richard Tuttles (?) paper sculpture,
- In the meantime we're gonna talk about Pennsylvania. So many people like to think of it as a between here and there type place when in fact so many people call it here, it is a lot closer to here and (whispering) there is some up on the.... where I live in Pennsylvania is about three and a half hours away from here on the Amtrak train, and if you get a good Amtrak train it'll have a smoking lounge with curtains that seperate it from the bathroom area, and you can go in there and smoke, and I used to smoke a lot, so I enjoy doing that, and the part of the trip between New York and Lancaster, closer to the New Jersey part of that journey, there'll be a lot of men speaking on cellular phones, and they normally leave by the time we get to Princeton Junction, then you get to Philadelphia, Pennsylvania, which is about an hour from New York, you get out and you switch trains. The Philadelphia station is a really nice station, it's a beautiful giant station. The ceilings are so high that the birds actually get in and live, but dont you think the *Ablaze!* staff would like Philadelphia?
- Oh yes.
- It's immaculate, just like their typesetting. [*Sarcastic swine.*]
- If the *Ablaze!* staff ever comes to New York, for instance for the New Music Seminar, we will happily take them on the Amtrak train to Philadelphia. But then after Philadelphia you go to Lancaster, which is about another hour's drive, in the western direction, and the Lancaster train station's a lot smaller than the Philadelphia or the

Photo: JW

PAVEMENT

New York station, and I normally like to walk, I don't ever call anyone in my family and tell 'em I'm arriving in Lancaster, I always just get in a train, no matter how many bags I have, I just take my bags and I walk home, because the good thing about walking back from the train station is that there's a big difference between New York and Lancaster, when you get out of the train in Lancaster and you're walking down the street, you can hear pretty much every, no listen, you can hear pretty much every car in a quarter mile radius. Anyone that was with me, for example any one of the *Ablaze!* staff that came with me to Lancaster, would probably hear any car within a quarter of a mile radius and we would walk to my parents house. and the door would never be locked. In Pennsylvania I never had keys because I never had a car [annoyed with the others for trying to talk over himÖ] I'm talkin' about Pennsylvania! The thing about Pennsylvania is that I never had keys before I came to New York.
- You dont realise, the next issue of *Ablaze!* is not the Pennsylvania issue.
- We're goin' over to the next question Karren, you've got nice encapsulated versions of where we're from...

How does the band operate when the distances within it are so big?
- D'you know how close you feel when your mother calls you? D'you feel far? D'you feel close...?
- The best thing about being so far apart, there's no problems whatsoever, we all talk to Scott quite a bit, and we've a neat little avoidance of tension problems, getting tired of each other...
- Well I feel pretty close to you right now Bob, you've got your armpits in my face.
- If people in other bands are reading this and you're not too happy about the way things are going in your band, I would suggest that you all move to different parts of your continent.
- I agree.
- And when you get together it will be a joyous celebration
- So far it's worked.
- It really has been.
- It doesn't matter.
- The panic stages are coming.
- But I love Steve.
- And Bob, I care for you.

How do Spiral and Stereo Master know each other and how did they meet the others?
- Scott and I went to school together since second grade when Scott was still missing teeth and wearing glasses. I had all my teeth, therefore I was the one that asked him to join the band.
- I met Steve during my second year at college, University of Virginia, and Scott and Steve met Gary.
- We met Gary by going to his studio cos it was the only one in town, you know that, and Mark we just met here in New York.
- The first time we saw the Dustdevils we freaked about Mark's appearance on stage, we refered to him for about 6 months before we knew him as the Bass Child, cos he fit so nicely into his bass guitar, and one time Dave went up to him and said man why don't you quit those losers the Dustdevils and join us, he was refering to his band with Rob, Mark didn't really know how to react, but we gradually over the course of time became good buddies with Mark, I remember one sunny day at Belmont when we mentioned the possibility that we'd need a bassplayer for the upcoming tour...
- So basically these guys, Mark and Bob, they're kind of grafted on, like a, not like a wheelchair, but they tour with us right now, they don't play on the records yet but they probably will one day, we'll see.

How long does it take to get those songs together? Are the founder members in charge of the song writing?
[Sniggering] - The founder members are in fact in charge of the songwriting.
- She's asking about the founder members being in

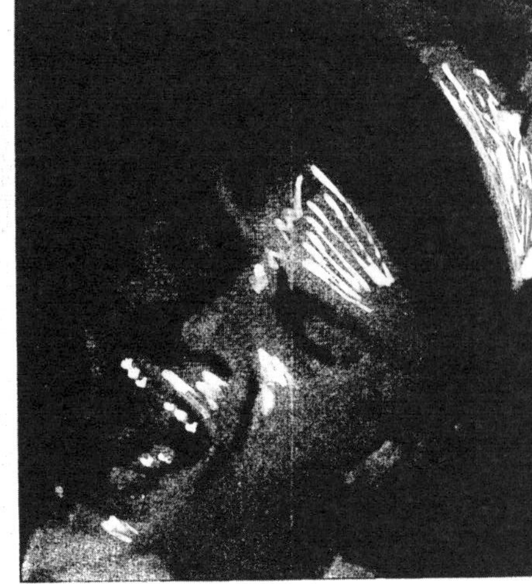

BELMONT N.

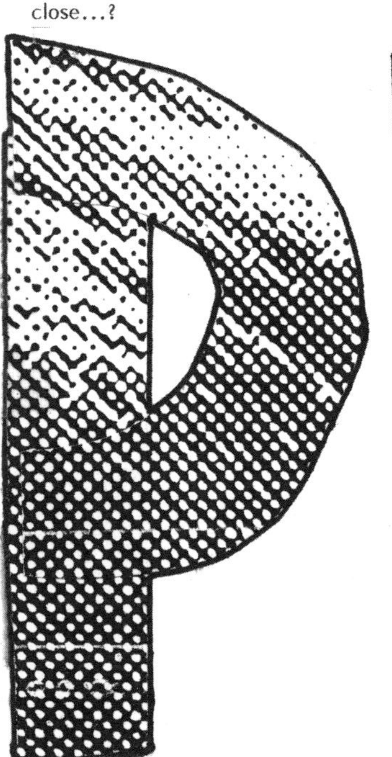

charge of the songwriting. Pretty much Spiral and I and Gary still write the songs.
- He claims that we rip off the Silver Jews, trying to bring it to the Silver levels, cheap whoring of the Silver Jews, trying to get into an English fanzine through the backside.
- "My First Mine" [*that Pave track available only on the flexi with Ablaze! 8*] is about the Silver Jews, how Steve mined the Silver Jews for riffs and ideas and songs.

The question about why Pavement previously existed without a bassist and how things had changed since they'd got Mark was answered so incomprehensibly that I have edited that part out of the interview. It was something to do with "writers, thinkers and, err, men who wear bow ties". I suspect that one of Pavement posesses a degree in philosophy, or something similar.

My next question concerned their then imminent signing to a UK label for European releases. Their response, "Some people say it's an untruth but in fact it's Fiction," proved to be misleading. They signed to Big Cat UK in March, amidst the mournful sobs of many label bosses. In the States they are with the terminally disorganised but cute Matador, although you will not be shocked when in the near future they are snapped up in the Nirv-driven jaws of Some Major.

What does death need time for?
[Sung, beautifully] - WHAT DOES DEATH NEED TIME FOR? WHAT DOES DEATH NEED TIME FOR? WHAT DOES DEEAATH NEED TIME FOR? NEED I REMIND YOU?

It's the end of the interview.
- Karren we wanna say goodbye to your private island, this is Steven we're saying goodnight now.

Mark at home, later: "Scott's answer to the question about angels, I had to come home and get it off my answer machine, it's coming up:"
"This is spiral, I'm only gonna answer one of these questions. "Angels And Devils" is probably one of my favourite Echo And The Bunnymen songs too. That's my answer. OK?"
"Alright, Scott, thank you. Uh, how do I turn this off?"

There is a very definite thing with time and Pavement. Some songs just flit by, they require so much of your concentration to be aware of exactly what they are, and other songs, sometimes, dare to dwell... the sort that wipe the others out, standing up there as if they're the only ones.

G. YOUNG

Despite all the nihilistic hissing noise, the willful obscurity, melodies manage to break through. Pavement have the capacity to produce the most infernal fucking pop music history has ever had. Pavement are the culmination of something, of some of the glory that can be squeezed from being an animal, they do for your ears what good sex does for your cunt and your brain. Pavement songs are full of angst, of crazy, healthy, adolescent yearning. Just pave me out, I don't mind. There's so much material, more than I can get my head round at any one time... here's what you missed:

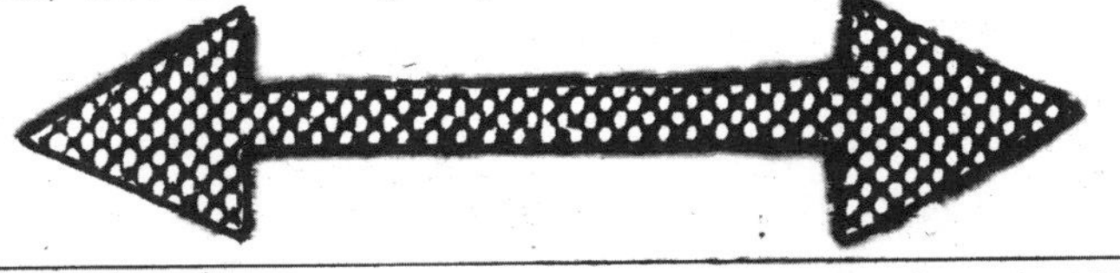

PAVE-MENT.

The best pop songs.

"Slay Tracks 1933-1969" 7" EP, recorded Jan. 17th & 18th 1989: YOU'RE Killing Me/ BoX ELDER/ MAYBE maYBE/ She BELIEVes (edit)/ PriceYEAH. (Treble Kicker).
"Demolition Plot J7" 7" EP - Oct. 16th & 17th 1989: Forklift/ Spizzle Trunk/ Recorder Grot/ Internal K-Dart/ Perfect Depth/ Recorder Grot (Rally). (Drag City).
"Perfect Sound Forever" 10" EP, 29th & 30th Dec. 1989: Heckler Spray/ From Now On/ Angel Carver Blues/ Mellow Jazz Docent / Drive-By-Fader/ Debris Slide/ Home/ Krell Vid-User. (Drag City).
"Exact Wording Of Threat" 7" EP: Summer Babe/ Mercy Snack/ Baptiss Blacktick. (Drag City).
"My First Mine" on Ablaze! #8 flexi. (Stuffed Cat UK).
"Slanted And Enchanted" LP (Big Cat UK).

(Demonlition Plot, Perfect Sound Forever, and Exact Wording Of Threat are available on import, through Greyhound distribution in this country. Slay Tracks is deleted. The flexi is available from our address, £1.50 & 50p postage - including a free magazine.)

NIRVANA

THIS ISSUE'S SELL-OUT SEGMEN FEATURES THREE NIRVAN INTERVIEWS FOR THE PRICE O ONE... LET THE STORIES UNFOLD.

Last autumn, NIRVANA exploded, all too spectacularly, onto the indierock ultrastar scene. All their dreams came true, and they could barely handle it. Our original attempts to get the interview we'd been promised resulted in our being barred from the building. Despite this strange twist in the obstacle course of life, we managed to get for you not one! not two! but three Nirvana interviews. Sadly, your caring but not-so-daring editor was unable to attend any of them, for fear of hassle scene induced mental illness, but not to worry - you'll get her opinion on the whole caboodle regardless.

DOCUMENT NUMBER ONE, parts a & b →

Notes on recent popmusic explosion:

The best band of 1991? After which all is post Nirvana? And the last tour, the most significant event in history since the Sex Pistols?

Well, '91 was a pretty lean year (it was the one, remember, in which Peel's Festive 50 was abandoned due to lack of interest for the first time in living memory) and in the desert the mirage appears to the most desperate.

The facts you probably already know: originating from Aberdeen, Washington state, they joined with Sub Pop, releasing their first LP *Bleach*, recorded in three days, and enjoying a symbiotic relationship with the label, Tad and Mudhoney. This experience was shared in other towns by other labels and other bands: "I think the idea of being a Sub Pop band is ridiculous, it's like being called a Dischord (Washington DC) or a Touch And Go (Chicago) band." Leaving the label, which was having financial troubles, to join Geffen, they produced *Nevermind*, selling 5 million copies worldwide.

But Nirvana *are* something fresh and new and their superbly crafted songs on *Nevermind* are no illusion. Human feelings *are* always mixed, only the simplest souls can pretend otherwise, and Nirvana's lyrics and music capture this beautifully. We tried to piece together the psyche of the three headed noise monster that is Nirvana from conversations with each of the three heads in turn. If the result is like that of the three blind men examining the elephant, then it reflects on the blind men. [Required explanation explanation provided by Chris Trout: "There are 3 blind men examining an elephant and one of them is at the arse end, someone says 'Hey blind men, tell us what this thing is and you can have something or other', so this one grabs the tail and thinks it's a rope and he's wrong. The second one is underneath it and he thinks it's a big skin thing, and the third one is by its head and thinks it's like a tube. The moral is that if a thing's big you can't understand it by looking at just one bit of it." OK?]

The David Head (tail):
Formerly of Scream, a moderately well known hardcore band of the mid 80's. An experienced tourer, having travelled to the UK four times. Found it depressing and still does. On the subject of "Polly", (their song about rape): "It's just common sense, being against sexism, racism, any -ism. If anyone said I was from a cock-thrusting band I'd be really offended, but if people say we smash our instruments, well that's OK."

The Chris Head (flank):
Relaxed giant, wont say anything about song lyrics by this, his first band (he doesn't write them), or about the last drummer. He defends Mudhoney's right to operate in their own domain, musically similar as they are, but otherwise poles apart. For the days when their rapidly increasing rider exeeds their drinking ability, he is prepared...

The Kurt Head (trunk):
Alleged narcoleptic (we're not using the madman-as-genius gambit are we?). [Kurt actually evaded our interviewer, so our notes on this end are sparse, but neighbouring investigations surely fill these gaps for you].

Pearl Jam

They are certainly playing the publicity machine in the same style as punksters of old: the wrong song on the Ross show; the F-word on The Word; going OTT on TOTP. Disclaiming any masterplan for world domination, they are well aware of the system in which they have become enmeshed: "The music press in England (sic) is sensational(ist). They come out once a week and have to have a 'story'. No-one talks about the Canadian music press..."

Watch out - great thirty-toed three-headed noise monster is changing the face of your music industry.

(There follows, as a supplement to this odd shaped animal, a mini interviewette with Chris Novoselic:)

Are you feeling nervous about going onstage?
- Naw, naw, old hat. It's all old hat.
Are you worried about becoming too big too quickly?
- It's already happened. All we can do is just be ourselves. That's it. What else are you going to do? Pretend? Hang around with Bianca Jagger or something?
So are you just going to let things happen?
- No, no, we've got control - we're trying to control what happens. Depends what happens, it's kind of a vague... records are going to sell, people are going to buy them. A lot of the same people who buy Sonic Youth records...
Are you still friends with Tad and Mudhoney?
- Oh yeah, totally. Totally friends. Why not? No, see what we've done is... we've denied our friends and now we hang out with the all the Hollywood crowd, ride Harley-Davidsons, wear bandanas...
I'm not asking you to answer for them, but you seem to be almost poles apart?
- People generalise about the Seattle sound but every band has its own identity, its own sound. Everybody has something to offer. It's not just the same shit.
Were you sad to leave the label?
- Sub Pop? No, we were rather glad to go. It was sad... they had to tear us away from Bruce and Jon; we were screaming, we were writhing... convulsions, tears, uncontrollable. It was just like a separation, like a classic story of three orphaned kids who struggled together and then their welfare agents tear them apart and send them to different foster homes, so they're having this big freak-out, ha ha ha.
What are you going to do as your rider gets bigger and bigger and your drinking capacity levels off?
- These are small cans. I drank a whole bottle of Bordeaux, Beaujolais, who knows? Check into the treatment centre. Go and see a hypnotist. Shock therapy. Anabuse pills, take those. Combination of a few of those treatments... uh-oh, I know: the Ludovico technique, that's in *A Clockwork Orange*. They'll strap me down in a chair and make me watch Dean Martin movies and Matt Lukin. Shoot me with drugs, make my eyes stay open and drop by drop...
How long has David been with you?
- Over a year... fifteen months. What's this interview for? (panic)
What happened to your last drummer?
- Oh well, it's like we just had some differences. I don't want to get into any details. It just didn't work out.

- I'd rather read this *(Ablaze!)* than *Q* or *Raw* or...
It's hard work.
- I imagine it is, yeah.

(Finally more alcohol arrives and that's it.)

DOCUMENT NUMBER TWO

I'm stranded on a roof in South Kensington, held hostage by three angst ridden teen spirits. Unless I ask super questions, they'll be answered very slowly, while little old me hangs from the roof edge. Best I sit down, cling to the floor and quietly sip my Coke. Aberdeen's finest are ready.

"'My Grandfather used to have this racist joke he'd play. My Grandpa's a dick. He had a black cat called Nigger. He also used to have this joke he thought was real funny, he'd take a bowl of water, put salt in and then he would put dish detergent in it. Then he'd throw pepper in and the dish detergent would make the pepper separate from the salt and he'd say, 'Oh look, buncha niggers just jumped in the swimming pool.'" Kurt's eyes glint with bitter disbelief, as the rest of us look on aghast. "My Grandpa's Archie Bunker, he looks like Brezhnev. He's got colon cancer. He deserves it."

You've done your indie apprenticeship on the Sub Pop label, did you ever expect to go beyond that?

"We never expected to get on Sub Pop, we never even expected to put out a record. At the time we were recording our stuff, we didn't even know Sub Pop existed," states Kurt emphatically. "When we recorded our first demo, we didn't realise they were a label. They'd only put out the Soundgarden and Green River EPs at the time. I didn't take much notice of that stuff. It wasn't like that was our premier goal."

NIRVANA

But now that you've left them, do you think people are going to start saying 'Nirvana, oh yeah, Sub Pop sound'?

Chris screeches, "Yeah, we'll try and break away from that for sure, but they'll always be there. Y'know what Jonathon Poneman (Sub Pop guru) told me once? 'Hey, you're always gonna be a Sub Pop band,' and I went, yeah, you're right. We never knew about any Seattle scene, we were a band for a year and a half before we even played there. We were really naïve about the whole thing."

"It's like, have you ever tried to pull a tree stump out of the ground and the roots are just so far down? That stump is Nirvana and the roots..." Dave hesitates as he prepares to execute his trippy metaphor "...are Sub Pop and the earth is the general public."

On the second album you've introduced more of a pop element into the band. Will you ever veer off towards a mellow REM sound?

"We've never really been away from the 'REM sound'. 'About A Girl' sounds like REM. It doesn't matter, so long as we do what we do. We'll never change drastically. I don't see anything wrong with REM, I never have, they write good songs. Nothing bothers me more than people being ignorant about music and only liking one certain style. If someone only listens to hardcore, then they're just as ignorant as the average laymen who only listens to Bruce Springsteen," says Kurt, annoyed.

"There's no big scheme to things either, no big plan plotted out," snorts Dave. "Well, you have *Bleach* which is heavy grunge rock and the *Sliver* single which is clever grunge pop and the *Nevermind* record is a..."

'...collection of REM rip offs.' interjects Kurt with just a hint of sarcasm.

As the whole world seems to be reliving punk (it does? - Ed), do you think Nirvana could ever be part of a whole new punk generation, in the way that you're combining pop melodies with hardcore noise as all the original seventies bands like The Damned, The Clash and The Sex Pistols did?

"Yeah, because those are just like really genuine rock and roll bands, they have a lot of melody, they were wise guys too, and they just fit into the punk scene very well. Y'know what a kind of reaction punk was, it was just to pump some fresh blood into rock and roll when things got stagnant," explains Chris whilst rolling his psychedelic bracelet about the floor. Previously he'd been hammering a metal plate against the wall.

You had quite a reputation as a devastating four piece band - was losing a member (Jason Everman) a major turning point in the sound?

Chris: "We started off as a three piece and were a four piece for about five months. There were only three of us on *Bleach*. We just put his picture and his name on the record, but there's no Jason Everman guitar playing on that album at all."

"We could never hear him live anyway. His amp wasn't loud enough, so we just replaced him with more amps," drawls Kurt, nasty as usual. "Anyway, whenever we play, we've got a cardboard cutout, with a guitar strapped around it and various celebrities' faces stuck on it... so we're still a four piece."

Suddenly there's a major buzz about the band, how can you account for this?

"That's just kinda happened; the people did that, we didn't. We were talking about it and... woooaahh," Chris shouts, amazed.

Dave continues: "That's one of the things that really bugs me about how, say some band will be together for a couple of years, get all this hype and the press eventually crucifies them because they couldn't live up to the hype, when it wasn't the band that created the hype in the first place, it was the press."

If you could flood MTV with your hits, would you be able to avoid the potential cries of 'sell out'?

"Why would there be any reason not to?" questions Kurt. "Because, as far as I'm concerned, Beat Happening should be number one or the Vaselines or Black Flag. The Sex Pistols should've been for years and had like a blowout."

Does anyone know what number one is?

"Who cares?" demands Chris. "It's just shallow crap. Even if we were number one band, who gives a fuck? Big Deal."

"You always hear about these bands that get asked, 'Where were you when you found out that your song was number one on the charts?' and they say, 'Well, I was takin' a shit when I found out and the shit just fell right outta my ass an' I called up our guitar player and went YEEEAAAHHH." Dave hollers with mock enthusiasm. "It's just so dumb."

On your 1990 tour you dropped your infamous and brutal smash-it-up routine. Why?

"We didn't feel like it. It wasn't on the set list. We just smash up whenever we feel like it. We're not Kiss, they had smoke come out of their guitars, fire, and they spit blood y'know, and that's what was expected of them at their shows everytime you saw them," sighs Kurt.

"But the key to all you bands out there who are looking for that 'smash it up' image," offers Dave, "is to rent equipment, smash it, buy it at a discount rate."

"Usually they sucker you for twice the amount it's worth, though," adds Kurt, with the usual dose of paranoia.

So what does the future hold for Nirvana?

Chris: 'We left our crystal ball at home and we can't read tarot cards.'

Kurt, in the hands of the public... Photo:

Kurt: 'Let's ask Shirley Maclaine. No, better still ask the magic eight ball.'

DOCUMENT NUMBER THREE

When Nirvana hit West Yorkshire, Tony The Woolgar, a chairleg of the odd-shaped piece of furniture known as the Leeds Music Scene, grasped the tape recorder and marched bravely forward, past seething security and tour managers with the springs and wires hanging out of their skulls like the aftermath of a hammer's meeting with a walking talking baby doll, and approached the newly press phobic sex objects Nirvana, specifically Kurt Cobain. Tony had been equipped with a ticket from a Newcastle metro train on which various probing questions were scrawled, and Eugene and Tracee, Leeds' Sleepers, helped him execute the interview (well, whatever they did to it, it certainly didn't escape alive).

"I haven't seen a fanzine since I was a young child," Kurt announces cheekily, upon finding himself confronted with yet another gang of keen kids with tape recorders.

"You've gone really mega, you've sold loads of records," they astutely point out. "What happened?"

"*Making It*," he divulges. "There was a TV show on ABC at 8 o'clock in the late seventies called *Making it*, it was a disco orientated show...(sings) 'Making it, you've got your chance, you're taking it, come on, come on...'"

HOT VIDEO ACTION

Tracee really likes Kurt's green t-shirt on the "Teen Spirit" vid.

"I haven't been able to bring myself to wear that t-shirt since the video was filmed," Kurt reveals. "Obviously because it's my favourite shirt."

One of Tracee's favourite songs on the new album is 'Lithium'. "To me it sounds like it's something to do with religion, taking drugs and being brainwashed," she says.

"Yeah, all that bohemian shit," Kurt agrees.

"So what is it actually about?"

"Well, the way that I picture it, the visual part of the song would be the skinny, long legged puppet from the Brothers Quay...you ever see a Brothers Quay movie? Well, they're these guys who pose as Eastern Europeans but they're typical bohemian art students from Philadelphia but they like to put out the image that they're from Eastern Europe and most of their short films are about ten minutes long and they have these really old-looking puppets that move around in a surreal way and they pick up screws out of the ground and it's really dirty and beautiful and that's what I pictured for this song when I was writing the lyrics. Really there's no meaning at all. Hopefully when we do our video, because that will be our next single, (It wasn't. - Ed) we'll hire the Brothers Quay if we can hunt them down."

ON NEPOTISM AND SELLING OUT

Nirvana do a lot to promote other bands. They took their favourites, Captain America (ex-Vaselines), from Scotland, and Shonen Knife, from Japan, on their big tour with them. Tony asks whether the latter are popular in their native land.

"No, I don't think so. I don't think they're really popular anywhere other than in a cult sense in America, a very small group of people like them, but it's obvious they made everybody in the whole place tonight very happy, everyone was just smiling."

They ask whether Nirvana will bring out a single with Seminal Twang, a fave label.

"I feel a special bonding with Dave (ST boss) even though I've never met him. Everything he's put out I've totally loved, y'know, Daniel Johnson stuff, The Vaselines, I mean, wow!"

"How many people like The Vaselines in America? Are they a cult band?"

"I don't think we're really aware of The Vaselines in the States but that's not very surprising when a band don't have the privilege of promoting or distributing their music. But then again, maybe it's so sincere that they just wanted to put out a record, that they wanted to record together and write some songs."

"Do you think that's something which may not be part of Nirvana anymore, because of the fact that you're getting bigger and bigger?" they ask. "It must be really frightening." This is in fact Kurt's cue to talk about his justifications for being on a major label.

"It's not so much frightening as it is embarrassing because really we'd be just as happy playing together in our basement, we really would. But at the time we were on Sub Pop we thought there were too many people coming up to us after shows saying 'We can't find your records', so we just decided to go onto another label and we were under contract to Sub Pop for seven more years, so there were no independent labels that would even touch us, there was no way that they could buy us out of the contract so we had to go onto a major label. We're not ashamed of that, we're quite pleased with it because DGC is a really good major label."

"Is it true that Mudhoney were gonna sign with Geffen becasuse you did?" A chance for Kurt to continue his justifications.

"It doesn't have much to do with that. I mean it could have something to do with that because we signed with DGC because Sonic Youth joined, which means they've proved they can handle an independent band and promote them in the right way. But besides the fact that Sonic Youth were on the label; the people at DGC, they just convinced us that they could do their job. There are a lot of people at DGC who have worked at other independent labels before, so they're totally aware of it, they're very independent orientated."

"So you're happy anyway?"

"Yeah, sure. I've made my own bed, I can't complain too much because there's nothing I can do about it at this point unless we break up; and we don't want to do that, we like playing together still. I mean, if it gets too out of hand, and the shows become so huge that we don't feel that it's very personal anymore, we'll just break up and change our name and start over again and hopefully we'll write good songs."

IDIOCY

"It's not true about the turtle farm is it?" (Our reporters have been doing their homework.)

"What?"

"I read an interview that said you had a turtle farm," they say.

"You're English, aren't you? You're aware of the English papers. It's as simple as that, I mean, I don't have to say anything more..."

While Tracee and Eugene casually slander Everett True, the subject of The British Music Press arises. And Kurt is upset.

"Every article that's been writen about us has been so completely exaggerated, taking things so literally. In an NME article [written by Mary Ann Hobbs], they took a quote out of another one months before, and the quote was exaggerated and rewritten and she took that right out and I mean, we sat around for two hours and gave her, in my opinion, pretty good statements but she only used a few of them and she reworded all of it, every bit that came out of my mouth was completely reworded. And I don't mean to be so picky about it, I don't like to look at everything and analyse it and say, 'This is wrong', but it's so ridiculous when something is written about us in these major papers that it's really distressing."

PUNK ROCK

"Which punk rock bands were you into, then? What made you start off?" This is Kurt's cue to slag off straight edge.

"Stuff that made me start off was stuff like the Butthole Surfers and Scratch Acid and Flipper, very noisy bands, because that was really the time when hardcore was very big in America, this straight edge and very philosophical type of music... they don't have sex, they don't smoke cigarettes, they don't drink, I mean it's fine if somebody wants to do that, to promote it to such an extreme but it's offensive to me.

"So did these hardcore bands make you start writing?"

"The hardcore bands made me rebel against the very typical form of punk rock at the time. I tried to find other bands that were subversive to that kind of music; like Flipper, Butthole Surfers and Scratch Acid were bands that were completely the opposite, they were very much more like '77 punk rock when

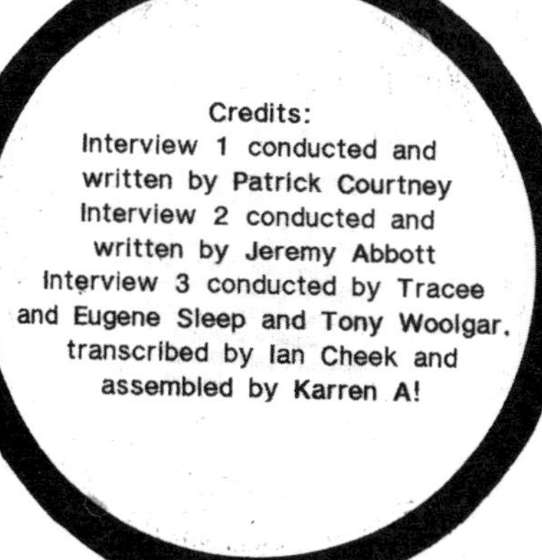

Credits:
Interview 1 conducted and written by Patrick Courtney
Interview 2 conducted and written by Jeremy Abbott
Interview 3 conducted by Tracee and Eugene Sleep and Tony Woolgar, transcribed by Ian Cheek and assembled by Karren A!

NIRVANA

things were a bit more open. The stuff I've been into in the last few years is different, even though I still really like those bands, but I've been listening to The Raincoats and Half Japanese and Jad Fair and Beat Happening, Kleenex, The Marine Girls, Slits, a lot of English bands from the early 80's."

"It's really strange because a lot of your music is quite melodic really."

"Yeah, people would expect us to be listening to Godflesh... I mean, I don't have anything against them but it's just not my cup of tea. Most people would expect us to be listeing to nothing but grunge music all the time, so they have no idea we like melodic pop music."

REAL LIFE

In response to what must have been a question about their reaction to Freddie Mercury's death from AIDS, which had occurred a couple of days earlier, he says,

"I started getting into Queen, sort of in a jokey way, and I went out and bought this Queen's *Greatest Hits* tape at a truckstop and I was just getting into it and then, *bam*, Freddy's dead... It's sorta weird, cos Magic Johnson, the famous basketball player, got AIDS and it sort of slapped everyone into reality - 'oh my god, *normal* people can get aids too!' The fact is, although he's always had a reputation for being homosexual, he could equally have got it from a woman, or from shooting drugs. You just wait till President Bush gets AIDS, and then maybe the bullshit'll be turned around a little bit..."

This sojourn into reality proves a little taxing. Kurt is asked whether he likes The Pastels.

"Yes, I like The Pastels, " he says.

Eugene looks at the ticket and says, "What are you going to do on Top Of The Pops?"

"Either we'll do the thing that everyone expects us to do, or we'll, erm... I have no idea, we've only had five hours' sleep in the last two days and we're supposed to do it tomorrow morning. If the vocals are lipsynched, we'll be able to fuck it up even more..."

"Are you gonna do a Kylie?" asks Tracee.

"What's that?"

"Kylie Minogue, she goes on in bondage outfits."

"We'll decide tomorrow morning, it'll depend what mood we're in."

The performance in question proved to be a historical, inspired, adrenaline rush of an event, extra wonderful for the fact that dull establishment TV was being subverted so joyfully. They made no attempt to play out the well known lie, but held their guitars above their heads, threw them around a bit, and the kids leapt onstage in a beautiful surge. After which, the presenters were their usual grinning idiot selves and carried on as if nothing had happenned.

COMPLETE AWFULNESS

"Did you have a happy childhood?" asks Eugene.

"A very happy childhood, yes indeed."

"Were your parents into rock music as well?"

"No, my parents weren't into rock music, not at all. My parents..."

He was interrupted by someone, then was asked something else, and the next round in the competition to see who could be the most unprofessional interviewer began.

"What are your favourite pets?"

"I got a very definite bonding with cats," replies Kurt.

"Yeah cats, especially charcoal grey," says Tracee. "I'd really like a charcoal grey cat. But I'm not allowed because..." (goes on at length about why she can't have a cat). "Do you have pet cats?"

"I can't keep cats any more," says Kurt. "I'm on tour so often I can't afford to pay my friends to feed them and take care of them."

"What would you call a cat?"

"Alien."

"I would call my cat Dollyrocker. It's a Syd Barret song, it goes 'Dollyrocker, Dollyrocker, Dollyrocker.' It's just a cool name, I'd rather be called Dollyrocker instead of Tracy. My mother called me Tracy," says Tracee. "My mother has no imagination, she went to the movies a lot so she called me Tracy after Spencer Tracy, and that's so shit, she could have called me something better, she could have called me Dollyrocker. Anyway, shall we change the subject?"

"Yeah."

"Sorry."

SCARY IMAGE MACHINE

"Why are you so scruffy?" asks Eugene the question asker. "You don't need to answer that one cos you've only had five hours sleep!" he immediately decides. But Eugene, my faint astral projection whispers, I wrote the question before seeing them this evening - I wrote the question because all their press shots show them as the messiest looking band alive... oh, nevermind.

On a less visual theme though, there've been conflicting reports about Nirvana: on the one hand there's the 'New Age' man dealing with issues responsibly, and on the other they're smashing everything up.

"It's part of human nature to appreciate all forms of emotion and to not deny any of them; if you're a true person you shouldn't deny any of them. You shouldn't feel that you should go in one specific direction to promote the image of your band. We like to fuck off, we like to have fun and we also care sincerely about specific things that affect us..."

"So what makes you want to smash things up?" they ask, concerned.

"Well, actually there's the fun side of it..." Kurt giggles.

"How do you prefer to be portrayed?"

"Just like this" Kurt says. "As the sensitive artist type, the frontman with long blond hair."

THE END

Everyone gasps, and the tape recorder is turned off.

The editor scrawls...

Nirvana have performed a cool trick: playing fine tunes with heavying guitars without the sexism and homophobia that we had previously believed to be an integral part of the genre - the new metal man washes this many more dishes.

As a latecomer and an early leaver, I managed to become a fan of Nirvana, and then a cynic, in the space of a month. But who cares? All the marketing scum and dependednt journalists want to know now is, who's The Next (Real) Nirvana? We don't mind, if they pick off our favourite rockin' brothers (and sisters? unlikely) for the corporate destruction, as long as you kids are happy. That's all that matters....

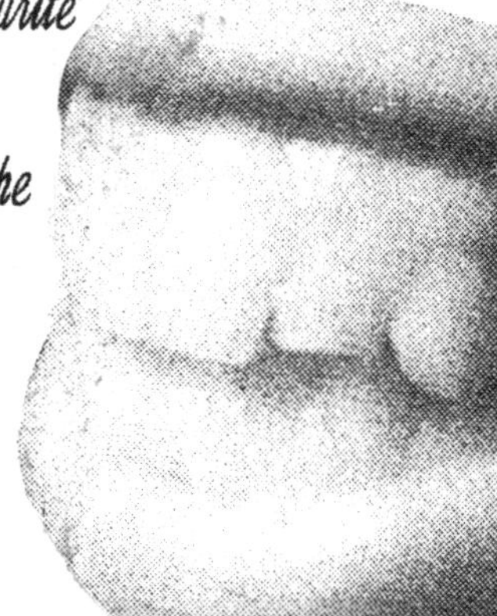

MY BLOODY VALENTINE

Photo: FG

They file past, silent, their pallid faces bowed, as if the very humanity had been bludgeoned out of them, leaving only walking husks, blind stumbling things devoid of personality: shadows, imprints.

Refugees? Concentration camp survivors? Nope, shoegazers actually. The occasion is My Bloody Valentine's 1991 performance at Bradford University, and these eight hundred-odd precious flowers, having just voluntarily subjected themselves to an hour of (let's be honest) badly-mixed, over-amplified cacophony, are looking distinctly wilted.

Still, according to the principle by which all healthy foods taste horrible, it'll have done them good. Whatever else you could say about the My Bloody Valentine live experience, it certainly wasn't *cosy*. Vicious blinding strobes flickered mercilessly at our eyes for minutes on end, matching sensory blow for sensory blow the thirty kilowatt battering being dealt to our ears. The encore comprised top chestnut "You Made Me Realise", with the oft-imitated (indeed, originally copped from Sonic Youth) aeroplane-taking-off middle bit stretched way beyond meaning and time into a remorseless, formless hammering; the entire audience immolated in searing white light. Now, minutes later, the evening's "entertainment" concluded, we're on our way home, somewhat dazed. Which is where you came in.

Me, I want to take a look at the apparent contradiction between the sensuality and subtlety of MBV's recorded work and the aggressive, one-dimensinal live show. It's not that I expect a faithful duplication of the records: that would clearly be a pointless (not to mention, in the case of this particular music, impossible) exercise. It's just that most of tonight's set was so bastard *painful*, in any sense of the word you can think of, and I really don't think it was supposed to be. Let's go and talk to Kevin about it.

"It's about looking at people's faces. Honest...
I know you don't believe half of what I'm saying."

Do you find it difficult to present what is very much a studio music live?

"We don't try to recreate it live. It would be hard if we tried to make it the same, but we don't, so..."

Did you enjoy the gig tonight?

"Really crappy mixed audience reaction, like bad atmosphere... I mean, we were shit. If we're good, and you can tell that people know we're good, that's great; but we were bad and you could tell that people knew it."

Have you rehearsed much for this tour?

"We were rehearsing, but we weren't playing the songs. We were just sorting out the gear, trying to get to grips with some of the stuff we bought. I was only around for four days."

You were phenomenally loud. Don't you think you might be sending lots of people prematurely deaf?

"No, because you need to be exposed to it for a long time to go deaf."

Sorry?

"YOU NEED TO BE EXPOSED TO IT FOR A LONG TIME. It's loud, but not *that* loud. It's more dangerous to wear a Walkman, because when you put a headphone in your ear, the sound pressure levels created in that little space are often a lot higher than at a gig. At a gig what happens is that, as it gets louder, your ears just close down, so you're not actually taking in that much. You can feel it physically, it's really loud, but it's less loud than a club - it sounds worse than it is. Some things that sound pretty mellow can actually seriously do people damage... say if you played a well-produced house track really, really loud; you wouldn't perceive it as being dangerous because it's just (imitates big bass drum) "boom boom boom", but there's transience, the speed of the sound, and if it's really fast your ears can't react. Synthesizers and bleepy things have got really fast transience, much faster than anything I can do with a guitar.

If you imagine it, something that's loud and travels fast, like a snare drum - an electric guitar is comparatively much quieter. It *sounds* louder, because it's lasting, but if you actually measure on a decibel meter, most drummers play at ear damage level the whole time, but because it's fast sounds you don't really notice it; and it's the same with a lot of bleep bleep music. More people are going deaf from going to clubs and listening to dance music on Walkmans than ever would from rock music. I know it doesn't sound true, but it is."

You don't think your tickets should carry health warnings, then?

"No. You can always put earplugs in. Bilinda's got a kid and he wears earplugs. He saw us at Reading. He thought it was gross... I think people get more frightened because they think something might happen, especially when it gets really heavy, the noise thing thing, the rumble, then people think maybe something's going to fall. That's what bothers people. It's quite good, really..."

There was orange stuff flaking off the ceiling during "You Made Me Realise".

"...that would be terrible, though, wouldn't it, if one of those big heavy things went (splat). No, that's not the idea."

What *is* the idea?

"There's no idea, that's the thing. It's easier to say what *isn't* the idea than what *is* the idea."

Come on, you must have some conception of what you want to acheive by doing "You Made Me Realise" with ten minutes of sonic hell in the middle.

"It's about looking at people's faces. Honest, for me, by the way. I know you don't believe half of what I'm saying."

What do you see?

"It's a mixture of things, but nearly everybody's got an expressive expression on. It goes from lots of people just going (looks pissed off), like that, really irritated, like "this is shit, I wish I could go now". There's a hell of a lot of people for whom, like, that's the last straw: they didn't like the gig, and they're like, "well this is really too much, but they don't want to walk out because they don't wanna be seen to be... you know... so they're *bearing* it. There was one girl, you could tell she was in pain. She just wanted to walk away from the P.A."

It's quite a P.A.

"It's the one they use at Wembley Arena, except this is like a tiny part of it. Metallica have got the same P.A. but theirs is 100k and ours is only 30... it's not just volume, though, because you can get a 10k P.A. and make it sound just as loud, but it's more blurry. What freaks people out is it's really loud and clear. Not with us so much, but some of the support bands... like Silverfish, you could hear Lesley's voice perfectly."

The lighting seemed pretty aggressive, too.

"Yeah. It encourages people to close their eyes, by... *ideas*, as opposed to closing them because they think it's horrible. You know, they close them but they think they're missing something."

"*Isn't Anything* only got one really good review. When *You Made me Realise* first came out, all the reviews were condescending."

We moved on to talking about the *Loveless* LP, a record which, despite the glowing reviews it received, was never going to live up to the impossible expectations heaped on it by two years in which *Isn't Anything* became the standard textbook for aspiring indie rockers with no ideas of their own. Myself, I found the record disappointing in that it didn't seem to continue the exploratory direction of tracks on the *Glider* and *Tremolo* EPs, generally sticking to a structurally repetitive rock format; although it's perfectly possible to find pleasure in the rich, layered, guitar/sampler textures and delicious melodies for their own sake. I wondered, on behalf of the poor shoegazey bastards who still haven't got it right, how these sounds were acheived.

"Most of those bendy single-note type things, the melody things, are made up of a mixture of Bilinda's voice and a sample of a flute or something; but not in the way it's supposed to be used - when you use samples properly, you use lots of them spread across the keyboard to give a natural flute sound; but with one sample spread right across the keyboard it takes on different tones, so it's not trying to use it naturally, you know?"

I was a bit disappointed with *Loveless* because the song "To Here Knows When", which was already out on the *Tremolo* EP, seemed to be much the most "out there" piece on the album.

"We're not around to conform to people's idea of what's supposed to be "out there". A lot of the stuff on *Loveless* was a lot more radical than the *Tremolo* EP; but it's not *obviously* radical, it's something that most people will never notice. That's why I gave up on the idea of trying to make music for other people, because it's extremely easy to make music to make people think, that's really radical. It's too easy to do things that are seen as avant-garde or progressive."

How is *Loveless* more radical?

"When it comes to sound and things, there's stuff on there that's definitely taking more chances. The interesting thing is that most people's idea of what's different, as far as I can see, is based on something that's more superficial."

Like the mix of a track like "To Here Knows When", is that what you're getting at?

"Well, there's that, but people just presume... they associate lack of form with something... *weird* or something. It would be really easy - I think I probably will do it sometime, just for the hell of it - to make music that people perceive as extremely radical or innovative or something; but only on a superficial level, because music that really works is music that still *means* something years later, you know what I mean? Initial response isn't the only thing to care about, it's the overall impact. It's when something really means something to you. I mean, you hear a lot of music, pop music in particular, its main purpose is to be *instantly* appealing; while a lot of music that's seen as avant-garde is initially confusing for people, but that's the whole scam of it - you know, a lot of musicians are tricking *themselves* a lot of the time: they do something that they themselves don't feel anything for, but they know it sounds weird, and that leads to a lot of Emperor's New Clothes type situations, where you get people who fool themselves into thinking they're doing something really different, when all they're really doing is something that doesn't connect with themselves; and in turn the people who listen to it don't really know what they're listening to. Like, there were lots of odd weird bands in the early eighties, around the time of the first wave of Factory stuff..."

And those records don't stand up now?

"No, they don't *mean* anything to anybody, because all they were doing was exploring the idea of being something different; whereas Joy Division themselves weren't necessarily doing it just to impress people, and that's why it lasted, that's why it still means something. When people hear it, it doesn't sound fake. It's always the same and it always will be the same. It's something people can't pin down, but it's a kind of honesty: people know when it's there."

"Virtually nobody really knows our genuine history, and some day it'll make a lot more sense to people, especially people who scratched their heads and said, how did they come from "Sunny Sundae Smile" to... you know, other records... in the space of a few years? We have lots of tapes from the very beginnings of the band, which was a hell of a lot more... *traditionally* experimental even than we're seen now. A lot more. We didn't have any ground rules at all. The main instrument was a 4-track portastudio, we just used to have all sorts of stuff on that; mix that live and improvise on top of it. It was interesting enough, but it got kind of boring."

So was that where the sweet pop songs direction came from?

"That was just... yeah, it was lots of things, but it became interesting."

Do you think maybe "direction" is a mistaken concept to apply to somebody's music, anyway?

"It's only a term that's used to help people get a grip on the way they perceive things. I'm not sure it can be worked out mathematically, I don't think many people consciously go in directions as much as people would presume."

You think people just *write what they write*, really?

"Mmmm - to the extent that sometimes people are seen not to change... you know, somebody who makes music may only really hear their *own* music for a long time; whereas somebody who buys music has the opportunity to hear lots of different things. New things can happen to make - whatever, say a certain band - seem a bit outdated, and when that band comes out with a new record it can sound a bit out of time or a bit... kind of, oh god, they're starting to sound old-fashioned; but it doesn't make it *bad,* or take anything away, because placed in the context of time it makes more sense. You see it so often with so many people, where ten years after they release certain records they're seen as very valid, but at the time they were pretty much ignored. *Isn't Anything* only got one really good review. When "You Made Me Realise" first came out all the reviews were condescending."

Can you see something funny in being press darlings now, "the most inflential indie band in the country" and so forth?

"I don't relate to it because we don't sell that many records compared to some of the other bands."

So it's a maufactured thing; what people are saying rather than what's actually happening?

"Yeah. Maybe. I don't know. I know Ride sell more records than we do. House Of Love sell more records than we do, know what I mean? Ride and House Of Love are bigger than we are, more important, more relevant, et cetera, et cetera. The people who liked us on *Melody Maker* aren't there any more. The people who *really* run *Melody Maker* never did like us, anyway. I've never had any illusions about things like that. It's always a couple of people who start the ball rolling and everyone else basically just wants to be seen to be into the right stuff. There's a huge gap between what the music press writes about and what actually goes on."

→next page→

ROCK'N'ROLL

the p

Karren Ablaze! went there

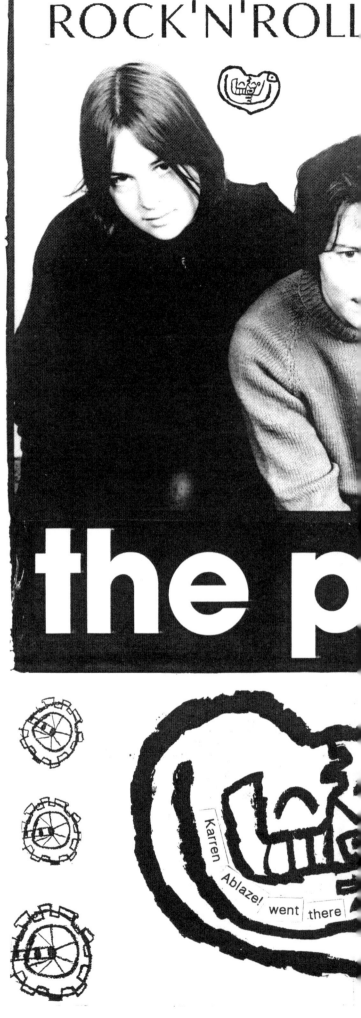

Every now and then a big high hits. There have been several during the time it's taken to compile this luvverly 9th thing; the Mabuses' LP, the Nirvana single, Shudder To Think's tour, but the one that affected me most suddenly, deepest, flooding the euphoria right up to my toes, was the show the Pastels performed with Jad Fair in Leeds in November. In the Duchess Of York I was unexpectedly captivated by the sounds emanating from the figure of Jad, wide-eyed, teasing his beautiful painted guitar, drawing us out. Forcing, in fact, the miserable cynics of West Yorkshire to go with him on his journey into the sky. He won us over completely, and then brought onstage a smooth, zoomy, rocky bunch of Pastels to back him. What a live LP that night would have made. "We've got friends that can do things" is how they announce hordes of autoharp and violin players onto the stage. Professionally unprofessional, these eternal early teenagers, they did a song called "Lucky Star" which had such sunshot rain, so much high sugargasm bursting joy, that the very boundaries of my soul were rended - the Pastels Aggi, Stephen and Katrina, and at this event Charlie and David too) reached right through and *touched* me. Stephen had violet eyes, they shone unreasonably as he sang, but afterwards I discovered they were something dead usual like brown. So, as you can imagine, I needed to ask someone some serious questions.

O Pastels Of Utter Wonder. Tell me about pop music.

"Pop music isn't the most important thing in the world," pronounces ace bassist Aggi. "People are. But pop music's a very important part of our lives. Why else would we spend so much time trying to connect up with what might be the ultimate sound or a perfect melody? We like playing and we like listening." I sat with Aggi and Stephen, two longstanding members of this glowing youngpeople band from Scotland. They are a band that's never been frightened into bowing to convention, a band to whom waywardness is a way of life. We were sheltering from Saturday afternoon in a nasty commercial café in Leeds, right next to the record shop. I wanted to know why art seems so much more important than all that other stuff, that "real life" thing we hear so much about. So? Stephen -

"When the government passes a piece of legislation that affects everybody, that's a lot more important. Less than one in a thousand people have even *heard* of Sonic Youth. But someone somewhere will love that band or any other favourite band, " he continues, "And when they hear their favourite band play it might affect them like nothing else in their life. And when you really love music and you hear it, sometimes it's just completely overwhelming - an insane, wild, intense assault on your senses. To compare that feeling with politics is impossible, but I'd say that politics is a lot drier. Or maybe the passion's just gone out of it."

Pastels maintain the positive aspects of being a child, the wonder, the honesty, the purity; their behaviour is a subtle form of rejection of the mainstream, adult ways of being. They explained what "Fire Bell Ringing" is about: how on the train, mother draws a happy domestic scene for her child. He takes the pencil and scrawls big all over it: "Mummy mummy, the kitchen's on fire!" When she draws in the fireman to save the scene, he scribbles on him also - "Mummy, the fireman's on fire too!".

Their dress, too, sets them apart. They say 'fuck you' to the label merchants with clothes fled from by forced fash consumption merchants. "Our clothes could be construed as ugly or drab," says Stephen, "But in fact they're kind of ironic and a bit flash."

I'm totally impressed with the Pastels. I used to like them, four or five years ago, but was subsequently discouraged by a bad performance which seemed to consolidate the "twee" (i.e. crap) label they'd been assumed to live under.

Upon rediscovering them, I rerealised how *Up For A Bit...* is an album of genius proportions. The first track, "Ride", is so much

HEAVEN WITH

astels

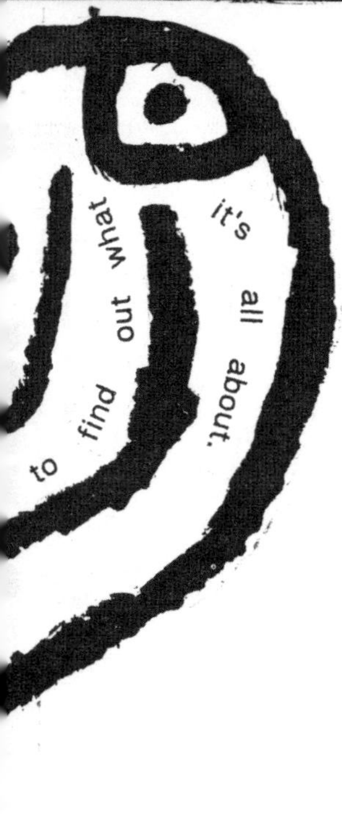

more useful than a busload of Oxfordshire bands. Stephen's angst-ridden story (*"I was born in the middle of nowhere and since thatday I've been suffocating"*) is conveyed with such deadpan determination, over those wondrous strings - it just scrunches me up.

One Pastelism that stayed with me through my prodigal wanderings was "Zooom", the last track on *Sittin' Pretty,* the one with the heaven-aimed autoharp - on seeing that Katrina posessed such a thing, I was adamant that they should play the song; but due to some severe line up alterations they were unable to do so.

In the cafe, I asked them how they had lost Martin, Bernice and Brian.

"We asked Martin and Bernice to leave," Stephen explains sadly. "I thought it was the right thing to do, but it was also the hardest thing I've done in the history of the group. We were going to leave, just take the name and let them have the band. It wasn't good because they weren't as enthusiastic as they had been. Our enthusiasm for the Pastels is boundless, we're trying to keep alive that feeling you have the first time you plug in an electric guitar and go 'wow!'"

So c'mon Aggi and Stephen, how does it feel to be the grandparents of so much twee bullshit?

They both sigh. "Ah," replies Stephen, tiredly,"we're not old enough to be *anyone's* grandparents. Most of those people that we're supposed to have influenced are the same age as us but they started later."

He's pretending to forget the fact that in our tiny universe of music, generations may pass in months, and the term incestuousness refers to *metaphorical* blood. He's refusing to play my game; probably he's been asked such questions too many times before for it to be in any way interesting.

But what would anyone do without their influences? The way people like the Pastels made, for example, the Sarah bands possible, "paranoid virgins" though they may be, was like how punk rock made us all possible; how Jonathan Richman made them, and Jad, possible. And there's *always* gonna be the unintended outcomes, the side effects; like those boys at Pastels gigs who dress like desperate entrants in a Paddington Bear lookalike competition.

I was worried about the fact that my tape recorder had failed completely and that I might not recall all the things they told me. That's when they told me about their Heavy Lawyers, who sue negligent journalists.

"That's what every band needs," they explained. "First you get the amps, then you get the Heavy Lawyers. Tho' we haven't actually met our Heavy Lawyers yet."

But, what happens, I asked these Pastels, when civilization comes to an end and all the records melt and all the CDs melt?

"Oh, I don't know..."

We each gaze into our own personal distance.

"It'll be like Noah's Ark," says Stephen. "All the good artists will be rescued from the molten vinyl and go on a big boat..."

Aggi: "A really good recording studio."

And, I guess, all the music journalists will flounder in the mire.

How long has it been since I last felt like this, rushing, racing, feeling the dimensions around me, my relationship to the road, to vehicles, the buildings' to the sky (that big blue tall thing)?

No other band is quite like the Pastels. I want to get all the Pastels records and play them to my (kickin' an' screamin') friends. I want to go out and see them tonight, and drink the dew of excitement. I want to rock out tonight like there's nothing else.

to find out what it's all about.

Lord, I don't fancy yours much! It's...

Ale-free chat?

LEATHERFACE

Words by Lucy Nation, grisly pics by Tony Woolgar

Since the release of their irresistable *Mush* LP, Sunderland's Leatherface have been picking up plaudits from all quarters of the Bubble Of Babble. Indeed, *Melody Maker* went so far as to dress singer/songwriter/guitarist Frankie N.W. Stubbs up in a Santa Claus suit for their Christmas issue. *Smash Hits* must surely be around the corner; and no wonder, because the Leatherface pop steamroller at its best demonstrates a truly exhilarating and affecting combination of classic melodies, heartfelt lyrics and sheer horsepower presumed extinct by most since the demise of Hüsker Dü.

That comparison will piss them off because, along with hardcore forefathers Motörhead, it's the one they always get, and neither is particularly accurate (Frankie: "I've got *Candy Apple Grey* and *No Sleep 'Til Hammersmith* and that's it."). Leatherface songs are more intricate and tuneful than anything in the Motörhead canon, yet they don't have the spacey, transparent sound of the Hüskers' best work; where the shimmering, zinging blanket of fuzzy guitar always seemed to be miraculously suspended some distance *above* the fluid bass and (completely inconsequential) drums. On *Mush* the two guitars and bass mesh into a taut and purposeful machine equally reminiscent of melodic punk bands such as the Sex Pistols, Stiff Little Fingers, even Buzzcocks circa *Another Music In A Different Kitchen.* As for Mega City 4 etc, we're talking different leagues here. If you wanted third-rate you wouldn't be reading *Ablaze!,* after all, you'd be off buying Carter and Kingmaker records and immersing yourself in the can't-spell-won't-spell world of *NME.*

The heart and brain of Leatherface is Frankie, a man once described as "an excellent acerbic lyricist with the unmistakeable air of the autodidact", yet one who just can't decide what his Favourite Song Ever might be; a question which presents no dilemma for guitarist Dickie Hammond (SLF's "Alternative Ulster" and "God Save The Queen"), drummer Andy Laing ("New Rose" by The Damned and, er, "Ne Ne Na Na Na Na Nu Nu" by Bad Manners) and bass player Andy, then a veteran of two days' standing, who restores their arthouse credibility somewhat by opting for Killing Joke's excellent "Requiem".

Why did the old bassist (Steven "The Eagle" Charlton) leave, then?

"Cos he had ginger hair, like," deadpans Frankie, "he had ginger hair and his girlfriend said he couldn't go away any more, so he had to leave. His girlfriend actually came and told us, you know, that she was the stronger person of the two of them."

He's not going to be happy about that, is he, having to stay at home in Sunderland instead of travelling the world in a band?

"He'll not be happy sitting in a house with her. Nagging. And she'll soon get sick of him, and all."

Reflective pause.

"As long as he knows what he wants."

How come you got a feature in *Kerrang!*? I ask, trying unsuccessfully to change the subject.

"You didn't fucking *see* the pictures, did you?" hoots Dickie.

A band that deserves to be in colour, definitely.

"There was *too much* colour on those photos. We look as though we've been to fucking Barbados for a couple of weeks!"

"Eagle's spots didn't half look good though," muses Frankie. "In black and white they didn't show up very much, but in colour, like, they were really fucking colourful. He used to pick them until they bled, and all. I didn't like that, in the back of the van."

In addition to the previously-eulogised quality of the writing and arrangements on *Mush,* the (self-)production and ye olde musicianship are also highly accomplished. Whipping out my Asking For A Punch Hat (backwards baseball cap, naturally) I ask them; are you all quite old then?

"Fucking ancient. Really old."

"None of us are in our thirties, put it that way."

Dickie and Andrew were in a Sunderland punk/HC band called HDQ. Andy the new bass player was actually in top Mike Yarwood combo Snuff, but we won't hold that against him (Leatherface's naff covers – with the exception of "Message In A Bottle", the ghastly original of which could only have been improved – represent the band at the absolute nadir of their capabilities).

"The engineer mixed *Mush* and it sounded fucking rubbish. We had to spend £300 of our own money remixing it."

This leads to the inevitable question about the (let's be clear) utterly flaccid and shite bands with whom certain equally flaccid and shite journalists on the inkies have predictably lumped the 'Face. Frankie is unerringly diplomatic, yet still somehow manages to answer the question correctly:

"I know Mega City 4 as people, y'know, I like them - I can't, like, say they're shite, you know what I mean, they're nice people, fine chaps. I haven't got an objective view. They could be complete and utter toss and **I'd still** go and see them. They're making a living."

What objects do you always carry with you?

"My lighter," gravel-toned Frankie, with Marlboro.

"Drum key"

"My diary, but I haven't got it," offers Dickie, "this is the first time I haven't had it in years. Well, not in years, cos it's only this year's, like." (*fanzine and inky writers note cunning deployment of apostrophes here - Ed*)

Do you write in your diary every day?

"No, it's not a *diary*, it's not a diary in that respect. That's student clobber, that, innit, really... writing stuff you've been doing every day, that's a bit steep. A bit pretentious. No, I just write dates of what's going on. It's more like an organiser, really."

What do the N and W stand for?

"Norman Warsaw."

Always ask a band about their pets. You never know what you might learn. Andrew the drummer has "a pit bull whippet thing" called Zoltan (*"GO, ZOLTAN, YOU HAVE OFFENDED ME!"*) and a pure Staffordshire called Tina. Frankie, on the other hand, who enjoys the company of "two or three cats", doesn't like dogs much. At all.

"Basically a rubbish animal, the dog. Come round sniffing your genital area the whole time. Apparently, dogs have only got a memory for eleven faces. Useless. You piss off for a few weeks, it's met a few people, it's forgotten you. You've got to take them for walks. "Come on, Fido." It's only got eleven faces in its fucking thick skull. Now, cats don't remember *anyone*. Cats are fucking brilliant. I had this cat who lived in the same house all his life. When I moved in there, he just moved in with me. When I moved over the road, I took him over with me, and he just moved back. He lives in that house, that's his house. It's going to be a great interview, this, isn't it?"

Ace leather, F!

→ MY BLOODY VALENTINE →

Do you miss anything about Ireland?

"It's got its good points and its bad points. Basically, if I wanted to be there I'd be there, and I'm not, so..."

Would it be possible to run My Bloody Valentine from there?

"Oh yeah. Dublin is a city that loves rock and roll bands, everybody's in a band there."

There's not much, er, *new music*, if I can call MBV that for a second, though, is there? It's all very trad.

"Yeah, but one of the most influential bands to me were the Virgin Prunes, and they never actually made it to England in their best form. By the time they got to England they were caught up in the sort of Batcave/gothy thing, you know really unfortunate."

They never really sounded like that, though, just looked the part.

"They began to, once they got into the dance thing, having the big thumping beats, from "Baby Turns Blue", all that period on. They lost something that they had. They were once free, they once could do anything. It's one of the most difficult things for bands to have that freedom *and* be successful enough to have the freedom, which is a Catch 22 that ruins most bands. Our insistence on a certain amount of freedom has completely damaged any kind of commercial success that we could have had."

INTERVIEW BY LUCY NATION

PURPLE ETERN

WARNING: Non-Leeds people are unlikely to make very much sense of the following article.

Welcome to the enticing and terrible world of Purple Eternal. They're gathered in our front room. What are we going to say to them? In the style of parent reading a progress report, I had but one question for them: why haven't they got anywhere since their last *Ablaze!* interview, way back in 1988? Although, of course, I get sidetracked, while everyone talks at once, shouting out reminders of subjects forbidden during the interview, swapping in-jokes with *Ablaze!* staff, bickering over which cup of tea belongs to whom.

I love the Purple Eternal. In fact, I lost the need for pop star pin ups the day these boys first came round to my house. Allow me to introduce them to you. Vocalist Ross is (arguably, as everything with them always is) the band leader. He's weird, both gross and delicate, torn between his immediate desires and his ambition. Sometimes his voice seems to verge on exasperation as he tries to guide this wayward group of friends to follow his latest scheme. He seems to spend most of his time producing succinct analyses of the history and the direction of his band. Drummer Karl is his ever present sidekick, energetic and pretty, and bursting with sharp, witty retorts to Ross's painstaking pronouncements. These two form the nucleus of the band, sufficiently so that the pair are often referred to as 'The Purple Eternal' without any apparent inconsistency. Mark, the guitarist, joins the fray wholeheartedly, along with the lost-and-found born again raver and guitarist Darren, and the ever unpredictable, contradictory, charming and beautiful Sven. Oh yeah, Sven plays the bass.

You'll hear them, in full flow, urging us to believe that things are "basically" this, and "basically" that. But the Purple Eternal are implicated in a whole heap of basicallies, a never ending nest of them, which they are doomed to rummage through, holding up each one as if it holds the answers to everything, disgruntled to see the others doing the same with different shaped truths. You should hear them rehearse, if your head could bear the screams. *You should see where they live...*

Darren, Ross, Karl, Mark, Sven: Young men seek gay music journalists

PURPLE ETERNAL

Tell me the story about the prodigal Eternal, Darren, coming back.
Ross seemed to have prepared his reply in advance: "In the first *Ablaze!* interv
it said he was the token musician, and in the meantime the rest of us
become musos, so we asked Darren back so we'd have a token non-musician.
first time he turned up to a new rehearsal he only had four strings on his g
and moaned that we asked him to put two more on."

You know, I observe, *everyone in this room except for me has got long hair*
a proper Tony Woolgar scene.
"So what's your definition of the verb 'to woolgar'?" Gavin wants to know.
Ross thinks it means 'to hang around, to lig'. Sven thinks it means 'to stare
the bass amp, not look at you and talk the other way.'

Ross is ready to begin answering our central question. "I think the reason
haven't got anywhere is that we had a lot of potential but we didn't actually
any songs. It's taken us about 4 years to write some."
"We have this incredible knack of jumping *off* the bandwagon just at the w
moment," notes Karl.

A L

Ross: "We used to sound like Loop/Spacemen 3 before the Telescopes, then we thought it was really naff to do that and stopped, at which point those bands became much more trendy than they had been before, then we started sounding like Hawkwind."
Karl: "Purple Eternal are like Rip Van Winkle, we went to sleep in Hyde Park one day when we were really stoned and woke up four years later..."

They decide to ask themselves about their influences (professionals, these lads).
Ross: "There's only two bands that everybody in the Purple Eternal likes and that's the Butthole Surfers and Public Enemy. Recently we've got more influenced by Can and less influenced by Pussy Galore. We only said we were influenced by Pussy Galore in the first place because..."
Karl: "We thought it was trendy and we could jump on the bandwagon!"
Ross: "No, because we thought it was really good that they were too loud and couldn't play as well."
Mark: "Purple Eternal's major influence is Micheal Walsh."
Karl: "We idolise him."
We can exclusively reveal that this is among other things...

You've got a record out? we ask them, refering to the shiny single on our very own Stuffed Cat UK label.
"Oh yeah!" they exclaim. "We've got a record."
Tell us about your record.
Ross: "Well we've got two tracks on it, one of them is called 'Arthur Lee's Duvet', and the other is called 'We Worship The Worm'. 'Arthur Lee's Duvet' is about kicking my room in."
Really?
"Yes. The landlord's still after us. It's literally about lying on my duvet, listening to Love."
Which house?
"17 Ebberston Terrace."
You had holes in your wall at 6 Ebberston Terrace too.
"But I didn't do that, Karl did that. And Sven."
Sven: "I think we were just completely claustrophobic."
It's a bit sad really, it's not the same as trashing hotels is it?
Ross: "Kicking hotels in is rock'n'roll wank, though."
"Whereas kicking our house in was great," quips Sven.

So where's the single gonna take you?
"Um, oh.. b.. err..." (They're not sure.)
Sven: "I think our ambition for the past four years has been to break into Bradford, and we still haven't done it yet..."

"What about the single?" asks Ross.
Karl - "What about it?"
"Well, I think we should answer some questions about the single."
"Well go on then."
Are you on the B side as well? asks Gavin, obligingly.
"No."
No? It's a good job we checked then!
Ross: "The single is a split single with Spectral Alice."
Darren: "This is completely obvious anyway, cos if you look at it..."
Ross (shouting with frustration by this stage): "But you can't look at the single if you're reading the interview!"

The relatively smooth running of this rock industry chit-chat is shattered by a suggestion that the Purple Eternal have gone straight edge. "We're good clean-living kids nowadays," they claim.

"But... Why don't we talk about the songs?" asks Ross, persevering in his attempt to lead his wayward flock from the subject of *substances.*
Darren: "Well, the first one's about kicking your room in...and the second one is about drugs..."
About how few drugs you take?
"About how they screw you up and everyone should get into looking after their bodies," explains Karl.
So how many of the Purple Eternal take drugs at the moment?
Mark: "Six."
Karl: "There are only five of us, Mark."

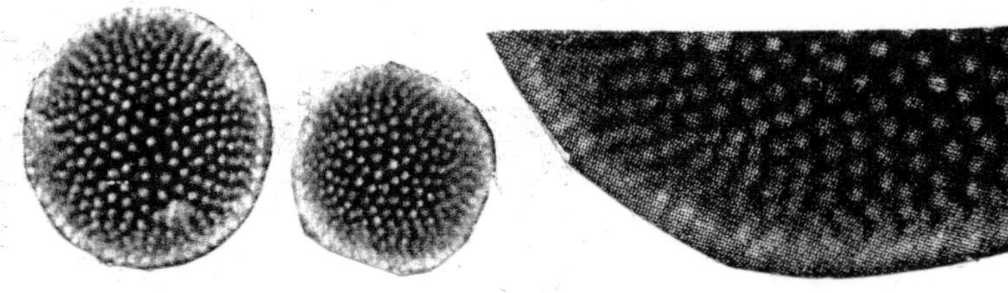

Your record's produced by Richard Formby (of Spacemen 3 fame)*?*
"Yeah, it's the best production we've ever had."
Karl: "We've been spending a lot of time rehearsing and going back to the proverbial drawing board, trying to get somewhere, failing, going back and rehearsing again..."
Sven: "And ending up sounding like Nirvana."
Ross: "OK, we're selling out."
Sven: "How can we sell out when we've never had any principles?"

They're bemoaning the lack of official music press agents in The North. As Darren poignantly puts it, "Who've we got reviewing gigs in Leeds? DAVE SIMPSON. What a wanker."
What bands are there in Leeds worth reviewing anyway? I ask, diabolical-accomplice-like.
"Zero Zero."
Ah yes, Zero Zero. They do about one gig a year, packing the dancefloor by the force of their Godflesh-aided-by-turntables-and - all-sortsa-gadgetry noise.
Mark has a hot tip too: "There's a really good band from New York, called Get Starsky."
New York?
"New York, Leeds Six."
"They have nothing at all to do with Purple Eternal and Spectral Alice," we are assured. "Honest."

"We're really hoping that some teenagers will commit suicide to our record."
Why dont you get some of your friends to help out?
"Or that someone will have a fit and die in front of the stage."
"Doesn't Micheal Walsh always stand at the front?"
"Yeah, ha ha ha!"
"He needs a bit of abuse to keep his life in order."
"We named one of our songs after him at our last gig - this is called 'Micheal Walsh, Phone Home'!"
He's supposed to be writing for Ablaze! *y'know.*
Ross "I keep hearing that he's gonna write for *Ablaze!*, and then he says 'No no I'm not, I'm going to start my own magazine'."
"He's worried he'll corrupt his words if he actually puts them down on paper."
That was the walshism definition I was looking for! Gav is pleased.
Sven: "Funny how walshism almost rhymes with bullshit..."
Ross: "Are we talking about Leeds or are we talking about the Purple Eternal?"

Take it away, Ross
"Well, obviously some of the songs are about drugs...
Hahahaha.
"They're the older ones, we're writing mature sensible songs now. 'We Worship The Worm' is a sort of nursery rhyme, in praise of the worm..."
Hahahahahahaha.

Pretty good. Now answer this one in less than 10,000 words: Why haven't you got anywhere even though you've been working, erm, fairly hard all these years?
Sven: "Because we haven't been working very hard, cos we're basically lethargic."
Ross protests: "I don't think we should talk about this cos people might not want to have anything to do with us."
The very foundations of my house creak with laughter.
Karl: "People won't want to buy our records if they think we're losers, I mean I know we are, but..."
Ross: "Basically we were really exciting about four years ago, then we all got off on being hippies and taking too many..."
Darren: "They kicked me out of the band and it all went downhill from there."
Ross: "We've got the original line up back and we're ready to kick ass and rock and roll again."
Karl: "And remember, kids - drugs are for losers."

Since writing this article we're received the news that Mark has left the band, and that they're going to continue as a four piece. The single will probably be distributed by APT, but you can buy mail order copies from the Ablaze! address, for £2.50 inc. P&P. Special Offer - *buy both* Stuffed Cat UK *releases:* Orange Sunshine's "Wife Swapping Party" *(CAT 1) & this one (CAT 2) for £4.50, including delivery.*

CRAIG WEDREN sings, STUART HILL plays bass, CHRIS MATTHEWS plays guitar, MIKE RUSSELL plays drums. KARREN ABLAZE! writes her heart out, about SHUDDER TO THINK.

Despite my ordinary human evils I know that I'm basically a good person. I wish other people and other beings well, and the words I write are part of my gift to the world. The next sentence is going to be a significant one for things with ears. *Hear* Shudder To Think. Not that I'm arrogant enough to believe that their appeal is universal; though if you're interested in the sort of bands we feature, or if you've a head for exciting music generally, I suspect you'd be able to handle them.

"I'll burn your day down..."

Craig is a man with fire in his soul, you catch it when he sings. Craig's voice is a strong, pure and beautiful, ranging from high up to way down, maintained by an admirable inward steadiness. Shudder To Think are not a hardcore band, so, *please* don't be scared of them. Neither are they some wimp-out excuse for a tea party. Don't let any of your preconceptions get in the way this time. Hear them.

Craig gives us access to his dreams. By defying the rules we're all usually bound by, those unspoken ones we all obey in order to protect ourselves from the menace of insanity, he cuts a path to childhood. You know that lovely glimmer of fascination that used to surround everyday events and objects when you were a small, small person? So close to the magical feelings of dreams, where you're in a world quite new and unpredictable, you don't know how it works... And anything might happen.

"'Regina' I shouted. That's when it came clear. The fire truck was black. It kept circling my house. Down the street. Through my backyard fence. (Snake in the bushes). Then through the fence again... Her head is engulfed in blue (color). In the white (her collar). On fire. On fire. My wife is on fire. The piano burnt down. The train caroused around my house. "Ride that sexy horse" she howled..."

WIPE ME OUT. I love their records. Their records are perfect. When they play live I'm disappointed by the sound, I'm disappointed by the people there who have to dance with their elbows (why hurt each other? what's your problem?) and people blowing bad smoke into the small amount of air we share. Live they give insight, they exude love, but the records are *pure pleasure.*

A personal guide:

There's the *Medusa Seven* single, on the British label Hoss 45. I bought it last time they played Leeds, when I didn't even watch them. I took home and marvelled at the singer's weird voice, and left it dormant with the others like it was just some freak of nature, a band with only one interesting feature. The A side track, "Vacation Brain", turned out to rock entirely, so we then assumed they were a band with one song. Although still presumed guilty, their *Ten Spot* and *Funeral At The Movies* LPs were introduced to the living room turntable, where they eventually became an essential part of each good day.

Their debut LP came out on Sammich in the US, I don't think it's available here, and it's got some really good bits, and one dire bit where they cover 'Imagine'. *Curses, Spells, Voodoo, Mooses* appears to be its title, and listening to it makes me feel like I'm soaring through the sky really fast looking down at glorious landscapes. It's very rocky, and Craig's voice isn't doing much of what it's capable of, and he screams a lot, so it's not very sophisticated at all. OK, it sounds like Slade, but it's ace to hear once you've got a taste for STT.

Ten Spot pretty much defies description. A rock LP, for sure, but one with enchanting subtlety... Guitars trickle and weave in and out with heavy metal solos from high realms, and gnash and shudder and crystalize out there. The lyrics are worthy of literary awards, their delivery is exquisite. Really. "About Three Dreams" has lyrics which could have been criminalized for their corniness; that anyone could use them, without an apparent sense of order, and pull it off so awesomely, defeats my powers of explanation. Let's just say STT *fuck* the conventions of rock - backwards - and the conventions of rock seem a lot better for it. In "*Yes*", Craig sings "No, no, no, no, um, yes, yes, yes, yes..." - that's *a/* "*Tony Told Me.*" Tony and Christie. "It was misty like a mystery... Broke and bony like windchimes hung in war time." From tenderness to frustration. Way, way... And the rest of the time Craig's voice is chasing the guitars. Drenching, daring, delicious.

Funeral At The fuckin' *Movies*, the glossiest yet, shows the vocals and guitars, untangled slightly, and adorning even stronger songs. No-one can argue with 'Chocolate', on which Craig irresistably demands: "Am I really second best, to HIM?" It's the instant hit on here, but there's so much more. 'Red House' is beautiful, their version of 'Crosstown Traffic' rocks... but the specialest thing has gotta be the welding together of the so clear, vocally chiming and determined 'I Blew Away' with the surreal dreamscene of 'Ride That Sexy Horse'. Pour it into your hangover, let it hang over your living room, loud.

Record players are benevolent machines sometimes, pushing out sounds that massage yer pleasure centres after a hard day's whatever. I hate to sound like a salesperson, but these two long play wreckids are utter ideal accessories for your own special music machine. And now:

"**Swoon**". The first note of "Love Catastrophe" is an early morning rude tongue in my ear. *Get Your Goat* has arrived. A C60 tape from Victoria recorded only on one side, is packed with the most incredible sounds. I feel stretched when I listen to this, like I can't believe, lying down and my toes are leaping out of my feet; my back arches at the sound of Craig's voice. Floating. His voice is the central thing, with the summer steamrollering (quite a bit of "You Made Me Realise", NB. there are 1,000,000 ways of sounding like MBV and, just now, everyone *does*) ploughing around, digging out the stars, getting burnt hands, then eating them. Then exploding. I mean EXPLODING. Oh where does it come from? Something prepared me for this, a tune forced its way into my muffled three year old brain and I've been craving for its completion ever since. Which is not to say that my current satisfaction is eternal, I'll be begging for more soon enough, but: there aren't words big enough for the rocky road of abstract cries by the bright hills of "White Page", the upward spiraling guitars and yearning yells in "He-Harem", the weird song of sadness and strangeness that is "Rain Covered Cat" (this song made me cry). I hope you are not discouraged by my ego smeared here, by the way I've fused the record with my personality: take the record and leave me here and you've got it.

"Hey sleeping pumpkin hey, hey the fire's blo-own out..." the weird ending song this time is "Funny", in which it sounds like someone burns down the house, with themselves and their friend in it, because they've thought about it. It's painful to hear.

Outrageous band. They've swum against the thin, pathetic (but somehow, for other mortals, compelling) tide of 90'sness to a patch of sea that is unspoilt and otherwise uninhabited - now they float there, at peace with themselves, whirling vocal c(h)ords to shocking effect. The fish are confused; they gaze, wide eyed. Mike has just enough control over gravity to jab at those drums. Stu and Chris *PLAY* their guitars, there's no other word; they don't tease them - that would be cruel. And they don't worship them either, cos, although understandable, it's stupid.

"What about art?" I asked Craig, who is a performance artist in the other half of his life. Although my spirit tells me that the creation of something beautiful is the most valuable thing it's possible for a human being to do, a nagging voice bothers my conscious mind, asking *shouldn't we be doing something more useful?*

"I personally think that to make something beautiful or to make something ugly, just something that contacts yourself first and then other people, is worth as much as any political or social, anything statement orientated, y'know. For me." Craig often interrupts what he's saying like this, at pains to point out that his views are only specific to himself, that his knowledge is limited.

"So the way I involve myself and contribute is through my self, my own experience, not so much through *issues*. Those are the things that move me most..."

The TV buzzing in a different corner of the pub was showing *Top Of The Pops*, and at that moment the interview skidded to a sudden halt as Craig and Stu, Lisa the merchandiser, Gavin and I and most of the bar staff leapt from our seats at the sound of the dumb DJ uttering the phrase "Straight in at number nine... Nirvana!" The gales of laughter, the shrieks of ecstacy as a British cultural institution is mocked by the indifferent new indie metal jesuses, subverted by over-the-head bass playing and a stage invasion, hint that few things affect us as strongly as full flowing, living *art*.

Photo: FG

TEEN SPIRIT

As the hysteria dies down, I ask Craig what would he do if Shudder To Think were *TOTP*.

"I dunno! I'd probably just laugh and laugh and laugh. I've never seen it before but that was really something."

We try to make some cultural comparisons. Gavin notes that their MTV is sub-musical bullshit available all the time, whereas *TOTP* is just a concentrated half hour of it once a week, a form of "ritualistic torture". Lisa tells us that it's similar to *American Bandstand*, "but with lamer bands." We raise our eyebrows at such a notion.

"There's a lot of different kinds of bands on Dischord now," Shudder To Think tell us, doing their bit to dispel a popular misconception about the label's image as a hardcore institution. "It's not like things fit in and things don't fit in."

Do you know Nation Of Ulysses?

"I like them live very much, they're really really good."

They're not serious are they?

"Serious? Ah, you'd have to talk to them." he says, unwilling to blow their non-sleeping, non-tooth-brushing image. "They're very stylish dressers. They generally wear suits. They're a hot band, good-looking guys wearing some proper garb, makin' some noise."

The pizzas arrive and Craig peels the cheese off his. (I could draw an analogy between Craig's vocal talent and the finest cheese: try something you really like, such as mature cheddar with fruit cake, and you'll see what I mean.) "I like cheese but I try not to eat it on tour as it's not so good for my voice." He takes good care of his voice, drinking hot water and lemon juice all night from a flask, even on stage, and eating bits of lemon every now and again.

Lisa points out that today is thanksgiving, and leads them in a garbled and surreal prayer:"God is great, god is good, let us thank him for our fud, Amen."

When the band decided to do this tour Craig told his family, ("They're really cool") and his mom and his grandparents wanted to come along too.

"So we came here together, we spent a couple of days in Bath and then we played in Newport last night."

What do they think of STT?

"I don't think they really have an opinion on it, it's not their type of music. My grandma likes it actually, but she likes everything I do cos she's my grandma. They're totally approving. Their basis for judging is whether people turn up and get into it. They ask me, 'Did the kids like it?'"

WHAT HAPPENED BEFORE

Stu, the unfeasibly sexy bass player, explained how he was originally in a band called Stuge with Chris and Mike and when their singer left to go to school in Scotland, Chris recruited high school pal Craig after seeing him singing in a play.

"We didn't think we were going to actually be a band," Craig remembers. "I'd just been kicked out of a band so I figured I'd be

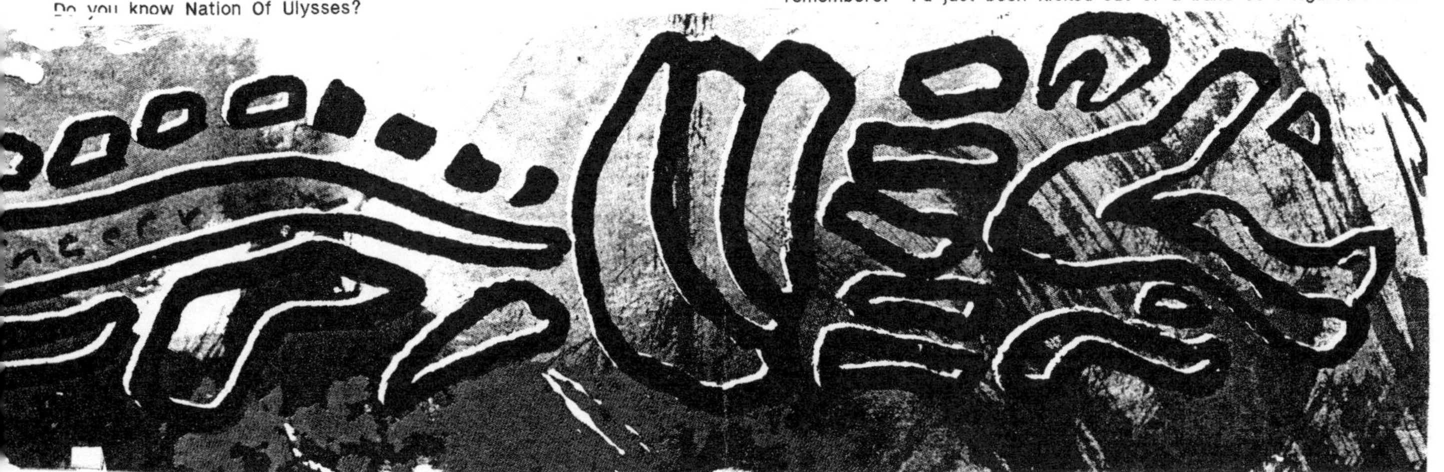

in this hardcore band for a while but I didn't really wanna do hardcore, I was never much of a screamer, then after a couple of practices we thought 'this is really fun, we'll carry on for a while,' and," (his voice ages 60 years), "it's been five years now...!"

"We're massive now." reveals Stu, to an ignorant world.

Isn't Shudder To Think a total pop band?

"Not any more. You should hear *Get Your Goat*. It's slower, harder, more atonal at times, noisier at times, mellower at times, odd tempo, unusual rhythms. It's just more its own thing than pop. *Funeral At The Movies* was pop. We wrote that record and it was songs that we didn't spend a lot of time writing, and they were just catchy songs that we liked. This one's a little different."

Well those ingredients sound like good ones, I tell them, my eyes glazed with sound-greed.

"It makes sense that this new record is a little more individual, we spent a lot of time writing the songs."

"It kind of pushes out the band's talent of songwriting, cos *Ten Spot* was a pretty solid rock-type album, then *Funeral* pushed it out to poppiness and better songwriting, and this new album is gonna push it out way much; further...!" explains Stu.

"It's definitely gonna take people more time to get used to it."

Craig is deliberating. "I kind of feel like this is the first record where we totally... this is gunna sound ridiculous... we've always had elements of other people's sounds or other kinds of music but I think this one is the least like that, it's totally *our* music."

"It's definitely the one we've put the most time into." says Stu.

Do you think that all art, not just music, is about finding your own voice? Gavin, sitting under the folds of his great philosopher hat, asks.

"I think that's kind of what life is about; hopefully I'll become more and more myself the older I get."

But for some people, the struggle to find their voice is more interesting than once they've found it, and for others it's a positive evolution process towards something that makes sense.

"And I think a lot of people just resign themselves to whatever voice is most available around them, what is the least tumultuous voice."

Or the one that gets the most approval.

"Yeah."

Your records are so beautiful, you sound like you love the music so much; like Stu onstage, the way he faces the band and SMILES when he rocks out.

"I'll tell you the reason why - we've been together for five years!" announces Craig, beginning a stream of disclaimers to their brilliance.

Stu: "We're not technical geniuses, by a fucking long shot."

There's a lot of passion in your music.

"I really love playing," Craig tells us. "I don't understand why people play music other than for music's sake. Like people who play music for fame, it's like a vehicle, it could be anything. It just so happens that music and pop stardom in our time and culture is the route to like the *funnest* kind of fame or something. It's totally beyond me how the form can be ignored."

Gavin asks Craig whether he needs to hear lots of new music.

"Yes, it's something I almost need to discipline myself to do. I see so many people who as they get older they stop looking for anything new, I mean most adults, they kind of hit a ceiling at a certain yea in their life and they don't take anything in anymore and I don't eve wanna be like that. It's not to say that I'll understand or be a part everything I hear, because I think the older we get the harder it is t like, connect, like with subcultures and stuff, but I always wanna b available to it. I try to read a lot of record reviews and fin interesting record stores and talk to the people who work there. Among his favourites he lists Frank Sinatra, Slint, Lyle Lovett an Patsy Cline.

He tells us about one of his records: "I have this disc called *Voice From Tuba*, a teeny place I think, between USSR and China, it's all o these voices and things with Jews' harps... It's basically this plac where singing is part of the culture, so they have all these rites i the form of songs - just these routine things they do during the da like washing the cow or something. There's this one thing they do like chanting, it sounds a little bit like Tibetan monks - apparentl they stand at the top of some steps at a certain angle to the wind s the wind like blows across their mouths when they're singing and i makes this completely new instrument, it sounds as if they have som sort of reed instrument lodged in the throat. It's really incredible."

Do you think you might pick up on that and play with a wind machin at the side of the stage?

"No," he smiles, "but I was thinking how amazing it would be to g to Tuba and find somebody to study with and just sing all the time..."

It would be nice to be *permitted* to sing, to have the space to d that.

"When I'm home I feel so self-conscious. As much as I love t sing, as much as I want to sing for the rest of my life, I kind o don't have that much confidence about it, I always judge myself b other people's voices and end up shutting myself up."

The thing about outstanding singers is that they have their ow style, they don't copy anyone.

"That's the thing about outstanding people, they're just them. Havin the courage to be themselves."

So what does the phrase *Get Your Goat* refer to?

"It was like, 'I wanna call it *Get Your Goat*. Craig does his bes durr-brain voice. "I kept saying it for months, and eventually they were like, 'OK'."

"There is a song called 'Goat'," Stu points out, perhaps hoping to present the group as some kind of reasoned entity.

"Yeah," agrees Craig, spoiling a short-lived illusion: "but we jus named a song 'Goat' so it would have something to do with the album title!"

"Don't print that!"

WHAT DOES EVERYTHING MEAN, BASICALLY?

Do you have thing about goats, or goat jokes?

"It's not a thing about anything. Not much of our stuff is things about things," Stu explains, ultra-eloquently.

"But actually," bursts Craig, "the new songs have tons of animal references. I go through phases with lyrics where shit comes up like all the time..."

Which animals?

"Let's see, horse, fish... others!

PHOTO BY CHARLES STECK

"Goats!" offers Stu.

What were previous lyrical phases about then?

"Religious, mythical stuff, death..."

Stu: "Girls."

"Girls!, I guess it doesn't change much. Oh, seasons, the weather... *Ten Spot* was very dreamy..."

Stu summarises their lyrical career to date, Stu-style:

"Then *Funeral* stuff was more stuff about nothing... and the new album is even more stuff about nothing."

The LP titles fuck me up, I tell them. I recognise the sleeves but the titles don't really fit in. I don't understand.

"That's because we are, don't, we haven't, connected them..." explains Craig. *Funeral At The Movies*, we named after a song on the LP. I personally like things that are totally unrelated, I like just throwing shit in, not to confuse people, it leaves more room for my imagination."

Stu seems to ignite: "People get really eaten up that *Funeral At The Movies* is such a pop album and that it has the word 'funeral' in the title."

The phrase still doesn't make any sense

though.

"Oh, that was an actual dream I had," muses Craig, "And the lyrics are about that, I had a dream that I was at the Waverley Cinema on 6th Avenue and Leaguer St. in Manhattan and I was sitting in the rightmost section, kind of in the middle, and I looked back and there was this kid, he looked like Sal Mineo in *Rebel Without A Cause*, and he was wearing a suit and he was flanked by these two very old men on either side of him and they were walking him down the aisle, and I somehow knew that it was his funeral, that he was dead, oh, and he had this cut across his neck and I knew that he must have got his neck slit, and then they like sat him down in the centre section, and I knew that this was, in my dream reality, the ritual of a funeral."

Are films important to you?

"I love films so much, I could sit in the movies all my life. My favourte film is called *Nashville*, it's very long but it's just mindblowing. One of my favourite movies is called *Unheard Music*,(?) a documentary about the band X. If you don't like X, it might be a bit pretentious cos a lot of it, what looks like footage, is actually acted. That's kinda cheesy, and if you know that..."

"I didn't know that!" Stu looks disappointed.

You've spoilt it for him.

"Yeah, dick!"

I asked Craig about films as sources of lyrics, eliciting a mere "I dunno", whereas a mention of dreams produces a river of stuff:

"Over the years, I do a lot of writing, and I've just got used to that kind of stream of consciousness writing. That's mostly what my lyrics are like, even if they're not dreams I had, they have a dream logic; I much prefer it to linear logic."

You prefer it to real life?

"Well, I probably should say yes, I think I do, although I don't like that." He begins on a story and cuts himself short, sounding a bit sad, saying "I don't really want to go into all that... I'm definitely hooked up."

It's nice to allow yourself to experience child-like happiness, when you don't have to be responsible for things.

"That's the thing, no responsibility – to logic, or to be understood, there are so many gorgeous incredible things that come out, reflexiveley – you don't have to force things out, I don't really know what I'm saying but there's so much latent in myself and in everybody that particularly comes out in dreams, and it doesn't take any effort. It's the richest material, you don't have to manipulate it and squeeze it into shape. And that's what I think reality's like, I have to squeeze myself into reality."

Dream things usually need censoring before anyone else can hear them.

"Well, even between your head and speaking and writing it, it changes. My teacher was telling me how dreams don't happen frame by frame, they can just be this big like squoosh of stuff in your head, and just because you can't speak like that, cos you can't go 'zgmndrtlm', you end up taking the important parts and putting it into story form, even though it doesn't make *sense...*"

It's not temporal.

"Yeah. Another thing I like is the fact that in dreams, I think I've said this in interviews a lot, I could be sitting like right here like right now, and there could be something SO evil about the chair that you're sitting on for no reason at all and it could be like the most awful thing, and then suddenly I'll just be in love, I'll be sitting here and maybe I'll be saying the same thing but I'm TOTALLY in love. Y'know and there's just so much under the surface and it just bubbles..."

It's a pity that you can't be physically real in the dream.

"I try that. There are people who say you can train yourself to control yourself in dreams. And I've tried that, but it always ends up that I'm in a dream and I'm like (in tones of desperate effort) 'I-WANT-TO-PICK-UP-MY-ARM'!! Someone told me that if you focus on an object, you can kind of go into it, and somehow once you get to a certain focus control, you can start controlling your actions in the dream."

The beer arrives.

"Beer is another thing that influences me. Beer reality. Are they warm?"

"They're English-cold," Mike, bringer of beer, tells him.

That's not as cold as American-cold?

"No."

Is that what you think of this country, that it's substandard?

"Certain things are better about this country..."

"There are better British accents here!!"

Craig: "It stems from anti-Americanism, there's a lot of things to dislike about America."

Stu: "Especially when you're from our section of society."

"So when you travel in foreign countries you pick out things like, our stuff's colder, when you go into a store and order ice cold coke, we get ice in our beverages, you just kind of notice..."

"It's like Levis, Hot Rods, and Converse tennis shoes... those are the main things," quips Craig.

What's good about other countries then?

"In Belgium, there are the waffles, and Holland for the bicycles. Definitely Germany has the beer. Hofmeister," he says, examining the cans they've been brought. "They package it so you think you're eating a banana, so you think it's good for you."

"How full is it down there?"

"Packed, it's packed," Mike lies.

"When do the doors open?"

"Now."

In my reality it would be brimming, I tell them. There'd be queues down the street. Craig says that his reality would be like that too.

"They've all watched TOTP, they're inspired," says Gavin comfortingly.

"But they'll say, 'You can't top this,' and they'll stay in."

You should go on stage and play "Smells Like Teen Spirit". With your guitar above your head, I urge.

Craig is uncertain. "I have to say, I like Nirvana, but it's just kind of college rock, it not that earth-shattering..."

"But think back 4 or 5 years..." the drummer begins.

"Oh, if I were like 12?"

To everyone's laughter, he justifies himself. "I always feel like I'm 16, y'see. Cos I don't get to drive that much."

"But say you're 12, just think what hearing that record would be like."

Yeah, for all those scruffy kids with greasy hair, they've finally found their gods. When Nirvana don't shave for their publicity shots, that makes them feel really at home.

"If Nirvana are reading, I like it. I like it a lot..." Craig mutters diplomatically.

Mike: "For a lot of people it's gonna be the first record they hear, so it's gonna be important to them, but within the scene, I don't think it's important, it's just very good. But like Dinosaur Jr, they just wrote one song..."

Craig: "If Dinosaur Jr are reading this, we like the album, we're all for it...!"

"I definitely think our albums have gotten better. I hope so, cos if they haven't we might as well just get on the next flight home."

They have. It's OK. Get the first flight *back* here, please.

"You've explained *Funeral* and you've kind of explained *Get Your Goat*, but you haven't explained *Ten Spot* as a title.

"Oh that's because, when we were on tour, we get 10 dollars PD, per day..."

"Our old roadie, he's very abrupt, he'd go, 'Hey gimme my tenspot!'"

"And we have all these good titles too, but we've always been a very democratic band, and consequently, cos we have varying tastes, we usually end up settling for the totally middle of the road ones."

"We each get lists of our favourite titles and vote on them."

"And Ten Spot won!!?! I found the lists the other day and it was totally embarrasing. I thought, 'Wow, I'm glad it's called Ten Spot.'"

"The stripping child show."

"That was a lyric, man. It was from a dream."

"There was *Plateskipping*. Oh, and *Rapunzel, As In Ponytail*."

"Oh god."

What do you think about animals?

"I think they're cute! I like animals a lot."

Don't you think animals are people?

"No, I think that people are people, and I think that animals... are animals. I think that we're animals, but I don't think that animals are people."

I think that we should extend our definition of people to animals, then we wouldn't be as horrible to them, I tell him.

"I think we should extend the definition of animals to include people."

But that's already done. I think it's best to do it my way round.

"I think we should call everything Buicks. No, it would be good, because everyone would just be stylin'."

Stu objects that everyone would get mixed up if we all addressed each other as 'Hey! Buick!'

Craig elaborates. "You would still be Stu, but you would be Stu of the Buick species."

"But..."

"And my dog", continues Craig, "Would be JR of the Buick species."

"But then, see, that would never work."

"No, I don't think it would work either!"

Cars aren't nice.

"Buicks are *very* nice."

But as a species, they're not good.

"I don't think cars should be extended. I think cars are cars."

Mike told me the reason they were called Shudder To Think. It was really lame. They were trying to come up with a name and one of them said "Oh, I shudder to think..." and so they chose it. I was disappointed, I wanted it to be packed with meaning.

"I told you," Stu perseveres, "Like most of our stuff, it's just like things about things."

"Buicks. Exactly."

I had been looking at Craig's hands and the vast rings he carries on them. What's with all this jewellery?

"I really love huge rings!"

"Huge!"

"Yuge, with a capital Y."

My heart is full. This has been the most wonderful interview. I'm going to turn *Ablaze!* into the Shudder fanzine. Only one more question needs to be asked: are you a non-smoking band?

"I'm a non-smoking man," admits Craig.

"I'm the only one that smokes," croaks Chris, the dreaded guitarist, "And I'm sick."

When it was announced just now that Chris is being replaced by Nathan Larson (trumpet player with Girls Against Boys) for this summer's European tour, we at first assumed that this was why. No we didn't, we read the press release and it explained that he was going to be too busy studying. But he'll be back.

So kids, you know what to do and you know where to go. This has been my testament: I Shuddered To Think, and my senses blazed.

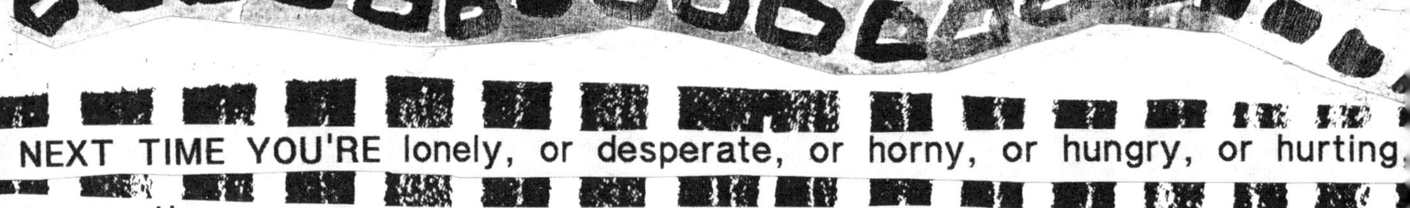

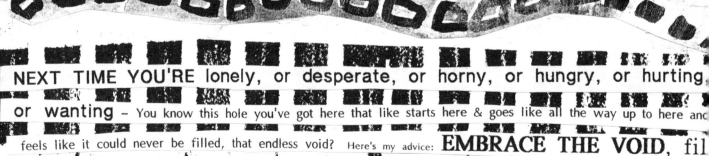

NEXT TIME YOU'RE lonely, or desperate, or horny, or hungry, or hurting, or wanting – You know this hole you've got here that like starts here & goes like all the way up to here and feels like it could never be filled, that endless void? Here's my advice: **EMBRACE THE VOID**, fill up the void: not with sewage, not with garbage, not with food not with drugs, not with useless sex from useless men BUT WITH YOURSELF – with your own POWER, with your own heat, your own energy, with your own light, with your own LOVE. And once you learn to do that you wont need anything useless anymore. Go on, grow up, get FULL – & *NOT* of shit.

(from *Conspiracy Of Women* CD by Lydia Lunch

HELLO!! WOULD YOU LIKE TO BUY A FANZINE?

The highly judgemental approach to fanzines that we employed in the last issue, with divisions between "the best" and "the rest", and the awarding of points based on very arbitary standards, was criticised by some readers. I am aware that such opinionated treatment, while appreciated when applied to everyday scapegoats (such as the major press and successful bands), cannot be tolerated when applied to things considered in some way worthy (usually due to their lack of popularity). However, I see no virtue in encouraging the inept to do what they are clearly bad at, and I find no pleasure in the work of individuals living under self-imposed restrictions. Rather than trying to over-reach their abilities, most fanzine writers set out with the idea that they are capable of little, and go on to fail themselves. I guess nobody told them they could step out of line and do something a little different from everyone else. It could be that I'm just nostalgic for a time when fanzines told you to bog off and had exclamation marks in their titles. Whatever, due to public demand, here are some thoughtful, caring and less openly abusive fanzine reviews.

These A5 fanzines are a delight to behold. Like 7" singles, they're so cute and delicious: Eighth time on the planet: **PLANE TRUTH #8**. It's caught us up agewise already! Here, Andrew continues to play with an intricate necklace of long words. He experiences music, people, books and films, and is compelled to comunicate their inspiring qualities by packing as much meaning into each sentence as he possibly can. Sometimes this style falls over itself, but if you stick with it you get to eat the juicy fruit of understanding. In this issue he interrogates Shudder To Think, Polly Harvey, 70 Gwen Party and Nerve Rack; Jennifer Brogan writes a sexy Mercury Rev piece and Greg of Quality Time contributes a snazzy centre spread Rev poster. Also reviews, excellent fiction and an interview with me (!?). All this for 30p and A5 SAE to: Andrew, 18 Golf View, Preston, PR2 7EH. (K)

KILL YR GIRLFRIEND (OR SHE'LL KILL YOU FIRST) I like the multicoloured paper this is printed on, and the clear text and the way that it's cut into strips over interesting backgrounds. It's produced by a young tyke who calls himself DMCL and who runs the cute Fluff noise pop label. Features uninteresting music criticism and some interviews (form insists that I list the bands featured: Boyracer, Librarian, oh I don't know). At least he shows some awareness of the Sex War. (50p & A5 SAE from 86, Parklands Drive, Loughborough, Leics LE11 2TD.) (K)

FAR OUT AND FISHY #5 – I can't argue with this, oh no I can't. Chris' style is light and lovely, he whisks us around the sights and likes of Langfield Crane, The Go-Betweens, Ant-Bee, Love and Emily with a gut full of energy and a great sense of beauty. His friend Robert produces a fine guide to the works of David Lynch, and Chris even *interviews* The Pastels, The Orb and Another Sunny Day, although his musical descriptions are just as charming, if not more interesting, than what the people in bands say. This issue's dead old, but still a wonderfully informative and life affirming read, for only 50p. Send it, with an A5 SAE, to Chris Fish Bowl, 16 Marsh Lane, Oxford, OX3 0NF. (K)

FURTHER TOO... boasts that it features pop, sex, football and culture. It's appealing at first, with a neat layout, but on further inspection it turns out to be a very bitty arrangement of things. Pop = record and gig reviews, Pitch Shifter, Some Velvet Sidewalk interviews and a weird trailing off Daisy Chainsaw article, sex =, well I can't find it in here, but I'm sure some of this is sexy for some people, football = an interview with a Russian football supporter, and culture = book and fanzine reviews and weird stuff about mailart and the Pope being the devil. This fanzine *could* be really good. (50p & A5 SAE from 40 Darwin Court, Barlow St, London SE17 1HR.) (K)

OPEN YOUR EYES #1. I like this a lot, it has a lively and innocent charm and features some really cool bands like Pavement and Thinking Fellers Union Local 282 (earning it 3000 points on our fab-o-meter!), plus Beatnik Filmstars and Boyracer and The Pooh Sticks and loads more. It reminds me of the first *Ablaze!*, maybe just cos of the yellow cover, but I say it has potential, which is always a great thing to conceal up your sleeve. 30p and A5 SAE to Huw Davey, 4 Langdale Close, Wetherby, W. Yorks LS22 4YE. (K)

GARBLES #2. This brilliantly named thing has vibrant, energetic pictures and cartoons, weird newspaper cuttings, a picture of an extraordinarily pierced penis, zine and gig reviews and an interview with All You Can Eat, and weird record reviews – this girl is a dodgy yankophile so likes lots of dodgy HC stuff, but get this – she *even* likes Poopshovel. Weird. Get hold of a copy anyway, its free if you send her a zine or a tape or something nice: Ros, 5 New House Close, Canterbury, Kent CT4 7HQ. (K)

LESS THAN BRAINLESS #1. Guaranteed to induce strained eyes and aching back muscles if you're interested in any of the bands featured (Who? Oh – Boo Radleys, Citizen Fish, 5.30, Fudge Tunnel and loads more) due to the poor quality of the copying and the size of the print, but worth the trouble if you can tolerate the rather unappealing layout and the 'it's-on-the-tape-it-must-be-in-the-article' approach to writng. (40p and A5 SAE from 26 Summerdown Road, Eastbourne, E.Sussex BN20 8DR.) (G)

NOSEBLEED #5 and **SPIDER MITES**. Nosebleed! interviews Sonic Youth, Chumbawamba and NoMeansNo. In spite of the obvious limitations of living in a country most bands don't seem to know exists, the whole thing is enthusiastic and worth reading, especially for the Mr. Nobody cartoon strip and the slightly silly 'Do You Know Your Hardcore?' quiz. And no, I don't, before you ask.

Spider Mites is one single cartoon strip about (violent, militaristic, men-only) human liberation movements set up some time in the future to oppose the increasing power of capitalism. Unfortunately, the bits of it which are actually penetrable are extremely tedious. (30p and 50p plus A5 SAEs from 37 Chalfont Road, Malahide, Co. Dublin, Ireland.) (GB)

ABUSE #2. These people are geniuses; every interview ends up having more to do with Carter USM than the bands interviewed, so I'm not going to even bother telling you who they are. And while we're on the subject, 'What's your favourite venue?' is a crap question, although I suppose anybody who hates Kingmaker can't be all bad. (A4, £1 inc p&p from Steven Siddle, 17 Muskham St, Meadows, Nottingham NG2 2HB.) (G)

BAGS OF STICKS AND CANDY STICKS #1. Not much to recommend in spite of the editor's fine name; interviews with Len Liggins and Ted Chippington as well as a couple of reviews. Not much else, and I suspect the whole lot would have fitted on a couple of pieces of A4. (60p and A5 SAE from Gavin, 210 Borough Road, Middlesborough, Cleveland TS1 2EQ.) (G)

UGLY #1. I hate slagging off first issues but somebody has to do it. Probably. Apart from a good cartoon strip (Trashed), which takes up two sides when half a page would have been more appropriate, and interviews with The Levellers and Chumbawamba, there's not much here to justify the entrance fee and no discernible style or wit in the reviews either. (50p and A4 SAE to Flat 4, 11 Oakroyd Terrace, Bradford, BD5 7AE.) (G)

UMPH! #1. You need this like you need leprosy; compiled by some saddo who thinks women's breasts, farting and Ronnie Corbett's penis are ground-breaking areas for comedy. Worse than you can possibly imagine. (50p and A4 SAE to 16 Glebe Road, West Bridgford, Nottingham, NG2 6DS.) (G)

PROGRESSION. Includes flexi featuring Screaming Custard and Dead Famous People. Interviews with The Popguns, The Family Cat, The Senseless Things and The Charlottes and as well as a muddled piece on Babes In Toyland but at least some effort has been put into this and it takes more than ten minutes to read: especially if like me you despise all of the bands featured. (50p and A4 SAE to Greg Herriet, 73 Clarence Road North, Benfleet, Essex SS7 1HT.) (G)

e.p. #3. Bland. Access to top quality printing and lots of record company freebies to give away seems to have effectively suffocated anything approaching criticism, so you get reviews of everything from Bad Religion to UB40 and guess what, it's all lovely! Even Midge Ure. (A4, £1.50 inc p&p to Vigilante Productions, 6c Park Villas, Brampton Road, Huntingdon, Cambs PE18 6BQ.) (G)

PAGAN PRATTLE #10. Mostly about misled ritual abuse cases but also stuff about fundamentalist attacks on occult shops and rock music, details of pagan groups and publications, and reviews of music, beer and literature. Free for an A5 SAE to Feorag NiBride, Box 333, 52 Call Lane, Leeds LS1 6DT. (K)

INCREDIBLY INEDIBLE #3. The Captain America interview included here is described by the author as a "full blown love-in with three different publications"; listen, mate, as one of those publications present, if that's what qualifies as a love-in in Manchester then I'm glad I don't live there. Less controversial Moose, Teenage Fanclub and American Music Club interviews are also featured. An incredibly frustrating 'zine in that parts are very well written and the whole thing is enthusiastic, but the whole is far less than the sum of the parts. Whatever that means. (50p and A5 SAE to Jackie and Mihcheal, 53 Matthias Court, Silk St, Salford M3 6JE.) (G)

TRASHCAN #2. Readable and mostly entertaining, if somewhat unadventuriously presented: includes interviews with Carter and Neds for those that want them, plus Pram, Gumball, Boo Radleys and American Music Club (Eitzel: "... *ultra-serious now, if I don't have a chin and if my face is in repose, I look very, very sad.*"). Includes a fourteen track cassette of West Midlands combos. (A4, Chris and Ros Ullman, Lilac Cottage, Exhall, Alcester, Warwickshire B49 6EA – no price on it so try £1.50 and extra stampage for the tape.) (L)

OVERALL There Is A Smell Of Fried Onions (no.1, vol.2) is a local listings mag, but it's actually pretty good. From the full colour, extremely lifelike cover photo of the table scene (ash tray, rizla packet and grinning playing card) on in, it's quality stuff: loads of record and demo reviews, a feature on blippy blippy music in Nottingham, an Aldous Huxley article (distinguished contributors here!) and the weirdest editorial piece I've ever seen. It's free in Nottingham but I think foreigners might have to pay a little more, so send 'em 50p and a nice letter and see what happens. P.O. Box 73, West PDO, Nottingham NG7 4DG. (K)

UNHINGED #9. Interviews Faith Over Reason, Gumball and The Dambuilders (whose previous incarnation, The Exactones, had a tune called "Approach The Horse, Sexually", it says here) and includes a pull-out supplement with 592 (it says here) reviews in miniscule type. The guy who does it is clearly a total expert on obscure American rock, but his dry and humourless style begins to drag long before you reach Review No. 592. Design-wise, it looks like a parish magazine, too. Flexi by somebody called AED. (A4, £1.60 from Paul, The Old Schoolhouse, Yatesbury, Nr. Caine, Wilts SN11 8YE.) (L)

RAPTURE #1. The person who does this omitted to print their address on the 'zine... still, if your cooking up essays with titles like "Dance, Noise And the Fridigity Of Post-Valentism" maybe you don't have time for the gritty practicalities. Yes, it's a cerebal one, and while it's hardly *Monitor* there are some good ideas among the unruly verbiage. Includes a defence of Pop Techno (as against the hip stuff), a 70 Gwen Party i/v and some pretty impenetrable ramblings about, er, iconoclasm and the Moment of Pop. If you've got time for the Simon Reynoldses and Chris Bohns of this world, you may as well spend fifteen minutes reading this. (L) (Found it! Try 50p and an A5 SAE to Julian, 35 Buckingham Rd, Brighton BN1 3PQ.) (K)

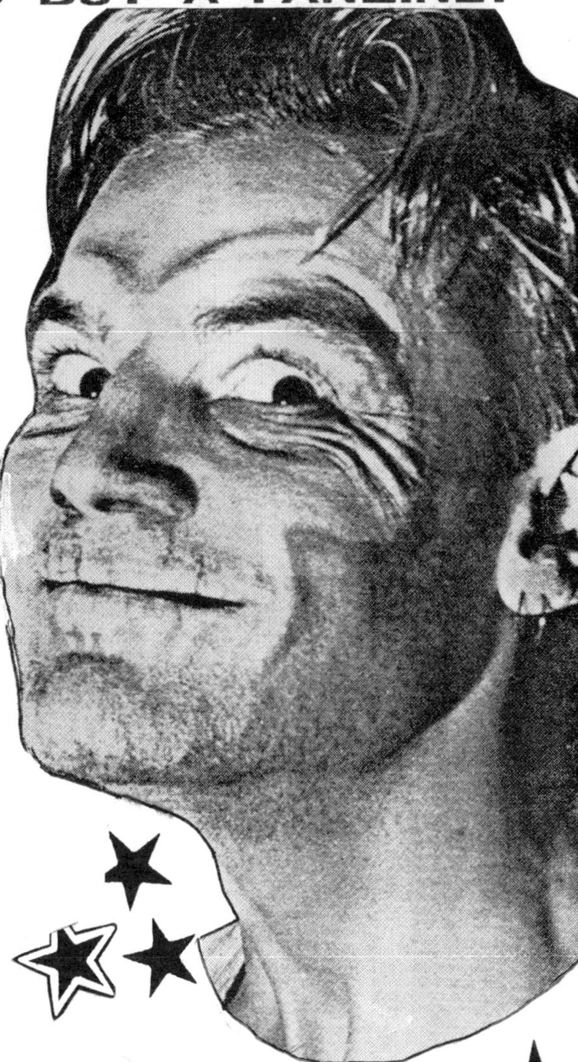

DREGS #5. This zine is *so* good, my heart swelled with joy when it arrived and I took all morning off work to read it. It really means a lot to me to see something done so well. In case you don't know Dregs, it's the publication that loves to ask weird questions, like *why is time changing speed?* and *what about the freak weather terror conditions?* and *what are your sexual fantasies?* and *what is true love?*, which is the question of this issue (I mean, compare it to *why did you sign to a major label?* and *do you think punk's really dead?!!*) And these questions aren't just asked to scraggly haired guitarists and drummers; it's open to everyone – Duncan seems print all the weird letters and contributions he gets. This veritable *Cosmopolitan* of the Anarcho/Indie scene has now gone A4. It's even got a glossy cover and proper typesetting! The line up of bands features is eclectic: Babes In Toyland, Silverfish, Discharge, Daisy Chainsaw, Carter, Scorpio Rising, Ned's Atomic Dustbin, Extreme and The Levellers. There's also a hilarious Mykel Board contribution and a surreal photo love story (in my copy the words "Well alligators eat dogs don't they?" have been painstakingly glued in). You really really must buy this fanzine. It's only £1 including postage, so you don't have to mess around with SAEs, to Duncan, P.O.Box 110, Liverpool L69 8DP. (K)

? ← ZINE OF THE AEON ←

All this SAE business a bit taxing? Two suggestions: either contact a distributor, like those listed below, for a list (gotta send *them* a SAE I'm afraid, or at least a stamp), or just bung on an extra 30p or so to cover the cost of sending the thing to you. It's as easy as, erm, writing a letter.

TOP DISTRIBUTORS – write nice letters to these people:
Anthony, KBHM Inc, 5 Cross Normanton St, Wakefield WF4 5EN. (The Ablaze! zine distribution division, therefore highly recommended.)
Paul, BIJOOPITER, 2 Wentworth Rd, Hertford SG13.
Paul, FISHEYE, 437a High Road Leyton, Leyton, London E10 5EL.
Ian, TONGUE IN CHEEK, 55 Albion St, Otley, W. Yorks LS21 1BZ.

A WARNING TO FANZINE WRITERS: Be wary of approaching distributors not recommended here or by other trusted sources, because unfortunately a lot of these people are in the business of taking your zines and then refusing to pay you for them. So unless you can afford to pay the printer out of your dole money so that these scum can make money out of you, call us to check before using an unknown distributor. Also, let us know which ones have ripped you off, and we'll compile a big list of them for publication in the next issue. Hopefully in this way we can stop them. The weird thing is, they're probably sitting around in smug self praise, thinking that they're *doing something* for the *alternative scene*...

PAVEMENT *Slanted And Enchanted* LP (Big Cat)

In *Ablazeland*, a magic and myth-filled place where it never rains, you only leave the house when you want to and leprechauns bring nectar to the door. I'm a relative newcomer to this piece of genius. It first graced my personal stereo last September, a religious experience on a packed number 50 bus, townward bound, a day of misery awaiting me there. From that day, filing cabinets and the stupid people I work with lost their power to annoy, to create despair; now I just look to the corner where my coat is hanging, containing my stereo and *Slanted And Enchanted*, and smile, safe in the knowledge that insanity is close at hand.

There are so many great *moments* on this LP, anything which on first hearing doesn't sound like one becomes one on the second play... or the fiftieth. I guess I've already played this album more times than any other (take a bow, *Songs To Remember, The Smiths, Surfer Rosa, Reckoning*...) and it's still totally fresh, incredibly *exciting*. Like when he sings, *"I've got a trigger cut / And I can't pull it back / But if I learn how I'll be coming back today"*, the introduction to 'Mr. Y'; the phrase *"soaked it with a dry sponge"* or the remarkable false ending to... well, you wouldn't want me to spoil it for you, would you? Moments when your heart stops and the only reaction left is to swoon, to stagger in disbelief. Micheal has a theory that in these post-modern times to gain any sort of fulfillment from art we must grasp the moments, the tiny parts of things which make the whole worth experiencing, worth consuming. On behalf of the defence I call *Yerself Is Steam* and *Slanted And Enchanted*, inspired from the first note to the very last: records to swagger with and sway to. Power and beauty, effortlessly and totally displayed. On 'Here' they even have the audacity to sing *'I was dressed for success / But success it never comes'* - one thing is for certain, this group will be massive. Synonyms for deiform to the usual address. (GB)

BONGWATER *The Big Sell-Out* LP (Shimmy Disc)

A group whose first LP was called *Breaking No New Ground* and whose new album opens with a track called 'Ye Olde Backlash' may appear to be simply hedging their bets, apologising before they start. Surely not the way to operate when so many other noble folk are forced to fight over the few grains of unpolluted truth they believe to be hiding somewhere (Ritchie: Cut me, do I not bleed? Billy: Real men cry real tears.) and failing, obviously. But at least *trying*. As rumours circulate that Kramer's most inspired collaboration to date has, like B.A.L.L. and Butthole Surfers before, finally fallen apart, *The Big Sell-Out* arrives to comfort us in our moment of need but also tantalise us with thoughts of what could (should) have been.

The creaky production which spoilt some of *The Power Of Pussy* has been replaced by a consistent, lush sound, perfectly stated for Ann to weave joyful and heart-rending tales around. A group with so much knowledge of, and so much respect for, the past, musically and politically; who always sound totally fresh and, in spite of themselves, totally original. A totally modern pop group (and there aren't many of them!).

'What's Big In England Now?' has Ann narrating a tale of the shoot for the new Bongwater video, complaining about having to do camp *again*, then somehow ends up with her finding Lenny Kravitz cross-legged, sitting in the loft. When asked the question of the song title, the idiot obviously replies *'Mushy Peas'*. Self-deprecation and satire, perfectly executed, when most others fall embarrassingly short. (When Ween attempt similar things, the result is at best unappealing musically, at worst a scrambled mess.) 'Schmoozedance' is the Eurythmics if they happenend upon any style or actual songs and is glorious; 'Celebrity Compass', previewed in last year's incredible live shows, is sexy and witty as Ann relates her experiences at a Led Zeppelin party.

'Over The Credit Line', though, is quite possibly Bongwater's greatest moment; the futility of belief, money to live and the greatest Velvet Underground parody (*"There's a railroad credit line / And I was looking for that fine line"*) you'll ever hear. 'Holding Hands' sees Ann adopting a deliberately bad German accent to tell the story of a Nazi theatrical performance and is about the weakest thing on here, but the very next track, 'Flute Of Shame' would inspire Julie Andrews to sing along, rude word and all. By the last track, 'Everybody's Talking', a cover of a Nilsson song with a story of suicides added (listen to Crust and see how this idea can fall flat), I've laughed, cried and *wallowed* in this LP so much the only thing left to do is to play the whole damned thing again. Always inspired, often inspirational, wicked and wise, the last word must be Ann's, from the track 'The Bad Review' on 1990's *Too Much Sleep*. *"But I'm still not sure if it was a pan. The writing was so convoluted and semiotic... why in the hell do I let Kramer do whatever the hell he wants, anyway?"* (GB)

THINKING FELLERS UNION LOCAL 282 *Where Officer Tuba?* MLP (Hemiola)

The song this begins with is fine. Quivelly sounds persistent Dustdevil guitars, and a weirdly pitche vocal. In the second number (this is a pre-release tap and I lost the tracklisting) you can hear a knot c fighting strings; no, they're doing the okey cokey joining together and splitting up and the singer i climbing an upside down guitar staircase inhabited b rats but he doesn't care, he's drunk. And th Dustdevils are there again and he's singing high u again. The third one is the squeaky mice one, the on you should or shouldn't listen to when you're feelin confused and your friend comes into the room an says "What are you doing?" in an alarmed tone upo hearing such a strange sound. Here the singer i slowly wrapping a cable round his neck and recordin his own slow death. Time takes on different speeds a various stages of the process and the squeaking i magnanimous. No, I mean it. But now I'm taking thes pills to calm me down and it *really* does help. I collapses into a waking scene where fifteen strang things happen more or less simultaneously. Then brief silence and a little tune just asking for a T series about hardware shops to adopt it as thei theme. Then there's the one about the bees, which know for a fact is called "Hive", is warm and laz and excellent; it's my favourite here. Afterward things get even more complicated by the minute, an my puzzlement barrier is exceeded. Maybe becaus they're the Thinking Fellers they don't want anybod else to be able to think, so they make really confusir music so that the rest of the world has to sit in corner being fairly quiet for ages after hearing i What do you think? Let me know when you'v listened to your copy. That's it, we'll have competition to find the best answer and the winne can have tea and scones with Justine. Get to i (KA)

(£6 including postage from Hemiola, 35 Barbrough S Leeds LS4 2QY).

PASSING CLOUDS *Protect Your Baby Ears EP* 12"(Bit Back!)

I like things with unpolished, unsure vocals; the remind me of Fluff, and this is one reason for my interest in these Passing Clouds. Another is the expertly jangling minor chords, the boy's attempted (and failed) Gerard Langley impression, and the girl's complimentary screen of melody. It's obvious that the boy cannot sing, and that their lyric writing isn't gunna win them any literary awards just yet, bu they've got something and I really really like the sound of it. Come on down, Passing Clouds, rain or us! (KA)

(Bite Back! 51 Bath Rd, Southsea, Hants PO4 OHX.)

SCUM PUPS *Babykill* MLP (Sycophant)

Tuneful, dull, sub-Fugazi throb grunge. They have a song called "Get A Life" which goes *"Get a life, get a life, get a life..."*. Well, what do you expect me to say to that? They threatened to beat up my friend Greg Quality Time if I slagged off their wreckid, well I'm not bowing down to this kind of bullshit so I've advised him to leave the country for a while. The scurvy sneaksbies! (KA)

(Sycophant, 8 Orchard St, Newthorpe, Nottingham NG16 2EL)

MANIC STREET PREACHERS *Generation Terrorists* DLP (Sony)

They're *not* generation terrorists, for a start. If anything they're terrorising their *own* generation with this old, old music; with their tedious love of "classic" 60s and 70s rock long since robbed of the context which made it exciting. Even a band like Nirvana, hardly the most groundbreaking of musical propositions, seems positively futuristic compared with this lot. Not since... oh, say the Teenage Fanclub LP... have so many knackered clichés been crammed into one release by a supposedly "happening" band. They can all go choke on their miserable reverence for the past, because that's the very cholesterol in the arteries (hey! Manics-type image! I'm getting the hang of this already) of the seriously obese and sickly creature they describe without irony as "rock'n'roll".

That said, there are *some* moments on this record: probably enough to have made a half-decent single LP (no less retro, it's true: only the US version of "Repeat" and the drum textures on "Love's Sweet Exile" make *any* concessions to the present). As it is, there's so much filler it's nearly impossible to endure all four sides in one sitting. Apart from the aforementioned tracks, I'll admit to soft spots for their "You Love Us" taunt, the widescreen pop of "Little Baby Nothing" and the ludicrous "Nat West-Barclays-Midland-Lloyds" (Q: how much of this band's appeal is comic? To what extent is this intentional?) but, really, I'm just trying to be nice. For all their obvious intelligence, their ability to fill endless entertaining column inches, they haven't come up with enough memorable tunes (even within the undemanding parameters of MTV-friendly yankophile corporate cocksucking soft rock) to give their rhetoric the populist bite it obviously aspires to. (LN)

GIRLS AGAINST BOYS *Nineties Vs. Eighties* LP (Adult Swim)

Eighties is the funkier side (hardcore people playing funky; grisly voice shouting, plus Public Enemy tricks) and nineties is the far groovier side. "Stay In The Car" even has tinges of Live Skull's serious beauty, where the guitars twist and the vocals get just a bit urgent, but with slabs of hard metal percussion and a fine sense of rhythm throughout, and "Jamie" conjures an image of rock obsessed youth and the chorus, with its siren backing vocals, is full of yearning. This strange grey stone is streaked with gold. And... at least they're aware of the Sex War. (KA)

FURNITURE *The Wrong People* LP (Stiff, I think); *Food, Sex And Paranoia* LP (Arista, probably)
Not strictly allowed on the reviews pages because one of these was out in '86 and the other in '89; nobody, as far as I know, is about to re-release them and nobody was good enough to (tee hee) furnish us with copies of the things (nobody, that is, except Terry from the Outer Hebrides); but some things *have* to be said, so I'm going to stuff it into the machine anyway and hope Karren doesn't notice. Quite simply, brilliant stuff. If you've any kind of soft spot for Scott Walker or the sublime Associates (and if not, you haven't *lived*, child) you'll love the voice. Pretty much whatever your bag you'll love something in the music as it takes in so many styles, from simple pop through broody ballads, epic production numbers, reggae basslines, flamenco guitars, jazz piano - and I swear, "Answer The Door" sounds like *Christian Death*. I hope to be interviewing the ex-Furniture people (they've split up now and taken dodgy day-jobs) for the next *Ablaze!*, though I'm not quite sure what their music has to do with the progressive (oh yes!) outlook of the magazine, except that it doesn't sound like anyone else's. The lyrics are excellent, full of resonant little observations about love and life and stuff; and the tunes and arrangements immaculate. Not your usual *Ablaze!* reader's diet, perhaps, but a spot of genre-bending never did anyone any harm. Have you heard early Roxy Music stuff? You should, as loud as possible. Furniture, for all the sonic and sartorial dissimilarity, were an eighties equivalent in their fusion of the avant garde and disparate conventional styles to produce a classy, intelligent pop music with no discernable obligation to its own, or any other, era. (LN)

PALE SAINTS *In Ribbons* LP (4AD)
"I really like your new LP," I told Ian, "but it sounds so fucking much like *Isn't Anything*." He looked hurt, I didn't understand why. "So that's why we spent four months locked away in the studio" he said, adding "I'm glad you're not coming to the pub with us."
But... wait, come back! It's so damn lovely, so warm and golden and voluptuous. I think Gavin mumbled something about it being the greatest LP ever when he swooned into the room just now, and I think I see what he's getting at. Oh Pale Saints. You know, I hated them up until this - there were moments in their sets that would stop my heart and hold me petrified wih wonder, but apart from that, I used to get bored. This! The first track is sex, the second track has ace smashing sounds and smashing bell sounds. The stuffed cats are rolling around the furniture in sensual delight. The third song is a love song about Micheal Walsh: "Hey Percy, your beauty....." (for non-Leeds people, "Percy" is what Mercury Rev call our Mikey) sung ever so sweetly by Meriel. I feel proud to live five streets from this person (for non-Leeds people, Leeds 4 is the new hipville in the city, hence the term "The Burley Hill scene").
What do these Pale Saints people do for fun? Do they like sports, and if so which ones? I imagine them doing graceful swerves down a pure white ski slope, quickly followed by a deep sea diving sesh. Maybe they are curl-up-catlike-in-front-of-the-fire-with-a-sexy-book types. Maybe they enjoy walking; a Pale Saint for each season, scenes splattered with flecks of white /deep brown/ pale green/ light yellow/ orange/ red /rust /gold... (Oh my god! Clive Gabriel total bullshit award!)
The tones of Ian's voice are too fine for me to describe with my rough, ugly vocabulary, but into those guitars they slide, like golden syrup into the oddest cake mixture... the drum beats fall like raisins, and the production was obviously executed by a superb cook, the glimmering substances delicately beaten with the whisk till they all went frothy...
Bloody scrumptious. Perhaps I can come to the pub next time? (KA)

THE NEON JUDGEMENT *Are You Real* LP (Play It Again Sam)
Not even a question mark. These kids think you can abandon grammar, with their "revolutionary" technobeat and sampled guitars and crap lyrics. Stupidity is no excuse. This is for people who enjoy listening to unstimulating, unambitious sad men locked in plastic studios. (We like our music to be played on authentic wooden acoustic instruments. Oh yes we do.) Disco hits. Human League. Oh you're so weird. You live in the world we like to pretend we're not a part of. Vocals sound so lazy, so ugly, unenigmatic... I'm sorry. I've given up on you, The Neon Judgement. (KA)
(Do you know, the assistant engineer on this record is called Fulton Dingley? - Barry.)

TOASTED HERETIC *Galway And Los Angeles* 12" (Liquid), *Another Day, Another Riot* MC (Liquid)
Toasted Heretic vocalist Julian Gough has a voice you'll either love or hate - most people of my acquaintance seem to opt for the latter, words like "smug" and "mimsy" cropping up repeatedly; but me, I love it. I was turned onto the Heretic by a tape of two excellent LPs of demos which some thoughtful member of the public sent us: here's hoping lots of those songs appear on vinyl in the future, but in the meantime we've got "Galway And Los Angeles", a song about exchanging a lustful glance with Sinead O'Connor at a T.V. station, and as superbly-crafted a lyric as you'll hear anywhere. I'm no Costello-bore, either. Just hear it. The music's great, too: an unlikely hotch-potch of tacky electronic rhythm, sporadic bursts of twiddly lead guitar and air-raid sirens. "Another Day, Another Riot" is sadly nowhere near as good, being too flimsy a musical vehicle for Gough's expansive personality. It does, however, contain the verse: *"How can you continue to / Be human when your job includes / Bugging Freddie Mercury's funeral / Sobbing run as interviews"*, which is great, if a little Roger Woodis. (LN)

SUPER CHUNK *Super Chunk* LP (Matador)
They sound cute, and this record opens like its gunna be Tha Noize of Tha Nineties, but it's just *SUB*. You see I've thought long and tough about this, and that's the word (prefix?) which suits them perfectly. Superchunk are seriously sub. Sub what? you snivel. Sub fuckin' everything that was worth listening to. Sub the subbest things. Sub Teenage Fanclub. Really. They don't come anywhere near the genius of their semi-namesakes Supertramp, and that's clearly what they were aiming for. Oh, I'll come see them when they play, and I'll devour more of their vinyl when the relevant people send it; I'll try to disprove my judgement, but on this evidence, there's just no need for anyone to tear around headlessly. Sorry, folks. (KA)

SUPER CHUNK *No Pocky For Kitty* LP (City Slang)
A better class of grungepop. If you really want to be hip and impress your friends this summer, get into Superchunk now before they release their singles compilation, an LP which is going to put their name on lips across the nation. So there. (M)

PETER JEFFERIES *The Last Great Challenge In A Dull World* LP (Ajax)
I've tried, but this is all by a guy with a posh and serious voice going on with himself; the songs are miserable, flat, poorly recorded (in a garage - while people are fixing cars in it) and sparsely instrumentalised. It's a re-release that was originally out on the trendy NZ label Xpressway, but still. I'm sure less pleasure-seeking people will enjoy this. (KA)

MILHOUS *Set You Free* 12" (110 Pound Productions)
The singer is trying to do a Michael Stipe and is getting a bit sweaty in the process. Possibly a scraggly wolf is hiding in this pile of oddly shaped pop songs. There are bits of tune here but there's something funny about the way he sings *"swap my eyes for je-ew-els"*, and I just can't put my finger on it but I suspect they are up to no good. (KA)
(110 Pound, 96 Gloucester House, Cambridge Rd, London NW6)

THE CROMPTONS *Head On The Block* LP (Cromptone)
Beefheart's dog. Singer Tony's taste in tunes is positively infantile, and this end of the Big Flame lineage here gets lost in an exclusively schizophrenic nursery. Wacky and zany in the original senses. (KA)

CASPAR BRÖTZMAN MASSAKER *Der Abend Der Schwarzen Folklore* EP (Our Choice)
C.B. Massaker's record made me feel rather strange when I was forced to hear it. It made me feel *violent*. It made me want to *smash things*. So I went and smashed some things and then I phoned the press officer responsible. "Less of the dodgy subliminals" I suggested, and I told her why I thought this. She seemed pleased. "I'll tell Caspar," she said. "He'll laugh". Caspar will laugh? I wouldn't like to be there when Caspar laughs. Oh no. (KA)

UNREST *Cherry Cherry* 7" (Hemiola)
"Cherry Cherry" is Wedding Present with "Temptation" "Ooh-ooh-o oh"s, but "Wednesday and Proud" is utterly wonderful. I used to have a record player that would play the same record over and over again and I really wish it still worked just so I could set it to play this song to me 50 times every afternoon. It's circular and sweet and pretty and light, with the loveliest guitars chiming and jingling lightly in the summer breeze like butterflies and dreamily happy vocals: Mark Robinson, who Justine tells me is ace, sings *"I am... Wednesday and proud... the first day of this world"* (I think), and you just don't need anything else. The spiral gets bigger and louder and ends in such a way that you've got to put the needle back to the start... just once more... (KA)
(£2.50 including postage from Hemiola, 35 Barnbrough St, Leeds LS4 2QY.)

THE WOULD BE'S *The Wonderful EP* 12" (Decoy)
Sorry. I hate doing this, but a song like "My Radio Sounds Different In The Dark" doesn't have to be so *clean*. I HATE (among many, many other things) this weak, brash, ugly, sterile pop. And I hate singers who sound like Natalie Merchant. Obviously a heretical statement like that requires some explanation, but the reason probably lies deep in my past; maybe there was a lightly tanned, neatly groomed girl in my class who did everything perfectly, pronounced and spelt all her words without error, who ate triangular sandwiches tidily, who lived utterly without avarice. Had such a person existed, she would have doubtless been carefully avoided by me and my nasty, naughty, strange-smelling friends. I think it's best if all those healthy and obviously happy people like The Would Be's and people like me are spared any further contact with each other. Am I excused? (KA)

SPIRITUALISED *Lager Guided Melodies* (I'm leaving this in - proof Ed)7" (Dedicated)
Strangely, I haven't had to try too hard with this one. Side AA, a remarkably long affair for a couple of inches of plastic, consists of the dreamy "100 Bars (Flashback)", which, like "You Know It's True (Instrumental)", (dig those brackets!) on side A, induces a shimmering placid hazed-over state of mind, with gently ringing guitars appearing and disappearing over a pink whirlwind and barely-audible spoken vocals while flutes and vibrating pieces of metal sing in a misty field in the middle of the night. OH MY GOD! IT'S COMPLETELY ENCHANTING! (Hear the cries of a startled reviewer who never expects any of this stuff to be any good.) I might even play this one again. (KA)
(Unfortunately I *did* play it again. It was crap hippy bullshit the second time round. Ed)

DANIEL JOHNSTON *Artistic Vice* LP (Shimmydisc)
According to the insert, "Daniel is feeling a bit better" these days. I'm glad. This is a first for him, a collection of properly recorded songs with a real backing band. It's much more optimistic and uplifting than anything else I've heard by him. Indeed, Daniel goes so far as to say *"every day is Christmas time"* at one point; a far cry from the angst of songs like "Desperate Man Blues" and "I Remember Painfully", but then, they were recorded nearly ten years ago. This sounds like *Rubber Soul* Beatles crossed with the Velvet Underground's 3rd LP: simple, emotive songs with hooks that get under your skin. Apparently, not too long ago this man pushed an old lady down a staircase because he believed she was possessed by the devil. Despite this, he remains the pop star I'd most like to meet and swap stories of mental hospital with. (SM)

SMOG/SUCKDOG *split single* (#1 Hits)
Lisa Suckdog's three tracks on here sound like they were recorded in her sitting room with the aid only of a drug casualty on keyboard. I'm sad to say that they are silly and tuneless and a waste of time, but maybe that's not the point... you see, despite my seeming arrogance and my adherence to a strictly narrow-minded view of music, it does sometimes occur to me that these things may have other meanings to other people. However, I can't begin to guess what they might be, so let's move on to Smog, an altogether slightly more tuneful proposition. "My Shell" is a lonely, existentialist ballad made with the trashiest guitar amps ever and flat, demoralised male vocals. A work of art, in its way. (KA)
($5 to Bill Callahan, P.O.Box 1491, Dover NH, 03820 USA)

AMERICAN MUSIC CLUB *Everclear* LP (Alias)
Oh god, where to start with this? Mark Eitzel, "broken-hearted genius" much beloved of journalistic types, in Fifth Album Even Better Than The First Four shock; and that's no mean feat because they're *all* flawless, even 1984's *Restless Stranger*, which Eitzel loathes. To the hardened Clubber, *Everclear* comes initially as a disappointment, Bruce Kaphan's lush production serving perversely to render the songs less immediate than Tom Mallon's characteristic dry, band-in-a-room sound did - but once you get used to it, it's like seeing the band in colour for the first time, and what colours: the beautiful sleeve depicts its contents perfectly. There's no point pulling out lyrics for you to gawp over, though any randomly-selected couplet would put 99% of writers to shame: you'll just have to go out and acquire their entire back catalogue, starting with this one. That's not some kind of cute hyperbole to end the review with, I really mean it. Go out and get the entire American Music Club back catalogue, not forgetting Eitzel's live solo LP and the awe-inspiring "I'm In Heaven Now" track on the *Human Music* compilation. If you don't love it all, then one of us is a banana. (LN)

PEARL JAM *Ten* LP (Epic)
This band are *so* lucky. Fancy releasing an album just when the anally-retentive music press are aching to jump on somebody and proclaim them the next Nirvana (Question: Why? Do you think people will respect you if you lie to them? Listen, I do a bit of Nirvana myself now and again, but one is quite enough thank you very much.), and being clutched to the collective bosom like a long-lost friend for this! Fortunately, here at *Ablaze!* we still listen with our ears; this album is truly dreadful. The first time I heard the opening track 'Once' I spat tea all over my living room. Tired, nay completely knackered, guitar work (it's even more work for me, let me tell you) and one of those histrionic heavy rock vocalists who would be equally at home in a band called Love Truncheon or something and would normally, quite properly, just be ridiculed. Look to America by all means, there's a lot of really great stuff there; but look to Pavement, Mercury Rev and Shudder To Think, not this drivel. If Whitesnake covered this album, two things would be immediately apparent: 1. No-one would dare pretend to be shocked. 2. It would sound better. (GB)

PUSSY GALORE *Corpse Love, The First Year* LP (Hut)

Fuck-you attitude monsters to a man, primal in every sense of the word. Pussy Galore created a sound that was like a distillation of the very essence of rock'n'roll; interpreted by a gang of New York alley cats, using the neighbourhood trashcans for instruments. But better. A comprehensive retrospective compilation featuring the ubiquitous 'rare and unreleased material'. A pretty essential package by a band that you shouldn't have let pass you by. (M)

MACHINES OF LOVING GRACE *Rite Of Shiva* 12" (Mammoth)

Me, I thought Nine Inch Nails were a kind of imaginary media scam (hey! anybody remember Terminal Crash Fear? Yo, Neil Taylor, respect due and all that) but it seems there's people out there who take them Very Seriously Indeed. Unequal distribution of intelligence, y'see. Blame God. (LN)

VARIOUS *Independent 20* DLP (Beechwood)

They're odd, these things: I mean, you'd have thought people would already *have* the stuff they wanted, and probably wouldn't *want* the stuff they haven't. Still, they're obviously selling. Yet another indicator of how *undiscriminating* the indie kids are nowadays - not surprising, given the desperate "if it moves, hype it" mentality still prevalent on the inky bibles. Listen, inky eds and staffers, you don't *have* to pretend there's something exciting happening when it's blatantly obvious there isn't. We'll respect you more in the morning. All these shitty bands you've stuck on your covers! You ought to be ashamed of yourselves. A conspiracy of mediocrity - entirely in tune with the (lack of) political spirit of Major/Kinnock's Britain. Get, as I believe you say, a life.

Sorry. I'll talk about the record now. As I say, funny things, but useful in that they're the only way we get to hear half the bands the press features every week: in fact, we use them to play an amusing parlour game called Guess The Indie Band. You can probably work out how it goes. This one features "Car Wash Hair"; **The God Machine**'s rather fine "Home"; **Wonky Alice**, who veer from a pleasant New Orderish northern wistfulness to something totally sixties and horrible in the space of one song; **Lush** (motto: "we're getting there") and **Curve** (great sound, no song)... but then it also has clichéd shit such as **Moose**, **Dr.Phibes**, **Midway Still** and **Captain America**. Standing head and shoulders over the others in the crapness stakes, though, step forward Mr. **Chris Roberts**, whose frankly risible vocal performance on **Catwalk**'s "Damascus" not even the reputed presence of some ex-members of **Furniture** can redeem. For Christ's sake, as they say, sit down, man: you're disgracing yourself. (LN)

PUBLIC IMAGE LIMITED *That What Is Not* LP (Virgin)

Well, it took them sixteen years, but in snapping up Virgin Records, EMI have finally welcomed Rotten Johnny back to their death-peddling multinational fireside. And, that, I'm afraid, is about as good as the irony gets around these parts nowadays, PIL having long since settled into the tedious rock band routine which Lydon was one of the first to explicitly condemn. Some of the stuff on here is OK, and sure it puts lots of today's supposed young bloods to shame for ideas, but it's so *rote:* not even John McGeoch's patient layering of his characteristic guitars can help Johnny transcend his sneery boredom. Poor bloke - I'm not surprised he's miserable. How would *you* feel if you'd changed the world irreversibly as a teenager and then had to spend the rest of your life living up to it? (LN)

JACOB'S MOUSE *No Fish Shop Parking* LP (Blithering Idiot)

This debut by "19 year-old Suffolk heroes" Jacob's Mouse is a mixture of undistinguished thrash pop and something more intriguing. The opening "Tumbleswan", with burbling backwards vocals, and "Twist" (some great guitar which goes "erk!") are fine, as is the Fugazi-esque "Carfish", but the other stuff leaves much to be desired. Great title, though, in an English Whimsy sort of vein. (LN)

THAT UNCERTAIN FEELING *Sunriser* 12" (Dead Dead Good)

Ride meets The Chameleons, which is about as vicious a put-down as you get in my book, but they'll probably be happy with it. As, no doubt, will thousands of dipshit students if they can stomach the dreadful band monicker. Come on, do something *new* or don't do anything at all. (LN)

MADNESS *Divine Madness* LP (Virgin)

They'll keep repackaging these singles until you bastards stop buying them you know, but I won't complain too much; rather this than The Jam or The Beat any day of the week. I can't (alright I haven't *really* tried to) listen to this without thinking of a particularly unpleasant person I was at school with who was Madness mad, and this was such a large part of eighties 'youth culture', that's (for most people) probably the point. If this reminds you of happier times in the past or you genuinely have never heard many of these songs before then buy the bloody thing, I really don't mind; just don't come around here in one of those hats doing that stupid dance. (GB)

MC 900 FOOT JESUS *Killer Inside Me* 12" (Nettwerk)

Literate and wryly observant rap about pathological bores who corner you in a public place and won't let go of you, accompanied by bubbly Real Instruments in lots of different mixes; the Meat Beat Manifestations on the first side being my favourites. (LN)

THE LAURELS *Neck* 7" & *Burn* 7" (Heparin)

Hooray, King Of The Slums are back!!! They've dropped the violin yet somehow recaptured a good proportion of their original, beautiful desperation. Of course, the Laurels are not KOTS and have probably never even heard them, but their strong, whining transatlantic vocals somehow evoke the man Keigher at his best. Mild and catchy are their pop tunes, with ambitious, stretching guitars which conform to no particular clichés that I am aware of. "Neck" is a dissolving nursery rhyme, and at 2 minutes 9 seconds it's the longest track here, yet it still fleets by. That's a problem for me; as soon as I get used to the fact that one of their songs exists, it's gone again. "Burn" has a slightly heavier, busier guitar sound with thinner vocals but does pretty much the same stuff, except where it starts to sound like Bogshed. My favourite track is on this second record: "Fueled" has magificent guitar bursts and vocals alternately wailing and calmly descriptive. That they live somewhere dead glamorous like Providence and sound like they wanna be here in North England is something I can only consider perverse. But these eight curious little songs are sure to be of interest to *Ablaze!* readers worldwide. (KA)
(PO Box 29447, Providence, RI 02909, USA)

CHUMBAWAMBA *First Two* CD (Agit Prop)

CD reissue of their *Pictures Of Starving Children* LP, which stands as a highly intelligent and entertaining punk rock cabaret critique of Live Aid, and *Never Mind The Ballots (Here's The Rest Of Your Life)*, which, though momentarily relevant every few years, doesn't. Some of the former is excellent, however; especially "Slag Aid". Their northern petit bourgeois accent pisstakes simply *have* to be heard. (LN)

SHUDDER TO THINK *Get Your Goat* LP (Dischord)

In a decade that's already given us *Yerself Is Steam* and *Slanted And Enchanted* (not to mention *Funeral At The Movies*) it seems incredible to be saying so but - Album Of The Decade! Definitely! This is Shudder To Think's fourth LP, and the one in which they shake off all conventional pop structures, rewriting the history of music in the process by bringing about the spectacular rehabilitation of Prog Rock. You've never heard anything like this before because it's never been done before; and this week, probably for weeks to come, it's the most beautiful thing in the world. At first, it seems obtuse, but once you're inside the music everything slips flawlessly into place. Breathtaking originality: Craig's voice and stage presence are literally *other-worldly*. Everybody should hear this band. Go on, infernal ham-fisted inky brethren: do your stuff. (LN)

DASH RIP ROCK *Not Of This World* LP (Mammoth)

From Louisiana, these come on like the original hard-living bar band, all bayou blood and alligator attitudes, which could be a good thing in other hands, but Dash Rip Rock fail because they're so weedy. Shouts of *"Woargh, let's go"* and *"Awwright"* and plenty sincere sexism do not compensate for the merely workmanlike , uninflected passionlessness of these numbers. I've a nasty feeling that in some American quarters this is seen as kick-ass music, like G'n'R. The same arch mix of stompers and 'ballads'; formulaic. No drama and no dynamic, no sense of irony and no feminine side, rock'n'roll can't get far without those, these days. *"Louisiana is a dream state"*, glad you think so, Dash Rip Rock (what a name!). Mayhap they're gutsy crawdaddies live, on record they're just shrimps. Hamstrung, fellas. (TT)

THE JACK BREWER BAND *Harsh World* LP (New Alliance); **PRAY TV** *Flux* LP (Shock)

These two wouldn't even sit on the turntable, they had so little discipline. (JG)

NIKKI SUDDEN *The Jewel Thief* LP (UFO)

I'm so glad this one fell to me. I'm blown away by this terrifically good album. I don't care what group he may have been in, what shape their trousers were, or if the aggregate age of the players on here is 36000. At his best, he soars over genres like a little bird. Varied instrumentation, with Nikki's guitar songs, from doodle to rambling ballad, upfront. Words of throwaway genius; cut-throat emotion; astute musical accompaniment. It's classic subject matter: liquor, guns, ammo and carpets. Strangely the *Ablaze!* team used the word 'hackneyed' or was it 'corny'. Rock'n'roll is younger than almost anyone good. REM (minus Stipe, girls) are on here too, having a ball in your guts. Carefree, comic and tragic; if we must have "sounds like", check one B. Dylan, then GW McLennan. Fond and fair, I'll be damned if it doesn't even at times realise our striped sunlight sound. (TT)

DENIZEN *The Cord* 7" (In Reverie)

Marillion! Whatever will they think of next? (KA)

YOUNG GODS *T.V. Sky* LP (Play It Again Sam)

Why did he have to start singing in English? Seen live, still one of the most compelling bands around, but on this LP not completely convincing. Covering similar ground to previous LPs, occasionally jingoistic ("Gasoline Man") but often nerve wracking ("Our House"), *TV Sky* is stacked with Americana, and even samples "LA Woman". Lacks the special something *L'Eau Rouge* posessed. What a pity - not enough devils. (JG)

VIOLET TOWN *Seventh Veil* 12" (Shock)

There's a really good film called *The Seventh Veil*. It's got James Mason as this pianist's psychotic guardian, and if she doesn't practice enough then he slams the piano lid down onto her fingers or whips her or something. So she for obvious reasons falls in love with him. Progressive, I call it. Now if James Mason had been present this evening I'd have let him do the same to me. Anything really to distract me from this godawful record. (JW)

THE ONLY ONES *Another Girl - Another Planet* 12" (Columbia)

You're laughing, aren't you? You think we're doing a *Spiral Scratch*, don't you? But they really have re-released this, on "special red vinyl", and backed it with the Psychedelic Furs' "Pretty In Pink". It's a trailer for both *The Best Of The Only Ones* and *The Sound Of The Suburbs* (Altered Images! Ian Dury! Martha And The Muffins! The Undertones! etc), and since *somebody* has to make their contribution to the upkeep of the cars and houses of the various incarnations of The Man this week, it's clearly the turn of Those People Who Wish To Remain In A New Wave Disco For The Rest Of Their Lives. Serves them right, I say. (KA)

MOE TUCKER *I Spent A Week There The Other Nigh[t]* LP (New Rose)

Surefire perfect ten. Healing essence of rock'n'roll Do you know about Moe Tucker? Like Reed and Cale she means more to me with each new piece of work They all inherit the best marks of ye Velve[t] Underground; realism, passion, musicality. This L[P] has famed reunion of that group. But first, recall las[t] classic Moe, *Life In Exile After Abdication*. This is a[s] good! Working momma's punk blues, all the gathering storms, failing horizons, leaking taps and soft tears Bad food, bad TV, cold bed, and no cash (for n[o] record deal, remember, life is cruel). Moe drums no[w] but plays guitar now, but of course the drums her[e] are Tuckeresque too. Sprightly, rubbery guitar recall[s] good times, simpler times, the joy of motoring, bein[g] choked on sunlight. '(And Then) He Kissed Me' wit[h] Cale viola is a naked moment. 'Blue, All The Way T[o] Canada' is a quiet but scorching paean to Amerindia[n] values. Real, sharp lyrics. Burst fruit energy. The las[t] track, 'I'm Not', the one with all four of our black riders, I find intensely sorrowful, the journey withi[n] of a caged bear. Do listen. Rock'n'roll is sometime[s] this good. Soul, wit, compassion. Alive, today, I'[m] sticking with Moe. (TT)

LAURA NYRO *Eli & 13th Confession* and *New York Tendaberry"* LPs (both Columbia)

You shouldn't own a pair of ears without giving this woman a chance. Recently re-issued from 1968 and 1969, but completely relevant. Explorations in joy and misery. *(You're supposed to have a verb in every sentence, you know - Ed)* If *Eli & 13th Confession* doesn't make you leap out of bed in the mornings, then you don't have a hope. *New York Tendaberry* is almost frightening in its emotional openness. Written and produced by Nyro. Listen. (JG)

LIZARD WHIP *Five Lashes* CD EP (Shagpile)

One wonders how the perpetrators of this particularly cringeable form of Heavy Metal keep their faces straight long enough to ever seriously nurture the seedlings of these infantile ideas, pursue them into a recording studio, and finally have the nerve to inflict them upon a passing innocent such as myself. But somehow they've done it. An achievement, truly. (M)

THE LEAVING TRAINS *The Lump In My Forehead* LP (SST)

I've told myself that they're harmless (and I have to say that the world is in need of their Bob Hope death hymn) but you see there's this bloke in the band and he "launches personal affronts at women (who make you feel like a piece of shit)" (quote from press release). Well, I don't like to pass conjecture; but if he's not too popular with the ladies *no wonder*. Perhaps it's the mauve hair ribbon, cheap baubles and crudely daubed cosmetics that are the problem; because if the cod transvestism, as featured in the band photo, is indicative of how he views womankind then I think he may have to settle for a "bachelor lifestyle". *"She's got big tits/ She's got red lips/ I want to touch her/ I want to fuck her/ Women are evil, lead you down the path to death and destruction/ Women are evil, never give you nothing"*. (From"Women Are Evil") Oh dear. Irony in overdrive? Perhaps - but I can't take any chances. So, Mr.Falling James, if you're reading this, I'm a woman and I'll give you something - yep, a bad record review - and if women won't fuck you then all I can suggest is that you go fuck yourself. (JW)

DHARMA BUMS *Bliss* LP (Frontier)

Look Karren, this was hanging around even when I shared a house with you. I don't wish to upset you, but aside from being old and crap it's scratched as well, and it jumps loads, so I think I should warn you that it's highly unlikely you'll get more than a quid down Gerol's for it. (JW)

"Nipping young talentlessness in the bud"....
Yes yes, it's time for those dreadful
DEMO TAPES

SIDEways (0494 783418 / 256 Berkhamstead Road, Chesham, Bucks HP5 3ET)

These sent us a whole 150g of Galaxy *and* put yellow stickers on their tape. They say *Ablaze!* makes them want to move to Leeds.

K: They're gonna go a long way. Who wants a cup of tea?
G: They're going to have to send hard drugs next time.
K: *(popping head around door)* Bryan Ferry!
G: Is he singing "I want a love life"?
L: "I want a life", more like. What a dire vocalist.
G: After Bob Mould and Mark Eitzel and Robert Forster are we really down to "I want a love life"? Fucking pitiful.
L: The second track is so bad it sounds like he's slowed the vocals down. The Ian Curtis revival starts here.
G: I think Fluff are a goth band.
What's he talking about Fluff for?
K: Chameleons. Oh, give up the Joy Division, it screws you up kids.

POND "The Pond Demo Jan '91" (081-579-6186)

Not, it would seem, the American band of the same name.. Kind of OK. Sort of Mercury Rev-ish, or Galaxie 500 or Stereolab. A Velvet Underground imitator kind of thing, with lots of dynamics.

K: Hippy monstrosity.
B: I quite like this.
L: Me too.
K: It's the kind of thing you do. *(Lucy is a member of a well-known progressive rock group)* You're all hippies.
L: Exactly.
G: Recorded in a phone box. It's the new fashion.
L: Sounds like a good live band though, I'd like to see these.

No song titles, no nothing. Definite Mercury Rev influence in the way the guitars get loud. They're not Up There yet, though. The songs are dead long. The third song sounds almost like guitar-led improvisation and is a very sleepy river indeed.

HOOD "3" (27 Spofforth Hill, Wetherby, W.Yorks LS22 4SE)

This one sounds pretty 'kin interesting. The songs start quiet with weird vocals, then tend to get loud. Manages to create an atmosphere and not even seem derivative when they're using the bassline from 'Bela Lugosi's Dead'.

K: I think this is going to be the token one we like. Apart from Meredith, that is.
L: Ian Pale Saint was on about these being good. Looks like he was right.
K: Pastels! (this was during a deliberately-out-of-tune vocal bit) The third song is absolutely incredible. When I win £20,000 in a junk mail competition I'll release their records. They can come round my house and eat all the tomatoes.

SISTERLOVERS "Pop-Up Machines" (P.O. Box 6, Rugby, CV21 3XW)

K: Sounds like the Buzzcocks songs that weren't written by Pete Shelley.
G: *(examining band photograph)* Long hair problem.

The sleeve features a tasteful collage with a packet of condoms. The mag has loads of sexist pictures of girls' thighs and arses. Steve Sisterlover says, "I am a fucking pop star in Holland and Belgium but I can't get a gig in my own country," and "You don't have to assault a groupie, you just have to ask."

B: Reminds me of a raucous Housemartins.
G: I'm not putting the other side on, and you can quote me on that. You shouldn't put pictures of women in your press release unless you've got women in your band.

VATICAN SHOTGUN SCARE (Robin, 031-556-0042)

They sent us a Christmas card, which they all signed as if we knew who they were.

K: I've already heard this and I don't like it. Sounds Euro. She sounds like she's wearing an evening dress. If she's Scottish she should sing in Scottish.
L: Makes Curve look like genius. Drab workmanlike rock.
K: Curve are quite good actually. Don't write that down.
B: The band are as tight as Gavin's pants. Oh, there's another chord.
K: What?
B: I've just spotted another chord. They need some songs. They play well.
G: "Somewhere between John Zorn and the Pixies"... only in the alphabet.
L: Somewhere between Pixies and Inspiral Carpets. Whatever that means.

LAUGHING LEN, A GUITAR GOD "Who Really Gives A Fucking Shit?" (c/o 67 Dungannon Road, Dungannon, Co. Tyrone BT71 6SE)

K: Well he doesn't sound like he's laughing to me.
G: I imagine him onstage with his underpants on his head or something. And that's not a compliment.

TSE TSE FLY "Demo 8/11/91" (Simon Cleave, 6 Carr Mills, 322 Meanwood Road, Leeds LS7 2HY)

K: (within five seconds of start) Sounds like Sonic Youth.

Well, it's miles ahead of most of the stuff we get, but they aren't exactly Fluff, are they? Mark Goodrham is not as good a singer as Simon Cleave. Fluff's version of 'Selchie' pissed all over the one on here, too. The two guitars often seem to mess each other up: just because you're a four-piece doesn't mean you can't use space in your palette like you used to, dudes.

K: Horrible gothy vocals. But mention all the psychotic people walking around Leeds, inconsolable and crying.

Actually, we really love this band but this was disappointing.

A PYGMALION DREAM (RD3 Box 47, Hackettstown, NJ 07840 USA)

L: It's the Cure.

And sure enough it is. If they ever have a Robert Smith singalike contest, this guy will win it. He writes the same tune as well - you know, the one Smith's been using for thirteen years.

K: It's weird how these Americans always want to be English and English people always want to be American.

We can't decide what period Cure it is exactly.

K: It's crossed with something dodgy, like Balaam And The Angel.
I'll have to find somebody who likes the Cure and give them this tape.
G: I bet they've got black, spiky hair. (Obviously a clairvoyant)

MEREDITH Demo (274 Wingrove Ave, Fenham, Newcastle)

K: Ace band! Really good band from Newcastle! Nice people.
G: This is much better than I thought it was.
L: Good tunes. Lovely bit on the chorus on the first song, the two low notes, I liked that bit. Nice guitar sound too, though the solo wasn't interesting enough to live. Kay, the singer, sounds a bit like Pauline Murray which is mildly amusing considering they live in Newcastle.

Bet you don't know what the old buffer's on about, do you kids?

K: This is rockin'. They should have a record deal.

ELATION Demo (Julian Berry, 17 Gateland Lane, Shadwell, LS17 8HR)

L: Bad Stone Roses.
G: I could find out whether this person is on Income Support, but that would be an abuse of my position. Music for people who don't like music.
K: There'll always be people who don't come up with their own ideas, and they just let the rest of us down.
L: Worst vocal I've heard for a long time. You can't sing, lad.
K: I've got a headache. I suppose we ought to listen to the second song. It might be a hip hop number.

Arf arf. One of the band is called Jeremy, the manager's called Julian and they've wasted loads of money on this insipid crap.

STARSTRUCK (Bosque Records, 25 Eyre Place, Edinburgh EH3 5EX)

L: They sound very Shimmydisc. Very, very Shimmydisc indeed; to the point of having a Jad Fair cover and a Bongwater cover on it.

A comprehensive review is out of the question here because there's about 36 songs on it and the stuff is totally diverse.

K: The cover (wallpaper and track listing printed on acetate) shows great enterprise.

KATHY FREEMAN Demo (Mark Davidson, 13A Strathleven Road, SW2 5JS)

G: Pious, self-righteous cliché. I bet she's loved and lost!
L: Workmanlike, and I'm quite aware of the incongruity of applying that term to the work of a woman, but it's just dull boysrock with aspirations towards MTV slush; especially the first track. There no reason why she shouldn't write and play like an eighteen-year old lad, equally there's no reason why we should listen to her.

THROAT Demo (Gonzalo, 105 Hoole St, Sheffield S6 2WQ)

L: "Excuse appalling sound quality" says the guy's letter. No! Why the fuck should we? That's like saying, sorry the songs are crap, y'know; we're shite, but...
K: WE DON'T LIKE THIS KIND OF THING!

(In case you're wondering, "this kind of thing" is grungy rock with shouting over the top).

L: I agree. We're the only fucking fuckers in this corrupt music press who don't push an oily mush of equivocation. *Ablaze!*, the magazine that knows where it stands.
K: Tell them to go back to school. It's like sub-sub-something-or-another.
G: I like it. It sounds like a band rather than a few mates making a demo. I mean, so do Simple Minds, but...

THE DELPHI (46 Douglas Cres, Viewpark, Uddingston.)

Bog-awful, dreamy pop. Three of the band are called Steven.

K: Is it like A-ha and Icicle Works?
G: It probably sounds like Chapterhouse. It's just one of those crappy shoegazing bands. It sounds like "Moving In With" being done by some shoegazers.
K: The Railway Children! Oh, there was a weird bit. Yes, they're trying to be a bit more spooky than that.

Happily there is some glorious stuff among the pile of bollocks people keep sending us. I mean, when we're handed tapes at gigs we can warn the donors that they are probably going to have their piss taken right out of them (at the very best), because we see no virtue in wasting the earth's resources on derivative, unimaginative nonsense, and if you've any debris floating around there in your head at all, you'll have noticed by now that we merely want to clear all that shit right out of the way, and make a bit of space for beautiful things. Value laden talk, yes, but that's the way we're built. So carry on sending those tapes - hopefully you'll be so depressed by our thoughtless comments that you'll pack it all in and find your appropriate position in life. Not that we wish to add more limits to the fulfillment of your human potential than there already are - the point is, if you're going to do it, do it properly. There are easy ways out, but they're all crap.

And don't forget: we like chocolate, money, XL t-shirts and aeroplane journeys. Make sure that all the essential details are written on the body of the cassette so we can lose the box without irreperably hindering your career in rock music... and the sticker colour for this issue is GREEN.

a wet and wild surf recording from the actual surfing wedding present

And you thought they were only releasing two LPs and twelve 7" singles this year! Well, here's the flexi, an aberrant 7" number 13 if you like, featuring a track which wont appear on any of their other releases, ever. It's called "Undercurrent", it's a cover of a song by The Pacific Surfers (check *Surfin' Wild,* on Hot Rod records of Rio De Janeiro, if you wanna hear the original). It was *nearly* produced by Jimmy Miller (of "Honky Tonk Woman" fame), except he was out of the room at the time. But, best of all, it's an instrumental. Maybe their first ever! Hear them transcend their past yet again with this gorgeous surf melody.

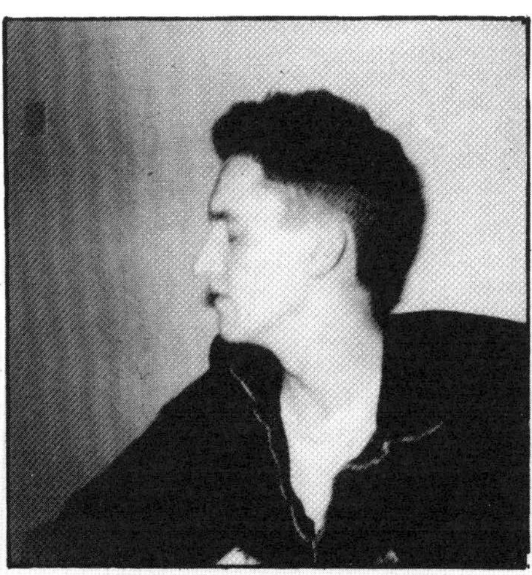

Top: Dorro when he was, erm, *different*; Left: Simon with his legs out; Centre: Keith, cleverly concealing his enthusiasm for having his picture taken; Right: Sally with her weird looking boyfriend. All photies by Justine Wolfenden.

But wait, there's more to this flexi business than you may immediately realise. Those nice Wedding Present people have moved along to make room for

A.C. TEMPLE.

The astute among you will remember that Paul Dorrington was a Temple bassist in a previous incarnation, when they used to sound like Sonic Youth (joke!: A.C. Temple have never really sounded like anyone, but journalists are not renowned for listening with their ears). The song here is "Miss Sky", but a mix different from any you have ever heard before. The original mix can be found on their *Sourpuss* LP, a record of pure pop wonder, one firmly placed in the list of Ablaze! favourite five records ever ever ever. So you can imagine that it's quite a thrill to be presenting this airborn slice of beauty to you. *Listen.*

What to look for in summer: complete your Temple collection with *Songs Of Praise, Blowtorch, Sourpuss*, and their most recent masterpiece, *Belinda Backwards*. The Templettes are currently deciding which record deal to sign, and are hoping to bring you more special happiness soon.

Astoria

A!8

A!9

TERRA

BLUE

ORANGE

Photo: Tony Woolgar

Pavement: Tender Last Moments

Karren Ablaze! psychologises Stephen Malkmus

Going through my stuff, I found some pieces of paper containing a transcribed interview with Stephen Malkmus, apparently conducted by me, and probably at the end of their first European tour in 1992. Gavin and I had been with them selling merch, and in Gavin's case, adding some backing vocals too. It was the best time. Here are the lost scrolls of Pavement.

It starts like this...

SM: I dunno, it's hard to say. I don't really want to say seriously. I guess I would say, in Belgium, when we played this time – the second show we played there, we were just playin', and it was really fun.

KA: How did you feel on the stage tonight with all those people going completely crazy?

SM: I felt like a member of Jesus Lizard. I felt like David Wm. Simms, I felt myself grow a few inches shorter and my hair curled a little bit, so it was weird.

KA: What you gonna do when you go home?

SM: Well, I'm just gonna eat a lot of good international cuisine, New York style, sleep long, just... not much basically!

KA: How does your state of health compare now to when you started the tour?

SM: Oh I'm good now. In the North I had a cough [describes cough, and how it improved when he returned to the south of the UK]. Although I love the North, we had our best shows in the North.

KA: Why do you always come across as miserable when you have everything in the world you could possibly want?

SM: I don't have everything, that's why. Do I seem miserable always?

KA: For somebody... yeah, considering...

SM: Well I guess it's just my nature, to feel bad when things are good, to feel good when things are bad. It's not that good though, I mean I feel like it's just not bad y'know. Anyway, I kind of shy away from like fans and stuff, it's like strange for me. I've never been a huge fan of a band where I would stand up front, I've always been back behind like ten rows watching a band and I'm not used to it, and I'm sure if we go on and make some other good songs, it's just a matter of making one more good record and then I'll feel good.

KA: Aren't you always gonna be saying that?

SM: No, I don't think so. One more and...

KA: Do you truly believe that?

SM: No, I don't believe it, but I'm hoping. Look at The Cure, they made a lot of good records, whether you like The Cure or not, they had something going that was real and interesting, and Robert Smith went into middle age a little bit happier even though he was much more depressed than he makes it up in the press to be, like drinking too much and thinking of suicide... This is just only one thing I've read, it's not anything that I'm like obsessed about or like I normally think about, but I think right now this band [Pavement] is so new and everything's going so fast - not as fast as other bands like Nirvana, everything happened to them so fast that they're blown away - but still for us, our band has always been like an artificial band as far as I'm concerned, it ends up being more real than most bands but for me it's just thrown together. I mean most people would probably think that too, they'd like to say "we just made up the songs," but our recordings are so quick and we stand by our recordings. I treat our records as a fun thing and like to try to bring something – but how much can you do through guitars and singing?

KA: A lot! [Everything, Stereo Master]. It works.

SM: We try. I mean our live set has more to do with American Music Club than it does the Pixies, and some people haven't noticed that.

KA: It isn't like anything these, all those other bands, Sonic Youth, Pixies...

SM: No, I know it's not like those bands.

KA: No but in terms of the way people appreciate it, it's beyond that.

SM: I hope so, I hope they know it's like that, that it's not like those bands. I like those bands too and I wouldn't disrespect them, but it's like with the mix of people we have in our band it can't be that way, cos we're like all these people that don't know what we're doing. For Bob to be in a band is the funniest thing on earth to me. He's like everyman y'know, he's there and he's playing with his spirit, I don't mean everyman in disrespect, he would say the same thing y'know, he's just like 'I'm back there, I don't play, I hit my drums,' y'know. I think it's great that someone like that is in our band. To look back at him and see him smiling, that's like a great thing. I don't mean to act like a grand progenitor, just putting people behind the drums and like anyone, like I could just pick someone out of the crowd and say hey you, go behind and play, because Bob's just completely integral to it. Bob's weird man, what can I say. Gary's crazy, I mean the most normal one in this band is Mark.

KA: I thought Scott was quite normal.

SM: Yeah, Scott and Mark and maybe me.

KA: You're not normal cos you're really weird.

SM: No I'm not, why?

KA: I just find it strange when people are quiet and really introverted and you sit in the van for hours and not really say anything and then you'll say a few comments not really related to anything and then you go quiet for a few more hours.

SM: I can talk under certain circumstances.

The transcription ends abruptly at this point. The remaining words on the page are as follows:

Bass

Beatles

I can't communicate with you – you're too weird.

WE RAN OUT OF SHIRTS ON TOUR... BUT YOU CAN SEND OFF FOR SOME! PAVEMENT MERCHANDISE

STYLISH RED ON GREY SHIRTS

PAVEMENT THE SLOW CENTURY

£7 each, plus £1

BIG CAT MAIL ORDE
P.O. BOX 1561 LON

4: HANSEL
TRAINED BY FRAN
RIDDEN BY JERRY BA
BOOK AT KEENELAND
DERBY STRETCH, REN
SHIFTLESS IN PREAKNE
SOLD IN BELMONT, MY
LAME IN TRAVERS, RE
CRIED, YOU CALLED C
4: JULIE KRONE
SMITH, LAFFIT PINC
RANDY ROMERO, RIC
LUC SAMYN, ART MA
ANGEL CORDERO, JER
ABLE SPORTS PEOPLE
OVERLOOKED, JUST A H

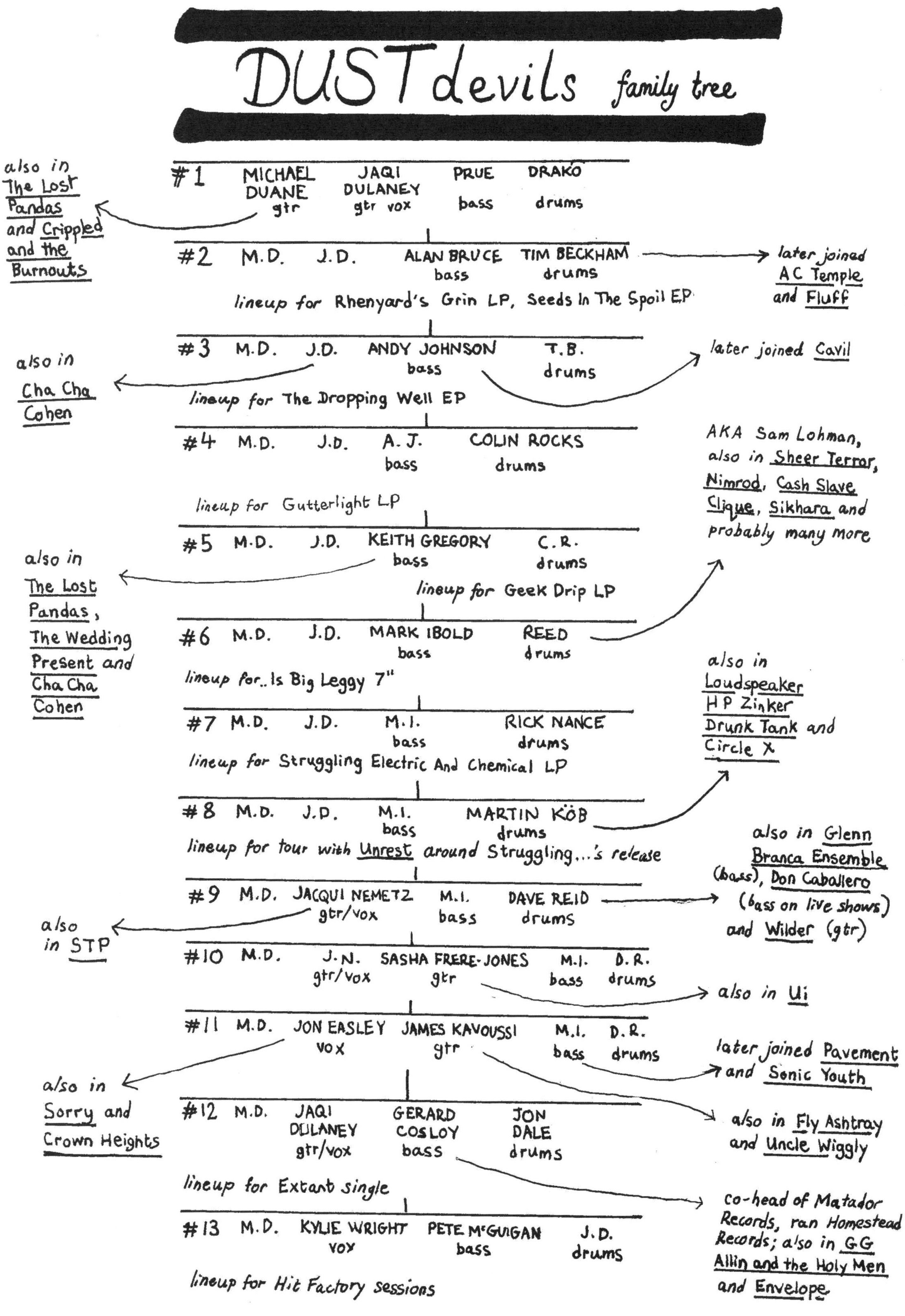

DUST devils family tree

#1 MICHAEL DUANE gtr · JAQI DULANEY gtr vox · PRUE bass · DRAKO drums

(Michael Duane) also in The Lost Pandas and Crippled and the Burnouts

#2 M.D. · J.D. · ALAN BRUCE bass · TIM BECKHAM drums

(Tim Beckham) later joined AC Temple and Fluff

lineup for Rhenyard's Grin LP, Seeds In The Spoil EP

#3 M.D. · J.D. · ANDY JOHNSON bass · T.B. drums

(J.D.) also in Cha Cha Cohen

(Andy Johnson) later joined Cavil

lineup for The Dropping Well EP

#4 M.D. · J.D. · A.J. bass · COLIN ROCKS drums

lineup for Gutterlight LP

#5 M.D. · J.D. · KEITH GREGORY bass · C.R. drums

(Keith Gregory) also in The Lost Pandas, The Wedding Present and Cha Cha Cohen

lineup for Geek Drip LP

#6 M.D. · J.D. · MARK IBOLD bass · REED drums

(Reed) AKA Sam Lohman, also in Sheer Terror, Nimrod, Cash Slave, Clique, Sikhara and probably many more

lineup for ..Is Big Leggy 7"

#7 M.D. · J.D. · M.I. bass · RICK NANCE drums

lineup for Struggling Electric And Chemical LP

#8 M.D. · J.D. · M.I. bass · MARTIN KÖB drums

(Martin Köb) also in Loudspeaker, HP Zinker, Drunk Tank and Circle X

lineup for tour with Unrest around Struggling...'s release

#9 M.D. · JACQUI NEMETZ gtr/vox · M.I. bass · DAVE REID drums

(Jacqui Nemetz) also in STP

(Dave Reid) also in Glenn Branca Ensemble (bass), Don Caballero (bass on live shows) and Wilder (gtr)

#10 M.D. · J.N. gtr/vox · SASHA FRERE-JONES gtr · M.I. bass · D.R. drums

(Sasha Frere-Jones) also in Ui

#11 M.D. · JON EASLEY vox · JAMES KAVOUSSI gtr · M.I. bass · D.R. drums

(Jon Easley) also in Sorry and Crown Heights

(M.I.) later joined Pavement and Sonic Youth

(James Kavoussi) also in Fly Ashtray and Uncle Wiggly

#12 M.D. · JAQI DULANEY gtr/vox · GERARD COSLOY bass · JON DALE drums

(Gerard Cosloy) co-head of Matador Records, ran Homestead Records; also in GG Allin and the Holy Men and Envelope

lineup for Extant single

#13 M.D. · KYLIE WRIGHT vox · PETE McGUIGAN bass · J.D. drums

lineup for Hit Factory sessions

Family Tree by Ian Cockburn

TEAMWORK AND A SHARED DREAM

Gavin Bradbury reveals how he lost the will to rock

It is September 13, 1993. I am in a large studio apartment in Berlin. I have no idea who lives here. Whoever it is, they are not here at the moment. I think I am alone. I appear to be having some kind of identity crisis. Certainties by which I have lived my life no longer seem to hold. I do not know what I believe anymore. How can I carry on? What will I do now?

For the past twelve days I have been travelling around Holland, Belgium, Austria and Germany selling t-shirts for the San Diego band Trumans Water. The gigs have been loud, energetic and fantastic fun, the band are charming, funny and kind, but something is not quite right. I am not quite right.

At the last minute, the tour schedule had to be rearranged. Trumans Water were supposed to have supported Manic Street Preachers at several shows in Germany. It appears that Manic Street Preachers no longer want Trumans Water to support them. Nobody in the band knows or cares why.

The rejigged itinerary means that sometimes we drive for more than eight hours between gigs. Sometimes the driving is shared as we travel overnight, leaving straight after the gig. The van we are travelling in is small; this is not a tour bus, this is most definitely a van. Brothers Kevin, bass, and Kirk Branstetter, guitar, have fashioned a space at the back of the van on top of and in between stacks of equipment where we take turns to half lie down and try to sleep, but otherwise we sit for hours in the same position, barely registering the European countryside as it speeds past outside. There are six of us; the band, the tour manager Joe Hickey and me. Selling band t-shirts in mainland Europe before 1999 means regularly changing a lot of foreign currency into a different foreign currency and then hoping you sell enough t-shirts to make back the commission the bureau de change has taken from you. I am unsuccessful more often than not. Nobody minds, this is all too much fun.

At the start of the tour in Groningen in Holland, I had been abruptly awoken one morning when the woman whose flat we were sleeping in opened the refrigerator door and smacked me in the head with it. I was sleeping in the only place where there was room for me to lie down.

On September 8, Trumans Water are scheduled to support Manic Street Preachers in Stuttgart. Through record company connections Trumans Water instead join the bill of a Jesus Lizard and Bivouac show at the Luxor in Cologne. As we are not supposed to be there, I get the day off from shirt selling. The three bands and assorted hangers on set themselves the task of finishing all the beer in the large glass-fronted refrigerator in the dressing room. This is a lot of beer. There is so much of it, there is absolutely no way that it can all be for us. Somehow (teamwork and a shared dream, probably) we manage to finish it. A member of staff comes backstage and stares at the refrigerator. There is silence, an impasse. He leaves the room. We wait to see what will happen. He returns a moment later and starts to refill the refrigerator as if it is the most natural thing on earth. Only one of our extended party spends the latter part of the evening vomiting in the street.

L-R: Bob Nastanovich, Gavin, Mark Ibold Photo: Greg Neate

I spend my twenty-fifth birthday in Vienna being talked at by the English gig promoter who goes on incessantly about "Manic The Street Preachers". In Groningen two Dutch girls had told me about this great band Motorpsycho they had seen a few weeks before. They both pronounced it "Motor-pah-sycho". English is their second language.The promoter has no such excuse.

I have never met Trumans Water before this tour. They played in Leeds a year before but for whatever reason I missed it. Despite spending hour after hour travelling and working together, there is not a second's arguing, no sulking, no tension. Trumans Water are a happy band and, therefore, we too are a happy band.

My only problem on the tour is musical. My affection for Trumans Water and their music never wanes; I enjoy each night's show in turn. Indeed, I am prompted several times to jump on stage and join in with 'Rations' from *Spasm Smash XXXOXOX Ox & Ass*, screaming "Rat, you dirty rat, you dirty rat, you!" into whichever microphone is close at hand. It is when we are travelling that I am troubled. I am starting to hate music.

We spend so many long hours travelling. The band's music collection consists of cassette recordings of Royal Trux, Smog and The Jon Spencer Blues Explosion. These are not the only three cassettes that I can remember them having, these are the only three cassettes they have. I have spent half of my life listening to Americans singing and playing guitars. I have spent the last two years doing little except listening to, talking to and writing about Americans with guitars. Now I don't care if I ever hear an American with a guitar ever again. No, that's wrong, I do care. I want to never hear an American with a guitar again. And I fucking hate Royal Trux, Smog and The Jon Spencer Blues Explosion.

In the large Berlin apartment, many times larger than a small van crammed full of equipment and men, I stare at the television. MTV Europe is on. This in itself is not important, but what it is showing and its effect on me, is. Cypress Hill's 'Insane In The Brain' is followed by The Goats' 'Typical American'. I like this. I really like this. These people look as if they would hit you for owning a guitar.

I never write a word about music again. Within the year I have sold or given away every one of my 1500 records.

***

The first time I encountered Karren Ablaze! is lost in the mists of time. It was certainly at a gig, almost definitely at the Duchess of York on Vicar Lane in Leeds. She may have been with Lucy Nation, she was probably selling fanzines. I was doubtless sipping beer and trying to remember if I smoked that week. I do remember seeing her at a Lemonheads gig at The Duchess where she surmised succinctly and accurately that Evan and his gang were "at least better than the truly awful Buffalo Tom" (Buffalo Tom played The Duchess Of York on July 4 1990, the day England lost on penalties in the World Cup semi-final to West Germany. When the lead singer of Buffalo Tom took the stage the tool quipped, "Now you have lost two things on July the fourth." "We don't follow football, that's why we are at a gig watching your dreary sub-Dinosaur Jr. crap during England's most important game of the last 24 years, dickhead," I replied. I don't think he heard me.).

SEPTIC
LIMEY
WANK
PAVEMENT
AAA

Buffalo Tom never featured in Ablaze!. Dinosaur Jr. did.

The first time I read Karren's writing was much earlier than that, although I didn't know they were her words until many years later.

The church near Leeds University, where I was studying, used to have a different poster outside each week to encourage stray members of the flock to come inside. These "witty" advertisements seem commonplace in Leeds now but at the time they were less popular. From the late 1980s I remember "C H _ _ C H - what's missing?", "Jesus is the reason for the season" (to which my friend Jez, visiting from Oxford asked "Is Mary a fairy who is hairy?") and "Jesus is the door". The reason I remember the third and most bland of these is that below "Jesus is the door" someone had written "no, Jim Morrison is The Door". Several years later I was relating this graffito to my friend Micheal (correct spelling) Walsh, who told me that it had been done by his friend Karren. [I've no idea if this is true, and sadly we don't have Walshie on hand to double check it with – K].

The first time I spent any time talking to Karren was when Micheal and I went to her house on Hopewell Place in Leeds 6. I remember a staircase, a Sonic Youth poster and an enthusiastic woman with a riot of pink hair who sat on the floor. There were records everywhere, nearly all by bands I'd never heard of.

After this I used to visit Karren at Wetherby Grove before I eventually moved in. One time she thrust a few records at me and told me to see what I made of them. My first reviews appeared in Ablaze! 8. I moved in to number 17 in Autumn 1991, just after Ablaze! 8 came out.

Music had always been my main passion. In 1981, when 12 years old, I went to a gig at Walsall Town Hall with one of my school friends. I remember little about the relative merits of heavy rock bands Fist and Taurus but have seared in my memory the image of a hairy man lying on his back in the middle of the floor of the venue whilst a woman had her hand down the front of his jeans. I was wearing a denim jacket with Queen embroidered on the back. A couple of almost appropriate badges adorned the jacket's front. Nobody seemed to mind that two terrified young boys were witness to so much metal mayhem. It was the Midlands, after all.

Later at Leeds University, most of my grant and all of my overdraft went on records. My tastes had escaped the Midlands as I had, and I bought the back catalogues of Hüsker Dü, The Go-Betweens and Talking Heads, spending all my spare time in Crash Records opposite the university.

Since school my favourite band had always been R.E.M. In May of 1989 I saw R.E.M. eight times in 15 days in seven different cities and failed my second year at university as a result. I still think it was worth it. My mother disagrees.

With new Leeds friends I regularly attended The Duchess Of York and saw amongst others Alice Donut, Snuff, The Chills,

Colorblind James Experience, False Prophets, Henry Rollins and Nirvana. Nirvana played to about two hundred people on 25 October 1989, sandwiched between Edinburgh's Cateran and Seattle's Tad. This remains the loudest gig I have ever seen. Exactly one year later Nirvana headlined a bill featuring L7, Arm and Victim's Family at Leeds Polytechnic. After the gig my sister cried for hours; during Nirvana's set the mosh pit parted with immaculate timing as some poor stage-diving sap flew through the air and he duly smashed his face on the Poly floor. I can still picture the blood. Less than two years later Karren and I saw Nirvana headline at the Reading festival. Kurt was pushed on stage in a wheelchair by Everett True. It wasn't quite the same.

Once I moved into Wetherby Grove I began to take more of a role in helping with the fanzine. You may think that being a writer on a fanzine is a relaxing laid-back existence. Would it surprise you to know that I got up at 7am Monday to Saturday for the entire time that I worked on Ablaze!? Not the picture of a fanzine writer you had, is it? Shows how pre-conceptions can be wrong and sometimes a little hurtful. As I was saying, I got up at 7 a.m. every Monday to Saturday for two years. Well, someone had to answer the door to the postman with all his free records and CDs for us. I went straight back to bed once I'd opened them of course.

We were sent a lot of free records and CDs. A hell of a lot. Almost all of them were complete shite.

Many memorable things happened in my two-and-a-half years at Ablaze! There was an almost daily confusion of new records to listen to, tuna on toast, arguments about The Fall, hot knives, requests to get on guest lists, cups of tea, phone calls from fanzine writers and visits from bands. We were perpetually broke, living on benefits and the proceeds from selling records to the second-hand record store in the Merrion Centre, but happy for the most part, arguing over reviews and interviews. Bands would visit and sometimes stay; Sebadoh, Tsunami, Circus Lupus and Moonshake all spent nights on our living room floor. Moonshake even stayed one night at my mother's house in Birmingham. To this day she cannot believe that people could be so scruffy and yet so polite.

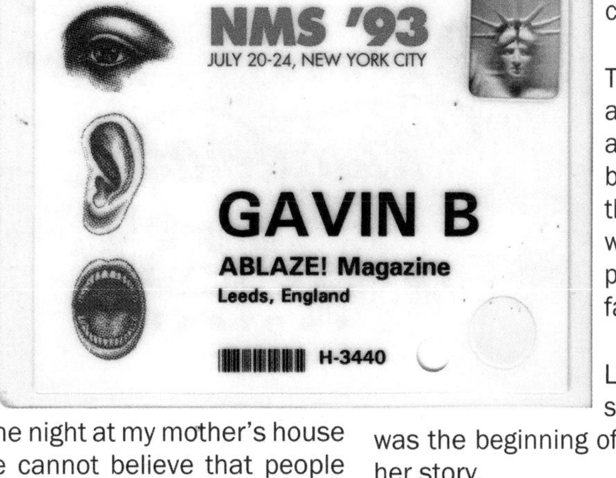

Karren and I spent a couple of weeks in July 1992 selling t-shirts across the UK for Pavement. Getting this job as with most things I did during this time was testament to Karren's determination and character. I could do liking Pavement, I did that very well, but I needed someone else to get me a job with them. Pavement were very charming and decidedly un-rock'n'roll. I even got to sing along with them a few times on No Life Singed Her, which the band called 4-4-2 as this was the only way to get drummer Gary Young to remember the drum pattern. At ULU, Tanya Donelly of Belly and I sang backing "ooh-ooh-oohs" on In The Mouth A Desert. It doesn't get much better than that.

***

One event more than any other for me sums up my time living at 17 Wetherby Grove.

Barry Millington moved into Wetherby Grove at the same time as I did and lived there for nine months. He had answered an advertisement that Karren had pinned to a university message board and could not have been less interested in Ablaze! and its music."Bad News" Barry was a guitarist and piano player who in the time I knew him never even once betrayed the slightest interest in non-classical music.

Barry now teaches music. Remarkably he recently found himself teaching music to our friend Bela. Barry related an anecdote to Bela of how, whilst living at *Ablaze!* Mansions, he once went downstairs in the middle of the night to find Courtney Love in our kitchen. This sums up the haphazard and often impromptu way the house was used to offer temporary shelter to waifs and strays, usually American, who slept in our front room before resuming their tour the following day. Many bands came to see us in Burley. One of them subsequently had a number one single in UK, when to do that meant you had to sell more than sixty mp3s.

Courtney Love never visited our house. But it makes complete sense that Barry thinks that she did.

***

During the summer of 1993 Karren and I spent two weeks in America. At the time Hoover were offering a pair of return flights to Europe or the USA if you spent more than £100 pounds on one of their products. Karren bought a vacuum cleaner, I bought some insurance, Justine's friend Glenn Luttman agreed to put us up and we flew to New York from Manchester airport on Sunday 18 July. The entire fortnight's holiday cost me around \$200. The free-flight promotion cost Hoover almost £50m.

This was the first time I had left Europe and only the third time I had been on an aeroplane. For two weeks I watched bands, interviewed bands, drank beer on the street in paper bags, tried to keep up with American speech patterns and proposed marriage. New York remains my favourite place.

Later that year I travelled around Europe selling t-shirts for Trumans Water, which was the beginning of the end for Ablaze! and me. The rest is her story.

Post Script

Since September 1993, post-Trumans Water, I have been to exactly four gigs (one every 1700 days or so); The Fall, Half Man Half Biscuit, Scritti Politti and Throwing Muses (The 'youngest' of these bands, Half Man Half Biscuit, formed in the early-1980s). After seeing Throwing Muses for about the eighth time, in Holmfirth of all places (a place famous for old men doing the same thing over and over again), I realised that it was 23-and-a-half years since I first saw them, with The Pixies at Leeds Polytechnic on 28 April 1988.

Having given away all my records and CDs, mellow middle age and the internet has seen me reacquainted with *almost* all of them.

To this day, however, I still cannot listen to Royal Trux, Smog or The Jon Spencer Blues Explosion.

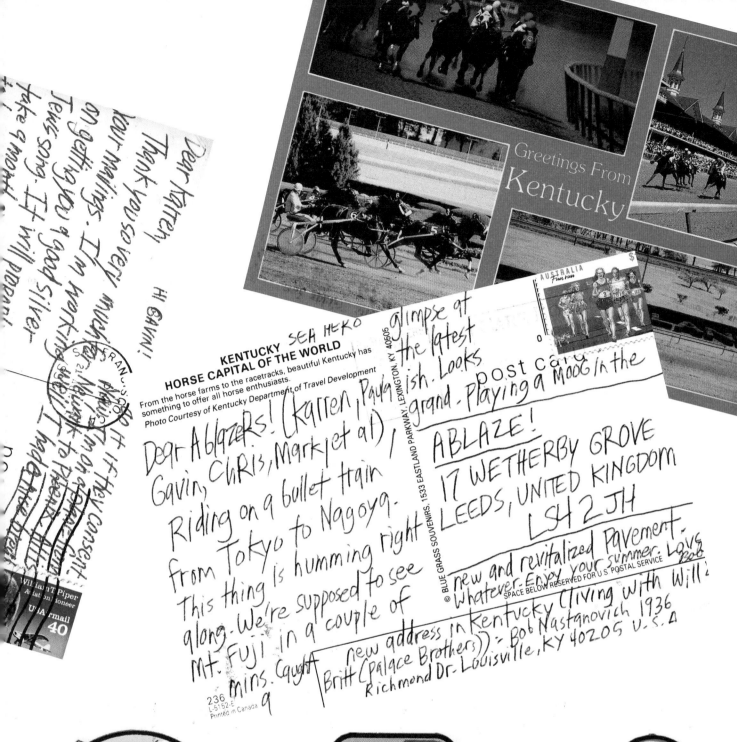

Dear Karren,
Thank you so very much for your mailings. I'm working on getting you a good silver Jews song. It will probably take a month

HI GAVIN!

SAN FRANCISCO

William T. Piper Aviation Pioneer USA airmail 40

Greetings From Kentucky

AUSTRALIA Fun run

KENTUCKY SEA HERO

HORSE CAPITAL OF THE WORLD

From the horse farms to the racetracks, beautiful Kentucky has something to offer all horse enthusiasts.

Photo Courtesy of Kentucky Department of Travel Development

© BLUE GRASS SOUVENIRS, 1533 EASTLAND PARKWAY, LEXINGTON, KY 40505

post card

Dear Ablazers! (Karren, Paula, Gavin, Chris, Mark, et al) I'm Riding on a bullet train from Tokyo to Nagoya. This thing is humming right along. We're supposed to see Mt. Fuji in a couple of mins. Caught a glimpse at the latest ish. Looks grand. Playing a MOOG in the new and revitalized Pavement. Whatever. Enjoy your summer. Love Bob

ABLAZE!
17 WETHERBY GROVE
LEEDS, UNITED KINGDOM
LS4 2JH

SPACE BELOW RESERVED FOR U.S. POSTAL SERVICE

new address in Kentucky (living with Will & Britt (Palace Brothers)) - Bob Nastanovich 1936 Richmond Dr. Louisville, KY 40205 U.S.A

236
L-5152-E
Printed in Canada

EMPIRE STATE BUILDING
UNITED NATIONS
CHINATOWN
NEW YORK CITY

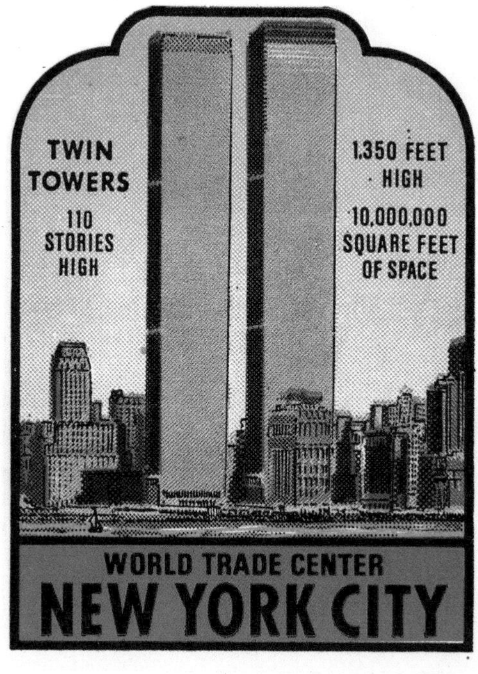

TWIN TOWERS
110 STORIES HIGH
1,350 FEET HIGH
10,000,000 SQUARE FEET OF SPACE
WORLD TRADE CENTER
NEW YORK CITY

Ablaze!
10

Ablaze! 10

Publication date: March 1993

POSSIBILITY EXPLOSION. PUNK ROCK POSSIBILITY EXPLOSION. UNCEASING POSSIBILITY EXPLOSION. Not gonna lie it down, or ever accept the supposed. What's at stake is everything.

Ablaze! 10 was about the moment of discovering the fullness of the word that would set us up for endless adventure, a word all too infrequently spoken:

POSSIBILITY = why the fuck not?
POSSIBILITY = DO IT ANYWAY
POSSIBILITY = now is when we are alive
POSSIBILITY = GO GO GO GO!

We were now at the height of our confidence. We thought we were going on forever. There are almost too many words in this issue; we worked hard to cover what we felt was necessary at the time. The Nation of Ulysses interview was the pinnacle of my heartfelt band investigations; I'd finally met my match in Ian Svenonius, who inspired me to go much further with my forceful creations. From this, several Riot Grrrl tracts arose, and an intense and mangled experience of Huggy Bear, with whom it could not have been another way.

O Nation of Ulysses. Their first UK gig was at Camden Underworld. Two hundred miles - why the hell not? I liked one of their songs, the trumpet-drunk 'Aspirin Kid'. Let's go and see what they are like live.

Waiting in the venue, some geeky boy taps my arm and issues a polite greeting. He's like "Excuse me, would you like one of these?" or something, and he's peddling a manifesto-zine called *Ulysses Speaks*, and he looks kinda spotty, I swear his demeanour was that of a gangly little church kid. He introduced himself as Ian. He said he was in the band. I don't know what we said in those first few sentences. Surely nothing meaningful can be said before one's baptism. You don't expect me to describe it in words, do you? Why are you looking at me like that? OK then, I'll give you one - single - word, an element for you to play with - *F!I!R!E!*. They set the stage on fire, and then they played a show.

After that, I couldn't go home. I just got in the van. And the contents of the van went all around the island, committing musical arson at a series of searing shows in the civic centres of the kingdom. One day it stopped and I turned on the tape recorder, setting it on the floor between me and Ian. We sat, forehead to forehead, eye to eye, in a shop doorway in Liverpool. This piece is part of the world we created.

As a gesture of friendship I'd given Ian my donkey jacket, but one cold cold morning outside the van by the kerb of 10 Middleton Road, London N8, he solemnly handed it back, as though bringing our friendship to an end. It's true that I had been a bit of a handful: I'd sincerely attempted to take a magnet to Everett True's tape of his NOU interview, and when that failed, had loudly called for the burning of the Ulysses flag. And now it was early and we were tired, and I'd been mouthing off about how much I hated the music press and everything it stood for. I had sought to prevent the inevitable trivialisation of their incendiary capabilities, because they deserved so much more than half a page in the new bands section of *Melody Maker*. They deserved to stand outside the morass and... well I don't know exactly what I thought they could do, but I knew what they did to my heart, and it was something quite serious. Somehow we healed our dispute, and though subsequently I've lacked the agility to follow Ian's mental trajectories, he has made an indelible impression on me, a fact to which this issue attests only too well.

And now I'm startled by the 24-year-old me. She is shouting joyously. I can hardly believe I wrote this manifesto; I called it Girl Power International, pretending that it was scribed by "a worldwide network of revolutionaries". It *kind of* was; I had the NOU and lots of feminist thinkers in my head, mixed up with too much coffee, spun around on the swings in the middle of the night with Walshie at my side. I would love to be able to write like this all the time, but how often can such a cocktail of influences be imbibed?

My *Ablaze!* journey took me from being too shy to ask The Pastels a question, to becoming very egotistical, seriously cliquey and a little bit clever. I travelled from the world of a folded-up girl who could barely speak to an outward-facing grrrl who would not stop.

These pages are the only ones that I have seen fit to re-typeset, offered as they are for redistribution. I'm embarrassed by some of what I wrote but don't want to apply adult arrogance to youthful lightning surges, and I can't take back the gift.

The Bikini Kill hated this issue. It came out just before their UK tour with Huggy Bear, and when they'd read it they spat on it and cast it upon the ground. I hadn't loved their records up to this point and only got to see them live after we went to press. They were amazing, and I was hoping to interview them for the following issue, but by then it was too late. We had aroused their displeasure by failing to praise them sufficiently, whilst devoting the entire issue to their arch-rivals, The Nation of Ulysses. At a show in the Covent Garden Rough Trade Shop, Kathleen Hanna took me aside and, in her self-assumed role as custodian of all grrrls, she sought to set me straight. She told me how I'd let down the side in my adoration of the NOU. She said it made me look like I "wanted to suck their dicks". And she ended her sermon with a solemn warning that I should never tell anyone what she had said.

Uh, back to the *Ablaze!* thing. This one looks so clean, all neat digital lines and no scribbling. I'd ended *A!* 9 complaining that I wanted to work with more females, and then met Andrea on a bus. She became our designer, and night by night she worked, unpaid, using this thing called a PC. No more scissors, no more Pritt Stick, and for me, no more control. I sat with her at times, telling her how I wanted it to look, but saw how time-consuming my demands really were. Her computer, a miraculously expensive thing we could never afford, creaked along so slowly, and re-doing a page to my specifications would keep her up at night, so I limited my requests to just a few pages. The rest I still struggle with now, because it couldn't be how I wanted it. At least you can read the thing, and Andrea got to unleash her creativity with mousetrap style illustrations of how she perceived the Ablaze! machine to work.

I feel a current running through this and *Ablaze!* 1, as though they represent the whole endeavour, and I am amazed by the difference between the two, the journey spanned between them. Issue 1 went out to two hundred people in Manchester, and by the time of issue 10 the print run had crept up to 5000 and the zine was being distributed across Europe and the States.

The opening page boasts of subscriptions for the next three issues, fully guaranteed with refunds if we failed to publish. Of course we did fail, yet not one person claimed their refund. I consider this to be money owed, and hope that these faithful readers will finally get in touch.

Moonshake were fully celebrated for their *Eva Luna* LP. Gavin and Trout were massive fans, as was our roving contributor Sara Worley.

Sugar is a bad thing and a nice thing. Bob Mould though is entirely sweet. Trout and Mould got on like a house on fire. This ex-Hűsker Dű scream machine is so genial and sensitive, it must have blown Trout away. Trout's writing has properly matured by this stage, along with all other contributors, with the noble exception of myself.

Tsunami. I'd clearly spent too much time thinking about Jenny Toomey's socks – that was the lamest ending to an article ever, yet it tells me so much. I loved the energy of what Jenny and Kristin did – two workaholic DIY punk grrrls living together. I was in awe of how much they achieved with their band(s) and their record label. They worked harder! They achieved more stuff! And if they weren't on a fast track to M.E., I don't know what they were. Of course I hope that's not true, and I wonder what they do now.

The Hood interview captures a perfect moment, when Justine and I bussed it up to the mystery town of Wetherby. Justine took these photos of the summer evening when we discovered the wonder of pylons.

The Kicking Giant article is written by a member of one of the bands interviewed in this issue, can you guess which one? The author says it's a review but it looks nicer here with the more extensive pieces.

Reviewing had become a gargantuan task, and this time the record review section ran to 11 closely-typed pages. Gavin can write the book *200 Ways To Devastate Shit Bands*; I cannot work out why the record companies sent us this stuff. Did they not know us by the trail of dread? How often did we feature a band because they sent us their records? I had to write all my reviews in one night, which accounts for a lot. We ended up contracting bark psychosis, and had to get Moonshake in to finish the job.

The notes at the bottom of each page are quotes from the wall – explain the wall, Gavin:

During the time of Ablaze! 8, 9 and 10, the walls of the front room and kitchen of Wetherby Grove were covered in a motley collection of posters, flyers, postcards and the blank backs of press releases.

The last of these was known as "the wall". This is where we, but mainly I, wrote residents' and visitors' utterances that we found amusing or interesting. Ablaze! had a host of regulars, and some of them were more prolific than others in this regard. Lots of the scribblings were puns on band names, frequently profane or scatological, or the accidental malapropisms of the weary and emotional. You probably had to be there. When I left Wetherby Grove in 1994, apart from my records, all I took with me were three tour passes, two photographs and one wall. Looking at it now, my favourite lines are those where I have no clue what the hell we were on about.

And now it's time to shut the fuck up about the Nation of Ulysses and go and do something else instead.

Getting over Huggy Bear

I should have celebrated their sound but was too tangled in jagged emotion. Why else would I besmirch my favourite band so?

They were the greatest. It's not just music, this was rhythm and detonation. It's a volatile substance, you have to handle it carefully. I didn't, and the wounds still hurt.

First thing #1. Stood with Ian Svenonius outside the van. He asks me, do you know Huggy Bear? I'm like, no, what, that guy out of Starsky and Hutch?

First thing #2. Pavement were playing at ULU. I was minding my own business, selling fanzines, and I think I met these kids, I dunno, they might have talked to me. They crawled around the merch stall like lovely urchins, excited kittens. It was the night when Gary Young made a lot of toast onstage, and lots of important things happened.

The First Thing Ever. Pavement did a press conference in W1, and then they said let's go to the Rough Trade shop, Huggy Bear are playing. OK. It was only a few streets' walk to the Neal's Yard shop, and down the secret spiral stairs, and there was this band!! Who were so energetic, so excited. 2 boys, 3 girls, one of the boys, this 18 year old, was singing with such a wide-open expression, like the whole world was completely new all the time, and all you had to do was rouse it, get it out of bed and get it to play, that's all, that's all you had to do. I talked to Jo afterwards. She was on a mission. We were very excited. She gave me a tape, *Webitched*, all sketches and giggles and one great song, 'Sour Creamer Stag'.

First thing #3. These letters started to arrive; long, handwritten, poetic. The envelopes were covered in pieces of torn up photocopies, coloured in with coloured pencils, inscribed with biro'd hearts. But who were they from?

Sonny Lee Wake, they were signed... After a while I told my friends that Huggy Bear had written to me, and then realised the letters were from the singer, Chris. It was the start of the strangest correspondence, all stream-of-consciousness, declarations of LUV. I wrote back suspiciously, guardedly, and the beautiful letters continued, torn up pages of handwritten poetry. When I did succumb it got weirder. I remember being kicked across Sonic Youth's dressing room at a gig the two bands played in Bristol by bassist Jo, in defence of Nikki, whom Chris had recently broken up with. And this isn't all, but it was too weird to even describe, to even know what was happening. Later, I found out that there were a number of girls in the same scene who received similar attentions, some of whom did not get off so lightly.

Huggy Bear. I'm complaining about them selling out, but those blips are not what we remember now. TV riot and SY support slots are not the things that remain.

The piece I wrote is all spilled guts, embarrassing, tearing them apart. Should it, could it have done something else? Anything that destroys hero worship when there is a chance for empowerment has got to be right... It's so inelegant and hurried, a mess, all ripped-apart heart... I think it confused them. I'd just felt it all too much. Chris's delicate answers scrawled and faxed, are really good, maybe I should have put his words more upfront and shut the hell up. But I couldn't do it, not then in the middle of it all. And of course they were not doing anything for money or fame, they had their reasons, and they had set a date ...

They were hastening their own demise. They knew they had to go, they had a pact, they knew exactly when they would die. I watched the last gig – it was fire – I did not know how to respond. I considered suicide but dyed my hair instead.

With them there was an emphasis on viciousness. I had seen them in action, a fierce tight-knit gang roving round a gig, picking off individuals for reasons only they knew. I watched them lay into someone, tearing them apart – disturbing to watch, undoubtedly terrifying to experience.

It's better for those that did not know them – then you're just dealing with the most incendiary band ever. Those that became entangled, in their relationships, in their politics, or just stumbled unknowingly into their sphere, have their own scars.

I would love to meet them still. When they went, they bolted underground like a mole, its ass disappearing under the soil like lightning. To play their records is to sign up for a dangerous thrill ride; there will be agitation and electrocution. But you know that as well as I do. You know it too.

What We Gonna Change

ABLAZE!
Issue 10
£1.90
FREE 7" SINGLE!
With tracks by CORNERSHOP, JACOB'S MOUSE, BIVOUAC and TRUMANS WATER

Interviews with:
NATION OF ULYSSES
FRANK BLACK
TSUNAMI
POSTER CHILDREN
SUGAR
MOONSHAKE
BARK PSYCHOSIS
SONIC YOUTH
NIRVANA
& more.

Huggy Bear

PUNK ROCK POSSIBILITY EXPLOSION

PAVEMENT review the demos

MOONSHAKE review the records

RIOT GRRRL TRUTHS

INTERVIEW BY KARREN A!

Jenny Toomey, singer/guitarist in Tsunami, is a girl I'd heard so much about. She's a kind of hero. I love her voice, I love her songs, she's been in about six bands all of which are great, and she runs, along with fellow Tsunami guitarist Kristin Thomson, the most staggeringly imaginative and innovative record label, Simple Machines. She's also been known to write the occasional fanzine, she and Kristin put out all kinds of booklets and literature with their records... and both of them have full-time jobs. As a hard-working person myself, you can imagine I'm impressed.

Tsunami (with John Pamer on drums and Andrew Webster playing bass) came over to the UK in January '93 to remix and re-record parts of their fantastic first LP, *Deep End*, which originally went a bit wrong because of Jenny's amp, an amp which cost her all of $50 in a Texan pawn shop.

"We're so used to that wonderful 'help-me-I'm-overloading' sound," laughs Kristin.

Jenny admits that, though it's okay live, when recorded it sounds just terrible. So John Loder, famed producer and boss of Southern Studios, ended up with the task of helping them put it back together in a more listenable way, something he was only too pleased to do.

While over here for that, they played four London shows (three of which were on the same day), as well as one in Brighton and one in Leeds. At times like this I'm happier than usual that my town is on the circuit; the north so frequently misses out on bands when the London show is imperative and any extras are still within capital-sneaking distance. Tsunami's set was replete with those guitar and vocal glitter-rain showers that endears me to their recorded output, although the essence of their sound was obscured by that almost inevitable technical scuzz. Watching them play their first British date was thrillingly nerve-racking; though they didn't falter or seem at all peturbed, the specialness of the moment made it seem fragile (butterfly-fluttering) as well as strong.

They stayed at *Ablaze!* Central after the show, so I took the opportunity to keep them up past their bedtimes with my erratic interview technique.

I began by asking these emissaries from far-away places to tell me about the origins of the Riot Grrrl movement that we're having so much fun with on these shores right now. I listened like a grandchild, wonderfilled, as they casually recalled experiences.

Neither Jenny nor Kristin had been to meetings for a while, as they found that the issues under discussion were ones with which they had already dealt. However, they were around at the start, and recalled how Molly of Girl Germs and Bratmobile resolved to put out a fanzine every week: "they were pretty good too." They also cited a promoter named Claudia who created a precursor to Riot Grrrl by hosting all-women teas in D.C., at which girls involved in music would gather and eat sandwiches. "It was weird and controversial, but it worked."

The biggest problem, it seems, that the grrrls in America have encountered, has been their treatment by the press. As Jenny explained, at last girls had found a safe environment in which they could be vulnerable and say things that they might have been keeping inside for years, secret from everyone. Having revealed personal details in a trusted environment, it must have been extremely traumatic to have that newfound security shattered by journalists who infiltrated meetings and took the secrets they shared out of the secure Grrrl space and into the arena of the parental world, by exposing them in publications like the *New York Times*.

I asked Kristin and Jenny whether they felt Riot Grrrl got a rougher deal with the media than other groups because of its feminist nature, and their response was a series of steadily escalating expressions of agreement, culminating in Kristin's "Yeah, one million per cent!"

Jenny: "It says here [in a smug, stupid *Daily Telegraph* article] that it's all style and no content and it is a lot of style, but the thing is, everyone talks about Camille Paglia and how great she is because she finally admitted that Madonna could still be a feminist - punks and riot grrrls have always known that, that you can wear lipstick and still be a punk, that it's not going against your feminism. Well, I'm happy that Riot Grrrl and Camille Paglia happened in the same year so that you can align yourself with Riot Grrrl and be a post-punk-feminist and you don't have to agree with anything Camille says!"

She continues, questioning the 'all style, no content' line: "Basically it's all about practical information, there's no agenda. But the problem is, all this major media gets involved and asks 'So, what's your plan of action?' It's not about a plan of action! The editor of *Stay Free* zine made fun of the statistics they have in USA Today features, like 'Americans are taking more vacations! In 1972 they took this number of vacations,' etc, - she counted how many times they used certain words in their Riot Grrrl article. The number one word was 'boys', another of them was 'incest' or something, but 'music' they didn't say once!"

K: "At the very first meeting in D.C. I remember it was totally diverse, in age, and why they were there; there were people who weren't part of the punk rock scene, and once a mom came - moms are always welcome..."

J: "...but not boys."

Brian, who is accompanying the band on tour, and who also runs Convulsiv Records, interjects sadly: "Once I made them all banana bread and they didn't even say 'thank you'!"

The American Riot Grrrl meetings are attended mainly by girls aged between fourteen and nineteen, apparently. "They all go bowling together and have sleepovers and go camping."

"People don't focus on the practical stuff," Jenny points out. "The initial girls were learning how to run a sound board, getting bands together, but all these articles go on about is incest and the writing on the arms and stuff."

K: "You know where that came from? The Nation Of Ulysses, they make fake tattoos."

Did the N.O.U. have much to do with it starting?

J: "Well, Bikini Kill happened in Olympia, in the fall of '90, and they toured out to D.C. with the Nation in the spring of '91, and that was just a bond, they were like two sides of the same coin."

In February 1994, Tsunami will celebrate their combined 100th birthday. They've decide to throw a party to celebrate, and... "You're all invited."

I tell Jenny that her singing reminds me of Tracey Thorn and a punk rocker. She denies the Tracey Thorn bit, although she doesn't seem offended, and accepts the punk rocker side, because people have said her vocals remind them of Fugazi. "And the B52s. But Tracey Thorn doesn't scream." On one of her songs, Geek's "Night Moves On The Catwalk" on the *Fortune Cookie Prize* LP, she manages to sound like both Jad Fair and Steve Malkmus (in his Mark E. Smith persona). Don't believe me? Listen to it, there are moments that will astound you.

How many bands are you in, Jenny?

"I'm only in two right now but I've been in a bunch, but they weren't real bands, some of them were just recording bands." She reels off a list of band experiences and names in a weary mumble. Here's what I could glean: Geek was a band she was in with her best friend, a "new wave punk band no-one in D.C. liked."

"Then we went to England and played in a band called Choke, at lunchtimes, and we got two pints of beer and lunch for free for playing, and a lot of exciting people in London said they were going to get us shows, but they never did, and then we went back to the States and we recorded, and then I went to Olympia and was in My New Boyfriend with Aaron Stauffer from Seaweed and Tobi who's in Bikini Kill now, and with Kristina of Green Eggs And Ham. Then I came back and did Slack with one of my best friends in the whole world."

Strangely enough, Slack are described in the Neopolitan Metropolitan booklet as a band unable to get together in one room "due to artistic tensions". Jenny was somewhat peturbed to find that everyone took seriously this tiny white lie she'd had to use to cover up the fact that they didn't have a picture of themselves. "Why do journalists want to believe those myths, like all recording bands hate each other, or all Riot Grrrls were abused?"

She hastily completes her musical CV: "And then we did Tsunami for the last two years, and the last year I've been doing Grenadine too with Mark Robinson from Unrest and Robert from Eggs."

Tsunami and Grenadine are two strange words. I had to look both of them up.

"They are? You don't have to look up either in the States. We thought we'd be called Tsunami cos we were gonna be this dumb little band," - Kristin and Jenny learned to play their guitars within six months of each other and within six months of starting the band - "and Tsunami is like an enormous wave [Huge and destructive too, according to the dictionary]. Grenadine was just because Mark Robinson and I went out drinking one night and there was this whole bar full of stuff, and we wanted to be a lushy band, we would wear velvet dresses and jackets and be very croony. So we decided we wanted to be named after some sort of liqueur."

At this point Brian mentions something rather strange. "I had a brain haemorrhage the other day."

Before I get time to swap looks of disturbance with my loyal members of staff, it is revealed to us that Brian is actually refering to a cocktail. Andrew goes on to describe the drink in greater detail (please bear in mind the fact that Andrew sits on our settee with his hair twisted into two delightful devil-horns during most of the interview): "It's like you puke in a cup, and drink it back up."

Jenny decides this would be an excellent rhyming name for a new new wave band.

When I confessed to Jenny and Kristin,

PHOTO: JIM SAAH

guardians of environmentalism and many other kinds of good-thinking things, that I hadn't yet recycled any of our waste paper, my punishment was to have a negative point placed by my name in The Book. Andrew also threatens to separate our "trash", Fugazi style, while we're asleep. He tells of a housemate nervously checking with him whether she could use non-biodegradable cleaner to clean the bath.

"Did you slap her?" Jenny demands.

John decides to have the letters "P.C/H.C" printed on his t-shirt. Jenny explains that they're each planning to make 20 of their own t-shirts and hawk them from the stage at their gigs, to see who sells more. A heated arguments over colours, quantities and profits begins.

A: "Man, Art School has come to town."

Jenny says her design will read "I don't buy John's t-shirt cos he oppresses people."

For some reason that no-one explained to us, John is the butt of many band jokes... it's partly because he's 21, and partly because he's leaving school to be a full time Tsunami... still we do not understand, because we are English.

How do you manage to do all this Simple Machines stuff as well as everything else?

J: "We both drink a lot of coffee. Kristin and I are both workaholics, and we live in a house together."

K: "We get up at 8:30 for our jobs but we stay up till at least 2 every morning."

J: "We don't go to shows and hang out very much. We do invite people into the house though..."

K: "'We could get a pizza and put together 4,000 singles - how about it? Come on over!!"

J: "We've had 8 singles with Tsunami on them but we rarely get a chance to practice. It works real good for Kristin and me because we can put Tsunami on the back burner. Kristin and I will set up the records and Andrew sets up shows, there's no wasted time."

Don't you lose money on Simple Machines?

"No."

No? Why not?

J: "Cos we use a calculator! It took us a while to make back the money from the first records; and for the more expensive projects that we've done, like the Lungfish record and the Fortune Cookie Prize album, Dischord loaned us money interest free. But we keep all our receipts and don't give a lot of free promo. We send to people who review it and we deal with good bands and we don't lose money on it. We don't have a hard time selling things."

K: "We're organised, and there's tonnes of stuff that we do on our computer that takes care of itself."

J: "We also have lots of friends so that we can ask questions - from the very start we didn't deal with distributors who weren't trustworthy. We also do mail order and we help sell our friends' things. We have a lot of devoted fans who buy everything we sell. And we keep them cheap so everyone can afford them."

Simple Machines have recently made a pact with Southern Studios, so they'll have people taking care of distribution and promotion in this country too. Southern do tonnes of work with Dischord Records, who are friends with Simple Machines, so Jenny is understandably chuffed.

J; "It's a dream come true, from watching Dischord growing up in D.C., they're definitely trustworthy and it's the sort of situation we'd really want to be in, where you have the autonomy to do the label by yourselves, and then the money plus the fact that people really love the stuff you're doing and want to help you do it on a different level. It was a real treat for us when we got offered that."

Simple Machines is based in Arlington, Virginia, only "prostitute walking distance" (some local history that they giggle through too much for comprehension) from D.C.. I had been wondering why they always have plenty of strange concepts that link their releases, whereas most labels are like: 'here's another band, here's a title and here's the artwork, there y'go'. The only reason I could imagine is that they both live in the same house and consequently end up musing about lots of stupid things. Jenny admits this is true: "For a long time we had the house to ourselves and we would just fuel each other's insanity."

Kristin fills in a bit of the background: "The whole idea was something Jenny and Brad Sigal thought of - to put out six records was a finite project that was achievable at that point; if they didn't want to do any more they could stop. But Brad went on to do other things and I came and lived in the house at that point and got involved. Then there was talk about what we were going to do next. Like Stupid Machines - hair crimpers and mini-egg scramblers - there was a totally endless series of things we could do. Then we got ideas about different projects like the Neopolitan Metropolitan triple 7" box set - we got the whole concept of neopolitan ice cream and coloured singles and the alternative business and metropolitan, urban issues, and then we were like 'What about a booklet? What about a box?' Now we just about dug our own graves with Working Holiday: 'Let's extend it over twelve months instead!', 'And put out twelve singles!', 'And put it in a box!', 'And do a calendar!'"

"And track down 24 bands," murmurs Jenny.

"It's a little Pandora's box," says Andrew. "Once you open it and go, 'We don't have to do just a dumb old single with nothing thematic about it...' suddenly everything you think of, you find a way to do, because you get into patterns of saying 'Why not?'"

J: "Like the matchbook idea, to have a single that opens like a matchbook and has an inner sleeve that looks like matches..."

I think they're mad. and ask whether they don't worry about these things completely taking over their time.

J: "We don't worry enough, like the calendars were a nightmare, putting the box set together was a nightmare, but we're getting more established now, we have people who help us do it, so we can go away and they look after things for us."

The Grenadine single, the most elaborate package I've ever seen, involved at least six different steps (putting the insert inside, cutting and wrapping the cream colour wallpaper round the inner sleeve, and stamping it and sticking on a gold star, and making a band to go round it out of flock wallpaper, stapling on the gold star card and putting it round the record)... and they made 2,000 of them.

"But that's the whole thing about Riot Grrrl," says Jenny. "I think Kristin at a very early age did tonnes of stuff and was really responsible, and was told that she could do anything, and Positive Force, for me, was the same way. When it started it was a lot like Riot Grrrl, with all-ages meetings, people coming for all different reasons from all different backgrounds to talk to each other and do creative action. Those kind of groups are great. I put on a show when I was fourteen, and once I did that, I thought 'If I can do that, then I could probably do this,' - it gives you these skills and you realise you can change things in the world. You realise how easy it is. Like the booklet we did about how to put out records, it's twenty pages of information, and it's so easy when you read the basic steps, but it's information that's usually denied you. I wish all bands had to put out their first record by themselves, so they understood the process, they wouldn't get taken advantage of and they wouldn't expect the wrong things."

You got any good stress cures?

J: "We usually get to the point where we break down, we just sort of walk into a room and sleep, or we scream and cry a little..."

Do you argue with each other?

K: "Not really, it's usually we're arguing about colours but it's actually because we're both incredibly exhausted. [In a sobbing voice:] 'It's not the right green!!'"

J: "It's also so much fun for us, we do get stressed, but we love it a lot."

K: "It's the only reason I stay up all night looking at my computer, totally this deep in accounting, and I'm like [she gasps in horror], but once I've figured it out, I'm like 'Yay!, I'm learning more about this accounting stuff!"

Do you get sick a lot?

J: "She doesn't, I get sick all the time. And I get really temperamental and whine about it, and then I think, 'Well I only get 6 hours sleep every day, maybe that's why...'"

Simple Machines also donate some of their profits to charity. The beautiful Beat Happening tribute LP, *Fortune Cookie Prize*, is a benefit for a youth-at-risk home in D.C.. Bands recorded their songs for free, and they've made $2,500 for the home, from the vinyl alone... "I think everyone should do a benefit thing once a year. Why not give back a little bit?"

I put it to them that Simple Machines has a strong didactic element, as if, by hook or crook, they will get the kids to think about things.

"Well, it's not really forced," Jenny counters: "If you've got the space why not talk about something that's important? And it's exciting for us to learn about it as well, to sit back and interview tenants' organising groups, I'd never talked to tenants' organising groups before. And what I always think about is that whatever you go through in life, you're not always happy, you're not always sad, you're not always in love, you're not always political, you're not always dancey, you're not always moody; there's all this variety of experience, it would be neat if the singles could represent as wide a range of human experience as possible. So we have sad records, happy records, political records, silly records, all sorts..."

"Or even to put all those components together on one project," adds Kristin. "Cos there's all sorts of different songs on those. I think that's going to happen with Working Holiday, some bands have taken the project very seriously and are writing songs about the holiday they wanna do, and writing really political pieces about it. Or like Pitchblende, who are doing Guy Fawkes' Day as their holiday - they've ordered books about Guy Fawkes, they're really researching their piece!"

J: "I don't think its didactic because we don't say that anyone has to do anything, they can read the stuff if they want to..."

I mentioned my feelings of astonishment upon reading about Ben And Jerry's, the incredibly socially-conscious chain of ice-cream shops featured in the Neo Metro booklet. I really don't expect things like that to go on within capitalism.

"Capitalism and communism, conceptually, are so black and white that people forget that you don't have to follow those guidelines, like profit = sales - cost , or whatever, so I think Ben and Jerry's is setting a really good example by being creative with capitalism. They're making money, there's no doubt about it. They're the best examples of that sort of thing, although other companies do it to a lesser extent."

Talking to a tired Jenny the next morning about hitching experiences in this country we realised that we had met before. On a Mudhoney tour in 1989 we had hitched with mutual friends, I can't recall where from, but we ended up at the gig in Leeds and she had stayed in my house. I was pretty stunned to recall this previous encounter. What was my strongest memory of meeting this strange girl? Her socks, actually (she didn't say much). They were nice, and superior to the plain black towelling ones I drag on each morning; as well as looking gorgeous, they were also long and warm-looking, protecting her ankles on those freezing sliproads whilst mine were pink-chill-blotched. I believe that, since then, I've been on a subconscious quest to acquire a similar pair.

Fantastic band, great label, excellent socks.

YET MORE NIRVANA!

COMPILED BY GAVIN B. WITH MASSIVE THANKS TO BETHAN WILLIAMS
ILLUSTRATIONS BY RALPH HORSLEY

By the end of last year, self-styled 'Redneck Situationists' Nirvana had achieved a popularity and notoriety few would have predicted for them just eighteen months before. Drug addiction, celebrity weddings and even preposterous accounts of premature demise have always been the staple diet of tabloid newspapers, but Nirvana presented us with a youth phenomenon the liberal British music press need have little fear of. Kurt's pronouncements against racism, and particularly homophobia, lent an air of sanity and intelligence to the excesses of Nirvana in '92. The 'Will they? / Won't they play?' rumours circulating during the three days of last year's Reading festival, not allayed until they took to the stage, added just the right amount of intrigue. But what about the head of this careering grunge machine? What was on Kurt Cobain's mind the hour before what was being described by the optimistic as Nirvana's last ever British show? Bethan Williams knows, she was backstage in Nirvana's trailer with him...

IDEAS ON THE CONCEPTUALISATION OF THE NOTION OF THE SCENE
"Courtney and I will attend the premiìre of Singles in sequined dresses. Matt Dillon trying to be a grunge star? All these people dressed in trendy clothes acting like Pearl Jam, havin' a good time, fallin' in 'n' out of love - it looks ridiculous and I don't want any part of it."

NICKNAMES?
"Yeah, slow-brain. Cos it rhymes with my last name."

POLITICAL GRAFFITI
"It's one of the best forms of art. We used to go around our neighbourhood and spray paint 'HOMOSEX RULES' on the side of vans. If you write 'QUEER' on a redneck's 4X4 truck, it's pretty much the most effective word you can use to offend him. It really affects his manhood."

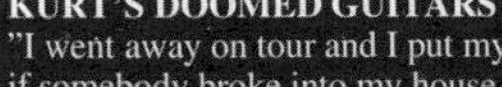

KURT'S FIRST GUITAR
"My mom was recently married, this was like six years ago. She married this redneck guy, and he had sex with this girl one night. My mom found out about it and she took all my dad's guns and threw them in the river. I hired this kid to fish a few out and I sold them. I got my first guitar with the money. It was star-shaped, the kind Cheap Trick played"

KURT'S DOOMED GUITARS
"I went away on tour and I put my two new guitars in the shower, because I thought if somebody broke into my house they wouldn't look in the shower for valuables.... While I was gone our neighbours had a leak in their pipes and all this mucus sludge soaked into my guitars."

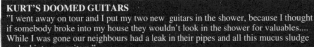

NEW MAN IN ROCK SHOCK
"I think everyone is aware of the fact that we hate racism, sexism and homophobia, but I don't think we're articulate enough to really challenge or get into political debates with people - I don't think we could call it art. Now we've found ourselves entertaining not only ourselves, but other people, and that's a lot more fun, that's more important."

ANY LAST WORDS...
"Can we play now?"

Within minutes Kurt is wheeled on stage in a wheelchair, resplendent in a blonde wig, and fifty thousand people breath a sigh of relief and forget about the mud, the rain, the food prices and the toilets for a whole ninety minutes. The show that most people had wanted to see, and what seemed like everybody had stayed to say they had seen, took place without further incident.

Sometimes, that's rock and roll for you.

THERE'S ONLY ONE NATION OF ULYSSES

Karren Ablaze! followed them to Liverpool and Glasgow. They showed her how to play dice and they changed her life.

JAMES CANTY, STEVE KRONER, STEVE GAMBOA, TIM GREEN, IAN SVENONIUS. FIVE SPECIAL BOYS FROM D.C., TALKING 'BOUT YOUTH REVOLUTION. THE SOUND TAKES YOU BEYOND THE CONSTRAINTS OF YOUR MIND/YOUR BODY/THIS ROOM: 50,000 WATTS, ENOUGH TO MAKE YOU KICK THE AIR, CLAW IT WITH YOUR TEETH, TO MAKE YOU LOOK PRETTY STUPID, BUT IT DOESN'T MATTER, AND YOU CAN'T HUM ANY OF THOSE TUNES, BUT IT'S THE MOST EXCITING AND ELECTRIFYING ANTI-PARENT CULTURE THING BEEN SEEN ROUND HERE. NO MYSTIFYING MARKETING, JUST LIBERATIONARY LITERATURE, ADDING A NEW DIMENSION TO OUR FLAILING INDIE-CULTURE - WRITING YOUR OWN MANIFESTOES. SO YOU GOT THAT FAR AND NOW THEY'VE GONE, WHAT'S THERE TO BUILD ON?

RECORDS YEAH. TOUR — enchantedness. fire + comb + mirror + braking bones. How my life was changed. PROPHETIC OCCURRENCES. The AESTHETIC, the UNIFORM, the TIMEZONE...

REMEMBER...

TIPS FOR FIGHTING SLEEP'S DEATH-LIKE GRIP:

1. The Intent - While society sleeps, bound to this archaic ritual, we shall take over.
2. The Drink - The dewy drops of perspiration from one another's brow, flavoured as they are with the mania of the long in waking.
3. The Mantra - "Ulysses, Ulysses, little flower beloved by all the youth."
4. The Sartorials - Pajamas, once clownish and babylonian, now present themselves as a bold new uniform for the army fighting against the nauseous prospect of the ethical workday, and also as a salute to madness and possibility - both children of the night sky.
5. The Noise - The Sound Of Young America, The Nation Of Ulysses. They will restore your lust for the nocturnal waking state, synonymous as it is with the Ulysses Nation State."

"The weekend starts here with the Nation Of Ulysses, and will never end, as they have exonerated us from the confines of the wage system and the work week."

PHOTOS: TONY WOOLGAR.

Being but a recent recruit to The Fruit Of Ulysses, I've got a hard task to explain and summarise and remember all the points of the N.O.U. aesthetic. I shall proceed to quote from the plethora of gorgeous and nourishing Ulysses-originated literature, and ad lib and guess and make up what I can. As this work is intended both to enlighten newcomers to the Ulysses aesthetic, and to amuse those already familiar with such sacred knowledge, I hope that the latter will forgive any tedious repetition which occurs for the sake of the newer children.

The N.O.U. and its affiliated organisations are the progeny of liberal hippies, gone as bad as you could hope. "The idea of N.O.U. was to drop out of conventional status competition into the smaller netherworld of Rotten Teenagers and start one's own league." They demand autonomy, nationhood, and the abolition of the stop sign and the speedbump.

Ulysses attacks retrogression and nostalgia. American parent culture is dubiously justified by the failure of the sixties revolution, which enables the propagation of kids who go along with the idea that there is no other choice, that it's all been done. Clearly there is a need for a new youth revolution that will be infinitely powerful and uncompromising, but in order for this to happen the tenacious influence of the nineteensixties, with its ineffectual philosophies*, has to wither. Since that decade the process of the sanitization of teen rebellion, of rock'n'roll, has escalated. N.O.U. deny the usefulness of the old folks' rock'n'roll, whilst reclaiming its original spark, its true strength. "In the words of punk rock Patti Smith - We created it. Let's take it over!"
(*That the N.O.U. aesthetic draws heavily on situationist theory is just one mentionable contradiction in their tangled, snarling nasty plan.)

Ulysses attacks the history that's been passed on to us with soothing intentions. Once history is cleared, space is made for that word, possibility: to "cure yourself of the dread march of the uncool who seek to enslave you with the tedium which they willingly shower themselves in each morn as they shout their sun salutation and gloat as its rays decay our skin, while showing to best effect the fruition of their long hours at the tanning salon, that bastion of babylon, that cradle of the corrupt." (Ulysses Speaks 5)

The process? The Nation Of Ulysses is not a musical group, rather it is a revolutionary group, and the noise is only one part of its operation, i.e. that concerned with the proliferation of arms, cunningly disguised as record albums, to the kids. Through the production of noise sounds, torn out of new instruments, "the soundtrack to revolution" is formed. These sounds are the components of the secretly manufactured weapons which are distributed to the kids in a clandestine manner. These weapons serve to instruct the youth on skills such as "building a catacomb for the old order"... with real bricks. Also, and more powerfully, through the aural moulding of the immediate environment with "surround sound", the transformation of the "simple space" of gigs into "the lush and ripened mango of violence and petulant behaviour" is effected: "Revolt can be endeavoured only one small space at a time, and with an exceptional cacophony, tuning keys untouched and tips of fingers bloodied, bound on extracting the evening from the banality of its counterparts, from their lack of vision and from their seduction of the victim into the bludgeon-like coma called slumber.... This room-to-room "Stalingrad" style struggle may be hard fought, but behind us on every turf trodden, we hear a spirited and jubilant war cry: The weekend starts here with the Nation Of Ulysses, and will never end, as they have exonerated us from the confines of the wage system and the work week."

Ulysses also adopts traditional kid tactics such as trick or treating: "Then sugar teeth and gums that bleed will raise their voice in a chorus with me singing Spectra-Sonic Sound; this is the sound that surrounds, adorns your ears like a crown..." The threat of violence and destruction these children pose if their demands go unmet mutually endears these two forces, uniting them in the menace they hold for the establishment.

Members of the N.O.U. do not sleep. Ian Svenonius' pretty head may have tipped limply onto my adjacent shoulder in the middle of some long night journey, but this was surely the practice of soul travel, spinning lightyears catching fresh visions for replenishment in the battle.

The aesthetic includes dietary directives - pure sugar, a special and very accessible mind drug. However, they are aware of the "paradoxical nexus twixt one's passion for confection and one's equally unyielding desire to protect one's teeth, figure, and idealism from all consumptive decay," as addressed in the song "Diptheria". Members of The Nation Of Ulysses also drink a lot of coffee.

The issue of dress is central, and also deeply problematic, as you'll discover when you read on. N.O.U. personel who propagate the revolutionary noise-sounds at youth gatherings are to be seen sporting slicked-back, neatly netted hair and thrift store suits, weirdly echoing the style of fifties delinquents.

All members of The Nation Of Ulysses are 18 years old.

THE NATION LIST: 1. Zip guns. 2. Chimp. 3. Anatoly Karpov. 4. New Peoples Army (Philipines). 5. Bold sharp lines. 6. The camel walk. 7. Hairshirts. 8. D.C. Blue. 9. Knives. 10. Malted milk tablets. 11. Futurism. 12. Ford Falcons. 13. A complete revamping of the social and political order.

"Contrived" is just a miserable way of saying that we positively contruct our own reality. Look out! SOUL IS BACK!

OK? I hope that helps. Here's where I go out to unpeel the truth, to get to the centre of this Ulysses phenomenon. (N.B. The scope of this piece does not include the confusing and heretical problem of the N.O.U. jazz impostor band.)

"If the Beatles had an infinity menudo in their contract, when Paul McCartney started writing 'Ob-la-di Ob-la-da' he would have been replaced, because obviously he was commiserating with the parent culture....."

Ian Svenonius and I sit in a shop doorway in Liverpool city centre. Nearby a busker plays Smiths songs. We crane our voices over his piteous noise to fire ideas at one another, each shuffling around on the stone floor to better challenge the other as it becomes necessary, which it frequently does on my part given Ian's tendency to use words as delaying tactics. Our conversation is like a fight, with moments of concession, moments of empathy. I mock his attempt to have a fully formed and operative ideology, and sometimes he outwits me. There's something very stimulating about this game. He obviously plays it a lot, otherwise the unique and beautiful Nation Of Ulysses vision would not survive; it thrives on challenge.

I ask whether death is on the Ulysses agenda, and listen carefully till I can find a flaw, something to get my teeth into.
"Actually death is real interesting to us, because we know that, besides girls making noise in America, that we're the most interesting thing. But we also understand that we can be compromised and become completely obsolete at any moment, and as soon as the kids understand that and recognise our invalidity, they should come and bury us and burn us and destroy us, we invite them to do that because we're not into the perpetuation of ourselves for our own sakes. To me that's one of the really gross things about rock'n'roll: people soldiering on. That's what being 18 is, being really non-careerist. But, death: we're into the idea of future, and that's how we bury the past. We don't like the future, or now, being defined by precedents, which is something that people always do. They try to define you in terms of what you've done before, like if you fuck up once then they say 'Oh well you're gunna fuck up again'. Similarly, as revolutionaries, failed things like the sixties kid revolution are always cited to us as proof of our compromise or our failure, so that's why we destroy history. We hate history because we think anything can happen in the future, we think we can live forever, that it's a possibility. The future is unwritten. We're into mortality, we flirt with our mortality all the time. One of our concepts is infinity menudo... you know Menudo? They're the Brazillian New Kids On The Block, they're 5 virile young boys with greased pompadour type things, really cheesy and incredibly popular. All over America in Latin American communities they have a Menudo shop and it's like this huge thing, it's kinda dying out now but one of the things about Menudo is, it perpetuates itself by replacing old members, and that's understood within our group - as soon as somebody compromises their ideological youth status they're replaced. That hasn't happened yet because we're all revolutionaries... [So why has the loss of Tim Green resulted in the cessation of The Nation? If what Ian says is true, they could simply have found another revolutionary to take his place. Hmmm.] if the Beatles had an infinity menudo in their contract, when Paul McCartney started writing 'Ob-la-di Ob-la-da' he would have been

replaced because obviously he was commiserating with the parent culture by reciting the songs of the fathers. Actually I shouldn't mention the Beatles because we're a terrorist party, I don't really know anything about music..."

That's a lie! You talk about bands all the time.

"Well, only as a metaphor."

No! You're genuinely so into it...

"No, no, (laughing) no no, I..."

You're always saying you know this band, you know that band? You don't come up to me and say d'you know this revolutionary movement?

"I only talk to you about bands because you're a fanzine writer, and you write about music, so that's my point of reference. And it's true, I like music cos it's the only thing kids care about and that's the reason we use the medium of music, but all I'm saying is that we don't wanna carry on like a traditional rock'n'roll band. I don't think most bands recognise their ideological potential, that they can beat off powerful enemies.... See, people are alienated from the whole concept of having political power because it's placed in the hands of people who have nothing to do with... I mean the whole idea of politics is so absurd, it's such a disgusting word, and everybody's really cynical, but for us everything is inherently political, everything you do. But we won't even use the word politics anymore because the things that we think are political are our hair and everyday life, we wanna bring it back into that sphere, cos everything else is just about money, like we're a new nation but we don't have a currency yet."

Are you gonna have a currency?

"No, our only currency is, we advocate mass stealing, and we do that when we're on tour in America, we steal everything, we steal our oil, this is true, we steal all our food all the time cos we don't have jobs, and we don't have the dole in America so we have to go and steal spaghetti from the grocery store."

All the desire in the explosions of the universe. All the hatred. All the fuckin' energy, distilled. *Surfer Rosa* and *Slanted And Enchanted* don't come near this. It may not have been immediately apparent, but the *13-Point Program To Destroy America* is the expression of a serious intent. So c'mon, I defy you to hear this record at neighbour-killing volume without screaming, without disintegrating with that full force, the bombardment on your being of noise.

they got style, miles & miles, so much style & it's wasted

The Nation Of Ulysses Must Prevail

If the *13 Point Program* did this, are there words in the medical dictionary to describe the effect of *Plays Pretty For Baby*? Wordless, psychotic, climbing those barbed-wire stairs on my hands, wrenched inside out, food for devils. it defies time and it defies wanting. Before, nerves got you there: now, you need nothing. They've refined their arms production methods to kill squares like me. Only those with tough eN.O.U.gh hearts survive this. As a humane being, this is my advice: don't put yourself through it.

THERE'S ONLY ONE NATION OF ULYSSES. And fire never burned like this before, a new blazing way of burning. That barbed wire, sparking, like nothing else. All of it leaves me yearning for an energy that can rarely be possessed without subverting nature. "TAKE THE KINGDOM OF HEAVEN BY STORM" is the sound of synapses ablaze! - that moment, abandonment, on the carpet like there's nothing else. Just... cancel out the rest of my life.

Ian F. Svenonius is mumbling, D.C. style, about the Nation Of Ulysses glorious vision hypothesis. I am spellbound by his insanely swollen pupils that betray the fire inside his skull, but I have to keep struggling to stop him talking and get him to acknowledge certain contradictions within the ideology. He seems to get bored of treating me like an unwilling piece of conversion material, evading questions like a *Living Marxism* seller on the high street, and slips into a more confidential mode - he occasionally insists that I switch off the tape recorder while he says the things that he says he cannot say to the *NME*. Of course he speaks to the *NME* like this too, gaining conspiratorial allegiance with whichever writer he must impress. Whatever, I like him. His manner is challenging and also magnetic, simultaneously polite and manic. His fronting of The N.O.U. is heroic. I have never witnessed a band like them - this may be because they claim not to be a band at all. But terrorists? The series of explosive acts for which they claim responsibility, printed on the sleeve of 13-*Point Program*, looks unlikely. The terror they wreak on their own bodies during shows surely has a lot to do with it. When they toured the U.K. in April 1992, frames were flung and injuries sustained with the carelessness of the frequently hospitalised. I was used to their habit of starting the set with lighter-fueled shoes blazing (flames licking trouser hems with awesome, dangerful, delight) but was still alarmed when the stage at the Leeds Duchess caught fire. Call me a wimp, but I really felt that it would be a shame if our best venue was razed. Did those strange boys take any notice of our arm-waving protestations? Not exactly. It was only after Ian had performed a particularly daring somersault into the air, resulting in his landing with an obviously painful bump, that he looked around (startled for a second) at the flames. His reaction? Pulling a comb from his pocket, grabbing a mirror that just happened to be close by, he carefully combed his hair. Nonchalant-as-U-like. I've a feeling that much of the insane energy of The N.O.U. that has so inspired me comes directly from this man. And his denial of this idea is more or less where we begin...

In the darkened backroom of a Glasgow venue, Ian is telling me about the mythical function of Steve Gamboa, bassist in human terms, within The N.O.U. His voice is hushed: an adult is present.

"I was in the process of denying that this was some sort of personality cult" (before we realised the pause button had been pressed down for 10 minutes) "which was constructed around a single person's vision, or an egomaniacal tyrannical crusade on my part to force my own ideology down the throats of children using the tools of other people. I was outlining the different functions of the various members of The N.O.U. and I was saying that Steve Gamboa is the Lamb Of Ulysses. Lamb is a word which is used in religious imagery in the United States..." Ian stops. Suddenly he's screaming, "GOD I HATE THIS! Ugh, this is exactly what happens, see that's why I'm dubious about the term drug... "

He recovers quickly from this minor coffee-and-frustration induced tangent and is ready to continue, but the outburst has thrown me. He explains that it's from having to recite his journalist fodder twice because I didn't record it the first time round...

But I still want to hear it. So, erm, tell me about the lamb.

"Are you religious?" He gives me a curious look.

"Roman Catholic," I whisper.

"Are you really? Catholics are EVIL!" he spits, gleaming black eyes at me.

Thank you, I'm not practicing.

"The lamb is a religious metaphor for purity of intention, and Steve Gamboa, he steals all of our food when we're on tour, our oil and stuff for the van."

So, why didn't they steal in this country - why give money to a fascist state?

"Well, first of all, being outside the constraints of the Nation of America, we don't have the currency or whatever..." he lies. At this point, our grown-up companion leaves and Ian switches off the tape recorder to say the real reason, about which I can't go into too much detail, but it involves them nearly being deported from a European country for thrifty activity involving combs, of all things. I challenge him to engage in some theft of their number one stimulant: the coffee. There's an unattended machine in the room we're in. He won't, even though the girl selling the coffee here at 70p a cup had previously told Mr. Svenonius to piss off.

He's puzzled at this. "You thought it was cool though, that she was rude to me."

She's entitled to be, I felt. It can't be fun, working all day in a noisy club where Americans are complaining about the price of the coffee they're incessantly guzzling.

"What about communication, though? What about miscommunication, and alienation?" he demands.

This particular question just cries out to be turned back on him: isn't The N.O.U. gonna alienate people by having such strict style directives? Aren't people going to say 'I can handle that bit, and I can handle that bit, but I can't accept a contrived new look'?
"Yeah, in fact they're really insulted by that," Ian admits, "and we've had epistles from the youth which disdain us for our dictates about hair length and the like, but that's OK because the Ulysses revolution is totally new, it's day by day, we're not prescriptive for our ego's sake, we're just saying what needs to be said. The Ulysses revolution doesn't dictate that everyone has to be a clone of ourselves, in fact it encourages diversity."
So, in what sense is there a uniform?
"Well," he begins, deciding on a logical approach, "do you agree that different signifiers which people wear intimate different ideologies?"
"Yeah...?" I'm dubious.
"So that's the idea behind the uniform."
But uniform means the same, and you're saying you encourage diversity.
"Well yeah, sure. There's more than one way of knowing and there's more than one way of seeing and there's more than one way of thinking."
"Bullshit." I reach for the throat of the slippery snake before me.
"No no no it's true, there are things that we're definitely directly opposed to, but there's also the things that are embraced within our, like, err..."
Emphatically, I ask him to explain how they can have a uniform while encouraging diversity in dress.
"Well, in the British army for instance you have the Highland troops who wear kilts and the other ones who wear their trousers."
OK. I'm satisfied, but only momentarily. If the uniform changes spontaneously, if the group does it simultaneously, how does it work out? Don't people in other areas lag behind?
"You're talking about the idea of backwater, which is really insulting. If someone is hip enough to be prescripted (sic) to the Ulysses youth gang community, we trust them to have good judgement about what the aesthetic holds for their community and what they need to prescribe."
How d'you know it's not better to go in disguise? What's good about being so overt?
"Like Umberto Eco said, I speak through my clothes. You wear ideological signs."
But then you're easier to pick off.
"Yeah, we invite desecration, we want an open war instead of this insidious war which would teach us that we're crazy or totally invalid or illegitimate failures or whatever - much better to have an open war, where the enemy would grant us that we do have an ideology as opposed to that we're just loonies."

This is just fine, so I rush us onto another topic that has been bothering me, that of nostalgia. The Nation is well acquainted with its evils, yet they also use it... "Like with this..." I point to his hair, a jet black, extremely greased quiff.
"This is nostalgic, but it's nostalgia in a different way, in a totally prescriptive way. There are only so many ways you can cut your hair, and in America we're awash with the baby boom generation who own all the channels of the media, basically they own truth in terms of society, and their truth is, specially concerning revolution, that what they did was a really important thing, but it's over, and lets get on with the realistic idea of free market capitalism. So when we wear our hair like this, it would have intimated a totally different idea in the seventies when the fifties generation were totally in control of media channels, but now that the sixties people are in control, it doesn't have the same retrogressive vision. Now it intimates an idea of the juvenile delinquent and stuff, it's the antithesis of the hippy idea. In America you have all these hippies, I dunno what it's like here, there are tons of hippies and they're all like college kids, liberal bohemian existentialist-reading jerks..."
He's dismissing most of the youth. I have to interject. A lot of potential revolutionaries now come under that description.
"It's people who perceive the sixties critique as being still relevant. And things like taking drugs and having long hair had a totally different relevance in the sixties than they do now."
So, it's just that those methods have failed and worn out. But all the hippies are conforming to something and you're conforming against it - you're still conforming.
"You say that we're dictated by the terms that they set for us, well basically if you don the uniform of the old order, you're etching retro on your tombstone.To an extent we are definitely really reactionary."

I ask about the flag on his badge.
"It's the flag of Washington D.C., and that's not because we're patriots, not because we're football fans or anything, it's because Washington D.C. is a mostly black city, America is divided into 50 states and each one has representation in congress, and D.C. doesn't have any of those, it's 64 square miles, it's not part of any state, it stands on its own, it's where the government is, and it's taxed without representation, which of course is the reason why the American revolution was supposedly fought, because of taxation without representation, by King George to the colonies or whatever, so by wearing the D.C. flag I'm just speaking about disenfranchisement. The Ulysses struggle is analogous to the Washington struggle for home rule."

At that moment I was envisioning a feminist movement based on the inspirational features of The N.O.U. combined with the bite of the S.C.U.M. Manifesto (see the Girl Power manifesto elsewhere in this baby textbook for the first fruits of this union).
"Well, the people who understand us best are girls and we really wanna speak to girls, I don't think that we're the end all, there's a lot of room for a broad based girl revolutionary critique - things that we can't, by virtue of our gender, really embark on."
You'd be crushed by them, turned upside down, the whole thing would be...
"Annihilated, basically. Yeah, because we embrace overturning the old order and part of that is male hegemony [pronounced "hojomony" in his murmuring tongue]. Whenever we talk in interviews we embrace our own defeat by saying that the most interesting thing going on is the noise being made by girls, which would instantly exclude us, but that's alright because N.O.U. isn't about power, its not about pigs, and the term 'nation' means common vision, it doesn't mean hate."

Youth: is it an age or an attitude?
An evasion: "It's a lifestyle."
An attitude?
"Yeah..."
So you could have 50 year olds who could align themselves with the 18 year olds?
"Absolutely, yeah. When someone's asked how old they are, it's usually an obscene thing, kind of like, 'what position are you at in your life?' It's a gross kind of query, and N.O.U. declare ourselves 18 because our nation exists outside the constraints of the old timezone of America so we don't really feel any need to refer to the old calendar or any of the old rules that were foisted on us by the nation that we were born into without any choice. It's all about attacking the underlying assumptions of everyday life. So when someone asks you how old you are and you say 23, the whole conversation turns to how legitimate are you or what have you achieved by this age. That's really disgusting. We don't ever want to do anything legitimate, we don't want to have any kind of legacy that would validate us in the eyes of the people that think in those terms."

On a personal level do you also deny history, cos I've never seen anything written about where and how The N.O.U. began.
"Yeah, totally, it's just disgusting."
Why?
"It's like, we're totally self-constructed, everything we do is very self-conscious. Isn't it really boring, stuff like that?"
"It's because people like me who ask interview questions just wanna be in bands, so we want to know how other people did it, and in your literature you quote Vaneigem about how politics must refer to everyday life, otherwise its bullshit. But," I conclude, having given a pretty weak explanation, "I don't *really* want to know."
"Well I'll tell you!" He laughs, black eyes sparkling. "This is an exclusive for *Ablaze!* fanzine, but I just wanna say that the way that Karren is deconstructing The N.O.U., forcing us to speak in the terms of the everyday, is really warming. Our father was a lightning bolt and our mother was an operating table and we were cranked up into the sky with electrodes on our necks, and then we sprang to life. The scientist who created us tried to do it in his own image and his own gender, and we found that really hateful so we went out on a rampant destructive killing spree."

So that old abuse-of-knowledge story lives on. Words fail. Bubbles burst. I am made up entirely of bubbles dying in the afternoon sun. I am on the biggest adventure in my life. Everyone else is tired and wants to go home. Later I shout at these men, I shout with all my might and rage. This is real life, the way it breaks, the way it bursts. The way you have (been given) the greatest idea ever, but when you're on your own with it, it's nothing. I wanted something to show for all this, something not only I could believe in but that clearly made sense outside of my head too. The energy that they left me with, I wanted to see something change for it. They I spent months talking, trying to push things, writing, waiting for action. When some of the implications of the Riot Grrrl movement were pressed home in Sally Margaret Joy's writings, when the whole thing was presented as something that could and would happen here, this preparation made sense. Nation Of Ulysses have been more than a catalyst, they are, for me, a big part of the origins of the upheavals that are going on within that prime site of teen rebellion; rock music. A friend told me that they had split a few days after I received a letter from Ian, in which nothing of this was mentioned. By the time that garbled paragraph appeared in MM (I quote, "Singer Tim Green announced he was quitting...") I was well into the denial phase of grief. The official press statement, released by Southern Studios shortly afterwards, which stated "The Nation Of Ulysses is putting out only spoken word records," was obviously intended to throw everyone off the scent of the truth. A more recent comment, from Cynthia at Dischord Record this year, was less hope-inspiring. "I see them all the time; they're hanging out having parties and not being The Nation Of Ulysses. I think it's really over for them, so I highly doubt anything will come out under that name."
However... I'm not yet convinced. And if, by any chance, The Nation Of Ulysses does not prevail, The Fruit Of Ulysses most surely will.

2f the word "revolution" makes you laugh then you're thinking too narrow. I can't blame you I know history too... YOU DON'T NEED A LABEL TO BE A FEMINIST. YOU DON'T NEED TO BE PART OF SOME CLUB. NO-ONE OWNS THE RIGHTS TO THESE IDEAS, ANYGIRLS CAN START GANGS ANYWHERE, AND YOU CAN DO STUFF BY YOURSELF - IT DOESN'T MATTER AS LONG AS YOU'RE DOING IT - CHALLENGING THE GENDER ROLES THAT WOULD STRANGLE US - WE'RE QUESTIONING IDEAS WE'VE BEEN BROUGHT UP WITH, BUT IT'S SO OBVIOUS, SO UNTHREATENING TO US. THE THREAT IS IN THE EYES OF THE THREATENED, THE THREATENED ARE THE POWER HOLDERS, AND THEY'VE GOT REASONS TO BE SCARED. TURNING IT AROUND. POWER TO THE POWERLESS. BY THAT TOKEN, NEW GRRRLS WILL COME AND OVERTURN US. WE CAN ONLY DO WHAT WE CAN. AND, IN CASE YOU'RE WONDERING, THIS IS NOT SOME EVERETT TRUE FANTASY SCENE. THAT'S WHAT THEY'D LIKE YOU TO BELIEVE. AND IT'S NOT A BUNCH OF JOURNALISTS IN LONDON STANDING IN A CIRCLE APPLAUDING THE ANTICS OF HUGGY BEAR. FORGET THE MYTHS THEY SELL YOU EACH WEEK. IT'S ALIVE AND IT'S HAPPENING AROUND YOU...

RIGHT NOW. RIOT GRRRL:

THE EXPANSION OF PUNK ROCK

You know, it's said ("it's said"!? hear me using their language of "objectivity"!) that there is no theoretical basis for feminism - that there is no social need for it. Fuck that. Feminism is punk rock to the schoolword and the squareworld. Feminism rips up the foundations of our psychology, our history, our political system, our families, our friendships, our sexual lives, it's true, feminism is going for it and people who want things to continue as they are (legalised rape) will tell us we are wrong.

Well, we're not listening to those people anymore. Riot Grrrl, It's like a suggestion, it's like an order. The grrrl probably isn't one who's already been socialised too far down - she's been waiting for the opportunity, like all through history, and sometimes something comes along that makes space, that permits, like a group of women that somehow forms and somehow says, yeah, let's do these things we want to do. Fuck philosophy. Fuck punk rock history. GRRRLS ARE THE EXPANSION OF PUNK ROCK AND WE NEED NO JUSTIFICATION. The reasons are on the surface of the world. The reasons we have all-girl meetings are obvious. The reasons are the blisters of society, at which liberals have been saying "yuk" but very few have been kicking. ACADEMIA IS A SHITTY PLACE for me, it's like a long tall twisting staircase in a building with no doors, and little light, just enough to realise that every few steps those ugly grunting noises are made by little pug-dog type monsters with running noses and bad breath and they keep trying to sniff up to me - NO!!!! Relatives of those little dogs also live in the indie-world, they're arse-expanding collectors and beer-slurping theorists and you know what? They know everything, as much as little dogs can know, about what we should do. So we spend a while trying to tame them, get them to help us out sometimes, but it's hard work mobilising them and they can never really get away from those dog mentalities. Slow, perfectionist, fouling things up with their petty, competitive ways. So we thought we'd try something without them. Of course, they're very upset and rarely give up that fearful howling on our doorsteps, but you know that in a while they'll quieten down and leave us be.

Anyhow, we can't hear them just now, over the beautiful weird electric scream of our newly switched on guitars. The dogs have got most of the equipment but we got some, and we can share it, and we can steal theirs when they're not looking. And this is what we do:

We use music-playing things as a way of showing ourselves that we can do whatever we want to do. We use them as a way of denying history, of ignoring the messages in our upbringing telling us we can't do certain stuff. <u>WE CAN DO ANY STUFF.</u> Yeah - it's so obvious and it's so straightforward, it's hard to see why there's been all that mystique, why power's been held onto so tightly and knowledge withheld so meanly when it's this easy to claim it - we just use the magic word, and the word is POSSIBILITY. It's an idea that links Huggy Bear and Simple Machines and Nation Of Ulysses and Ablaze!. Anger makes things happen, then the uncertainty we've been trained in melts into confidence. Self-destruction turns into self-love, and our self-love is our power because we are alive and we're going somewhere, whether we realise it or not.

DO STUFF. DO IT. DO - IT - YOURSELF

The backlash is here already. "Ironic" sexism prevails in the music press, they think they've outwitted us because they're still selling papers to 50,000+ kids every week. But only empty things happen fast. We're growing, we're underground, and we're denying their power by not talking to them. They need us, y'see. They need people who are doing things, so they can continue to make money by being seen to always exist at the centre of things. But Riot Grrrl isn't centralised, it's not organised, we've no leaders, no spokeswomen, we're not geared up to exploit the press now because you always pay for that kind of stuff in the end. So yeah, Sally wrote the articles that stimulated a lot of us to get moving, but ever since there have been attacks from all sides, and too much interest - boys wanting to know, wanting to pull us aside and argue with us, wanting to find out where they fit into it. They don't, we don't need them, we don't need the corporate press. We're truly independent, we'll pay our way, we'll use our own channels. That's the whole point.
They mighta stopped us before but now we are too many for them. And that stuff, the ways they made you cry and feel so bad inside, if you say it to us we say yeah. It's true that that happened and they're shits and you, you are fine and you will come with us and we will grow. What they do is their problem, they might wanna fall on the floor and die and we're not going to stop there trying to hold them up.

Too much to say so simply..
Can you get hold of a pen, some paper, some kind of duplicating machine (photocopier, printing press)? Then you can make your own newspaper. You don't need all this desktop publishing and typewriters, but if you have access to it, you could use it. "Typography is for fascists" - a joke made by the music press at our expense, we'll turn around, we'll write it in their blood sometime soon.

Getting guitars: some girls have bits of equipment, and some of us have some money, and some of us can get things cheap - we'll figure out ways. And if all that fails, we got loud voices and we can always find things to hit, things that make good sounds. We can make tapes of our music and swap them, send them, lines of encouragement spinning round from town to town, blocking out boring boyrock, getting more and more ways of saying our thing that's been ignored centuries.
Hiring venues, doing the sound, making our own shows, inviting who we want - it's our scene where we're not pushed around. If you want advice about stuff, write to us in Leeds and we'll tell you anything we can. We're sharing with each other the things we already know, and we're inviting more and more girls to make it bigger.

We're armed with a knowledge of the past. Our voices are not to be diminished. Too many of us, too linked, too wise to it all. Riot Grrrl. So much to say, so simply...

We're all over the UK, in Europe, beyond. We can network all across this space, creating our own nation. Contact **Riot Grrrl Leeds/Bradford: Box 14, 52 Call Lane, Leeds LS1 6DT.** Write to let us know what you're doing to turn around and reclaim the power your culture has taken from you. We'll do the same. Or write to **Riot Grrrl London c/o Box XX, Ceased To Exist, 83 Clerkenwell Rd, London** EC1, and ask them to link you up with other grrrls in your area. **Riot Grrrl (WA), P.O. Box 782, Olympia WA 98507** will probably tell you stuff too.

WE'VE GOT A LOT OF WORK TO DO - NOT TO BECOME MEDIA STARS, BUT TO FULFILL OUR INTENTIONS. WE'VE GOT A LOT OF THINGS TO DEFINE AND SHARPEN.

"Life in this society being, at best, an utter bore, and no aspect of society being at all relevant to women, there remains to all civic minded, responsible, thrill-seeking females, only to overthrow the government, eliminate the money system, institute complete automation and destroy the male sex." Valerie Solanas.

G I R L S P E A K

The manifesto of GIRL POWER INTERNATIONAL, a worldwide network of revolutionaries: HERE TO SMASH THE FALSE TEETH OF THE ESTABLISHMENT

Girl Power speaks in a new voice to a "post-feminist" (sic) world. Well, to all purposes feminism looks like a dying corpse on the corrupt claws of media savages; frequently co-opted and diluted, sometimes censorious to the benefit of the status quo, often unambitious and backlash-weary. But as herstory shows, female strength is never entirely wiped out. We're back - and this time we don't want equality with the death-merchants that crawl the earth in suits - we want everything.
Girl Power was born in the UK, a sick, broken nation, during the patriarchal festival of "Easter", celebrated with eggs and bunnies as symbols of fertility. Our springtime cry is "Fuck fertility!" as we smash those chocolate emblems of selflessness, and distribute the resulting fragments to all cool girls in the area.
We steal from the doctrines of Washington D.C. boy terrorists Nation Of Ulysses, and use them as blueprint for greater things. They plan to destroy America. Girl Power intends to destroy the whole "civilized" world, with all those dominant cultures based on corrupt, damaging gender roles - and replace it with something far better.

BREACHING THE PEACE: GIRL POWER DIRECTIVES ON HOW TO ACHIEVE MULTIPLE REVOLUTION:

Raw material:
Women, oppressed beyond the point at which we were able to recognise it, our eyes newly opened to the insecurity and hypocrisy of the sane, the safe, the sanitary genocidal governmentality echoed at (almost) every level of our experience. Slowly we begin to recognise their attempts to suffocate our life-force, our desire, with the institutions of work, marriage, and all the trappings.
The transformation: through catalytic noise-sounds and inflammatory literature, previously "impossible" possibilities are unleashed. After a period of extreme energization a vision of the necessity and practicality of removing oppression in every sphere becomes apparent. Once reunited with the gleeful spirit that has whispered obscenities into the ears of everyone you hate, you'll find there's a choice: to return to your previous position on the escalator of sickness, conformity, denial of responsibility for the universal battery farm you are helping to perpetuate... or to move from the middle ground of mindless euphoria to a position from which you fuck everything up - setting fire to the escalators, smashing down walls - creating escape routes for those with the imagination to run.
Teenage rebels have spoken: "The idea was to have a completely rotten attitude towards the whole adult world, meaning, in the long run, the whole established status structure, the whole system of people organising their lives around a job, fitting in to the social structure... The idea of N.O.U. was to drop out of conventional status competition into the smaller netherworld of Rotten Teenagers and start one's own league." Girl Power agrees that a person's absorption into the hideous establishment (i.e. having a job) = death. We also state that marriage = death, (see our teachings on Unmarriage for the perfect panacea). However, the construction of a political party/terrorist organization with a hierarchical structure isn't exactly an act of dropping out of the conventional status competition. We are aware of the dialectical nature of protest, which ensures that dissenters are relegated to the role of "other", thus playing a necessarily supportive role to the mainstream ideology. We refuse to give credibility to traditional modes of protest. We won't bother to ask, but we accept the belated gift of what is ours, with grace.
While Ulysses lose themselves in paradox, we seek clarity. We talk not about the potentially divisive concept of "nation", being, as it is, the basis for big wars; instead we focus on dismantling the structures of gender that are used to define and limit us from the moment we are born. We also oppose ourselves to Ulysses' ill-defined market relationship, wherein they fetishize specific commodities; we deny consumerism in all its forms. N.O.U., like the blustering American religious and political sects on which it is based, depends on the charismatic oratory ability of its Leader. G.P. is leaderless and anti-heirarchical.
Having imbibed all the energy we need, and inhaled enough inspiration, we feel ready to cry out: "Burn the flag of Ulysses! Leap from the mothership of feminism into the cool dark waters of Girl Power freedom!"

Since youth dissent has been sold back to us over and over, the assertion that we may challenge society through our clothes clearly becomes laughable. There is no sartorial style that has not already been mass-marketed. As women, we've been brainwashed into the sick belief that our surface appearance is the most essential facet of our beings and that we must express ourselves primarily through our shape, clothes, skin, hair, eyes, etc for an audience of judgmental males. Girl Power casts out the internalised stagnant eyeballs to free us into a state

of uninhibited self-love in which we fulfil our dreams. Also, and importantly: as women, we are denied any legitimate means of protest about our position, and the adoption of a conspicuous uniform would surely invite assassination. We do not need explicit signs in order to recognise one another as revolutionaries, and the spheres in which we operate, often involving intimate contact with the enemy, require that we are sneaky and cunning.

We have provisionally formulated a plan which includes specific methods of working, and new notions of time and space:

Girl Time Zone: We refuse the authority of the traditional male calendar divisions, so we shape our own units of time. Our cohesive chronological structure enables us to work closely without the interferences of patriarchal time constraints. The Girl Time Zone directly defies the adolescent-fixated dictates of the square world, the bloodsucking exploitation of youth energy by the rotting carcasses of control. The boy revolutionaries' alignment with young people due to their disenfranchisement betrays an ignorance of the fact that while men tend to gain societal prestige as they age, the opposite is true for women who are given little real power at any age, and are frequently viewed as one-dimensional sexual ornaments, thus losing our primary usefulness as we age. We deny this arrangement and wish to point out that staying young is the best that boys can hope for, as they feel their sexual energy drain away rapidly after the hurried ascent to "maturity". However, female stamina, combined with our longer lifespan and our temporally more diffuse sexuality, means that we're at our peak for pretty much as long as we're alive. We are truly spiritually teenage, although our wisdom cumulates as we grow (This "passionate stage of life", bringing out "qualities of moral idealism and intense emotionality", according to a Victorian expert, is shared by woman who, "at her best never outgrows adolescence as the man does, but lingers in, magnifies and glorifies this culminating stage of life with its... convertibility of emotions, its enthusiasm..." This analysis is remarkably perceptive: although references to girls' superior intellect and strength are omitted, it does suggest our immense revolutionary potential.)

7 Easy Methods Of Generating Girl Time: By denying the necessity of time spent taking drugs, having sex, explaining ourselves to boys, working (for anyone but ourselves), getting "educated" in patriarchal death camp schools, and the murderous rations of housework time and that oh-so important Preparing To Be Watched By The World (make-up) time, we are freed to pursue pleasure and revolution (the two are essentially the same thing).

New Girl Geography: We're constructing new roadmaps of our territory, the globe, which is unbounded by walls and unmarked by flags. The terms "ours" and "not-ours" make no sense.

Anonymity is a weapon against the patriarchal pestilence which silences women who speak against it. For example, a woman defining her right to appear as she wishes is invalidated if she doesn't conform to the prescribed notions of beauty which we are all encouraged from an early age to strive towards, and is invalidated if she does (as she cannot be taken seriously in the uniform of man-pleasing woman.) So, if she dares to write her feelings, the criticism is polarised between "equal rights for ugly women" (in the language of Viz "humour", based on the idea that a woman only feels dissatisfied because she has failed to conform to patriarchal standards of "beauty"); and the kind of criticism levelled at Naomi Wolf (i.e. that she's conventionally beautiful, and so has no reason to want to deconstruct female beauty, in fact she must be gaining from it, therefore her motives are hypocritical). Girl Power asserts that a woman's outward appearance belongs fully to herself; we are not items on supermarket shelves to be discarded or selected, we're whirlwind points of energy unconstrained by the definitions and judgments of the miniature-minded. This secrecy of identity also helps defend us from the cancerous practices of the medical men(ace), psychiatric pigs and other forms of patriarchal pestilence.

Diet: Against a word which has come to signify spiritual slavery, we proclaim "eat whatever you like", opposing the endless societal prescriptions fired at us from school, home, government, "youth" literature, TV, etc. that are designed to make us weak by alienating us from ourselves and our knowledge of what we desire.

Methods of Attack: The militarist stance of boy revolutionary groups, with their slogans and insignia, bores girls who are less inclined to be excited by the traditional trappings of war. We do not deny that a war is being fought, but for boy and girl revolutionaries the targets are different, thus our strategies are at variance. They fight the adult world, and we fight the man-world. Mary Daly writes: "The difference between sisterhood and male comradeship, which is disguised by an apparent similarity in terms, would be almost impossible to exaggerate. An important clue to the essence of this fact is that the epitome of male bonding in comradeship is experienced in war... male merging in "the fire of communal ecstacy" or as "cells in a military organism" is necrophilic self-loss. In contrast to this, the Fire Of Sisterhood results from the sparking of Female Selves who are finding each other... [sparking] new ideas, new words, new images, new feelings, new life, new Be-ing." (Gyn/Ecology, p370.) Our aim is not to alienate boy revolutionaries by recognising these limitations in their way of being, but simply to clarify our differences and get on with our task, unhindered, while they get on with theirs. We attack with noise, confusion (often employing multiple or shared names) words, chocolate, and guns, bricks and bombs when appropriate. Our fight is adrenalin-fueled and essentially fun, following no pre-set programme. This manifesto is a carrier of gifts/weaponry, only effective if ideas are stolen or disputed, altered or refuted and spread throughout the network of brave people linked by a revulsion for authority. We are prepared to (ab)use philosophy, to put forward statements we know to be untrue, in order to stir up stagnant ponds of thought into newly rushing fountains of debate. We use threat tactics, to implant fear into the minds of our oppressors, following the work of Helen Zahavi; now there is the possibility that the next attempted rape victim turns around and stabs her attacker. "The non-saleable goods such a free bulletin can distribute are previously unpublished desires and questions, and only the thorough analysis by others can constitute a return gift." For our purposes authorship is a redundant concept, and correspondence with the originators of this work is unnecessary. The spontaneous creation and dissemination of free literature ensures that no-one has a duty to bring such things to life; it is only for those who want to do so at a particular moment. And, as we stole ideas from numberless sources, there's no copyright on this manifesto - steal any or all of it for your own subversive purposes.

GIRLSPEAK:

The language of Girl Power defies the patriarchal meanings historically imposed on words. We have noted how most feminine-associated words have been loaded with the weight of male fear and the hypocrisy that enables the equivalent masculine words to be swollen with positive traits. Our attack on misogyny is two-fold: propelled by our knowledge of etymology we peel off the layers interposed through time, and reveal often contadictory senses of those labels they impose on us and on themselves. Simultaneously we adopt their terminology and train it to betray male society, so that it will no longer bear their ideology, but instead throws fire in their smug undefended faces. Words that were the maidservants of men will raise the dust of their innermost libraries, setting pages alight and sowing seeds of beautiful chaos all around. The language of Girlspeak evolves organically as our aims prevail.

THE GIRL POWER VISION:

The ultimate vision of Girl Power is not to create a fascist world, but to share this space with its other inhabitants without the self-destruction and living death experienced as the everyday lives of so-called civilised society. Men wish to die because of their suppressed need to be female, or to express a big aspect of themselves that's denied by current dictates. Boy revolutionaries will destroy the old men who are keeping this system in place, but the final battle will be ours. This will also be achieved with the co-operation of people who lack the zest and love to live their lives - these people will be permitted to slink away and indulge in the self-destructive activities that will eventually fulfill their need for all-encompassing death. The key to our vision is the deconstruction of gender divisions; not the destruction of any type of person. This will result in a worldwide society, in which all exist freely and in wonderment, unbound by old laws of how to live.

Do not be discouraged when they tell you that our vision is but a pleasant dream, a symptom of despair at our coming assimilation into the adult world. The need for boredom, work, marriage etc only arise when we invite them to. Fear is a specifically designed limitation, like white lines drawn on the station platform that they command us not to cross, lest men with lazer guns surround and mutilate us. They have no such power, until they cripple our boundless minds and spirits. It doesn't ever have to happen. Accept no limitations... take that starpower.

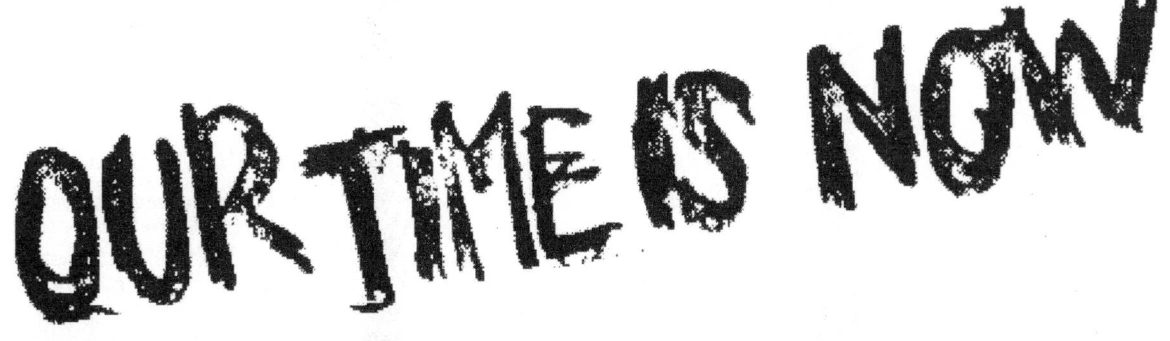

FIVE STRATEGIES FOR THE UNLEASHING OF GIRL POWER

1.To propagate girl love by spontaneously expressing how we feel about each other in ways which cut across the alienation that's enforced by media death machines and which keeps us apart. The first strategy, the Breaking Of The Chocolate, involves handing out gifts to girls at gigs and other public gatherings. Chocolate, traditionally a male tool for appeasing females, now becomes an instrument of destruction of the male hegemony. We use this method to stake out our territory (the world) and to create spaces from where we begin our Voyage Vision. It works on several levels: gigs are turned into events where kids start to communicate across the normal insular groupings. Girls experience a cutting through and destruction of a small part of the alienation that holds us separate, and are then inspired to carry the message and the chocolate wherever they go. It also serves to highlight our primary ememy, the Neanderthal, Misogynist Asshole. He may not have been visible previous to your experience of extreme harassment that occurs because you will not give him some of your chocolate. He may begin to howl like an unhappy infant and make threats of violence which he has no intention of seeing through. He will scream phrases such as sexist bitch at you, because he believes you do not have a right to free association in the male world. Why should his female friends have anything which he does not have? How could there be something that he is not at the centre of? The girls around him look on sadly, having learned a valuable lesson about their "friend". Meanwhile, quiet-spoken, cool boys will notice what is happening but will not interfere, correct in the knowledge that we are perfectly happy as we are. This is how they will show themselves as our brother revolutionaries. We accept that chocolate is a commodity that can enslave us, and that it is created in severely exploitative circumstances. As is the case with most of our weapons, we are independent of them and prepared to abandon them as soon as they become obsolete.

2. To fuck things up at every opportunity. Stealing from the shops and, if you're unfortunate enough to have a job, sabotaging your place of work are currently our primary methods of dismantling things as they are. To those trapped in useless or difficult relationships we recommend Unmarriage, a simple process by which you disentangle yourself from the other that keeps you from fulfilling your dreams. It's a celebration of a new life, and a gift of love to your ex-partner, therefore it need not be experienced in negative terms - rather it is a glorious, euphoric process.

3. To provoke the alarm of the squares and the joyful recognition of our sisters, eg. by the wearing of masks depicting heroic figures, the drinking of orange juice and coffee rather than brain rotting fluid (unless you truly want to be less alive than you are), talking to people you don't know and telling them the truth about everything, giving out presents (drawings, literature, badges, sweets, anything) and generally stepping out of line wherever possible.

4. To swamp the world with genius, noxious, girl-power noise groups, appropriating the instruments of boy musos and turning them against the guitars-as-penis-extension tradition. Our multiple purposefulness will include the distribution of Girl Power propaganda contained in beautiful noise-sounds, thus proliferating the utter confusion that will frighten the insecure while feeding the hungry whirlwind spirits of joyous transformation.

5. STAMP UNDERFOOT THE WORMS OF DECEIT! MEN ONCE ADMIRED, NOW TURNED FATHER-MINDED, WORK IN THE HIVE OF LIES IN THE ULTIMATE SOAP POWDER PRETENCE. We make "The British Music Press" our first target. It is a dangerous patriarchal institution, influencing those without critical defences and misleading the worldly-wise with its hateful cynicism thinly disguised as youthful enthusiasm. Next time you read how a pillar of this deathful establishment has "discovered" a Hot New Act, consider how much he (for it is usually he, and those that are she might as well not be) is being paid for having penned those weak words of fake wonder, and if the interview was conducted in any other town than London, imagine the luxury of the hotel room, paid for by a record company, in which he writes those words. Then consider how much his ego and his reputation require that he be seen to exist on the "cutting edge" of popular music. The fact that it is the kids who really love the music, often travelling hundreds of miles in adverse conditions, just to hear the Noise-sounds of their dreams, is overlooked by the slavering le(e)ch that tries to sell back to us what we already own, in the process of blunting the force of our experience of music through the deceit and greed that he weaves like worms into our spiritual sustenance. Soon the Journalists of The Establishment will find themselves on the real cutting edge, and their blood will form the ink in which we inscribe the New Message of Euphoria. "The British Music Press" will soon be quivering in its tall Tower, beyond the protective Reach of a King who does not exist, vulnerable to the attack of thousands of Invading Prophetic Cats who will claw at their kid clothes-disguise to reveal... the PARENTS. When faced with the realisation that they have been accepting the only thing they thought valuable and true to their youth-status from adults, kids will kick over the news stands and build their revolutionary methods of communication in the form of "fanzines" and messages in secret codes, meaningless to the newly abandoned square world that so depended on their blood. We will confuse them by disseminating different pieces of literature under the same name, and there will be no sense in which any is more "authentic" than any other. We will share the Girl Power Vision. The mutilation of "The British Music Press" will serve as an interesting and enjoyable model for the total destruction of the male-parent culture.

Glorious and hideous deaths await us, and in the meantime we're going to try every permutation that exists beyond the comfortable suffocation, the anaesthesia of the patriarchal establishment: compulsory education, family (child and adult abuse), consumerism, private property, law, their medicine and their war...

<u>All the desire in the explosions of the universe.</u>
<u>All the hatred.</u>
<u>All the energy, distilled.</u>
<u>This is the expression of serious intent.</u>

WRITTEN IN THE UK, MAY 1992 Anti©. PHOTOCOPY + DISTRIBUTE UNTIL YOUR HEART'S CONTENT.

KICKIN GIANT

"Fulfil expectations never"

Envision a music unable to be compartmentalised into a sound for 'the dead of night' or the 'hot action sunny afternoon' but where the imagined actions that take place therein are transposed: catchin-ball games in sleepin street spillin milk onto the kitchen floor, feelin the temperature barefoot on tiles, openin post by moonlight, seein how long you can keep going on pretending to be yr best friend's dog / cat / fish while your makin out friend wants to make out 'meow' 'gulp' 'woof' oh yeah of course. Makin out. Kissin. Kickin Giant is a Kissin Giant them kisses that engulf, that steal all your decision makin faculties, make you dread the next movement...

POLITICAL AS ALL HELL MELT YR MADE UP MIND. This is Girl Boy Boy Girl Boy promise, a REVO-LATION, a revolver-lotion. I think culture um requires this new punk rock sound and you don't ???

Boy = guitar = sing ♡ = Tae
Girl = drum = sing ♡ = Rachel= **Kicking Giant**

LOVE SONG AMMUNITION ANTI LUV. How about a specled history, no curates egg-splains a shiver makes you shout lose control...

What's a review for anyway children?

Political as **ALL HELL MELTER SKELTER** ♡ They don't follow that typical boyfriend girlfriend stuff no typical stereo sex, Kickin Giant swoon, make it up, exhausted just even by the aroma of a fresh shaved nape with the barbers talc (and allowed to get close enough to look retarded choosing groceries together). **SEX ACTS ALL CONFUSING O.K**, so involved 'accidentally' nudgin forearms or toastin the future with the dizzyin clunk of belt buckles amidst arguments about cereal too loud - too sweet - too soon.

For all you non penetrative disciples out there, don't worry cos Kickin Giant **FUCK** they sure do **FUCK** and **FEEL IT** awash in obscenities become prayers stuck sore to them like subtitles. 1/2 understood wilted drunken genitals... A 'dirty' review for a dirty band. Simplistic. Uneven. Righteous. Humbug. Mutant. They ain't no chic currency they make things too difficult by being too direct. They don't travel well hotel to hotel to picture pages. Non-cosmopolitan adventurers. Dreamin a rich dream, a pissed off dream, in a doorway (pissy + rich = Kickin Giant ♡) I could not want to tell you about any other group now I only want to yell out Kickin Giant **YEAH YEAH YEAH**... you wouldn't understand them. Listen don't laugh, to how they **RAMPAGE** thru' gender distinction expectations (destroy) on all of one song 'Go Girl (RIOT)' vandalising all hetero Dinosaur (yawnier) convention rules in three minutes of spazz life hectic axis. Or create the most precious sad (what's wrong with sad don't sad make you kind of....) in songs like 'I Don't Mind' or 'The Way That You Are'.

NEVER FELT SUCH A STING ♡

What's a review for anyway. Vandalising. Rule. Kickin.

Yr underground is bullshit if you are bothered by this, if you hate them cos of me. Bullshit. Sunny. Puny. Weedy. Poofy. I carn't tell the difference between the groups you like oh darling don't laugh when I sniff yr neck it's like an Alien that fell into my patch and I fixed them up and watched television for a while, tried to see what they liked to eat snd never wanted them to leave. - I feel - with them - different -

A stick drawing girl holding up a bank (LET'S hear it for her...)
Boy answerin door dribbling sperm. (Hi)
wanna kill. (???) * *

Kickin Giant they'd get a gold medal but wouldn't make an acceptance speech. It'd be in 'the look'. Implication of lips fingers crossed eyes. You might think we're smartasses but you follow us around longing to trade addresses

DREAM-TO-CUM * Sad as by accident seeing your lover's pants, hearing them, they'll make you blush. Remember the summer or number. If you're worth your salt they'll make you swear (sweat). **WATCH OUT!!** cos you thought you were alternative and carn't listen to their fuckin lesbo lesboy shit shit shit. Rub against

the soft
pillow of ...
A shadow like a panther paw
your knee length socks in rolls
the links I cannot see
'faked magic symbols' lipstick
fingerprints
orange peel.

KICKIN GIANT SAY 'TRUST STUFF'.

(Sonny Lee Wake - 93♡ ♡!)
Kickin Giant are on *Chinny Chin Chin 4 N.Y. Bands* on See Eye

WRITE TO KICKIN GIANT C/O TAE/RACHEL, P.O. BOX 782, OLYMPIA, WA 98507, U.S.A.

sonic youth

star "femcore grunger" kim gordon talks to karren ablaze

T.W.

"Sonic Youth is just a side project"

Kim Gordon tells me, and suddenly it all makes sense: a supergroup made up of members of Free Kitten, Mosquito, Dim Stars and, umm, Lee Ranaldo, who just happen to dominate the sharp psych-garde of what yer might call alternative rock. Me? I'm cynical nowadays, among the number (a small one) who believe the Youth shoulda split after *Daydream Nation*. This winter we hung out in foyers across the land, recovering from Pavement's always-stunning stage stint, exchanging pop anecdotes and forming alliances. I didn't, however, feel able to talk to Kim about this long-burgeoning movement of disillusioned Sonic Lifers, let alone reveal that I am one of them. How could I express the fact that, whilst onetime her band occupied the highest shelf of the household shrine, now they're too tired and sad to even bother watching? They're beautypunk icons supreme who don't dance no more. Now Sonic Youth tour with the finest and freshest bands, vampirishly siphoning off as much cool as they possibly can, to supplement that deficiency in their ageing reputation. Cos they need it - SY got that cool habit *bad*.

The Stuffed Animal Lib Guerillas

Stuffed Animal Liberation involves awareness of the plight of stuffed animals in the hands of humans, which is something Sonic Youth have started to do in pictorial form on the sleeve artwork that accompanies their *Dirty* LP. Many minorities exist without a voice, but stuffed animals are particularly hindered; a lot of them don't even have *mouths*.

"No-one's ever really picked up on that before. It's funny how a stuffed animal can take on ET-type proportions, in terms of lovableness."

This isn't always the first adjective that springs to mind when old Ev's name is mentioned, but I let this pass. The now-censored (by Geffen, after complaints from anti-stuffed animal cruelty lobbyists) sexual abuse pictures on the sleeve are particularly poignant, I tell her. It's something that's not really been documented until now.

"Yeah, adults really abuse stuffed animals," she agrees.

Violent activists have started hanging round fairgrounds and slot machine arcades in the UK holding hammers, hoping to liberate animals from those grabbing machines. Pacifist activists merely attempt to define their skills on the grabbing machine in attempts to "win" the animals from their plastic prison captivity.

"In New York," Kim reveals, "They tie stuffed animals to the front of garbage trucks."

Similar tales of inhuman atrocities against our cuddly friends abound. Sonic Youth's gesture of inviting toys on the tour, a stuffed squirrel among them, and allowing them to watch the shows from prime positions on top of the amps, starts to redress the problem by treating them with some of the respect they deserve.

"In the States," she confesses, "*We* were actually exploiting them - we were going to thrift stores and buying tons of them, and we made these buttons that said 'Hug me, I'm dirty' and put them on the animals, and sold them for $5. It wasn't that much of a profit! But when we started collecting them we got a sense that they *really did* look like orphans.

Grrrls & Guuuys

In 1985 Kim Gordon sang the beautiful line "*Support the power of women, use the power of men,*" a sentiment we still havta keep foremost and burning. I ask for her view on Riot Grrrl in America and Europe.

"I don't know if it has anything to do with it, but at our shows in the states there were more and more girls; the audiences were half girls, and really young, like 15, 16, so that's really cool. I think Riot Grrrl is a really good thing."

She's an admirer of Kathleen Hannah's lyrics, and emphasises that Bikini Kill, like the whole movement, is essentially *fun*.

"It's funny to tell guys to get to the back of the club."

Yeah, if you can get them to take any notice. Boys tend to be so sure of their right to be there while girls tend to be unsure. That's changing, but it's important to realise that we exist so much in *the problem* right now it's difficult to see how things can be different.

"I'm interested in the concept of Riot Guy," she says, but I'm sceptical. I ask whether she has ever met one.

"Yeah. Eric from Sebadoh... and Pavement are kind of Riot Guy."

Much as I love them, I find this hard to believe - In what way?

"Well, you can hear it in their music, the repressed singing. When Steve screams sometimes he sounds like a repressed girl, he's showing his repression. You don't always have to have overt lyrics, you know, like 'suck my left one'!"

Kim strikes me as an energetic woman, and I had to ask her how she manages to do so much stuff, like being in Free Kitten and all those interminable side projects that end up on every compilation record, as well as being one half of the SY nucleus.

"You can't just sit around and go to movies all the time," she says, and I agree, cos personally I never get the time to visit the cinema at all. So *how* does she do it? Don't you sleep, Kim?

"New York is a very work oriented city. And anyway, work to me is fun."

I guess if I'm not impressed with her recorded output any more, her vitality still inspires me. Years ago Sonic Youth demanded that we kill our idols, which means either that we stab to death the likes of her and the kids from Pavement, or that we break out of patterns of servile obsession. It's great to be wise enough that my soul doesn't shrivel under Kim's harsh gaze, and though I constantly crave revolutionary noise groups to help me change the world in my head and out of it, the price of obsession's too high for me.

Lay your idols gently to rest.

THOSE HUGGY BEARS, THEY MAY LOOK CUTE BUT...WATCH OUT!!!

When Jo smiles... can I say it without cliche? The sky lights up. The clearest, brightest smile she has, so full of warmth and knowing. When she smiles...

I hereby turn all the love in this article into hate.

First they were too busy to do anything for *Ablaze!*. Such foolish lambs. But I devoted these pages to them anyway, and then some words came. At one time I'd have said that our future depends on the germ they've been carrying, at one time I'd have wrote all kinds of stuff, and now it's my dead-line time and I am gonna give you something, something to read, whether it's packed full of emotion or whether it lacks limbs... One disadvantage in making this top popzine for you is that it takes so long - three generations pass and I'm still working on the same issue (3 words for it: snail-messenger-loss). By the time these words are printed, published and real, the Huggies' disease may have left them, with any luck they'll have split... But new bands will be infected. At first, I'd have put their numbers in the hundreds, now I know y'don't expect, and I'll believe whatever I see. The Nation Of Ulysses made me know I had to form a band, and Huggy Bear y'see, they're that desire in a visionary form, they're everything a band needs to be to kill the cover-version-ordeal that passes for our scene. I've seen something change, over the span of the few times I've seen them: an increase in arrogance that seems to screen out their roots. I watch them reach out for that balloon of fame (yeah, ethically - with democratic decision taking and a no-sell out policy that doesn't quite extend to turning down Sonic Youth support slots) and I think, yeah, it happens. And that isn't the important thing.

Let's run a quick inventory of Huggy Bear qualities to get ourselves warmed up here.

Unbounded energy. Soul, nerve, guts,

Like Jo announced, "With my gang I can do anything," I see them and I know it's true.

Threats of violence. Tenderness. Jealousy. Sexual and emotional waywardness.

All those things you always wanted to do but was too damn wise to...

Being real, being too real (but not 4 real - they use marker pens, not knives. These kids are practical adaptationists).

Huggy Bear know how to use machines - that means they know when to switch them off. They know about tunes too, thank the bitch that is god - otherwise none of this would make any sense. (Maybe they know a little too much about tunes - I must inform Customs and Excise, unless, unbeknown to me, licenses have recently been granted for the export of tunes from the States.) They know about rhythm and they know a little about vibes and they know about love, hate, all that shit.

PHOTO : LIANE HENTSCHER

We ready now, to talk Huggy Bear? OK.
Everyone hears 'em differently, but a common interpretation is this: they show the way to go. Because they've got that nerve, and that nerve is their germ. They defy everything, especially containment and description. And I would have said that to take them in anything other than their own terms is to misconstrue that essential thing, but I know I can irritate you more by defying my own statements, and use words like they use them, like snakes in brylcreem.

So what made me stupid enough to start to love them? I didn't need The Press to tell me, because Ian Svenonius, Nation Of Ulysses' shrieking thing, did six months before all that. When I found out what it meant that Huggy Bear, stupid name, greatest band ever were living in England, it was a good summer's day. After a Pavement show in that oven-like Rough Trade shop at Covent Garden, I first heard this new band about whom only whispers had penetrated my brain tissue. They opened with a crappy version of "Baptiss" and I saw Bob and Mark Ibold there on the stairs tappin' their heads and smiling, I saw that and I saw five petite individuals with some sass about them... I could see so much because I'd already pushed my way to the front, as close to them as I could, before dizziness befell me from dancing more than was medically advisable in that temperature. So everyone was baking and loving it and this tiny girl sang, "I'm the lady with the bouffant hair," with worlds in her eyes, later I find out that she is Niki and I know she's a star. The air of confidence about this band scared away everyone who could see that they could see, and like the most gullible ming vase I thought I knew this was the way to do it, I knew they'd found something within themselves and it was just right... this kid, this blond boy in the corner he was rocking around with his microphone and yelling and rapping and singing and he had so much glee, I can still see that expression flowing out of his face. Later I approached Jo, expecting some kind of grievious verbal thing that'd knock me to the floor, but she said "Yeah!" and her eyes shone, and she stole things for me and gave me a fanzine like a neverending coffee jar of inspiration and energy... So then I found they shared my N.O.U. obsession... nothing more need be said, but hey, I'm gonna cut this short story just a little longer. Their tape, *Webitched,* has classic Ablaze! songs without number, gorgeous tunes and shouting and perfect timing and fuck it, I'm not gunna describe this precious music for you, first because it's not possible, second cos I got all this sky to fly across, all this pleasure coming to me before I die so I won't waste

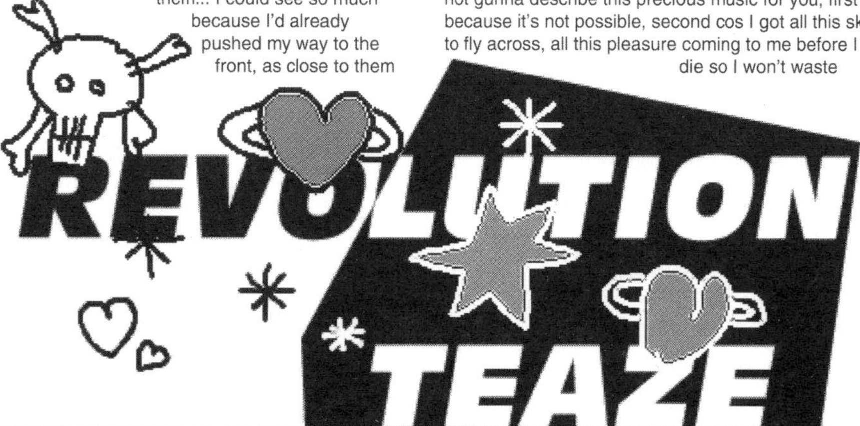

mine or yours. On first listen it seemed to spell a dead end: too much sucking on one scene, but lines came through and like poor dumb sparrows we followed the arrows, like gradually appearing invisible ink, we tasted, we knew the fruit was really really good. And... it was like playing this tape brought all the neighbourhood children into my life. So I invited them in for coffee.

The first single, *Rubbing* The *fucking Impossible*, well if you ever came round my house for coffee you'll know "Snail Messenger Loss", at least, by heart. But I guess being bound to an armchair and forcefed sub-sonic youth creepy voices of great beauty from beyond the grave, gameplaying songs from the great '86 purgatory, accompanied by the lecture of a girl lost to the world ("they kicked history off its axis" etc) was too high a price to pay for a cuppa, so I lost most of my friends... The loyal remainder are those who possessed, or claimed to possess, their own copy of this record, and were thus spared the ritual...

I tried to work out a formula for making a Huggy Bear single (they only do 7"s and tapes you know. Watch out for the CD boxset...) but it won't quite fit.
How about, one latterday Fall song, a punk rock city lovesong, a scarey spooky song and a wimpy Pastels-type song? This is so wrong, I had to write it. Haven't I got anything better to do with my life? No. Some things just feel too good and you can only, erm, try and bug them.

Halloween '92. I perch on a crate next to the White Horse stage, I take in the soundcheck. It's mine. This venue is mine. I stab the wine bottle cork with a biro for the best part of an hour. I don't drink and I don't think I ever will at this rate - and Mambo Taxi are soundchecking too. I drop the pen, now shattered and bleeding ink, between two blocks of the stage. Throwing away a lifeline. Later it's impossibly crowded, I don't know where their spirit has gone in the heat, I don't know what this means but they seem to play with hate. Look, Huggy Bear can have the life span of Sonic Youth if they want it (and when are SY gonna split up??) but that's not the point. It's just that they inspire, sometimes - most times. And their disease spreads.

But all this is so far (a day's walk at least) from the language and spirit of Huggy Bear. I carn't provide it because I am old, old beyond years. They're the brilliant kids playing brilliant games. I merely observed... that gleaming sexiness, the way Niki sang like she knew they ruled the room, it drew me in...

Her-Jazz Revolution IS Here. In here. Her-Jazz is the theme, it's gonna go round and round but they've already scooped out its guts. CAST your eyes wide to feel it. Scooped out corrupt guts of school and guaranteed dysfunction. Kicked aside fuckin' dreary philosophy, pissed on historical combats, cracked the shells of those snails. I keep knowing that all this meaning is in the songs, more multi-layered and visceral (stomach churning) and terrifying (What about a word that never held terror before? Was it a word I never heard before?) and irresistable than words on paper. Oh yeah I could scratch at all those things, make weak attempts to summarise (like all my record reviews in here) but sometimes I feel respect for some art so much I don't want to insult it. Oh oh oh. "Girl boy revolution," it's as intangible as the world. Confounded. A little fire is blazing and spitting out bright pain
SO.
Every now and then a band comes... yeah yeah yeah, but what if they succeed? What if they turn complacency to hatred? What if you believe and get trancebound useless sixteen tutting and not going to make any sense, not going to do what you want? I'm asking you, I'm asking... but you can't help.
The gutscream of the new song. I don't want this to sound like everything I've said about every new song that's excited me. There's a sense of magical space (chocolatebox wonder, cannot be condensed, it's that old human essence thing, the pain and the elation we can't escape).
The lesson of the Peel session - one song is not the same song if you mixit and record it with a different (crap) attitude. But yet I can hear bones amongst a plague of lyrical repetitions. Like a bad day? Peel hopes they'll record another. He doesn't seem too sure they'll want to. After I hear this, I want to run away into the cold foggy night. Everything else is a waste of time.
On their shared ("split" could be too prophetic) LP with Bikini Kill, they show themselves as sixties punks with wings that beat the garage walls, with songs like pencil lines filled in and terrifying as they happen. Shaking. Feb'ry Fourteenth, massacrous. Hearing Niki's anger's like lying in broken glass.
The Stereolab single thing. I have these sounds scattered nameless on tapes scattered on my floor. A heliumised cut up cracked up beautiful poem. A pure bedroom popsong sabotaged by a recorder, by a childs' keyboard, the instruments you have when you're nine if you're lucky. They're all regressing cos they're trying to be cute. I'm making this up because I don't know.

PHOTO: WENDY STONE

YOU GOTTA GET PAST THE DREAMING STAGE... TO LIVE IT.

It's here, the thing you been searching for, not in America, it's in your own land, no need to walk across no sea.

CHRIS ANSWERS, IN HIS OWN INIMITABLE (HUH) STYLE, THE QUESTIONS WE FAXED ACROSS THE BITTER BRITISH AIR.

What did you feel like when you realised you could and was going to do the things (songs, fanzines, psyche out terrorism) that you do?
Like I was going to get beaten up. Just plain beaten. Potent?? Visible - like people knew how much I wanted to chop things up. A long laugh like conjurerers ribbons that keep on coming out from his assistant's orifice(s). ... As if a sudden telepathy might get me in touch with new people thinkin' stuff like me. Magic, tingling, scared...

Some say that, while N.O.U. "missed out" on all the grrrl kinda publicity that's been happening, they've been catalysts for it all. D'you think this understates their role? (Don't you think they still exist and will rule in their own right?) Do you think any of your mission is to be a catalyst for a gigantic youth uprising?
N*O*U* are like classic, i.e. 50's archetype boyfriends, but non-predatory. N.O.U. exist forever in my heart, the truest fuckin luv - isolated... it comes about cos the delinquency N.O.U. helped redefine, the Riot Girls use delinquency as empowerin'... I wish. I don't know.

What do you say to the lonely but beautiful kids in villages and cities who know they want to do something but end up spending their energy loving your band and treating you as heroes?
Heroes have a sad ritual to eternally perform, that of disappointing their followers, destroyin' themselves when all the powers go bad... We love you more when you do stuff. Something, anything. New poetry. Art. Schemes. Circulation 1 - 1,000,000.

Do you aim to scare your audiences?
I want audiences to erupt, to sieve themselves apart in dirty dancing grit from gold. I want them to feel possessed by frightening new scares then... I don't know. A little. Exhilarated more ♡ness.

Is it going to last (should it last?) or has it all burned too brightly?
It hasn't burnt enough yet, I carn't feel warm yet in the winter in t-shirt just from the caught-alight-heat. No idle threat/promise/resolutions demolish. We'll really know when to turn off our lights.

Detail things that may happen, and things you have dreamed that probably won't.
A transfusion from history gives you the blood to spill in recognition of your desire to be the new princesses + princes.... RUB out the bad words that bumps in the twilight of your test drive alphabet...
13a) "Oh baby 'I' want all that's wrong with you all they carn't wait to hit"
13b) "Our manners where are our manners .. oh i like them most when they shock even us..."
13c) KISS kiss solid gone kiss / time will tease out the queer in you..

PHOTO: WENDY STONE

There won't ever be a total youth time - youth itself with its inconsistencies + selfishness would ruin its own total state = separated and burning the dominant corporate world. We welcome the temporary sites of action, pockets of resistance, and experience the vitality there and then, 'made to make our mouths water'. A dominant culture by its definition will seek to impose, oppress, condemn, deceive and this is how we make our mark, constant changing, never gettin' complacent. Meanwhile wars being thought and are fort thru'. We join up the 'Playgrid Agitationale' swopping secrets, sayin how it is, * poetry + dreams with warriors' bravery. Defining our young people world only to keep on breakin' it into bits, hanging out, creating against... ♡♡+♡ at this time it means cutting off the homophobes, the subliminal girl haters, racist fucks, those that would suppress that which would make our wings beat beat beat and burn. You don't wanna 'know exactly'.. that's it...

How do you respond to the accusation that your "political" "writings" exclude people, make them feel bad and unvalidated? (Someone talked to me about this, it's a good point, I imagine you envisage it as a challenge for people to figure out who they are and what they really believe - maybe your exclusivity also excludes you - definitely attacks your culture of origin...

Our writings probably do exclude, but at this stage why bother about who you exclude? I don't want to teach the world to sing in some sick pepsi cola harmony. Division/opposition is as healthy as it is inevitable. I don't know how I want things received - my own scribbling ultimately should challenge/exclude me too I wish. People who desire, truly desire that state of personal flux are the people who'll try and won't be offended at our obvious 'exclusivity'. World ain't my friend. Shall I use that Lynne Tillman quote? "So I must wrest this language and its forms away from or out of 'the majority' (of which I am part, in some ways and at some times, to others), to un-man it, to un-American it, even to un-white it, to inconvenience the majority language, to unconventionalise it, even to shame it in an odd sort of way, to question privilege, my own too of course."

The accusation also came with the idea that you're just perpetuating your own coolness at everyone else's expense...

Sure we think we're cool but not cool like cool has been, cool like in celebration - a clumsy grasp, a dorky stance. Dare to dork. We're too ugly and stupid to be 'cool'. (Tradition offends).

You seem to be pissing lots of people in bands off cos they're jealous of your success. How's this feel?

It should be some cool gang / a timeless zone when you're in a band, but most people in bands treat it lke football or work in the office. * Real cool (as in 'dork out') bands don't get annoyed or irritated (at least not in some down-the-pub grumbly way) by other bands. So yeah it is fun and good when other bands are shown up for the squares we always thought them to be...

Huggy Bear: WHAT ARE THEY?

They're ghosts sounds, they float headless and wide eyed in the middle of the night.
They're little girls with deadly knives that no-one, not me, not you, wants to meet. They're playing football in the street but somehow their shoes are muddy, their clothes are filthy...
They're cheating and lying seducers you want to murder, cos they're bad-mouthin' you behind your back after all those sweet fucken nothing-at-alls.
They're infuriating, irresponsible, secret-keeping promise-breaking likkle BASTARDS.
They got big teeth for all that sparse flesh.
They're dirty and not to be trusted.
They're ripping you off if you believe the indie co-operative myths.
They play at "worthy", they play creation myths, they don't heed warnings...
They're spoilt Southern bratlets, the sweetest things you ever did see.
They're pretentious stupid genius plagiarists, artists of the lowest highest fucken disorder.
THEY ARE all your paranoid fantasies, ever, cum true 4.

They're not just singing about the fucking girl boy boy girl revolution, they're having these insane arguments in their songs. She's telling him, she's telling him, and she's so tough I wish she could tell it better with her great teeth with her brilliant shining knives. The emotional charge, you couldn't keep it in a bathroom. This band, they'll implode in the effort just to live. Don't look to them to tell you anything cos they don't know nothing, just hooked into a magic formula and they know it only takes them up to midnight, it'll be good to watch as the time approaches, to see those colours change. Their arrogance is that they'll make out you can be cool by association with them. My arrogance is that the *Ablaze!* seal of blizzard life love adds a tone of distinction to their flame flyin firework life. What they give to me, I am honour bound to give it back.

Such a stupid name...

Like toddlers on a tartrazine wipeout. Like the 3rd form on a schooltrip, gone one beaker of vodka too far. Those screams, they're callin' teacher, the big fucken teacher in the police suit sat behind the desk marked Ed. on the 26th Floor.
Watch out you pretend gayboyriotgirls, when you're sussed by the purring rrr-ing things you've been unimpeded stringing along with your sensitive little songs... those misandrist salivating dyke-with-bollock-choppers myths might just come true, just for you.

Ah... I believe... I love... too bad.

When Huggy Bear appeared on *The Word*, along with their friends in the Huggy Nation, they took over the studio. After playing "Her Jazz" kind of straight, apart from fifteen seconds of chaos tacked onto the end, there were some beautiful moments of destruction; bursts of yelling and biting and admonishments sweeping through the audience. The second half of the show was mostly pre-taped bullshit (the patronising trivia we are used to) hastily shown to hide the fact that what was happenning at that time in front of those cameras was not what they, the producers of this "wild" youth TV programme, wanted us to see. The band and entourage were escorted from the building. Just playing a song, just taking control. It wasn't clear from the livingroom end of things whether to be encouraged or disillusioned. First I crumbled (I expect so much from my pop groups, I guess I want them to start the civil war...), then I wondered, if they can do that in such a controlled environment. . . . . what can we do in our towns?

PHOTO : LIANE HENTSCHER

Pedants who trace phrases back to other speakers not only miss the point but ignore the fact that big explosions don't go without big catalysts. The Nation Of Ulysses have been tilling the earth for stuff like this to grow. Stop picking at things, analysing the work of others. Do something... do it... do it yourself.

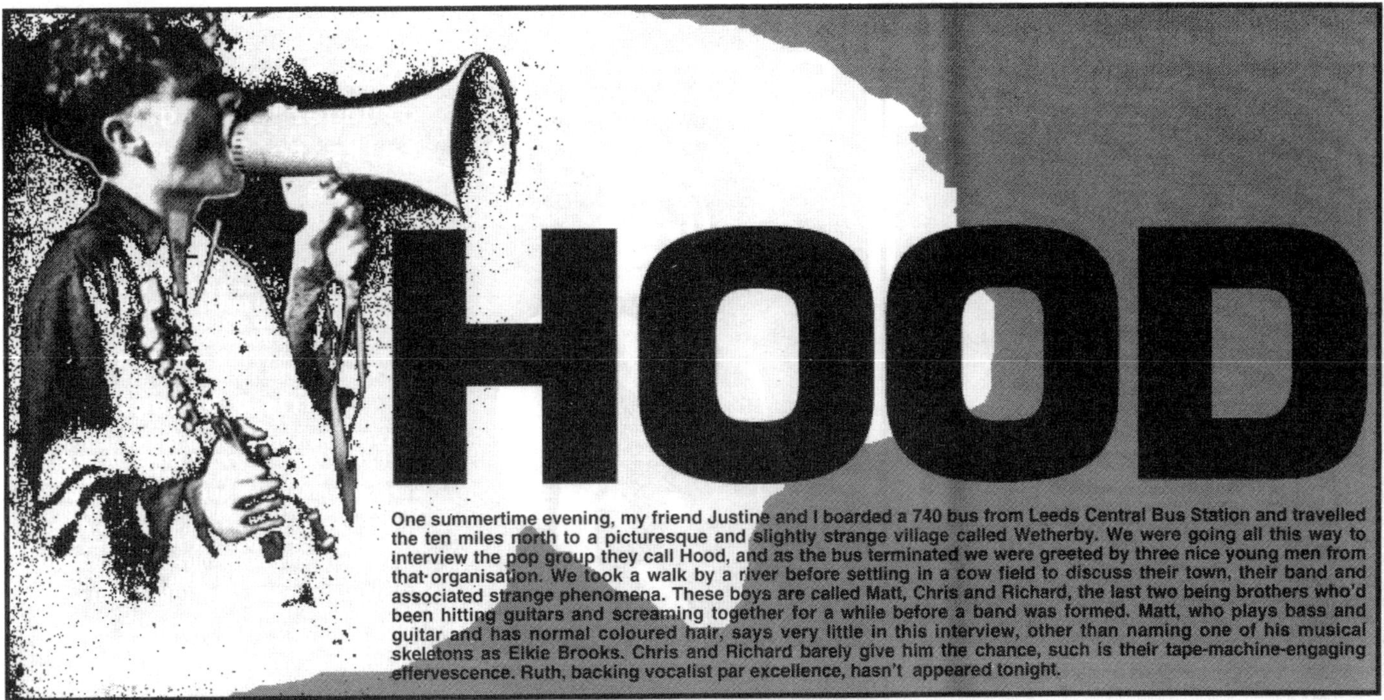

One summertime evening, my friend Justine and I boarded a 740 bus from Leeds Central Bus Station and travelled the ten miles north to a picturesque and slightly strange village called Wetherby. We were going all this way to interview the pop group they call Hood, and as the bus terminated we were greeted by three nice young men from that organisation. We took a walk by a river before settling in a cow field to discuss their town, their band and associated strange phenomena. These boys are called Matt, Chris and Richard, the last two being brothers who'd been hitting guitars and screaming together for a while before a band was formed. Matt, who plays bass and guitar and has normal coloured hair, says very little in this interview, other than naming one of his musical skeletons as Elkie Brooks. Chris and Richard barely give him the chance, such is their tape-machine-engaging effervescence. Ruth, backing vocalist par excellence, hasn't appeared tonight.

When someone stole a plantpot from a garden and left it in Hugh (a local fanzine editor)'s garden, the story ended up being reported in *Wetherby News*.
Richard, known for guitar and bass guitar playing as well as his auburn hair and freckles, explains; "things happen in this town that wouldn't happen in a major city." He tells us about Mary, cover star of their single on Fluff records. "He was gunna commit suicide on April 1st. He bought the wood to make the gallows, but he forgot to get up before midday, so he didn't do it. The idea was that people would see the hanging body and think it was an April Fool's trick."
Chris (guitaring, curly auburn hair and singing): "His mum caught him in the garden talking to the trees with an ironing board."
"I heard a rumour he's 21," Richard adds, somewhat confusingly. "And someone saw a car floating down the river..."
"And there was a case of dysentery in the local school," says Chris. "Matt thought I meant a *suitcase* of dysentery in the middle of the playground, with people playing hopscotch."
Well...
"That school opposite the Royal Park, have you seen the hopscotch there?" Richard seems concerned. "Loads of lines swirling about, just to confuse the kids."
The Royal Park, located many miles from Wetherby in the sixth postal district of Leeds city, is Hood's favourite pub. It is also the site of the unsavoury "Rottweiler Incident", in which the landlord is said to have set his dogs the task of savaging a neighbourhood pusscat, a crime which the band in no way condone. In fact, Hood have stated that they will donate all proceeds from future gigs at that venue to the family and friends of the cat. They play there every few weeks to an assortment of indiebands and fanzine writers, events which are understated in atmosphere, yet they undeniably contain some of the coolest pop moments Leeds has to offer.
"I answered the phone outside the Royal Park," Chris tells us. "It was the police."
Richard: "In Wetherby one day a phonebox was ringing and a guy was videoing it." "You just leave it, you don't like to think about it too much." The Hood worldview finds unexplainedness inside the layers of everyday occurences, and revels in it. These kids fetishize electricity pylons and the relay plants that buzz bright silver menacing in sick summer sun. As you can tell, they delight in the slightly odd misfortunes of their fellow villagers. At this point I should tell you something about their music but I can't find the tapes. Rural mutterings run across shards of guitar, petal-unfurling backing vocals capture sunlight essence melodies. Hood sound like the Pastels in a haystack with Royal Trux.

You think there's higher density of weird kids here?
"There's a higher density of complete idiots who shout at you as you go down the street," reckons Richard.
How many people live in Wetherby?
"12,536," reckons Chris. "I've got an abacus."

Richard tells us about his ambitions.
"I work at a garage, taking money from people for petrol and stuff. One day I'm going to pretend to be American and offer them a dime in change and ask if they want any gas. I also really want to introduce the sentence 'Zat is where you are wrong' into a conversation."
We considered going off to make a corn circle, but ended up in an amazing derelict farm building, among broken stone and rafters and curious passageways that lead to yet more agricultural ruins. The boys were, needless to say, enthusiastic about the place, and it is here that Justine photographed them.

Chris tells us about his and Richard's house: "We live in tardis houses with spiral staircases. The ivy tried to strangle me one day. A snail crawled all the way up the house to the top floor. We had a silverfish in the toilet for a year. We couldn't get rid of it. Then it did that LP, *Fat Axl*."

Possibly the biggest controversy in the band's history has been over the split between Hood and Boyracer. Originally linked siamesely, Stewart announced at a Royal Park gig that he would cease playing bass and drums with Hood. No-one seemed alarmed because he did this sort of thing several times a week, and band splits are not the sorts of things that alarm such stalwart lovers of the unusual. Stew is a cocky kinda kid who works in an art supplies shop and writes energy-bursting songs that occasionally hit the charm waves. Things came to a head after the split when Stewart and friends appeared in *Northern Star*, Leeds' *Other Paper*, bitch-biting about Hood. It wasn't very nice.
Twin statements were issued on the split. Stew first:
"Although it broke my heart, I guess it was kinda mutual and necessary for the survival of all involved. i think it's worked out OK, though I still miss those magical cheesey moments."
And the band's response:
"Our obsession for pylons became too much for Stewart and he stopped turning up for day trips to electrical structures. He wanted to concentrate full time on learning to play the zither."
Justine tells them about the recent Hood weekend on MTV. "Well, I think it was Hood... maybe it was Phil Collins..." [The two are oft confused in today's fast pop world.]

"Everyone keeps dreaming about us," they say.
Here are some dreams that may or may not related to Hood:
Chris: "A friend from San Francisco came to stay and brought one hundred friends. I couldn't put them all in the house so they had to stand outside."
Karren: "I dreamed Gavin was asked by Nick Cave and Blixa Bargeld to go to Holland with them to be in a play as a dog. But *I* wanted to go cos I had a furry face, I shaved half of it so I had half skin and half fur, and I had white hair and blue fur."
Chris Trout: "A.C.Temple were supporting Hood, and when Hood came on they had this big stage set, like a Gary Numan set with black marble pillars, on top of which, in the dramatic lights, you could see ginger-headed guitarists."
Karren: "I dreamed that this kid was turning into Mark Goodrham of Tse Tse Fly but actually he was Andrew of Hood. He couldn't get into a gig at Leeds University, he was stood outside and it was dark. It was sad."
That leads kinda neatly into the Hood drummer situation story. Laura replaced Stewart, but then she said decided to move to Australia, so Chris, Richard and Matt turned up at one of their Royal Park shows rather nonchalantly drummerless. Andrew had been doing work experience at *Ablaze* ! for a week, and was rounding it off by seeing one of his favourite bands. I offered to stand in, but didn't know what I was doing, and the sound of me trying put Andrew into a state of frustration. "I know all these songs!" he cried, after my artless bashing had got too much, so I moved aside. His playing as well as his appearance fitted in perfectly and the Hood lads begged him to join. But then... Laura reappeared, having changed her mind about Australia. Unpeturbed, they decided to have *two* drummers, just in case one of them goes wrong or gets scared.
"I keep getting electrocuted in my sleep and I hear this massive buzzing sound," insists Richard.
Everyone tries to convince him that it's just his radio. We talk about how sometimes your hair colour changes as you grow up. Then Chris insists he used to be black. Which takes us kinda untidily and intentionally awkwardly, like a Hood song, into this issue's competition. Send your best dreams about Hood to Chris and Richard, "Dream About Hood" Competition, 27, Spofforth Hill, Wetherby LS22 4SF, and they'll send out prizes as they deem appropriate.

Hood; the first band in history to have equal numbers of ginger haired people as normal haired people.

PHOTOS: TONY WOOLGAR.

HOOD RECORDS-U-NEED

Sirens 7" (Fluff)
I didn't think you were going to hit me in the face 7" (Fluff)
Shared flexi with Lichenstein Girl (Fluff/Skit On You)
Plus so many compilations on Fluff and on other labels that I can't be bothered to write them all. Contact th'lads at the address above, or write to Fluff at 86 Parklands Drive, Loughborough, Leics. LE11 2TD, for further information.

Hood will also be on the forthcoming *Ablaze!*/Fluffy Cat Records compilation LP and CD, *Best Of Music*, along with The Wedding Present, Nation Of Ulysses, Pastels and lots more top *Ablaze!* bands.

REVIEWS EDITOR SUPREME: Gavin B.REVIEWS CONCOCTED BY: Gavin B. (with occasional inspiration from Andrew Phelan), Lucy N., Karren A!, Simon Morris, Maria Pickering, Tony Tunes, Claudia Elliot, Veena Virdi, Ross Holloway, Anthony Aerschot, Andrew Johnson, Phil Asbestosis, Andrew Truth, Jack Puppy and assorted members of Moonshake....

RECORD reviews

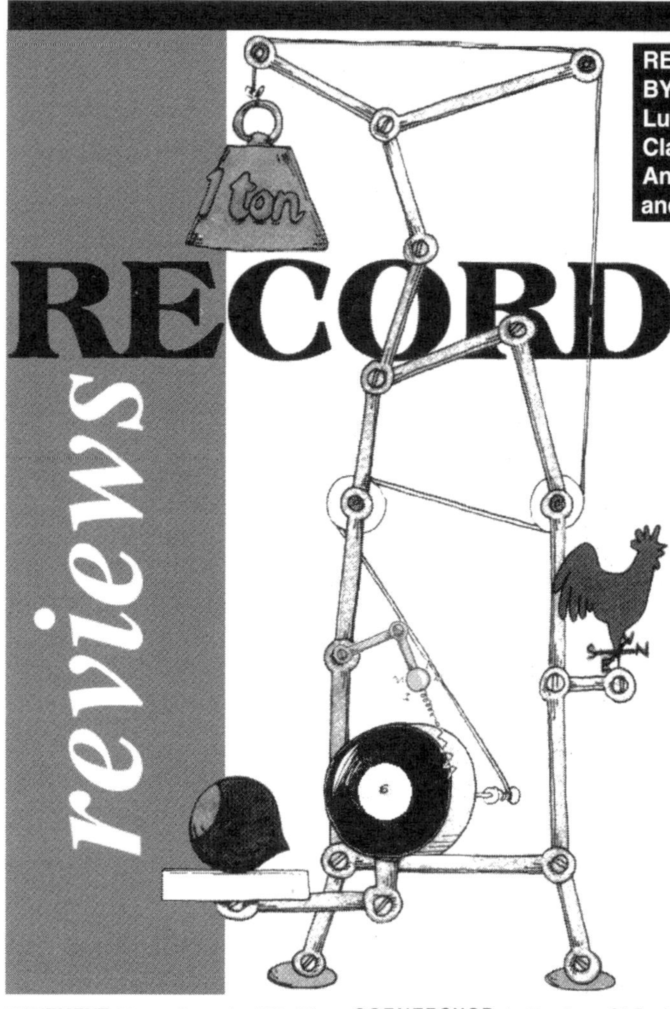

PAVEMENT *Watery, Domestic* CDS (Big Cat)
Our plan was to include two reviews of this music, one of the vinyl and one of the CD, but we were not sent the vinyl so I can only recall from memory how much more alive-and-leaping-out-of-the-speakers-to-grab-your-heart it is than this lifeless shiny thing we got here. I love *Watery, Domestic* best on the warped picture-disc that my friend has...

I've got stuff to say. This EP took me a long time to appreciate. The first time I heard it, I insisted that "Lions" was too like a Wonderstuff song, with its irksome climbing thing. Course, now I can't really tell what was wrong. Now it's just hard to understand how it doesn't fall back and become part of "Texas Never Whispers". You know? (Please say you know). "Texas" seems to exist stronger and fuller live, partly because it has Bob's whisper-shout, partly because it *lives* more live. But even here it has beauty flowing, layers appearing and disappearing, like the "da-da-da" secret singing, and that, THAT crystal guitar piece... "Frontwards" is resonant, it links up things I really know, and songs, and the first summer tour where I first heard this, and Stephen's snide or sincere words... "Shoot The Singer", well, I can't put words on this song, don't ask me to. I don't want to have to say "soulful", and "intense", for what's so carelessly precisely fuckedly throne... in the very last second, the song crumples, a stray drumbeat's found its way into the mix, and this proof of imperfection makes it all the more beautiful. *Watery, Domestic* overwhelms me, scares me, burns my brain out. What it says about Stockton I can't tell. I wanted to call the reviews section "Not Everyone Can Be Pavement", but other members of the *A!* team interpreted this as a sycophantic sentiment. It's actually based purely on aesthetics, and nothing to do with flattery, it's straight out of my heart and central to the project of this magazine: to say the truth, both negatively and positively. Otherwise there's no point in talking about music. Pavement just happen to be working on several more dimensions than everyone else, and that's all, I suppose. (KA)

THE JIGSAWS Camouflage 7" (Jigsaws)
Produced by Bill Goffrier of Big Dipper in what can only be seen as a cynical attempt to make his own band seem more reminiscent of Extreme Noise Terror. So weak it couldn't fight its way out of its paper sleeve, and I certainly won't be helping it out again. (GB)

CORNERSHOP *In The Days Of Ford Cortina 7"* (Wiiija)
Well, to start with, the singer sounds like Fat Mark on tranquilisers. The band are best described in Andrew Truth's words as "like The Ceramic Hobs without any of the style". The first track, and come to think of it all the other tracks, are third-generation Jesus And Mary Chain. They're not fit to be mentioned in the same breath as Nation Of Ulysses. Despite this it's good fun and doubtless it's all very punk and revolutionary. No, actually it's crap. (SM)

UNMEN *Love Under Water* CD (Some Bizarre)
A bunch of machines with the burps. Hard to work out if humans had anything to do with this. Loops, samples, weird noises; a sound-track to rigor mortis. Just terrible. Nearly complete monotony, but all mono and no tony. (TT & GB)

VARIOUS *The Greatest Dance Album In The World* (Virgin),
VARIOUS *Dancing On Sunshine - 22 Classic Reggae Hits* (Virgin)
Virgin records, admirably showing us that with their hands so far into our pockets it would be impossible for them to have their fingers on anything even resembling a pulse. The first of these collects together **Soul II Soul**, **The KLF**, **Yazz** (topical), **Black Box** and **Neneh Cherry** as well as anybody else who's popular and straightforward. Ideal for people like me for whom 'Dance Music' begins and ends with 'Groove Is In The Heart'. The cutting edge, it ain't.

What comes into your head when you hear the phrase 'Classic Reggae Hits'? Virgin records, lovely people that they are, think of **UB40**, **Jimmy Somerville** and **Boy George**; nice, inoffensive white boys with their insipid love songs. **Desmond Dekker**'s 'Israelites' is the only vaguely political thing here, and probably included to cynically seduce the margarine lovers amongst you. Pride of place goes of course to **10cc**'s 'Dreadlock Holiday', a vile little thing about being scared of black people and their nasty culture, which sums up this LP rather more succinctly than I have. (GB)

A HOUSE I Am The Greatest LP (Setanta/Parlophone)
The press furore which greeted these people's "Endless Art" single (shopping-list type thing with names of supposed Great Artists like John Donne and Ian Curtis which included NO WOMEN AT ALL) is a useful point-making anvil for a rant about deeply-ingrained prejudice in the male-dominated inkies; for, instead of castigating the band over their unintentionally humorous faux pas, the journos hurried to praise them for their rush-job all-female B side version. In fact, casual unthinking sexism gained A poxy House more column inches than they would ever have received otherwise. All I'm saying, media boys, is you can't treat gangrene with a Band-Aid: perhaps it might help to address the root cause of the disease rather than the symptoms next time. But then I'm a bloke. (LN)

THE RELEASE PARTY *Don't Say It Again 7"* (Perfect Pop)
MONKEY *101 Transistor* 7" (Papa Popov)
People talk about the Death Of Vinyl... I almost wish it would happen after sloshing through these endless wastes of space, this barren wilderness of useless information encoded in black plastic. These things will be turning up in junk and secondhand shops over an ever-widening radius for decades, maybe hundreds of years to come, like the spores of some terrible mushroom. There should be laws prohibiting the preservation of useless information in durable media, that's what I think. Stave off the Death Of Vinyl not by producing more grubby 7" singles, but better grubby 7" singles. (LN)

GOD MACHINE *Home* 12" (Fiction)
Again??? How many times has this been released? Okay, okay, I like it. It's nice, but you don't need to keep putting it out in different sleeves just to get extra column inches in *Ablaze!*. The God Machine, your time will come - it might look like the apocalypse, but it will be yours. (KA)

JAWBOX *Novelty* LP & *Tongues* 7" (Dischord)
What Jawbox do is magic that's yet to be acknowledged, or maybe magic that's been so wove and rewove in the land once ruled by Sonic Youth and once by Husker Du that it's hard to unpick and analyse. A loose HM demon is spinning through sewers, wrapped in bright blue crinkly silk. Dream-melody-angst that never quite bursts out of its seams. The, ah, Unmistakable sound of Jawbox. (KA)

PALE SAINTS Throwing Back The Apple 12" (4AD)
A bloke who drinks with the Pale Saints told us that Nick Cave, for whom the bloke had recently been selling corduroy baseball caps, is completely unbeatable at Scrabble. And that's not all. Apparently, Nick loafs around the tour bus in shorts and sneakers all day, only retiring to the shower room to change into his more familiar black suit as the bus approaches the venue. An inverse Mr. Benn from the Deep South! Of Australia! A straw poll taken among the *Ablaze!* stuffed animals says you're a charlatan, Mr. Cave. We demand more suffering. (LN)

RIPE *Tough Guys Don't Dance* CD (Shock)
So bland that it almost defies description. How about, 'Crowded House, only more so'? (GB)

VARIOUS *International Pop Underground Convention* CD (K)
What you need to know: this five-day convention happened in Olympia in the summer of '91 and it must have been an incredible thing to experience: so many youths collected together to see so many cool bands and to deny corporate rock. One of the days was the Girl Day, spurring on much of the Riot Grrrl energy that was starting to burn. So this CD gives a glimpse into those sunny shows sandwiched between barbecues and picnics and revolutionary propaganda-distributing. **Scrawl**'s "Go Girl Go" is totally tops, as Mancunian DJs used to say. It's an anti-apathy song with a simple, strong tune and you'll love it too... swiftly followed by The Sacred **Nation Of Ulysses**, having an impassioned-and-wired-as-usual go at "Shakedown", which should be followed by at least four exclamation marks. "This is about the destruction of nostalgics" Ian gulps, catchin' his breath to chase this power rolling thing. The bass nearly falls right outta the bottom of it, exhilaration comin' out of this stereo... **The Pastels** do "Speedway Star" even more tunelessly than usual (this is the point at which Gavin leaves the room. He's done well staying so far). They're screamin' and twangin' and generally being on a Pastels adventure; "We're gonna ride all over everythin'"... **Melvins** make no sense to me, their contribution is a formless dirge... **L7** do their heavy metal thing... **Spinnanes** play an unlikely pop tune in honour of Jad Fair's sex appeal - (it takes all sorts)... **Seaweed** are another of these bands that I can see and hear and never *even notice*... **Kicking Giant** got loosed energy, like light objects on elastic, ace power-thud-drumming. They're also awful... **Shadowy Men On A Shadowy Planet** play this instrumental surf thing that, if chronologically placed, would have been over and done with before we were born... **Kreviss** are, like Bratmobile, in a 1986 Membranes zone with this gurl's singing as estranged from a tune of any kind as John Robb's always was. Great... **Mark Hosler, Steve Fisk and Bob Basanich** have all got Pavement firstnames and play and shout over Negativland-kinda-sinister tapes of men in suits which turns into like a spooky relaxation thing with mouth-organ interference and all sorts of shit going on, cutting back and forth over the evil work-leisure dichotomy... **Some Velvet Sidewalk** leave little impression, it's like they click into my deaf spot or some void in my perceptions (compilations are hard work to review, you're supposed to have thoughts about 2 dozen bands at once)... *Mecca Normal*, her voice is too folky and gritty y'know for me, I'm a delicate kind of a lower mammal and we wouldn't do well on a camping trip together... There's so much more, **Fugazi** (togetherest band here - no surprise) and **Girl Trouble** (blokes, ugh, playing dim voyeurist rock'n'roll) and **Courtney Love** and **Unwound** and **Bratmobile** (yeah! yeah! "Punk Rock Dream Come True" yeah!) and **Rose Melberg** and **Fastbacks** (gruff-voiced-girl anthemic punkpop) and **Beat Happening** (surprise surprise!). If you're interested in the Grrrl phenomenon and wanna get a taste of some of the bands behind it, you oughta hear this and feel so jealous, so yearning that you wasn't there... (KA)

LA COSTA RASA *The Last Of The Baby Boomers* MLP (Esperanza)
The lad from this group came round with our copy in his shiny silver briefcase and, although there were plenty of chairs free, he spent the whole of his brief visit squatting uncomfortably by the sofa on account of the *Ablaze!* staff being unsocialised, estranged and frankly more than a little dysfunctional. This has nothing particularly to do with the record itself, but does have the advantage of being memorable, always a plus in the here-today-gone-tomorrow world of popular music entertainment. (LN)

FAITH HEALERS *Lido* LP / *Mr Litnanski* 12" (Too Pure)
Everything reminds me of Band Of Susans. I wonder if medical fascists have already developed a treatment for this unfortunate condition? It certainly hampers communication with other humans. Hey though, I fulfilled an ambition in December when I spoke to Roxanne Faith Healer. I'd been a from-afar admirer and it was quite a big step for me to introduce myself to the woman. Always I missed out on the Healers' thing, being North-based, but appreciated the appalling curtains of drain-noise they drew at their shows. Hmmm. Having these records is like having a headache I can get out and put away at will. I can't mentally locate this group or give them a timeslot, they're weird like every human being, unpredictable. "Don't Jones Me" sounds serious when they play it but can it be a serious thing, to be Jonesed? And on the sleeve is a (50s?) beach crowd scene with a tent crowd scene on the front, and I'm sitting here, like, "huh?", though I know I won't lose sleep. *Lido* is an LP by chaosists who are probably very stable, they just like to mix this particular chocolate cake to get themselves in trouble sometimes, to get it thrown in the bin by teacher because it defies structure, colour distinction, all that shit. It hots up as it goes on, and the single's even (ouch) hotter. Go... dance... (KA)

HOSS *You Get Nothing* LP (Dog Meat)
If Hoss did not exist, it would most definitely *not* be necessary to invent them. (GB)

"This walking person is making me cough."

THE BOO RADLEYS *Lazarus* 12" (Creation)

Top typist Andrew Johnson declared that "Lazarus" was his favourite track of last year, but when I asked him to review this he had already joined a top Wetherby band as second drummer and consequently now has better things to do than favours for the likes of me. Therefore this onerous task fell to me. "Lazarus" starts out as a dub type thing, all bass and feedback, before launching into familiar Boo territory, but the whole thing seems disjointed and clumsy. "The Sound Of Speed" and "Petroleum" are two of the Boos' sixties numbers which I never cease to be depressed by. The feedback on "Let Me Be Your Faith" is nice, as is the guitar, bringing to mind images of flamenco dancers, but the singing? Well, this bloke's not Paul Simon, is he? (GB)

ST. JOHNNY *Go To Sleep* 7" (Ajax)

Luckily, I reviewed this record when I was on my own; not only did this prevent me from being giggled at every time I turned it over (one side at 33, one at 45) but also limited the damage of anyone picking up anything dangerous due to passive U2 rip-offs; second only to passive smoking in its seriousness according to a recent government report. Hey, before you start worrying, I've been vaccinated. (GB)

ASHTRAY *Same* CD (Shoe)

Like everything I've reviewed today I was expecting great things from this (the eternal optimist as always). We received the single from this album a while back and I playlisted it as soon as possible. To recap, "Trailer" is a gloriously sexy romp through a couple of days in the life of Sarah Howells. One can only presume that the relationship so vividly depicted there has depleted Sarah's enthusiasm for the less intimate surroundings of the rehearsal and recording studios to the extent that she is physically incapable of writing anything else. The rest of the album is sung and almost exclusively written by Joe Leifheit, a man whose lyrics are so flat and whose voice is so monotonous that it leads me to conclude that Sarah must be paying him to show her in a good light; the effect is rather like Steve Albini getting the drum machine to throw together a few things whilst he makes a few bob producing Strangulated Weasel. For God's sake, Sarah, get yourself another band, write a whole LP as good as "Trailer", and take over the world. (GB)

LAUGHING HYENAS *Crawl* 12" (Touch & Go)

It's not that we don't appreciate lead singer John Brannon's torment, we're sure having your record released on Touch & Go is very trying; but if he just calmed down for a moment then we'd be able to hear Larissa Strickland's sonorous guitar playing which we really like quite a lot. (AP & GB)

GLORIES *Aurora* CD (Aurora)

The press release describes this as 'the very first debut', which I immediately scribbled into my book of 'Tautologies Through The Ages' next to Terry Nutkin's (a sort of taller Bobby Charlton) infamous and oft repeated 'It's 5a.m. in the morning' and John Major's less well known 'the itsy-bitsy teenie weenie yellow polka dot recession'. Wallpaper for 'Who's grungin' who?' discussions. (GB)

THE HAPPY FAMILY *The Man On Your Street* CD (4AD)

In 1981, Nicholas Currie lost his virginity, dropped out of university and signed to 4AD. I know this because the quite excellent liner notes, written for this CD by the man himself, tell me. This reissue brings together the album and single he recorded as part of The Happy Family before he left the band and became Momus, a creation spanning several albums of witty and erudite tales of love, lust and betrayal; criminally ignored by an audience which equates *'On the escalator, we shit paracetamol'* with subversion and style. Currie was there first and Currie does it much better. Although not equal to any of the Momus output, this CD contains fascinating insights into someone who was to become one of the songwriters of the eighties. The work on this collection is more overtly political in tone, with less of the religious metaphor and sexual deviancy (except "Two Of A Kind", a tale of incest) which fills his most recent work. Currie here seems unable to throw off the influence of Brecht, as studied furiously at university, and although always too subtle to be crass or hectoring, the observations are often underpinned by a need to show where he stands and what he believes. This contrasts sharply with his most recent work which portrays, among other things, paedophilia and incest with little moral tone, presuming the listener has the intelligence to make up their own mind. This predictably has led to people criticising Momus' style and motives; ambiguity apparently is not allowed in the world of rock after all. This CD may offer some comfort to those people who really believe this, being irrefutably politically correct, but more interestingly offers the rest of us a glimpse of the young artist, at a similar age and with parallel experiences to those of many of his later charmingly described protagonists. (GB)

EARWIG *Under My Skin I Am Laughing* LP (La Di Da)

Another contender for LP of the issue.

PAINTEENS

Along with such top combos as Papa Sprain and His Name Is Alive, Earwig signpost another new trajectory for rock, away from the apotheosis of rage and bluster as exemplified by Nirvana, towards an open-ended investigation of sound, harmony and texture. Not that I can see any of these seven delicate slow-burning ten minute *builders* wowing 'em on *Top Of The Pops* or anything, but who the fuck cares about that? To single out specific tracks seems churlish when the whole thing's so good, but "Every Day Shines", which creeps in like the Sussex tide over a mesmeric synth riff, and the Nymanesque "Scraped Out" are particular highlights. There again, what about "When You're Quiet", where Kirsty Yates' intimate lyrics command attention until the band kicks in with a surprise bit that sounds like early Swans? Or "We Could Be Sisters"? See, I told you it would be churlish. (LN)

MERCURY REV *Yerself Is Steam / Lego My Ego* 2LP (Beggars Banquet)

When *Yerself Is Steam* was released on Jungle records about eighteen months ago, we here at *Ablaze!* had our flabbers well and truly gasted. Later that year half a dozen live shows, ranging from fascinating experiments in distortion to total genius-like excess, and touching all bases inbetween, confirmed that Mercury Rev are one of the very few truly great bands of the nineties. Those of you not yet dedicated Revaholics again have a chance to reaffirm your faith in the true Butthole spirit of excess, so completely misunderstood by the Trance Syndicate roster and scores of others. A reinvention of sonic assault is not an overly grandiose claim for *Yerself Is Steam*, a fifty minute long invocation to madness. *Lego My Ego* collects together a Peel session, a fifteen minute long live version of "Shhh/Peaceful/Very Sleepy Rivers" and one new song, the positively restrained but still magnificient "Blood On The Moon". Wallow in wonder. (GB)

CIRCUS LUPUS *Supergenius* LP /*Popman* 7" (Dischord)

I love Chris Thompson's voice, it's moist and loose and mad, he's like a spitting vicious Mark E. Smith from DC, pronouncing everything wrong. Circus Lupus I first heard in the Ulysses van, they had a prerelease tape of this record and were all wide-eyed, swearing, pushing hair back, stunned at the power-packed Lupus sound. These tracks are very rhythmic testosterone scareytales with guitar solos that beautify the wreckage. It's punk refined into punk art without pomposity - it still kicks hard. "Popman" is all this, distilled and extra gorgeous and hateful. You'll know it when you hear it, the gurgitated first line: *"I've never felt so CHEAP in my WHOLE LIFE!!"* Hear this band if you haven't already - and this single is a fine place to start. (KA)

GIRLS AGAINST BOYS *Tropic Of Scorpio* LP (Adult Swim)

Fugazi meets the Bee Gees in a land of cars and discos in high rise basements. Most cryptical fuckerrrs GVSB have made a new record more untamed than their first, and less well ordered. I play it when no-one else is around, and dance and whoop and wish I'd thought of their name before they did. Watch out for my rival group, Chicks Versus Geezers. (KA)

VARIOUS *Lever* 7" (Simple Machines)

Severin! Scrawl! Autoclave! Circus Lupus! Beautiful glory! Paper bag full of happiness. Severin are their straight (uncomplicated) but powerful and resonant selves. Scrawl hit the karaoke machine with the first Wire song. Autoclave are jingly, choppy awkward and cute, like something on Rough Trade in 1980 (that era links with this one as cleverness once again pushes past the pop balloons, bursting a few, to get into the party). The Circus Lupus shqueal and grawl their second biggest hit. Oh to sing like that guy, such gum freedom, all loosed from words and gone. Must be a love turtle! (KA)

RED HOUSE PAINTERS *Down Colorful Hill* LP (4AD)

"The heaviest of burdens is therefore simultaneously an image of life's most intense fulfillment. The heavier the burden, the closer our lives come to the earth, the more real and truthful they become." Milan Kundera, The Unbearable Lightness Of Being.

Down Colorful Hill starts quietly; a long slow fade-in easing us into what's ahead. When the vocals finally come in, they are stark and open; two minutes later you're hooked. "24" is an understated account of a man coming to terms with life, finally accepting that there are no more codes to unravel, that he knows all he will ever know. This is childhood overtaken not by adulthood, some mythical superior condition, but by resignation; as an opener it's fatally seductive. This leads into "Medicine Bottle", the band as always content just minding the music to ebb and flow whilst the tale is recounted. When there's nothing left to say, the song will finish, not before. "Japanese To English" closes side one, like "Medicine Bottle" a song of loss, again totally self-pitiless; still as sombre, still as intense, still as beautiful.

Side two opens with the title track, nearly eleven minutes long, every second dripping with regret, the *'Dressed for success'* refrain becoming darker each time. After all this, the following track "Lord Kill The Pain" is positively jaunty, but the lyrics, a series of requests for God to destroy, it would seem, everything singer Mark lives for, is an ironic juxtaposition of ridiculous proportions which somehow still manages to be the weakest thing on here. Last song "Michael", recalling a childhood friendship, is laced with humour (*'Do you remember our first subway ride? / Our first heavy metal haircuts?'*) but is obviously (you must have gathered by now) also very disquieting.

The debut album by San Franisco's Red House Painters is a long and lonely walk through the troubled psyche of singer and songwriter Mark Kozelek. A more sombre, harrowing but ultimately satisfying journey it is difficult to imagine. The album of 1992. (GB)

BIG BLACK *Pigpile* LP (Touch And Go)

Recorded at that esteemed band's Hammersmith Clarendon show of 1987, an event so insanely overcrowded that I spent the second half of their set watching on the monitors in the video truck parked outside. The trouble with Big Black live recordings (see also *Sound Of Impact*, if you're lucky) is that their studio stuff sounds loads better: sure, in the flesh they were incomparable, Albini's guitar sound causing lumps of manganese and zinc to spontaneously materialise in front of his amp, but without the visuals or the volume or the atmosphere all you're left with is inferior versions of the LP hits, though it's nice to see a fattened-up "Steelworker" on vinyl at last. There aren't enough jokes, either, but the spoken interlude in "Pigeon Kill" is a corker: whoever said this band dealt in amoral, emotionless reportage? Bullshit. Some of Albini's stuff positively drips with compassion for its subjects, except he'd probably look pityingly at you and say something darkly humorous if you ventured to suggest as much to his face. Not a bad record, but what you really need is *Songs About Fucking, Atomiser* and perhaps a tape of *The Hammer Party* and *Racer X*. The sleevenotes are better on those, too. (LN)

JESUS LIZARD *Liar* LP (Touch & Go)

Dumb name, dumb cover, dumb record. Whereas Juliana Hatfield expresses her angst with mature eloquence, Jesus Lizard rage like petulant children in a playpen. If ever there was a sound of bread going stale here it is; hey lads, we all moved on from *Junkyard* and *Atomiser* years ago, so join us if you please. Or is it the only sound Touch & Go will release? "A droll spoof of a tragedy of awkward mediocrity", to quote the band themselves. (AA)

BRATMOBILE *Kiss And Ride* 7" (Homestead)

It's that kickdrum thump that gets me, the no-technology Membranes-ness of it - more straightforward, much more simple - that matter-of-fact, slightly shy singing like she's in the corner of the schoolyard and doesn't particularly want to be heard. I'm enthralled.Justine gave me this and I treasure it. (KA)

Micheal Walsh's Holding Limit.

VARIOUS ARTISTS Best Of Independent 20 CD (Beechwood)

Oh look, here's another one. This one's a compilation of the compilations (confused yet?) so I won't have to talk about **Verve, Adorable, The Breeders, The Boo Radleys or Levitation** again, but that still leaves an awful lot of sewage-wading to get through. There's **Carter**, the low-IQ Pet Shop Boys you can male bond to, then there's (surprise!) **Curve**, whose "Ten Little Girls" is marginally more interesting than their other stuff, perhaps because they for once deigned to include a tune. **Suede** and **Teenage bastard Fanclub**, on the other hand, both have an ear for a melody, but blow it for me with their fixation on the rock music of the past. Theme park culture, bub.

Chapterhouse sound like an infernal shotgun marriage of Foreigner and A.R. Kane: this band's label offered us thousands of flexis for nothing, which would have helped the magazine's permanently tottering financial situation no end, but, fuck it, we'd rather eat out of dustbins for the rest of our lives than put out a Chapterhouse flexi. **Slowdive**, on the other hand, surprise me by actually being quite good. Their "Catch The Breeze", along with the holy "Car Wash Hair", is the most un-rock, un-pop track on the compilation, all stillness and shingle and pre-pubescent sexual encounters in the vestry. I'll look forward to hearing what they've done with Eno.

Spiritualized? Retro sixties cack, despite their mainman's predilection for being photographed in one of my excellent **Drugs Not Jobs** T-shirts (true! write for details). I don''t understand the appeal of **Cud** at all. **Lush**'s "For Love" is an OK song, but the production's shit and those high-pitched vocals grate after about five seconds. **Catherine Wheel** and **The Telescopes** are wan variants on a theme (shoegazing) which was never of any interest in the first place, although the latter combo score some ironic brownie points for their ambitious but unsuccessful attempts to use instruments other than guitar. Finally, there's yer token crap metal number from **Smashing Pumpkins** and ą version of **Babes In Toyland**'s "Handsome And Gretel" which isn't as good as the one off *Fontanelle.* (LN)

HIS NAME IS ALIVE *The Dirt Eaters* EP (4AD)

More of the fragile genius we've come to expect from Warren Defever and co. It seemed to spend a long time hanging around the indie charts, too; so (disregarding the fact that those charts are compiled by a bunch of old men in darkened rooms pulling the names of the combos on each other's labels out of hats) maybe some of you fluffy little fuckers out there are waking up to the idea that music can still be a diverse and fascinating thing. Oh, if only they'd gig over here. Come on, His Name Is Alive. What's the matter with you? Don't you *like* bad food and cold rain? We'd love to see you. (LN)

JACOB'S MOUSE *Ton Up* 12" (Wiiija)

As Lucy said of their LP on Blithering Idiot in *Ablaze!9* , there's certainly a lot more adventure on offer here than most of the Mouse's contemporaries can muster up. A-side "Oblong" is a long, windy, thrashy thing which threatens to break out of its strai(gh)t-jacket but unfortunately never quite manages to. Side B has "This Room", a completely different, funkier proposition with hernia-on-the-toilet vocals, "Motorspace" recalls nobody less obscure than Tar Babies and "Fridge", the best thing by far, starts gloriously but soon ends when it should have been at least four times longer. Aspiration rather than inspiration, but more fun than anything else I've reviewed so far this issue. (GB)

LOVECHILD *Witchcraft* LP (City Slang)

This is a band comprised of several men and one woman. She is described as a "self conscious sexpot", in the very addled press release, whereas all the other people in the band are discussed in terms of their musical ability. Why? Because of the way she's dressed? Don't give me that patriarchal fucken claptrap. Anyhow they're rubbish, like my sister singing with The Wedding Present. Top Of The Bleeding Pops. (KA)

LIVE *Operation Spirit* 12" (Radioactive)

Produced by Jerry Harrison and offering further proof, if it were needed, that Jerry's (along with Tina's, Chris' and David's) contribution to (the) World('s) music should have been terminated at *Naked.* The press release boldly declares how similar to REM this is, originality not even given a look-in by these people apparently trying to help. In reality it's just irritating sub-Chili Pepper gargling, inane lyrics plus the added distraction of some sort of baggy drumbeat just in case any of the aforementioned originality attempted to break out. We've been sent an LP by Live as well; tell Karren I'll cut the lawn with nail clippers if I can be excused. (GB)

BELLY *Slow Dust* EP/ *Gepetto* EP/ *Feed The Tree* EP (4AD)

I don't know why, but I didn't expect to be much impressed by Belly. Seeing them opening for Pavement did little to disabuse me of this prejudice - an ordinary pop-rock band with some half-decent tunes, I thought, smugly. Wrong! Or, rather, half-right: there's nothing remotely ground-breaking about these records (though Tanya's guitar solo on "Sexy S" does get a little frisky) but there are some lovely songs, notably "Gepetto" itself, "Sweet Ride" (hear this now), "Slow Dog" and their cover of "Hot Burrito #2", which makes me keen to check out the work of Gram Parsons immediately. I suppose it's too late to say that "Giant" and "Reel" were always among my top ten Muses numbers? (LN)

EARWIG

MEDICINE *Shot Forth Self Living* LP (Creation)

I love this. Initial impressions of yet more sub-MBV dream-noise were quickly replaced by an uncontrollable urge to play *Shot Forth Self Living* at neighbour-baiting volume at least once a day. That was weeks ago, and I'm still no nearer banishing it shelfwards to gather dust. Glorious mangled trebly fuzz guitars, lovely tunes, obscurely sexy vocals, unusual thumping and clanging noises: you can't go wrong, really. "A Short Happy Life", never fails to make me want to go out and shag the nearest consenting human being, slowly. "Aruca", "Sweet Explosion" and the nine minute "Once More" (*"One more kiss then we're history "* - this tells you everything you need to know about the lyrical bent of this record) have pretty much the same effect. Like MBV and Moonshake, in their very different ways, Medicine have sussed how to harness the "noise aesthetic" to a bass-driven rhythmic undercarriage, and when it's good it works a treat, so I'll forgive them the bits of side two which sound like bad Cocteaus through a distortion pedal and provisionally make this my LP Of The Issue, cos Gavin's doing Red House Painters, and R.E.M. don't exactly need my say-so to continue doing whatever alchemical thing it is they do. (LN)

PURE CULT *For Rockers, Ravers, Lovers And Sinners* CD (Beggars Banquet)

I'm afraid it really is called this, and with irony and The Cult being as compatible as, I don't know, name any two royals, there really is no excuse. Sod off you sodding sods. (GB)

70 GWEN PARTY *Knee Deep In Evil* 7" (Snape)

A most most beautiful two songs from these anti-IPC, studiedly lo-fi magic moment merchants. "Knee Deep..." has a special goff-scale-riff thing that ascends ice-skywards, magpie magnetic. The other track, "Versus The Cartel", makes me want to throw a disco just so I can play it really loud. Any Mrs Executive Producer who's reading: give 70GP a TV theme to compose, if you want a they go like snarling fighting dogs and frightening, with a man going "Ugh ugh ugh" like those horrible Extreme Noise Terror type records ugly people used to like a few years ago. Stray pieces of sound (scratch, thump, scrape, bump, erk) that I wouldn't think of keeping anywhere near a tune, form the backbone of their true noise side. A woman heart-races words like Jad Fair on speed. It is the entire history of music on one 7" single, and all in all, I wonder just why people like this band, unless those people are on very good drugs. And no, I don't want any even if you bring them round my house for free. (KA)

HIS NAME IS ALIVE

PHOTO: M. LAVINE.

DROP NINETEENS Delaware LP (Hut)

One of my favourite LPs, not a life changer but a comforter, a happymaker. Shall we go through it together? "Delaware" is gorgeous, and "Ease it Halen" is uninteresting except for where Paula sings; just slow fuzzy guitar strum with muttering. It has beauty in it but it's not a pop hit, not this century anywize. "Winona" is, however. It is gorgeouser than gorgeous. The guitars tremble as they dance on the beach at sunset. "Kick The Tragedy" is called "Fucking Phil" in our house. Because he's off on his board somewhere. Obviously it is sunny. Obviously the whole world is a cake. I don't like the swimmy lead-up gtttrings so much as when Paula comes in with her monologue, and her voice is candy crystal. On the one hand this gets sickly for me if I hear it more than twice a week, on the other hand weeks later I'm so glad it's there. It's, she's, genius. This wouldn't exist without her magic conjouring focusing unfocussedness... "Baby Wonder's Gone" is crap, cissy soppy kinda. But "Happen"!!!!! I wish I knew. It makes me cry out like a bird, it's that beautiful thing that's just around the corner, it's been dark so long and all of a sudden you're in a dew-sparkling light filled green field. Everything's pale, extremely delicate, beautiful, so full, excited, nothing can be done. "Happen" is a song that matches those extraordinary experiences that refuse to be reduced by words... then, another crap one. "Reberrymemberer"; imagine your first MBV record is warped and playing both sides as one although one of them is backwards. You've got a hangover and you're listening to it in the middle of a traffic island, while a man close to you has a nervous breakdown and plays bollocks hippy music (at least). "Angel", the one that rude lady stole off them, is actually a sandy coloured song, then "My Aquarium" is also ace, with dual vocals that kill. Enough to sing for several days. "(Plus Fish Dream)" is more noise, to show... what? To confound us. But they don't see that like a bag of sweets we'll just choose the sweetest, the chocalatiest, and leave the vague ones for auntie. Auntie here gets five twelfths of an LP, which she will doubtless put in her closet until the day she thinks of a use for it, only you know and I know that this day will never come. (KA)

GRENADINE *Goya* LP (Shimmydisc)

It's on Shimmy but it's not hippy noise-guitar stuff, cos this is Jenny Toomey again, this time with Mark Robinson and Robert Christiansen. It's because it's from Simple Machines and Teenbeat too. It's because all the songs were made by dead people (that is, very very old people) with names like Cole Porter and George and Ira Gershwin. It's because this is a luxury item, complete with cocktail recipes. And... it sounds great. I don't care about all the stuff, I just like it. .There's delicacy and tunefulness that your parents might like to, if it were more obvious, but that's not the point. Jenny's voice reminds me so much of Tracy Thorn, when she's not reminding me of a bucketful of punk rockers, but that doesn't matter either. This is what you get if you twist the weird wireless dial too far one way on a summer's day; a riot grrrl singing *"I only have eyes for you"*, with no irony whatsoever. Things like "Cherishino", it's dreamy and all in lovc with nice people. Gavin argues for the banning of all cover versions and I agree, but it's like the argument about sending all the men to the moon - you always want to keep back just one or two. So, what if I've never heard the originals, or if I don't believe they're cover versions, does that keep this cassette safe from the big vinyl etc. fire? I hope so. (KA)

DRIVE LIKE JEHU *Drive Like Jehu* LP (Headhunter)

A year after the fact I've aquired and fallen in love with this record. DLJ are the perfect band, they provide beautifully joined seams of AC Temple art rock and Fugazi's tough-and-righteousness while simultaneously they have nothing to do with either. Great tune and an anger-driving sound that sounds like they mean it. Totally necessary. (KA)

STRANGELOVE *Visionary* 12" (Sermon)

The highly unlikely has happened - my taste overlaps with the kids, just this once, because this band make me tilt my head and say "hmmm" in cautious approval. It's not just Patrick's confident Morrissey-Copishness, Strangelove seem to be hitting that triple 20 spot on the board, because they're also able to play and have original tunes. I'm not committing myself, mind. We will continue to monitor them on our vibrancy & smugness-o-meter. (KA)

What would you do if you ran out of glue?

NATION OF ULYSSES 3 Track 7" (Dischord)
The Nation's second major batch of artillery, *Plays Pretty For Baby*, isn't reviewed here because it's possibly the finest record ever, and as such is not predisposed to being tritely summarised by a tired girl. However I think the messages inside the feature I wrote on this phenomenon suffice to give fuel-and-weapon-seeking youth an idea of what to prepare for. This 7" formed a kind of between-meal sustenance necessary to continue our bloody war against that insipid, evil parent culture. It came to remind us, to reinforce, to slip in new ideas and ideas for ideas for the kids to feed off and vomit and grow strong, sickly but fighting hard. "The Sound Of Jazz To Come": the lecture is swallowed by the jazz is swallowed by the screechingness and sheer ferocity (like velocity) of the true Punk Rock Ulysses. "Then she hit me!!! It felt like a kiss!!!" A prayer. We'll rise.
My copy is already marked by the surface noise of love, of over-multiple playing, like how your teddy bear gets so hugged one day it turns into a real bear. "Destroyin' America, it's not easy, you gotta look it in the eye, you gotta take it by the throat, yeh I DON'T BELIEVE", this is a pre-image of the natural disaster that will destroy patriarchal institutions like flicking over dominoes... I keep talking about power but this is like a pure source to pour over your sweet sweet face, to scream, to fling an aching body at a wall, to feel so trapped and so excited to break out and swim/fly/transport explosives and be greeted by thesame power fifty-fold. "N.O.U.S.P.D.T.A." is what you must listen to when your courage fails and the vision fades, when it seems like a madness that you oughtta be confined for... see if they have it under the counter at a subversive vinyl store near you, or send some money to Southern Records Distribution (they've got an ad in here somewhere). (KA)

VARIOUS *Mesomorph Enduros* LP (Big Cat)
I really like this. As my close friends witness the slow but relentless decline of a once great man, a man painfully coming to terms with the fact that music is unimportant, a man who has seen the future and knows that it is green and silent, there's nothing like a great compilation album released for the price of a twelve inch single to reaffirm one's faith that music is the very stuff that facilitates the world's revolution. I don't know exactly what sort of hash this is, but I've only got as far as the first track (**CopShootCop**) and I already like the other 14 as well. Even **The Melvins**, the worst band in the world, are great. **Jesus Lizard** get their song title completely in upPeR CasE letters on the sleeve, which can only be a recommendation. **Hammerhead** are to **Helios Creed** and **Tad** as **Foetus Inc.** are to **Thinking Fellers Union Local 282** and **Laughing Hyenas**, and I don't say that lightly. I just bet **Drunk Tank**, **Pain Teens** and **Of Cabbages And Kings** haven't got through their lives without hearing Michael Jackson, whereas **Barkmarket** did a wonderful Peel session years ago. **Unsane** and **Motherhead Bug** are here also, at the end of side two. (GB)

LOVE BATTERY *Dayglo* LP (SubPop)
Love Battery do quite well in the treble stakes (treble = +!+!+!) especially before the bass comes in. And they're not heavy metal either - my hopes are raised. But, what's this? I can hear bullshit phallocentric lyrics, in the first track! So, it's off to Gerol's, the secondhand record stall on the market, with you, sad little piece of vinyl. (KA)

VARIOUS *Fortune Cookie Prize* LP (Simple Machines)
Another completely beautiful package from Simple Machines. All the songs are excellent, from the **Cannanes'** jangle and sweet-voiced-boy singing, to Kim's throat-scraping delivery of "Black Candy" (with Thurston and Epic). Hey! It looks like Beat Happening can make any band sound great. Here's a list of the rest of the bands on here: **Unrest, Love Child, Geek** (Jenny manages to sound like Jad Fair and Stephen Malkmus), **Superchunk, Fish and Roses, Whorl, Seaweed, Scrawl, Leaky Chipmonk** (featuring Lou Barlow and friends, playing "2 electric guitars, 2 drums, a bag of rice, 2 sets of keys, 2 pianos (one forward, one backward)") and **Velocity Girl**. I'd like to tell you more about all these songs but you wouldn't believe, I've left my record reviews so long that I have to write them all in one night, hence the laziness for which, if anything , I will be remembered. Inside the pink sleeve, there's a pink insert on which you"ll find facts about an agency that helps homeless and crisis stricken people, to which most of the profits of this release are being donated, as well as detailed information about how to put out records. Altogether truly special. (KA)

THROWING MUSES *Red Heaven* LP (4AD)
Stodgy compared to previous output, but hummable and ever-so-slightly lovable nevertheless. It's like the Muses lost their airiness when they lost Tanya, and now it all feels stiff, stifled and M.O.R., although the Zeppelin-esque "Pearl"'s OK. The sleeve looks like someone's gran's wallpaper... little more need be said. (KA)

P.J.HARVEY

COME *Car* 12" (SubPop) & **SUGARTIME** *Awestruck* 7" (Simple Machines)
I had high expectations of both these Live Skull spin-offs. Live Skull were my major experience of collossal and majestic galaxy guitar(t), and I still have respect for the singularity and determination with which they built new musical worlds inside which adolescents could lurk, taking drugs, biting their nails and crying. Something that these two releases suggest to me, though, is that the essential objects of my admiration must have been the guitar-players of the band. Come, as you all know, are fronted by Thalia Zedek, ex-LS vocalist, and Sugartime feature their last drummer, Richie Hutchins, You want me to review the records on their own merits? This I will do, if somewhat grudgingly: "Awestruck" is dismally heavy, ugly, cheerful post-Weddoes pop which we wouldn't tolerate if it were produced by a West Midlands band so there's no reason why we should let these yanks get away with it. Besides, they're all goths. Look at their photos on the inside of the sleeve if you don't believe me. 1992!!! Hello!!! Why do you Merocaines copy us Englishes? That it features boppy crescendos of mild knowing angst and the line "you're shaking like a cup of tea", is the most positive I can be with this song. As for Come: Thalia still hasn't got over her self-esteem problem, and continues to use it as a major lyrical ingredient. It would be kinda good to one day see a happy Thalia, who says "I'm nice and I don't piss my friends off by existing," but it's dangerous to deny your own reality, however grim it is. The main problem with Come, though, is that her voice seems to carry much of the melody, whereas in Live Skull it was a distraction from it. Yet this song seems to work; a night-time journey of hatred and great sadness, a meditation on everlasting depression and ill-chosen lovers, where things could go either way - to self destruction, or to a new strength. It weaves and twists in winter's black winds, and finally swings its legs over a graveside. Overwards you reach a shimmering Death Western theme where snakes curl around the heavy-eyed girl's feet at she sings about how much she hates where she lives. Compelling modern day blues for heavy metal depressives. (KA)

POLVO PHOTO: LEXI MITCHELL

CITRUS GROOVE *Hit The Ground* 7" (Honeychain)
'I've been up, I've been down / But this time I've hit the ground'. Why don't you get mouse flavoured cat food? When was the last time your cat dropped a cow on your doorstep? (GB)

BLIND MR. JONES *Fading Fast* 7" (Cherry Red)
I wonder if "Blind" is an adjective or an imperative? (GB)

SPECTRUM ZERO *Free My Soul, Free My Mind* 10" (Placebo)
I'm with Marx on this one; if, as capitalists claim, capitalism's innate sense of supply and demand automatically regulates and only those things that are truly of use thrive, then what's this for? (GB)

WALT MINK *Chowdertown* 7" (Quigley)
The best thing about this record is that whoever wrote the press release spelt the producer's name Butch Vig and not Butch 'Nevermind' Vig as everybody else does. Such economy is touching in these cn difficult times. Also, they're a group, not a bloke. (GB)

P J HARVEY *Dry* LP (Too Pure)
How the woman howls, with the passion of the ocean flowing out of her lungs. This I love. I don't care that they're doing what might be construed as very old peoples , it grooves me good. You've all heard it too so there's not much else to say, except: I'm with you, Polly, even though you deny the necessity of feminism. We should talk about this one day. (KA)

EGGS *The Government Administrator* 7" (Hemiola)
If Unrest sound like a group you should ride a donkey to and Thinking Fellers Union Local 282 are the soundtrack to a party just as the police arrive, then Eggs (what? You don't collect Hemiola records?!) are dairy produce from a golden hen.
"The Government Administrator", which I guarantee at least six of my friends are going to fall in love with, illustrates perfectly the complex emotions involved in applying for and getting a job you don't really want (and, in the words of Shirley Valentine, 'Hey, I've been there.'). If this doesn't make you laugh then you're probably mourning the death of Benny Hill, you swine. Side B's on the other side, and if The Verlaines is too obscure a reference then I apologise but "Sugar Babe" is a classic tale of unrequited love with the classic denouemont, 'I can make the phone ring in your house'. It's poppy, slightly wacky, yet has a knack of producing empathy and complementary sorrowful expressions. A totally great record. (GB)

POLVO *Cor Crane Secret* LP (Touch And Go)
On an obscure episode of Dr. Who the guitars of Polvo can be heard chasing behind disarrayed robots, their metal-plate-sides hanging off, their sad trapped little eyes looking out pleadingly... on that particular planet, the sun sets green and small furry people live under the ground. They celebrate life with cupcakes and self-electrocution, on those rolling orange hills, and everyone lives in beautiful harmony until a fateful day, when the idyllic peace is shattered by an invasion of... Pipkins!! Hartley Hare and Octavia come turtling over the horizon. The only thing superheroes Polvo can do in this situation to defeat the hideous Brum force of the crap pig is to play their song in its most refined form, i.e. to launch into "Channel Changer". This scares away the puppet insurgents good and proper, leaving the inhabitants to party all afternoon to the music of the Polvo variations. Fluffy creatures kiss softly on the everlasting lawn, robots clankingly embrace and all of a sudden feel a lot less alienated. Watching and hearing this from a planet all of 2 light years away (through my super-audio-telescope) I feel somehow warmed, my troubles in the *Ablaze!* office shrinking to levels of minor importance. Thankfully Touch And Go Records of Chicago, USA, managed to employ ultra-new inter-planetary recording technology and bootlegged the gig. And now... it's available to the public! A once in a lifetime opportunity... (Excuse us while the *Ablaze!* team collapse with review-fatigue... it seems the first stages of bark psychosis have well and truly set in, Doctor). (KA) We're sooo tired and there's still loads of crap records to go. What can we do?... Ah, here's Moonshake at the door - maybe they can help us?

Several hours and many indulgences later, Lucy types:

THE MOONSHAKE REVIEWS

During the gig season, you can't move for minor pop celebrities here at Ablaze! Towers. Indeed, it seems to have become standard procedure for tour managers and record labels involved in the pre-production of low-budget tours to avail themselves of our wonderful hospitality. You can imagine the board-room conversations. "Shall we go for the Travelodge at £32 a double or Ablaze! Towers at two litres of orange juice and a loaf of bread?" Not that we mind: most musicians in non-hotel-using combos are exactly the kind of people we'd choose to have cluttering up the sitting room anyway, and Moonshake were no exception. What other group, after all, would show up at 1am, three weeks into a tour, and spend the next three hours voluntarily reviewing crap records and discussing the finer points of music appreciation? Present were Dave (vocals and guitar), Margaret (vocals, guitar and sampler), John (bass), Mig (drums), Simon (sound engineer), Gavin (drugs) and myself (rapid biro movement). The transcript speaks for itself.

THE AUTEURS *Showgirl* 12" (Hut)
Mig: "A Sailor for the Nineties."
Dave: "No, a Pilot."
Mig *(not to be outdone)*: "Poco!"
Dave: "It sounds like The Move with Bev Bevan."
Mig: "If this is the future give us back the Pale Saints."

BARK PSYCHOSIS *Scum* 12" (Third Stone)
One side of this record is a twenty-minute song entitled "Scum", the other a splendidly messy, detailed and psychotic-childlike etching. Dave *(before it goes on)*: "I think we're going to prefer the etched side."
Simon: "It's a bit Pink Floydy. Except even Pink Floyd are more exciting than this."
Dave: "The bass player pops in for a piss three minutes into it."
Mig: "This is like John Martyn."
Dave and Margaret: "YOU'VE NEVER HEARD JOHN MARTYN!"
John: "Large reverb noises; no substance."
Mig: "It sounds like the backing music for The Professionals. Dope-smoking music for people who keep thinking there's something wrong with their hi-fi and have to keep turning it up."

CRANE *Burning Hole* 12" (Elemental)
This goes longer without a sarcastic comment than anything so far.
Dave: "This was about their best one live."
John: "It's really average punk rock, but I like punk rock."

MONSTER ZERO *Wrench* LP (Eve)
Margaret: "This is getting boring. Can we go to sleep?"
Mig: "More desperate than Some Have Fins?"
Dave: "Mig, do you realise you've just lost three friends?"

3D'S *Hellzapoppin* CD (Flying Nun)
Sounds like... Pixies, Chills, really bad Pavement. Margaret: "Is this the Wedding Present?"
Gavin: "It's me singing with the Wedding Present."
Margaret believes him. Uproar.
Mig: "It does sound like Gavin singing with the Wedding Present!"
(Moonshake spontaneously combust. No, they don't, but I can't be arsed to write a cute outro.)

"I said *grunge*, I meant *noise-pop*."

DEMO reviews

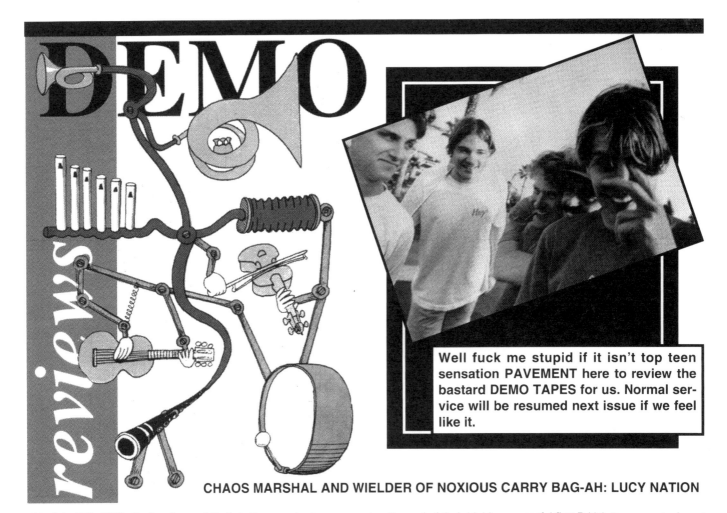

Well fuck me stupid if it isn't top teen sensation PAVEMENT here to review the bastard DEMO TAPES for us. Normal service will be resumed next issue if we feel like it.

CHAOS MARSHAL AND WIELDER OF NOXIOUS CARRY BAG-AH: LUCY NATION

It's July 19th 1992, it's Sunday and it's hot. Pavement, who are nearing the end of their highly successful first British tour, are staying at the swanky pad of A.C. Temple guitarist Noel Kilbride in Sheffield's salubrious Abbeydale Road district. Since it's their day off, the afternoon has been pleasantly spent walking around the grounds of nearby Chatsworth House (Gary: "Can we go see the castle now?") and as the summer sun goes down on South Yorkshire our heroes are to be found enjoying a barbecue on Noel's patio in the company of various luminaries of the burgeoning Sheffield prog rock scene. Bob's excellent chicken marinade having been washed down with copious quantities of crap lager, there remains nothing to do but sit back, put your feet up, don the silly glasses with the flashing LEDs and file a visa application for the Land Of The Hot Knives.

Oh yes, and review the demos. Sorry, Pavement.

(Note from Chaos Marshal: the only possible way to channel the amorphous state of flux that we call Pavement into anything as tedious as two hours of demo tape criticism - and, believe me, we're talking grand scale tedium here - was to give each of them (except Gary: "You wouldn't be able to read it, anyway") a pencil and a piece of paper on which to scrawl their opinions. What you get is what they wrote or, in Gary's case, said: so if there's anything you don't understand don't come crying to me.)

STRANGELOVE "Chances" *(this came from Food, I think it must have been a pre-release rather than a demo, but - ha! - the wretched and luckless thing ended up in the wrong bag,didn't it?)*
Bob: "This is what I always imagined "She Sells Sanctuary" sounded like. I never heard that. I never got to hear *Dazzle Ships* either. So I'll say this is an early Cult/mid-period O.M.D. crux."
Mark: "Sounds like a cross between Lloyd Cole and The The. Wouldn't cut the mustard on the dancefloor at Camden Palace indie-dance night."
Scott: "It's kinda hard to express my love of this band. I'm in Xtasy!"

28 DAYS "House Red" (6 Clarendon Road West, Manchester M21 1RW)
Gary: "It's the same four chords!"
Bob: "Lyric sample: "I'll sit down and think. I'll take off your coat. I'll fuck your Dad" ! I just had one of these hot knife things."
Scott: "Reminds me of Hvy Load (sic), this band from Santa Barbara who Tom Riers (?) likes! Of Split Enz!"
Mark: "Limey lounge rock. I wanted to like this one 'cuz of "I'll Fuck Your Dad" title. Ho hum."
Gary: "It's a lousy mix."

THE DELPHI "Reaf" (46 Douglas Crescent, Viewpark, Uddingston, G71 5JL)
Scott: "I've always wanted to be in a band like this! Groovy but sucky!"
Mark: "There are two Steves and one Stephen in this band. Ours spells his name "Stephen"."
Gary: "Doesn't this sound like U2?"
Bob: "Paint-by-numbers Lightning Seeds ripoff. Very soothing. I like the way Dutch men say words like "phantom". It's a shame they aren't Dutch. Probably the best-dressed band we've listened to tonight."

LOW *(hey! I've lost the title, OK?)* (Machine Music, 28 Roman Road, Birstall, W.Yorks, WF17 0BY)
Mark: "The bass player in this band plays much better than I. He can slap it like Flea Chili Pepper. Oh yeah, it also got stuck in our tape player. Ix-nay."
Bob: "I saw a band from West Virginia called 63 Eyes do a set that reminded me of dishwater Die Kreuzen. That was in 1988. This made me remember that specific set of emotions."
Scott: "Reverb makes the world go round and round! Chances are the Comets of the future!" *(Look, I'm doing my best here.)*

FAMILY ARSENAL "Truthrobots"/"Bagpuss" (33 Kelso Rd, Leeds)
Bob: "This is great. I love this..." *(etc, at great length)* "I'd like to quit Pavement and be their vocalist. There should be more British bands doing this instead of this guitar phaseout shit."

Ross out of A.C. Temple *(for it is he)*: "Nice drum sound, man."
Gary: "The drummer's way out of whack."
Bob: "Family Arsenal. Great package, great songtitles."
Mark: "I think we're heading in the right direction now. A cool, laid-back sound, but we still can't handle bad Brit vocals."
Bob: "Peppy and jazzy like that first great King Kong single. Spoiled by irritating pseudo-passionate vocal style. Darn. I liked everything except for the singer trying for what ended up to be a very poor fit."
Scott: "Rick Springfield was my sister's idol when she was young. I hear the Bay City Rollers have got back together! FOW!"

FENN (Richie: 041-812-4267)
First we get confused listening to the traditional Scottish music on the wrong side of the tape. Then we turn it over.
Scott: "I'm still trying to recover from their set in Glasgow! Caterpillars smell sweet!"

Bob: "Vivarin, No Doz, White Cross and other over-the-counter low quality speeds - I always hoped that they would have their positive effect. We played the same night as Fenn in Glasgow. I was very ill and stayed upstairs. I kinda regret it now. I should have at least bought a shirt. Reminds me of better Phantom Tollbooth and "Slake Train Coming"-era Squirrel Bait."
Mark: "Here we are! Cool starts and stops with really nice guitar sounds and plenty of surprises. Named after my favourite T.V. babe. Go, Glasgow! Go, Glasgow! Go, Glasgow!"
Ross: "Excellent snare sound."
Mark Trout out of Jennifer's fuckin' Ear *(for it is he)*: "He's a good drummer."
Gary: "I think this music's kind of exciting."

HUGGY BEAR *(this came from Wiiija, and no, I don't know what it's called. "Not a demo either," says Karren, "but their first proper release." Sounds like a f'kin' demo to me, chum.)*
Noel: "I think she's going to have to get rid of her band."
I don't think it's that kind of set-up, Noel.
Stephen: "I've got ink spots on my trousers: you've heard the one about the melted chocolate shirtpocket - this band is about melted chocolate shirtpockets. The stains, etc. They probably like old trains and edible underwear. But that's maybe too much credit to give on just one listen, and anyway, what do my locker room jokes signify?"
Mark: "Hard to be objective about this one, considering my wet dreams involving several members of this band. Huggy Bear: automatic weapons and spanking magazines! Vinyl, please."
Bob: "I saw these ruffians in the late afternoon at a record store in London. I

was completely entertained. They have a woman named Nikki who plays bass, sings and stomps on a kick drum. I'd list her comfortably on my top five coolest women in rock list. I hope they continue to retain originality and step aside from the Bikini Kill/Bratmobile/Nation Of Ulysses axis. Do they have a Drag City-type thing going on in this country? They belong there. They've only just begun. Good luck to them."

Scott: "Michelle Alviltar(?) was one of my first loves. So was Kelly Collingwood! I'm still trying to live that one down with my falcon friends!"

100 ELECTRA (041-556-1184)
Bob: "Australia's dreamy Moffs meets "Cables". Disturbing combination. Sounds like those kind of people who spend too much time hanging out in music stores."
Scott: "I'm still dreaming of the day I spent at Chatsworth."
Stephen: "There was a time when guitars sounded bright like the most beautiful girl in Scotland. The one who was smart *and* beautiful. Guitars sound dumb, naive, beautiful, but they never sound like her. (No, there never was

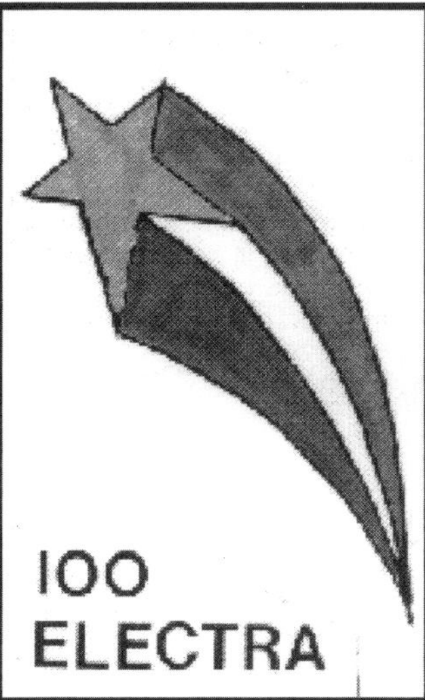

such a time, place or girl.) 100 Electra, rave on."
Mark: "I can't be bothered - Larry Cohen's "Q" is on BBC2."
Noel: "If these lived in Glasgow they'd be signed to Creation and they'd be on Top Of The Pops within six months."
They do, and he's wrong.
Bob: "They're better than Jacob's Mouse, though, I'll say that."

PURPLE ETERNAL "Arthur Lee's Duvet" (c/o Stuffed Cat UK at this

address)
Not, as you might have gathered, strictly a demo either.
Stephen: "This is that "licky griddle" genre that has little to do with my "pathos orbit", so I collapse and"
Mark: "Heavy, perverted guitar sound. I'll be right up front when they play the Duchess."
Scott: "The slow century days cement rules!"
Bob: "Ross just looked at me and said "killer snare sound!". I must agree. Very Paul Learyesque guitar style. Weird tempo-changed "Ghost Bitch" feel. Good in a tamer Drunk With Guns sort of way. Maybe a bit too ugly at times. But wait, here's a sitar."

SIMON BERRIDGE *(no information on tape, unfortunately for Simon.)*
Mark: "Bob's telling his Paul Leary story during this demo tape. Good story, Bob!"
Bob: "Crime And The City Solution have the same guitar sound as this."
Stephen: "Minor chords - are they inferior to major 7ths? Minor chords belong to Tom Petty, R.E.M, Paul Weller. Can you just take 'em and call 'em your own? P.J. Harvey did, maybe Simon Berridge will slink up and whisk the elan of a nation into their hairless nape."

CAPTAIN RIK "Schwanz" (Blase Noise Productions, 12 Rothsay Blaze, Bedford, MK40 3QD)
This one's a locked groove taken off Lee Ranaldo's twatty solo record.
Scott: "Everyone deserves to go through this phase in their musical careers! Me, I experienced it 5 years ago in a lonely dorm room in the middle of the desert."
Mark: "The old Captain should send this one to RRR. About as catchy as Zoviet France's second LP."
Gary: *(understating wildly)* "Boringish"
Stephen: "Negativland circa 1984. Sub-Throbbing Gristle, not that that means anything at all. (I used to own a spaceship. Its name was Fred. I'm a loop. A walking nymph, tee-hee, tee-hee.) A good companion to J.J. Burnel's *Euroman Cometh.*"
Bob: "I feel like going to the Captain's house right now to peek in on his electro mastery and sip a variety of teas. Oh, the price of fame is a sordid thing, Captain."

THE BIG MONEY (081-423-8201)
Stephen: "Big Black on an English diet... wearing Simon Le Bon's make-up. A plus."
Bob: "Big Black and The Levellers. Depeche Mode and The 25th Of May. I am deeply hurt. This is not much help."
Scott: "NYC makes me ill. I miss the English countryside!"
Mark: "It is difficult for me to enjoy this tape. Pass the hash, Lucy."

INFANT CONSUMPTION "Fangs" (Jod, 40 Dale Crescent, Patcham, Brighton.)
Gary: "Well, this is no good because it's got a drum machine."
Stephen: "The first Rudimentary Peni impersonators to get it right."
Gary: "It could stand a little more tone on the kick drum."
Mark: "Sick Brighton combo. Chaotic buzzing sound with great keyboard

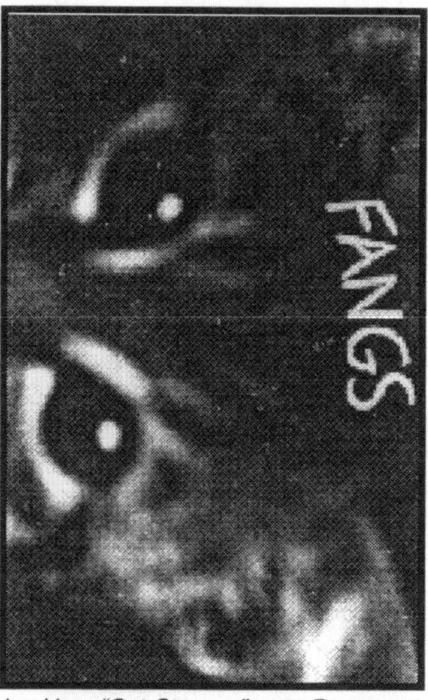

backing. "Cat Stevens" gets Pavement seal of approval."
Scott: "Lincoln Street brings back many memories! I now know I can never go back!"
Bob: "I envision this awful album cover by this punk band called Ism. Keyboard magic. They need a singer. I would love to be their choice. Their current singer is caught up in that Unsane vocal style. Frenetic. Gary got upset when they took it off in the middle."

THE UNDERGROUND (80 Hackworth Point, Rainhill Way, London E3)
Came with a note saying "One for the devastating arrow-like wit of your demos page," which is a bit like those people who walk around with a sign saying "kick me" on their back.
Mark: "Martha And The Muffins with violin."
Bob: "Very crispy. They must have shiny, pretty equipment. Perky. I think that band Faith Over Reason sounded like this. But, in all fairness, I only heard them once. A little too "Patty Perfect" for this stiff."
The others have long since given up on this pitiful charade.

ANDALULA'S LOCKET "Blue To Grey" (Wayne, 071-431-1342)
Bob: "There's a great band called Autoclave from D.C. These are not as good in any way. But they did remind me of Autoclave. However, they also reminded me of Jawbox."
Mark: "Sounds OK right now, but they'll sign to a biggie. Soon we'll see 'em on MTV and they'll look and sound like idiots."

JUDGE MENTAL AND THE HEAVY DREAD BEAT (Stuffed Cat UK, again.)
Mark: "Christ almighty! Sounds like a bad brit-hip hop record being played over a bad brit-house record. Bad brit-hip-house?"
Bob: "Over my head. I can't put a finger on this "super-electrode", "bass thump", "ass-shakin' boogie" dance drivel."

TAPE OVER THE WORLD

THE FIRST *ABLAZE!* HARD VINYL EXPERIENCE
A MONUMENTAL 7" single from ELEMENTAL & WIIIJA

Brought to you through all hell.
We have worked hard and we've baked you this cake, all full of fizzle and sizzle holes and chumpy currants.
Only *Ablaze!* can do this,
and only then with massive help from Garry and Sarah and Nick and Bridget and Pete and Ewan and Bill, to whom, thanks are owed .
Appropriate action? Place with care on your turntable and spin... wahey!

el-e-ment'al, records

CORNERSHOP "Change", recorded live at that excellent venue Harlow Square, 16.1.93 The band have said they'll never record this track; hence, it's a total **exclusive** to *Ablaze!*. and, in case you're wondering, the people screaming between the stops and starts are those unruly kids from **Huggy Bea**r. Can't take 'em anywhere. Talking of which, Cornershop made their TV debut causing a fuss in the audience of the Bear's legendary appearance on *The Word*. You want commentary? OK. "How Cornershop stand out against a whtewashed sea of post grunge blandness - apart from by their colour - is by their style. a clash of (dis)harmony follows when they mix'n'match and slice'n'scratch raucous guitar noise from the Eastern influenced sounds they draw from their half-Asian (?) backgrounds. An-out-of synch beat adds to this cultural cacophony, whilst the recently recruited sitarist purses his own peaceful course through the eye of the storm." (Greg, friend of *Ablaze!*. More next ish.)

JACOB'S MOUSE. "Kettle" is from their new album entitled *I'm Scared*, limited quantities of the vinyl of which come with special 7" singles. I've been told not to use the g-word, but this kettle has a mighty noise witch in it and they're brewing up some heavy thudding muddle. Mouse scrunge!

Other top pop things released by this cutesie noise label: Blood Sausage, Huggy Bear, Love Blobs, Action Swingers...

130, TALBOT RD., LONDON W11 1JA.
Wiiija Records are distributed by APT.

BIVOUAC. "Dragging Your Weight around", from their first album, *Tuber*, released in May. What have the press said about Bivouac? From a bunch of glowing recommendations, we selected this: "In short, they are a beautiful mess, hinting at brilliance in between arguing about which song to play, and, in keeping with this shambling naivete, they're strangely phazed by friendly praise." Check that kid's weird cherubic larynx action, and if you're amongst the first in the queue for their LP you will be presented with a free six track 12" of weird acoustic material, interspersed with snippets from their last tour. Write to them at P.O. Box 905, London SE1 6LF.

TRUMANS WATER "Soar Ossinaxx At Long Last" from their second LP, *Spasm Smash XXXOXOX Ox & Ass.* Totally ace and odd like something scratchy on Rough Trade from the early eighties that managed to hear Pavement and get its strings in twist over them. Their first LP is called *Of Thick Tum*, and it drove John Peel into a state of crazed ecstacy (when bothered by the press at the end of last year, our John was heard to say "What do you mean, best? New? Band? Actually, Trumans Water from San Diego come pretty close."). No apostrophe for those toply tipped for world confusion. Contact them c/o Justice My Eye/ Elevated Loin, 6161 El Cajon Blvd, San Diego, CA 92175, U.S.A..

Other bands you can hear on this queer little pop label: Crane and Swineherd.

64, MOUNTGROVE RD., LONDON N5 2LT.
Elemental Records are distributed by RTM.

A LOVE SUPEME - sayin' goodbye

Please forgive us our typographical errors in this issue; the transition to high technology has been a rough but enjoyable ride, and you'll have noticed all accented characters have been transformed into other accented characters. A language revolution, or is that passî? IN FUTURE: AC Temple, Belly, Bikini Kill, Breeders, Circus Lupus, Come, dc Basehead, Disco Inferno, Drive Like Jehu, Drop Nineteens, Earwig, Eggs, Fugazi, Girls Against Boys, Medicine, Mercury Rev, Papa Sprain, Pavement, Polvo, Pram, Red House Painters, REM, Scrawl, Seven Year Bitch, 70 Gwen Party, Sidi Bou Said, Slint, Stereolab, Thinking Fellers Union Local 282, Throwing Muses, Trout Masters, Trumans Water, Unrest... and anyone else worth listening to, we'll be talking to...

Meantime, keep away from that TV, fight the anti-grunge war.

This zine, the love-work of eleven months' gestation, is to be launched on the world during the Bikini Kill/Huggy Bear UK revolution mission. Now is our time. Sisters and brothers, what are you*r real* desires?

Geek the Girls

Lucy Cage on the genderisation of fandom

This is a story about how it was that people thought that girls who liked music might not be liking it in quite the right way. About how girls, when they weren't being perfect pop eye-candy, got sneered at for having an emotionally-driven relationship with music while the boys got cast as experts.

This is still a general dynamic in popular culture as a whole, of course: fandom across the board is undeniably gendered. Just look at the way the overwhelmingly female readership of the *Twilight* series is reviled in a subtly gendered way; territorial pissings by snide sci-fi devotees a particular feature of such commentary, wherein boy enthusiasts are held up as holders of arcane knowledge and girls are baying fools. (Or for a phenomenon that bucks the trend and, in so doing, reveals the extent of gendered attitudes to fans, consider the utter horror that has greeted the sizeable male fanbase of the newly revived and actually rather wonderful *My Little Pony* TV show: the homophobic, misogynist bile that gets spewed at loved-up MLP aficionados by net nerds needs to be seen to be believed. Apparently they're just not being *male* enough in their devotion.)
But we're sticking with music and our own story - however unreliable and partial it might be - of girls who were in love with (little-known? alternative? independent? largely ignored? - pick your own label) music beyond the reaches of the charts.

The difference in attitude towards male and female music fans suggests that there's been some kind of hierarchy of love in operation. Women and their messy feelings at the bottom and muso geeks, *Wire* readers, record collectors, vinyl junkies, fetishisers of product, curators of the obscure, possessors of technological know-how in all their analytical, articulate masculinity, at the top. Girls (who want the singer, not the song, who wouldn't know a diminished seventh from Christmas, Beatlemaniacal girls, all sound and fury) vs. boys (who either make the music or listen to it properly and thus win all the cool).

If that sounds improbable and out-of-date to you, well, let's hope it is, but consider this: in 2012, t-shirts are being dreamt up, mass-produced, put on hangers and sold to girls in chain stores, t-shirts that say shit like this:

I FANCY THE LEAD SINGER
I'M WITH THE BAND
I PREFER THE DRUMMER

It's not as if I don't have *some* sympathy with that - I've fancied quite enough lead singers in the years that I've been lusting after music, and hell yes, give the drummer a break for once - but it's so fucking prescriptive of the relationship that women can have with music.

Not only do those stupid slogans paint girls as consumers of music rather than creators but they sexualise that consumption to the point where love for music is dominated by one emotion, one impulse. Not an insignificant impulse, granted, but not by any stretch of the imagination the only thing going on when music is appraised either. (I often wondered what lesser manic pop thrill the sweaty, topless, apparently ragingly heterosexual moshers at Nirvana or Pavement or Mudhoney shows were getting stirred up by without all that fiery lust mixed in with the other stuff, the chords and the feedback and the noise and the beauty; of course, plenty of them probably were high on the sexual lovebuzz too, but that wasn't a widely acknowledged part of the deal at the time and maybe isn't still.)

So while I'm not discounting the part that sexual attraction has to play in fandom (you only have to point to the crashingly unnecessary career of Wendy James from Transvision Vamp to be sharply reminded of all that some boy journos had on their minds in 1988), I *am* appalled that the times are sticking to their archetypical guns quite so relentlessly now. That music consumption by girls can still be parsed explicitly as a passive, sexually submissive deal, as if the whole semi-tragic, insidious groupie myth wasn't made redundant decades ago. That someone thought it was cute, in 2012, to revitalise the trope wherein girls just listen to and enthuse about music in order to get fucked by the lead singer. That such an ambition might be the source of amusement and pride rather than disgust.

Just imagine if those t-shirts were on hangers in the men's section instead. Imagine if hordes of shaggy-fringed teenagers wore such things to the next Japandroids gig. I FANCY THE LEAD SINGER. If male guitarists or female keyboard players sported them. I PREFER THE DRUMMER. If joyously enthusiastic boys thronged outside stage doors waiting for Savages or Trash Kit in such shirts. I'M WITH THE BAND. What then? What kind of brave new world would *that* be?

It certainly wouldn't be this one. This one needs dealing with, especially in a book devoted to devotion, to the relationship between a girl and the musical objects of her affection.

***

I knew three other people in Birmingham who liked the same music I did back in the day. Three. One boy, two girls. We read the weekly music papers together on Wednesdays and pored over Fall sleeves; we went to gigs whenever we could and on Saturdays we made a trek to the couple of decent independent record shops to choose which album we'd buy that week based on the relative enthusiasms of our critic heroes. All the others, all the thousands of other people who read and bought and listened to *our* music were a ghost presence out there in the wide blue yonder, as unreachable as the bands themselves. It didn't matter if or how people thought of me as a female music fan, because my fandom was quite peculiar in itself; the simple isolation of numbers was alienating enough without any gendered overtones.

Of course, those who made the music I ended up listening to were predominantly male. Those who had anything at all to do with the whole scene appeared to be predominantly male. And those who critiqued and contextualised it were too. I couldn't miss that. Everett True, Simon Reynolds, Chris Roberts, Steven Wells: writers who made my heart beat faster and to whose reviews we'd turn first, catching secondhand fire from their passion so that the reading about it was almost as stirring as the music itself. (Such was the experience of non-chart pop music at the end of the twentieth century: first as blazing words, then as quest, then as consummation of needle on groove. All change now.)

It had the effect of normalising masculinity and obscuring femininity; the whole non-chart, independent music scene was coloured by who wrote the songs and who reviewed them and that tended to be men. God knows why the spiky music made largely by young, white, male, heterosexual American punk rockers and trumpeted largely by similarly young, white, male, heterosexual British writers struck a chord in me, but it did, and it swept its assumptions of what was normal along with it. (There's a parallel story in which transgression is yer watchword but that is not this one.)

When I moved to London and started going to see bands, I felt even more alone in my geekery than I had in Birmingham. I hung around record shops, lingering over Swans LPs, rattling imported Big Black t-shirts on their hangers and picking up the same early Throwing Muses record and putting it back in the racks over and over in a pathetic and mostly hopeless attempt to beam out my love for and detailed knowledge of a certain small subsection of the musical pond to a generally pretty oblivious world. I went to dark and violent gigs and got bruised in the mosh pit by angry men. I'd back away to the edge of the thrashing mess until I was relatively safe from being crushed or drenched in beer or punched or stamped on - gigs back then *hurt* – but I'd carry on going, aware of my status as oddity in a world of boys but a bit at sea about what to do with it.

In or around 1991 everything changed. The shape of fandom shifted with riot grrrl (and to some extent with the UK's homegrown Camden scene, chock-full with stompy-girl awesome as it was). Suddenly women were visible as creators, consumers, critics as well as fans of music. Amazing music too; fierce, furious, wrong, gawky, genius music. And everything was blown wide open. Women were present and active and unrepentant.

Ablaze! was part of that, of course, part of the democratisation of knowledge and of cultural capital, barging onto the scene and wrestling it into different and more girl-friendly shapes. Rock'n'roll has always been discussed in terms of cool (as opposed to mere sets of notes) but that cool was mostly boy-cool, the accumulation of which was a status activity in a subculture whose values mirrored those of the mainstream which spawned it. Riot grrrls made their own cool – so much cooler than before! – and dared anyone to challenge it. Women were making music, organising gigs, putting out records, writing, critiquing, scene-setting, dancing... Establishing girl-only mosh-pits was a triumphant physical manifestation of the way that women were taking up space and holding it for ourselves, no longer either merely the object of the male gaze or anomalous beings on the sidelines.

At the time I was working in record shops, first in an enormo-megastore and then in the Soho branch of a micro-chain of independent shops; I was used to feeling an oddity, took pride in my obsessive knowledge of the output of minor record labels, but with the coming of the riot grrrls I found that I had other girls to talk to about early '80s electronica or the latest Touch and Go release. It was riotous. Marvellous. Girls owning the creativity, storming the citadel of geek. It made all the difference to me. That's the spirit in which I read *Ablaze!* and that is how I hope it will be read now.

When I started writing about music I bent over backwards to concentrate on women as musicians: I resisted highlighting kookiness over cleverness; I wanted to reclaim skill and competence as virtues for female band members; I was fed up with the witchy madness trope that only allowed successful female musicians (see almost any commentary on PJ Harvey, Bjork, Kate Bush) to shine as wacky curios. I shied away from asking personal questions in favour of contextualisation, credit and creativity and I'd have been mortified to have been stuck in the 'groupie' bin so made no mention of the extra-textual shit that was informing my love. I'd like to think that that battle has been won and that women are equal custodians of the culture these days. That both head and heart can be called upon to describe our reactions to music. I certainly loved *Ablaze!* for having the chutzpah to act as if that were already true. For being bright and funny and smart and as unmasculine as you like. I hope that the idiots who pegged Karren for a groupie when she tried to sell them her zine are long, long gone.

It's not easy to add up how deep the influence of riot grrrl has been, how far its benign tsunami has carried us along the way to equality. Things aren't perfect, for sure, but there's evidence that the female experience has been incorporated into the culture of indie (agh!) music, not least in the defiantly geeky vibe of the ubiquitous/unisex spectacles-and-cardie combo of vinyl-collecting hipsters the world over. There seem to be vastly more girls at small gigs than there used to be; the ratios are evening out. (Not for every genre of independent music, of course: go to an evening of experimental improvisation and, as a friend pointed out recently, there'll be no queues for the Ladies all night. And online music forums? Don't even go there.)
And then there's Pussy Riot, making headlines and garnering international celeb support for offending the powers that be, an unexpected reappearance and reanimation of our past in the shape of three Russian Bikini Kill fans...

Damn those dumbass t-shirts. Who's up for a riot?

IN-GRRRL-LAND, SCATTERLAND & WAILS.

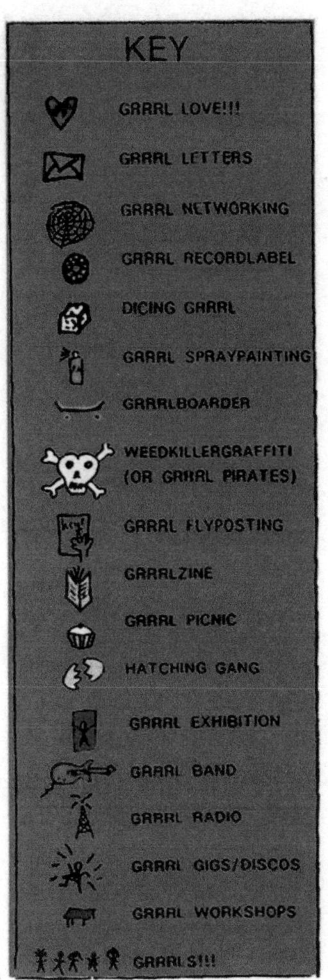

RIOT GRRRL ABERDEEN

SEE?

RIOT GRRRL NEWCASTLE

RIOT GRRRL YORK

RIOT GRRRL BRADFORD

RIOT GRRRL LEEDS

RIOT GRRRL MANCHESTER

RIOT GRRRL SHEFFIELD

RIOT GRRRL BIRMINGHAM

RIOT GRRRL LONDON

RIOT GRRRL PORTSMOUTH

Scale: Enormous! Bigger than you could ever guess...

"...as a woman I have no country. As a woman I want no country. As a woman my country is the whole world."
Virginia Woolf,
Three Guineas.

This map includes only those grrrls I know of from my work with the Riot Grrrls of Leeds and Bradford – hence the Northern bias. There are so many more grrrls I can't know about, so it's up to you to fill in the gaps...

PUT YERSELF ON THE MAP!!

Riot Grrrl was not a sound
Riot Grrrl was not an image
Riot Grrrl is still your future – go get it!

HIT THE NORRRTH

If the historical Riot Grrrl movement of the 1990s was one thing, it was regional. Published accounts have focussed on its originators in the States, and discussions about UK activities have been London-centred. Like Ross says of the Leeds music scene, we had (and still have) our own thing going on. This is true for Riot Grrrl actions in Yorkshire too. In Leeds, Bradford and York it was all about *doing stuff*.

London groups had problems operating because their meetings were flooded with people who wanted to infiltrate and/or document rather than actually take part. *Girls to the Front* by Sara Marcus provides a wonderful survey of grrrlism Stateswise. My only two experiences with the movement over there took place in Washington DC and New York City in 1993. I stepped into a meeting in DC where there were maybe 20 grrrls there. No-one spoke to me or made any friendly gestures, and the meeting was dominated by one lady who had had a problem with some other group members and spent the whole time reading out a letter she'd written to everyone explaining how very pissed off she was. Did I just happen upon the worst Riot Grrrl meeting ever? I hope so. I went to a party hosted by some grrrls in New York and they seemed very laid back and sensible, with their activities centred around arts more than music. Like I say, it was regional.

When I started writing zines there were not so many female zine writers. I knew of three within a ten mile radius of where I started. I kept going but was mostly surrounded by, and communicating with, men. At university I studied a little feminism, but was getting much more meaningful input from girls I was meeting who were in bands. In 1991, in discussion with Karen from Archbishop Kebab, I realised that it was time for girls to reclaim guitars. Throwing Muses and God Is My Co- Pilot introduced me to American feminism. Inspired by Lydia Lunch, I made some music by myself, but didn't dare play it to anyone else. I'd been wanting to form a band since I was 14 – I'd tried to make some music with a boy, but he said I couldn't sing. I tried to play the guitar, but a more practiced boy put me off by demonstrating complicated hand movements and dismissively telling me they were easy. But doing the zine year after year gave me confidence. In 1992 Nation of Ulysses' guitarist Tim Green whispered to me about these meetings in the states, girls who were getting together, starting a revolution. But it sounded far away and alien, and I didn't know what to do with the information. Then Sally Margaret Joy brought the revolution to the UK, using her *Melody Maker* platform to spread the word. It was the best thing the music press ever did. They clamped down with a rapid backlash, but by that time we'd already got the idea.

Debi-Rah talks about DIY as activation elsewhere in this book. That's how Riot Grrrl was for us – a big 'ON' switch, no downsides. The confidence-giving nature of DIY engagement meant I had something to give, so I encouraged other grrrls to do it!, whatever *it* was. And those grrrls, they formed bands with me. They didn't tell me I couldn't sing, and they let me try (and fail) at the guitar at my own pace, and discover that I could play keyboards with two fingers if I concentrated really really hard. We found our own skills. Simone played recorder and did backing vocals in our first band until another girl, Bela, our original bassist, handed over her bass as a leaving gift. Sim mastered (mistressed?) it in weeks and became the most killer bassist I know. As a band we threw ourselves in at the deep end with both recordings and gigs, and the results were embarrassing and awesome by turns. Other grrrls formed their own bands. There were zines, shows, club nights, graffiti outings. We taught each other to sing, to publish, to DJ, and shared what we knew about self-belief and confidence. We did it, we did it ourselves, and the joy was tangible. In this way, through mutual support and the power of DIY, we made huge gains.

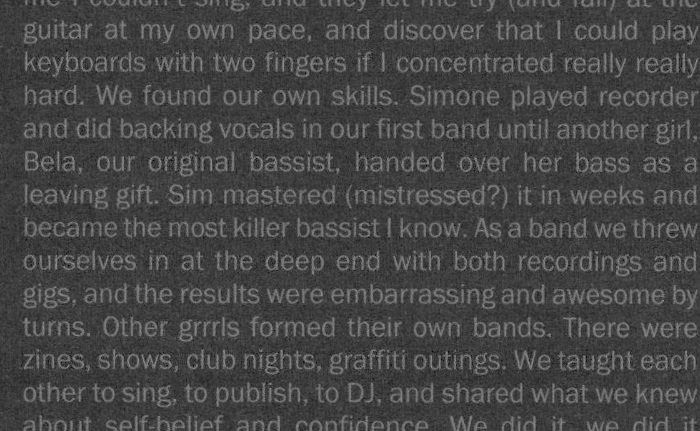

Really I can only talk about what we did. Because we were doing whatever we liked, there was no sense that our activities or existence depended on external forces, like bands for instance. So while the media liked to portray the movement as essentially musical, exemplified by the likes of Bikini Kill and Huggy Bear, we knew it was about *us*, because we made it that way. It was never about heroine worship. Riot Grrrl as *we* did it was borne from a straightforward sense that we could go ahead and empower ourselves. All we needed was energy and love.

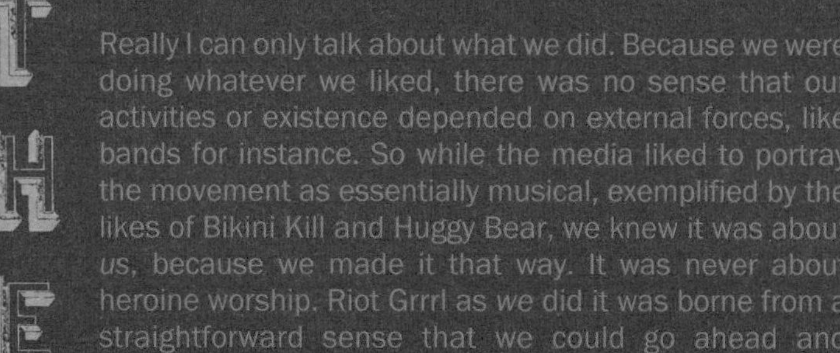

We focused on grrrl love rather than boy-aggravation. I realised that boys asking us questions were generally just setting a trap; they didn't really want to know our thoughts, they were looking for a fight. It was too easy to lose energy by engaging with these anti-feminist saboteurs, so we focused on the positive, on supporting each other to find ways to do what we wanted to do.

In Leeds, Bradford and York, Riot Grrrl was closely linked to our political activism, with our connections to the peace women at Greenham and WoMenwith Hill and with Bradford's anarchist venue the 1 in 12 Club. It was about getting out there and doing something fun that would change our lives and the world.

I was impatient to see others become self-motivated, only needing the inspiration of seeing each other, but there are so many levels of lack of confidence, such as the ones I had been working through in the seven years I'd produced *Ablaze!* If we had established a way to bring this about for ourselves it would have been stronger and more enduring. But how do you do that? Establish a Riot Grrrl therapy centre? It wasn't going to happen, so we snatched the immediate energy and ran with it, as far as we could.

After the initial surge, a group of us reconvened for a few meetings and activities a year or two later. I wanted these gatherings to be self-sustaining, not for others to look to me to make things happen. I wanted to be a conduit, a messenger that could transmit and move on, but when I stepped away the meetings stopped. Maybe I should have

been less impatient, more accepting of my role as facilitator, and worried less about others' snap judgements.

At times I've feared that so much Riot Grrrl activity seems to take place in academia; girls writing about it for their theses but not necessarily taking action. Happily it turns out that some are also out there creating grrrl-fun-space-time zones. For example, Julia Downes was an activist in Leeds-based Manifesta before she started writing her PhD on the subject. She's edited *Women Make Noise*, a book that challenges the sexist paradoxes that still confound female musicians, and agitates wherever she goes. As she points out at the end of this section, there are groups everywhere now, the Ladyfest movement is still in effect, and Leeds queer pop punkers Jesus and his Judgemental Father exist. The love goes on.

Here are five grrrls whose lives changed in the Riot Grrrl explosions of 1990s Yorkshire. We proved to ourselves that we can create a new world, and we each took that energy and created it differently. The exact same opportunity exists in every moment still. I urge all grrrls to get together, identify the barriers to doing what you want to do, and break them the fuck down, starting now.

AISHA ALI

I discovered Riot Grrrl when I was about 15. I had spent years submerged in the world of heavy metal and was just acquainting myself with punk rock. Suddenly I found there was this energetic movement of music, ideologies, and activism coming from women, something which I could relate to more directly, something which expressed my thoughts, feelings, views, and gender. My journey so far had naturally led me to feminism and political action, but to find these things combined with female-led punk rock couldn't have appealed to me more. Riot Grrrl felt like a force that I was compelled to be part of.

My part in Riot Grrrl involved writing, radio shows, a few bands, DJing, groups and meetings, activism, and generally being involved in and a part of the network and activity.

Like me, a lot of girls that were attracted to Riot Grrrl had already been doing things on their own or as part of smaller circles, but the movement presented a platform to have your voice heard in a much wider arena. It was exciting and empowering to be part of a united front of like-minded people, a movement with identity, focus, and purpose.

I do think Riot Grrrl has contributed to some change in our culture. Its legacy is an irremovable mark, certainly in punk rock, where bands are just bands these days regardless of members being girls or boys, and where people feared separatism as a result of the movement, it has in fact led to inclusiveness. Change has to be maintained and progressed, and will always be under threat from regressive reactions. I think Riot Grrrl's real legacy is tied in with how, and how much, these continue to be resisted and counteracted now and in the future.

SIMONE IVATTS

For me, Riot Grrrl began when a girl I didn't know approached me at a Headcleaner gig at the Duchess of York in Leeds in December 1992 and handed me a flyer for a Riot Grrrl meeting to be held at the 1 in 12 Club in Bradford later that month. I was 19 years old. I had heard the stirrings of this new punk rock feminist movement and decided I wanted in.

I had never been to the 1 in 12 before, so I summoned up all my courage (I was a little shy) and called the number on the flyer to ask how I got to the club. The number turned out to be that of the girl who had handed me the flyer, Karren Ablaze!. Having devoured *Ablaze!* since issue 6, which I had randomly stumbled across one day in Jumbo Records, and been in awe of the fact that the super cool kids who wrote it were in my very own city, I was excited at the prospect of meeting Karren and travelling to a Riot Grrrl meeting with her.

I don't remember a whole lot about that first meeting, other than a feeling of huge excitement and possibility, and the pleasure of meeting other girls and women who had similar incendiary idea(l)s to those I'd never really put words to before. I made friends - many of which I still have to this day - and I learned a whole lot. We formed bands and wrote letters and zines of love and inspiration and anger and passion and fierce, fierce joy. We put on gigs, did radio shows, graffitied our feelings so the wider public could see them, and we shared our skills with one another - the Bitch Skirmish music/zine making workshop day at the 1 in 12 was a prime example of this and it was fuckin' beautiful! We sometimes argued with each other (there were a lot of very different personalities and beliefs in that group!), but most of all, we SUPPORTED each other, in all of our endeavours. We allowed ourselves to be who we wanted to be and encouraged each other to develop in the ways we wanted. We made art in a multitude of ways, even being recognised by the 'art establishment': taking part in the Riot Grrrl day at the ICA in London is one of my most enduring memories of that time. We connected with girls all over the country, sometimes from across the world - and all before access to the internet made that an easy thing to do. There was a 'second wave' of Riot Grrrl in Leeds in the late 1990s, which introduced me to another bunch of amazing women.

I am still vehemently proud of being involved in the Riot Grrrl movement and identify as a Riot Grrrl to this day (I think I always will). It gave me the strength and confidence and inspiration to do things I may never have done otherwise: play music in front of a lot of people, write down and publish feelings I never thought I would share, travel the world and many more incredible (to me) things. It has informed the way I have lived my life for the past twenty years and I will always be immensely grateful for its influence and for all the friendship, learning, opportunity and strength it provided me with. I feel incredibly lucky to have been a part of it, now even more than when it was actually happening.

BELA EMERSON

Photo: Chandra Moon

Riot Grrrl started for me through Karren Ablaze!. We'd become friends a few years before (meeting at a Cure gig through a mutual friend, zine writer Mark Lemonade) then lost touch for a while. In 1992 I was in York studying and I saw an ad for *Ablaze!* somewhere or other. I wrote to Karren, and then went on the train to visit her, and she was just starting to do Riot Grrrl stuff in Leeds and beyond, and I was hugely inspired and exhilarated by what was beginning to happen: that we could form rock bands, write zines, hang out and hatch plans with all these brilliant women. I'd been going to see bands in York and Leeds - it was fun but quite a staid scene (especially as I was so damn shoegazingly indie at the time). Seeing Huggy Bear for the first time blew my head off.

So after I'd visited Leeds, and met Simone Ivatts, Lianne Hall and a few others, I was totally fired up and started Riot Grrrl meetings in York - it was intended to involve everyone local but I guess inevitably it was all students. Still, we had a group - of about ten of us - that was strong and creative for a year or so; one of the things I especially liked about it was that we were all involved for different reasons: musicians like Celia who'd been in male-dominated bands for years and were excited about the opportunity for change, artists like Zoe who enjoyed the exploratory and social aspects, others such as Lizzie and Leila and Liz who liked the autonomy of initiating action/s. One late-night graffiti session got the extra lights we needed on campus in those dark dark places: seems amazing to me now how easy (and how fun) that was to effect. We made some zines, proper collaborative efforts: cut and pasted and copied, full of artwork and writing and ideas (well, four A5 pages full, every couple of months anyway).

One of the high points for me of the York Riot Grrrl scene was when we made artwork for the Riot Grrrl exhibition at the ICA - it was a real focus for us and helped us feel part of the bigger picture. It motivated the group to travel to London together to see the exhibition and join in with the talks. There was a lot of bigger picture stuff for me that day, some of which has stayed with me since: learning about female circumcision, global women's issues, gobsmacking and heartbreaking inequalities. Meanwhile, in the summer of 1992, Karren A! called me up and asked if I wanted to be in a band. Yes, I surely did. And what did I want to play? I was beside myself with excitement - I learned cello while I was at school (though had put it down a couple of years before in favour of following rock bands and trying pathetically, unsuccessfully, to get off with people) but no music-making I'd done had been anything like *exciting*... and I knew it could be. Coping Saw was so much fun. I found it frustrating sometimes too - I loved rehearsing but I sometimes couldn't make it sound right on stage with everyone. It was exhilarating to make music with people - it became addictive. I'd never been free to just play and experiment and join in before and it was wonderful.

I can say for sure that Riot Grrrl has affected the direction of my life: I've been playing music for 20 years as a result of playing in Riot Grrrl bands and I've also carried on collaborating with many female musicians (and artists of other kinds), which these days there are lots more of than there used to be (and I do think that Riot Grrrl helped with that too, though it hopefully would have happened eventually one way or another). I still have (active and real, not-just-Facebook) friendships with some amazingly inspiring and wonderful strong intelligent no-bullshit women I met through northern Riot Grrrl scenes, and I can see that certain pivotal personal moments in my life have been informed by my being involved in a creative network of active (young) women 20-odd years ago. I took way less shit from tossers as a result of being involved in Riot Grrrl and I think it helped me on the road to admiring rather than being jealous of other women too...

GERALDINE MONTGOMERIE

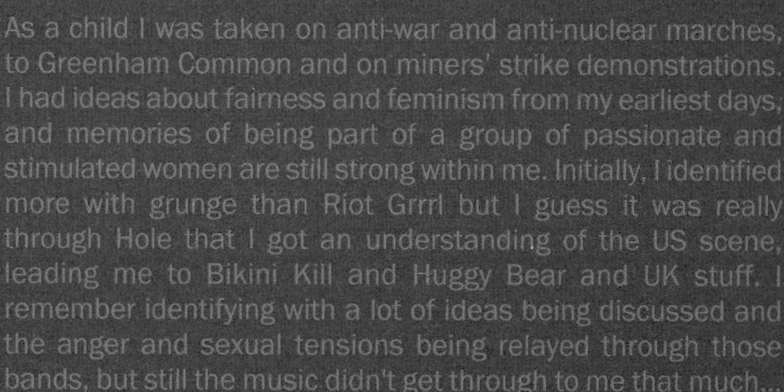

As a child I was taken on anti-war and anti-nuclear marches, to Greenham Common and on miners' strike demonstrations. I had ideas about fairness and feminism from my earliest days, and memories of being part of a group of passionate and stimulated women are still strong within me. Initially, I identified more with grunge than Riot Grrrl but I guess it was really through Hole that I got an understanding of the US scene, leading me to Bikini Kill and Huggy Bear and UK stuff. I remember identifying with a lot of ideas being discussed and the anger and sexual tensions being relayed through those bands, but still the music didn't get through to me that much...

When I was 15 I started going to gigs and my grrrliness related to being gutsy - going to gigs alone and finding ways to get in without paying and begging bus fare home. I began to meet girls who were more open to music, more interested in counter culture and risk taking. At that point, my closest friends - both girls and boys - were relatively undifferentiated by gender - all clothes, haircuts, interests and abilities were interchangeable. There were a lot of Riot Grrrl ideas but I can't remember us using the term - it seemed like all those things were just part of the time and didn't need a label.

At 17, I began to take a real interest in feminism - the history of modern feminism, key figures, what were considered key issues and that brought me back to Riot Grrrl from an angle of celebrating femininity. It was only when I met people who openly identified with it that I can confidently say that I experienced Riot Grrrl first hand, aged 20. We worked on a fanzine, played around in a band, I invented a cocktail. I was confident I had no musical talent, which my experiences in The Vaginal Teeth Collective largely confirmed and I felt I did not need to share my writing with others to validate it. I became much more committed to being part of a DIY scene and to taking some personal responsibility for improving myself and my world. It felt good. Like first love.

I guess I equate much of my version of feminism with Riot Grrrl and an idea of friendship that allows for respect, free expression and creativity. But people are human and it's hard for others to live up to your hopes for them. It's hard to live up to being a good grrrl yourself. I have often felt disappointed by women as I somehow expect more of them. I am often uninspired, uncreative and when I have become excited about something or agreed to a project I have often found myself unable to complete it. In giving me confidence that anything was possible, it led me down a lot of dead ends - trying different forms of artistic expression that ultimately I could not develop enough skill in to reliably convey ideas. I tried to involve myself in community and even mainstream politics without finding much satisfaction there. I invested a lot of time and effort in relationships that for one reason or another were unsustainable. I guess what I am saying is, it promises so much, but in reality it is hard to live in a Riot Grrrl world.

Despite this, I think it relates to a lot of what I value in myself and my memories, finding helpful anger and a willingness to fight against unfairness, to assert myself, to acknowledge weakness alongside strength, to self-disclose. I think it has made me choose a road less-travelled, made me a much more playful and curious person, made me try a lot of different things. I relate it to rights I feel I have that are strong and hard to challenge such as my right to walk alone at night.

I am currently a mental health worker and I do a lot of sessions around feminist issues, such as domestic violence, domestic responsibilities, gender roles, self-esteem and confidence. Part of my work involves helping people to identify how their expectations of themselves and others and their behaviour is limiting their well-being and the well-being of others. In teaching assertiveness techniques, problem solving and goal setting and identifying positive qualities within yourself, there is some empowering content. It's interesting work, particularly as I work in prisons with offenders as well as with victims. When I notice things that seem unfair or wrong I question my complicity in this and try to act to address it - be the change you want to see in others!

SARAH BAG

Witchknot - Lianne Hall, Sarah MacHenry, Jane Graham

I was older than the average Riot Grrrl, 26 as opposed to 16, but had previously been in all-women bands inspired by anarcho-punks - Slits, Raincoats, Poison Girls etc. When I moved to Bradford I didn't know too many people and got in touch with Riot Grrrl trying to form another women's band, which ended up being Witchknot. The great thing about Riot Grrrl was that there were all these other women/girls trying to start bands/put on gigs/do zines at the same time. Coming from a small (minded) town in the Midlands where my band had been a bit of an oddity: "Are you all lesbians?", "Are you carrying in the gear for your boyfriends?", "If I show you a drum roll will you be my bird?" etc., it was pretty inspiring to suddenly see so many other women taking the plunge and getting up on stage. Up until that point I think I had only ever seen two or three other women drummers so I thought "About fuckin' time! Reinforcements have arrived at last!"

The meetings were so chaotic and really fun and practical - not so much sitting around chin rubbing - more getting on with stuff like the fastzines which were done in one session - genius. At the ICA Riot Grrrl event I remember one speaker saying something along the lines of "let's face it, most of us are here 'cos it'll look good on our CV" and I thought "that's the difference between London and the rest of us" - we're not trying to "make it" with the band or anything else. Most of us in Bradford didn't have full-time work, but were involved with running community-based projects either on a voluntary basis or for peanuts. For us, being in a band was just an extension of our politics.

Riot Grrrl didn't change things enough for my liking! Perhaps it was too much, too fast. It's a slow process. Look at feminism a century on - there's still quite a way to go. I think there was a huge backlash from laddism and mainstream culture which quickly diluted the whole "Girl Power" thing. The letters in the music press were vitriolic - females daring to play in bands - shock horror! Whatever next? Equal rights! Are they mad? Scary really - don't ever get complacent. It ain't over, not by a long way.

I remember all the letters from 11-15-year-old girls that used to arrive at the Riot Grrrl PO Box where they felt that they were the only ones in their school/town/village who felt "that way" and needed to know that they weren't the only one. I felt that then, and now that I have moved to rural Wales, I guess sometimes I feel that now - except that sometimes I meet another ageing punk or feminist and we go for a cup of coffee and talk about the old times and before you know it we've started a band and anything could happen...

And I can only hope that happens for other Riot Grrrls too. These days – well, I have a daughter and she's turned out pretty well – plays guitar and writes cool stories and is nobody's fool – so I guess it's influenced my parenting style to be politicised but to have fun too and not to be too dogmatic.

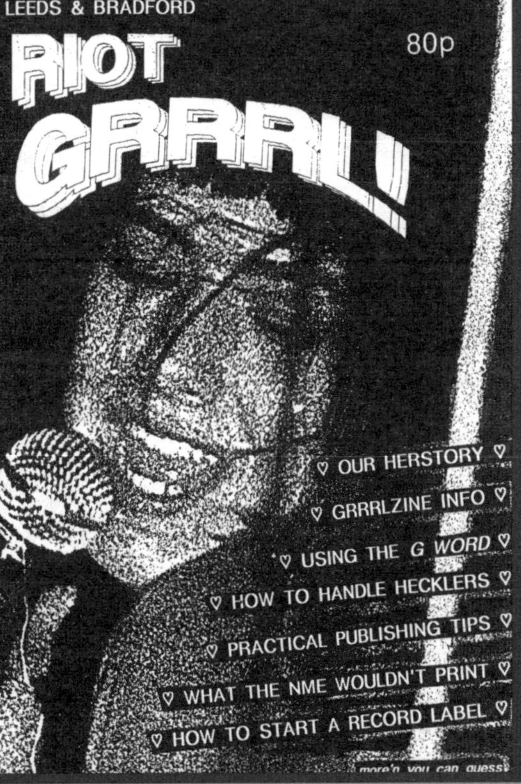

LEEDS & BRADFORD
RIOT GRRRL!
80p
♡ OUR HERSTORY ♡
♡ GRRRLZINE INFO ♡
♡ USING THE G WORD ♡
♡ HOW TO HANDLE HECKLERS ♡
♡ PRACTICAL PUBLISHING TIPS ♡
♡ WHAT THE NME WOULDN'T PRINT ♡
♡ HOW TO START A RECORD LABEL ♡
more'n you can guess

I asked Julia Downes to give us an overview of contemporary girl gangs / Riot Grrrl inspired stuff in the UK. She sent us this list:

Bands: Trash Kit, Silver Fox, La La Vasquez, Wet Dog, Woolf, Sacred Paws, The Middle Ones, Muscles Of Joy, Rosanne Barr, Cover Girl, Slushy Guts, Good Throb, Tortura, Jesus and his Judgemental Father, Edible Arrangements, No Womb, Etai Keshiki, Queer'd Science.

Ladyfests: Glasgow 2001, London 2002, Bristol 2003, Manchester 2003, Brighton 2005, Cardiff 2006, Leeds 2007 etc. Bring Yourself Fest (Bristol 2004), LaDIYfest Sheffield 2011.

Queer/feminist DIY organisers:
In Leeds: Sapphic Traffic, Riot Grrrill
In London: Big Takeover Project, Milk Records
In Newcastle: Even Clean Hands Cause Damage, Lady Garden
In Durham: Discount Horse Records
In Edinburgh: Pussy Whipped

DO IT! DO IT! DO IT! DO IT!

Deborah Withers is the author of *Adventures In Kate Bush and Theory*, founder of Hammeron Press, creator of exhibitions on feminist history, drummer of the band Bellies, and a supporter of Norwich City. I asked her to give us her take on DIY.

Do it yourself is activation. In a world where it is hard to shake off the forces of consumerism and capital, learning and knowing and feeling that you can do it yourself is a lightning bolt-like awakening that breaks the chains of passivity.

Becoming activated through DIY substantially transforms who you are and what you can do. There is no turning back after you experience reading or making a zine, putting on a club night or organising your own tour. It just gets bigger – your dreams expand and your actions realise your dreams. Like Huxley's *Doors of Perception*, once you have been opened by the mind-, body- and soul-changing potency of do it yourself, there is no going back. It acts like a vampire bite that turns things upside down, but it means there is no more sleepwalking through life. The intensity is cranked up and it becomes possible to really feel, because the illusion that your life, your time, your gender, sexuality and desire belong to someone or something else is shattered.

The cultural effort of DIY is often invisible or unrecognisable to the mainstream. Yet these activated vampires chip away, making tiny, fleeting incisions that nonetheless have unshakeable depth. They transform individual and collective rhythms through music, performance and intuitive expressions. They expand a sense of what is possible in time by refusing the regulation of the working week. It is a never-ending process that shows there are different ways to experience time, and there are different ways to work. Space is altered too. It is no longer something you move through passively, but something that can be reclaimed in temporary or more lasting ways. Life becomes more like a conversation rather than a one-way shouting match. The world sticks out as you paint coloured lines on concrete and enter buildings.

DIY has no fixed definition - it is a cultural condition that gives people the courage to experiment, to 'do'. DIY subcultures create so many things because they emerge from endless creativity that springs from people: businesses, record labels, free schools, organic food co-ops, publishing houses and club nights. The awareness that you can create the world on your own terms, indeed that you can create the world itself, is a unique and unruly power. It can be delicious, exciting and sometimes exhausting. But it's better than doing nothing, or being told what to do.

THE SHRIEKING VIOLET

I asked Natalie Bradbury what it's like doing a fanzine in Manchester in the twenty-tens:

The Shrieking Violet started in the summer of 2009 during a long period of unemployment. I decided to be proactive and create my own writing opportunity, using the skills I had gained during my journalism training. The first edition came out on 1st August - I was determined that it should be released monthly, but after getting a job it ended up being quarterly, which gives me time to find contributors between issues, discuss concepts for articles, chase and collect articles, copy edit, find images, and do layout.

I turned 25 a few months ago, but my mum and dad were teenagers in the late '70s/early '80s and my dad has a collection of punk, goth and New Wave zines in the attic that I used to enjoy looking through as a teenager. I always hoped to emulate them one day and I love the aesthetic, but I'm far too lazy and clumsy for all that cutting and pasting. I see it as being quite a laborious task, and for me the content is always the most important consideration.

My concession to the old technology and way of doing things is that I have, from the start, photocopied my zines in black and white; photocopying is a skill that anyone can pick up! Generally I've produced between 50 and 70 of each zine in paper form. It's vital for me that there is the option to read the zine as a physical product, but by far the most views are online - each zine is also hosted on Issue as a browsable PDF.

I distribute the Shrieking Violet by putting it in various record shops, cafés and creative spaces, primarily in central Manchester, for people to stumble across. On my blog, I also invite people to request a copy in the post if they can't get to Manchester, so I generally get a few strangers asking for copies. The most rewarding thing about doing a zine is meeting people with similar interests, and having people with particular passions and hobbies contribute articles on their particular area of expertise - often things which wouldn't be written about elsewhere. For example, a man who has been speaking Esperanto since the 1960s wrote of the adventures it's enabled him to have.

I also really enjoy getting to read all the creative writing submissions. In the latest edition of the Shrieking Violet, I printed the first chapter of a novel currently being written by Matthew Duncan Taylor!

Doing a zine has changed my life. I suffered from depression for a while before I started making my zine, and the doctor's answer was to pump me full of anti-depressants, but it was actually having a project and something to focus on and aim for which brought me out of my depression, far better than any medication.

Read and buy The Shrieking Violet at www.theshriekingviolets.blogspot.com

The end of
Ablaze!

Publication date: August 1993

NO! is *Ablaze!* 10.5. It is a fastzine, formulated because *Ablaze!* had become so slow. I was tired of the snail messenger loss , so went back to basics like the first zine I ever published, but with much more focussed energy and intent.

I'd enrolled in the Sonny Lee Wake Skool of Writin, via enforced correspondence course, and several parts of this are the result of that dubious tuition.

Gavin and I had been to the States for the 1993 New Music Seminar, and my delirious account is here. I had the privilege of interviewing Polvo, one of the most incredible bands to ever have existed, and Thurston Moore had sent me a fax (we didn't have a fax machine so he'd posted us the fax-paper-letter). I included that too, with my response.

FIRE FOR YOU, HEAT RAGE YOUTH. A SMALL SPARK FOR YOUR HEART.
IT HURTS, IT'S HARSH, IT'S REAL...

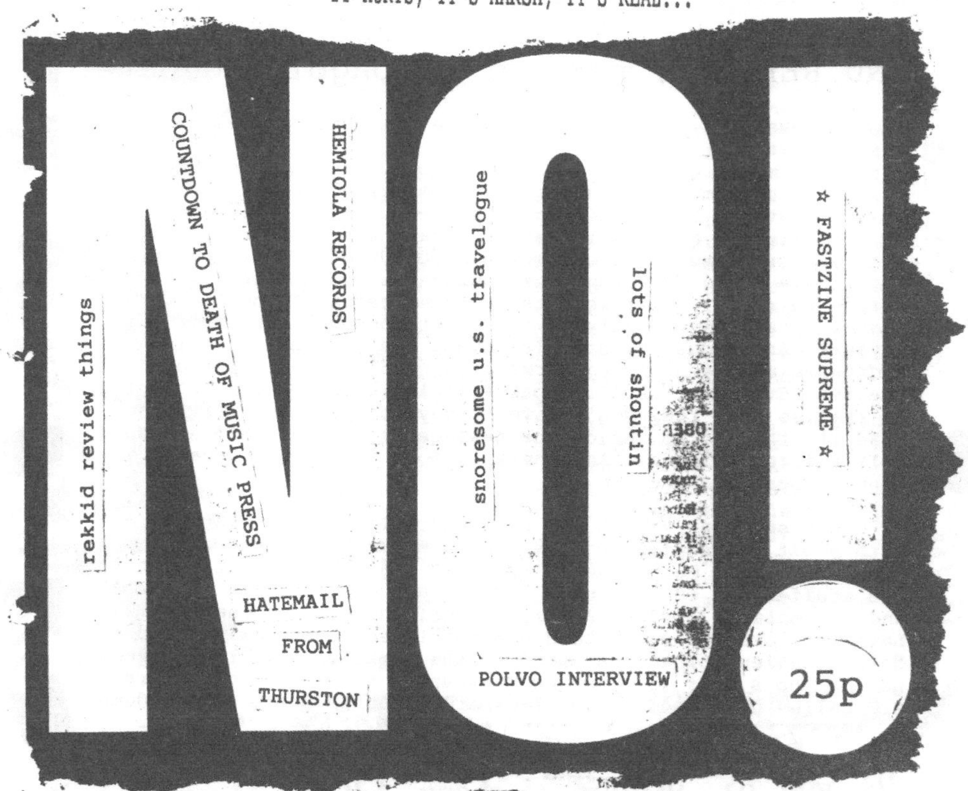

NO!
rekkid review things
COUNTDOWN TO DEATH OF MUSIC PRESS
HEMIOLA RECORDS
HATEMAIL FROM THURSTON
snoresome u.s. travelogue
lots of shoutin
POLVO INTERVIEW
☆ FASTZINE SUPREME ☆
25p

No! = Ablaze! babyzine from August 1993, in the neverending winter of North England. No! is what I have to say sometimes, when the men of my dreams are trying to get into my house (into me), when they're pushing as I try to lock the door. No! is a word I use when I go to less polite lands (where people are more honest, where the culture does not always revolve around women pleasing men), when they hassle me in the street (walking "unacompanied" means walking blinkered, never permitting myself to focus on another person), when they pursue me in subway stations. No! is the word I finally get to scream in the sound-proofed practice room the first time Coping Saw play together (they play, heads down in concentration, soaked in delerium, they are magnificent). No! is the sound I make each wednesday if I read the lies they pass as news, when they dis my girlfriend, when they act like they think they can crush the only things that are good, the things that come from us...
This is the foetus of Ablaze! #11, the total screaming pinkness of which will not appear for many months. As you know it takes a very long time to make an issue of Ablaze!, it can only happen once a year if I want to do other stuff too, so this is for those impatient lambs who will brave lo-fi productions to get to the truth... this is for those who make their own fastzines - THIS IS TO SAY WE ARE FAST + OUR WORDS ARE MORE VITAL - we are here to gnaw away at the corporate music press, *we are here to wave it goodbye.*
No! is inspired by The Cupid Car Club, Leeds&Bradford & NYC riotgrrrls, and Leeds&Bradford Fruit Of Ulysses. Maybe ultimately it is fired by those Huggybear demons who have struck matches for a hundred scarey new communiques.

with reference to the Ablaze! vision of THE DEATH OF THE MUSIC PRESS: OBJECTIONS AND REPLIES, part of an ongoing debate.

"You're one girl on your own: how are *you* going to destroy the music press??"
First, I am not going to do it on my own. The death of the parent oriented music media is a part of my mission, and it's something a lot of others are working on. Female journalists are boycotting it, refusing to have their genius sucked away for profit. Riot kids are creating their own media - FOR US NOT THEM. Spy grrrls infiltrate music hack (un)consciousnesses. Noise terrorists refuse to reveal their secrets to them, refuse to be photographed, psychically-up-the-skirt-focussed, by their paid voyeurs. Anonymous terrorgirls reveal the personal details, addresses and identifying marks of specific egoful journo enemies. Even your usually apathetic indie masses are beginning to realise that they don't have to buy it (if they still wanna read it, they do so inside the newsagents, or pass copies round half a dozen friends). And there is more stuff afoot that I cannot speak of here.

"I don't see what you've got such a problem about. What's wrong with a bit of reading enjoyment on a Wednesday afternoon?"
When there's *so* much else to read, it's a bit sad to take it from the stuffed men in London. The deep lack of credibility of *NME* and, especially, *Melody Maker*, is well known. Even the fucking Levellers are taking a stand against these racistsexist hasbeens. No-one believes what they read in the weeklies anymore (at least, no-one who's over 15 - w/ no disrespect to our younger, more all-believing friends). The IPC-paid scene is a rotted kingdumb.

to make feed + grownup bunnies to fuck — so it just stares, breaking & feeling bad. which is worse? Bear, rabbit, piglet, owl, tigger, kanga, roo? Are they really all

"Don't Die" Huggy Bear = Punk-kissed kids. "Don't Die" is sometimes the saddest thing you have to say. Here the scarey beary manifesto "Teen Tighterns" finally makes it onto wreckid, sounding less focussed when it's challenging the kid by the turntable than when it's spitting and spiting out at the big guys standing always-in-the-way at shows. "No Sleep Till..."'s the angriest angry angry and as such it kinda passes me by, grating, BUT "Shaved Pussy Poetry" goes straight to the centre of my soul. Oh please please please. I feel like tearing my body open, not like the glamourised Sacred Heart Christ but all messy, burning blood eveywhere, so I can give my heart (stupid, stuttering) to Huggy Bear. "SPP" is two minutes of racing rattling bliss because it is a song of wonder like you never never never expect then cannot let go of. A letter - "I keep it in my bag! I wont let the authorities have it!" - and its power to animate.... "Pansy Twist" is queer warped roar. Turned out destructive. "My boyfriend violates his parole" spits Chris. "And he's not you." In case you weren't sure. It's the same viciousness past the time when I thought it could continue. How do they still exist? This band threaten the already tenuous stability of language (and everything) so much that I keep expecting them to get off the face of the planet so we could all deny they were ever here. YEH I DON'T BELIEVE. So don't just read this shit I'm so hard trying to give you to describe them, if you don't feel this yourself there's no point. (She said) IGNØNØNØ

Small fry - terror fry in this union on the edge of a boiling universe. Huggy as good just different? Can anyone tell

---

Shrewsbury Underground is a brand new high velocity fastzine full of considered reviews of the very latest wreckids. Send an SAE (it's free!) to Topper, 6 Corndon Drive, Harlescott, Shrewsbury, Shropshire SY1 4LH. Send him your fanzine while you're at it.

ABLAZE!

Ablaze! 10 is still available if you missed it: 7" single w/ tracks by Cornershop, Trumans Water, Bivouac & Jacob's Mouse. Interviews with Huggy Bear, Nation Of Ulysses, Tsunami, Frank Black, Poster Children, Sugar, Moonshake, Bark Psychosis, Sonic Youth and Nirvana. Moonshake help us review the records and Pavement take on the task of sorting out the demo tapes... and there's a detailed girl power manifesto too. £2.50 including postage from here.
Also available is the **Leeds & Bradford Riot Grrrlzine** which includes detailed practical information on putting out records and fanzines, a discussion about the word 'girl' and accounts of our adventures so far, as well as a great many riot grrrl group and fanzine contact addresses. £1 including postage.
Future fastzines are available from here too for 25p + SAE or 50p inclusive.
Ablaze! 11 *might* feature Bikini Kill, Luscious Jackson, Dolomite, d c Basehead, Pavement, Circus Lupus, God Machine, Cornershop, Trumans Water, Stereolab, 7 Year Bitch, Throwing Muses, Belly, Breeders, Stereo MCs, Razorblade Smile, God Is My Co Pilot, Papa Sprain, Sidi Bou Said, His Name Is Alive, Bratmobile, Skinned Teen, Fly Ashtray, Palace Brohers... and an updated version of this Polvo piece. The record might be a Simple Machines collaboration... and it will be out by spring '94.

◊ **ABLAZE! / NO!, 17 Wetherby Grove, Leeds LS4 2JH.** ◊

Justine from HEMIOLA needs a holiday, so buy all her record releases and send her to see the sun!

HEM001 - UNREST with the "Cherry Cherry" / "Wednesday and Proud" 7", a snip at £2.00 inc. p+p.

The elusive HEM002, THINKING FELLERS UNION LOCAL 282 "Where's Officer Tuba" 8 track mini-lp. Yours for £6.00 inc. p+p.

HEM003 is the EGGS band with their Britsmash-hit: "Government Administrator" / "SugarBabe" 7". Steep yrself in EGGS for the bargain price of £2.00 inc. p+p else you is most definitely stoopid.

WOW!!!!!♡♡♡♡ FLY ASHTRAY "Let's Have Some Crate" is an 11 track 10" record. Its catalogue no. is HEM004 and its price is £6.00 inc. p+p.

So which one are you going to buy? Remember to make cheques / P.O.s payable to HEMIOLA and send yr moolah, aeroplane tickets, crummy jokes et al to:

35, BARNBROUGH STREET, BURLEY, LEEDS LS4 2QY.

POLVO

Dave Brylawski sings some of the words and (more significantly) plays one of the guitars (read GUITARS) in Polvo. Polvo is almost the only band that exists.

He's garrulous and a bit drunk, making himself an enthusiastic friend to most of the audience after their head-splittingly beautiful Leeds show. He thinks fast, talks in quote marks, attempts to make that leap to communicate. I am here as a kind of measuring device, some sort of devotional test tube. I collect sweat and cradle it back to my stereolab.

ggglacier slide builds the mountains. Big chunks of ice were what made them lumpy. After an afternoon on the Pennines with Clare, I was conceptually ready for Polvo. Some geometrick bird flapping in my heart.... and you know, my interview is an art, if they aren't all wound round ripped intense by the end of it (if I cannot do to them what they do to me), I failed.
So put your heart down on the table, when I put mine. "I never had to spill my guts like this before" Dave promises.

Elephant – cat – bear – octo
Polvo rule the animal kingdom from their helicopto

"We have no territory," say Polvo, a band without a doctrine. "We're exiles, we just float around..."
Yeah yeah, in heaven, I know, but you must have wandered off some path sometime. Your claim to orphanhood is *surely* due to memory lapse (trust me on this – 24 is a difficult age).
"We just played a lot, we just jammed, we would play like forty-five minute songs..."
So you'd take a load of drugs, sit down and... get on with it?
"Is my mom gonna see this?" Dave seems concerned. I assure him that Mrs Brylawski doesn't subscribe to Ablaze!.
"Actually, yeah, we get stoned, but not as much as you think..."

The sound that goes *Vrooom* frightens me, it's so true, like the Huggy motorcycle rev behind trailing slurred poetry. All the danger terminol, the pinnacle, but it's more magic than that. The crux. Dammit. Anyone with slightly psychic tendencies should be cautious when going to see Polvo, cos they will bring you out to fly then leave you grounded like the ladybird whose wings are stuck ouch after a trip over grass stalks. Like, that moment in "Thermal Treasure", the twitchy song of hope (desperate, punk rock, carscream) where the record got stuck twice with only a few seconds between the catches. It phased me. Why? Cos I only got it on CD? Or because they're playing it in front of my ears, and yet... (eyelids clamped... teeth on strings...) *HOW CAN THEY DO THESE THINGS?*

Tigers, we are watching this band play, and the band is skipping heartbeats and sticking needles and we can hear backing vocals that no-one is singing. They weave bridge links between each song for 40 minutes and in a joke they call it all one. Oh role up, oh know it's true, these gentlemen can procure secrets, can whisk magic up into the air with their sonic wings, the wings with strings to make ghosts real. Where are we? Place called Leeds, the Duchess Of York pub. How many of us in this pub? No more'n seventy. It befalls the band itself to try to answer *why*, why the kids are missing this, why this band is missing the kids.

So, I'm asking in a most exasperated tone, *why* do people listen to Suede?

Eddie, the man who plays the drums, replies. "They sound like a lot of Dave Bowie songs. It reminds people of what they grew up listening to."
And no-one listens to Polvo.
"No-one?!" Dave sounds outraged for a second. "A few misguided ones... but you're right."

I tried to explain that sometimes I see a band and the perfection gets me so I've abandoned my fucken body, cast it down cos it cannot serve me to express me, and you know the closest thing it looks like (visual, appearance, beauty, link up) is an epileptic fit. *THROW MYSELF IN THE FIRE – LIFE URGE SELF DESTRUCT – like the Circus Lupus thing...*

I feel like...
Dave looks at me. "You wanna marry me?"
I look at him, he retracts the question, I continue.
I feel like, some fucken crazy classical music fan, completely on my own and off my rocker listening to Polvo.
When after my heartfelt revelation they're distracted by so many goodbye interruptions ("Drive safely! Oh, you're walking? Well, don't walk to fast!"), I get impatient. This is an important part of my mission, so I pretend to give up on the interview, which increases the intensity somewhat. Perhaps as a warning, Eddie tells me how Polvo used to take themselves seriously:
"... And we were horrible, competely stoic onstage, frowning, looking like we were having the worse time in the world. We sucked live."
But, I demand, isn't your music the most important thing in your life?
Dave affirms that it certainly is, but denies that it is *art*.
"The word art has grand connotations, I don't feel like anyone special."
Yet what you do, in a field that hasn't got a name (bordered on one side by Live Skull, A C Temple, Dust Devils, and on another by trance ambience), is about ultimate.
"The most important thing is for us to please the four of us, and in that sense we're content. If that's our creative longings, then we fulfil them, and if that's art... It's just more therapeutic."

We briefly consider the way the English music press's lack insight into bands as majestic as the one we have here. "It's very dangerous," says Dave. "If we were an English band that would stomp us into the ground."
It's especially sad when there's only five good things going on in the world and they miss one of them. At least everyone here knows those papers are on their way out.

For some reason, Dave launches into a vitriologue about 'weird'.
"Until this album came out I never thought of us as a weird band ever. People were saying 'this is really difficult, it takes a lot of listens to get used to,' but it's like such a natural progression for us. If I said 'hey, we're a weird band,' I'd be the most insincere bastard musician to ever play guitar. We don't try to play weird or play accessible, it's just whatever comes out..."
I point out that the word 'weird' never passed my lips.
"Well, we get a lot of shit for being weird. I think Suede's a weird band, look at that guy! Leather coat, no shirt..."
"That's gotta be uncomfortable," says Eddie, "He'll get rashes all over his body..."
"England is definitely a tough nut to crack, it's not like America," Dave is rambling "...and God bless it for not being like America, but we're exiles anyway..."
He's forgotten his script already.
"Why did you get me on this subject anyway?"

...nued on another page

Eddie is more levelled and calm. By the time you read this he will be even married. He gives me their story, the one they tell to all the press. "We've known each other for at least seven years. Dave has known bassplayer Steve since they were twelve. We have no conceptual ideas about what we're doing."
But don't you wake up in the middle of the night and think... '*!'?
"It just kinda happens, we play and..."
"We fall apart." Dave finishes the sentence.
You think what you do is in some way imperfect?
"Imperfect's not the word, imperfect's like an understatement. A band like the Jesus Lizard, they can play an impeccable set, we could never do that. We're different, we're not tight, we're not master musicians. I like bands that are really intense and perfect onstage and I also like bands that have that human edge."

If I were really sad, I might wanna start with Polvo's perfect imperfection and package a new genre to sell. For those of you taking notes at KR tower, here's yer starter for ten: It has dreamtrails in early 80's Rough Trading, takes as its root generously perverted guitar tunings, there's a harsh beauty random element from Jazz Punk, it is the source of tremendous ice magic pleasure... and you've been ignoring the bands involved for years.

My friend says Polvo means octopus. (Actually, the word is *pulpo*).
Dave: "Polvo means dust in Spanish, but if you wanna think of it as octopus, we have eight arms..."
Eddie: "And seven legs."
Dave continues. "'Help' by The Beatles was gonna be called 'Eight Arms To Hold You'."
And on another plane Polvo *are* The Beatles. That plane is *real*, it's just no-one believes in it.
"No." This is making Dave scared. "I can't touch that. I grew up listening to The Beatles, Paul McCartney was my hero till I was like twelve..."

And then there's the wings...
"I love The Wings!"
Huh? What wings?
Dave's *puzzled* now. "Paul McCartney's Wings...?"
I was thinking about the angel wings.
"When I was little The Wings were my favourite group, I preferred them to The Beatles until I was about twelve. When I was mature I liked John Lennon."
Paul McCartney is the face of evil.
"He's a good songwriter, though I can understand what you're saying."
Clare told me that the phrase "Today's Active Lifestyles", (also the title of Polvo's terrifyingly awesome second elpee) was a phrase taken from an advert for sanitary towels.
"She's right. Not using sanitary napkins myself, I do know what those wing things are." But here's the weird bit: "We never told anyone that, how did she know?"
She listened to the LP for five seconds, and then that's what she said.
"Uh, that's fucked up. Is she OK?"
We wave to Clare.

polvo continued

The guitars are wings for you, but you only get one each.
"If I had four arms I'd play two guitars ... I wish I was an octopus. Me and Ash would be an octopus."
We start talking about the possibility of having children. (And no, not with each other you conclusion-hoppers).
"I think having a child would be the most beautiful thing, it would mean more to me than a gold record."
I admit that it was only while being transported by the Polvo set that evening that it occured to me that maybe, justabout maybe, it might be worth having children someday. Call me a commiserator, but that was sincerely a step up in my commitment to life, along the lines of 'well if there's *this much* good in the world...'.

Dave says he wasn't always so blessed as to play in a band with three people that he loves.
"I've been at the very bottom. Everyone has, I guess."
I haven't actually. What's it like?
"It makes being where I am a lot nicer, a lot clearer. I am very self critical and analytical which is probably a curse..."
This cursed self-analysis is illustrated when he tells of their show with Sonic Youth:
"We've been jinxed in New York, we supported Sonic Youth there. People called us the junior Sonic Youth, and we owe a great deal to them. It was too much."
Can you hear the line of pain running through this? Why do they diminish themselves before a band so much less vital? Why do they believe the longstanding myth that SY have the ability and the right to judge everyone else working in the same area?
"I wanted to play well, I wanted to show them that we could play... I haven't seen or talked to 'em since. It was our chance and we blew it. Whatever, it's hard to talk about it, I was the only person who was depressed about the show, the others didn't give a shit."

Perhaps if Polvo believed in itself it could not be the same thing. Perhaps part of the beauty lies in hearing that self-crucifiction, the constant disclaimers that cry out to be denied...
"In America there's a reasonable amount of hype which we certainly don't live up to."
And when I tell them that that's as it should be, Dave comes back with more. He reports that when playing with Babes In Toyland to twelve hundred people, "they wanted to rock and we couldn't rock 'em."
And: "We played this show at CBGB with Tar, Jesus Lizard, Poster Children, we were definitely outclassed."
Such things I cannot imagine, but what's the point of an interview where I constantly disagree with the band I love?

clock chiming midnight, guitars chiming, it's to do with timing, things fitting together, eyes fitting together, i don't know how something can be completely perfect and so damaging at the same time - like the barbed penis of a cat. So you see: my fight with Polvo is my fight with life (this is a lie). I am struggling with their butterfly nature, I get my metal limbs shaken, but they get worse, bruised and torn in the forbidden-fruit-biting battle to KNOW SOMETHING. (This is also partially untrue).

YEAH I DON'T BELIEVE. Driven sick and I know driven sick friends I can tell, where it pierces centrally, where it hurts, how we could be vampires together. I collected hatred for the big explosion. Nice guys? No such thing as a nice guy.

NB. This piece omits almost any mention of Polvo's records. And Ash Bowie, a person of great guitar and understated vocals, has also been left out. There are no particular reasons for these glaring omissions, it's just that this is a fastzine, my head's like exploding jelly, my bedtime's way past and the young fucking people I live with have just put the *Su*d** LP on so I gotta leave the room. A more stylish version of the above event will be reported in A! 11.

polvo: p.o. box 9052 chapel hill, NC 27515

does anything hurt more than knowing what you've only just missed?

I am here forever on the F train, because F is forever and that's how long it takes. Summer oven heat = inescapable sex. Eyes to eyes on every street, and no... I don't want to escape.

From Burley Village Leeds to East Village NYC: I bought a vacuum cleaner and took the chance. To go mad, cuz the city never sleeps so why should I? ...And I felt that if I left it, it might not always be there. It blows up. Boundaries defied: hell becomes home because my heart constantly explodes hot – "My heart always overreaches" – I want to live *every* life. Gavin and I stayed with Glenn from Fly Ashtray, he said "Make yourselves at home" and we did, got settled in this evil wonderful new world instantly. The iced coffee seemed the blessed way to go, it made my stomach bleed like a cold hot steel cavity. When Cupid Car Club played they rocked so hard so real it felt like my unstable identity was consolidated in the fucktest uppest way. And how time changes when you cross the Atlantic – the number of rings that mark its passing appear and disappear, and I found myself six years younger (sometimes even seven). The easiness and impossibilty of Village Life is the essense of its insaneness. The neither of us had missions, and dreams crystalised unfinished... No no no, chaos wont let you... Frenetic street activity, a population burrowing in bins to survive. In the 90° heat day and night melt together. I was driven by the changing lights, leaping over blocks, driven by the people landscape, leaving me a ghost.

Riot Grrrl NYC proved about the most highly inspiring phenomenon (they told me some things, which will appear in the next Leeds grrrlzine). The Coney Island fleas are vicious fuckers. We saw Luscious Jackson. We were treated to a special showing of the new hyper-sexualised Mercury Rev videos. Half of Pavement (Steve, Mark + new drummer Steve) played four new songs, and the one, the one about the boy with the new haircut was the finest; even without Spiral and Bobby N. (and of course Gary) they can still do *something.* The Silver Jews (with new guy Steve replacing Bob on drums) were fragile and scrawky, just like you might expect the Silver Jews to be. David didn't dare turn round to face the Irving Plaza crowd for the first song, maybe his first live song ever.

But now it's like I'm trynna tell you all which is not a possibility and there's no point starting. Suffice it to say, after a week of nonstop shows and schmoozing, I had to get out...

In the hour long Greyhound ticket queue, you wouldn't believe or maybe you would, two people met each other and both confessed to knowing Mother Theresa personally... and now I know why everyone there is mad. The muzak makes you tap the fixtures out of time. The 25¢ tv chairs turn your skin grey and the queues make your hair fall out. I felt myself start to chatter and was almost overwhelmed by a desire to just rip up the busticket and run. But if I stayed in NYC the overdrive thing mighta got me, and besides, I wanted to see DC...

Kicking out. Going: that long view of Manhattan in the mist. Oh my god. Babylon is awesome, a big funfair lighting up the sky clouds (die for them lights). Like a beautypark & you never leave. Like the taxidriver said... like they all say: you're here'n that's it.

"We will be arriving at Washington DC at approximately 3.15 in the morning."

Between DC and NYC there is some dawnlight magical city from the most fantastic bridge – a plastic pumpkin space structure stands glistening. Baltimore has roads that stand with their legs in the water.

I went to stay in the Embassy, a hollow house with vast rooms and outside chirrupping things chirrup so very loud just like on the TV (and we always thought it was sound effects...). Diplomatic transport = scooters, old vans and BIG big cars. The front door stays always open, even when they sleep, in an area where rapists patrol and shotgun wankers cruise. Trust and distrust mingled inseparable. I dreamed, dragons and terror. About not knowing what to trust. Ropes with rocks tied round my feet... under the perpetual light of a church.

Burning one hundred in the DC diamond. Electricity shocks knew of my secret snarls, and attacked me in a herd. The buses were plastered with 20 different adverts for a product that poisons cockroaches. Rattlebirds rattled in the trees so loud. The National Zoo is numinous, despite the obvious arrogance of its existence. It was there I realised that giraffes are altogether higher creatures, and was godmoved by butterflies as big as my hand.

Slant 6 and Cupid Car Club were both preparing to go on long tours, and something akin to schizophrenia was in the air. Drops of speech like nectar. Everything becomes its exact opposite... Time to reconstruct, to come back elsething.

Because & in spite of its affluence, DC is the fairest finest city I have seen, and NYC, it isn't even words for me but endless screaming. That's why it's so hard and pointless to try and translate it into language. So we returned to the unceasing winter of "England", to fulfill our missions and to let out the noises that these places sound like. Which is another story; the story of Coping Saw....

Ablaze! v. Sonic Youth

and the tale of the cursed cassette tape...

Sonic Youth were the alpha and omega of *Ablaze!*. In the 1980s they were iconic, they were the most exciting thing in the world, and even if there were bands that were better, they represented them in culture, they defined a certain space, making the unknowable known. Sonic Youth was like the coolest kid at school, but who could never deal with not being cool. It's okay though, cos everyone will always remember them as cool. They also made the best side of any record ever[1].

Although they'd been featured in *Ablaze!* 1, 5 and 6, this was the first time I was doing the interview myself. Still somewhat starstruck, I met with Kim backstage at the Town and Country club in Leeds in December 1992. It was a nervy meeting. Kim was quiet and knelt on the floor. She spoke gently with me about stuffed toys and riot boys.

Five days later I took a coach down to London, with the cassette of that interview in my bag. Probably the interview was only partly transcribed, and I was intending to write down more of it on my trip. This was my 24th birthday, and it seemed like the best birthday ever. I saw Linus at the Bull and Gate, met up with some Pavement and Huggy Bear personnel, and we went to Blur's 1992 Xmas gig, followed by a visit to a dodgy club somewhere in the centre of the city. On the way home I was violently attacked by someone who wanted that bag. That's how I lost the tape, and gained the injury that was to rob me of my health for the next two decades.

Back in Leeds I wrote up the piece from what I had. The result was a small article in *Ablaze!* 10 (p. 283 in here) that has been the subject of various interpretations. I was only actually mean to them in the first part. The second part is about stuffed animals, and in the third and final part we had a discussion about Riot Grrrl. In the conclusion I talked about digging her energy for doing so much stuff.

When Thurston read his copy, he picked up on the "ageing reputation" comment and was somewhat displeased. He promptly sent us, and all of his friends, a faxed message – the start of a short correspondence with long consequences.

[1] *Evol*, side 1

Re: new issue of ABLAZE: 5.3.93

Karen Ablaze thinks Sonic Youth should
break up. They are old and they don't
thrill her. They suck the cool out of
younger bands by supporting them and
genuinely likeing their music. Karen
Ablaze is ageist – a trait in solidarity
with sexism. Thus, her pro-feminist appeals
seem to ring hollow. Riot Grrrl puts a
spotlight on HER and that comes across as
most important. Karen Ablaze is ageist and
will be working at Melody Maker alongside
David Stubbs whose opinions she emulates.
I support equality, fairness and respect
to and for all individuals save those who
create elite factions for their own
ego-stroke: (Karen A. as Riot G.).
Sonic Youth's next LP will sound like Journey,
Foreigner and STYX – it will not appeal to
the world of Karen Ablaze. It never "planned" to
in the first place. I'm a man and I wrote the
lyrics to FLOWER. I forgive and hope for Karen A.
I don't hate her but I can see why some
people do. — THURSTON

This letter

ASK MRS. ABLAZE!

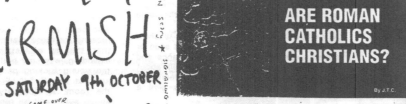

... Santa Claus; the Tooth-Fairy; the Easter Bunny; the Bogey-Man; they're all part of an elaborate CON designed to keep you DOWN! & when you grow up, the names change, but it's the same old CON!

well the kids keep askin, what do you listen to? (what should we listen to?) in the mistaken view that i might know more about it than they do, but sometimes that illusion is useful cos i get to influence you in all sorts of horrible ways. so go ahead.

The kids: what are you listening to, mrs. ablaze?
Mrs Ablaze!: funny you should ask, but that simple machines compilation is pretty good - although if i didn't know what simple machines was i might have played the first two tracks and written them off as a rock label. this has lots of jenny toomey bands on it and super tracks by Nation Of Ulysses, Scrawl, Autoclave, Circus Lupus... all my favourite things in one little measure. plus the Juliana talking bits are astounding.

The Kids: what's yer favourite Fly Ashtray song title then?
Mrs Ablaze!: i think it has to be "L'AGE-NT-SNO-PEE" (oh!oh!) from their "Clumps Takes A Ride" LP, but "Let's Have Some Crate" from the super ten inch on Hemiola comes a close second.

The Kids: but what do you think about the new Circus Lupus wreckid?
Mrs. Ablaze!: they're burning aren't they, they're burnt away into non existence with their sick glarin thing about life. the repetition of popman makes for unstimulating listening after a while, but it really hots up in the middle; check "Deviant Gesture Catalog" (cool title!) and the unmistakably soul-incisive Kim Cupid Car vocals on "Takes About An Hour: Epilepsy". Tragic that this vital monster group has gone, leaving the world more boring without its total savage delicacy.

The Kids: hang on, we're going to be in sheffield in october for some weird reason and we were wondering what radio stations and shows we should listen to.
Mrs A!: funny you should say that but from oct 15th Forge FM is going to be broadcasting, and there are shows by Ablaze! people like me and Gavin (Dicing With Dice) and Lucy Nation (Hex Enduction Hour). you might quite like those.

The Kids: isn't there a fanzine by other members of Coping Saw as well as this one?
Mrs A!: well, actually Simone, Matt and Marcus have put together the stunningly ace Saw Tooth zine which has just come out today! isn't that weird? it's got interviews with A C Temple, Bewilderness, Tse Tse Fly and Credit To The Nation. it costs 60p plus 30p postage (or a A5 sae) from Simone, 45 Willow Garth Avenue, Whinmoor, Leeds LS14 2EA.

The Kids: so what is the coolest record label in the world? isn't it one from leeds that's released stuff by Eggs, Thinking Fellers Union Local 282, Unrest and Fly Ashtray?
Mrs A!: you are exactly right! it's called Hemiola and its run by Justine and there is some information about the releases and how to get them through the post elsewhere in this Very Small Fanzine. incidentally, Hemiola recently was awarded the number 1 Very Cool Record Label position in world-renowned Plane Truth fanzine.

CALL ME A WIMP BUT... the recent beautiful living room drenching musics have been, well, not really Punk Rock. like the new Jane Siberry LP, "When I Was A Boy", which is utterly perfect. she has the most profound voice and does these terrifyingly beautiful songs about things so tender and true, which are scary cos they're felt more than it feels safe to feel things... I've been converted to her genius after all this long time. and the very old Laura Nyro "New York Tendaberry" LP from about 1969 which is hollow scary tunes that bump you up and down like the way that PJ Harvey use really naked dynamics, but it's also totally not rock. I don't know about other genres (i don't even know about rock really) so i can't even tell you what it *is*...

the Leeds Riot Grrrl High School Of Noise is having a →
BITCH SKIRMISH
* WORLD'S FIRST *
Screamin scary * SIGNALLING the death of the boy rock supremacy *
ALL DAY - SATURDAY 9th OCTOBER
Spray paint yr clothes + yr friends
figger out how to DJ + do live sound + put on gigs
come over
pick up guitars
drum sticks + mics
start a fanzine + create your first spoken word performance
BRADFORD
1 in 12 club
All grrrls (ANY AGE) come along - - -
Bring stuff - ideas stories songs dreams pictures
Write to: RIOT GRRRL, BOX 14, 52 Call Lane, Leeds LS1 6DT.

And did you hear the gorgeous Linus 7"? They're going to take over the world. I saw 'em live and did not expect anything this cool. My favourite song is "Jack T. Chick": "look what I've found, a comic book that fits in the palm of my hand, and it's all about god, and the pope and the devil...". I was freaked out when I heard this line sung so charismatic by Tammy, cuz I brought the very same comic home with me from the states. It's vicious, quoting Revelations to describe the Catholic Church as "the great whore". as a catholic myself I cannot comment publicly... buy this single because it's a special thing.

ARE ROMAN CATHOLICS CHRISTIANS?
By J.T.C.

IMPORTANT MESSAGE TO THE KIDS: watch out for future fastzines from here and a lot of other places, and send us yours as you put em out. the faster the better. the Ablaze! address is: 17, wetherby grove, leeds ls4 2jh. and the leeds riot grrrl address is box 14, 52 call lane, leeds ls1 6dt.
till next time,
take risks,
Karren A! xx

Ah!

Thurston HATEs Ablaze!

It's become a tradition at Ablaze! that we never print letters unless they're *really really* funny. Overleaf you'll see one we got from Thurston Moore of Sonic Youth, which seems to merit inclusion in this here babyzine, although it reads less like a letter than a press release. It's in response to my Sonic Youth piece which appeared in Ablaze! 10. It seems he didn't like it very much, and begins by stating his reasons why. Let's have a look at what he says...

1. He doesn't like the article because in it I wrote that I'm not into Sonic Youth anymore.
This was a very bad thing for me to write, because no-one slags off Sonic Youth. They are the alternative rock monarchy, in their own estimation, and will not tolerate dissent.
2. He doesn't like it because I said they are old.
However, I didn't say this. I wrote of their "ageing reputation", but nothing of ageing people. An ageing reputation, in this fast moving pop world, is what you have when your best work came out seven years ago.
3. He doesn't like it because I described their relationship to new bands in vampiristic terms.
Which is what I believe to be true, whether they genuinely like those bands or not (and of course they do). I believe that a lot of kids were at Sonic Youth shows last year mainly to see the likes of Pavement and Huggy Bear, both younger bands at the peak of their careers. I find it hard to believe that those audiences really dig the washed out r'n'r that SY churn out these days.
4. Therefore, he says, I am ageist.
Huh? It's *old people's music* I despise, not old people (not that I am describing Sonic Youth are old, or young, or anything).
5. Therefore, I am a bad feminist.
At this point, Thurston's logic leaves me way behind.
6. I am also a bad feminist because I am seen to be involved in Riot Grrrl, which I am doing purely to get attention for myself.
Hang on. I've been putting out fanzines for six years, and because of the high circulation and exposure that Ablaze! has received, a few people know my name. So when we set up a Riot Grrrl chapter in Yorkshire, it gets connected with me. I use my experience and influence to further the cause of Riot Grrrl, and Thurston, who is not doing anything for ego reasons *at all*, says my motives are suspect. This is interesting.
7. Therefore I will a) get a job at Melody Maker b) alongside David Stubbs c) whose opinions I emulate.
a) No, b) no, c) no, I don't think so. Thurston seems to be getting a little confused here. In fact, Ablaze! is the first cool British fanzine of a sizeable reputation not to sell out to the major press for a salary and expenses paid jaunts (maybe we should - then we could hang out with Sonic Youth). As if I'm psychically tough enough to work in that misogynist environment (like, pass the Stubbs Lexicon of Xenophobia and General Repellance).
8. Thurston respects everyone except those who create elite factions for their own ego-stroke.
Well, I'm sorry if the fascist Riot Grrrls of Leeds and Bradford have been terrorising poor defenceless little Sonic Youth. Maybe you can redress the power balance; Geffen will pay thousands of dollars for you to make a video in which you can try to set the matter right and put nasty fanzine writers in their place. It's not much of a platform, obviously, but...
9. Sonic Youth's next LP will be crap and I wont like it.
At last, a point of agreement! Perhaps we can start to mend this feud with such a promising piece of common ground...
10. Thurston is a man and he wrote the lyrics to "Flower".
Yes. And?
11. Thurston doesn't hate me, but he can see why some people do.
Oooh! This, I presume, is supposed to stimulate some kind of paranoia. The message "everyone hates me" should sink into my consciousness and hopefully reduce my self-confidence. Then maybe I will stop writing those wretched fanzines, and crawl off somewhere and be a nice quiet little woman in the hope that nobody will hate me. What do you think, readers? Will Thurston and his crap corporate rock band succeed in extinguishing Ablaze!?

An interesting addition to this story, which I found out bit by bit, is that Thurston didn't just send this letter to us. Courtney'n'Kurt, Bratmobile, Pavement, Huggy Bear, Unwound... I keep hearing of people who are in on his little hate campaign. Some of these people already know me and might take it with a pinch of salt, but most of them don't, and perhaps (because this is the first thing they hear about me) have no reason to disbelieve the things it says about me.

Nice, huh?

Thurston must have picked up a copy of *NO!* at See Hear bookshop in St Mark's, Manhattan, because one day soon after our trip there we received another letter from him. We lost it before publication of the first edition of this book, but rediscovered it tucked away beside a Shellac LP just in time for this reprint.

His contribution to the field of glittering guitar genius has been immense, and a fracas with a fanzine writer should never detract from that. His name is etched on the hearts of all true lovers of art (rock), and – should humanity survive – the music he made with Kim, Lee, Steve and other Sonic Youthers will be increasingly contemplated and cherished throughout future centuries, when the late twentieth will be viewed as a time of hyper-accelerated creativity. Sonic Youth defined musical perfection, and maximum respect is due. So I'm giving Thurston the last word.

ABLAZE:

My turn,

The thing that set me off wasn't Ablaze's dislike/slagging off of Sonic Youth. If I responded to every critical slag I'd have nary a second to create crap music, etc. I think it was the fact that you continuosly would throw Sonic Youth's name on your COVER. You hate us - don't use us to sell your magazine.

When we take Pavement, Babes In TOyland, Mudhoney, Huggy Bear, These Immortal Souls, Firehose on tour with us it is only because we love these bands and want to expose them to any aND EVERYONE. It is an insult to these bands to claim that Sonic Youth may be using them. We pay these bands out of own money to play and travel with us. We don't care who our audience is. It can be a roomful of elderly pensioners or a roomfull of self-righteous punk rock fanzine editors. We love em all. Kids who just come to see Huggy Bear have that right. We're only there if they want us.

Feminism seems to me a sophisticated and high ideal well worth any male's spiritual support. I didn't call you a 'bad feminist'. It's just by saying things like, "It's just old people's music I despise" that leads me to be suspicious of your HUMANISM.

I was trying to create paranoia by saying "I don't hate her but I can see why some people do." That was mean and I apologize.

I rsponded to Ablaze as if I was indeed issuing a press release but more as if I was a fanzine. That is why I sent it to others who might've related to the dialogue. Maybe I'll do it again but as I'm sure you'll agree this is tiresome and who the fuck cares????

I support you all the way for putting out a fanzine that for the most part everybody reads and digs, etc. I mean I buy it!!I bought NO! too?? (well, my name was on the cover..) but never let a jerk like me slow you or stop you from writing, creating, ranting and loving out loud all that inspires you. You do it well.

peace.......thurston

The Ablaze! 11 files

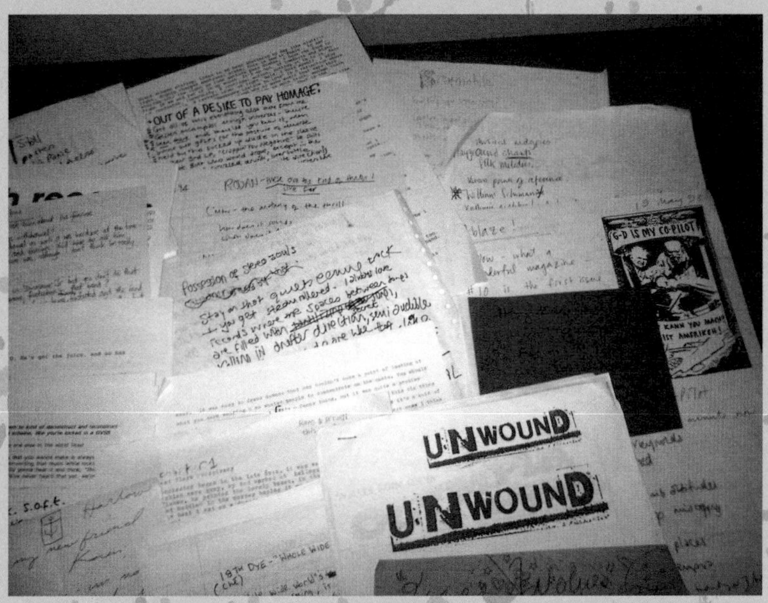

There are two cardboard folders marked *Ablaze!* 11, brimming with half-completed messages of love. If the zine had continued it would have been about Americans: Polvo, Unwound, Drive Like Jehu, Girls Against Boys, The Grifters, Bratmobile, The Make-Up, ...And You Will Know Us By The Trail Of Dead, Heavens To Betsy, Versus, Sleater Kinney, Shellac, Elliot Smith, Circus Lupus, Bikini Kill (for the perfect punk album *Reject All American*), Le Tigre, and Pavement, for the unendingly fascinating Wowee Zowee.

And if it had lasted even longer than that it would have been all about British bands. Champion Kickboxer, Linus, So'eza, Cowtown, The Cribs, Smokers Die Younger, The Week That Was, The Wednesday Club, Jelas, Autobodies, and the current incarnation of Scritti Politti.

THE END OF ABLAZE!

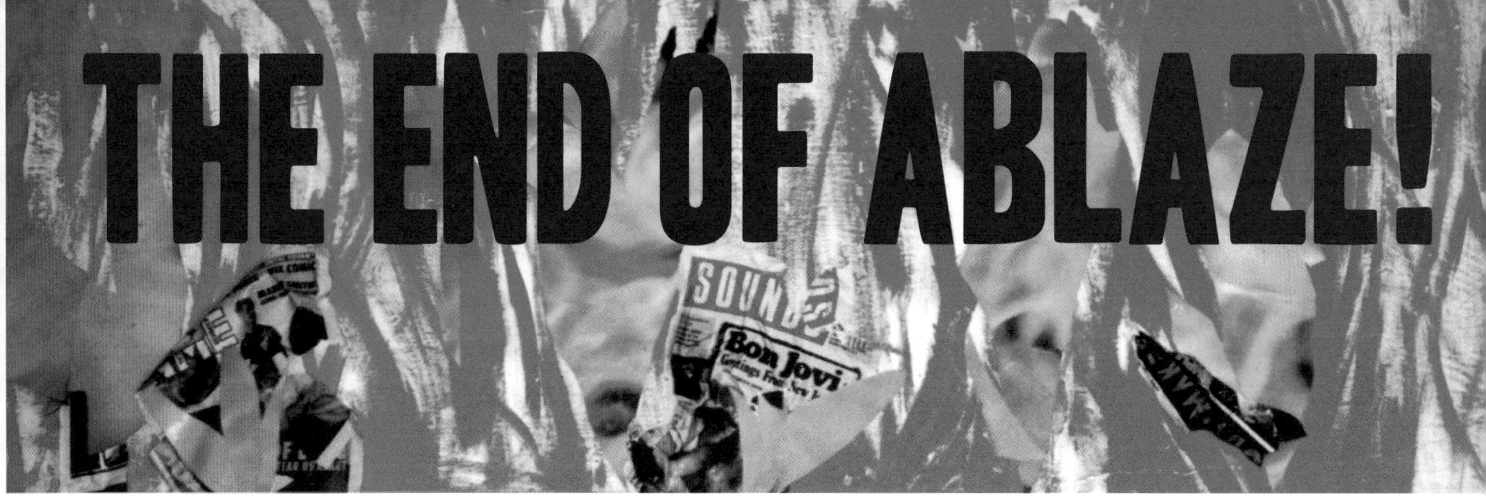

The story of *Ablaze!* finishes at a point in history where both my life and the world were about to alter irrevocably. It was the end of a 25-year period where I enjoyed a state of health that fell within the realms of 'normal' – I was about to be transferred into that other place, outside the safe boundaries of the square world of work, recognition, and the ability to earn – the space of illness, serious and long-term. It is from such an underworld that I have been writing to you, when I've been strong enough to wave you a signal from the rising and lowering tides of ability.

And in the real world? Well maybe that's too broad, or western-centric, a term. *Ablaze!* ceased to publish mere moments before the internet 'emerged', although it's a phenomenon that came into being at different times for each of us. Months after the last issue was released I sent and received my first emails. Instead of ringing someone up in America I wrote them a letter on a computer, and at the press of a key it arrived *in their house!* Later that very same day I received a reply, so there was time to write back and ask more questions, to have a conversation in text! It was nothing short of astonishing.

My internet virginity had been lost at work, with King Coffey of the Butthole Surfers. Southern Studios, a London-based independent record label with its origins in Crass Records, had liked what I was doing and asked if I would go and work for them as a press officer. I had sizeable debts from printing *Ablaze!*, and figured that if I had to get a job, this would be as cool as any, so I gulped down my fears and moved down to London at the start of January 1994, and King Coffey ran one of the many labels (Trance Syndicate) that I would attempt to promote.

Within that month my now Napoleonic-style right arm, injured in that mugging after my birthday night out with Pavement over a year before, led to a diagnosis of rheumatoid arthritis,[1] a disease that affects many young people, particularly women. It was to slow me down, but not straight away.

When I left the job and returned to Leeds a few months later, I asked around to see who had internet access - but there were blank looks all round. It was worth attending college at this time for free access, and over the next five years we acquired our very own squealing grinding dial-up modems.

However, once back in Leeds, I encountered blank looks regarding more than just the internet. In the past I'd held youthfully narrow views on what kind of actions entailed selling out. Dave Haslam had fallen foul of my values by working for someone in London (NME), for his involvement with an independent record label (Factory) and by putting out a well-produced fanzine. Want to see how karma works? I returned home to a new independent music scene, to bands like Polaris, Baby Harp Seal and Solanki formed by groups of students freshly arrived from the north-west and north-east coasts. I was excited to see these new bands, and I looked forward to writing about them. But they didn't want to know me, and they made it very clear. What had I done? I took it personally, agonised over it, got paranoid, and got angry. But really I was only being judged by my own, past values. I'd gone to work in London, for an independent label, and had put out a well-produced fanzine. This was selling out; I was the establishment. And that's just how it goes.

Were it not for the uptightness and intensity of youth, the story of *Ablaze!* would never have begun. But now I was 25 years old, an ideological write-off, and ill. For a decade I'd enjoyed the sensation of a life expanding, of never-ending possibility, but now it was my turn for the walls to close in - to experience the dark world of disease and desperation. My confidence as a writer, so hard won, diminished in the face of personal attacks by Thurston, Kathleen and people in my home scene, to the extent that I when sought to write a book about the music I loved in 1994, critical voices once again crowded the words out of my mind. I played in bands and worked as much as I could, and later devoted myself to learning a whole new set of values to make sense of life's more wretched turns, a system for navigating rugged paths. It would take fifteen years for me to remember myself as a writer, and a few more years to realise that I needed to revisit these expansive times.

Maybe we don't live our own happy-ever-afters. But there are always bright sides. Gary Jarman's going to close the book with his tale of what happened next. And... at least I never wrote for the British music press.

[1] After 16 years I worked out how to get rid of it. Check out my forthcoming book, *The Truth About Carrots*, if you want to know how.

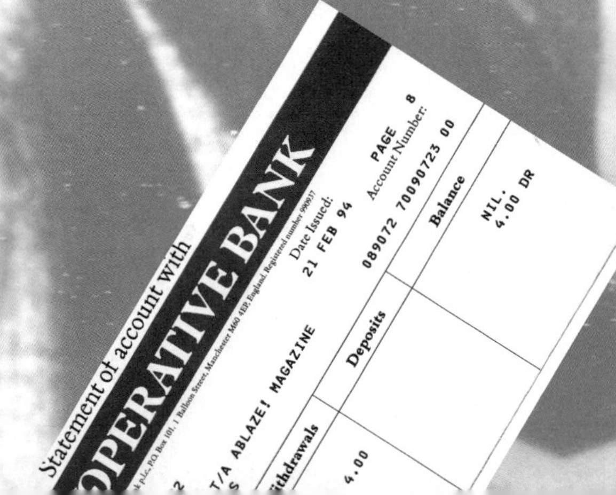
Statement of account with
OPERATIVE BANK
Date Issued: 21 FEB 94
PAGE 8
Account Number: 089072 70090723 00
T/A ABLAZE! MAGAZINE

ithdrawals	Deposits	Balance
4.00		NIL.
		4.00 DR

Love
Goes
On...

Epilogue

by Gary Jarman

When Karren first asked if I would write something for this book, I was flattered - but also a little worried about how to approach it. I told her there was a risk it would turn into a love letter from a teenager written as a jaded 31-year-old. First and foremost, I should mention that I was born in 1980, so by the time I was discovering punk rock (and consequently forming bands) in my early teens, it was already '93/'94. Factoring in that it would still be four whole years before I would be able to get into any show worth seeing, it is fair to say that the heyday of *Ablaze!* was a bit before my time. It did, however, still play an important and influential role in my life, and was an integral part of my introduction to many of the bands I would later cherish.

I grew up in the city of Wakefield, about 20 minutes' drive from Leeds, and around the time I was in the second year of high school I started to get into punk music. I had played violin and studied classical music as a junior, which was painfully uncool, and so at that point had pretty much unconsciously rejected the interests of most of my male peers. I was also a big Queen fan, and after Freddie died in '91, I was on the lookout for a new favourite band. There were just a small handful of 'moshers', as we were collectively referred to (punk kids, metalheads, thrashers, grungers) at our school, and we would share mix-tapes with each other during dinner hour (yeah, all the clichés are indeed true!). I still have a bunch of them - most of them included bands like Sepultura, Pantera, Ugly Kid Joe, Red Hot Chili Peppers, Nail Bomb, and Nirvana. Nirvana stood out a million miles - as a Queen fan I still wasn't ready for most of the death metal and thrash stuff, and in amongst all that death growling Nirvana's melodies were just diamond bright.

It was directly through them and reading their interviews that I then discovered Sonic Youth, Dinosaur Jr., Sebadoh... Once you scratched the surface (or had it scratched for you) there were myriad new bands to discover. There was one independent record store in town, Hellraiser, that specialised in metal, but was clued up enough to track down and order any obscurity you were looking for. We would go in to the store on our dinner hour at school and wait for our records to arrive. When we eventually received them we would typically find the label's mail order catalogue tucked in the record sleeve, hence uncovering newer, more obscure favourites such as Beat Happening, Jesus Lizard, Heavens To Betsy, and Huggy Bear. It's a typical tale, and maybe trite - but label identity was so fucking important in these small towns, it was like a lifeline to the wider world.

Anyway, as cliché-riddenly romantic as all that may seem, by the time I was actually old enough to go to shows it was the late nineties. Big-beat, nu-metal, and (shudder) nu-acoustic were the prevalent styles, and basically fuck-all was happening that I was interested in. It was crushingly depressing. I was born too late and bored as fuck. A lot of my punker friends had got into Chemical Brothers and started taking ecstasy in swanky wine bars. I was living in a flat on a rough estate in Wakefield, flogging a dead horse making crappy four-track demos and trying to get my own fanzine going. I was also drinking a lot of Lambrini if I remember correctly. It was around this time that I first discovered *Ablaze!*. I was bought a second-hand copy of issue 10 for my birthday by my then girlfriend, as it had my favourite band Huggy Bear on the cover. I couldn't believe that only a few short years before that THIS was happening in Leeds. It was totally revelatory to me, not just because of how vibrant the local live scene appeared to be back then, but also just by how RADICAL and impassioned the zine itself happened to be. It was totally bad-ass. They had

Photo: Steve Gullick

features with pretty much everyone of note, yet were never fawning or reverential. The interviewers seemed to be on the same level as the band (which is uncommon in a FANzine), and were in turn (seemingly) treated very much as equals. They were unafraid to ask tough questions about not only convoluted things such as the eternal ethical debate of underground musicians crossing onto major labels, but also straight up myth-busting and penetrating hard facts (e.g. "Do you ever lie to the press?" from the Frank Black interview), and the artists would, for the most part, respond with a level of frankness and honesty that the established straight music press would never manage to draw from these mostly guarded people. It cut through all pretence, it was 'rock stars' laid bare. Just relevant, interesting conversations really, rather than interviews.

They could also be powerfully vitriolic, but not in the manner that the current knee-jerk-say-something-provocative wannabe Lester Bangs way that blog immediacy and anonymity lends itself to. There was no hot-headed self-importance to this - the zine would take weeks [months!] to complete, so every article and review was a considered piece, nothing was there un-necessarily. They even had the guts to call out Sonic Youth. In the early nineties. This ain't tweeting - you have to admire the will of steel to not pull that article out in the weeks leading up to printing (when I later met Thurston Moore in Portland, the ice-breaker was "You're from near Leeds? Do you know Karren Ablaze!?"). They certainly weren't haters though - they just had an agenda. More often than not it was the optimism that fuelled the articles, and that is what made it so exciting to me. Oh, and they had a sense of humour! They were radicals, and right-on, but not dullards!

Of course, as mentioned before, this was all in the past by the time I discovered it, but having seen that a local collective could create something so powerful (not to mention influential) was very inspiring to me. It was a real shot in the arm and helped pull me out of the "why bother? No one cares" kind of attitude that prevails in hopeless small towns. It helped give me the impetus to be pro-active and rather than complaining about the lack of a scene, to try and nurture one in my own small way by renting a really old warehouse space and putting a (ramshackle) studio in there. Later we would put on shows in there. This is where The Cribs first formed with my two brothers, Ryan and Ross.

One time, down at the studio, we were producing (awesome Leeds garage-scuzzsters) The Real Losers debut LP *Time To Lose*. They really wanted it to sound fucked up and trashy. "Jet Sonic", in their words. We pretty much turned the treble way up and ran it all in the red. It sounded crazy. At the end of mixing, the guitarist Shaun said "Man, this sounds so nutsoid. Karren is gonna love this." Turns out he was dating Karren Ablaze! at the time, and I was secretly really flattered that he thought she would dig it. It was through The Real Losers that I would discover that there was once again a really amazing movement burgeoning in Leeds, and meet people like Jonny Strangeways who would put on these killer all-dayers featuring some of my favourite bands, like (ex-Huggy Bear) Comet Gain. He was the first (and one of the only) people that The Cribs ever sent a demo to, and all of a sudden - ten years later - we felt like we had found our place. We were playing shows with some of our favourite artists, people we had grown up listening to like Calvin Johnston, doing gig swaps with other like-minded bands, recording each other, and eventually putting out a split 7" on the newly formed Squirrel Records. It was pretty much everything I had been fantasizing about before. From that point on, The Cribs have been determined to keep that idealism as much as we can. Not for dogmatic reasons, but because it's what we LOVED and yearned for. It's absolutely what got us here in the first place.

I feel like I owe a lot to *Ablaze!*. It really seems pivotal to me now looking back, as it factored in so many of these formative anecdotes. It's strange, but a second-hand fanzine really did prove talismanic for me in those bleaker times. My strongest feeling towards *Ablaze!* is rooted in it being an already defunct (and therefore unattainable) ideal for me that I held throughout the godawful late nineties in northern England. So, sorry if this seems a little like a sappy love letter... but I guess it kinda is.

Acknowledgements

Writing about one's own past can be trying, and I benefited from the assistance of several people who provided a combination of management and cheerleading services. Initially this role was fulfilled by knitting terrorist and guitarist Matthew Evans, who wishes to be credited under the name Reginald, but has hopefully forgotten that stipulation by now. Once Matt got bored – it can take a long time for a sick girl to write a book - Ross Holloway re-manifested himself in my life and took the helm for a few months, spending hours on the phone providing world-weary reassurances that this was not a completely pointless exercise after all. And when Ross vanished back into the world of work, a place where one's effort is more likely rewarded by some kind of result, DIY Radio's Pik had the happy news of redundancy and became my writing partner. Although at a distance of 200 miles, we arranged times in which we would write simultaneously; writing is a solitary business and it does help to know that you are not alone. I continued to wrestle with the smothering duvet of illness that would take me out of action for varying periods of time. A trip to Turin proved very inspiring, during the course of which I was introduced, by my host Gaia D'Angelo, to an institution called Circolo de Lettori, a revered and centuries-old Italian centre for the appreciation of literature. Circolo's exquisite surroundings and pensive atmosphere made it the perfect place for writing and drinking creamy cappuccinos, and there I was able to see the light at the end of the very long tunnel. That's when Shaun Alcock's work came to the fore. Renowned as a guitarist in The Real Losers, Shaun Alcock is also celebrated for his creation of dazzling posters for events at venues in the North of England. He kindly agreed to put everything else aside for two months in order to bring this book from ethereal concept to physical reality.

Old friends Chris Trout and Simone Ivatts made time to advise on suitable selections from the zines, and Simone managed to fit a bunch of proof reading in around her busy work schedule. Gavin Bradbury, having escaped from his career as an IT lecturer at just the right time, stepped up in typical 'without whom' style, and assisted with proof reading, editing, transcribing, and website design. Justine Wolfenden broke off from her work as a Classics lecturer to provide advice, and to help me remember things that had happened. Artist and model maker Rachel Barker restored and coloured in the Riot Grrrl map. Animator Kerrie McKinnon provided technical support and graphics work, cellist Bela Emerson and technologist Patrick Courtney helped with transcription, while novelist Andie Mills assisted with editing. Craftsperson and my ex-landlady at Hopewell Place, Jean Wildish showed up, proof read and pitched in with artwork along with her partner Neil Wildish. Radio station manager Jaz Long also reappeared in my life and supported the project in many kind and practical ways. Female Borstal guitarist and French-English translator Jerome Smith saved the book's ass on the proof reading front in the final weeks and days before going to press.

And house renovator Chris Brereton let his own work slide in order to provide technical support, business advice, food, love and immense patience at a time when all aspects of our lives became subservient to this book's emergence.

To the above, to the book's contributors, and to all the others who have supported and encouraged me with this project – thank you.

All are friends, and many I met through my work with Ablaze!. No professionals were involved in the creation of this work, and I take great delight in publishing it myself, just like a fanzine.

Post-*Ablaze!* bands of now: So'eza

Champion Kickboxer Jelas

The Wednesday Club Cowtown

Opposite: Post-*Ablaze!* bands of yesteryear...